Expert C# 2008 Business Objects

Rockford Lhotka

Apress®

Expert C# 2008 Business Objects

ISBN-13 (pbk): 978-1-4302-1019-1

ISBN-13 (electronic): 978-1-4302-1020-7

Printed and bound in the United States of America (POD)

Editor: Matthew Moodie
Technical Reviewers: James Miller, Andrés Villanueva, Joe Fallon
Editorial Board: Clay Andres, Steve Anglin, Mark Beckner, Ewan Buckingham, Tony Campbell, Gary Cornell, Jonathan Gennick, Michelle Lowman, Matthew Moodie, Jeffrey Pepper, Frank Pohlmann, Ben Renow-Clarke, Dominic Shakeshaft, Matt Wade, Tom Welsh
Project Manager: Richard Dal Porto
Copy Editors: Nicole Abramowitz, Jennifer Whipple
Associate Production Director: Kari Brooks-Copony
Production Editor: Laura Esterman
Compositor: Susan Glinert
Proofreader: Nancy Bell
Indexer: John Collin
Artist: April Milne
Cover Designer: Kurt Krames
Manufacturing Director: Tom Debolski

Distributed to the book trade worldwide by Springer-Verlag New York, Inc., 233 Spring Street, 6th Floor, New York, NY 10013. Phone 1-800-SPRINGER, fax 201-348-4505, e-mail orders-ny@springer-sbm.com, or visit http://www.springeronline.com.

For information on translations, please e-mail info@apress.com, or visit http://www.apress.com.

Apress and friends of ED books may be purchased in bulk for academic, corporate, or promotional use. eBook versions and licenses are also available for most titles. For more information, reference our Special Bulk Sales–eBook Licensing web page at http://www.apress.com/info/bulksales.

The source code for this book is available to readers at http://www.apress.com.

To my Mom and Dad. Thank you for all you've taught me through the years!

Contents at a Glance

Contents

CHAPTER 15 Persistence and the Data Portal 419

About the Author

ROCKFORD LHOTKA is the author of numerous books. He is a Microsoft Regional Director, a Microsoft Most Valuable Professional (MVP), and an INETA speaker. He contributes to several major magazines and presents regularly at major conferences around the world, including Microsoft Tech Ed and VS Live. Rockford is the Principal Technology Evangelist for Magenic (`www.magenic.com`), one of the nation's premier Microsoft Gold Certified Partners that is focused on delivering business value through applied technology. For more information, go to `www.lhotka.net`.

About the Technical Reviewers

JAMES MILLER is a senior architect and technical evangelist specializing in enterprise solutions. He has worked in multiple industries and capacities in both the public and private sectors, and he has more than 25 years of programming experience under his belt. He has embraced CSLA since 2002 and has been an active proponent of the framework in his career and on the CSLA forums. He is currently working with an ISV, leading an international group of developers to upgrade their products to the latest .NET technologies, practices, tools, and techniques, while espousing the virtues of OOP, SOA, TDD, agile development, and CSLA. Jim is a proud graduate of the University of Michigan, is Microsoft certified in both VB .NET and C# for Windows and Web-based applications, and jumped at the chance to contribute to the next version of the CSLA framework.

Jim lives in a rural area outside Ann Arbor, Michigan, with his wife, five children, four cats, and three dogs. He fills much of his limited free time as the head coach of his local high school's junior varsity boys' lacrosse team. Jim still has an electric guitar plugged in over in a corner, a bookshelf filled with tech books, and a comfortable chair on the deck, perfect for viewing the deer as they meander by.

ANDRÉS VILLANUEVA is a consultant/developer living in Argentina. After a start in IT at age 15, he moved to the software industry, coding with Visual FoxPro and Visual Basic 6. In 2004, Andrés moved on to .NET and hasn't looked back. His early software experiences were in the banking industry, where he quickly rose as a leader, helping his firm improve consistency by implementing the CSLA framework. Since those days, he has made the leap into the consulting world and now provides software services from his office in Argentina to various clients around the world. He is an open source software fan and the current lead on the CslaGenerator project—an open source code-generation tool that targets development on the CSLA framework. In his little free time, Andrés enjoys playing soccer and relaxing with jazz music.

JOE FALLON is the Director of Framework Development at PurchasingNet, Inc., and is responsible for the development and implementation of the.NET Framework for PNet products. Prior to joining PurchasingNet, he worked at Nestle Chocolate and Confection as an assistant plant engineer after completing five years of service in the U.S. Army as a captain in the field artillery. During his tenure at Nestle USA, he held various positions in industrial engineering and IT.

Joe graduated from the United States Military Academy at West Point, New York, and was the 1981 recipient of the General Omar Bradley Award as the Academy's no. 1 mathematics major. He has been a Microsoft MVP for eight years in a row.

Acknowledgments

This book is a major update to the previous edition. This book, and CSLA .NET 3.6, exist thanks to a lot of work from many people.

I need to acknowledge the support, patience, and love from my wife and sons over the past many years. Without you, this would have been impossible.

I'd also like to thank Greg Frankenfield and Paul Fridman for making Magenic such an awesome place to work. The support that you and the rest of Magenic have provided has been great, and I appreciate it very much. It is an honor to work with everyone there.

CSLA .NET 3.6 is the result of a lot of work by several Magenic colleagues, including Sergey Barskiy, Justin Chase (now at Microsoft), Aaron Erickson, and Nermin Dibek. Jon Stonecash, Mark Steinberg, Grant Breems, and Chris Williams contributed as well. Sandy Fougerousse created the CSLA .NET for Silverlight logo.

A number of people outside Magenic also contributed to CSLA .NET 3.6, including Ricky Supit, Mark Chesney, and Miguel Castro. The CSLA .NET for Windows logo was contributed by Chris Russi.

The Apress editorial team went above and beyond to help shape this book into what you see here and to help get it done as rapidly as possible. I owe them all a debt of gratitude for their fine work.

Finally, I'd like to thank the scores of people who've sent me emails, posted on the forum and my blog with messages of support and encouragement, or just plain asked when the book would be done. The great community that has grown around these books and the CSLA .NET framework is wonderful, and I thank you all. I hope you find this book to be as rewarding to read as it has been for me to write.

Code well and have fun!

Introduction

I have a passion for frameworks. In more than 20 years as a professional developer, I've never worked on a computing platform that did everything I needed it to do to build applications productively. The Microsoft .NET platform is wonderful, but it doesn't always do quite what I want or need. To address those needs, I'm always looking for tools and frameworks, and sometimes I end up creating them myself.

A framework is simply the codification of an architecture or design pattern. Before you can have a good framework, you need to have an architecture. That means you need to have a vision and a set of goals both for the architecture and the kinds of applications it should enable.

This book is about application architecture, design, and development in .NET using object-oriented concepts. The focus is on creating *business objects* and implementing them to work in various distributed environments, including web and client/server configurations. The book makes use of a great many .NET technologies, object-oriented design and programming concepts, and distributed architectures.

Much of the book walks through the thought process I used in designing and creating the CSLA .NET framework to support object-oriented application development in .NET. This includes a lot of architectural concepts and ideas. It also involves some in-depth use of advanced .NET techniques to create the framework.

The book also shows how to make use of the framework to build a sample application with several different interfaces. If you wish, you could skip the framework design chapters and simply make use of the framework to build object-oriented applications.

One of my primary goals in creating the CSLA .NET framework was to simplify .NET development. Developers using the framework in this book don't need to worry about the details of underlying technologies such as remoting, serialization, or reflection. All of these are embedded in the framework, so that a developer using it can focus almost entirely on business logic and application design rather than on getting caught up in "plumbing" issues.

This book is a major update to the previous edition, *Expert C# 2005 Business Objects*. This updated book takes advantage of new features of .NET 3.5 and applies lessons learned by using .NET 2.0 and 3.0 over the past few years.

This book is the most recent expression of concepts I've been working on for more than a dozen years. My goal all along has been to enable the productive use of object-oriented design in distributed n-tier applications. Over the years, both the technologies and my understanding and expression of the concepts have evolved greatly.

From CSLA .NET 2.0 to 3.6

Over the past eight years, the CSLA .NET framework has become one of the most widely used development frameworks on the Microsoft .NET platform. Since I introduced the .NET version in 2001, the framework has grown and evolved quite a lot, in part due to changes to the .NET platform itself, and in part due to feedback from the vibrant community surrounding CSLA .NET.

The CSLA .NET framework is a reflection of an underlying architecture I call *CSLA*, for component-based, scalable, logical architecture. Over the years, I've received hundreds of emails from people who have used CSLA as a basis for their own architectures, as they've built applications ranging from small, single-user programs to full-blown enterprise applications that power major parts of their businesses.

This framework addresses two primary areas of object-oriented software development:

- How to use business objects to efficiently build Windows, web, and service-oriented applications
- How to enable the use of object-oriented design in a distributed computing environment

While .NET supports the use of objects, the author of an object has to do a lot of work to fully support important .NET concepts such as data binding. Much of the focus of CSLA .NET and of this book is on enabling objects to fully support data binding, as well as on other important concepts such as validation and authorization. For most users of CSLA .NET, these are the primary benefits that the framework provides.

Many people build distributed n-tier or service-oriented applications. Using object-oriented design and business objects in a distributed environment has its own challenges, and CSLA .NET uses various techniques to overcome those challenges. For n-tier client/server applications, the framework supports the idea of *mobile objects*—objects that actually move between computers in an n-tier environment. Mobile objects provide a powerful way to implement object-oriented designs in distributed environments. For service-oriented applications, CSLA .NET can be used to build both edge applications and services. The framework is compelling for edge application creation and is often useful for creating services or workflow activities as well.

As the .NET platform and the CSLA .NET framework have evolved, I've made a great many changes and added many new features. In some cases, using the new concepts and features has required making changes to existing business objects and user interface code. I don't take backward compatibility lightly, yet it is important to advance the concepts to keep up with both changes in technology and my views on both object-oriented and distributed computing.

When possible, I have minimized the impact on existing code, so the transition shouldn't be overly complex for most applications. Although there are a few breaking changes from version 3.0 to 3.6, *most* existing code should upgrade easily. Even version 2.1 code should upgrade with relative ease. Business classes written with CSLA .NET versions 1.x or 2.0 will require quite a bit of effort to bring forward.

Over the years, I've received a handful of emails from people for whom CSLA .NET *wasn't* successful, but this isn't surprising. To use CSLA .NET effectively, you must become versed in object-oriented design, understand the concept of mobile objects, and develop a host of other skills. The mobile object architecture has many benefits, but it's not the simplest or the easiest to understand.

However, over that same period of time, I've received countless emails from people who have had tremendous success in building applications using CSLA .NET. These applications range from Windows to web, from small to enterprise, from retail to manufacturing to military environments. I am amazed, pleased, and humbled by these emails and by all the cool places where CSLA .NET has helped organizations and individuals around the world.

Designing CSLA .NET

One of the characteristics of .NET is that it often provides several ways to solve the same problem. Some of the available approaches are better than others, but the best one for a given problem may not be immediately obvious. Over the past eight years, I've spent a lot of time researching many of these options and techniques. Although a variety have proven to work, in the end I've arrived at the one that best matches my original goals.

I have a specific set of goals for the architecture and the book. These goals are important, because they're key to understanding why I made many of the choices I did in terms of which .NET technologies to use and how to use them. The goals are as follows:

- To support a fully object-oriented programming model
- To allow the developer to use the architecture without jumping through hoops
- To enable high scalability
- To enable high performance
- To enable developer productivity when using business objects, including:
  - Support for data binding in Windows and Web Forms
  - Support for many types of UIs based on the same objects
  - Management of validation rules
  - Management of authorization rules
  - N-level undo on a per-object basis (edit, cancel, apply)
  - Integration with distributed transaction technologies such as Enterprise Services and `System.Transactions`
- To support the use of object-oriented design in a distributed environment through the use of mobile objects
- To simplify .NET by handling complex issues such as serialization, reflection, and network communication
- To use the tools provided by Microsoft—notably IntelliSense and the Autocomplete feature in Visual Studio .NET

Of these, saving the developer from jumping through hoops—that is, allowing him or her to do "normal" programming—has probably had the largest impact. To meet all these goals without a framework, the developer would have to write a lot of extra code to track business rules, implement n-level undo, and support serialization of object data. All this code is important, but it adds nothing to the business value of the application.

Fortunately, .NET offers some powerful technologies that help to reduce or eliminate much of this "plumbing" code. If those technologies are then wrapped in a framework, a business developer shouldn't have to deal with them at all. In several cases, this goal of simplicity drove my architectural decisions. The end result is that the developer can, for the most part, simply write a standardized C# class and have it automatically enjoy all the benefits of n-level undo, business rule tracking, and so forth.

It has taken a great deal of time and effort, but I've certainly enjoyed putting this architecture and this book together, and I hope that you will find both valuable during the development of your own applications.

Framework License

LICENSE AND WARRANTY

The CSLA .NET framework is Copyright 2008 by Rockford Lhotka.

You can use this Software for any noncommercial purpose, including distributing derivative works.

You can use this Software for any commercial purpose other than you may not use it, in whole or in part, to create a commercial framework product.

In short, you can use CSLA .NET and modify it to create other commercial or business software, you just can't take the framework itself, modify it and sell it as a product.

In return, the owner simply requires that you agree:

This Software License Agreement ("Agreement") is effective upon your use of CSLA .NET ("Software").

1. Ownership.
   The CSLA .NET framework is Copyright 2008 by Rockford Lhotka, Eden Prairie, MN, USA.
2. Copyright Notice.
   You must not remove any copyright notices from the Software source code.
3. License.
   The owner hereby grants a perpetual, non-exclusive, limited license to use the Software as set forth in this Agreement.
4. Source Code Distribution.
   If you distribute the Software in source code form you must do so only under this License (i.e. you must include a complete copy of this License with your distribution).
5. Binary or Object Distribution.
   You may distribute the Software in binary or object form with no requirement to display copyright notices to the end user. The binary or object form must retain the copyright notices included in the Software source code.
6. Restrictions.
   You may not sell the Software. If you create a software development framework based on the Software as a derivative work, you may not sell that derivative work. This does not restrict the use of the Software for creation of other types of non-commercial or commercial applications or derivative works.
7. Disclaimer of Warranty.
   The Software comes "as is", with no warranties. None whatsoever. This means no express, implied, statutory or other warranty, including without limitation, warranties of merchantability or fitness for a particular purpose, noninfringement, or the presence or absence of errors, whether or not discoverable. Also, you must pass this disclaimer on whenever you distribute the Software.
8. Liability.
   Neither Rockford Lhotka nor any contributor to the Software will be liable for any of those types of damages known as indirect, special, consequential, incidental, punitive or exemplary related to the Software or this License, to the maximum extent the law permits, no matter what legal theory it's based on. Also, you must pass this limitation of liability on whenever you distribute the Software.
9. Patents.
   If you sue anyone over patents that you think may apply to the Software for a person's use of the Software, your license to the Software ends automatically. The patent rights, if any, licensed hereunder only apply to the Software, not to any derivative works you make.
10. Termination.
    Your rights under this License end automatically if you breach it in any way. Rockford Lhotka reserves the right to release the Software under different license terms or to stop distributing the Software at any time. Such an election will not serve to withdraw this Agreement, and this Agreement will continue in full force and effect unless terminated as stated above.
11. Governing Law.
    This Agreement shall be construed and enforced in accordance with the laws of the state of Minnesota, USA.
12. No Assignment.
    Neither this Agreement nor any interest in this Agreement may be assigned by Licensee without the prior express written approval of Developer.

13. Final Agreement.
    This Agreement terminates and supersedes all prior understandings or agreements on the subject matter hereof. This Agreement may be modified only by a further writing that is duly executed by both parties.

14. Severability.
    If any term of this Agreement is held by a court of competent jurisdiction to be invalid or unenforceable, then this Agreement, including all of the remaining terms, will remain in full force and effect as if such invalid or unenforceable term had never been included.

15. Headings.
    Headings used in this Agreement are provided for convenience only and shall not be used to construe meaning or intent.

What You Need to Use This Book

The code in this book has been verified to work against Microsoft Visual Studio 2008 Professional Edition SP1 and against version 3.5 SP1 of the .NET Framework. The database is a SQL Server Express database, which is included with Visual Studio 2008 Professional. The Enterprise version of Visual Studio 2008 and the full version of SQL Server are useful but not necessary.

In order to run the tools and products listed previously, you'll need at least one PC with Windows Vista, Windows XP SP2 (or higher), Windows Server 2003, or Windows Server 2008 installed. To test CSLA .NET's support for multiple physical tiers, of course, you'll need an additional PC (or you can use Virtual PC or a similar tool) for each tier that you wish to add.

How This Book Is Structured

This book covers the thought process behind the CSLA .NET for Windows version 3.6 architecture. It describes the construction of the framework that supports the architecture, and it demonstrates how to create WPF, Web Forms, and WCF service applications based on business objects written using the framework.

If you are reading this book to understand the process of designing and constructing a development framework for the .NET platform, then you should read all chapters. If you are reading this book to understand how to use the CSLA .NET framework and are less interested in how the framework itself is designed and implemented, then you should read Chapters 1 through 5 and Chapters 17 through 21.

Chapter 1 introduces some of the concepts surrounding distributed architectures, including logical and physical architectures, business objects, and distributed objects. Perhaps more importantly, this chapter sets the stage, showing the thought process that results in the remainder of the book.

Chapter 2 takes the architecture described at the end of Chapter 1 and uses it as the starting point for a code framework that enables the goals described earlier. By the end of the chapter, you'll have seen the design process for the objects that will be implemented in Chapters 6 through 16; but before that, there's some other business to attend to.

In Chapter 3, I discuss the basics of responsibility-driven object-oriented design. As an example, this chapter lays out the requirements and design for a sample application.

Chapters 4 and 5 discuss how to use each of the primary base classes in the CSLA .NET framework to create your own business objects. I discuss in detail the object-oriented stereotypes supported by the CSLA .NET base classes, along with the code structure for editable and read-only objects, and collections and name/value lists.

Chapters 6 through 16 are all about the construction of the CSLA .NET framework itself. If you're interested in the code behind property declarations, validation rules, authorization rules, n-level undo, mobile object support, and object persistence, then these are the chapters for you. In addition, they make use of some of the more advanced and interesting parts of the .NET Framework, including data binding, serialization, reflection, dynamic method invocation, WCF, .NET security, Enterprise Services, `System.Transactions`, strongly named assemblies, dynamically loaded assemblies, application configuration files, and more.

Chapters 17 and 18 create the business objects for the application. These chapters illustrate how you can use the framework to create a powerful set of business objects rapidly and easily for an application. The end result is a set of objects that not only model business responsibilities, but also support data binding, validation, authorization, n-level undo, and various physical configurations that can optimize performance, scalability, security, and fault tolerance, as discussed in Chapter 1.

Chapter 19 demonstrates how to create a WPF interface to the business objects. Chapter 20 covers the creation of an ASP.NET Web Forms interface with comparable functionality.

Chapter 21 shows how to build WCF services using business objects. This approach enables service-oriented development by providing a programmatic interface to the business objects that any web service or WCF client can call.

By the end, you'll have a framework that supports object-oriented application design in a practical, pragmatic manner. The framework implements a logical model that you can deploy in various physical configurations to optimally support Windows, web, and XML service clients.

Downloading the Code

The code that reflects the contents of this book is available in the Source Code/Download area of the Apress website (`www.apress.com`). For the latest version of the framework and the example application, visit `www.lhotka.net/cslanet/download.aspx`.

Contacting the Author

You may reach Rockford Lhotka on his website, `www.lhotka.net`, which contains his blog, information about the framework and book, and his contact information.

CHAPTER 1

Distributed Architecture

Object-oriented design and programming are big topics—entire books are devoted solely to the process of object-oriented design or to using object-oriented programming in various languages and on various programming platforms. My focus in this book isn't to teach the basics of object-oriented design or programming, but rather to show how you may apply them to the creation of distributed .NET applications.

It can be difficult to apply object-oriented design and programming effectively in a physically distributed environment. This chapter is intended to provide a good understanding of the key issues surrounding distributed computing as it relates to object-oriented development. I'll cover a number of topics, including the following:

- How logical n-layer architectures help address reuse and maintainability
- How physical n-tier architectures impact performance, scalability, security, and fault tolerance
- The difference between data-centric and object-oriented application models
- How object-oriented models help increase code reuse and application maintainability
- The effective use of objects in a distributed environment, including the concepts of anchored and mobile objects
- The relationship between an architecture and a framework

This chapter provides an introduction to the concepts and issues surrounding distributed object-oriented architecture. Then, throughout this book, I'll be exploring an n-layer architecture that may be physically distributed across multiple machines. I'll show how to use object-oriented design and programming techniques to implement a framework supporting this architecture. I'll create a sample application that demonstrates how the architecture and the framework support development efforts.

Logical and Physical Architecture

In today's world, an object-oriented application must be designed to work in a variety of physical configurations. Even the term *application* has become increasingly blurry due to all the hype around service-oriented architecture (SOA). If you aren't careful, you can end up building applications by combining several applications, which is obviously confusing.

When I use the term *application* in this book, I'm referring to a set of code, objects, or components that's considered to be part of a single, logical unit. Even if parts of the application are in different .NET assemblies or installed on different machines, all the code will be viewed as being part of a singular application.

This definition works well when describing most traditional application models, such as single-tier or 2-tier rich client applications, n-tier smart client applications, web applications, and so forth. In all those cases, the application consists of a set of objects or components that are designed to work together within the context of the application.

You can contrast this with an SOA model, where multiple services (each essentially a separate application) interact through message-based communication. In an SOA model, the idea is to build an enterprise system that is composed of applications and services. In this context, both applications and services are stand-alone, autonomous units of functionality, which means they both meet the definition of an application. Confusingly enough, this means a service is merely an application that has an XML interface instead of an HTML or graphical interface.

If you're thinking about service-oriented systems as you read this book, the term *application* means one of two things. First, it may refer to a service implementation. Second, it may refer to an application on the edge of the system that allows users to interact with the system. Edge applications are much like traditional applications, except they typically interact with services instead of databases for retrieving and storing data.

You can contrast the traditional and SOA models with a workflow model, which you're likely to encounter when using Windows Workflow Foundation (WF). In this environment, an application is often implemented (in whole or part) in the form of a workflow. However, the workflow itself merely orchestrates a set of *activities*, and each activity should be an autonomous, stand-alone unit of functionality. This means that an activity must meet the definition of an application. An activity is merely an application that has no real user interface beyond the data-binding infrastructure built into WF.

Traditional, service-oriented and workflow applications *might* run on a single machine. However, it's very likely that they will run on multiple machines, such as a web server or a smart client and an application server. Given these varied physical environments, you're faced with the following questions:

- Where do the objects reside?
- Are the objects designed to maintain state, or should they be stateless?
- How is object-relational mapping handled when retrieving or storing data in the database?
- How are database transactions managed?

Before discussing some answers to these questions, it's important that you fully understand the difference between a *physical architecture* and a *logical architecture*. After defining these terms, I'll define objects and mobile objects, and show you how they fit into the architectural discussion.

When most people talk about n-tier applications, they're talking about physical models in which the application is spread across multiple machines with different functions: a client, a web server, an application server, a database server, and so on. And this isn't a misconception—these are indeed n-tier systems. The problem is that many people tend to assume there's a one-to-one relationship between the layers (tiers) in a logical model and the tiers in a physical model, when in fact that's not always true.

A *physical* n-tier architecture is quite different from a *logical* n-layer architecture. An n-layer architecture has nothing to do with the number of machines or network hops involved in running the application. Rather, a logical architecture is all about separating different types of functionality. The most common logical separation is into an Interface layer, a Business layer, and a Data layer. These may exist on a single machine or on three separate machines—the logical architecture doesn't define those details.

■ **Note** There is a relationship between an application's logical and physical architectures: the logical architecture always has at least as many layers as the physical architecture has tiers. There may be more logical layers than physical tiers (because one physical tier can contain several logical layers), but never fewer.

The sad reality is that many applications have no clearly defined logical architecture. Often the logical architecture merely defaults to the number of physical tiers. This lack of a formal, logical design causes problems because it reduces flexibility. If a system is designed to operate in two or three physical tiers, then changing the number of physical tiers at a later date is typically very difficult. However, if you start by creating a logical architecture of three layers, you can switch more easily between one, two, or three physical tiers later on.

Additionally, having clean separation between these layers makes your application more maintainable, because changing one layer often has minimal impact on the other layers. Nowhere is this more true than with the Interface layer (sometimes called the UI or Presentation layer), where the ability to switch between Windows Presentation Foundation (WPF), Windows Forms, Web Forms, ASP.NET MVC, and workflow and service-based interfaces is critical.

The flexibility to choose your physical architecture is important because the benefits gained by employing a physical n-tier architecture are different from those gained by employing a logical n-layer architecture. A properly designed logical n-layer architecture provides the following benefits:

- Logically organized code
- Easier maintenance
- Better reuse of code
- Better team-development experience
- Higher clarity in coding

On the other hand, a properly chosen physical n-tier architecture can provide the following benefits:

- Performance
- Scalability
- Fault tolerance
- Security

It goes almost without saying that if the physical or logical architecture of an application is designed poorly, there will be a risk of damaging the things that would have been improved had the job been done well.

N-Tier and SOA

It is important to realize that a physical service-oriented architecture is *not* the same as an n-tier architecture. In fact, the two concepts can be complementary. It is also important to know that the concept of a *logical n-layer* architecture is the same in SOA as in any other type of application model.

In logical n-layer models, a service should have the same layers as any other application: Interface, Business, and Data. In a logical n-layer model, the Interface layer consists of XML messages, but that's not a lot different from the HTML used in a web-based Interface layer. The Business layer is much the same as in any other application; it contains the business logic and behaviors that make the service useful. The data layer is also much the same as in any other application, in that it stores and retrieves data as necessary.

However, the physical n-tier model might not appear to translate to the SOA world at all. Some people would say that SOA makes n-tier concepts totally obsolete, but I disagree. SOA has an important set of goals around loose coupling, reuse of functionality, and open communication. An n-tier client/server architecture has a complementary set of goals around performance, avoiding duplication of code, and targeted functionality. The reality is that *both models are useful*, and they complement each other.

For example, you might use a service-oriented model to create a service that is available on the Internet. However, the service *implementation* might be n-tier, with the service interface on the web server and parts of the business implementation running on a separate application server. The result is a reusable service that enjoys high performance and security and avoids duplication of code.

Complexity

Experienced designers and developers often view a good n-tier architecture as a way of simplifying an application and reducing complexity, but this isn't necessarily the case. It's important to recognize that n-tier designs are typically *more* complex than single-tier designs. Even novice developers can visualize the design of a form or a page that retrieves data from a file and displays it to the user, but novice developers often struggle with 2-tier designs and are hopelessly lost in an n-tier environment.

With sufficient experience, architects and developers do typically find that the organization and structure of an n-tier model reduces complexity for large applications. However, even a veteran n-tier developer will often find it easier to avoid n-tier models when creating a simple form to display some simple data.

The point here is that n-tier architectures only simplify the process for large applications or complex environments. They can easily complicate matters if all you're trying to do is create a small application with a few forms that will be running on someone's desktop computer. (Of course, if that desktop computer is one of hundreds or thousands in a global organization, then the *environment* may be so complex that an n-tier solution provides simplicity.)

In short, n-tier architectures help to decrease or manage complexity when *any* of these are true:

- The application is large or complex.
- The application is one of many similar or related applications that, *when combined*, may be large or complex.
- The environment (including deployment, support, and other factors) is large or complex.

On the other hand, n-tier architectures can increase complexity when *all* of these are true:

- The application is small or relatively simple.
- The application isn't part of a larger group of enterprise applications that are similar or related.
- The environment isn't complex.

Something to remember is that even a small application is likely to grow, and even a simple environment often becomes more complex over time. The more successful your application, the more likely that one or both of these will happen. If you find yourself on the edge of choosing an n-tier solution, it's typically best to go with it. You should expect and plan for growth.

This discussion illustrates why n-tier applications are viewed as relatively complex. A lot of factors—both technical and nontechnical—must be taken into account. Unfortunately, it isn't possible to say definitively when n-tier does and doesn't fit. In the end, it's a judgment call that you, as an application architect, must make, based on the factors that affect your particular organization, environment, and development team.

Relationship Between Logical and Physical Models

Some architectures attempt to merge logical n-layer and physical n-tier concepts. Such mergers seem attractive because they seem simpler and more straightforward, but typically they aren't good in practice—they can lead people to design applications using a logical or physical architecture that isn't best suited to their needs.

The Logical Model

When you're creating an application, it's important to start with a logical architecture that clarifies the roles of all components, separates functionality so that a team can work together effectively, and simplifies overall maintenance of the system. The logical architecture must also include enough layers so that you have flexibility in choosing a physical architecture later on.

Traditionally, you would devise at least a 3-layer logical model that separates the interface, the business logic, and the data-management portions of the application. Today that's rarely sufficient, because the "interface" layer is often physically split into two parts (browser and web server), and the "logic" layer is often physically split between a client or web server and an application server. Additionally, various application models have been used to break the traditional Business layer into multiple parts—model-view-controller (MVC) and facade-data-logic being two of the most popular at the moment.

This means that the logical layers are governed by the following rules:

- The logical architecture includes layers in order to organize components into discrete roles.
- The logical architecture must have at least as many layers as the anticipated physical deployment will have tiers.

Following these rules, most modern applications have four to six logical layers. As you'll see, the architecture used in this book includes five logical layers.

Cross-Layer Communication

Just because an application is organized into layers doesn't mean those layers can be deployed arbitrarily on different tiers. The code in one layer communicates with the layer immediately above or below it in the architecture. If you don't design that communication properly, it may be impossible to put a network (tier) boundary between the layers.

For example, the boundary between the Business layer and the Data layer is often highly optimized. Most applications have a network boundary between the Data layer and the rest of the application, so modern data access technologies are good at optimizing cross-network communication in this scenario.

The boundary between the Interface layer and the Business layer is often not optimized for this purpose. Many applications make use of data binding, which is a "chatty" technology involving many property, method, and event calls between these two layers. The result is that it is often impractical and undesirable to put a network boundary between these layers.

Not all layer boundaries should be designed to enable a tier boundary. You should design an architecture up front to enable the potential for tier boundaries in certain locations and to disallow them in other cases. If done properly, the result is a balance between flexibility and capability.

The Physical Model

By ensuring that the logical model has enough layers to provide flexibility, you can configure your application into an appropriate physical architecture that will depend on your performance, scalability, fault tolerance, and security requirements. The more physical tiers included, the worse the performance will be; however, there is the potential to increase scalability, security, and/or fault tolerance.

Performance and Scalability

The more physical tiers there are, the *worse* the performance? That doesn't sound right, but if you think it through, it makes perfect sense: *performance* is the speed at which an application responds to a user. This is different from *scalability*, which is a measure of how performance changes as load (such as increased users) is added to an application. To get optimal performance—that is, the fastest possible response time for a given user—the ideal solution is to put the client, the logic, and the data on the user's machine. This means no network hops, no network latency, and no contention with other users.

If you decide that you need to support multiple users, you might consider putting application data on a central file server. (This is typical with Access and dBASE systems, for example.) However, this immediately affects performance because of contention on the data file. Furthermore, data access now takes place across the network, which means you've introduced network latency and network contention, too. To overcome this problem, you could put the data into a managed environment such as SQL Server or Oracle. This will help to reduce data contention, but you're still stuck with the network latency and contention problems. Although improved, performance for a given user is still nowhere near what it was when everything ran directly on that user's computer.

Even with a central database server, scalability is limited. Clients are still in contention for the resources of the server, with each client opening and closing connections, doing queries and updates, and constantly demanding the CPU, memory, and disk resources that other clients are using. You can reduce this load by shifting some of the work to another server. An *application server*, possibly running Enterprise Services or Internet Information Services (IIS), can provide database connection pooling to minimize the number of database connections that are opened and closed. It can also perform some data processing, filtering, and even caching to offload some work from the database server.

■ **Note** It is important to realize that modern database servers can often easily handle hundreds of concurrent users in a 2-tier architecture. For most applications, scalability is *not* a good reason to move from a 2- to 3-tier model.

These additional steps provide a dramatic boost to scalability, but again at the cost of performance. The user's request now has *two* network hops, potentially resulting in double the network latency and contention. For a single user, the system gets slower; however, it is able to handle many times more users with acceptable performance levels.

In the end, the application is constrained by the most limiting resource. This is typically the speed of transferring data across the network—but if the database or application server is underpowered, it can become so slow that data transfer across the network won't be an issue. Likewise, if the application does extremely intense calculations and the client machines are slow, then the cost of transferring the data across the network to a relatively idle high-speed server can make sense.

Security

Security is a broad and complex topic, but by narrowing the discussion solely to consider how it's affected by physical n-tier decisions, it becomes more approachable. The discussion is no longer about authentication or authorization as much as it is about controlling physical access to the machines on which portions of the application will run. The number of physical tiers in an application has no impact on whether users can be authenticated or authorized, but physical tiers *can* be used to increase or decrease physical access to the machines on which the application executes.

For instance, in a 2-tier Windows Forms or ASP.NET application, the machine running the interface code must have credentials to access the database server. Switching to a 3-tier model in which the data access code runs on an application server means that the machine running the interface code no longer needs those credentials, potentially making the system more secure.

Security requirements vary radically based on the environment and the requirements of your application. A Windows Forms application deployed only to internal users may need relatively little security, but an ASP.NET application exposed to anyone on the Internet may need extensive security.

To a large degree, security is all about surface area: how many points of attack are exposed from the application? The surface area can be defined in terms of domains of trust.

Security and Internal Applications Internal applications are totally encapsulated within a domain of trust: the client and all servers are running in a trusted environment. This means that virtually every part of the application is exposed to a potential hacker (assuming that the hacker can gain physical access to a machine on the network in the first place). In a typical organization, hackers can attack the client workstation, the web server, the application server, and the database server if they so choose. Rarely are there firewalls or other major security roadblocks *within* the context of an organization's local area network (LAN).

■ **Note** Obviously, there *is* security. It is common to use Windows domain or Active Directory security on the clients and servers, but there's nothing stopping someone from attempting to communicate directly with any of these machines. Within a typical LAN, users can usually connect through the network to all machines due to a lack of firewall or physical barriers.

Many internal applications are coming under increasing security requirements due to government regulations and other business pressures. The idea of having the database credentials on a client workstation is rapidly becoming unacceptable, and this is driving organizations to adopt a 3-tier architecture simply to move those credentials to a separate application server. This is an easy way to quickly improve an application's security.

Of course, the result is that the clients have the credentials to the *application* server. If they know how to find and call the application server's services, they can use an application's own services to access its servers in invalid ways. This problem was particularly acute with DCOM, because there were browsers that end users could use to locate and invoke server-side services. Thanks to COM, users could use Microsoft Excel to locate and interact with server-side COM components, thereby bypassing the portions of the application that were *supposed* to run on the client. This meant that the applications were vulnerable to power users who could use server-side components in ways their designers never imagined.

This problem is rapidly transferring to XML-based services, as Microsoft Office and other end-user applications start to allow power users to call XML-based services from within macros. I expect to find power users calling XML-based services in unexpected ways in the very near future.

The services in this book are designed to prevent casual usage of the objects, even if a power user were to gain access to the service from his application.

In summary, security has replaced scalability as the primary driver for moving from 2- to 3-tier architectures. But you must be careful when designing your services to ensure you haven't simply shifted the problem down a level.

Security and External Applications For external applications, things are entirely different. This is really where SOA comes into play. Service orientation (SO) is all about assembling a system that spans trust boundaries. When part of your system is deployed outside your own network, it certainly crosses at least a security (trust) boundary.

In a client/server model, this would be viewed as a minimum of two tiers, since the client workstation is physically separate from any machines running behind the firewall. But really, SO offers a better way to look at the problem: there are two totally separate applications. The client runs one application, and another application runs on your server. These two applications communicate with each other through clearly defined messages, and neither application is privy to the internal implementation of the other.

This provides a good way to deal with not only the security trust boundary, but also with the *semantic* trust boundary. What I mean by this is that the server application assumes that any data coming from the client application is flawed: either maliciously or due to a bug or oversight in the client. Even if the client has *security* access to interact with your server, the server application cannot assume that the semantic meaning of the data coming from the client is valid.

In short, because the client workstations are outside the domain of trust, you should assume that they're compromised and potentially malicious. You should assume that any code running on those clients will run incorrectly or not at all; in other words, the client input must be completely validated as it enters the domain of trust, even if the client includes code to do the validation.

■ **Note** I've had people tell me that this is an overly paranoid attitude, but I've been burned too many times: any time an interface is exposed (Windows, web, XML, and so on) so that clients outside your control can use it, you should assume that the interface will be misused. Often, this misuse is unintentional—for example, someone may write a buggy macro to automate data entry. That's no different than if they made a typo while entering the data by hand, but user-entered data is always validated before being accepted by an application. The same must be true for automated data entry as well, or your application will fail.

This scenario occurs in three main architectures: Windows smart clients, rich Internet applications (RIAs), and SOA systems.

If you deploy a WPF or Windows Forms client application to external workstations, you should design it as a stand-alone application that calls your server application through services. Chapter 21 shows how you can do this with the object-oriented concepts in this book.

You may create an RIA with Asynchronous JavaScript and XML (Ajax) technologies or newer technologies such as Silverlight. In either case, the RIA often validates data or otherwise provides a richer experience for the user, but your server code should assume that the RIA didn't do anything it was supposed to. It is far too easy for a user to subvert your client-side JavaScript or otherwise bypass client-side processing—as such, nothing running in an RIA can be trusted. The code running in the browser should be viewed as a *separate* application that is not trusted by the server application.

Service-oriented systems imply that there's one or more (potentially unknown) applications out there consuming your services. The very nature of SOA means that you have no control over those applications, so it would be foolish to assume they'll provide valid input to your services. A healthy dose of paranoia is critical when building any service for an SOA system.

As you'll see, you can use the object-oriented concepts and techniques shown in this book to create smart client applications that call services on your servers. You can use the same concepts to create the services themselves. You can also use them to create web applications ranging from simple Web Forms to Ajax to Silverlight.

Fault Tolerance

You can achieve fault tolerance by identifying points of failure and providing redundancy. Typically, applications have numerous points of failure. Some of the most obvious are as follows:

- The network feed to your user's buildings
- The power feed to your user's buildings
- The network feed and power feed to your data center
- The primary DNS host servicing your domain
- Your firewall, routers, switches, etc.
- Your web server
- Your application server
- Your database server
- Your internal LAN

In order to achieve high levels of fault tolerance, you need to ensure that if any one of these fails, some system will instantly kick in and fill the void. If the data center power goes out, a generator will kick in. If a bulldozer cuts your network feed, you'll need to have a second network feed coming in from the other side of the building, and so forth.

Considering some of the larger and more well-known outages of major websites in the past couple of years, it's worth noting that most of them occurred due to construction work cutting network or power feeds, or because their ISP or external DNS provider went down or was attacked. That said, there are plenty of examples of websites going down due to local equipment failure. The reason why the high-profile failures are seldom due to this type of problem is because large sites make sure to provide redundancy in these areas.

Clearly, adding redundant power, network, ISP, DNS, or LAN hardware will have little impact on application architecture. Adding redundant servers, on the other hand, *will* affect the n-tier application architecture—or at least the application design. Each time you add a physical tier, you need to ensure that you add redundancy to the servers in that tier. Thus, adding a fault-tolerant physical tier always means adding at least *two* servers to the infrastructure.

The more physical tiers, the more redundant servers there are to configure and maintain. This is why fault tolerance is typically expensive to achieve.

Not only that, but to achieve fault tolerance through redundancy, all servers in a tier must also be logically identical at all times. For example, at no time can a user be tied to a specific server, so no single server can ever maintain any user-specific information. As soon as a user is tied to a specific server, that server becomes a point of failure for that user. The result is that the user loses fault tolerance.

Achieving a high degree of fault tolerance isn't easy. It requires a great deal of thought and effort to locate all points of failure and make them redundant. Having fewer physical tiers in an architecture can assist in this process by reducing the number of tiers that must be made redundant.

To summarize, the number of physical tiers in an architecture is a trade-off between performance, scalability, security, and fault tolerance. Furthermore, the optimal configuration for a web application isn't the same as the one for an intranet application with smart client machines. If an application framework is to have any hope of broad appeal, it needs flexibility in the physical architecture so that it can support web and smart clients effectively, as well as provide both with optimal performance and scalability. Beyond that, it needs to work well in a service-oriented environment to create both client and server applications that interact through message-based communication.

A 5-Layer Logical Architecture

This book will explore a 5-layer logical architecture and show how you can implement it using object-oriented concepts. Once you learn how to create the logical architecture, you'll discover how to configure it into various physical architectures in order to achieve optimal results for WPF, Windows Forms, ASP.NET, and service-oriented and workflow interfaces.

■ **Note** If you get any group of architects into a room and ask them to describe their ideal architecture, each one will come up with a different answer. I make no pretense that this architecture is the only one out there, nor do I intend to discuss all the possible options. My aim here is to present a coherent, distributed, object-oriented architecture that supports all these different interfaces.

In the framework used in this book, the logical architecture comprises the five layers shown in Figure 1-1.

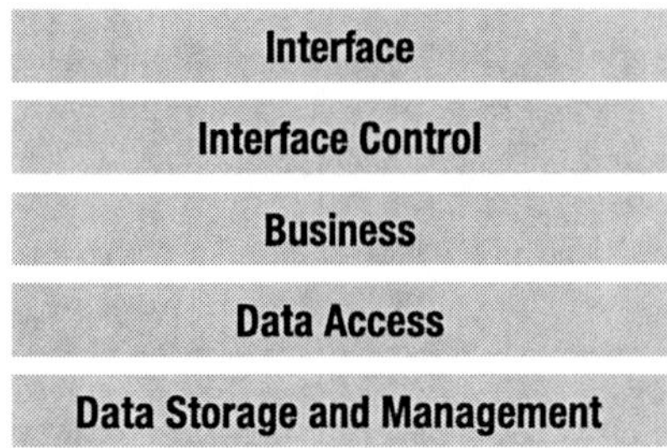

Figure 1-1. *The 5-layer logical architecture*

Remember that the benefit of a logical n-layer architecture is the separation of functionality into clearly defined roles or groups, in order to increase clarity and maintainability. Let's define each of the layers more carefully.

Interface

The Interface layer is often referred to as the UI or Presentation layer. I am using the more generic term *Interface*, because this architecture supports service-oriented applications that have no user, as well as WPF, Web Forms, Windows Forms, and other application types that *do* have a user.

At first, it may not be clear why I've separated Interface from Interface Control. Certainly, from a smart client perspective, the interface and the control of the interface are one and the same: they are graphical user interface (GUI) forms with which the user can interact.

From a web perspective, the distinction is probably quite clear. Typically, the browser merely provides an interface for the user, displaying data and collecting user input. In that case, all of the actual interaction logic—the code written to control the interface, to *generate* the output, or to *interpret* user input—runs on the web server (or mainframe) and not on the client machine.

Of course, in today's world, the browser might run Ajax or Silverlight. But as discussed earlier in the chapter, none of this code can be trusted. It must be viewed as being a *separate* application that interacts with your application as it runs on the server. So even with code running in the browser, *your* application's interface code is running on your web server.

The same is true for an SOA system, where the consuming application is clearly separate and thus can't be trusted. Your application's interface is composed of XML messages, and your interface control code (the service implementation) is running on your server.

Knowing that the logical model must support both smart and web-based clients (along with even more limited clients, such as cell phones or other mobile devices), it's important to recognize that in many cases, the interface will be physically separate from the interface control logic. To accommodate this separation, you need to design the applications around this concept.

■ **Note** The types of interface technologies continue to multiply, and each comes with a new and relatively incompatible technology with which you must work. It's virtually impossible to create a programming framework that entirely abstracts interface concepts. Because of this, the architecture and framework will merely *support the creation* of varied interfaces, not automate their creation. Instead, the focus will be on simplifying the other layers in the architecture, for which technology is more stable.

Interface Control

Now that I've addressed the distinction between the Interface and the Interface Control layers, the latter's purpose is probably fairly clear. This layer includes the logic to decide what the user sees, the navigation paths, and how to interpret user input. In a WPF or Windows Forms application, this is the code behind the form. Actually, it's the code behind the form in a Web Forms application, too, but here it can also include code that resides in server-side controls; *logically*, that's part of the same layer.

In an ASP.NET MVC application, the view and controller are both part of the Interface Control layer. The HTML, JavaScript, and other content produced by the view comprise the Interface. Finally, the Business layer is the model.

In many applications, the interface control code is very complex. For starters, it must respond to the user's requests in a nonlinear fashion. (It is difficult to control how users might click controls or enter or leave the forms or pages.) The interface control code must also interact with logic in the Business layer to validate user input, to perform any processing that's required, or to do any other business-related action.

Basically, the goal is to write interface control code that accepts user input and then provides it to the Business layer, where it can be validated, processed, or otherwise manipulated. The interface control code must then respond to the user by displaying the results of its interaction with the Business layer. Was the user's data valid? If not, what was wrong with it? And so forth.

In .NET, the interface control code is almost always event-driven. WPF and Windows Forms code is all about responding to events as the user types and clicks the form, and ASP.NET code is all about responding to events as the browser round-trips the user's actions back to the web server. Although WPF, Windows Forms, and ASP.NET technologies make heavy use of objects, the code that is typically written for the Interface Control isn't object-oriented as much as procedural and event-based.

That said, there's great value in creating frameworks and reusable components that support a particular type of interface. When creating a WPF or Windows Forms interface, developers can make use of numerous object-oriented techniques to simplify the creation, display, and management of the forms. When creating a web interface, developers can use ASP.NET master pages, user controls, and custom server controls to provide reusable components that simplify page development.

Because there's such a wide variety of interface styles and approaches, I won't spend much time dealing with interface development or frameworks in this book. Instead, I'll focus on simplifying the creation of the business logic and data access layers, which are required for any type of interface.

Business Logic

Business logic includes all business rules, data validation, manipulation, processing, and authorization for the application. One definition from Microsoft, which has since been taking down from MSDN, is as follows: "The combination of validation edits, login verifications, database lookups, policies, and algorithmic transformations that constitute an enterprise's way of doing business."

■ **Note** Again, while you may implement validation logic to run in a browser or other external client, you can't trust that code. You must view the logic that runs under your control in the Business layer as being the only *real* validation logic.

The business logic *must* reside in a separate layer from the interface code. While you may choose to duplicate some of this logic in your interface control code to provide a richer user experience, the Business layer must implement all the business logic, because it is the only point of central control and maintainability.

I believe that this particular separation between the responsibilities of the Business layer and Interface Control layer is absolutely critical if you want to gain the benefits of increased maintainability and reusability. This is because any business logic that creeps into the Interface or Interface Control layers will reside within a *specific* interface and will not be available to any other interfaces that you might create later.

Any business logic written into, say, a WPF interface is useless to a web or service interface, and must therefore be written into those as well. This instantly leads to duplicated code, which is a maintenance nightmare. You can separate these two layers through techniques such as clearly defined procedural models or object-oriented design and programming. In this book, I'll show how to use object-oriented concepts to help separate the business logic from the interface.

It is important to recognize that a typical application will use business logic in a couple of different ways. Most applications have some user interaction, such as forms in which the user views or enters data into the system. Most applications also have some very non-interactive processes, such as posting invoices, relieving inventory, or calculating insurance rates.

Ideally, the Business layer will be used in a very rich and interactive way when the user is entering data directly into the application. For instance, when a user is entering a sales order, she expects that the validation of data, the calculation of tax, and the subtotaling of the order will happen literally as she types. This implies that the Business layer can be physically deployed on the client workstation or on the web server to provide the high levels of interactivity users desire.

To support non-interactive processes, on the other hand, the Business layer often needs to be deployed onto an application server, or as close to the database server as possible. For instance, the calculation of an insurance rate can involve extensive database lookups along with quite a bit of complex business processing. This is the kind of thing that should occur behind the scenes on a server, not on a user's desktop.

Fortunately, it is possible to deploy a logical layer on multiple physical tiers. Doing this does require some up-front planning and technical design, as you'll see in Chapter 2. The end result, however, is a single Business layer that is potentially deployed on both the client workstation (or web server) and on the application server. This allows the application to provide high levels of interactivity when the user is working directly with the application, and efficient back-end processing for non-interactive processes.

Data Access

Data access code interacts with the Data Storage and Management layer to retrieve, insert, update, and remove information. The Data Access layer doesn't actually manage or store the data; it merely provides an interface between the business logic and the database.

Data access gets its own logical layer for much the same reason that the interface is split from interface control. In some cases, data access will occur on a machine that's physically separate from the one on which the interface and/or business logic is running. In other cases, data access code will run on the same machine as the business logic (or even the interface) in order to improve performance or fault tolerance.

■ **Note** It may sound odd to say that putting the Data Access layer on the same machine as the business logic can *increase* fault tolerance, but consider the case of web farms, in which each web server is identical to all the others. Putting the data access code on the web servers provides automatic redundancy of the Data Access layer along with the Business and Interface layers.

Adding an extra physical tier just to do the data access makes fault tolerance harder to implement, because it increases the number of tiers in which redundancy needs to be implemented. As a side effect, adding more physical tiers also reduces performance for a single user, so it's not something that should be done lightly.

Logically defining data access as a separate layer enforces a separation between the business logic and any interaction with a database (or any other data source). This separation provides the flexibility to choose later whether to run the data access code on the same machine as the business logic, or on a separate machine. It also makes it much easier to change data sources without affecting the application. This is important because it enables switching from one database vendor to another at some point.

This separation is useful for another reason: Microsoft has a habit of changing data access technologies every three years or so, meaning that it is necessary to rewrite the data access code to keep up (remember DAO, RDO, ADO 1.0, ADO 2.0, ADO.NET, and now LINQ and the ADO.NET Entity Framework?). By isolating the data access code into a specific layer, the impact of these changes is limited to a smaller part of the application.

Data access mechanisms are typically implemented as a set of services; each service is a procedure that the business logic calls to retrieve, insert, update, or delete data. Although these services are often constructed using objects, it's important to recognize that the designs for an effective Data Access layer are really quite procedural in nature. Attempts to force more object-oriented designs for relational database access often result in increased complexity or decreased performance. I think the best approach is to implement the data access as a set of methods, but encapsulate those methods within objects to keep them organized logically.

■ **Note** If you're using an object database instead of a relational database, then of course the data access code may be very object-oriented. Few of us get such an opportunity, however, because almost all data is stored in relational databases.

Sometimes the Data Access layer can be as simple as a series of methods that use ADO.NET directly to retrieve or store data. In other circumstances, the Data Access layer is more complex, providing a more abstract or even metadata-driven way to get at data. In these cases, the Data Access layer can contain a lot of complex code to provide this more abstract data access scheme. The framework created in this book doesn't restrict how you implement your Data Access layer. The examples in the book use LINQ to SQL, but you could also use ADO.NET or use some other metadata-driven Data Access layer directly if you prefer.

Another common role for the Data Access layer is to provide mapping between the object-oriented business logic and the relational data in a data store. A good object-oriented model is almost never the same as a good relational database model. Objects often contain data from multiple tables, or even from multiple databases; or conversely, multiple objects in the model can represent a single table. The process of taking the data from the tables in a relational model and getting it into the object-oriented model is called *object-relational mapping* (ORM), and I'll have more to say on the subject in Chapter 2.

Data Storage and Management

Finally, there's the Data Storage and Management layer. Database servers such as SQL Server and Oracle often handle these tasks, but increasingly, other applications may provide this functionality, too, via technologies such as XML-based services.

What's key about this layer is that it handles the physical creation, retrieval, update, and deletion of data. This is different from the Data Access layer, which *requests* the creation, retrieval, update, and deletion of data. The Data Storage and Management layer actually *implements* these operations within the context of a database or a set of files, and so on.

The business logic (via the Data Access layer) invokes the Data Storage and Management layer, but the layer often includes additional logic to validate the data and its relationship to other data. Sometimes, this is true relational data modeling from a database; other times, it's the application of business logic from an external application. What this means is that a typical Data Storage and Management layer will include business logic that is also implemented in the Business layer. This time the replication is unavoidable because relational databases are designed to enforce data integrity, and that's just another form of business logic.

In summary, whether you're using stored procedures in SQL Server, or service calls to another application, you typically handle data storage and management by creating a set of services or procedures that you can call as needed. Like the Data Access layer, it's important to recognize that the designs for data storage and management are typically very procedural.

Table 1-1 summarizes the five layers and their roles.

Table 1-1. *The Five Logical Layers and the Roles They Provide*

Layer	Roles
Interface	Renders display and collects user input.
Interface Control	Acts as an intermediary between the user and the business logic, taking user input and providing it to the business logic, then returning results to the user.
Business Logic	Provides all business rules, validation, manipulation, processing, and security for the application.
Data Access	Acts as an intermediary between the business logic and data management. Also encapsulates and contains all knowledge of data access technologies (such as LINQ to SQL), databases, and data structures.
Data Storage and Management	Physically creates, retrieves, updates, and deletes data in a persistent data store.

Everything I've talked about to this point is part of a *logical* architecture. Now it's time to move on and see how you can apply it in various *physical* configurations.

Applying the Logical Architecture

Given this 5-layer logical architecture, it should be possible to configure it into one, two, three, four, or five physical tiers in order to gain performance, scalability, security, or fault tolerance to various degrees, and in various combinations.

■ **Note** In this discussion, I assume that you have total flexibility to configure which logical layer runs where. In some cases, technical issues may prevent the physical separation of some layers. As I noted earlier, you need to strike a balance between flexibility and capability.

I want to discuss a few physical configurations to illustrate how the logical model works. These are common and important setups that are encountered on a day-to-day basis.

Optimal Performance Smart Client

When so much focus is placed on distributed systems, it's easy to forget the value of a single-tier solution. Point of sale, sales force automation, and many other types of applications often run in stand-alone environments. However, the benefits of the logical n-layer architecture are still desirable in terms of maintainability and code reuse.

It probably goes without saying that everything can be installed on a single client workstation. An optimal performance smart client is usually implemented using WPF or Windows Forms for the interface, with the business logic and data access code running in the same process and talking to a Microsoft SQL Server Express or a Microsoft SQL Server Compact Edition database. The fact that the system is deployed on a single physical tier doesn't compromise the logical architecture and separation, as shown in Figure 1-2.

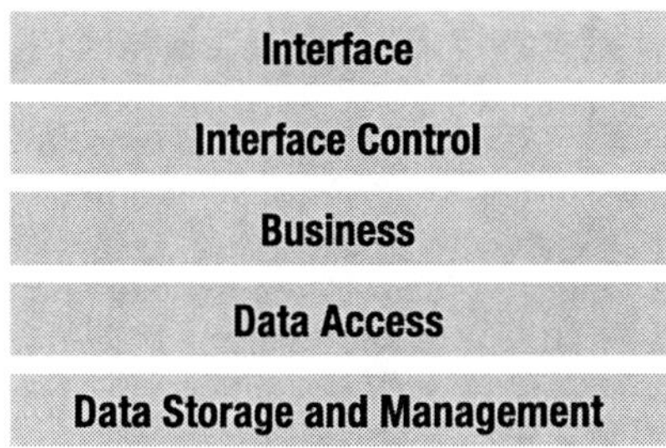

Figure 1-2. *The five logical layers running on a single machine*

It's important to remember that n-layer systems can run on a single machine in order to support the wide range of applications that require stand-alone machines. It's also worth pointing out that this is basically the same as a 2-tier, "fat-client" physical architecture; the only difference is that in a 2-tier physical architecture, the Data Storage and Management layer would be running on a central database server, such as SQL Server or Oracle, as shown in Figure 1-3.

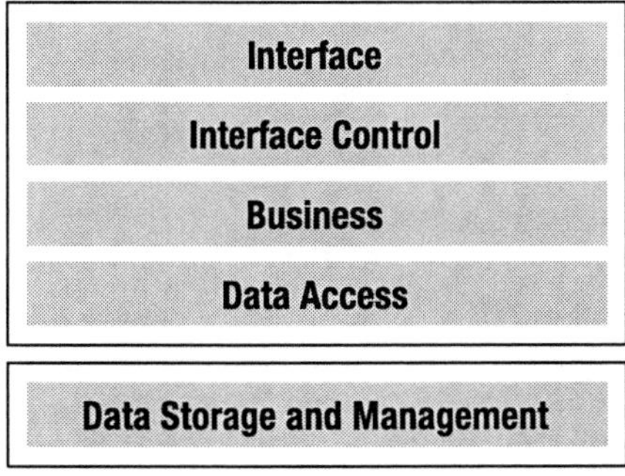

Figure 1-3. *The five logical layers with a separate database server*

Other than the location of the data storage, this is identical to the single-tier configuration, and typically the switch from single-tier to 2-tier revolves around little more than changing the database connection string.

High-Scalability Smart Client

Single-tier configurations are good for stand-alone environments, but they don't scale well. To support multiple users, it is common to use 2-tier configurations. I've seen 2-tier configurations support more than 350 concurrent users against SQL Server with very acceptable performance.

Going further, it is possible to trade performance to gain scalability by moving the Data Access layer to a separate machine. Single-tier or 2-tier configurations give the best performance, but they don't scale as well as a 3-tier configuration would. A good rule of thumb is that if you have more than 50 to 100 concurrent users, you can benefit by making use of a separate server to handle the Data Access layer.

Another reason for moving the Data Access layer to an application server is security. Since the Data Access layer contains the code that interacts directly with the database, the machine on which it runs must have credentials to access the database server. Rather than having those credentials on the client workstation, they can be moved to an application server. This way, the user's computer won't have the credentials to interact directly with the database server, thus increasing security.

It is also possible to put the Business layer on the application server. This is useful for non-interactive processes such as batch updates or data-intensive business algorithms. Yet, at the same time, most applications allow for user interaction, so there is a definite need to have the Business layer running on the client workstation to provide high levels of interactivity for the user.

As discussed earlier in the chapter, it is possible to deploy the same logical layer onto multiple physical tiers. Using this idea, you can put the Data Access layer on an application server, and the Business layer on *both* the client workstation and the application server, as shown in Figure 1-4.

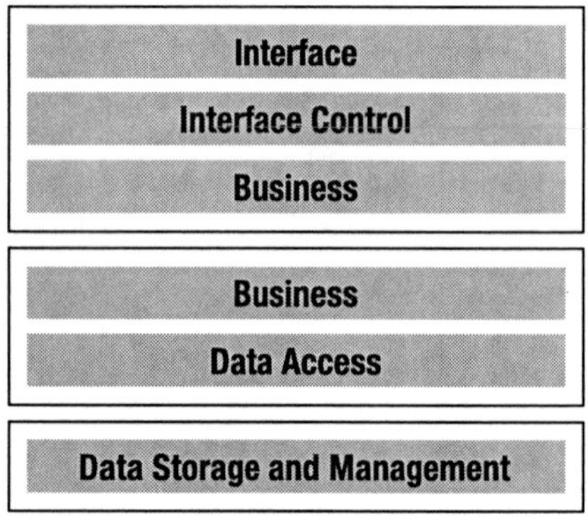

Figure 1-4. *The five logical layers with separate application and database servers*

Putting the Data Access layer on the application server centralizes all access to the database on a single machine. In .NET, if the connections to the database for all users are made using the same user ID and password, you'll get the benefits of *connection pooling* for all your users. What this means immediately is that there will be far fewer connections to the database than there would have been if each client machine had connected directly. The actual reduction depends on the specific application, but often it means supporting 150 to 200 concurrent users with just two or three database connections.

Of course, all user requests now go across an extra network hop, thereby causing increased latency (and therefore decreased performance). This performance cost translates into a huge scalability gain, however, because this architecture can handle many more concurrent users than a 2-tier physical configuration.

With the Business layer deployed on both the client and server, the application is able to fully exploit the strengths of both machines. Validation and a lot of other business processing can run on the client workstation to provide a rich and highly interactive experience for the user, while non-interactive processes can efficiently run on the application server.

If well designed, such an architecture can support *thousands* of concurrent users with adequate performance.

Optimal Performance Web Client

As with WPF or Windows Forms applications, the best performance is received in web-based applications by minimizing the number of physical tiers. However, the trade-off in a web scenario is different: in this case, it is possible to improve performance and scalability at the same time, but at the cost of security, as I will demonstrate.

To get optimal performance in a web application, it is desirable to run most of the code in a single process on a single machine, as shown in Figure 1-5.

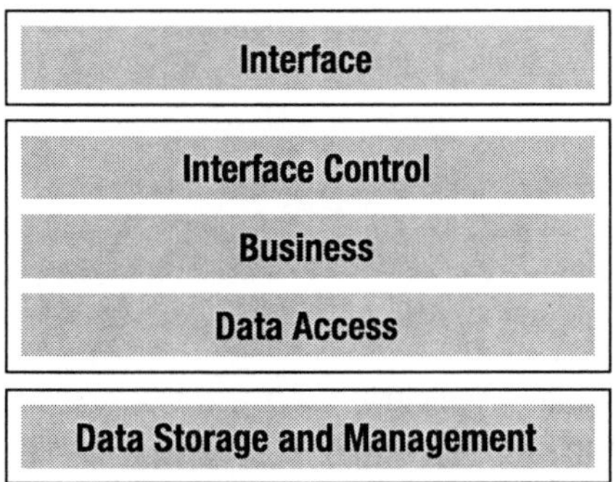

Figure 1-5. *The five logical layers as used for web applications*

The Interface layer must be physically separate because it's running in a browser, but the Interface Control, Business, and Data Access layers can all run on the same machine, in the same process. In some cases, you might even put the Data Storage and Management layer on the same physical machine, though this is only suitable for smaller applications.

This minimizes network and communication overhead and optimizes performance. Figure 1-6 shows how it is possible to get good scalability, because the web server can be part of a web farm in which all the web servers are running the same code.

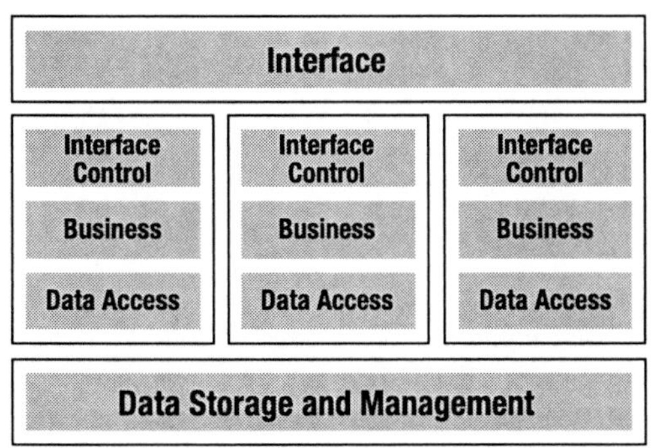

Figure 1-6. *The five logical layers deployed on a load-balanced web farm*

This setup provides good database-connection pooling, because each web server will be (potentially) servicing hundreds of concurrent users, and all database connections on a web server are pooled.

Unless the database server is getting overwhelmed with connections from the web servers in the web farm, a separate application server will rarely provide gains in scalability. If a separate application server is needed, there will be a reduction in performance because of the additional physical tier. (Hopefully, there will be a gain in scalability, because the application server can consolidate database connections across all the web servers.) It is important to consider fault tolerance in this case, because redundant application servers may be needed in order to avoid a point of failure.

Another reason for implementing an application server is to increase security, and that's the topic of the next section.

High-Security Web Client

As discussed in the earlier section on security, you'll have many projects that dictate that a web server can never talk directly to a database. The web server must run in a demilitarized zone (DMZ), sandwiched between the external firewall and a second internal firewall. The web server must communicate with another server through the internal firewall in order to interact with the database or any other internal systems.

As with the 3-tier Windows client scenario, there is tremendous benefit to also having the Business layer deployed on both the web server and the application server. Such a deployment allows the web interface control code to interact closely with the business logic when appropriate, while non-interactive processes can simply run on the application server. This deployment is illustrated in Figure 1-7, in which the dashed lines represent the firewalls.

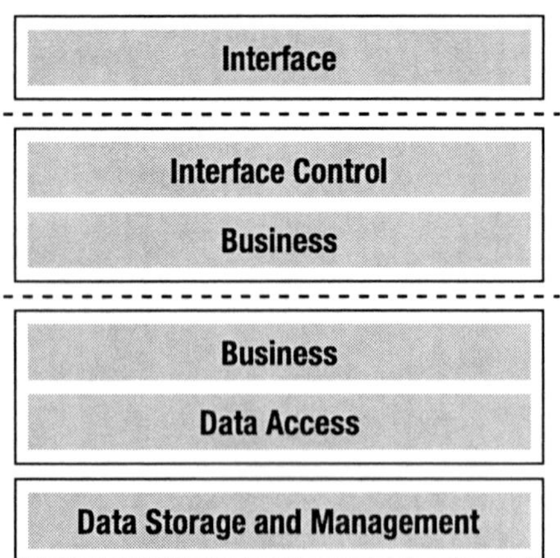

Figure 1-7. *The five logical layers deployed in a secure web configuration*

Splitting out the Data Access layer and running it on a separate application server increases the security of the application. However, this comes at the cost of performance—as discussed earlier, this configuration will typically cause a performance degradation of around 50 percent. Scalability, on the other hand, is fine: like the first web configuration, you can achieve scalability by implementing a web farm in which each web server runs the same interface control and business logic code, as shown in Figure 1-8.

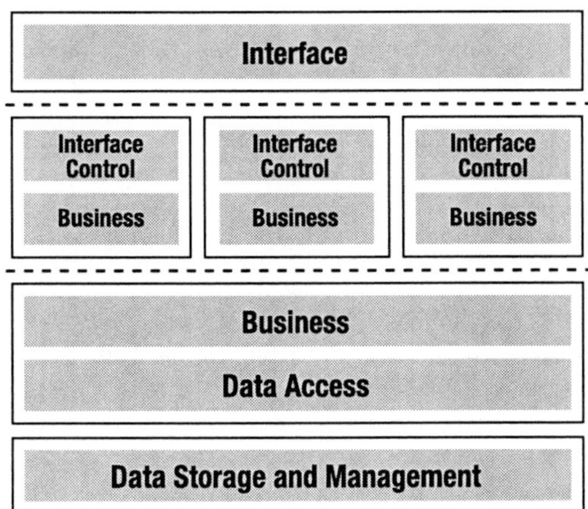

Figure 1-8. *The five logical layers in a secured environment with a web farm*

The Way Ahead

After implementing the framework to support this 5-layer architecture, I'll create a sample application with three different interfaces: WPF, web, and XML-based Windows Communication Foundation (WCF) services. This will give you the opportunity to see firsthand how the framework supports the following models:

- High-scalability smart client
- Optimal performance web client
- Optimal performance web service

Due to the way the framework is implemented, switching to any of the other models just discussed will require only configuration file changes. The result is that you can easily adapt your application to any of the physical configurations without having to change your code.

Managing Business Logic

At this point, you should have a good understanding of logical and physical architectures and how you can configure a 5-layer logical architecture into various n-tier physical architectures. In one way or another, all of these layers will use or interact with the application's data. That's obviously the case for the Data Storage and Management and Data Access layers, but the Business layer must validate, calculate, and manipulate data; the Interface Control layer transfers data between the Business and Interface layers (often performing formatting or using the data to make navigational choices); and the Interface layer displays data to the user and collects new data as it's entered.

In an ideal world, all of the business logic would exist in the Business layer, but in reality, this is virtually impossible to achieve. In a web-based application, validation logic is often included in the Interface layer, so that the user gets a more interactive experience in the browser. Unfortunately, any validation that's done in the web browser is unreliable, because it's too easy for a malicious user to bypass that validation. Thus, any validation done in the browser must be rechecked in the Business layer as well.

Similarly, most databases enforce data integrity, and often some other rules, too. Furthermore, the Data Access layer often includes business logic to decide when and how data should be stored or retrieved from databases and other data sources. In almost any application, to a greater or a lesser extent, business logic gets scattered across all the layers.

There's one key truth here that's important: for each piece of application data, there's a fixed set of business logic associated with that data. If the application is to function properly, the business logic must be applied to that data at least once. Why "at least"? Well, in most applications, some of the business logic is applied more than once. For example, a validation rule applied in the Interface layer can be reapplied in the Interface Control layer or Business layer before data is sent to the database for storage. In some cases, the database includes code to recheck the value as well.

Now, I'd like to look at some of the more common options. I'll start with three popular (but flawed) approaches. Then I'll discuss a compromise solution that's enabled through the use of mobile objects, such as the ones supported by the framework I'll create later in the book.

Potential Business Logic Locations

Figure 1-9 illustrates common locations for validation and manipulation business logic in a typical application. Most applications have the same logic in at least a couple of these locations.

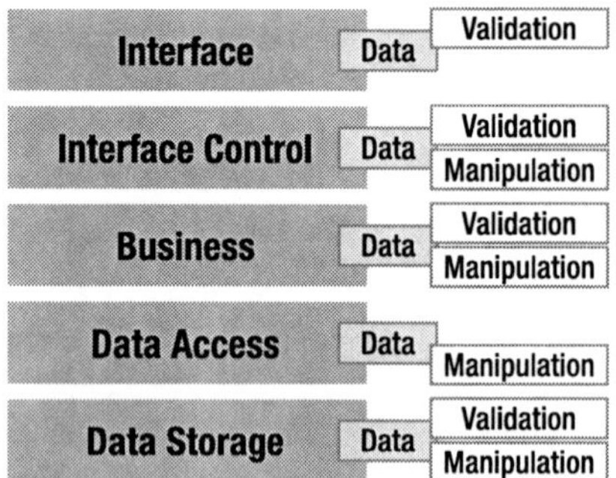

Figure 1-9. *Common locations for business logic in applications*

Business logic is put in a web Interface layer to give the user a more interactive experience—and put into a Windows Interface layer for the same reason. The business logic is rechecked on the web server because the browser isn't trustworthy. And database administrators put the logic into the database (via stored procedures and other database constructs) because they don't trust any application developers.

The result of all this validation is a lot of duplicated code, all of which has to be debugged, maintained, and somehow kept in sync as the business needs (and thus logic) change over time. In the real world, the logic is almost never *really* kept in sync, and so developers must constantly debug and maintain the code in a near-futile effort to make all of these redundant bits of logic agree with each other.

One solution is to force all of the logic into a single layer, thereby making the other layers as "dumb" as possible. There are various approaches to this, although (as you'll see) none of them provide an optimal solution.

Another solution is to dynamically generate the validation logic for the Interface or Interface Control layer based on metadata provided from the Business layer. This requires more work in the interface layers, but can increase maintainability overall.

Business Logic in the Data Storage and Management Layer

The classic approach is to put all logic into the database as the single, central repository. The interface then allows the user to enter absolutely anything (because any validation would be redundant), and the Business layer now resides inside the database. The Data Access layer does nothing but move the data into and out of the database, as shown in Figure 1-10.

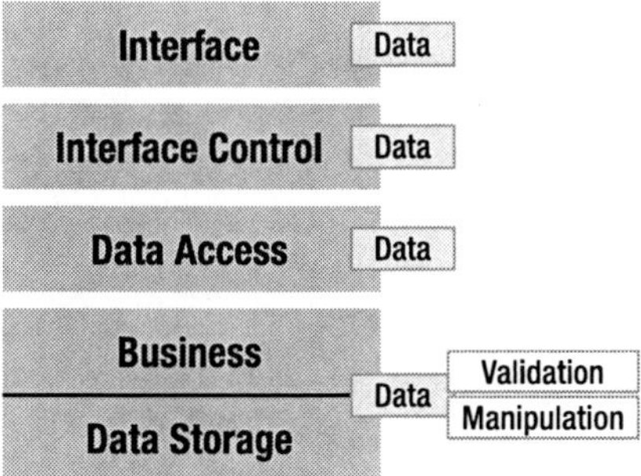

Figure 1-10. *Validation and business logic in the Data Storage and Management layer*

The advantage of this approach is that the logic is centralized, but the drawbacks are plentiful. For starters, the user experience is totally non-interactive. Users can't get any results, or even confirmation that their data is valid, without round-tripping the data to the database for processing. The database server becomes a performance bottleneck, because it's the only thing doing any actual work. Unfortunately, the hardest physical tier to scale up for more users is the database server, since it is difficult to use load-balancing techniques on it. The only real alternative is to buy bigger and bigger server machines.

Business Logic in the Interface Control Layer

Another common approach is to put all of the business logic into the interface control code. The data is validated and manipulated by the interface control code, and the Data Storage and Management layer just stores the data. This approach, as shown in Figure 1-11, is common in both Windows and web environments, and has the advantage that the business logic is centralized into a single tier (and of course, one can write the business logic in a language such as C# or VB .NET).

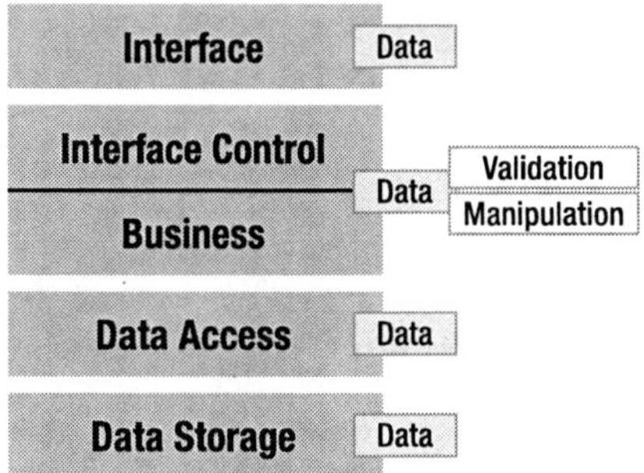

Figure 1-11. *Business logic deployed with only the Interface Control layer*

Unfortunately, in practice, the business logic ends up being scattered throughout the application, thereby decreasing readability and making maintenance more difficult. Even more importantly, business logic in one form or page isn't reusable when subsequent forms or pages are created that use the same data. Furthermore, in a web environment, this architecture also leads to a totally non-interactive user experience, because no validation can occur in the browser. The user must transmit his data to the web server for any validation or manipulation to take place.

■ **Note** ASP.NET validation controls at least allow for basic data validation in the interface, with that validation automatically extended to the browser by the ASP.NET technology itself. Though not a total solution, this is a powerful feature that does help.

Business Logic in the Middle (Merged Business and Data Access Layers)

Still another option is the classic UNIX client/server approach, whereby the Business and Data Access layers are merged, keeping the Interface, Interface Control, and Data Storage and Management layers as "dumb" as possible (see Figure 1-12).

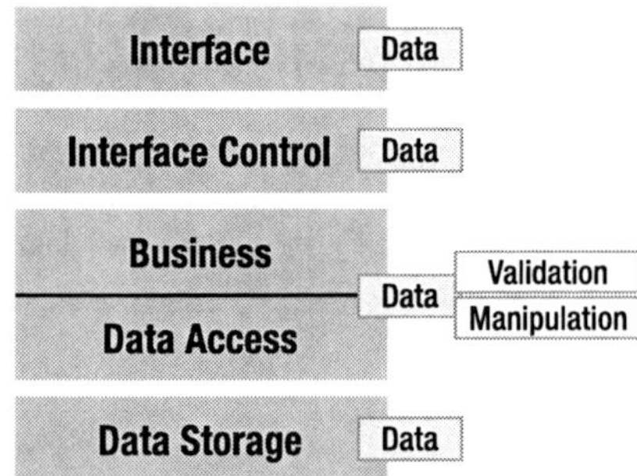

Figure 1-12. *Business logic deployed only on the application server*

Unfortunately, once again, this approach falls afoul of the non-interactive user experience problem: the data must round-trip to the Business/Data Access layer for any validation or manipulation. This is especially problematic if the Business/Data Access layer is running on a separate application server, because then you're faced with network latency and contention issues, too. Also, the central application server can become a performance bottleneck, because it's the only machine doing any work for all the users of the application.

Sharing Business Logic Across Tiers

I wish this book included the secret that allows you to write all your logic in one central location, thereby avoiding all of these awkward issues. Unfortunately, that's not possible with today's technology: putting the business logic only on the client, application server, or database server is problematic, for all the reasons given earlier. But something needs to be done about it, so what's left?

What's left is the possibility of centralizing the business logic in a Business layer that's deployed on the client (or web server), so that it's accessible to the Interface Control layer, and in a Business layer that's deployed on the application server, so that it's able to interact efficiently with the Data Access layer. The end result is the best of both worlds: a rich and interactive user experience and efficient high-performance back-end processing when interacting with the database (or other data source).

In the simple cases in which there is no application server, the Business layer is deployed only once: on the client workstation or web server, as shown in Figure 1-13.

Ideally, this business logic will run on the same machine as the interface control code when interacting with the user, but on the same machine as the data access code when interacting with the database. (As discussed earlier, all of this could be on one machine or a number of different machines, depending on your physical architecture.) It must provide a friendly interface that the interface developer can use to invoke any validation and manipulation logic, and it must also work efficiently with the Data Access layer to get data in and out of storage.

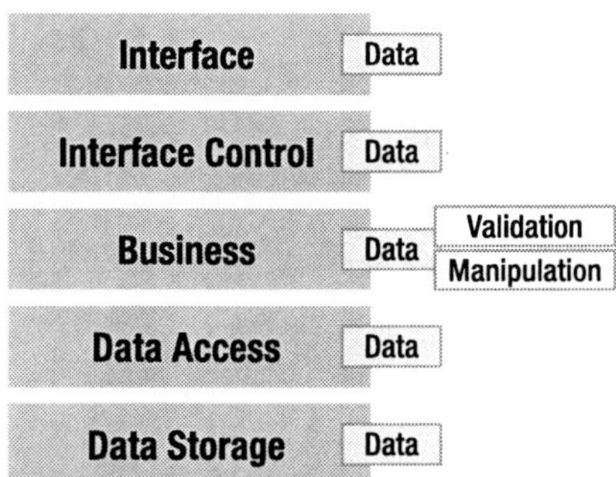

Figure 1-13. *Business logic centralized in the Business layer*

The tools for addressing this seemingly intractable set of requirements are *mobile business objects* that encapsulate the application's data along with its related business logic. It turns out that a properly constructed business object can move around the network from machine to machine with almost no effort on your part. The .NET Framework itself handles the details, and you can focus on the business logic and data.

By properly designing and implementing mobile business objects, you allow the .NET Framework to pass your objects across the network *by value*, thereby copying them automatically from one machine to another. This means that with little extra code, you can have your business logic and business data move to the machine where the Interface Control layer is running, and then shift to the machine where the Data Access layer is running when data access is required.

At the same time, if you're running the Interface Control and Data Access layers on the same machine, then the .NET Framework won't move or copy your business objects. They're used directly by both tiers with no performance cost or extra overhead. You don't have to do anything to make this happen, either—.NET automatically detects that the object doesn't need to be copied or moved, and thus takes no extra action.

The Business layer becomes portable, flexible, and mobile, and adapts to the physical environment in which you deploy the application. Due to this, you're able to support a variety of physical n-tier architectures with one code base, whereby your business objects contain no extra code to support the various possible deployment scenarios. What little code you need to implement to support the movement of your objects from machine to machine will be encapsulated in a framework, leaving the business developer to focus purely on the development of business logic.

Business Objects

Having decided to use business objects and take advantage of .NET's ability to move objects around the network automatically, it's now time to discuss business objects in more detail. I will discuss exactly what they are and how they can help you to centralize the business logic pertaining to your data.

The primary goal when designing any kind of software object is to create an abstract representation of some entity or concept. In ADO.NET, for example, a `DataTable` object represents a tabular set of data. `DataTables` provide an abstract and consistent mechanism by which you can work with *any* tabular data. Likewise, a Windows Forms `TextBox` control is an object that represents the concept of displaying and entering data. From the application's perspective, there is no need to have any understanding of how the control is rendered on the screen, or how the user interacts with it. It's just an object that includes a `Text` property and a handful of interesting events.

Key to successful object design is the concept of *encapsulation*. This means that an object is a black box: it contains logic and data, but the user of the object doesn't know *what* data or *how* the logic actually works. All the user can do is interact with the object.

■ **Note** Properly designed objects encapsulate both behavior or logic and the data required by that logic.

If objects are abstract representations of entities or concepts that encapsulate both data and its related logic, what then are *business objects*?

■ **Note** Business objects are different from regular objects only in terms of what they represent.

Object-oriented applications are created to address problems of one sort or another. In the course of doing so, a variety of different objects are often used. Some of these objects will have no direct connection with the problem at hand (`DataTable` and `TextBox` objects, for example, are just abstract representations of computer concepts). However, others will be closely related to the area or *domain* in which you're working. If the objects are related to the business for which you're developing an application, then they're business objects.

For instance, if you're creating an order entry system, your business domain will include things such as customers, orders, and products. Each of these will likely become business objects within your order entry application—the `Order` object, for example, will provide an abstract representation of the order being placed by a customer.

■ **Note** Business objects provide an abstract representation of entities or concepts that are part of the business or problem domain.

Business Objects As Smart Data

I've already discussed the drawbacks of putting business logic into the Interface Control layer, but I haven't thoroughly discussed the drawback of keeping the data in a generic representation such as a `DataSet` or data transfer object (DTO). The data in a `DataSet` (or a DTO, array, or XML document) is unintelligent, unprotected, and generally unsafe. There's nothing to prevent anyone from putting invalid data into any of these containers, and there's nothing to ensure that the business logic behind one form in the application will interact with the data in the same way as the business logic behind another form.

A `DataSet` or an XML document with an XSD (XML Schema Definition) might ensure that text cannot be entered where a number is required, or that a number cannot be entered where a date is required. At best, it might enforce some basic relational-integrity rules. However, there's no way to ensure that the values match other criteria, or that calculations or other processing is done properly against the data, without involving other objects. The data in a `DataSet`, array, or XML document isn't self-aware; it's not able to apply business rules or handle business manipulation or processing of the data.

The data in a business object, however, is what I like to call *smart data*. The object not only contains the data, but it also includes all the business logic that goes along with that data. Any attempt to work with the data must go through this business logic. In this arrangement, there is much greater assurance that business rules, manipulation, calculations, and other processing will be executed consistently everywhere in the application. In a sense, the data has become self-aware and can protect itself against incorrect usage.

In the end, an object doesn't care whether it's used by a WPF interface, a batch-processing routine, or a web service. The code using the object can do as it pleases; the object itself will ensure that all business rules are obeyed at all times.

Contrast this with a `DataSet` or an XML document, in which the business logic doesn't reside in the data container, but somewhere else—typically, a Windows or web form. If multiple forms or pages use this `DataSet`, there is no assurance that the business logic will be applied consistently. Even if you adopt a standard that says that interface developers must invoke methods from a centralized class to interact with the data, there's nothing preventing them from using the `DataSet` directly. This may happen accidentally, or because it was simply easier or faster to use the `DataSet` than to go through some centralized routine.

■ Note With consistent use of business objects, there's no way to bypass the business logic. The only way to the data is through the object, and the object always enforces the rules.

So, a business object that represents an invoice will include not only the data pertaining to the invoice, but also the logic to calculate taxes and amounts due. The object should understand how to post itself to a ledger and how to perform any other accounting tasks that are required. Rather than passing raw invoice data around and having the business logic scattered throughout the application, it is possible to pass an `Invoice` object around. The entire application can share not only the data, but also its associated logic. Smart data through objects can dramatically increase the ability to reuse code and can decrease software maintenance costs.

Anatomy of a Business Object

Putting all of these pieces together, you get an object that has an interface (a set of properties and methods), some implementation code (the business logic behind those properties and methods), and state (the data). This is illustrated in Figure 1-14.

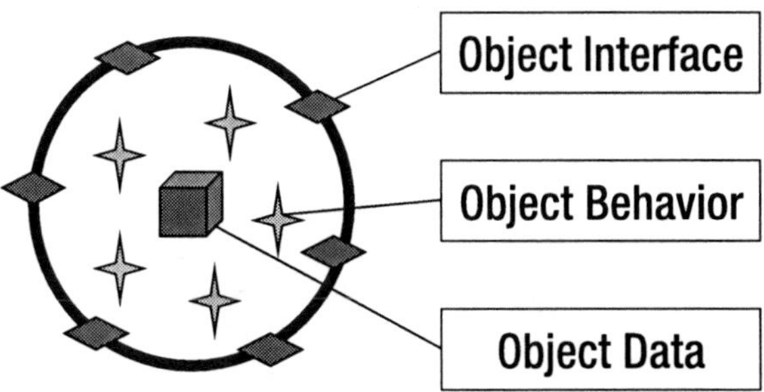

Figure 1-14. *A business object composed of state, implementation, and interface*

The hiding of the data and the implementation code behind the interface are keys to the successful creation of a business object. If the users of an object are allowed to "see inside" it, they will be tempted to cheat and to interact with the logic or data in unpredictable ways. This danger is the reason why it is important to take care when using the `public` keyword as you build your classes.

Any property, method, event, or field marked as `public` is available to the users of objects created from the class. For example, you might create a simple class such as the following:

```
public class Project
{
  private Guid _id = Guid.NewGuid();
  public Guid Id
  {
    get { return _id; }
  }

  private string _name = string.Empty;
  public string Name
  {
    get { return _name; }
    set
    {
      if (value == null) value = string.Empty;
      if(value.Length > 50)
        throw new Exception("Name too long");
      _name = value;
    }
  }
}
```

This defines a business object that represents a project of some sort. All that is known at the moment is that these projects have an ID value and a name. Notice, though, that the fields containing this data are `private`—you don't want the users of your object to be able to alter or access them directly. If they were `public`, the values could be changed without the object's knowledge or permission. (The `_name` field could be given a value that's longer than the maximum of 50 characters, for example.)

The properties, on the other hand, are `public`. They provide a controlled access point to the object. The `Id` property is read-only, so the users of the object can't change it. The `Name` property allows its value to be changed, but enforces a business rule by ensuring that the length of the new value doesn't exceed 50 characters.

■ **Note** None of these concepts are unique to business objects—they're common to all objects and are central to object-oriented design and programming.

Mobile Objects

Unfortunately, directly applying the kind of object-oriented design and programming I've been talking about so far is often difficult in today's complex computing environments. Object-oriented programs are almost always designed with the assumption that all the objects in an application can interact with each other with no performance penalty. This is true when all the objects are running in the same process on the same computer, but it's not at all true when the objects might be running in different processes or even on different computers.

Earlier in this chapter, I discussed various physical architectures in which different parts of an application might run on different machines. With a high-scalability smart client architecture, for example, there will be a client, an application server, and a data server. With a high-security web client architecture, there will be a client, a web server, an application server, and a data server. Parts of the application will run on each of these machines, interacting with each other as needed.

In these distributed architectures, you can't use a straightforward object-oriented design, because any communication between classic fine-grained objects on one machine and similar objects on another machine will incur network latency and overhead. This translates into a performance problem that simply can't be ignored. To overcome this problem, most distributed applications haven't used object-oriented designs. Instead, they consist of a set of procedural code running on each machine, with the data kept in a `DataSet`, an array, or an XML document that's passed around from machine to machine.

This isn't to say that object-oriented design and programming are irrelevant in distributed environments—just that it becomes complicated. To minimize the complexity, most distributed applications are object-oriented *within a tier*, but between tiers they follow a procedural or service-based model. The end result is that the application as a whole is neither object-oriented nor procedural, but a blend of both.

Perhaps the most common architecture for such applications is to have the Data Access layer retrieve the data from the database into a `DataSet`. The `DataSet` is then returned to the client (or the web server). The code in the forms or pages then interacts with the `DataSet` directly, as shown in Figure 1-15.

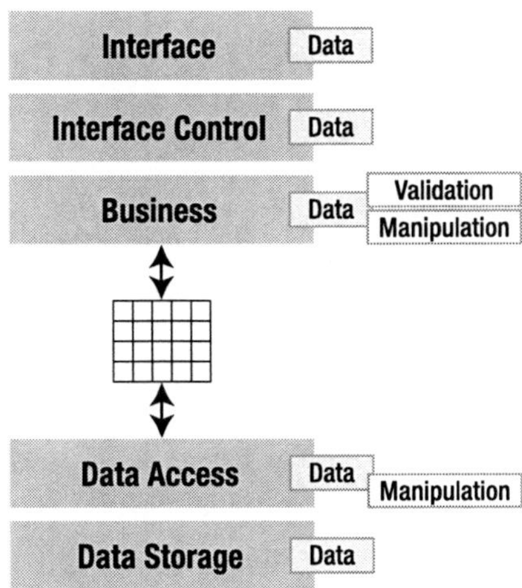

Figure 1-15. *Passing a DataSet between the Business and Data Access layers*

This approach has the maintenance and code-reuse flaws that I've talked about, but the fact is that it gives pretty good performance in most cases. Also, it doesn't hurt that most programmers are pretty familiar with the idea of writing code to manipulate a `DataSet`, so the techniques involved are well understood, thus speeding up development.

A decision to stick with an object-oriented approach should be undertaken carefully. It's all too easy to compromise the object-oriented design by taking the data out of the objects running on one machine, sending the raw data across the network, and allowing other objects to use that data outside the context of the objects and business logic. Such an approach would break the encapsulation provided by the logical Business layer.

Mobile objects are all about sending smart data (objects) from one machine to another, rather than sending raw data.

Through its WCF, serialization, and deployment technologies, the .NET Framework contains direct support for the concept of mobile objects. Given this ability, you can have your Data Access layer (running on an application server) create a business object and load it with data from the database. You can then send that business object to the client machine (or web server), where the interface control code can use the object (as shown in Figure 1-16).

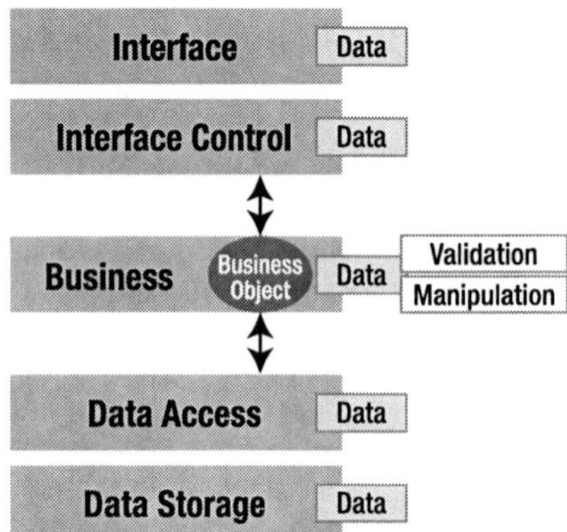

Figure 1-16. *Using a business object to centralize business logic*

In this architecture, smart data (in the form of a business object), rather than raw data, is sent to the client. Then the interface control code can use the same business logic as the data access code. This reduces maintenance, because you're not writing some business logic in the Data Access layer, and some other business logic in the Interface Control layer. Instead, all of the business logic is consolidated into a real, separate layer composed of business objects. These business objects will move across the network just like the `DataSet` did earlier, but they'll include the data *and* its related business logic—something the `DataSet` can't easily offer.

■ **Note** In addition, business objects will typically move across the network more efficiently than the `DataSet`. The approach in this book will use a binary transfer scheme that transfers data that is about 30 percent of the size of data transferred using the `DataSet`. Also, the business objects will contain far less metadata than the `DataSet`, further reducing the number of bytes transferred across the network.

Effectively, you're sharing the Business layer between the machine running the Data Access layer and the machine running the Interface Control layer. As long as there is support for mobile objects, this is an ideal solution: it provides code reuse, low maintenance costs, and high performance.

A New Logical Architecture

Being able to access the Business layer from both the Data Access layer and the Interface Control layer directly opens up a new way to view the logical architecture. Though the Business layer remains a separate concept, it's directly used by and tied into both the Interface Control and Data Access layers, as shown in Figure 1-17.

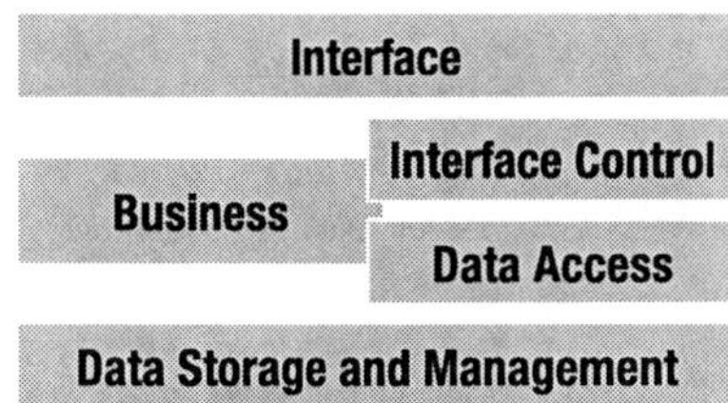

Figure 1-17. *The Business layer tied to the Interface Control and Data Access layers*

The Interface Control layer can interact directly with the objects in the Business layer, thereby relying on them to perform all validation, manipulation, and other processing of the data. Likewise, the Data Access layer can interact with the objects as the data is retrieved or stored.

If all the layers are running on a single machine (such as a smart client), then these parts will run in a single process and interact with each other with no network or cross-processing overhead. In more distributed physical configurations, the Business layer will run on both the client *and* the application server, as shown in Figure 1-18.

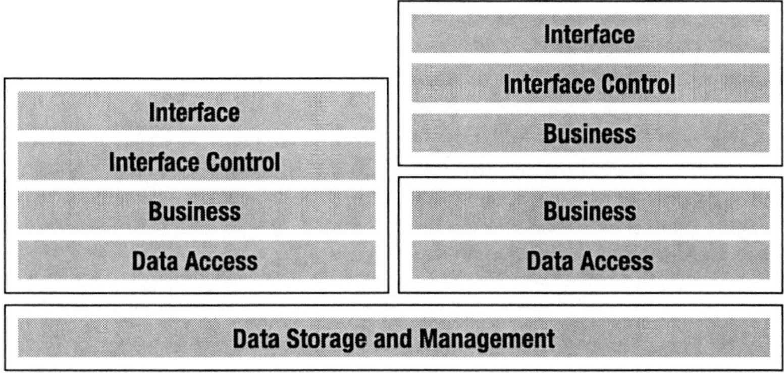

Figure 1-18. *Business logic shared between the Interface Control and Data Access layers*

Local, Anchored, and Mobile Objects

Normally, one might think of objects as being part of a single application, running on a single machine in a single process. A distributed application requires a broader perspective. Some of the objects might only run in a single process on a single machine. Others might run on one machine, but might be called by code running on another machine. Still others might be mobile objects, moving from machine to machine.

Local Objects

By default, .NET objects are *local*. This means that ordinary .NET objects aren't accessible from outside the process in which they were created. Without taking extra steps in your code, it isn't possible to pass objects to another process or another machine (a procedure known as *marshaling*), either by value or by reference.

Anchored Objects

In many technologies, objects are always passed *by reference*. This means that when you "pass" an object from one machine or process to another, what actually happens is that the object remains in the original process, and the other process or machine merely gets a pointer, or reference, back to the object, as shown in Figure 1-19.

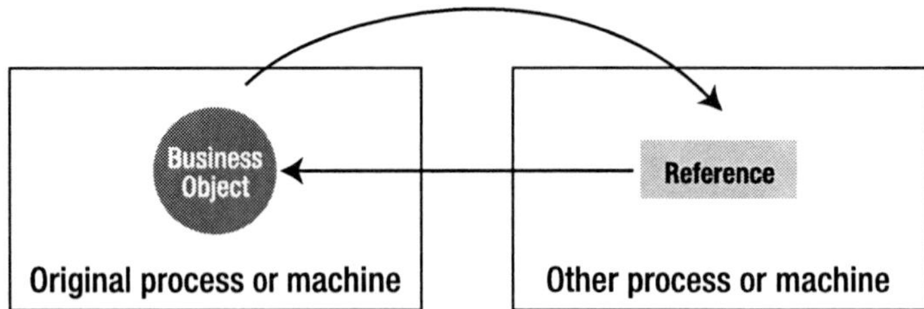

Figure 1-19. *Calling an object by reference*

By using this reference, the other machine can interact with the object. Because the object is still on the original machine, however, any property or method calls are sent across the network, and the results are returned back across the network. This scheme is only useful if the object is designed so it can be used with very few method calls; just one is ideal.

The recommended designs for Enterprise Services objects call for each method on the object to do all its work in a single method call for precisely this reason, thereby sacrificing "proper" object-oriented design in order to reduce latency. The same is effectively true for objects exposed to the network through WCF. Each method on a service object should do all its work, not relying on the client to have called other methods before or after calling this method.

These types of objects are stuck, or *anchored*, on the original machine or process where they were created. An anchored object never moves; it's accessed via references.

In .NET, you can create an anchored object in a couple different ways. If you're using WCF, the object will implement a service contract:

```
[ServiceContract]
public interface IMyService
{
  [OperationContract]
  void MyOperation();
}

public class MyServiceImplementation : IMyService
{
}
```

If you're using the older .NET Remoting technology, you create an anchored object by having it inherit from `MarshalByRefObject`:

```
public class MyAnchoredClass: MarshalByRefObject
{
}
```

Either way, the .NET Framework takes care of the details. Code running in another process or on another machine across the network can call the anchored object.

Mobile Objects

The concept of mobile objects relies on the idea that an object can be passed from one process to another, or from one machine to another, *by value*. This means that the object is physically copied from the original process or machine to the other process or machine, as shown in Figure 1-20.

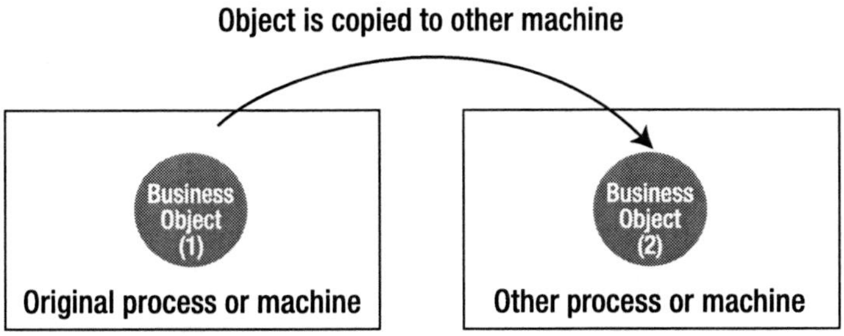

Figure 1-20. *Passing a physical copy of an object across the network*

The object starts on the left (instance 1) and is copied, or cloned, across the network to the right (instance 2).

Because the other machine gets a copy of the object, it can interact with the object locally. This means that there's effectively no performance overhead involved in calling properties or methods on the object—the only cost was in copying the object's data across the network in the first place.

Note One caveat here is that transferring a large object across the network can cause a performance problem. Returning a `DataSet` that contains a great deal of data can take a long time. This is true of all mobile objects, including business objects. You need to be careful in your application design in order to avoid retrieving very large sets of data.

Objects that can move from process to process or from machine to machine are *mobile objects*. Examples of mobile objects include the `DataSet` and the business objects created in this book. Mobile objects aren't stuck in a single place, but can move to where they're most needed.

To create one in .NET, add the `[Serializable]` attribute to your class definition. You may also optionally implement the `ISerializable` interface. I'll discuss this further in Chapter 2, but the following illustrates the start of a class that defines a mobile object:

```
[Serializable]
public class MyMobileClass
{
  private string _data;
}
```

When using WCF, you might choose instead to use the `DataContract` and `DataMember` attributes:

```
[DataContract]
public class MyMobileClass
{
  [DataMember]
  private string _data;
}
```

Either approach works, but the `Serializable` attribute is often better for this scenario because it uses an opt-out approach. All fields of the object are serialized unless you explicitly prevent the serialization. The `DataContract` approach is opt-in, so you must remember to mark every field for serialization. Forget one, and you've just introduced a hard-to-find bug.

Again, the .NET Framework takes care of the details, so an object of this type can be simply passed as a parameter to a method call or as the return value from a function. The object will be copied from the original machine to the machine where the method is running.

It is important to understand that the *code* for the object isn't moved across the network automatically. Before an object can move from machine to machine, both machines must have the .NET assembly containing the object's code installed. Only the object's serialized data is moved across the network by .NET. Installing the required assemblies is often handled by ClickOnce or other .NET deployment technologies.

When to Use Which Mechanism

The .NET Framework supports all the mechanisms just discussed, so you can choose to create your objects as local, anchored, or mobile, depending on the requirements of your design. As you might guess, there are good reasons for each approach.

WPF, Windows Forms, and ASP.NET objects are all local—they're inaccessible from outside the processes in which they were created. The assumption is that other applications shouldn't be allowed to just reach into your program and manipulate your interface objects.

Anchored objects are important because they will always run on a specific machine. If you write an object that interacts with a database, you'll want to ensure that the object will always run on a machine that has access to the database. Because of this, anchored objects are typically used on application servers.

Many business objects, on the other hand, will be more useful if they *can* move from the application server to a client or web server, as needed. By creating business objects as mobile objects, you can pass smart data from machine to machine, thereby reusing your business logic anywhere the business data is sent.

Typically, anchored and mobile objects are used in concert. Later in the book, I'll show how to use an anchored object on the application server to ensure that specific methods are run *on that server*. Then mobile objects will be passed as parameters to those methods, which will cause those mobile objects to move from the client to the server. Some of the anchored server-side methods will return mobile objects as results, in which case the mobile object will move from the server back to the client.

Passing Mobile Objects by Reference

There's a piece of terminology here that can get confusing. So far, I've loosely associated anchored objects with the concept of *passing by reference*, and mobile objects as being *passed by value*. Intuitively, this makes sense, because anchored objects provide a reference, though mobile objects provide the actual object (and its values). However, the terms *by reference* and *by value* have come to mean other things over the years.

The original idea of passing a value by reference was that there would be just one set of data—one object—and any code could get a reference to that single entity. Any changes made to that entity by any code would therefore be immediately visible to any other code.

The original idea of passing a value by value was that a copy of the original value would be made. Any code could get a copy of the original value, but any changes made to that copy weren't reflected in the original value. That makes sense, because the changes were made to a copy, not to the original value.

In distributed applications, things get a little more complicated, but the previous definitions remain true: an object can be passed by reference so that all machines have a reference to the same object on a server. And an object can be passed by value, so that a copy of the object is made. So far, so good. However, what happens if you mark an object as `Serializable` or `DataContract` (that is, mark it as a mobile object) and then *intentionally* pass it by reference? It turns out that the object is passed by value, but the .NET Framework attempts to provide the illusion that the object was passed by reference.

To be more specific, in this scenario, the object is copied across the network just as if it were being passed by value. The difference is that the object is then returned back to the calling code when the method is complete, and the reference to the original object is replaced with a reference to this new version, as shown in Figure 1-21.

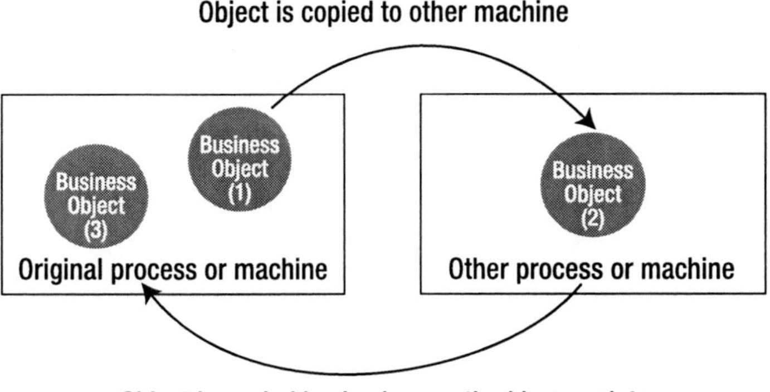

Figure 1-21. *Passing a copy of the object to the server and getting a copy back*

The original object (instance 1) starts on the left and is copied (cloned) to the right (instance 2). The right-hand process or machine has full access to a local copy of the object and can interact with it freely. When that's done, the object is "returned" to the left, meaning it is copied back across the network into a new object on the left (instance 3).

This is potentially very dangerous, since *other* references to the original object continue to point to that original object—only this one particular reference is updated. You can end up with two different versions of the same object on the machine, with some references pointing to the new one and some to the old one.

■ **Note** If you pass a mobile object by reference, you must always make sure to update *all* references to use the new version of the object when the method call is complete.

You can choose to pass a mobile object by value, in which case it's passed one way: from the caller to the method. Or you can choose to pass a mobile object by reference, in which case it's passed two ways: from the caller to the method and from the method back to the caller. If you want to get back any changes the method makes to the object, use *by reference*. If you don't care about or don't want any changes made to the object by the method, use *by value*.

Note that passing a mobile object by reference has performance implications—it requires that the object be passed back across the network to the calling machine, so it's slower than passing by value.

Complete Encapsulation

Hopefully, at this point, your imagination is engaged by the potential of mobile objects. The flexibility of being able to choose between local, anchored, and mobile objects is very powerful, and opens up new architectural approaches.

I've already discussed the idea of sharing the Business layer across machines, and it's probably obvious that the concept of mobile objects is exactly what's needed to implement such a shared layer. But what does this all mean for the *design* of the layers? In particular, given a set of mobile objects in the Business layer, what's the impact on the Interface Control and Data Access layers with which the objects interact?

Impact on the Interface Control Layer

What it means for the Interface Control layer is simply that the business objects will contain all the business logic. The interface developer can code each form, page, service, or workflow activity using the business objects, thereby relying on them to perform any validation or manipulation of the data. This means that the interface code can focus entirely on displaying the data, interacting with the user, and providing a rich, interactive experience.

More importantly, because the business objects are mobile, they'll end up running in the same process as the interface control code. Any property or method calls from the interface control code to the business object will occur locally without network latency, marshaling, or any other performance overhead.

Impact on the Data Access Layer

A traditional Data Access layer consists of a set of methods or services that interact with the database and with the objects that encapsulate data. The data access code itself is typically outside the objects, rather than being encapsulated within the objects. This, however, breaks encapsulation, since it means that the objects' data must be externalized to be handled by the data access code.

The framework created in this book allows for the data access code to be encapsulated within the business objects, or externalized into a separate set of objects. As you'll see in Chapter 7, there are both performance and maintainability benefits to including the data access code directly inside each business object. However, there are security and manageability benefits to having the code external.

Either way, the concept of a Data Access layer is of key importance. Maintaining a strong logical separation between the data access code and business logic is highly beneficial, as discussed earlier in this chapter. Obviously, having a totally separate set of data access objects is one way to clearly implement a Data Access layer.

Architectures and Frameworks

The discussion so far has focused mainly on architectures: logical architectures that define the separation of responsibilities in an application, and physical architectures that define the locations where the logical layers will run in various configurations. I've also discussed the use of object-oriented design and the concepts behind mobile objects.

Although all of these are important and must be thought through in detail, you really don't want to have to go through this process every time you need to build an application. It would be preferable to have the architecture and design solidified into reusable code that could be used to build all your applications. What you want is an *application framework*. A framework codifies an architecture and design in order to promote reuse and increase productivity.

The typical development process starts with requirements gathering and analysis, followed by a period of architectural discussion and decision making. Next comes the application design: first, the low-level concepts to support the architecture, and then the business-level concepts that actually matter to the end users. With the design completed, developers typically spend a fair amount of time implementing the low-level functions that support the business coding that comes later.

All of the architectural discussions, decision making, designing, and coding can be a lot of fun. Unfortunately, it doesn't directly contribute anything to the end goal of writing business logic and providing business functionality. This low-level supporting technology is merely "plumbing" that must exist in order to create actual business applications. It's an overhead that in the long term you should be able to do once and then reuse across many business application–development efforts.

In the software world, the easiest way to reduce overhead is to increase reuse, and the best way to get reuse out of an architecture (both design and coding) is to codify it into a framework.

This doesn't mean that *application* analysis and design are unimportant—quite the opposite! People typically spend far too little time analyzing business requirements and developing good application designs to meet those business needs. Part of the reason is that they often end up spending substantial amounts of time analyzing and designing the plumbing that supports the business application, and then run out of time to analyze the business issues themselves.

What I'm proposing here is to reduce the time spent analyzing and designing the low-level plumbing by creating a framework that you can use across many business applications. Is the framework created in this book ideal for every application and every organization? Certainly not! You'll have to take the architecture and the framework and adapt them to meet your organization's needs. You may have different priorities in terms of performance, scalability, security, fault tolerance, reuse, or other key architectural criteria. At the very least, though, the remainder of this book should give you a good start on the design and construction of a distributed, object-oriented architecture and framework.

Conclusion

In this chapter, I've focused on the theory behind distributed systems—specifically, those based on mobile objects. The key to success in designing a distributed system is to keep clear the distinction between a logical and a physical architecture.

Logical architectures exist to define the separation between the different types of code in an application. The goal of a good logical architecture is to make code more maintainable, understandable, and reusable. A logical architecture must also define enough layers to enable any physical architectures that may be required.

Physical architectures define the machines on which the application will run. An application with several logical layers can still run on a single machine. You also might configure that same logical architecture to run on various client and server machines. The goal of a good physical architecture is to achieve the best trade-off between performance, scalability, security, and fault tolerance within your specific environment.

The trade-offs in a physical architecture for a smart client application are very different from those for a web application. A Windows application will typically trade performance against scalability, and a web application will typically trade performance against security.

In this book, I'll be using a 5-layer logical architecture consisting of the Interface, Interface Control, Business, Data Access, and Data Storage and Management layers. Later in the book, I'll show you how to use this architecture to create Windows, web, and service-oriented applications, each with a different physical architecture. The next chapter will start the process of designing the framework that will make this possible.

CHAPTER 2

Framework Design

In Chapter 1, I discussed some general concepts about physical and logical n-tier architecture, including a 5-layer model for describing systems logically. In this chapter, I take that 5-layer logical model and expand it into a framework design. Specifically, this chapter will map the logical layers against the technologies illustrated in Figure 2-1.

The CSLA .NET framework itself will focus on the Business Logic and Data Access layers. This is primarily due to the fact that there are already powerful technologies for building Windows, web (browser-based and XML-based services), and mobile interface layers. Also, there are already powerful data-storage options available, including SQL Server, Oracle, DB2, XML documents, and so forth.

Recognizing that these preexisting technologies are ideal for building the Presentation and UI layers, as well as for handling data storage, allows business developers to focus on the parts of the application that have the least technological support, where the highest return on investment occurs through reuse. Analyzing, designing, implementing, testing, and maintaining business logic is incredibly expensive. The more reuse achieved, the lower long-term application costs become. The easier it is to maintain and modify this logic, the lower costs will be over time.

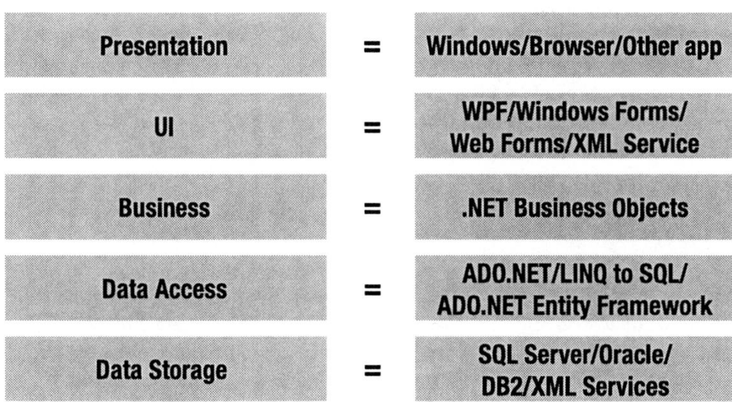

Figure 2-1. *Mapping the logical layers to technologies*

Note This is not to say that additional frameworks for UI creation or simplification of data access are bad ideas. On the contrary, such frameworks can be very complementary to the ideas presented in this book; and the combination of several frameworks can help lower costs even further.

When I set out to create the architecture and framework discussed in this book, I started with the following set of high-level guidelines:

- The task of creating object-oriented applications in a distributed .NET environment should be simplified.
- The interface developer (Windows, web service, or workflow) should never see or be aware of SQL, ADO.NET, or other raw data concepts but should instead rely on a purely object-oriented model of the problem domain.
- Business object developers should be able to use "natural" coding techniques to create their classes—that is, they should employ everyday coding using fields, properties, and methods. Little or no extra knowledge should be required.
- The business classes should provide total encapsulation of business logic, including validation, manipulation, calculation, and authorization. Everything pertaining to an entity in the problem domain should be found within a single class.
- It should be possible to achieve clean separation between the business logic code and the data access code.
- It should be relatively easy to create code generators, or templates for existing code generation tools, to assist in the creation of business classes.
- An n-layer logical architecture that can be easily reconfigured to run on one to four physical tiers should be provided.
- Complex features in .NET should be used, but they should be largely hidden and automated (WCF, serialization, security, deployment, etc.).
- The concepts present in the framework from its inception should carry forward, including validation, authorization, n-level undo, and object-state tracking (`IsNew`, `IsDirty`, `IsDeleted`).

In this chapter, I focus on the design of a framework that allows business developers to make use of object-oriented design and programming with these guidelines in mind. After walking through the design of the framework, Chapters 6 through 16 dive in and implement the framework itself, focusing first on the parts that support UI development and then on the providing of scalable data access and object-relational mapping for the objects. Before I get into the design of the framework, however, let's discuss some of the specific goals I am attempting to achieve.

Basic Design Goals

When creating object-oriented applications, the ideal situation is that any nonbusiness objects already exist. This includes UI controls, data access objects, and so forth. In that case, all developers need to do is focus on creating, debugging, and testing the business objects themselves, thereby ensuring that each one encapsulates the data and business logic needed to make the application work.

As rich as the .NET Framework is, however, it doesn't provide all the nonbusiness objects needed in order to create most applications. All the basic tools are there but there's a fair amount of work to be done before you can just sit down and write business logic. There's a set of higher-level functions and capabilities that are often needed but aren't provided by .NET right out of the box.

These include the following:

- Validation and maintaining a list of broken business rules
- Standard implementation of business and validation rules
- Tracking whether an object's data has changed (is it "dirty"?)
- Integrated authorization rules at the object and property levels

- Strongly typed collections of child objects (parent-child relationships)
- N-level undo capability
- A simple and abstract model for the UI developer
- Full support for data binding in WPF, Windows Forms, and Web Forms
- Saving objects to a database and getting them back again
- Custom authentication
- Other miscellaneous features

In all of these cases, the .NET Framework provides all the pieces of the puzzle, but they must be put together to match your specialized requirements. What you *don't* want to do, however, is to have to put them together for every business object or application. The goal is to put them together *once* so that all these extra features are automatically available to all the business objects and applications.

Moreover, because the goal is to enable the implementation of *object-oriented* business systems, the core object-oriented concepts must also be preserved:

- Abstraction
- Encapsulation
- Polymorphism
- Inheritance

The result is a framework consisting of a number of classes. The design of these classes is discussed in this chapter and their implementation is discussed in Chapters 6 through 16.

■ **Tip** The Diagrams folder in the Csla project in the code download includes `FullCsla.cd`, which shows all the framework classes in a single diagram. You can also get a PDF document showing that diagram at `www.lhotka.net/cslanet/download.aspx`.

Before getting into the details of the framework's design, let's discuss the desired set of features in more detail.

Validation and Business Rules

A lot of business logic involves the enforcement of *validation rules*. The fact that a given piece of data is required is a validation rule. The fact that one date must be later than another date is a validation rule. Some validation rules involve calculations and others are merely toggles. You can think about validation rules as being either broken or not. And when one or more rules are broken the object is invalid.

A similar concept is the idea of *business rules* that might alter the state of the object. The fact that a given piece of text data must be all uppercase is a business rule. The calculation of one property value based on other property values is a business rule. Most business rules involve some level of calculation.

Because all validation rules ultimately return a Boolean value, it is possible to abstract the concept of validation rules to a large degree. Every rule is implemented as a bit of code. Some of the code might be trivial, such as comparing the length of a string and returning `false` if the value is zero. Other code might be more complex, involving validation of the data against a lookup table or through a numeric algorithm. Either way, a validation rule can be expressed as a method that returns a Boolean result.

Business rules typically alter the state of the object and usually don't enforce validation at the same time. Still, every business rule is implemented as a bit of code, and that code might be trivial or very complex.

The .NET Framework provides the *delegate* concept, making it possible to formally define a method signature for a type of method. A delegate defines a reference type (an object) that represents a method. Essentially, delegates turn methods into objects, allowing you to write code that treats the method like an object; and of course they also allow you to invoke the method.

I use this capability in the framework to formally define a method signature for all validation and business rules. This allows the framework to maintain a list of validation rules for each object, enabling relatively simple application of those rules as appropriate. With that done, every object can easily maintain a list of the rules that are broken at any point in time and has a standardized way of implementing business rules.

■ **Note** There are commercial business rule engines and other business rule products that strive to take the business rules out of the software and keep them in some external location. Some of these are powerful and valuable. For most business applications, however, the business rules are typically coded directly into the software. When using object-oriented design, this means coding them into the objects.

A fair number of validation rules are of the toggle variety: required fields, fields that must be a certain length (no longer than, no shorter than), fields that must be greater than or less than other fields, and so forth. The common theme is that validation rules, when broken, immediately make the object invalid. In short, an object is valid if *no* rules are broken but is invalid if *any* rules are broken.

Rather than trying to implement a custom scheme in each business object in order to keep track of which rules are broken and whether the object is or isn't valid at any given point, this behavior can be abstracted. Obviously, the rules *themselves* are often coded into an application, but the tracking of which rules are broken and whether the object is valid can be handled by the framework.

■ **Tip** Defining a validation rule as a method means you can create libraries of reusable rules for your application. The framework in this book includes a small library with some of the most common validation rules so you can use them in applications without having to write them.

The result is a standardized mechanism by which the developer can check all business objects for validity. The UI developer should also be able to retrieve a list of currently broken rules to display to the user (or for any other purpose).

Additionally, this provides the underlying data required to implement the `System.ComponentModel.IDataErrorInfo` interface defined by the .NET Framework. This interface is used by the data binding infrastructure in WPF and Windows Forms to automate the display of validation errors to the user.

Some validation rules may interact with the database or could be very complex in other ways. In these cases, you may want to allow the user to move on to editing other data while a validation rule is running in the background. To this end, you can choose to implement a validation rule (though not a business rule) to run asynchronously on a background thread.

The reason this only works with validation rules is that an async rule method won't have access to the real business object. For thread safety reasons, it is provided with a copy of the property values to be validated so it can do its work. Since a business rule manipulates the business object's data, I don't allow them to be implemented as an async operation.

Tracking Whether the Object Has Changed

Another concept is that an object should keep track of whether its state data has been changed. This is important for the performance and efficiency of data updates. Typically, data should only be updated into the database if the data has actually changed. It's a waste of effort to update the database with values it already has. Although the UI developer *could* keep track of whether any values have changed, it's simpler to have the object take care of this detail and it allows the object to better encapsulate its behaviors.

This can be implemented in a number of ways, ranging from keeping the previous values of all fields (allowing comparisons to see if they've changed) to saying that *any* change to a value (even "changing" it to its original value) will result in the object being marked as having changed.

Rather than having the framework dictate one cost over the other, it will simply provide a generic mechanism by which the business logic can tell the framework whether each object has been changed. This scheme supports both extremes of implementation, allowing you to make a decision based on the requirements of a specific application.

Integrated Authorization

Applications also need to be able to authorize the user to perform (or not perform) certain operations or view (or not view) certain data. Such authorization is typically handled by associating users with roles and then indicating which roles are allowed or disallowed for specific behaviors.

■ **Note** Authorization is just another type of business logic. The decisions about what a user can and can't do or can and can't see within the application are business decisions. Although the framework will work with the .NET Framework classes that support authentication, it's up to the business objects to implement the rules themselves.

Later, I discuss authentication and how the framework supports both integrated Windows and AD authentication and custom authentication. Either way, the result of authentication is that the application has access to the list of roles (or groups) to which the user belongs. This information can be used by the application to authorize the user as defined by the business.

While authorization can be implemented manually within the application's business code, the business framework can help formalize the process in some cases. Specifically, objects must use the user's role information to restrict what properties the user can view and edit. There are also common behaviors at the object level—such as loading, deleting, and saving an object—that are subject to authorization.

As with validation rules, authorization rules can be distilled to a set of fairly simple yes/no answers. Either a user can or can't read a given property. Either a user can or can't delete the object's data. The business framework includes code to help a business object developer easily restrict which object properties a user can or can't read or edit and what operations the user can perform on the object itself. In Chapter 12, you'll also see a common pattern that can be implemented by all business objects to control whether an object can be retrieved, deleted, or saved.

Not only does this business object need access to this authorization information but the UI does as well. Ideally, a good UI will change its display based on how the current user is allowed to interact with an object. To support this concept, the business framework will help the business objects expose the authorization rules such that they are accessible to the UI layer without duplicating the authorization rules themselves.

Strongly Typed Collections of Child Objects

The .NET Framework includes the `System.Collections.Generic` namespace, which contains a number of powerful collection objects, including `List<T>`, `Dictionary<TKey, TValue>`, and others. There's also `System.ComponentModel.BindingList<T>`, which provides collection behaviors and full support for data binding, and the less capable `System.ComponentModel.ObservableCollection<T>`, which provides support only for WPF data binding.

A Short Primer on Generics

Generic types are a feature introduced in .NET 2.0. A generic type is a template that defines a set of behaviors but the specific data type is specified when the type is *used* rather than when it is created. Perhaps an example will help.

Consider the `ArrayList` collection type. It provides powerful list behaviors but it stores all its items as type `object`. While you can wrap an `ArrayList` with a strongly typed class or create your own collection type in many different ways, the items in the list are always stored in memory as type `object`.

The new `List<T>` collection type has the same behaviors as `ArrayList` but it is strongly typed—all the way to its core. The type of the indexer, enumerator, `Remove()`, and other methods are all defined by the *generic type parameter*, `T`. Even better, the items in the list are stored in memory as type `T`, not type `object`.

So what is `T`? It is the type provided when the `List<T>` is created:

```
List<int> myList = new List<int>();
```

In this case, `T` is `int`, meaning that `myList` is a strongly typed list of `int` values. The public properties and methods of `myList` are all of type `int`, and the values it contains are stored internally as `int` values.

Not only do generic types offer type safety due to their strongly typed nature, but they typically offer substantial performance benefits because they avoid storing values as type `object`.

Strongly Typed Collections of Child Objects

Sadly, the basic functionality provided by even the generic collection classes isn't enough to integrate fully with the rest of the framework. The business framework supports a set of relatively advanced features such as validation and n-level undo capabilities. Supporting these features requires that collections of child objects interact with the parent object and the objects contained in the collection in ways not implemented by the basic collection and list classes provided by .NET.

For example, a collection of child objects needs to be able to indicate if any of the objects it contains have been changed. Although the business object developer could easily write code to loop through the child objects to discover whether any are marked as dirty, it makes a lot more sense to put this functionality into the framework's collection object. That way the feature is simply available for use. The same is true with validity: if any child object is invalid, the collection should be able to report that it's invalid. If all child objects are valid, the collection should report itself as being valid.

As with the business objects themselves, the goal of the business framework is to make the creation of a strongly typed collection as close to normal .NET programming as possible, while allowing the framework to provide extra capabilities common to all business objects. What I'm defining here are two sets of behaviors: one for business objects (parent and/or child) and one for collections of business objects. Though business objects will be the more complex of the two, collection objects will also include some very interesting functionality.

N-Level Undo Capability

Many Windows applications provide users with an interface that includes OK and Cancel buttons (or some variation on that theme). When the user clicks an OK button, the expectation is that any work the user has done will be saved. Likewise, when the user clicks a Cancel button, he expects that any changes he's made will be reversed or undone.

Simple applications can often deliver this functionality by saving the data to a database when users click OK and discarding the data when they click Cancel. For slightly more complex applications, the application must be able to undo any editing on a single object when the user presses the Esc key. (This is the case for a row of data being edited in a `DataGridView`: if the user presses Esc, the row of data should restore its original values.)

When applications become much more complex, however, these approaches won't work. Instead of simply undoing the changes to a single row of data in real time, you may need to be able to undo the changes to a row of data at some later stage.

■ **Note** It is important to realize that the n-level undo capability implemented in the framework is *optional* and is designed to incur no overhead if it is not used.

Consider the case of an `Invoice` object that contains a collection of `LineItem` objects. The `Invoice` itself contains data that the user can edit plus data that's derived from the collection. The `TotalAmount` property of an `Invoice`, for instance, is calculated by summing up the individual `Amount` properties of its `LineItem` objects. Figure 2-2 illustrates this arrangement.

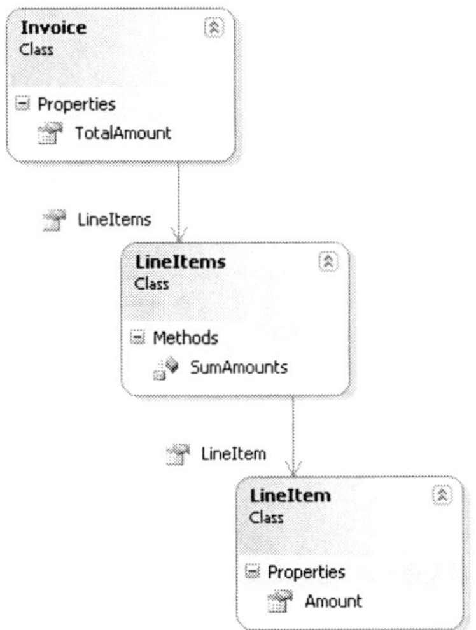

Figure 2-2. *Relationship between the Invoice, LineItems, and LineItem classes*

The UI may allow the user to edit the `LineItem` objects and then press Enter to accept the changes to the item or Esc to undo them. However, even if the user chooses to accept changes to some `LineItem` objects, she can still choose to cancel the changes on the `Invoice` itself. Of course, the only way to reset the `Invoice` object to its original state is to restore the states of the `LineItem` objects as well, including any changes to specific `LineItem` objects that might have been "accepted" earlier.

As if this isn't enough, many applications have more complex hierarchies of objects and subobjects (which I'll call *child objects*). Perhaps the individual `LineItem` objects each has a collection of `Component` objects beneath it. Each `Component` object represents one of the components sold to the customer that makes up the specific line item, as shown in Figure 2-3.

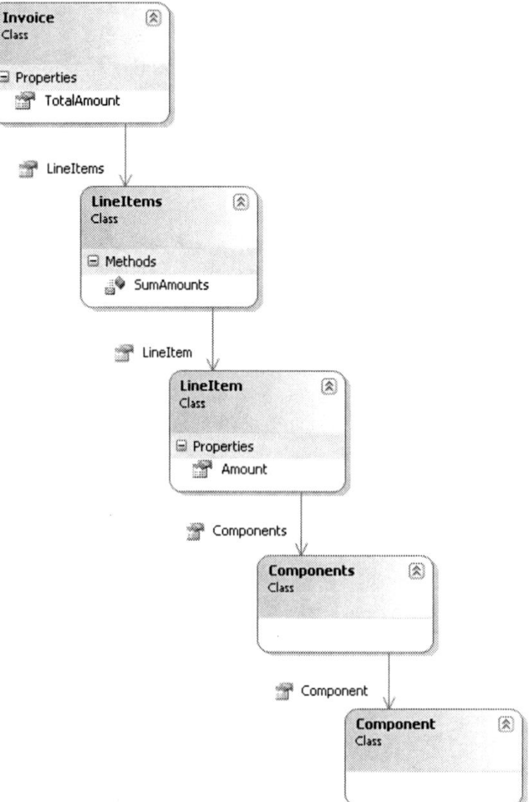

Figure 2-3. *Class diagram showing a more complex set of class relationships*

Now things get even more complicated. If the user edits a `Component` object, the changes ultimately impact the state of the `Invoice` object itself. Of course, changing a `Component` also changes the state of the `LineItem` object that owns the `Component`.

The user might accept changes to a `Component` but cancel the changes to its parent `LineItem` object, thereby forcing an undo operation to reverse *accepted* changes to the `Component`. Or in an even more complex scenario, the user may accept the changes to a `Component` and its parent `LineItem` only to cancel the `Invoice`. This would force an undo operation that reverses all those changes to the child objects.

Implementing an undo mechanism to support such n-level scenarios isn't trivial. The application must implement code to take a snapshot of the state of each object before it's edited so that changes can be reversed later on. The application might even need to take more than one snapshot of an object's state at different points in the editing process so that the object can revert to the appropriate point, based on when the user chooses to accept or cancel any edits.

■ **Note** This multilevel undo capability flows from the user's expectations. Consider a typical word processor, where the user can undo multiple times to restore the content to ever earlier states.

And the collection objects are every bit as complex as the business objects themselves. The application must handle the simple case in which a user edits an existing `LineItem`, but it must also handle the case in which a user adds a new `LineItem` and then cancels changes to the parent or grandparent, resulting in the new `LineItem` being discarded. Equally, it must handle the case in which the user *deletes* a `LineItem` and then cancels changes to the parent or grandparent, thereby causing that deleted object to be restored to the collection as though nothing had ever happened.

Things get even *more* complex if you consider that the framework keeps a list of broken validation rules for each object. If the user changes an object's data so that the object becomes invalid but then cancels the changes, the original state of the object must be restored. The reverse is true as well: an object may start out invalid (perhaps because a required field is blank), so the user must edit data until it becomes valid. If the user later cancels the object (or its parent, grandparent, etc.), the object must become *invalid* once again because it will be restored to its original invalid state.

Fortunately, this is easily handled by treating the broken rules and validity of each object as part of that object's state. When an undo operation occurs, not only is the object's core state restored but so is the list of broken rules associated with that state. The object and its rules are restored together.

N-level undo is a perfect example of complex code that shouldn't be written into every business object. Instead, this functionality should be written *once*, so that all business objects support the concept and behave the way we want them to. This functionality will be incorporated directly into the business object framework—but at the same time, the framework must be sensitive to the different environments in which the objects will be used. Although n-level undo is of high importance when building sophisticated Windows user experiences, it's virtually useless in a typical web environment.

In web-based applications, users typically don't have a Cancel button. They either accept the changes or navigate away to another task, allowing the application to simply discard the changed object. In this regard, the web environment is much simpler, so if n-level undo isn't useful to the web UI developer, it shouldn't incur any overhead if it isn't used. The framework design takes into account that some UI types will use the concept while others will simply ignore it.

Simple and Abstract Model for the UI Developer

At this point, I've discussed some of the business object features that the framework will support. One of the key reasons for providing these features is to make the business object support Windows and web-style user experiences with minimal work on the part of the UI developer. In fact, this should be an overarching goal when you're designing business objects for a system. The UI developer should be able to rely on the objects to provide business logic, data, and related services in a consistent manner.

Beyond all the features already covered is the issue of creating new objects, retrieving existing data, and updating objects in some data store. I discuss the *process* of object persistence later in the chapter, but first this topic should be considered from the UI developer's perspective. Should the UI developer be aware of any application servers? Should he be aware of any database servers? Or should he simply interact with a set of abstract objects? There are three broad models to choose from:

- UI-in-charge
- Object-in-charge
- Class-in-charge

To a greater or lesser degree, all three of these options hide information about how objects are created and saved and allow us to exploit the native capabilities of .NET. In the end, I settle on the option that hides the most information (keeping development as simple as possible) and best allows you to exploit the features of .NET.

■ **Note** Inevitably, the result will be a compromise. As with many architectural decisions, there are good arguments to be made for each option. In your environment, you may find that a different decision would work better. Keep in mind though that this particular decision is fairly central to the overall architecture of the framework, so choosing another option will likely result in dramatic changes throughout the framework.

To make this as clear as possible, the following discussion assumes the use of a physical n-tier configuration, whereby the client or web server is interacting with a separate application server, which in turn interacts with the database. Although not all applications will run in such configurations, it is much easier to discuss object creation, retrieval, and updating in this context.

UI in Charge

One common approach to creating, retrieving, and updating objects is to put the UI in charge of the process. This means that it's the UI developer's responsibility to write code that will contact the application server in order to retrieve or update objects.

In this scheme, when a new object is required, the UI will contact the application server and ask it for a new object. The application server can then instantiate a new object, populate it with default values, and return it to the UI code. The code might be something like this:

```
Customer result = null;
var factory =
  new ChannelFactory<BusinessService.IBusinessService>("BusinessService");
try
{
  var proxy = factory.CreateChannel();
  using (proxy as IDisposable)
  {
    result = proxy.CreateNewCustomer();
  }
}
finally
{
  factory.Close();
}
```

Here the object of type `IBusinessService` is anchored, so it always runs on the application server. The `Customer` object is mobile, so although it's created on the server, it's returned to the UI by value.

■ **Note** This code example uses Windows Communication Foundation to contact an application server and have it instantiate an object on the server. In Chapter 15, you'll see how CSLA .NET abstracts this code into a much simpler form, effectively wrapping and hiding the complexity of WCF.

This may seem like a lot of work just to create a new, empty object, but it's the retrieval of default values that makes it necessary. If the application has objects that don't need default values, or if you're willing to hard-code the defaults, you can avoid some of the work by having the UI simply create the object on the client workstation. However, many business applications have configurable default values for objects that must be loaded from the database; and that means the application server must load them.

Retrieving an *existing* object follows the same basic procedure. The UI passes criteria to the application server, which uses the criteria to create a new object and load it with the appropriate data from the database. The populated object is then returned to the UI for use. The UI code might be something like this:

```
Customer result = null;
var factory =
  new ChannelFactory<BusinessService.IBusinessService>("BusinessService");
try
{
  var proxy = factory.CreateChannel();
  using (proxy as IDisposable)
  {
    result = proxy.GetCustomer(criteria);
  }
}
finally
{
  factory.Close();
}
```

Updating an object happens when the UI calls the application server and passes the object to the server. The server can then take the data from the object and store it in the database. Because the update process may result in changes to the object's state, the newly saved and updated object is then returned to the UI. The UI code might be something like this:

```
Customer result = null;
var factory =
  new ChannelFactory<BusinessService.IBusinessService>("BusinessService");
try
{
  var proxy = factory.CreateChannel();
  using (proxy as IDisposable)
  {
    result = proxy.UpdateCustomer(customer);
  }
}
finally
{
  factory.Close();
}
```

Overall, this model is straightforward—the application server must simply expose a set of services that can be called from the UI to create, retrieve, update, and delete objects. Each object can simply contain its business logic without the object developer having to worry about application servers or other details.

The drawback to this scheme is that the UI code must know about and interact with the application server. If the application server is moved, or some objects come from a different server, the UI code must be changed. Moreover, if a Windows UI is created to use the objects and then later a web UI is created that uses those same objects, you'll end up with duplicated code. Both types of UI will need to include the code in order to find and interact with the application server.

The whole thing is complicated further if you consider that the physical configuration of the application should be flexible. It should be possible to switch from using an application server to running the data access code *on the client* just by changing a configuration file. If there's code scattered throughout the UI that contacts the server any time an object is used, there will be a lot of places where developers might introduce a bug that prevents simple configuration file switching.

Object in Charge

Another option is to move the knowledge of the application server into the objects themselves. The UI can just interact with the objects, allowing them to load defaults, retrieve data, or update themselves. In this model, simply using the `new` keyword creates a new object:

```
Customer cust = new Customer();
```

Within the object's constructor, you would then write the code to contact the application server and retrieve default values. It might be something like this:

```
public Customer()
{
  var factory =
    new ChannelFactory<BusinessService.IBusinessService>("BusinessService");
  try
  {
    var proxy = factory.CreateChannel();
    using (proxy as IDisposable)
    {
      var tmp = proxy.GetNewCustomerDefaults();
      _field1 = tmp.Field1Default;
      _field2 = tmp.Field2Default;
      // load all fields with defaults here
    }
  }
  finally
  {
    factory.Close();
  }
}
```

Notice that the previous code does *not* take advantage of the built-in support for passing an object by value across the network. In fact, this technique forces the creation of some other class that contains the default values returned from the server.

Given that both the UI-in-charge and class-in-charge techniques avoid all this extra coding, let's just abort the discussion of this option and move on.

Class-in-Charge (Factory Pattern)

The UI-in-charge approach uses .NET's ability to pass objects by value but requires the UI developer to know about and interact with the application server. The object-in-charge approach enables a very simple set of UI code but makes the object code prohibitively complex by making it virtually impossible to pass the objects by value.

The class-in-charge option provides a good compromise by providing reasonably simple UI code that's unaware of application servers while also allowing the use of .NET's ability to pass objects by value, thus reducing the amount of "plumbing" code needed in each object. Hiding more information from the UI helps create a more abstract and loosely coupled implementation, thus providing better flexibility.

■ **Note** The class-in-charge approach is a variation on the Factory design pattern, in which a "factory" method is responsible for creating and managing an object. In many cases, these factory methods are `static` methods that may be placed directly into a business class—hence the class-in-charge moniker.[1]

In this model, I make use of the concept of `static` factory methods on a class. A `static` method can be called directly without requiring an instance of the class to be created first. For instance, suppose that a `Customer` class contains the following code:

```
[Serializable()]
public class Customer
{
  public static Customer NewCustomer()
  {
    var factory =
      new ChannelFactory<BusinessService.IBusinessService>("BusinessService");
    try
    {
      var proxy = factory.CreateChannel();
      using (proxy as IDisposable)
      {
        return = proxy.CreateNewCustomer ();
      }
    }
    finally
    {
      factory.Close();
    }
  }
}
```

The UI code could use this method without first creating a `Customer` object, as follows:

```
Customer cust = Customer.NewCustomer();
```

A common example of this tactic within the .NET Framework itself is the `Guid` class, whereby a `static` method is used to create new `Guid` values, as follows:

```
Guid myGuid = Guid.NewGuid();
```

This accomplishes the goal of making the UI code reasonably simple; but what about the `static` method and passing objects by value? Well, the `NewCustomer()` method contacts the application server and asks it to create a new `Customer` object with default values. The object is created on the server and then returned back to the `NewCustomer()` code, which is running *on the client.* Now that the object has been passed back to the client by value, the method simply returns it to the UI for use.

---

1. *Design Patterns: Elements of Reusable Object-Oriented Software* (Addison-Wesley, 1995) by Erich Gamma, Richard Helm, Ralph Johnson, and John Vlissides

Likewise, you can create a static method in the class in order to load an object with data from the data store as shown:

```
public static Customer GetCustomer(string criteria)
{
  var factory =
    new ChannelFactory<BusinessService.IBusinessService>("BusinessService");
  try
  {
    var proxy = factory.CreateChannel();
    using (proxy as IDisposable)
    {
      return = proxy.GetCustomer (criteria);
    }
  }
  finally
  {
    factory.Close();
  }
}
```

Again, the code contacts the application server, providing it with the criteria necessary to load the object's data and create a fully populated object. That object is then returned by value to the GetCustomer() method running on the client and then back to the UI code.

As before, the UI code remains simple:

```
Customer cust = Customer.GetCustomer(myCriteria);
```

The class-in-charge model requires that you write static factory methods in each class but keeps the UI code simple and straightforward. It also takes full advantage of .NET's ability to pass objects across the network by value, thereby minimizing the plumbing code in each object. Overall, it provides the best solution, which is used (and refined further) in the chapters ahead.

Supporting Data Binding

For more than a decade, Microsoft has included some kind of data binding capability in its development tools. Data binding allows developers to create forms and populate them with data with almost no custom code. The controls on a form are "bound" to specific fields from a data source (such as an entity object, a DataSet, or a business object).

Data binding is provided in WPF, Windows Forms, and Web Forms. The primary benefits or drivers for using data binding in .NET development include the following:

- Data binding offers good performance, control, and flexibility.
- Data binding can be used to link controls to properties of business objects.
- Data binding can dramatically reduce the amount of code in the UI.
- Data binding is sometimes faster than manual coding, especially when loading data into list boxes, grids, or other complex controls.

Of these, the biggest single benefit is the dramatic reduction in the amount of UI code that must be written and maintained. Combined with the performance, control, and flexibility of .NET data binding, the reduction in code makes it a very attractive technology for UI development.

In WPF, Windows Forms, and Web Forms, data binding is *read-write*, meaning that an element of a data source can be bound to an editable control so that changes to the value in the control will be updated back into the data source as well.

Data binding in .NET is very powerful. It offers good performance with a high degree of control for the developer. Given the coding savings gained by using data binding, it's definitely a technology that needs to be supported in the business object framework.

Enabling the Objects for Data Binding

Although data binding can be used to bind against any object or any collection of homogeneous objects, there are some things that object developers can do to make data binding work better. Implementing these "extra" features enables data binding to do more work for you and provide a superior experience. The .NET `DataSet` object, for instance, implements these extra features in order to provide full data binding support to WPF, Windows Forms, and Web Forms developers.

The IEditableObject Interface

All editable business objects should implement the interface called `System.ComponentModel.IEditableObject`. This interface is designed to support a simple, one-level undo capability and is used by simple forms-based data binding and complex grid-based data binding alike.

In the forms-based model, `IEditableObject` allows the data binding infrastructure to notify the business object before the user edits it so that the object can take a snapshot of its values. Later, the application can tell the object whether to apply or cancel those changes based on the user's actions. In the grid-based model, each of the objects is displayed in a row within the grid. In this case, the interface allows the data binding infrastructure to notify the object when its row is being edited and then whether to accept or undo the changes based on the user's actions. Typically, grids perform an undo operation if the user presses the Esc key, and an accept operation if the user presses Enter or moves off that row in the grid by any other means.

The INotifyPropertyChanged Interface

Editable business objects need to raise events to notify data binding any time their data values change. Changes that are caused directly by the user editing a field in a bound control are supported automatically—however, if the object updates a property value through *code*, rather than by direct user editing, the object needs to notify the data binding infrastructure that a refresh of the display is required.

The .NET Framework defines `System.ComponentModel.INotifyPropertyChanged`, which should be implemented by any bindable object. This interface defines the `PropertyChanged` event that data binding can handle to detect changes to data in the object.

The INotifyPropertyChanging Interface

In .NET 3.5, Microsoft introduced the `System.ComponentModel.INotifyPropertyChanging` interface so business objects can indicate when a property is about to be changed. Strictly speaking, this interface is optional and isn't (currently) used by data binding. For completeness, however, it is recommended that this interface be used when implementing `INotifyPropertyChanged`.

The `INotifyPropertyChanging` interface defines the `PropertyChanging` event that is raised before a property value is changed, as a complement to the `PropertyChanged` event that is raised *after* a property value has changed.

The IBindingList Interface

All business *collections* should implement the interface called `System.ComponentModel.IBindingList`. The simplest way to do this is to have the collection classes inherit from `System.ComponentModel.BindingList<T>`. This generic class implements all the collection interfaces required to support data binding:

- `IBindingList`
- `IList`
- `ICollection`
- `IEnumerable`
- `ICancelAddNew`
- `IRaiseItemChangedEvents`

As you can see, being able to inherit from `BindingList<T>` is very valuable. Otherwise, the business framework would need to manually implement all these interfaces.

This interface is used in grid-based binding, in which it allows the control that's displaying the contents of the collection to be notified by the collection any time an item is added, removed, or edited so that the display can be updated. Without this interface, there's no way for the data binding infrastructure to notify the grid that the underlying data has changed, so the user won't see changes as they happen.

Along this line, when a child object within a collection changes, the collection should notify the UI of the change. This implies that every collection object will listen for events from its child objects (via `INotifyPropertyChanged`) and in response to such an event will raise its own event indicating that the collection has changed.

The INotifyCollectionChanged Interface

In .NET 3.0, Microsoft introduced a new option for building lists for data binding. This new option only works with WPF and Silverlight and is not supported by Windows Forms or Web Forms. The `System.ComponentModel.INotifyCollectionChanged` interface defines a `CollectionChanged` event that is raised by any list implementing the interface. The simplest way to do this is to have the collection classes inherit from `System.ComponentModel.ObservableCollection<T>`. This generic class implements the interface and related behaviors.

When implementing a list or a collection you must choose to use either `IBindingList` or `INotifyCollectionChanged`. If you implement both, data binding in WPF will become confused, as it honors *both* interfaces and will always get duplicate events for any change to the list.

You should only choose to implement `INotifyCollectionChanged` or use `ObservableCollection<T>` if you are absolutely certain your application will only need to support WPF or Silverlight and never Windows Forms.

Because CSLA .NET supports Windows Forms and Web Forms along with WPF, the list and collection types defined in the framework implement `IBindingList` by subclassing `BindingList<T>`.

Events and Serialization

The events that are raised by business collections and business objects are all valuable. Events support the data binding infrastructure and enable utilization of its full potential. Unfortunately, there's a conflict between the idea of objects raising events and the use of .NET serialization via the `Serializable` attribute.

When an object is marked as `Serializable`, the .NET Framework is told that it can pass the object across the network by value. As part of this process, the object will be automatically converted into a byte stream by the .NET runtime. It also means that any other objects *referenced* by the object will be serialized into the same byte stream, unless the field representing it is marked with the `NonSerialized` attribute. What may not be immediately obvious is that *events create an object reference behind the scenes.*

When an object declares and raises an event, that event is delivered to *any* object that has a handler for the event. WPF forms and Windows Forms often handle events from objects, as illustrated in Figure 2-4.

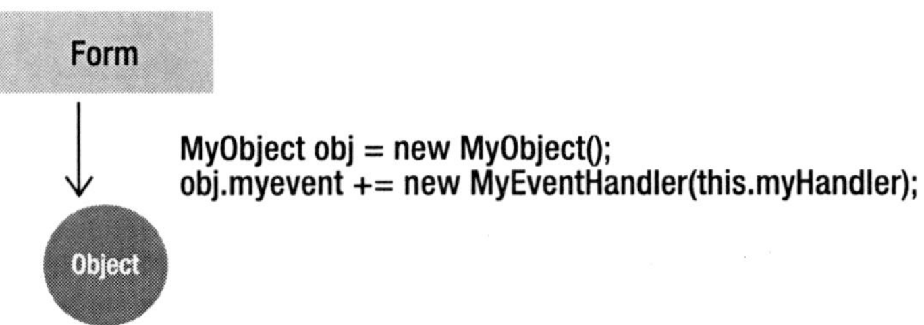

Figure 2-4. *A Windows form referencing a business object*

How does the event get delivered to the handling object? It turns out that behind every event is a delegate—a strongly typed reference that points back to the handling object. This means that any object that raises events can end up with bidirectional references between the object and the other object/entity that is handling those events, as shown in Figure 2-5.

Figure 2-5. *Handling an event on an object causes a back reference to the form.*

Even though this back reference isn't visible to developers, it's completely visible to the .NET serialization infrastructure. When serializing an object, the serialization mechanism will trace this reference and attempt to serialize any objects (including forms) that are handling the events. Obviously, this is rarely desirable. In fact, if the handling object is a form, this will fail outright with a runtime error because forms aren't serializable.

Note If any nonserializable object handles events that are raised by a serializable object, you'll be unable to serialize the object because the .NET runtime serialization process will error out.

Solving this means marking the events as `NonSerialized`. It turns out that this requires a bit of special syntax when dealing with events. Specifically, a more explicit block structure must be used to declare the event. This approach allows manual declaration of the delegate field so it is possible to mark that field as `NonSerialized`. The `BindingList<T>` class already declares its event in this manner, so this issue only pertains to the implementation of `INotifyPropertyChanged` and `INotifyPropertyChanging` (or any custom events you choose to declare in your business classes).

The IDataErrorInfo Interface

Earlier I discussed the need for objects to implement business rules and expose information about broken rules to the UI. The `System.ComponentModel.IDataErrorInfo` interface is designed to allow data binding to request information about broken validation rules from a data source.

We will already have the tools needed to easily implement `IDataErrorInfo`, given that the object framework already helps the objects manage a list of all currently broken validation rules. This interface defines two methods. The first allows data binding to request a text description of errors at the object level, while the second provides a text description of errors at the property level.

By implementing this interface, the objects will automatically support the feedback mechanisms built into the Windows Forms `DataGridView` and `ErrorProvider` controls.

Object Persistence and Object-Relational Mapping

One of the biggest challenges facing a business developer building an object-oriented system is that a good object model is almost never the same as a good relational data model. Because most data is stored in relational databases using a relational model, we're faced with the significant problem of translating that data into an object model for processing and then changing it back to a relational model later on to persist the data from the objects back into the data store.

■ **Note** The framework in this book doesn't *require* a relational model, but since that is the most common data storage technology, I focus on it quite a bit. You should remember that the concepts and code shown in this chapter can be used against XML files, object databases, or almost any other data store you are likely to use.

Relational vs. Object Modeling

Before going any further, let's make sure we're in agreement that object models aren't the same as relational models. Relational models are primarily concerned with the efficient storage of data, so that replication is minimized. Relational modeling is governed by the rules of normalization, and almost all databases are designed to meet at least the third normal form. In this form, it's quite likely that the data for any given business concept or entity is split between multiple tables in the database in order to avoid any duplication of data.

Object models, on the other hand, are primarily concerned with modeling *behavior*, not data. It's not the data that defines the object but the role the object plays within your business domain. Every object should have one clear responsibility and a limited number of behaviors focused on fulfilling that responsibility.

■ **Tip** I recommend the book *Object Thinking* by David West (DV-Microsoft Professional, 2004) for some good insight into behavioral object modeling and design. Though my ideas differ somewhat from those in *Object Thinking*, I use many of the concepts and language from that book in my own object-oriented design work and in this book.

For instance, a `CustomerEdit` object may be responsible for *adding and editing customer data*. A `CustomerInfo` object in the same application may be responsible for *providing read-only access to customer data*. Both objects will use the same data from the same database and table, but they provide different behaviors.

Similarly, an `InvoiceEdit` object may be responsible for *adding and editing invoice data*. But invoices include some customer data. A naïve solution is to have the `InvoiceEdit` object make use of the aforementioned `CustomerEdit` object. That `CustomerEdit` object should only be used in the case where the application is adding or editing customer data—something that isn't occurring while working with invoices. Instead, the `InvoiceEdit` object should directly interact with the customer data it needs to do its job.

Through these two examples, it should be clear that sometimes multiple objects will use the same relational data. In other cases, a single object will use relational data from different data entities. In the end, the same customer data is being used by three different objects. The point, though, is that each one of these objects has a clearly defined responsibility that defines the object's *behavior*. Data is merely a resource the object needs to implement that behavior.

Behavioral Object-Oriented Design

It is a common trap to think that data in objects needs to be normalized like it is in a database. A better way to think about objects is to say that behavior should be normalized. The goal of object-oriented design is to avoid replication of *behavior*, not data.

At this point, most people are struggling. Most developers have spent years programming their brains to think relationally, and this view of object-oriented design flies directly in the face of that conditioning. Yet the key to the successful application of object-oriented design is to divorce object thinking from relational or data thinking.

Perhaps the most common objection at this point is this: if two objects (e.g., `CustomerEdit` and `InvoiceEdit`) both use the same data (e.g., the customer's name), how do you make sure that consistent business rules are applied to that data? And this is a good question.

The answer is that the behavior must be normalized. Business rules are merely a form of behavior. The business rule specifying that the customer name value is required, for instance, is just a behavior associated with that particular value.

Earlier in the chapter I discuss the idea that a validation rule can be reduced to a method defined by a delegate. A delegate is just an object that points to a method, so it is quite possible to view the delegate itself as the rule. Following this train of thought, every rule then becomes an object.

Behavioral object-oriented design relies heavily on the concept of *collaboration*. Collaboration is the idea that an object should collaborate with other objects to do its work. If an object starts to become complex, you can break the problem into smaller, more digestible parts by moving some of the sub-behaviors into other objects that collaborate with the original object to accomplish the overall goal.

In the case of a required customer name value, there's a `Rule` object that defines that behavior. Both the `CustomerEdit` and `InvoiceEdit` objects can collaborate with that `Rule` object to ensure that the rule is consistently applied. As you can see in Figure 2-6, the actual rule is only implemented once but is used as appropriate—effectively normalizing that behavior.

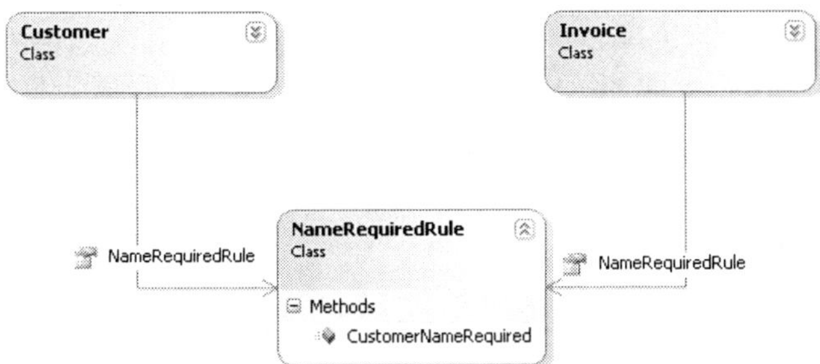

Figure 2-6. *Normalizing the customer name required behavior*

It could be argued that the `CustomerName` concept should become an object of its own and that this object would implement the behaviors common to the field. While this sounds good in an idealistic sense, it has serious performance and complexity drawbacks when implemented on development platforms such as .NET. Creating a custom object for every field in your application can rapidly become overwhelming, and such an approach makes the use of technologies such as data binding very complex.

My approach of normalizing the rules themselves provides a workable compromise: providing a high level of code reuse while still offering good performance and allowing the application to take advantage of all the features of the .NET platform.

In fact, the idea that a string value is required is so pervasive that it can be normalized to a general `StringRequired` rule that can be used by any object with a required property anywhere in an application. In Chapter 11, I implement a `CommonRules` class containing several common validation rules of this nature.

Object-Relational Mapping

If object models aren't the same as relational models (or some other data models that we might be using), some mechanism is needed by which data can be translated from the Data Storage and Management layer up into the object-oriented Business layer.

■ **Note** This mismatch between object models and relational models is a well-known issue within the object-oriented community. It is commonly referred to as the *impedance mismatch problem*, and one of the best discussions of it can be found in David Taylor's book, *Object-Oriented Technology: A Manager's Guide* (Addison-Wesley, 1991).

Several object-relational mapping (ORM) products from various vendors, including Microsoft, exist for the .NET platform. In truth, however, most ORM tools have difficulty working against object models defined using behavioral object-oriented design. Unfortunately, most of the ORM tools tend to create "superpowered" `DataSet` equivalents, rather than true behavioral business objects. In other words, they create a data-centric representation of the business data and wrap it with business logic.

The differences between such a data-centric object model and what I am proposing in this book are subtle but important. Responsibility-driven object modeling creates objects that are focused on the object's behavior, not on the data it contains. The fact that objects contain data is merely a side effect of implementing behavior; the data is not the identity of the object. Most ORM tools, by contrast, create objects based around the data, with the *behavior* being a side effect of the data in the object.

Beyond the philosophical differences, the wide variety of mappings that you might need and the potential for business logic driving variations in the mapping from object to object make it virtually impossible to create a generic ORM product that can meet everyone's needs.

Consider the `CustomerEdit` object example discussed earlier. While the customer data may come from one database, it is totally realistic to consider that some data may come from SQL Server while other data comes through screen scraping a mainframe screen. It's also quite possible that the business logic will dictate that some of the data is updated in some cases but not in others. Issues such as these are virtually impossible to solve in a generic sense, and so solutions almost always revolve around custom code. The most a typical ORM tool can do is provide support for simple cases, in which objects are updated to and from standard, supported, relational data stores. At most, they provide hooks by which you can customize their behavior. Rather than trying to build a generic ORM product as part of this book, I'll aim for a much more attainable goal.

The framework in this book defines a standard set of four methods for creating, retrieving, updating, and deleting objects. Business developers will implement these four methods to work with the underlying data management tier by using the ADO.NET Entity Framework, LINQ to SQL, raw ADO.NET, the XML support in .NET, XML services, or any other technology required to accomplish the task. In fact, if you have an ORM (or some other generic data access) product, you'll often be able to invoke that tool from these four methods just as easily as using ADO.NET directly.

■ Note The approach taken in this book and the associated framework is very conducive to code generation. Many people use code generators to automate the process of building common data access logic for their objects, thus achieving high levels of productivity while retaining the ability to create a behavioral object-oriented model.

The point is that the framework will simplify object persistence so that all developers need to do is implement these four methods in order to retrieve or update data. This places no restrictions on the object's ability to work with data and provides a standardized persistence and mapping mechanism for all objects.

Preserving Encapsulation

As I noted at the beginning of the chapter, one of my key goals is to design this framework to provide powerful features while following the key object-oriented concepts, including *encapsulation*. Encapsulation is the idea that all of the logic and data pertaining to a given business entity is held within the object that represents that entity. Of course, there are various ways in which one can interpret the idea of encapsulation—nothing is ever simple.

One approach is to encapsulate business data and logic in the business object and then encapsulate data access and ORM behavior in some other object: a persistence object. This provides a nice separation between the business logic and data access and encapsulates both types of behavior, as shown in Figure 2-7.

Figure 2-7. *Separation of ORM logic into a persistence object*

Although there are certainly some advantages to this approach, there are drawbacks, too. The most notable of these is that it can be challenging to efficiently get the data from the persistence object into or out of the business object. For the persistence object to load data into the business object, it must be able to bypass business and validation processing in the business object and somehow load raw data into it directly. If the persistence object tries to load data into the object using the object's public properties, you'll run into a series of issues:

- The data already in the database is presumed valid, so a lot of processing time is wasted unnecessarily revalidating data. This can lead to a serious performance problem when loading a large group of objects.
- There's no way to load read-only property values. Objects often have read-only properties for things such as the primary key of the data, and such data obviously must be loaded into the object, but it can't be loaded via the normal interface (if that interface is properly designed).
- Sometimes properties are interdependent due to business rules, which means that some properties must be loaded before others or errors will result. The persistence object would need to know about all these conditions so that it could load the right properties first. The result is that the persistence object would become *very* complex, and changes to the business object could easily break the persistence object.

On the other hand, having the persistence object load raw data into the business object breaks encapsulation in a big way because one object ends up directly tampering with the internal fields of another. This could be implemented using reflection or by designing the business object to expose its private fields for manipulation. But the former is slow and the latter is just plain bad object design: it allows the UI developer (or any other code) to manipulate these fields, too. That's just asking for the abuse of the objects, which will invariably lead to code that's impossible to maintain.

What's needed is a workable compromise, where the actual data access code is in one object while the code to load the business object's fields is in the business object itself. This can be accomplished by creating a separate data access layer (DAL) assembly that is invoked by the business object. The DAL defines an interface the business object can use to retrieve and store information, as shown in Figure 2-8.

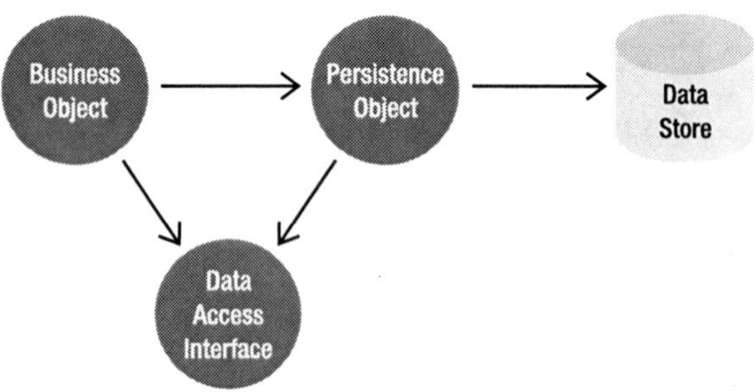

Figure 2-8. *Business object interacting with a data access layer*

This is a nice compromise because it allows the business object to completely manage its own fields and yet keeps the code that communicates with the database cleanly separated into its own location.

There are several ways to implement such a DAL, including the use of raw ADO.NET and the use of LINQ to SQL. The raw ADO.NET approach has the benefit of providing optimal performance. In this case the DAL simply returns a DataReader to the business object and the object can load its fields directly from the data stream.

Creating the DAL using LINQ to SQL or the ADO.NET Entity Framework provides a higher level of abstraction and simplifies the DAL code. However, this approach is slower, because the data must pass through a set of data transfer objects (DTOs) or entity objects as it flows to and from the business object.

■ **Note** In many CSLA .NET applications, the data access code is directly embedded within the business object. While this arguably blurs the boundary between layers, it often provides the best performance and the simplest code.

The examples in this book use a formal data access layer created using LINQ to SQL, but the same architecture supports creation of a DAL that uses raw ADO.NET or many other data access technologies.

Supporting Physical N-Tier Models

The question that remains then is how to support physical n-tier models if the UI-oriented and data-oriented behaviors reside in *one* object.

UI-oriented behaviors almost always involve a lot of properties and methods, with a very fine-grained interface with which the UI can interact in order to set, retrieve, and manipulate the values of an object. Almost by definition, this type of object *must* run in the same process as the UI code itself, either on the Windows client machine with WPF or Windows Forms or on the web server with Web Forms.

Conversely, data-oriented behaviors typically involve very few methods: create, fetch, update, delete. They must run on a machine where they can establish a physical connection to the data store. Sometimes this is the client workstation or web server, but often it means running on a physically separate application server.

This point of apparent conflict is where the concept of *mobile objects* enters the picture. It's possible to pass a business object from an application server to the client machine, work with the object, and then pass the object back to the application server so that it can store its data in the database. To do this, there needs to be some black-box component running as a service on the application server with which the client can interact. This black-box component does little more than accept the object from the client and then call methods on the object to retrieve or update data as required. But the object itself does all the real work. Figure 2-9 illustrates this concept, showing how the same physical business object can be passed from application server to client, and vice versa, via a generic router object that's running on the application server.

In Chapter 1, I discussed anchored and mobile objects. In this model, the business object is mobile, meaning that it can be passed around the network by value. The router object is anchored, meaning that it will always run on the machine where it's created.

In the framework, I'll refer to this router object as a *data portal*. It will act as a portal for all data access for all the objects. The objects will interact with this portal in order to retrieve default values (create), fetch data (read), update or insert data (update), and remove data (delete). This means that the data portal will provide a standardized mechanism by which objects can perform all *create, read, update, delete* (CRUD) operations.

The end result will be that each business class will include a factory method that the UI can call in order to load an object based on data from the database, as follows:

```
public static Customer GetCustomer(string customerId)
{
  return DataPortal.Fetch<Customer>(
    new SingleCriteria<Customer, string>(customerId));
}
```

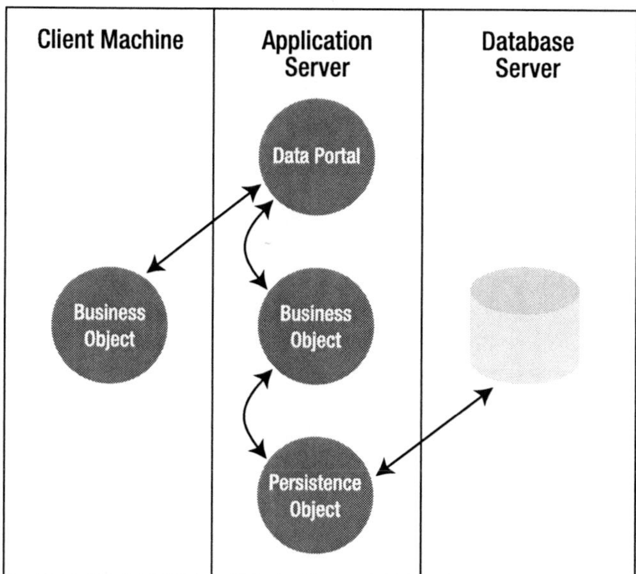

Figure 2-9. *Passing a business object to and from the application server*

Notice how the data portal concept abstracts the use of WCF, and so this code is far simpler than the WCF code used earlier in the chapter.

The actual data access code will be contained within each of the business objects. The data portal will simply provide an anchored object on a machine with access to the database server and will invoke the appropriate CRUD methods on the business objects themselves. This means that the business object will also implement a method that will be called by the data portal to actually load the data. That method will look something like this:

```
private void DataPortal_Fetch(SingleCriteria<Customer, string> criteria)
{
  // Code to load the object's fields with data goes here
}
```

The UI won't know (or need to know) how any of this works, so in order to create a `Customer` object, the UI will simply write code along these lines:

```
var cust = Customer.GetCustomer("ABC");
```

The framework, and specifically the data portal, will take care of all the rest of the work, including figuring out whether the data access code should run on the client workstation or on an application server.

Using the data portal means that all the logic remains encapsulated within the business objects, while physical n-tier configurations are easily supported. Better still, by implementing the data portal correctly, you can switch between having the data access code running on the client machine and placing it on a separate application server just by changing a configuration file setting. The ability to change between 2- and 3-tier physical configurations with no changes to code is a powerful and valuable feature.

Custom Authentication

Application security is often a challenging issue. Applications need to be able to authenticate the user, which means that they need to verify the user's identity. The result of authentication is not only that the application knows the identity of the user but that the application has access to the user's role membership and possibly other information about the user. Collectively, I refer to this as the user's *profile data*. This profile data can be used by the application for various purposes, most notably authorization.

CSLA .NET directly supports integrated security. This means that you can use objects within the framework to determine the user's Windows identity and any domain or Active Directory (AD) groups to which they belong. In some organizations, this is enough; all the users of the organization's applications are in AD, and by having users log in to a workstation or a website using integrated security, the applications can determine the user's identity and roles (groups).

In other organizations, applications are used by at least some users who are *not* part of the organization's NT domain or AD. They may not even be members of the organization in question. This is very often the case with web and mobile applications, but it's surprisingly common with Windows applications as well. In these cases, you *can't* rely on Windows integrated security for authentication and authorization.

To complicate matters further, the ideal security model would provide user profile and role information not only to server-side code but also to the code on the client. Rather than allowing the user to attempt to perform operations that will generate errors due to security at some later time, the UI should gray out the options, or not display them at all. This requires that the developer has consistent access to the user's identity and profile at all layers of the application, including the UI, Business, and Data Access layers.

Remember that the layers of an application may be deployed across multiple physical tiers. Due to this fact, there must be a way of transferring the user's identity information across tier boundaries. This is often called *impersonation*.

Implementing impersonation isn't too hard when using Windows integrated security, but it's often problematic when relying on roles that are managed in a custom SQL Server database, an LDAP store, or any other location outside of AD.

The CSLA .NET framework will provide support for both Windows integrated security *and* custom authentication, in which you define how the user's credentials are validated and the user's profile data and roles are loaded. This custom security is a model that you can adapt to use any existing security tables or services that already exist in your organization. The framework will rely on Windows to handle impersonation when using Windows integrated or AD security and will handle impersonation itself when using custom authentication.

Designing the Framework

So far, I have focused on the major goals for the framework. Having covered the guiding principles, let's move on to discuss the design of the framework so it can meet these goals. In the rest of this chapter, I walk through the various classes that will combine to create the framework. After covering the design, in Chapters 6 through 16 I dive into the implementation of the framework code.

A comprehensive framework can be a large and complex entity. There are usually many classes that go into the construction of a framework, even though the end users of the framework—the business developers—only use a few of those classes directly. The framework discussed here and implemented in Chapters 6 through 16 accomplishes the goals I've just discussed, along with enabling the basic creation of object-oriented n-tier business applications. For any given application or organization, this framework will likely be modified and enhanced to meet specific requirements. This means that the framework will grow as you use and adapt it to your environment.

The CSLA .NET framework contains a lot of classes and types, which can be overwhelming if taken as a whole. Fortunately, it can be broken down into smaller units of functionality to better understand how each part works. Specifically, the framework can be divided into the following functional groups:

- Business object creation
- N-level undo functionality
- Data binding support
- Validation and business rules
- A data portal enabling various physical configurations
- Transactional and nontransactional data access
- Authentication and authorization
- Helper types and classes

For each functional group, I'll focus on a subset of the overall class diagram, breaking it down into more digestible pieces.

Business Object Creation

First, it's important to recognize that the key classes in the framework are those that business developers will use as they create business objects but that these are a small subset of what's available. In fact, many of the framework classes are never used *directly* by business developers. Figure 2-10 shows only those classes the business developer will typically use.

Figure 2-10. *Framework classes used directly by business developers*

Obviously, the business developer may periodically interact with other classes as well, but these are the ones that will be at the center of most activity. Classes or methods that the business developer shouldn't have access to will be scoped to prevent accidental use.

Table 2-1 summarizes each class and its intended purpose.

Table 2-1. *Business Framework Base Classes*

Class	Purpose
`BusinessBase<T>`	Inherit from this class to create a single editable business object such as `Customer`, `Order`, or `OrderLineItem`.
`BusinessListBase<T,C>`	Inherit from this class to create an editable collection of business objects such as `PaymentTerms` or `OrderLineItems`.
`EditableRootListBase<C>`	Inherit from this class to implement a collection of business objects, where changes to each object are committed automatically as the user moves from object to object (typically in a data bound grid control).
`CommandBase`	Inherit from this class to implement a command that should run on the application server, such as implementation of a `Customer.Exists` or an `Order.ShipOrder` command.
`ReadOnlyBase<T>`	Inherit from this class to create a single read-only business object such as `OrderInfo` or `ProductStatus`.

Table 2-1. *Business Framework Base Classes*

Class	Purpose
`ReadOnlyListBase<T,C>`	Inherit from this class to create a read-only collection of objects such as `CustomerList` or `OrderList`.
`NameValueListBase<K,V>`	Inherit from this class to create a read-only collection of key/value pairs (typically for populating drop-down list controls) such as `PaymentTermsCodes` or `CustomerCategories`.

These base classes support a set of object *stereotypes*. A stereotype is a broad grouping of objects with similar behaviors or roles. The supported stereotypes are listed in Table 2-2.

Table 2-2. *Supported Object Stereotypes*

Stereotype	Description	Base Class
Editable root	Object containing read-write properties; object can be retrieved/stored directly to database	`BusinessBase<T>`
Editable child	Object containing read-write properties; object is contained within another object and *cannot* be retrieved/stored directly to database	`BusinessListBase<T,C>`
Editable root list	List object containing editable child objects; list can be retrieved/stored directly to database	`BusinessBase<T>`
Editable child list	List object containing editable child objects; list is contained within another object and *cannot* be retrieved/stored directly to database	`BusinessListBase<T,C>`
Dynamic root list	List object containing editable root objects; list is retrieved directly from database	`EditableRootListBase<C>`
Command	Object that executes a command on the application server and reports back with the results	`CommandBase`
Read-only root	Object containing read-only properties; object can be retrieved directly from database	`ReadOnlyBase<T>`
Read-only child	Object containing read-only properties; object is contained within another object and *cannot* be retrieved directly from database	`ReadOnlyBase<T>`
Read-only root list	List containing read-only child objects; list can be retrieved directly from database	`ReadOnlyListBase<T,C>`
Read-only child list	List containing read-only child objects; list is contained within another object and *cannot* be retrieved directly from database	`ReadOnlyListBase<T>`
Name/value list	List object containing read-only name/value objects	`NameValueListBase<K,V>`

Let's discuss each stereotype in a bit more detail.

Editable Root

The BusinessBase class is the base from which all editable (read-write) business objects will be created. In other words, to create a business object, inherit from BusinessBase, as shown here:

```
[Serializable]
public class CustomerEdit : BusinessBase<CustomerEdit>
{
}
```

When creating a subclass, the business developer must provide the specific type of new business object as a type parameter to BusinessBase<T>. This allows the generic BusinessBase type to expose strongly typed methods corresponding to the specific business object type.

Behind the scenes, BusinessBase<T> inherits from Csla.Core.BusinessBase, which implements the majority of the framework functionality to support editable objects. The primary reason for pulling the functionality out of the generic class into a normal class is to enable *polymorphism*. Polymorphism is what allows you to treat all subclasses of a type as though they were an instance of the base class. For example, all Windows Forms—Form1, Form2, and so forth—can be treated as type Form. You can write code like this:

```
Form form = new Form2();
form.Show();
```

This is polymorphic behavior, in which the variable form is of type Form but references an object of type Form2. The same code would work with Form1 because both inherit from the base type Form.

It turns out that generic types are not polymorphic like normal types.

Another reason for inheriting from a non-generic base class is to make it simpler to customize the framework. If needed, you can create alternative editable base classes starting with the functionality in Core.BusinessBase.

Csla.Core.BusinessBase and the classes from which it inherits provide all the functionality discussed earlier in this chapter, including n-level undo, tracking of broken rules, "dirty" tracking, object persistence, and so forth. It supports the creation of *root objects* (top-level) and *child objects*. Root objects are objects that can be retrieved directly from and updated or deleted within the database. Child objects can only be retrieved or updated in the context of their parent object.

■ **Note** Throughout this book, it is assumed that you are building business applications, in which case almost all objects are ultimately stored in the database at one time or another. Even if an object isn't persisted to a database, you can still use BusinessBase to gain access to the n-level undo and business, validation, and authorization rules and change tracking features built into the framework.

For example, an InvoiceEdit is typically a root object, though the LineItem objects contained by an InvoiceEdit object are child objects. It makes perfect sense to retrieve or update an InvoiceEdit, but it makes no sense to create, retrieve, or update a LineItem without having an associated InvoiceEdit.

The BusinessBase class provides default implementations of the data access methods that exist on all root business objects.

■ **Note** The default implementations are a holdover from a very early version of the framework. They still exist to preserve backward compatibility to support users who have been using CSLA .NET for many years and over many versions.

These methods will be called by the data portal mechanism. These default implementations all raise an error if they're called. The intention is that the business objects can opt to override these methods if they need to support, create, fetch, insert, update, or delete operations. The names of these methods are as follows:

- `DataPortal_Create()`
- `DataPortal_Fetch()`
- `DataPortal_Insert()`
- `DataPortal_Update()`
- `DataPortal_DeleteSelf()`
- `DataPortal_Delete()`

Though `virtual` implementations of these methods are in the base class, developers will typically implement strongly typed versions of `DataPortal_Create()`, `DataPortal_Fetch()`, and `DataPortal_Delete()`, as they all accept a criteria object as a parameter. The `virtual` methods declare this parameter as type `object`, of course; but a business object will typically want to use the actual data type of the criteria object itself. This is discussed in more detail in Chapters 15 and 18.

The data portal also supports three other (optional) methods for pre- and post-processing and exception handling. The names of these methods are as follows:

- `DataPortal_OnDataPortalInvoke()`
- `DataPortal_OnDataPortalInvokeComplete()`
- `DataPortal_OnDataPortalException()`

Editable root objects are very common in most business applications.

Editable Child

Editable child objects are always contained within another object and they cannot be directly retrieved or stored in the database. Ultimately there's always a single editable root object that is retrieved or stored.

`BusinessBase` includes a method that can be called to indicate that the object is a child object: `MarkAsChild()`. Normally this method is invoked automatically by CSLA .NET as the object instance is created by the data portal. This means that a child object might look like this:

```
[Serializable]
public class Child : BusinessBase<Child>
{
}
```

Notice that there's no different from the previous root object. If for some reason you do not use the data portal (discussed later in the "Data Portal" section) to create instances of your objects, you may need to call `MarkAsChild()` manually in the object's constructor:

```
[Serializable]
public class Child : BusinessBase<Child>
{
  private Child()
  {
    MarkAsChild();
  }
}
```

The data access methods for a child object are different from those of a root object. The names of these methods are as follows:

- Child_Create()
- Child_Fetch()
- Child_Insert()
- Child_Update()
- Child_DeleteSelf()

The BusinessBase class does not provide virtual implementations of these methods; they must be explicitly declared by the author of the child class. These methods are called by the data portal to notify each child object when it should perform its data persistence operations.

BusinessBase provides a great deal of functionality to the business objects, whether root or child. Chapter 6 covers the implementation of BusinessBase itself, and Chapters 17 and 18 show how to create business objects using BusinessBase.

Editable Root List

The BusinessListBase class is the base from which all editable *collections* of business objects are created. Given an InvoiceEdit object with a collection of LineItem objects, BusinessListBase is the base for creating that collection:

```
[Serializable]
public class LineItems : BusinessListBase<LineItems, LineItem>
{
}
```

When creating a subclass, the business developer must provide the specific types of his new business collection, and the child objects the collection contains, as type parameters to BusinessListBase<T,C>. This allows the generic type to expose strongly typed methods corresponding to the specific business collection type and the type of the child objects.

The result is that the business collection automatically has a strongly typed indexer, along with strongly typed Add() and Remove() methods. The process is the same as if the object had inherited from System.ComponentModel.BindingList<T>, except that *this* collection will include all the functionality required to support n-level undo, object persistence, and the other business object features.

Note BusinessListBase inherits from System.ComponentModel.BindingList<T>, so it starts with all the core functionality of a data-bindable .NET collection.

The BusinessListBase class also defines the data access methods discussed previously in the section on BusinessBase. This allows retrieval of a collection of objects directly (rather than a single object at a time), if that's what is required by the application design. Typically only the following methods are implemented in a list:

- DataPortal_Create()
- DataPortal_Fetch()

There is a DataPortal_Update() method, but BusinessListBase provides a default implementation that is usually sufficient to save all objects contained in the list.

Editable Child List

The BusinessListBase class also defines the MarkAsChild() method discussed in the previous "Editable Child" section. This is typically called automatically when an instance of the class is created by the data portal and indicates that the list is a child of some other object.

When creating a child list, the developer will typically implement the following data access methods:

- Child_Create()
- Child_Fetch()

There is a Child_Update() method but BusinessListBase provides a default implementation that is usually sufficient to save all objects contained in the list.

Dynamic Root List

The EditableRootListBase class is the base from which collections of editable root business objects can be created. This stereotype and base class exist to support a very specific scenario where the list is data bound to a Windows Forms grid control, allowing the user to do in-place editing of the data in the grid.

In that data bound grid scenario, when using a dynamic root list, all changes to data on a row in the grid are committed as soon as the user moves off that row. If the user deletes a row, the object is immediately deleted. If the user edits a value and moves up or down to another row, that change is immediately saved.

This is fundamentally different from an editable root list, where the user's changes to items in the list aren't committed to the database until the UI saves the entire list.

Given a CategoryList object with a collection of CategoryEdit objects, EditableRootListBase will be the base for creating that collection:

```
[Serializable]
public class CategoryList : EditableRootListBase<CategoryEdit>
{
}
```

When creating a subclass, the business developer must provide the specific type of the objects the collection contains. The contained objects should be editable root objects, with one variation. Rather than implementing DataPortal_Fetch(), they will typically implement Child_Fetch() so they can be loaded into memory by the containing collection.

Like BusinessListBase, EditableRootListBase inherits from BindingList<T> and so supports all the rich data binding behaviors provided by .NET.

A dynamic root list will usually implement only one data access method: DataPortal_Fetch(). Again, this stereotype and base class exist to serve a very specific function; but when dynamic in-place editing of data in a Windows Forms grid is required, this is a very useful approach.

Command

Most applications consist not only of interactive forms or pages (which require editable objects and collections) but also of non-interactive processes. In a one- or two-tier physical model, these processes run on the client workstation or web server, of course. But in a three-tier model, they should run on the application server to have optimal access to the database server or other back-end resources.

Common examples of non-interactive processes include tasks as simple as checking to see if a specific customer or product exists and as complex as performing all the back-end processing required to ship and order or post an invoice.

The CommandBase class provides a clear starting point for implementing these types of behaviors. A command object is created on the client and initialized with the data it needs to do its work on the server. It is then executed on the server through the data portal. Unlike other objects, however, command objects implement a special execute method:

```
DataPortal_Execute()
```

The optional pre-, post-, and exception data portal methods can also be implemented if desired. But the DataPortal_Execute() method is the important one, since that is where the business developer writes the code to implement the non-interactive back-end processing.

I make use of CommandBase in Chapter 17 when implementing the sample application objects.

Read-Only Root and Child

Sometimes applications don't want to expose an editable object. Many applications have objects that are read-only or display-only. Read-only objects need to support object persistence only for retrieving data, not for updating data. Also, they don't need to support any of the n-level undo or other editing-type behaviors because they're created with read-only properties.

For editable objects, there's BusinessBase, which has a property that can be set to indicate whether it's a parent or child object. The same base supports both types of objects, allowing dynamic switching between parent and child at runtime.

Making an object read-only or read-write is a bigger decision because it impacts the *interface* of the object. A read-only object should only include read-only properties as part of its interface, and that isn't something you can toggle on or off at runtime. You can make objects read-only, and consequently more specialized and with less overhead, by implementing a specific base class.

The ReadOnlyBase class is used to create read-only objects, as follows:

```
[Serializable]
public class StaticContent : ReadOnlyBase<StaticContent>
{
}
```

Classes shouldn't implement any read-write properties. If this were to happen, it would be entirely up to the code in the object to handle any undo, persistence, or other features for dealing with the changed data. If an object has editable properties, it should subclass from BusinessBase.

Read-only objects include authorization rules so the object can control which users can view each property. Obviously they don't implement business or validation rules because such rules are only invoked when a property changes, and that won't happen with read-only properties.

ReadOnly Root and Child List

Not only do applications sometimes need read-only business objects, they also commonly require immutable *collections* of objects. The ReadOnlyListBase class lets you create strongly typed collections of objects, whereby the object and collection are both read-only:

```
[Serializable]
public class StaticList : ReadOnlyListBase<StaticList, ChildType>
{
}
```

As with ReadOnlyBase, this object supports only the retrieval of data. It has no provision for updating data or handling changes to its data. While the child objects in such a collection may inherit from ReadOnlyBase, they don't have to. More commonly, the child objects in a read-only collection are just simple .NET objects that merely expose read-only properties.

Name/Value List

The `NameValueListBase` class is designed specifically to support the idea of lookup tables or lists of read-only key/value data such as categories, customer types, product types, and so forth. The goal of this class is to simplify the process of retrieving such data and displaying it in common controls such as drop-down lists, combo boxes, and other list controls. The following shows the beginnings of a custom name/value list:

```
[Serializable]
public class CodeList : NameValueListBase<int, string>
{
}
```

While the business developer does need to create a specific class for each type of name/value data, inheriting from this base class largely trivializes the process.

There are a couple similar types in the `System.Collections.Specialized` namespace: `NameObjectCollectionBase` and `NameValueCollection`. These types don't automatically integrate with the rest of the CSLA .NET framework for tasks such as object persistence and don't fully support data binding.

N-Level Undo Functionality

The implementation of n-level undo functionality is quite complex and involves heavy use of reflection. Fortunately, you can use inheritance to place the implementation in a base class so that no business object needs to worry about the undo code. In fact, to keep things cleaner, this code is in its *own* base class, separate from any other business object behaviors, as shown in Figure 2-11.

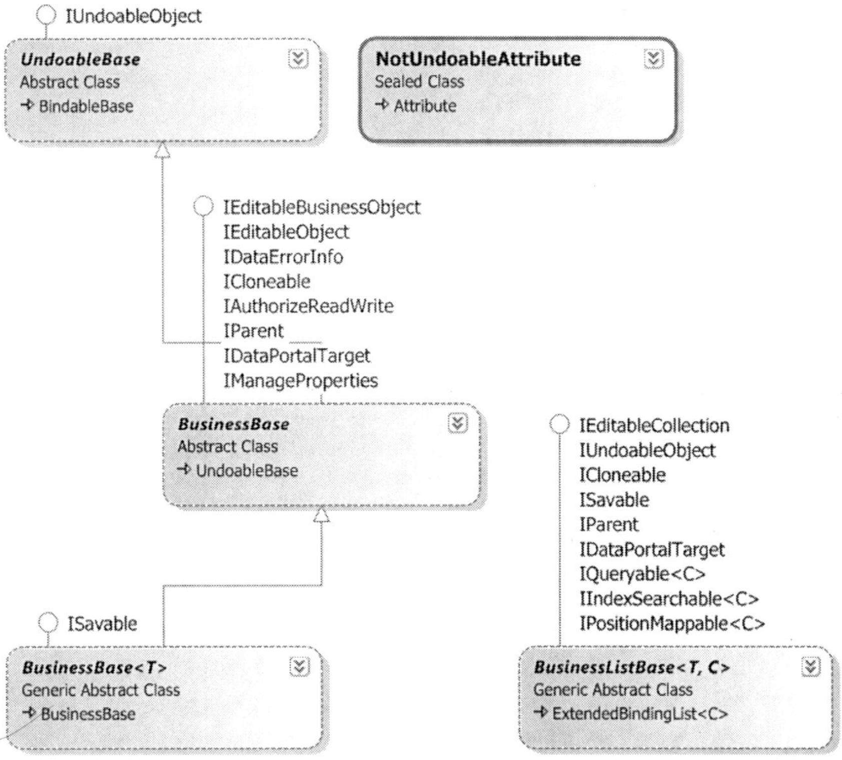

Figure 2-11. *Separating n-level undo into Core.UndoableBase*

At first glance, it might appear that you could use .NET serialization to implement undo functionality: what easier way to take a snapshot of an object's state than to serialize it into a byte stream? Unfortunately, this isn't as easy as it might sound, at least when it comes to restoring the object's state.

Taking a snapshot of a Serializable object is easy and can be done with code similar to this:

```
[Serializable]
public class Customer
{
    public byte[] Snapshot()
    {
      using (var buffer = new MemoryStream())
      {
        var formatter = new BinaryFormatter();

        formatter.Serialize(buffer, this);
        buffer.Position = 0;
        return  buffer.ToArray();
      }
    }
}
```

This converts the object into a byte stream, returning that byte stream as an array of type byte. That part is easy—it's the restoration that's tricky. Suppose that the user now wants to undo the changes, requiring that the byte stream be restored back into the object. The code that deserializes a byte stream looks like this:

```
[Serializable]
public class Customer
{
    public Customer Deserialize(byte[] state)
    {
      using (var buffer = new MemoryStream(state))
      {
        var formatter = new BinaryFormatter();

        return (Customer) formatter.Deserialize(buffer);
      }
    }
}
```

Notice that this function returns a *new customer object*. It doesn't restore the existing object's state; it creates a new object. Somehow, you would have to tell any and all code that has a reference to the existing object to use this new object. In some cases, that might be easy to do, but it isn't always trivial. In complex applications, it's hard to guarantee that other code elsewhere in the application doesn't have a reference to the original object; and if you don't somehow get that code to update its reference to this new object, it will continue to use the old one.

What's needed is some way to restore the object's state *in place*, so that all references to the current object remain valid but the object's state is restored. This is the purpose of the UndoableBase class.

UndoableBase

The BusinessBase class inherits from UndoableBase and thereby gains n-level undo capabilities. Because all business objects inherit from BusinessBase, they too gain n-level undo. Ultimately, the n-level undo capabilities are exposed to the business object and to UI developers via three methods:

- BeginEdit() tells the object to take a snapshot of its current state, in preparation for being edited. Each time BeginEdit() is called, a new snapshot is taken, allowing the state of the object to be trapped at various points during its life. The snapshot will be kept in memory so the data can be easily restored to the object if CancelEdit() is called.
- CancelEdit() tells the object to restore the object to the most recent snapshot. This effectively performs an undo operation, reversing one level of changes. If CancelEdit() is called the same number of times as BeginEdit(), the object will be restored to its original state.
- ApplyEdit() tells the object to discard the most recent snapshot, leaving the object's current state untouched. It accepts the most recent changes to the object. If ApplyEdit() is called the same number of times as BeginEdit(), all the snapshots will be discarded, essentially making any changes to the object's state permanent.

Sequences of BeginEdit(), CancelEdit(), and ApplyEdit() calls can be combined to respond to the user's actions within a complex Windows Forms UI. Alternatively, you can totally ignore these methods, taking no snapshots of the object's state. In such a case, the object will incur no overhead from n-level undo, but it also won't have the ability to undo changes. This is common in web applications in which the user has no option to cancel changes. Instead, the user simply navigates away to perform some other action or view some other data.

The Csla.Core.ISupportUndo interface exists to allow UI developers and framework authors to polymorphically invoke these three methods on any object that supports the concept. The BusinessBase and BusinessListBase classes already implement this interface.

Supporting Child Objects

As it traces through a business object to take a snapshot of the object's state, UndoableBase may encounter child objects. For n-level undo to work for complex objects as well as simple objects, any snapshot of object state must extend down through all child objects as well as the parent object.

I discussed this earlier with the InvoiceEdit and LineItem example. When BeginEdit() is called on an InvoiceEdit, it must *also* take snapshots of the states of all its LineItem objects because they're technically part of the state of the InvoiceEdit object itself. To do this while preserving encapsulation, each individual object takes a snapshot of its own state so that no object data is ever made available outside the object, thus preserving encapsulation for each object.

However, to complicate matters, a BeginEdit() call on a parent object does *not* cascade to its child objects when BeginEdit() is called through the IEditableObject interface. This is because data binding, which uses IEditableObject, gets confused if that happens and the child objects will end up out of sync with the parent, resulting in very hard to debug issues with data bound interfaces.

In that case, UndoableBase simply calls a method on the child object to cascade the BeginEdit(), CancelEdit(), or ApplyEdit() call to that object. It is then up to the individual child object to take a snapshot of its own data. In other words, each object is responsible for managing its own state, including taking a snapshot and potentially restoring itself to that snapshot later.

UndoableBase implements Core.IUndoableObject, which simplifies the code in the class. This interface defines the methods required by UndoableBase during the undo process.

A child object could also be a collection derived from BusinessListBase. Notice that BusinessListBase implements the Core.IEditableCollection interface, which inherits from the Core.IUndoableObject interface.

NotUndoableAttribute

The final concept to discuss regarding n-level undo is the idea that some data might not be subject to being in a snapshot. Taking a snapshot of an object's data takes time and consumes memory; there's no reason to take a snapshot if the object includes read-only values. Because the values can't be changed, there's no benefit in restoring them to the same value in the course of an undo operation.

To accommodate this scenario, the framework includes a custom attribute named NotUndoableAttribute, which you can apply to fields within your business classes, as follows:

```
[NotUndoable]
private string _readonlyData;
```

The code in UndoableBase simply ignores any fields marked with this attribute as the snapshot is created or restored, so the field will always retain its value regardless of any calls to BeginEdit(), CancelEdit(), or ApplyEdit() on the object.

You should be aware that the n-level undo implementation doesn't handle circular references, so if you have a field that references another object in a way that would cause a circular reference, you must mark the field as NotUndoable to break the circle.

Data Binding Support

As I discuss earlier in the chapter, the .NET data binding infrastructure directly supports the concept of data binding to objects and collections. However, an object can provide more complete behaviors by implementing a few interfaces in the framework base classes. Table 2-3 lists the interfaces and their purposes.

Table 2-3. *.NET Data Binding Interfaces*

Interface	Purpose
IBindingList	Defines data binding behaviors for collections, including change notification, sorting, and filtering (implemented by BindingList<T>)
ICancelAddNew	Defines data binding behaviors for collections to allow data binding to cancel addition of a new child object (implemented by BindingList<T>)
IRaiseItemChangedEvents	Indicates that a collection object will raise a ListChanged event to show that one of its child objects has raised a PropertyChanged event (implemented by BindingList<T>)
INotifyCollectionChanged	Defines a CollectionChanged event to be raised by a list when the list or its items have changed (implemented by ObservableCollection<T>)
IEditableObject	Defines single-level undo behavior for a business object, allowing the object to behave properly with in-place editing in a DataGridView
INotifyPropertyChanged	Defines an event allowing an object to notify data binding when a property has been changed
INotifyPropertyChanging	Defines an event allowing an object to notify listeners when a property is about to be changed
IDataErrorInfo	Defines properties used by the DataGridView and ErrorProvider controls to automatically show descriptions of broken validation rules within the object

The IBindingList interface is a well-defined interface that (among other things) raises a single event to indicate that the contents of a collection have changed. Fortunately, there's the System.ComponentModel.BindingList<T> base class that already implements this interface, so virtually no effort is required to gain these benefits.

As mentioned earlier, INotifyCollectionChanged and the corresponding ObservableCollection<T> class are WPF-only replacements for IBindingList and BindingList<T>. You should only implement one or the other solution, and CSLA .NET uses BindingList<T> to gain support for Windows Forms as well as WPF.

The System.ComponentModel.INotifyPropertyChanged and INotifyPropertyChanging interface members are a bit more complex. These interfaces define events that a business object should raise any time a property value is changing or changed. As discussed earlier, in a serializable object, events must be declared using a more explicit syntax than normal so the delegate references can be marked as NonSerialized.

The BindableBase class exists to encapsulate this event declaration and related functionality. This acts as the ultimate base class for BusinessBase<T>, while BindingList<T> is the base class for BusinessListBase<T,C>, as shown in Figure 2-12.

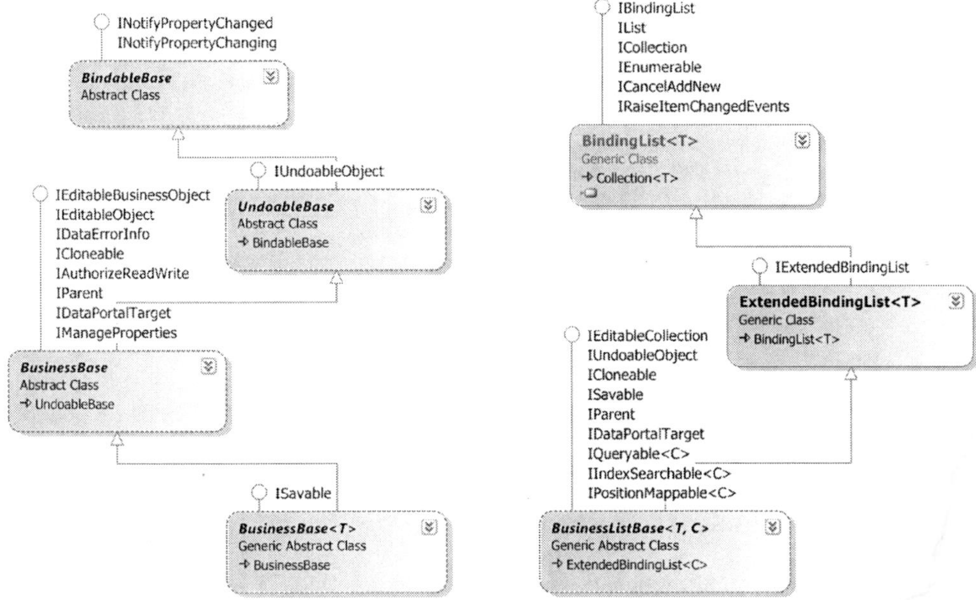

Figure 2-12. *Class diagram with BindableBase and BindingList<T>*

Combined with implementing System.ComponentModel.IEditableObject and System.ComponentModel.IDataErrorInfo in BusinessBase, the objects can fully support data binding in WPF, Windows Forms, and Web Forms.

The CSLA .NET list base classes don't support sorting of a collection through IBindingList. They do provide support for LINQ, however, which means you can use LINQ to CSLA queries to sort or filter the items in any CSLA list.

Note CSLA .NET does include SortedBindingList and FilteredBindingList classes that provide sorted and filtered views against any collection derived from IList<T> (which in turn means any BindingList<T>). These solutions are obsolete with LINQ but remain in the framework for backward compatibility.

ExtendedBindingList Class

The list base classes inherit from ExtendedBindingList<T>, which is a specialized subclass of BindingList<T> that adds a couple important features "missing" from the standard .NET base class.

Most notably, it adds the RemovingItem event, which notifies a business object author that a child object is being removed, including providing a reference to the child object. The standard ListChanged event is useful, but it is raised after the child has been removed, and so there's no way to get a reference to the removed child.

This class also implements a ChildChanged event. Unlike the PropertyChanged or ListChanged events, the ChildChanged event bubbles up through all parent objects to the root object. This means the UI developer can handle the ChildChanged event on any editable root object to be notified when any child object has been changed.

The ExtendedBindingList class also adds an AddRange() method, which makes it easier for a business developer to add multiple items to a collection. This feature is particularly useful when using LINQ to SQL or LINQ to Entities to initialize a collection with data from the data store.

Finally, the class implements the IsSelfBusy and IsBusy properties and related functionality required to support the asynchronous object persistence behaviors discussed in Chapter 15. The IsBusy property returns true while any asynchronous operation is in progress for this object or objects contained in the collection. The IsSelfBusy property returns true while any asynchronous operation is in progress for this object (but not the child objects it contains).

While BindingList<T> does nearly everything required to support data binding, the ExtendedBindingList<T> adds some important features that improve the usability of all CSLA .NET collection base classes.

Business and Validation Rules

Recall that one of the framework's goals is to simplify and standardize the creation of business and validation rules. It also automates the tracking of broken validation rules. An important side benefit of this is that the UI developer will have read-only access to the list of broken rules, which means that the descriptions of the broken rules can be displayed to the user in order to explain what's making the object invalid.

The support for tracking broken business rules is available to *all* editable business objects, so it's implemented at the BusinessBase level in the framework. To provide this functionality, each business object has an associated collection of broken business rules. Additionally, a *rule* is defined as a method that returns a Boolean value indicating whether the business requirement is met. In the case that the result is false (the rule is broken), a rule also returns a text description of the problem for display to the user.

To automate this process, each business object has an associated list of rule methods for each property in the object.

Figure 2-13 illustrates all the framework classes required to implement both the management of rule methods and maintenance of the list of broken rule descriptions.

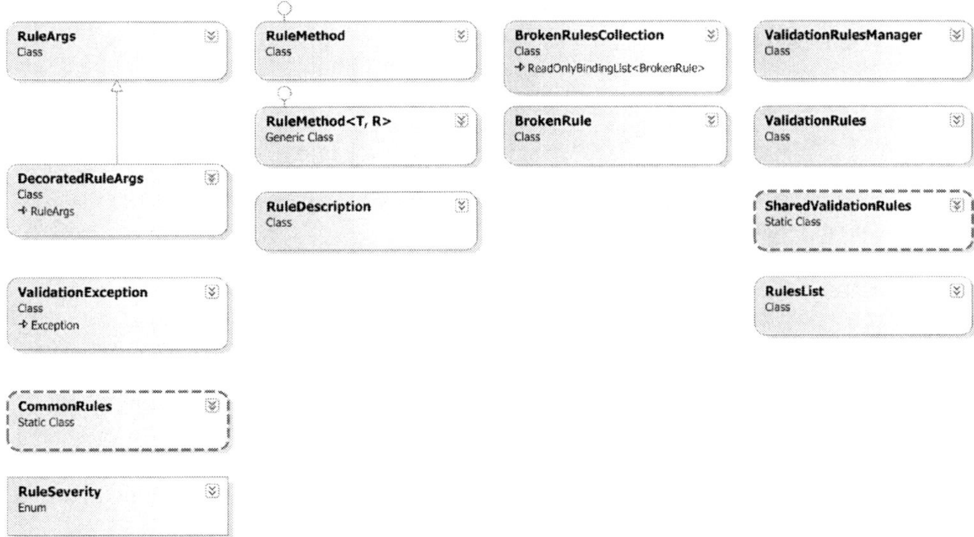

Figure 2-13. *Classes implementing the validation rules behavior*

A business object taps into this functionality through methods exposed on `BusinessBase`. The end result is that a business property is always coded in a consistent manner. In the following example, the highlighted line of code triggers the validation rules behavior:

```
private static PropertyInfo<string> NameProperty =
  RegisterProperty<string>(new PropertyInfo<string>(typeof(Customer), "Name"));
public string Name
{
  get  { return GetProperty<string>(NameProperty); }
  set  { SetProperty<string>(NameProperty, value); }
}
```

Behind the scenes, the `SetProperty()` method calls a `ValidationRules.CheckRules()` method to trigger all rules associated with this property. You can call that method directly if you need to force rules to be checked at other times during the object's life cycle.

You'll see more complete use of the validation rules functionality in Chapter 17, during the implementation of the sample application.

There are three types of functionality displayed in Figure 2-13. The `ValidationRules`, `RuleHandler`, `RuleArgs`, and `ValidationException` classes manage the rule methods associated with the properties of an object. The `BrokenRulesCollection` and `BrokenRule` classes maintain a list of currently broken validation rules for an object. Finally, the `CommonRules` class implements a set of commonly used validation rules, such as `StringRequired`.

Managing Rule Methods

Business rules are defined by a specific method signature as declared in the `RuleHandler` delegate:

```
public delegate bool RuleHandler(object target, RuleArgs e);
```

There are also two generic variations on this signature:

```
public delegate bool RuleHandler<T>(T target, RuleArgs e);
public delegate bool RuleHandler<T, R>(T target, R e);
```

Each business object contains an instance of the ValidationRules object, which in turn maintains a list of rules for each property in the business object. Within ValidationRules there is an optimized data structure that is used to efficiently store and access a list of rules for each property. This allows the business object to request that validation rules for a specific property be executed, or that all rules for all properties be executed.

Each rule method returns a Boolean value to indicate whether the rule is satisfied. If a rule is broken, it returns false. A RuleArgs object is passed to each rule method. This object includes a Description property that the rule can set to describe the nature of a broken rule.

As ValidationRules executes each rule method, it watches for a response. When it gets a negative response, it adds an item to the BrokenRulesCollection for the business object. On the other hand, a positive response causes removal of any corresponding item in BrokenRulesCollection.

Finally, there's the ValidationException class. A ValidationException is *not* thrown when a rule is broken, since the broken rule is already recorded in BrokenRulesCollection. Instead, ValidationException is thrown by BusinessBase itself in the case that there's an attempt to save the object to the database when it's in an invalid state.

Maintaining a List of Broken Rules

The ValidationRules object maintains a list of rule methods associated with an object. It also executes those methods to check the rules, either for a specific property or for all properties. The end result of that process is that descriptions for broken rules are recorded into the BrokenRulesCollection associated with the business object.

The BrokenRulesCollection is a list of BrokenRule objects. Each BrokenRule object represents a validation rule that is currently broken by the data in the business object. These BrokenRule objects are added and removed from the collection by ValidationRules as part of its normal processing.

The BusinessBase class uses its BrokenRulesCollection to implement an IsValid property. IsValid returns true only if BrokenRulesCollection contains no items. If it does contain items, the object is in an invalid state.

The primary point of interest with the BusinessRulesCollection is that it is designed to not only maintain a list of current broken rules but also to provide read-only access to the UI. This is the reason for implementing a specialized collection object that can change its own data but is seen by the UI as being read-only. On top of that, the base class implements support for data binding so that the UI can display a list of broken rule descriptions to the user by simply binding the collection to a list or grid control.

Additionally, the implementation of IDataErrorInfo makes use of the BrokenRulesCollection to return error text for the object or for individual properties. Supporting this interface allows WPF data binding and the Windows Forms DataGridView and ErrorProvider controls to automatically display validation error text to the user.

Implementing Common Rules

If you consider the validation rules applied to most properties, there's a set of common behaviors that occur time and time again. For example, there's the idea that a string value is required, or that a string has a maximum length.

Rather than requiring every business application to implement these same behaviors over and over again, you can have them be supplied by the framework. As you'll see in Chapter 11, the implementation makes use of reflection—so there's a performance cost. If you find in your particular application that performance cost to be too high, you can always do what you would have done anyway—that is, write the rule implementation directly into the application. In most cases, however, the benefit of code reuse will outweigh the small performance cost incurred by reflection.

Data Portal

Supporting *object persistence*—the ability to store and retrieve an object from a database—can be quite complex. This is covered earlier in the chapter during the discussion about basic persistence and the concept of ORM.

As you'll see in Chapter 18, data access logic is encapsulated within the formal data access layer assembly, which is invoked by the business objects. This data access assembly must be deployed to the physical tier that will execute the data access code.

At the same time, however, you don't want to be in a position in which a change to your physical architecture requires every business object in the system to be altered. The ability to easily switch between having the data access code run on the client machine and having it run on an application server is the goal, with that change driven by a configuration file setting.

On top of this, when using an application server, not every business object in the application should be directly exposed by the server. This would be a maintenance and configuration nightmare because it would require updating configuration information on all client machines any time a business object is added or changed.

Note This is a lesson learned from years of experience with DCOM and MTS/COM+. Exposing large numbers of components, classes, and methods from a server almost always results in a tightly coupled and fragile relationship between clients and the server.

Instead, it would be ideal if there were one consistent entry point to the application server so that every client could simply be configured to know about that single entry point and never have to worry about it again. This is exactly what the data portal concept provides, as shown in Figure 2-14.

The data portal provides a single point of entry and configuration for the server. It manages communication with the business objects while they're on the server running their data access code. Additionally, the data portal concept provides the following other key benefits:

- Centralized security when calling the application server
- A consistent object-persistence mechanism (all objects persist the same way)
- Abstraction of the network transport between client and server (enabling support for WCF, remoting, web services, Enterprise Services, and custom protocols)
- One point of control to toggle between running the data access code locally or on a remote application server

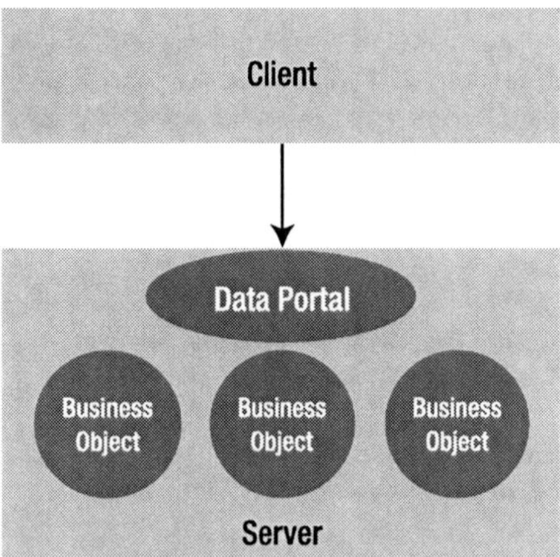

Figure 2-14. *The data portal provides a consistent entry point to the application server.*

The data portal functionality is designed in several parts, as shown in Table 2-4.

Table 2-4. *Parts of the Data Portal Concept*

Area	Functionality
Client-side `DataPortal`	Functions as the primary entry point to the data portal infrastructure, for use by code in business objects
Client-side proxy classes	Implements the channel adapter pattern to abstract the underlying network protocol from the application
Message objects	Transfers data to and from the server, including security information, application context, the business object's data, the results of the call, or any server-side exception data
Server-side host classes	Exposes single points of entry for different server hosts, such as WCF, remoting, `.asmx` web services, and Enterprise Services
Server-side data portal	Implements transactional and nontransactional data access behaviors, delegating all actual data access to appropriate business objects
Server-side child data portal	Implements data access behaviors for objects that are contained within other objects
Object factory	Provides an alternate model for the data portal, where the data portal creates and invokes a factory object instead of interacting directly with the business object

Let's discuss each area of functionality in turn.

Client-Side DataPortal

The client-side `DataPortal` is implemented as a `static` class, which means that any `public` methods it exposes become available to business object code without the need to create a `DataPortal` object. The methods it provides are `Create()`, `Fetch()`, `Update()`, `Delete()`, and `Execute()`. Business objects and collections use these methods to retrieve and update data, or in the case of a CommandBase-derived object, to execute server code on the server.

The client-side DataPortal has a great deal of responsibility, however, since it contains the code to read and act on the client's configuration settings. These settings control whether the "server-side" data portal components will actually run on the server or locally on the client. It also looks at the business object itself, since a RunLocal attribute can be used to force persistence code to run on the client, even if the configuration says to run it on the server.

Either way, the client-side DataPortal always delegates the call to the server-side data portal, which handles the actual object-persistence behaviors. However, if the client configuration indicates that the server-side data portal really will run on a server, the configuration will also specify which network transport should be used. It is the client-side DataPortal that reads that configuration and loads the appropriate client-side proxy object. That proxy object is then responsible for handling the network communication.

As an object is implemented, its code will use the client-side DataPortal to retrieve and update the object's information. An automatic result is that the code in the business object won't need to know about network transports or whether the application is deployed into a 1-, 2-, or n-tier physical environment. The business object code always looks something like this:

```
public static Customer GetCustomer(string id)
{
  return DataPortal.Fetch<Customer>(new SingleCriteria<Customer, string>(id));
}
```

An even more important outcome is that any UI code using these business objects will look something like this:

```
var cust = Customer.GetCustomer(myId);
```

Neither of these code snippets changes, regardless of whether you've configured the server-side data portal to run locally or on a remote server via WCF, remoting, web services, or Enterprise Services. All that changes is the application's configuration file.

Client-Side Proxies

While it is the client-side DataPortal that reads the client configuration to determine the appropriate network transport, the client-side proxy classes actually take care of the details of each network technology. There is a different proxy class for each technology: WCF, remoting, web services, and Enterprise Services.

The design also allows for a business application to provide its own proxy class to use other protocols. This means you can write your own TCP sockets protocol if you are so inclined.

The WCF proxy can use any *synchronous* channel supported by WCF. The data portal requires synchronous communication between client and server but otherwise doesn't care which WCF channel is actually used (HTTP, TCP, etc.). Additionally, you can configure WCF using any of its normal options, such as encryption.

The remoting and web services proxies use the HTTP protocol for communication across the network. This makes both of them firewall and Internet friendly. The Enterprise Services proxy uses DCOM for communication across the network. This is often faster than HTTP but harder to configure for firewalls or the Internet. Both HTTP and DCOM can be configured to encrypt data on the wire and so provide quite high levels of security if needed.

Every client-side proxy has a corresponding server-side host class. This is because each transport protocol requires that both ends of the network connection use the same technology.

The client-side DataPortal simply creates an instance of the appropriate client-side proxy and then delegates the request (Create, Fetch, Update, Delete, or Execute) to the proxy object. The proxy object is responsible for establishing a network connection to the server-side host object and delegating the call across the network.

The proxy must also pass other message data, such as security and application context, to the server. Similarly, the proxy must receive data back from the server, including the results of the operation, application context information, and any exception data from the server.

To this last point, if an exception occurs on the server, the full exception details are returned to the client. This includes the nature of the exception, any inner exceptions, and the stack trace related to the exception. This exception information will often be used on the client to rethrow the exception, giving the illusion that the exception flows naturally from the code on the server back to the code on the client.

Message Objects

When the client-side `DataPortal` calls the server-side data portal, several types of information are passed from client to server. Obviously, the data method call (`Create`, `Update`, `Insert`, etc.) itself is transferred from client to server. But other information is also included, as follows:

- Client-side context data (such as the client machine's culture setting)
- Application-wide context data (as defined by the application)
- The user's principal and identity security objects (if using custom authentication)

Client-side context data is passed one way, from the client to the server. This information may include items such as the client workstation's culture setting, thus allowing the server-side code to also use that context when servicing requests for that user. This can be important for localization of an application when a server may be used by workstations in different nations.

Application-wide context data is passed both from client to server and from server back to client. You may use this context data to pass arbitrary application-specific data between client and server on each data portal operation. This can be useful for debugging, as it allows you to build up a trace log of the call as it goes from client to server and back again.

CSLA .NET also includes the concept of local context, which is *not* passed from client to server or server to client. Local context exists on the client and the server, but each has its own separate context.

If the application is using custom authentication, the custom principal and identity objects representing the user are passed from client to server. This means the code on the server will run under the same security context as the client. If you are using Windows integrated or AD security, you must configure your network transport technology (WCF, remoting, etc.) to handle the impersonation.

When the server-side data portal has completed its work, the results are returned to the client. Other information is also included, as follows:

- Application-wide context data (as defined by the application)
- Details about any server-side exception that may have occurred

Again, the application-wide context data is passed from client to server and from server to client. If an exception occurs on the server, the details about that exception are returned to the client. This is important for debugging, as it means you get the full details about any issues on the server. It is also important at runtime, since it allows you to write exception handling code on the client to gracefully handle server-side exceptions—including data-oriented exceptions such as duplicate key or concurrency exceptions.

The preceding information is passed to and from the server on each data portal operation. Keeping in mind that the data portal supports several verbs, it is important to understand what information is passed to and from the server to support each verb. This is listed in Table 2-5.

Table 2-5. *Data Passed to and from the Server for Data Portal Operations*

Verb	To Server	From Server
`Create`	Type of object to create and (optional) criteria about new object	New object loaded with default values
`Fetch`	Type of object to retrieve and criteria for desired object	Object loaded with data
`Update`	Object to be updated	Object after update (possibly containing changed data)
`Delete`	Type of object to delete and criteria for object to be deleted	Nothing
`Execute`	Object to be executed (must derive from `CommandBase`)	Object after execution (possibly containing changed data)

Notice that the `Create`, `Fetch`, and `Delete` operations all use criteria information about the object to be created, retrieved, or removed. A criteria object contains any data you need to describe your particular business object. A criteria object can be created one of three ways:

- By using the `SingleCriteria` class provided by CSLA .NET
- By creating a nested class within your business class
- By creating a class that inherits from `CriteriaBase`

The `SingleCriteria` class is a generic type that passes a single criteria value to the server. You specify the type of the value and the value itself. Since most objects are identified by a single unique value, this class can be used to create, fetch, and delete most objects.

If your object has more complex criteria, perhaps a compound key in the database or a set of filter values, you'll need to create your own custom criteria class, either as a nested class or by subclassing `CriteriaBase`.

When a criteria class is nested within a business class, the .NET type system can be used to easily determine the type of class in which the criteria is nested. The `CriteriaBase` class, on the other hand, directly includes a property you must set, indicating the type of the business object.

In either case, your custom criteria class should include properties containing any specific information you need in order to identify the specific object to be created, retrieved, or removed.

Server-Side Host Objects

I've already discussed the client-side proxy objects and how each one has a corresponding server-side host object. In Chapter 15, I show how the WCF host object is created. You can look at the CSLA .NET code to see how the other three host objects work for remoting, web services, and Enterprise Services. It is also possible to add new host objects without altering the core framework, providing broad extensibility. Any new host object would need a corresponding client-side proxy, of course.

Server-side host objects are responsible for two things: first, they must accept inbound requests over the appropriate network protocol from the client, and those requests must be passed along to the server-side data portal components; second, the host object is responsible for running inside the appropriate server-side host technology.

Microsoft provides server-side host technologies for hosting application server code: Windows Activation Service (WAS), Internet Information Services (IIS), and Enterprise Services.

It is also possible to write your own Windows service that could act as a host technology, but I strongly recommend against such an approach. By the time you write the host and add in security, configuration, and management support, you'll have recreated most or all of WAS, IIS, or Enterprise Services. Worse, you'll have opened yourself up for unforeseen security and stability issues.

The WCF host object is designed to run within the WAS or IIS hosts. This way, it can take advantage of the management, stability, and security features inherent in those server hosting technologies. Both WAS and IIS provide a robust process model and thread management and so supply very high levels of scalability.

Server-Side Data Portal

At its core, the server-side data portal components provide an implementation of the message router design pattern. The server-side data portal accepts requests from the client and routes those requests to an appropriate handler—either a business object or a factory object.

■ **Note** I say "server-side," but keep in mind that the server-side data portal components may run on either the client workstation or on a remote server. Refer to the "Client-Side DataPortal" section of this chapter regarding how this selection is made. The data portal is implemented to minimize overhead as much as possible when configured to run locally or remotely, so it is appropriate for use in either scenario.

For `Create`, `Fetch`, and `Delete` operations, the server-side data portal requires type information about your business object. For update and execute operations, the business object itself is passed to the server-side data portal.

But the server-side data portal is more than a simple message router. It also provides optional access to the transactional technologies available within .NET, namely the new `System.Transactions` namespace and Enterprise Services (MTS/COM+).

The business framework defines a custom attribute named `TransactionalAttribute` that can be applied to methods within business objects. Specifically, you can apply it to any of the data access methods that your business object might implement to create, fetch, update, or delete data, or to execute server-side code. This allows you to use one of three models for transactions, as listed in Table 2-6.

Table 2-6. *Transaction Options Supported by Data Portal*

Option	Description	Transactional Attribute
`Manual`	You are responsible for implementing your own transactions using ADO.NET, stored procedures, etc.	None or `[Transactional (TransactionalTypes.Manual)]`
`Enterprise Services`	Your data access code will run within a COM+ distributed transactional context, providing distributed transactional support.	`[Transactional(TransactionalTypes. EnterpriseServices)]`
`System. Transactions`	Your data access code will run within a `TransactionScope` from `System.Transactions`, automatically providing basic or distributed transactional support as required.	`[Transactional(TransactionalTypes. TransactionScope)]`

So in the business object there may be an update method (overriding the one in BusinessBase) marked to be transactional:

```
[Transactional(TransactionalTypes.TransactionScope)]
protected override void DataPortal_Update()
{
  // Data update code goes here
}
```

At the same time, the object might have a fetch method in the same class that's *not* transactional:

```
private void DataPortal_Fetch(Criteria criteria)
{
  // Data retrieval code goes here
}
```

Or if you are using an object factory (discussed in the next section), the Transactional attribute would be applied to the Update() method in the factory class:

```
public class MyFactory : Csla.Server.ObjectFactory
{
  [Transactional(TransactionalTypes.TransactionScope)]
  public object Update()
  {
    // Data update code goes here
  }
}
```

This facility means that you can control transactional behavior at the method level rather than at the class level. This is a powerful feature because it means that you can do your data retrieval outside of a transaction to get optimal performance and still do updates within the context of a transaction to ensure data integrity.

The server-side data portal examines the appropriate method on the business object before it routes the call to the business object itself. If the method is marked with [Transactional (TransactionalTypes.TransactionScope)], the call is routed to a TransactionalDataPortal object that is configured to run within a System.Transactions.TransactionScope. A TransactionScope is powerful because it provides a lightweight transactional wrapper in the case that you are updating a single database; but it automatically upgrades to a distributed transaction if you are updating multiple databases. In short, you get the benefits of COM+ distributed transactions if you need them, but you don't pay the performance penalty if you don't need them.

If the method is marked as [Transactional(TransactionalTypes.EnterpriseServices)], the call is routed to a ServicedDataPortal object that is configured to require a COM+ distributed transaction. The ServicedDataPortal then calls the SimpleDataPortal, which delegates the call to your business object, but only after it is running within a distributed transaction. Either way, your code is transactionally protected.

If the method doesn't have the attribute, or is marked as [Transactional(TransactionalTypes. Manual)], the call is routed directly to the SimpleDataPortal, as illustrated in Figure 2-15.

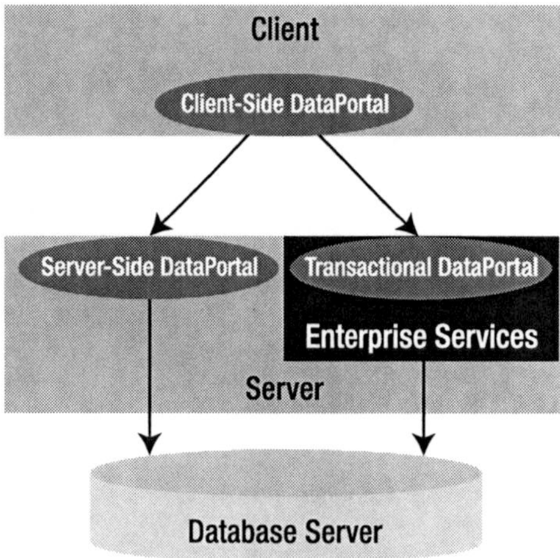

Figure 2-15. *Routing calls through transactional wrappers*

Object Factory Model

By default, the server-side data portal components route calls to methods of an instance of the business object itself. In other words, the business object becomes responsible for initializing itself with new data, loading itself with existing data, and inserting, updating, or deleting its data.

That approach is very simple and efficient but may not offer the best separation between business and data access logic. The `ObjectFactory` attribute and `ObjectFactory` base class provide an alternative, where the data portal creates an instance of an *object factory class* and interacts with that factory object, instead of the business object.

In the default model, the data portal does a lot of work on behalf of the business developer. It creates instances of the business object, manages the object's state values, and generally shepherds the object through the data persistence process.

In the object factory model, the data portal leaves all those details to the factory object, which is created by the business developer. The result is that the business developer has a lot of flexibility but assumes a lot more responsibility. If the business developer doesn't properly manage the business object's state, other areas of CSLA .NET (such as data binding or n-level undo) may not function correctly.

I discuss the details around object factories in Chapters 4 and 5 and the underlying implementation in Chapter 15.

Data Portal Behaviors

Now that you have a grasp of the areas of functionality required to implement the data portal concept, let's discuss the specific data behaviors the data portal will support. The behaviors were listed earlier in Table 2-5.

Create

The create operation is intended to allow the business objects to load themselves with values that must come from the database. Business objects don't need to support or use this capability, but if they do need to initialize default values, this is the mechanism to use.

There are many types of applications for which this is important. For instance, order entry applications typically have extensive defaulting of values based on the customer. Inventory management applications often have many default values for specific parts, based on the product family to which the part belongs. Medical records also often have defaults based on the patient and physician involved.

When the Create() method of the DataPortal is invoked, it's passed a criteria object. As I've explained, the data portal will either use reflection against the criteria object or will rely on the type information in CriteriaBase to determine the type of business object to be created. Using that information, the data portal uses reflection to create an instance of the business object itself. However, this is a bit tricky because all business objects have private or protected constructors to prevent direct creation by code in the UI:

```
[Serializable]
public class Employee : BusinessBase<Employee>
{
  private Employee()
  {      /* prevent direct creation */     }
}
```

Business objects will expose static factory methods to allow the UI code to create or retrieve objects. Those factory methods will invoke the client-side DataPortal. (I discuss this "class-in-charge" concept earlier in the chapter.) As an example, an Employee class may have a static factory method, such as the following:

```
public static Employee NewEmployee()
{
  return DataPortal.Create<Employee>();
}
```

Notice that no Employee object is created on the client here. Instead, the factory method asks the client-side DataPortal for the Employee object. The client-side DataPortal passes the call to the server-side data portal. If the data portal is configured to run remotely, the business object is created on the server; otherwise, the business object is created locally on the client.

Even though the business class has only a private constructor, the server-side data portal uses reflection to create an instance of the class. The alternative is to make the constructor public, in which case the UI developer will need to learn and remember that they must use the static factory methods to create the object. Making the constructor private provides a clear and direct reminder that the UI developer *must* use the static factory method, thus reducing the complexity of the interface for the UI developer. Keep in mind that *not* implementing the default constructor won't work either, because in that case, the compiler provides a public default constructor on your behalf.

Once the server-side data portal has created the business object, it calls the business object's DataPortal_Create() method, optionally passing a criteria object as a parameter. At this point, code *inside* the business object is executing, so the business object can do any initialization that's appropriate for a new object. Typically, this will involve going to the database to retrieve any configurable default values.

When the business object is done loading its defaults, the server-side data portal returns the fully created business object back to the client-side DataPortal. If the two are running on the same machine, this is a simple object reference; but if they're configured to run on separate machines, the business object is serialized across the network to the client (i.e., it's passed by value), so the client machine ends up with a local copy of the business object.

The UML sequence diagram in Figure 2-16 illustrates this process.

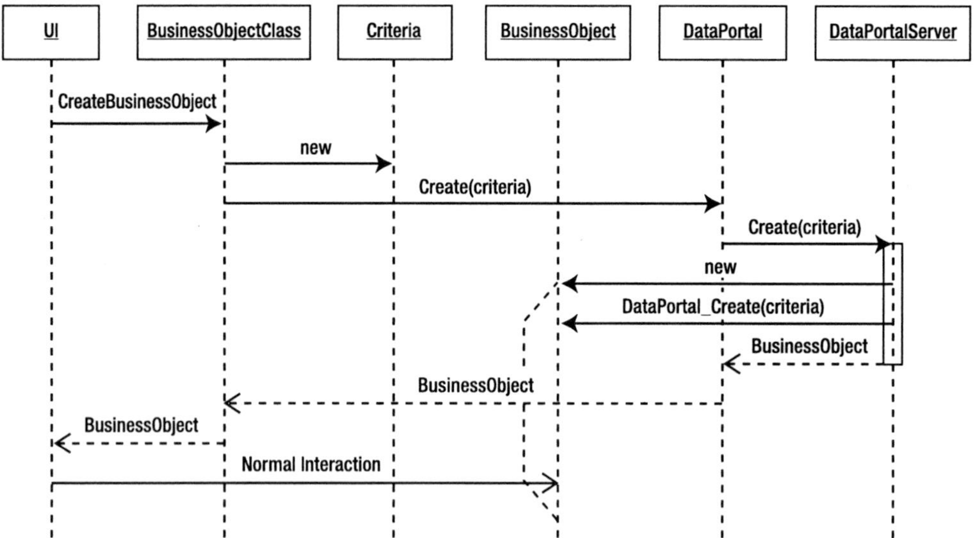

Figure 2-16. *UML sequence diagram for the creation of a new business object*

You can see how the UI interacts with the business object *class* (the `static` factory method), which then creates a criteria object and passes it to the client-side `DataPortal`. The client-side `DataPortal` then delegates the call to the server-side data portal (which may be running locally or remotely, depending on configuration). The server-side data portal then creates an instance of the business object itself and calls the business object's `DataPortal_Create()` method so it can populate itself with default values. The resulting business object is then ultimately returned to the UI.

Alternatively, the `DataPortal_Create()` method could request the default data values from a persistence object in another assembly, thus providing a clearer separation between the Business Logic and Data Access layers.

In a physical n-tier configuration, remember that the criteria object starts out on the client machine and is passed by value to the application server. The business object itself is created on the application server where it's populated with default values. It's then passed back to the client machine by value. This architecture truly takes advantage of the mobile object concept.

Fetch

Retrieving a preexisting object is very similar to the creation process just discussed. Again, a criteria object is used to provide the data that the object will use to find its information in the database. The criteria class is nested within the business object class and/or inherits from `CriteriaBase`, so the server-side data portal code can determine the type of business object desired and then use reflection to create an instance of the class.

The UML sequence diagram in Figure 2-17 illustrates all of this.

The UI interacts with the factory method, which in turn creates a criteria object and passes it to the client-side `DataPortal` code. The client-side `DataPortal` determines whether the server-side data portal should run locally or remotely and then delegates the call to the server-side data portal components.

The server-side data portal uses reflection to determine the assembly and type name for the business class and creates the business object itself. After that, it calls the business object's `DataPortal_Fetch()` method, passing the criteria object as a parameter. Once the business object has populated itself from the database, the server-side data portal returns the fully populated business object to the UI.

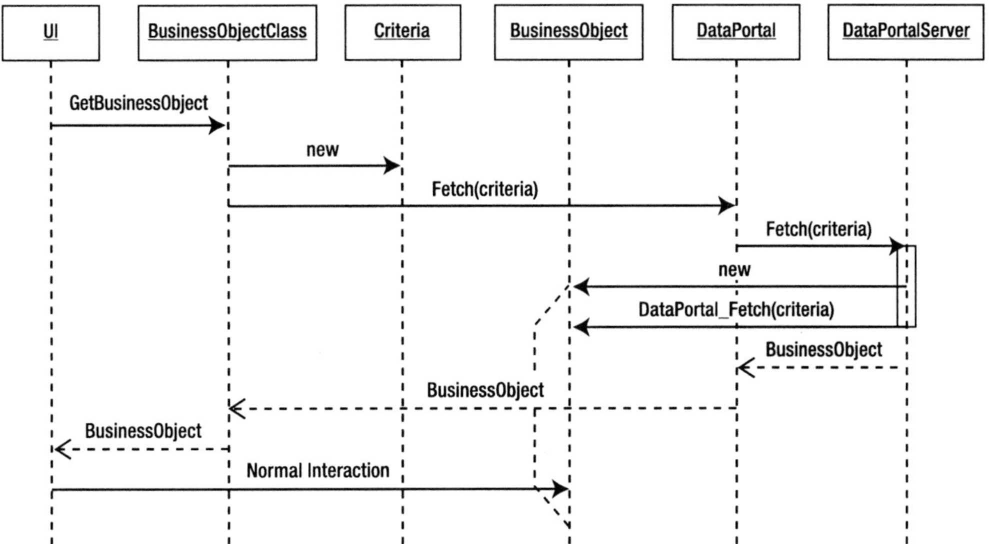

Figure 2-17. *UML sequence diagram for the retrieval of an existing business object*

Alternatively, the `DataPortal_Fetch()` method could delegate the fetch request to a persistence object from another assembly, thus providing a clearer separation between the Business Logic and Data Access layers.

As with the create process, in an n-tier physical configuration, the criteria object and business object move by value across the network as required. You don't have to do anything special beyond marking the classes as `Serializable`; the .NET runtime handles all the details on your behalf.

You may also choose to use the `DataContract` and `DataMember` attributes instead of `Serializable`, but only if you exclusively use WCF for serialization. I discuss this in Chapter 6 but generally recommend using `Serializable` as the simplest option.

Update

The update process is a bit different from the previous operations. In this case, the UI already has a business object with which the user has been interacting, and this object needs to save its data into the database. To achieve this, all editable business objects have `Save()` and `BeginSave()` methods (as part of the `BusinessBase` class from which all business objects inherit). The save methods call the `DataPortal` to do the update, passing the business object itself, `this`, as a parameter.

The `Save()` method is synchronous, while the `BeginSave()` method is asynchronous and reports that it is completed by raising an event. This event is automatically raised on the UI thread in WPF and Windows Forms. In Web Forms or other technologies you'll need to provide your own thread synchronization if you use `BeginSave()`.

The thing to remember when doing updates is that the object's data will likely change as a result of the update process. Any changed data must be placed back into the object.

There are two common scenarios illustrating how data changes during an update. The first is when the database assigns the primary key value for a new object. That new key value needs to be put into the object and returned to the client. The second scenario is when a time stamp is used to implement optimistic first-write-wins concurrency. In this case, every time the object's data is inserted or updated, the time stamp value must be refreshed in the object with the new value from the database. Again, the updated object must be returned to the client. This means that the update process is *bidirectional*. It isn't just a matter of sending the data to the server to be stored but also a matter of returning the object *from* the server after the update has completed so that the UI has a current, valid version of the object.

Due to the way .NET passes objects by value, it may introduce a bit of a wrinkle into the overall process. When passing the object to be saved over to the server, .NET makes a copy of the object from the client onto the server, which is exactly what is desired. However, after the update is complete, the object must be returned to the client. When an object is returned from the server to the client, a new copy of the object is made on the client, which isn't really the desired behavior.

Figure 2-18 illustrates the initial part of the update process.

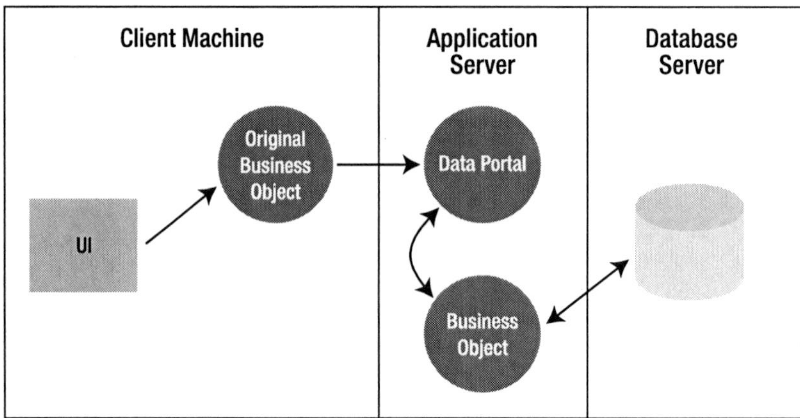

Figure 2-18. *Sending a business object to the data portal to be inserted or updated*

The UI has a reference to the business object and calls its `Save()` method. This causes the business object to ask the data portal to save the object. The result is that a copy of the business object is made on the server, where it can save itself to the database. So far, this is pretty straightforward.

The business object has a `Save()` method, but the data portal infrastructure has methods named `Update()`. Although this is a bit inconsistent, remember that the business object is being called by UI developers; and I've found that it's more intuitive for the typical UI developer to call `Save()` than `Update()`, especially since the `Save()` call can trigger an `Insert`, `Update`, or even `Delete` operation. However, once this part is done, the updated business object is returned to the client and the UI must update its references to use the *newly updated* object instead, as shown in Figure 2-19.

This is fine, too—but it's important to keep in mind that you can't continue to use the old business object; you must update all object references to use the newly updated object. Figure 2-20 is a UML sequence diagram that shows the overall update process.

You can see that the UI calls the `Save()` or `BeginSave()` method on the business object, which results in a call to the client-side `DataPortal`'s `Update()` method, passing the business object as a parameter. As usual, the client-side `DataPortal` determines whether the server-side data portal is running locally or remotely and then delegates the call to the server-side data portal. The server-side data portal then simply calls the `DataPortal_Update()` method on the business object so that the object can save its data into the database. `DataPortal_Insert()` would be called if the object is a new object; `DataPortal_DeleteSelf()` would be called if the object is marked for deletion.

These methods may implement the code to insert, update, or delete the object directly within the business class, or they may delegate the call to a persistence object in another assembly.

At this point, two versions of the business object exist: the original version on the client and the newly updated version on the application server. However, the best way to view this is to think of the original object as being obsolete and invalid at this point. Only the newly updated version of the object is valid.

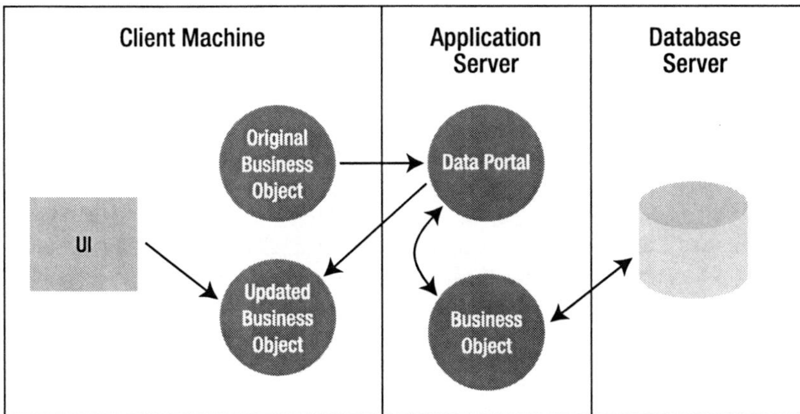

Figure 2-19. *Data portal returning the inserted or updated business object to the UI*

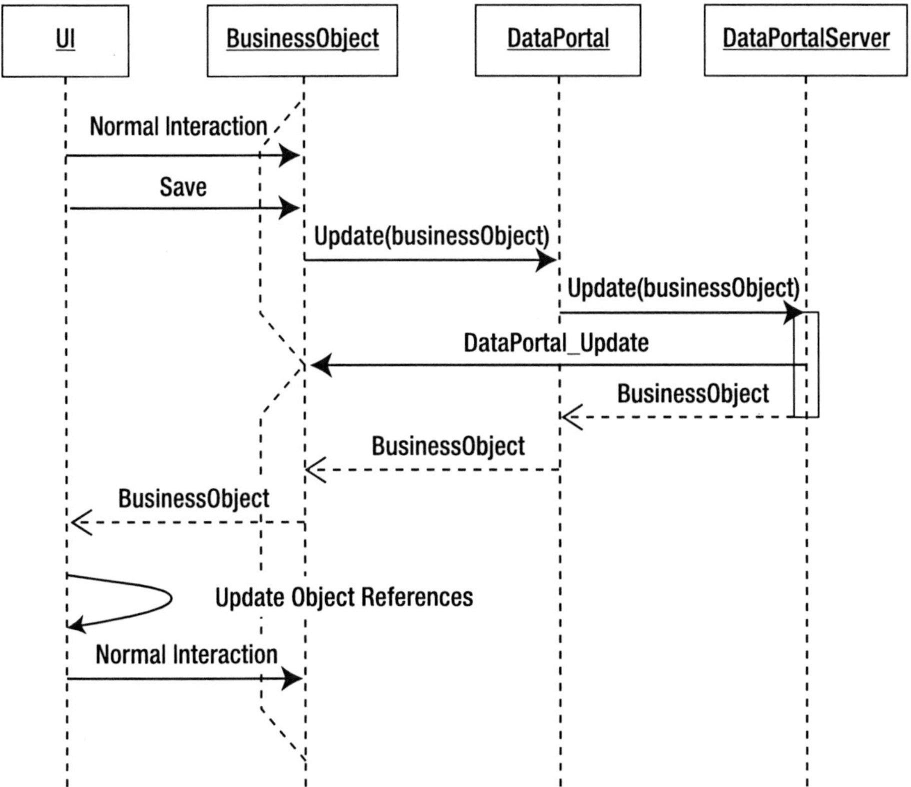

Figure 2-20. *UML sequence diagram for the updating of a business object*

Once the update is done, the new version of the business object is returned to the UI. The UI can then continue to interact with the new business object as needed.

■ **Note** The UI must update any references from the old business object to the newly updated business object as soon as the new object is returned from the data portal.

In a physical n-tier configuration, the business object is automatically passed by value to the server and the updated version is returned by value to the client. If the server-side data portal is running locally, however, the object is cloned and the clone is updated and returned to the calling code. This is necessary because it is possible for the update process to fail halfway through. If your business object contains other business objects, some might have been changed during the update process, while others are unchanged. The database transaction will ensure that the database is in a consistent state, but your object model can be left in an inconsistent state. By saving a clone, if the update fails, the UI is left referencing the *original unchanged object*, which is still in a consistent state.

Delete

The final operation, and probably the simplest, is to delete an object from the database. The framework actually supports two approaches to deleting objects.

The first approach is called *deferred deletion*. In this model, the object is retrieved from the database and is marked for deletion by calling a `Delete()` method on the business object. Then the `Save()` or `BeginSave()` method is called to cause the object to update itself to the database (thus actually doing the `Delete` operation). In this case, the data is deleted by the `DataPortal_DeleteSelf()` method.

The second approach, called *immediate deletion*, consists of simply passing criteria data to the server, where the object is deleted immediately within the `DataPortal_Delete()` method. This second approach provides superior performance because you don't need to load the object's data and return it to the client. Instead, you simply pass the criteria fields to the server, where the object deletes its data.

The framework supports both models, providing you with the flexibility to allow either or both in your object models, as you see fit.

Deferred deletion follows the same process as the update process I just discussed, so let's explore *immediate deletion*. In this case, a criteria object is created to describe the object to be deleted and the data portal is invoked to do the deletion. Figure 2-21 is a UML diagram that illustrates the process.

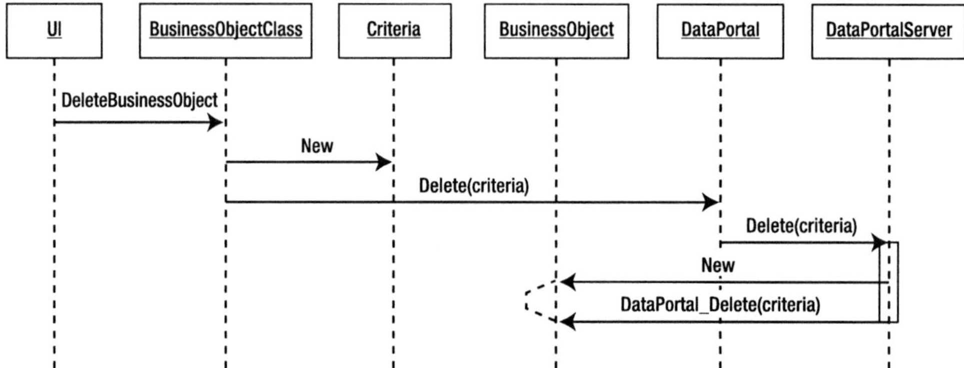

Figure 2-21. *UML sequence diagram for immediate deletion of a business object*

Because the data has been deleted at this point, you have nothing to return to the UI, so the overall process remains pretty straightforward. As usual, the client-side `DataPortal` delegates the call to the server-side data portal. The server-side data portal creates an instance of the business object and invokes its `DataPortal_Delete()` method, providing the criteria object as a parameter.

The business logic to do the deletion itself is encapsulated within the business object, along with all the other business logic relating to the object. Alternatively, the business object could delegate the deletion request to a persistence object in another assembly.

Custom Authentication

As discussed earlier in the chapter, many environments include users who aren't part of a Windows domain or AD. In such a case, relying on Windows integrated security for the application is problematic at best, and you're left to implement your own security scheme. Fortunately, the .NET Framework includes several security concepts, along with the ability to customize them to implement your own security as needed.

The following discussion applies to you only in the case that Windows integrated security doesn't work for your environment. In such a case, you'll typically maintain a list of users and their roles in a database, or perhaps in an LDAP server. The custom authentication concepts discussed here will help you integrate the application with that preexisting security database.

Custom Principal and Identity Objects

The .NET Framework includes a couple of built-in *principal* and *identity* objects that support Windows integrated security or generic security. You can also create your own principal and identity objects by creating classes that implement the `IPrincipal` and `IIdentity` interfaces from the `System.Security.Principal` namespace.

Implementations of principal and identity objects will be specific to your environment and security requirements. However, CSLA .NET includes a `BusinessPrincipalBase` class to streamline the process.

When you create a custom principal object, it must inherit from `BusinessPrincipalBase`. Code in the data portal ensures that only a `WindowsPrincipal` or `BusinessPrincipalBase` object is passed between client and server, depending on the application's configuration.

In many cases, your custom principal object will require very little code. The base class already implements the `IPrincipal` interface, and it is quite likely that you'll only need to implement the `IsInRole()` method to fit your needs.

However, you will need to implement a custom identity object that implements `IIdentity`. Typically, this object will populate itself with user profile information and a list of user roles from a database. Essentially, this is just a read-only business object, and so you'll typically inherit from `ReadOnlyBase`. Such an object might be declared like this:

```
[Serializable]
public class CustomIdentity : ReadOnlyBase<CustomIdentity>, IIdentity
{
  // implement here
}
```

You'll also need to implement a `Login` method that the UI code can call to initiate the process of authenticating the user's credentials (username and password) and loading data into the custom identity object. This is often best implemented as a `static` factory method on the custom principal class. In many cases, this factory method will look something like this:

```
public static void Login(string username, string password)
{
  CustomIdentity identity = CustomIdentity.GetIdentity(username, password);
  if (identity.IsAuthenticated)
  {
    IPrincipal principal = new CustomPrincipal(identity);
    Csla.ApplicationContext.User = principal;
  }
}
```

The GetIdentity method is a normal factory method in CustomIdentity that just calls the data portal to load the object with data from the database. A corresponding Logout method may look like this:

```
public static void Logout()
{
  CustomIdentity identity = CustomIdentity.UnauthenticatedIdentity();
  IPrincipal principal = new CustomPrincipal(identity);
  Csla.ApplicationContext.User = principal;
}
```

The UnauthenticatedIdentity() method is actually a variation on the factory concept, but in this case, it probably doesn't use the data portal. Instead, it merely needs to create an instance of CustomIdentity, in which IsAuthenticated returns false.

Integrated Authorization

Virtually all applications rely on some form of authorization. At the very least, there is typically control over which users have access to the application at all. But more commonly, applications need to restrict which users can view or edit specific bits of data at either the object or property level. This is often accomplished by assigning users to roles and then specifying which roles are allowed to view or edit various data.

To help control whether the current user can view or edit individual properties, the business framework allows the business developer to specify the roles that are allowed or denied the ability to view or edit each property. Typically, these role definitions are set up as the object is created, and they may be hard-coded into the object or loaded from a database, as you choose.

With the list of allowed and denied roles established, the framework is able to implement authentication in the GetProperty() and SetProperty() helper methods. Behind the scenes there are CanReadProperty() and CanWriteProperty() methods that are called to do the actual authentication. Rather than using the GetProperty() and SetProperty() helper methods, you could choose to make explicit calls to the authentication and validation subsystems in CSLA .NET. The result would be a property that looks like this:

```
private string _name = string.Empty;
public string Name
{
  get
  {
    CanReadProperty("Name", true);
    return _name;
  }
```

```
    set
    {
      CanWriteProperty("Name", true);
      if (string.IsNullOrEmpty(value)) value = string.Empty;
      if (_name != value)
      {
        _name = value;
        PropertyHasChanged("Name");
      }
    }
  }
```

Obviously the helper methods discussed earlier in the chapter result in a lot less code and are the preferred approach for coding properties.

The `CanReadProperty()` and `CanWriteProperty()` methods check the current user's roles against the list of roles allowed and denied read and write access to this particular property. If the authorization rules are violated, a security exception is thrown; otherwise, the user is allowed to read or write the property.

The `CanReadProperty()` and `CanWriteProperty()` methods are `public` in scope. This is important because it allows code in the UI layer to ask the object about the user's permissions to read and write each property. The UI can use this information to alter its display to give the user visual cues as appropriate. In Chapter 19, you'll see how this capability can be exploited by a custom WPF control to eliminate most authorization code in a typical application. While the story isn't quite as compelling in Web Forms, Chapter 20 demonstrates how to leverage this capability in a similar manner.

Helper Types and Classes

Most business applications require a set of common behaviors not covered by the concepts discussed thus far. These behaviors are a grab bag of capabilities that can be used to simplify common tasks that would otherwise be complex. These include the items listed in Table 2-7.

Table 2-7. *Helper Types and Classes*

Type or Class	Description
`ConnectionManager`	Enables easy reuse of an open database connection, making the use of `TransactionScope` transactions more practical
`ContextManager`	Enables easy reuse of a LINQ to SQL data context, making the use of `TransactionScope` transactions more practical
`SafeDataReader`	Wraps any `IDataReader` (such as `SqlDataReader`) and converts all `null` values from the database into non-`null` empty or default values
`DataMapper`	Maps data from an `IDictionary` to an object's properties, or from one object's properties to another object's properties
`SmartDate`	Implements a `DateTime` data type that understands both how to translate values transparently between `DateTime` and string representations and the concept of an empty date

Let's discuss each of these in turn.

ConnectionManager

The TransactionScope class from System.Transactions is typically the preferred technology for implementing data update transactions because it results in simpler code and good performance. Unfortunately, TransactionScope automatically invokes the Distributed Transaction Coordinator (DTC) if your code opens more than one database connection and that results in a substantial performance penalty (often around 15 percent). If you avoid opening multiple database connections, TransactionScope uses a lightweight transaction scheme that is just as safe but is much faster.

The result is that you should reuse one open database connection across all your objects when using a TransactionScope object for transactional support. This means you must write code to open the connection object and then make it available to all objects that will be interacting with the database within the transaction. That can unnecessarily complicate what should be simple data access code.

The Csla.Data.ConnectionManager class is intended to simplify this process by managing and automatically reusing a single database connection object. The result is that all data access code that uses a database connection object has the following structure:

```
using (var ctx = ConnectionManager<SqlConnection>.GetManager("DatabaseName"))
{
  // ctx.Connection is now an open connection to the database
  // save your data here
  // call any child objects to save themselves here
}
```

If the connection isn't already open, a connection object is created and opened. If the connection is already open it is reused. When the last nested using block completes, the connection object is automatically disposed of.

ContextManager

When using LINQ to SQL, your code won't typically interact with the underlying database connection object directly. To share an open database connection you must really share the LINQ data context object. Csla.Data.ContextManager is intended to simplify this process by managing and automatically reusing a single data context object. The result is that all data access code that uses a data context object has the following structure:

```
using (var ctx = ContextManager<SqlConnection>.GetManager("DatabaseName"))
{
  // ctx.Context is now an open data context object
  // save your data here
  // call any child objects to save themselves here
}
```

If the connection isn't already open, a connection object is created and opened. If the data context is already open, it is reused. When the last using block completes, the data context object is automatically disposed of.

SafeDataReader

Most of the time, the difference between a null value and an empty value (such as an empty string or a zero) is not important in regard to applications, though it is in databases. When retrieving data from a database, an application needs to handle the occurrence of unexpected null values with code such as the following:

```
if(dr.IsDBNull(idx))
  myValue = string.Empty;
else
  myValue = dr.GetString(idx);
```

Clearly, doing this over and over again throughout the application can get very tiresome. One solution is to fix the database so that it doesn't allow nulls when they provide no value, but this is often impractical for various reasons.

Note Here's one of my pet peeves: allowing nulls in a column in which you care about the difference between a value that was never entered and the empty value ("", or 0, or whatever) is fine. Allowing nulls in a column where you *don't* care about the difference merely complicates your code for no good purpose, thereby decreasing developer productivity and increasing maintenance costs.

As a more general solution, CSLA .NET includes a utility class that uses SqlDataReader (or any IDataReader implementation) in such a way that you never have to worry about null values again. Unfortunately, the SqlDataReader class isn't inheritable; it can't be subclassed directly. Instead, it is wrapped using containment and delegation. The result is that your data access code works the same as always, except that you never need to write checks for null values. If a null value shows up, SafeDataReader will automatically convert it to an appropriate empty value.

Obviously, if you *do* care about the difference between a null and an empty value, you can just use a regular SqlDataReader to retrieve the data. Starting in .NET 2.0, you can use the Nullable<T> generic type that helps manage null database values. This new type is very valuable when you do care about null values: when business rules dictate that an "empty" value such as 0 is different from null.

DataMapper

In Chapter 20, you will see how to implement an ASP.NET Web Forms UI on top of business objects. This chapter makes use of the data binding capabilities introduced in Web Forms 2.0. In this technology, the Insert and Update operations provide the data from the form in IDictionary objects (name/value pairs). The values in these name/value pairs must be loaded into corresponding properties in the business object. You end up writing code much like this:

```
cust.Name = e.Values["Name"].ToString();
cust.Address1 = e.Values["Address1"].ToString();
cust.City = e.Values["City"].ToString();
```

Similarly, in Chapter 21, you'll see how to implement a WCF service interface on top of business objects. When data is sent or received through a web service, it goes through a *proxy object*, an object with properties containing the data but no other logic or code. Since the goal is to get the data into or out of a business object, this means copying the data from one object's properties to the other. You end up writing code much like this:

```
cust.Name = message.Name;
cust.Address1 = message.Address1;
cust.City = message.City;
```

In both cases, this is repetitive, boring code to write. One alternative, though it does incur a performance hit, is to use reflection to automate the copy process. This is the purpose of the DataMapper class: to automate the copying of data to reduce all those lines of code to one simple line. It is up to you whether to use DataMapper in your applications.

SmartDate

Dates are a perennial development problem. Of course, there's the DateTime data type, which provides powerful support for manipulating dates, but it has no concept of an "empty" date. The trouble is that many applications allow the user to leave date fields empty, so you need to deal with the concept of an empty date within the application.

On top of this, date formatting is problematic—rather, formatting an ordinary date value is easy, but again you're faced with the special case whereby an "empty" date must be represented by an empty string value for display purposes. In fact, for the purposes of data binding, you often want any date properties on the objects to be of type `string` so that the user has full access to the various data formats as well as the ability to enter a blank date into the field.

Dates are also a challenge when it comes to the database; the date data types in the database don't recognize an empty date any more than .NET does. To resolve this, date columns in a database typically *do* allow `null` values, so a `null` can indicate an empty date.

■ **Note** Technically, this is a misuse of the `null` value, which is intended to differentiate between a value that was never entered and one that's empty. Unfortunately, you're typically left with no choice because there's no way to put an empty date value into a date data type.

You may be able to use `DateTime?` (`Nullable<DateTime>`) as a workable data type for your date values. But even that isn't always perfect because `DateTime?` doesn't offer specialized formatting and parsing capabilities for working with dates, nor does it really acknowledge an empty date; it isn't possible to compare actual dates with empty dates, yet that is often a business requirement.

The `SmartDate` type is an attempt to resolve this issue. Repeating the problem with `SqlDataReader`, the `DateTime` data type isn't inheritable, so `SmartDate` can't just subclass `DateTime` to create a more powerful data type. Instead, it uses containment and delegation to create a new type that provides the capabilities of the `DateTime` data type while also supporting the concept of an empty date.

This isn't as easy at it might at first appear, as you'll see when the `SmartDate` class is implemented in Chapter 16. Much of the complexity flows from the fact that applications often need to compare an empty date to a real date, but an empty date might be considered very small or very large. You'll see an example of both cases in the sample application in Chapter 17.

The `SmartDate` class is designed to support these concepts and to integrate with the `SafeDataReader` so that it can properly interpret a `null` database value as an empty date.

Additionally, `SmartDate` is a robust data type, supporting numerous operator overloads, casting, and type conversion. Better still, it works with both `DateTime` and the new `DateTimeOffset` type.

Namespace Organization

At this point, I've walked through many of the classes that make up CSLA .NET. Given that there are quite a few classes and types required to implement the framework, there's a need to organize them into a set of *namespaces* for easier discovery and use. Namespaces allow you to group classes together in meaningful ways so that you can program against them more easily. Additionally, namespaces allow different classes to have the same name as long as they're in different namespaces. From a business perspective, you might use a scheme such as the following:

```
MyCompany.MyApplication.FunctionalArea.Class
```

A convention like this immediately indicates that the class belongs to a specific functional area within an application and organization. It also means that the application could have multiple classes with the same names:

```
MyCompany.MyApplication.Sales.Product
MyCompany.MyApplication.Manufacturing.Product
```

It's quite likely that the concept of a "product" in sales is different from that in manufacturing, and this approach allows reuse of class names to make each part of the application as clear and self-documenting as possible. The same is true when you're building a framework. Classes should be grouped in meaningful ways so that they're comprehensible to the end developer. Additionally, use of the framework can be simplified for the end developer by putting little-used or obscure classes in separate namespaces. This way, the business developer doesn't typically see them via IntelliSense.

Consider the `UndoableBase` class, which isn't intended for use by a business developer; it exists for use within the framework only. Ideally, when business developers are working with the framework, they won't see `UndoableBase` via IntelliSense unless they go looking for it by specifically navigating to a specialized namespace. The framework has some namespaces that are to be used by end developers and others that are intended for internal use.

All the namespaces in CSLA .NET are prefixed with `Csla`. Table 2-8 lists the namespaces used in the CSLA .NET framework.

Table 2-8. *Namespaces Used in the CSLA .NET Framework*

Namespace	Description
`Csla`	Contains the types most commonly used by business developers
`Csla.Core`	Contains the types that provide core functionality for the framework; not intended for use by business developers
`Csla.Data`	Contains the optional types used to support data access operations; often used by business developers, web UI developers, and web service developers
`Csla.DataPortalClient`	Contains the types that support the client-side `DataPortal` behaviors; used when creating a custom data portal proxy
`Csla.Linq`	Contains types that implement the LINQ to CSLA functionality; not intended for use by business developers
`Csla.Properties`	Contains code generated by Visual Studio for the `Csla` project; not intended for use by business developers
`Csla.Reflection`	Contains types that abstract and enhance the use of reflection; not intended for use by business developers
`Csla.Security`	Contains the types supporting authorization; used when creating a custom principal object
`Csla.Serialization`	Contains code to abstract the use of the .NET `BinaryFormatter` or `NetDataContractSerializer` serialization technologies
`Csla.Server`	Contains the types supporting the server-side data portal behaviors; not intended for use by business developers
`Csla.Server.Hosts`	Contains the types supporting server-side data portal hosts; used when creating a custom data portal host
`Csla.Validation`	Contains the types supporting validation and business rules; often used when creating rule methods
`Csla.Web`	Contains the `CslaDataSource` control; used by web UI developers

Table 2-8. *Namespaces Used in the CSLA .NET Framework (Continued)*

Namespace	Description
`Csla.Web.Design`	Contains the supporting types for the `CslaDataSource` control; not intended for use by business developers
`Csla.WebServiceHost`	Contains the web services data portal host; not intended for use by business developers
`Csla.Windows`	Contains controls to assist with Windows Forms data binding; used by Windows UI developers
`Csla.Workflow`	Contains types to assist with the use of Windows Workflow Foundation (WF); used by workflow developers
`Csla.Wpf`	Contains controls to assist with WPF data binding; used by WPF UI developers

The primary base classes intended for use by business developers go into the `Csla` namespace itself. They are named as follows:

- `Csla.BusinessBase<T>`
- `Csla.BusinessListBase<T,C>`
- `Csla.ReadOnlyBase<T>`
- `Csla.ReadOnlyListBase<T,C>`
- `Csla.NameValueListBase<K,V>`
- `Csla.CommandBase`

The rest of the classes and types in the framework are organized into the remaining namespaces based on their purpose. You'll see how they all fit and are implemented in Chapters 6 through 16.

The end result is that a typical business developer can simply use the `Csla` namespace as follows:

```
using Csla;
```

All they'll see are the classes intended for use during business development. All the other classes and concepts within the framework are located in other namespaces and therefore won't appear in IntelliSense by default, unless the developer specifically imports those namespaces.

When using custom authentication, you'll likely import the `Csla.Security` namespace. But if you're not using that feature, you can ignore those classes and they won't clutter up the development experience. Similarly, `Csla.Data` and `Csla.Validation` may be used in some cases, as you'll see in Chapters 17 and 18. If the types they contain are useful, they can be brought into a class with a `using` statement; otherwise, they are safely out of the way.

Conclusion

This chapter examines some of the key design goals for the CSLA .NET business framework, including the following:

- Validation and maintaining a list of broken business rules
- Standard implementation of business and validation rules
- Tracking whether an object's data has changed (is it "dirty"?)

- Integrated authorization rules at the object and property levels
- Strongly typed collections of child objects (parent-child relationships)
- N-level undo capability
- A simple and abstract model for the UI developer
- Full support for data binding in WPF, Windows Forms, and Web Forms
- Saving objects to a database and getting them back again
- Custom authentication
- Other miscellaneous features

You've also walked through the design of the framework itself, providing a high-level glimpse into the purpose and rationale behind each of the classes that make it up. With each class, I discuss how it relates back to the key goals to provide the features and capabilities of the framework.

The chapter closes by defining the namespaces that contain the framework classes. This way they're organized so that they're easily understood and used.

Chapter 3 covers some important object-oriented design concepts. Though you can use the ideas in this book in many ways, Chapter 3 describes the thought process I use and the one I'm trying to support by creating the CSLA .NET framework.

Then Chapters 4 and 5 provide details on how a business developer can use CSLA .NET to build business classes based on the stereotypes in Table 2-2.

Chapters 6 through 16 detail the implementation of the concepts discussed in this chapter. If you are interested in the thought process and key implementation techniques used to build the framework, these chapters are for you.

Then Chapters 17 to 21 walk through the design and implementation of a sample application using object-oriented concepts and the CSLA .NET framework. These chapters, combined with Chapters 3 through 5, explore how the framework functions and how it meets the goals set forth in this chapter.

CHAPTER 3

■ ■ ■

Object-Oriented Application Design

Chapters 1 and 2 discussed the concepts behind distributed, object-oriented systems and the .NET technologies that make them practical to implement with reasonable effort. They also introduced the concepts and goals for the CSLA .NET framework. Before getting into the implementation details of the CSLA .NET framework, I think it is important to discuss the object-oriented design philosophy the framework is intended to support, and this is the focus of this chapter.

Chapters 4 and 5 will give you a quick preview of the types of business objects you'll be able to create with the framework. Being aware of the OO design philosophy and types of objects the framework is intended to help you create will make Chapters 6 through 16 easier to digest.

While it is possible to discuss OO design purely in theoretical terms, I find that most people understand it best in the context of a more concrete example. This chapter will cover a little theory, but will primarily focus on the object-oriented application design process, using a sample scenario and application that will be implemented in Chapters 17 through 21. The design process in this chapter will result in a design for the business objects and for an underlying database.

Obviously, the challenge faced in designing and building a sample application in a book like this is that the application must be small enough to fit into the space available, yet be complex enough to illustrate the key features I want to cover. To start with, here's a list of the key features that I want to focus on:

- Creation of a business object
- Implementation of business validation rules
- Implementation of business authorization rules
- Transactional and nontransactional data access
- Parent-child relationships between objects
- Many-to-many relationships between objects
- Use of name/value lists
- Use of custom CSLA .NET authentication

In this chapter, I'll focus on the design of the application by using some example user scenarios, which are generally referred to as *use cases*. Based on those use cases, I'll develop a list of potential business objects and relationships. I'll refine this information to develop a class design for the application. Based on the scenarios and object model, I'll design a relational database to store the data.

As I mentioned in Chapter 2, object-oriented design and relational design aren't the same process, and you'll see in this case how they result in two different models. To resolve these models, the business objects will include ORM when they are implemented in Chapters 17 and 18. This ORM code will reside in a specific data access assembly (project), created using LINQ to SQL. The business objects will invoke that data access code to retrieve and update the objects' data. This chapter will not focus on the data access mechanism; instead, it will leave those details for Chapter 18.

Responsibility-Driven Design

Object-oriented design has been around for many years. Unfortunately, there is no unified approach to doing OO design, and this often leads to confusion. Just because someone says he's doing OO design doesn't necessarily mean he's following a similar process to another person who *also* says he's doing OO design.

Many people want to use objects primarily so they can use dot notation to get at their database. They want to write code like this:

```
int qty = Customer[9].Order[4].LineItem[11].Product.Inventory.Quantity;
```

Each "object" here is actually some table or data entity that is hopefully loaded automatically and efficiently when it is used. The dot-notation motivation for using objects is not a bad one, but it is not what most people consider object-oriented.

Use-Case or Story-Based Analysis

Ideally, your objects exist to serve the needs of a specific *use case*, or user story, or user scenario. In many cases, this means that the objects exist to provide the required business logic and data for each form the user will use to complete a task. That user task is the use case.

Following this approach first means that you need to identify the use cases for your application. This is an analysis process where you interview the business stakeholders and end users of the application to identify the specific tasks that the application must accomplish for the users.

Each task is a use case. Of course, some tasks are big and some are small. If a task is big and complex, you might need to subdivide it into a set of smaller tasks, each of which is a use case. This means that some use cases may rely on, or interact with, other use cases. Your ultimate goal, however, is for each low-level use case to be a stand-alone task—a scenario you can clearly describe.

What I'm describing here is the basic concept of *decomposition*, where complex problems are decomposed into simpler subproblems. Eventually, you get to the point that the individual subproblems (low-level use cases) are simple enough that you can design and implement them without getting lost in the overall complexity.

Objects with Responsibilities

Once you have a low-level use case, you can start to identify the objects that are required to implement that use case. One important thing to remember is that *you should not focus on data at this time*. Don't worry about the data in each object. Instead, *focus on what the object does*. What is its job or role within the use case?

Some objects are responsible for collecting data from the user. Others may be responsible for validating data or calculating values. Notice how I'm phrasing this: each object is *responsible* for doing something. Objects are not passive; they are actors that have a job to do within the use case.

In fact, objects should have a *single responsibility*. This is called single-responsibility design and is the goal for this object design technique. Each object should have exactly one job—one responsibility—within the use case. An object may have numerous behaviors (properties, methods, and so on), but all those behaviors should exist so the object can meet its responsibility.

Objects Exist for Use Cases

An important side effect of what I'm talking about here is that objects are designed for use cases—not for an enterprise, not even for an application. They are designed for a *specific use case.*

This might appear to be a problem, because it could reduce reuse. I suggest that this is not a problem. Reuse is not a goal for software; it is one tool we use to achieve the real goals of maintainability and lower cost of development.

In fact, reuse is often counterproductive. Most reuse causes a side effect called *coupling,* where code becomes overly dependent on other code. Coupling is perhaps the ultimate enemy of maintainability, and it's a primary driver for increasing the cost of software development. Figure 3-1 illustrates how reuse causes code to become interdependent.

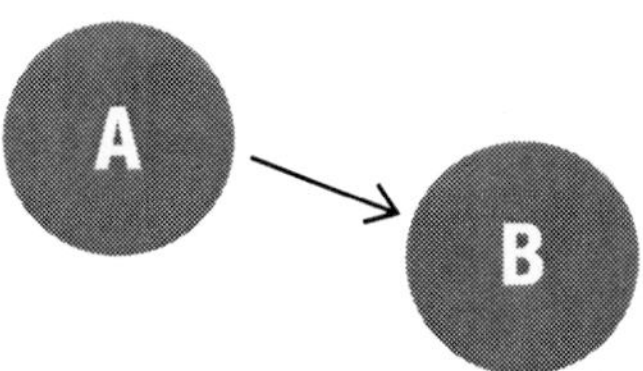

Figure 3-1. *Object A reusing code in object B*

Let's imagine that objects A and B from Figure 3-1 are in different use cases within the same application. Then let's imagine that object B has some useful behavior that object A also needs. It is natural to have object A reuse the behavior provided by object B.

Unfortunately, there is a very real risk that object B might change at some point in the future, probably due to a change in the use case to which it belongs. And changing object B will very likely break object A, often in a way that you may catch only if you have *extensive* unit and integration testing in place. Coupling leads to unintended consequences and fragile code.

■ **Tip** You should only pursue reuse if you can avoid coupling.

Designing objects for specific use cases might eliminate some reuse, but it also helps minimize coupling, and thus it helps reduce the cost of development by increasing maintainability.

Please note, however, that I am not suggesting that reuse itself is bad. All I'm saying is that you can't blindly pursue reuse. Instead, you should reuse code whenever you can do so without causing tight coupling. It is important to realize that you can't have reuse without coupling, so it isn't like you can avoid coupling. All you can do is control the coupling.

Normalization of Behavior

One powerful technique you can use to achieve reuse and control coupling is *normalization of behavior.* The idea is to move the code to be reused into its own object, so objects that contain reusable code are somewhat isolated from most other objects.

Figure 3-2 illustrates how you can use normalization of behavior to accomplish the same result as Figure 3-1, but with controlled coupling.

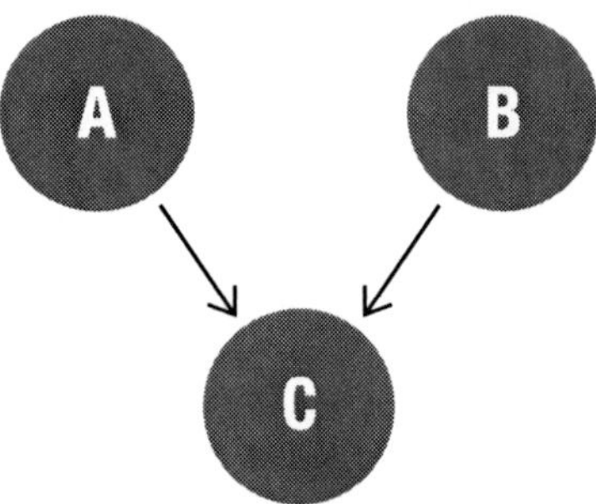

Figure 3-2. *Common behavior normalized into object C*

In this case, the behavior originally contained in object B that is needed by object A is moved to a *new object* called C. Object C only contains the common behavior required by both objects B and A, and both A and B collaborate with C to use that behavior.

This requires more work than simply having A call B, but it is better, because it avoids having A depend on B. Instead, the dependency is shifted so both A and B are dependent upon C. More work is required, because some refactoring of B is required to achieve this result.

This is a better solution because C is highly focused, in that it only contains the code common to both A and B. While coupling still exists, the coupling is clearer and more easily managed.

Object-oriented design works best when objects are designed for a specific use case and when each object has a single responsibility within that use case. To achieve reuse, utilize normalization of behavior by refactoring common code into its own object and have other objects collaborate with this new object to leverage the behavior.

Given this brief conceptual background, I'll put the ideas into practice by walking through the design of a reference application called Project Tracker.

Application Requirements

There are many ways to gather application requirements, but in general, you can choose from these three main areas of focus:

- Data analysis and data flow
- UI design and storyboarding
- Business concept and process analysis

The first option is the oldest of the three. It's the idea that an application can be designed by understanding the data it requires and how that data must flow through the system. While this approach can work, it isn't ideal when trying to work with object-oriented concepts, because it focuses less on business ideas and more on raw data. It's often a good analysis approach when building applications that follow a data-centric architecture.

Note The data-focused analysis approach often makes it hard to relate to users well. Few users understand database diagrams and database concepts, so there's a constant struggle as the business language and concepts are translated into and out of relational, data-oriented language and concepts.

The idea of basing application analysis around the UI came into vogue in the early-to-mid 1990s with the rise of rapid application development (RAD) tools such as Visual Basic, PowerBuilder, and

Delphi. It was subsequently picked up by the web development world, though in that environment the term *storyboarding* was often used to describe the process. UI-focused analysis has the benefit of being accessible to end users, who find it easy to relate to the UI and how it flows.

The drawback to this approach is that there's a tendency for business validation and processing to end up being written directly into the UI. This doesn't *always* happen, but it's a very real problem—primarily because UI-focused analysis frequently revolves around a UI prototype, which includes more and more business logic as the process progresses, until developers decide just to use the prototype as the base for the application, since so much work has been done already.

Tip Obviously, people can resist this trend and make UI-focused design work, but it takes a great deal of discipline. The reality is that a lot of great applications end up crippled because this technique is used.

Another drawback to starting with the UI is that users often see the mocked-up UI in a demonstration and assume that the application is virtually complete. They don't realize that the bulk of the work comes from the business and data access logic that must still be created and tested *behind* the UI. The result is that developers are faced with tremendous and unrealistic time pressure to deliver on the application, since from the user's perspective, it's virtually complete already.

The third option is to focus on business concepts and process flow. This is the middle road in many ways, since it requires an understanding of how the users will interact with the system, the processes that the system must support, and (by extension) the data that must flow through the system to make it all happen. The benefit of this approach is that it's very business focused, allowing both the analyst and the end users to talk the language of business, thereby avoiding computer concepts and terminology. It also lends itself to the creation of object-oriented designs, because the entities and concepts developed during analysis typically turn into objects within the application.

The drawback to this approach is that it doesn't provide users with the look and feel of the UI or the graphical reinforcement of how the system will actually work from their perspective, nor does it produce a clear database design. It leaves the database analyst to do more work in order to design the database.

Personally, I use a blend of the business concept and UI approaches. I place the strongest emphasis on the business concept and process flow, while providing key portions of the UI via a prototype, so that the user can get the feel of the system. Since end users have such a hard time relating to database diagrams, I almost never use data-focused analysis techniques, instead leaving the database design process to flow from the other analysis techniques.

In this chapter, I'll make use of the business concept and process-flow techniques. It's difficult to storyboard the application at this stage, because we'll be developing both WPF and Web Forms user interfaces, along with a WCF service application interface. The starting point, then, is to create a set of use case descriptions based on how the users (or other applications) will interact with the system.

Use Cases

Let's create a set of imaginary use cases for the project-tracking system. In a real application, you would develop these by interviewing key users and other interested parties. The use cases here are for illustration purposes.

Note This application is relatively simple. A real project-tracking system would undoubtedly be more complex, but it is necessary to have something small enough to implement within the context of this book. Remember that my focus is on illustrating how to use CSLA .NET to create business objects, child objects, and so forth.

Though not mentioned specifically in the following use cases, I'm designing this system to accommodate large numbers of users. In Chapter 19, for instance, the WPF UI will use the mobile object features of CSLA .NET to run the application in a physical n-tier deployment with an application server. This physical architecture will provide for optimum scalability. In Chapter 20, the Web Forms UI will make use of the CSLA .NET framework's ability to run the application's UI, business logic, and data access all on the web server. Again, this provides the highest scaling and best-performing configuration, because you can easily add more web servers as needed to support more users.

Project Maintenance

Since this is a project-tracking system, there's no surprise that the application must work with projects. Here are some use cases describing the users' expectations.

Adding a Project

A project manager can add projects to the system. Project data must include key information, including the project's name, description, start date, and end date. A project can have a unique project number, but this isn't required, and the project manager shouldn't have to deal with it. The project's name is the field by which projects are identified by users, so every project must have a name.

The start and end dates are optional. Many projects are added to the system so that a list of them can be kept, even though they haven't started yet. Once a project has been started, it should have a start date but no end date. When the project is complete, the project manager can enter an end date. These dates will be used to report on the average lengths of the projects, so obviously the end date can't be earlier than the start date.

Every project also has a list of the resources assigned to it (see the "Assigning a Resource" section later in this chapter).

Editing a Project

Project managers can edit any existing projects. Managers choose from a list of projects and can then edit that project. They need the ability to change the project's start and end dates, as well as its description. They also need to be able to change the resources assigned to the project (see the "Assigning a Resource" section later in this chapter).

Removing a Project

Project managers or administrators must be able to remove projects. There is no need to keep historical data about deleted projects, so such data should be removed completely from the system. Users should just choose from a list of projects and confirm their choice, and the project should be removed.

Resource Maintenance

At this point, the system not only tracks projects, but also tracks the resources assigned to each project. For the purposes of this simple example, the only project resources tracked are the people assigned to the projects. With further questioning of the users, a set of use cases revolving around the resources can be developed, without reference (yet) to the projects in which they may be involved.

Adding a Resource

We don't want to replicate the Human Resources (HR) database, but we can't make use of the HR database because the HR staff won't give us access. We just want to be able to keep track of the people we can assign to our projects. All we care about is the person's name and employee ID. Obviously, each person must have an employee ID and a valid name.

Project managers or supervisors can add resources. It would be nice to be able to assign a person to a project at the same time as the person is being added to the application (see the "Assigning a Resource" section later in this chapter).

Editing a Resource

Sometimes, a name is entered incorrectly and needs to be fixed, so project managers and supervisors need to be able to change the name.

Removing a Resource

When an employee is let go or moves to another division, we want to be able to remove him from the system. Project managers, supervisors, and administrators should be able to do this. Once they're gone, we don't need any historical information, so they should be totally removed.

Assigning a Resource

As we were talking to the users to gather information about the previous use cases, the users walked through the requirements for assigning resources to projects. Since this process is common across several other processes, we can centralize it into a use case that's referenced from the others.

The project managers and supervisors need to be able to assign a resource to a project. When we do this, we need to indicate the role that the resource is playing in the project. We have a list of the roles, but we might need to change the list in the future. We also want to know when the resource was assigned to the project.

Sometimes, a resource will switch from one role to another, so we need to be able to change the role at any time. Equally, a resource can be assigned to several projects at one time. (We often have people working part-time on several projects at once.)

Last, we need to be able to remove an assignment. This happens when an employee is let go or moves to another division (see the "Removing a Resource" section earlier in this chapter); people also often move around from project to project. There's no need to keep track of who used to be on a project, because we only use this system for tracking current projects and the resources assigned to them right now.

Maintaining a List of Roles

Resources are assigned to projects to fill a specific role. The list of possible roles needs to be maintainable by end users, specifically administrators.

External Access

During conversations with users, we discovered that a number of them are highly technical and are already skeptical of our ability to create all the UI options they desire. They indicated high interest in having programmatic access to the database, or to our business objects. In other words, we have some power users who are used to programming in Access and know a bit of VBA, and they want to write their own reports and maybe their own data entry routines.

Note This same scenario would play out if there were a requirement to provide access to the application to business partners, customers, vendors, or any external application outside our immediate control.

Obviously, there are serious issues with giving other people access to the application's database—especially read-write access. Unless *all* the business logic is put into stored procedures, this sort of access can't be provided safely.

Likewise, there are issues with providing direct access to the business objects. This is safer in some ways, because the objects implement the business logic and validation, but it's problematic from a maintenance perspective. If other people are writing code to interact directly with the business objects, then the objects can't be changed without breaking their code. Since the other people are outside of our control, it means that the Project Tracker application can never change its object model.

Of course, this is totally unrealistic. It is a virtual guarantee that there will be future enhancements and requests for changes to the system, which will undoubtedly require changes to the business objects. Fortunately, XML services offer a clean solution. If XML services are treated just like any another interface (albeit a programmatic one) to the application, they can be used to easily provide access to the application without allowing external programs to interact directly with the application's database or business objects.

In Chapter 21, I'll revisit these ideas, showing how to implement a set of XML services using WCF so that external applications can safely interact with the application in a loosely coupled manner.

Object Design

At this point, the key requirements for the application have been gathered from the use cases. Based on these use cases, it is possible to create an object-oriented design. There are a variety of techniques used in object-oriented design; you may have heard of Class Responsibility Collaborator (CRC) cards and decomposition, in addition to others. In this chapter, I'll use ideas from both decomposition and CRC cards. A form of decomposition will be used to identify the "nouns" in the use cases and then narrow down which of these are actual business objects. These objects will be described in terms of their CRC.

Initial Design

The first step in the process, then, is to assemble a list of the nouns in the use case write-ups. By using a bit of judgment, you can eliminate a few nouns that are obviously not objects, but still end up with a good-sized list of potential business objects or entities, as shown in Table 3-1.

Table 3-1. *Potential Entities Discovered in the Initial Design*

Project manager	Project	Project number
Project name	Start date	End date
Administrator	List of projects	Employee
Resource	Employee name	Employee ID
Supervisor	List of assignments	Role
List of roles	Assignment	Date assigned
List of resources	List of assigned resources	

Using your understanding of the business domain (and probably through further discussion with business users and fellow designers), you can narrow the options. Some of these entities aren't objects, but rather data elements or security roles. These include the following:

- Project manager
- Administrators
- Supervisor

■ **Tip** I am assuming there's already an object to deal with a user's role. Such an object will be created by subclassing the `Csla.Security.BusinessPrincipalBase` class later in the chapter. However, these security roles should not be confused with the role a resource (person) plays on a project—they're two very different concepts.

Pulling out these nouns, along with those that are likely to be just data fields (such as project name and employee ID), you can come up with a smaller list of likely business objects, allowing you to start creating a basic class diagram or organizing the classes using CRC cards. Table 3-2 lists the high-level CRC data for each potential object.

Table 3-2. *Potential Objects and Their Associated Class Names*

Potential Class	Responsibility	Collaborators
`Project`	Adds and edits a valid project	`ProjectResources`
`Resource`	Adds and edits a valid resource	`ResourceAssignments`, `Employee`
`Employee`	Adds and edits a valid employee	None
`ProjectList`	Gets a read-only list of projects	`Project`
`ResourceList`	Gets a read-only list of resources	`Resource`
`ProjectResources`	Maintains a list of resources assigned to a project	`Resource`, `RoleList`
`ResourceAssignments`	Maintains a list of projects to which a resource is assigned	`Project`, `RoleList`
`RoleList`	Gets a read-only list of roles	`Role`
`Role`	Provides read-only role data	None
`RoleEditList`	Maintains a list of roles in the system	`RoleEdit`
`RoleEdit`	Adds and edits a valid role	None

One key aspect of CRC-based design is that an object's responsibility should be short and to the point. Long, complex responsibility descriptions are an indication that the object model is flawed and that the complicated object should probably be represented by a set of simpler objects that collaborate to achieve the goal.

The diagram should also include relationships between the entities in the diagram. For the most part, these relationships can be inferred from the use case descriptions—for instance, we can infer that a "list of projects" will likely contain `Project` objects, and that a `Project` object will likely contain a "list of assigned resources," which in turn will likely contain `Resource` objects.

Note that I use the word *likely* here, rather than *will*. We're still very much in a fluid design stage here, so nothing is certain yet. We have a list of potential objects, and we're inferring a list of potential relationships.

Figure 3-3 illustrates how these objects relate to each other. Looking at the CRC list and this diagram, there is some indication that there's more work to do. You should look for and address several issues, including duplicate objects, trivial objects, objects that have overly complex relationships in the diagram, and places that can be optimized for performance.

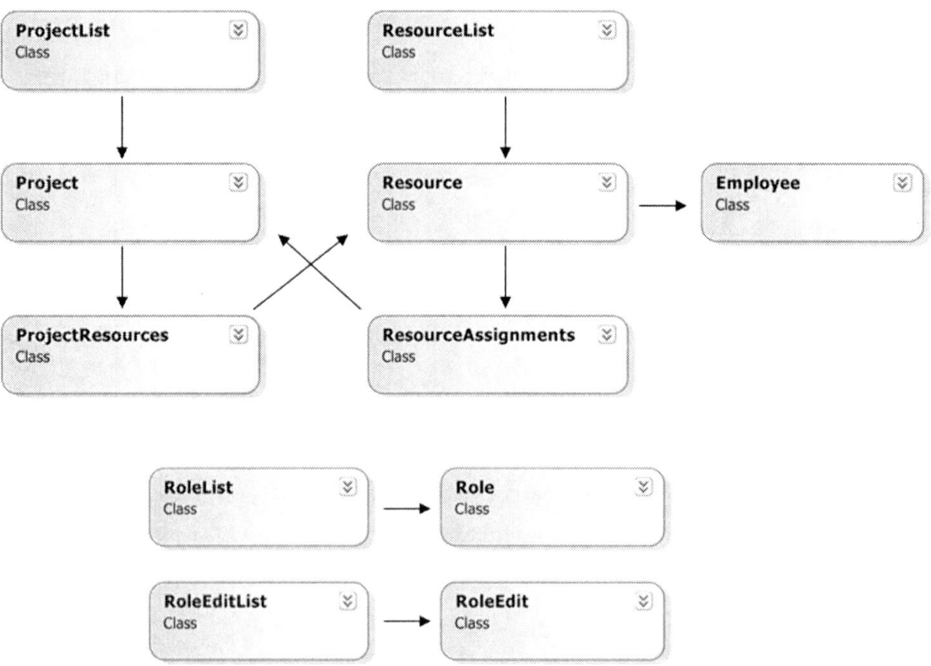

Figure 3-3. *Possible class diagram for the Project Tracker application*

Revising the Design

The following list indicates some of the things to address:

- `Resource` and `Employee` could be duplicates. It isn't clear that `Resource` adds anything to `Employee`, so the two can probably be merged into one class.
- Based on the use case description, we know that `RoleList` is a name/value list, which directly implies the `Role` is just a name/value placeholder. Given `Csla.NameValueListBase`, this can be simplified.
- The relationship between `Project`, `ProjectResources`, `Resource`, and `ResourceAssignments` is very complex. In fact, it forms a loop of references, which is always a danger sign.
- The `RoleList` object isn't used by any other objects in the model. Given that the use cases indicate that resources are assigned to projects based on a specific role, this is suspicious.

- The use cases for `ProjectList` and `ResourceList` indicate that they're used primarily for selection of objects, not for editing all the projects or resources in the system. Actually loading all the `Project` or `Resource` objects just so the user can make a simple selection is expensive, performance-wise, so this design should be reviewed.
- It is clear that when the list of roles is edited, any `RoleList` objects need to know about the changes so they can read the new data. This is not explicitly stated in a use case, but is an inferred requirement.

In the early stages of *any* object design process, there will be duplicate objects or potential objects that end up being mere data fields in other objects. Usually, a great deal of debate will ensue during the design phase, as all the people involved in the design process thrash out which objects are real, which are duplicates, and which should be just data fields. This is healthy and important, though obviously some judgment must be exercised to avoid *analysis paralysis*, whereby the design stalls entirely due to the debate.

Let's discuss this in a bit more detail.

Duplicate Objects

First, you should identify duplicate objects that have basically the same data and relationships (like `Resource` and `Employee`). In this case, `Employee` can be eliminated in favor of `Resource`, since that term is used most often in the use case descriptions (and thus, presumably, most used by the end users).

In most scenarios, the end users will have numerous terms for some of their concepts. It's your job, as part of the analysis process, to identify when multiple terms really refer to the same concepts (objects) and to clarify and abstract the appropriate meaning.

Trivial Objects

The `Role` object may not be required either. Fundamentally, a `Role` is just a string value, presumably with an associated key value. This is the specific scenario for which the `NameValueListBase` class in the CSLA .NET framework is designed. That base class makes it easy to implement name/value lists.

■ **Tip** My characterization of the `Role` value is based on the use cases assembled earlier. If you intuitively feel that this is overly simplistic or unrealistic, then you should revisit the use cases and your users to make sure that you haven't missed something. For the purposes of this book, I'll assume that the use cases are accurate and that the `Role` field really is a simple name/value pair.

Note that I'm not suggesting the elimination of the `RoleEdit` class. While you can use `NameValueListBase` to create read-only name/value lists, you use `RoleEdit` and `RoleEditList` to *edit* the role data. They can't be automated away like a simple name/value pair.

Like the process of removing duplicates, the process of finding and removing trivial objects is as much an art as it is a science. It can be the cause of plenty of healthy debate!

Overly Complex Relationships

Although it's certainly true that large and complex applications often have complex relationships between classes and objects, those complex relationships should always be reviewed carefully.

As a general rule, if relationship lines are crossing each other or wrapping around each other in a diagram like Figure 3-3, you should review those relationships to see if they need to be so complex. Sometimes, it's just the way things have to be, but more often, this is a sign that the object model needs some work. Though relying on the aesthetics of a diagram may sound a bit odd, it is a good rule of thumb.

In this case, there's a pretty complex relationship between `Project`, `ProjectResources`, `Resource`, and `ResourceAssignments`. It is, in fact, a circular relationship, in which all these objects refer to the other objects in an endless chain. In a situation like this, you should always be looking for a way to simplify the relationships. What you'll often find is that the object model is missing a class: one that doesn't necessarily flow directly from the use cases, but is required to make the object model workable.

The specific problem caused by the circular relationship in Figure 3-3 becomes apparent when an object is to be loaded from the database. At that time, it will typically also load any child objects it contains. With an endless loop of relationships, that poses a rather obvious problem. There must be some way to short-circuit the process, and the best way to do this is to introduce another object into the mix.

In the object model thus far, what's missing is a class that actually represents the assignment of a resource to a project. At this point, there's no object responsible for assigning a resource to a project, so an entire behavior from the use cases is missing in the object model.

Additionally, data described in the use cases isn't yet reflected in the object model, such as the role of a resource on a particular project, or the date that the resource was assigned to a project. These data fields can't be kept in the `Project` object, because a project will have many resources filling many different roles at different times. Similarly, they can't be kept in the `Resource` object, because a resource may be assigned to many projects at different times and in different roles.

Adding an Assignment Class

The need for another object—an `Assignment` object—is clear. This object's responsibility is to *assign a resource to a project.*

Figure 3-4 shows an updated diagram, including the changes thus far.

However, we're still not done. The `Assignment` class itself just became overly complex, because it's used within two different contexts: from the list of resources assigned to a project, and from the list of projects to which a resource is assigned. This is typically problematic. Having a single object as a child of two different collections makes for very complicated implementation and testing, and should be avoided when possible.

Beyond that, think about its responsibility in the diagram in Figure 3-4. `Assignment` is now responsible for assigning a resource to a project *and* for associating a project with a resource. When used from `ProjectResources`, it has the first responsibility, and when used from `ResourceAssignments`, it has the second responsibility. Sure, the responsibilities are similar, but they are different enough that it matters.

There's also an issue with data. A `Project` object uses the `ProjectResources` collection to get a list of resources assigned to the project. This implies that the `Assignment` object contains information about the resource assigned to the project. Yet a `Resource` object uses the `ResourceAssignments` collection to get a list of projects to which the resource is assigned. This implies that the `Assignment` object contains information about the project to which the resource is assigned. The fact that both behavioral and data conflicts exist means that the object model remains flawed.

There are two possible solutions. You could combine the list objects (`ProjectResources` and `ResourceAssignments`) into a single list of `Assignment` objects, or you could have two different objects representing assignments. To resolve this, you need to think about the different behaviors that are required when approaching the concept of assignments from `Project` and from `Resource`.

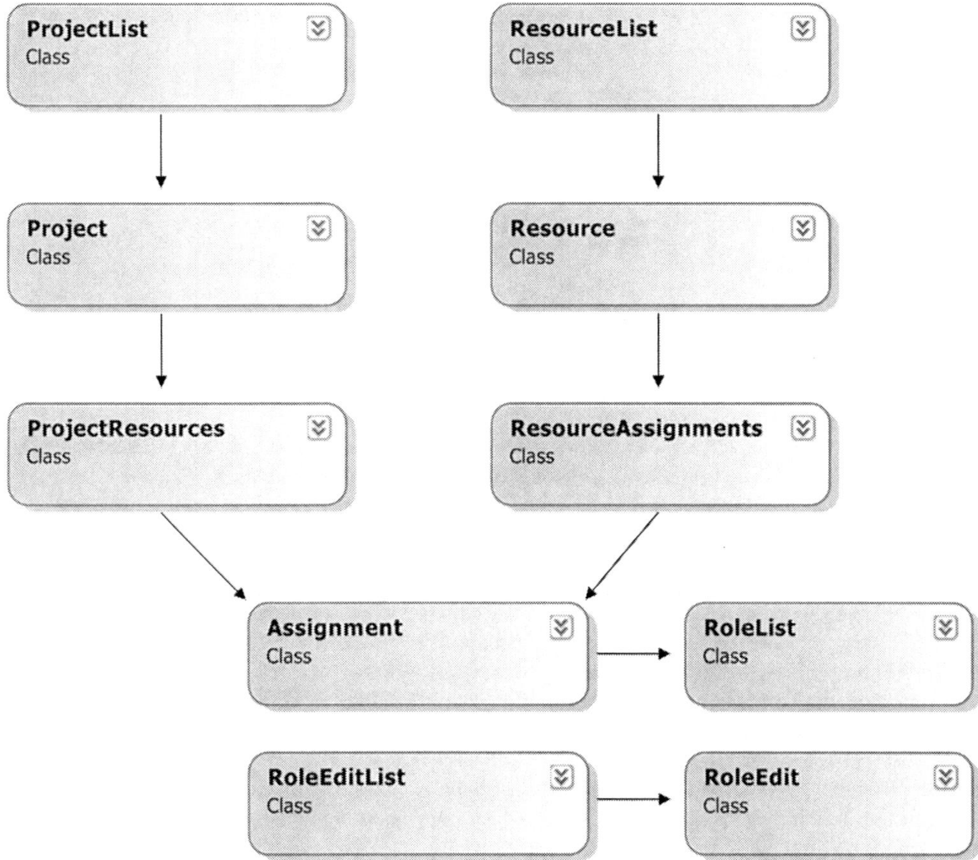

Figure 3-4. *Revised class diagram for the Project Tracker application*

Assigning a Resource to a Project

Based on the use cases, you can assign resources to projects. This implies that the user has identified the project and wishes to assign a resource to it. It also implies that a project has a collection of assigned resources: hence, the `ProjectResources` collection in the object model.

But what behavior and information would a user expect from the items in the `ProjectResources` collection?

Certainly, one behavior is to return the list of resources assigned to the project. Another behavior is to allow a new resource to be assigned to the project, implying something like an `Assign()` method that accepts the `Id` property from a `Resource`.

It is also worth considering what information should be provided to the user. When viewing or editing a `Project`, the list of assigned resources should probably show something like this:

- Resource ID
- Resource name
- Date assigned to the project
- Role of the resource on the project

This means that `ProjectResources`, and the items returned by `ProjectResources`, might look something like Figure 3-5.

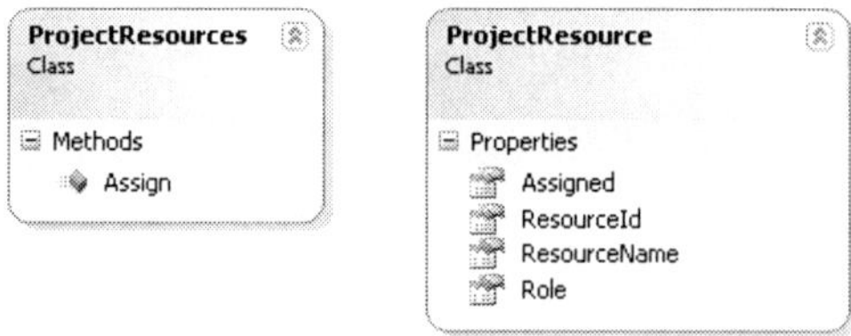

Figure 3-5. *The ProjectResources collection and the ProjectResource child object*

Though not visible in Figure 3-5, the `Assign()` method accepts a `resourceId` parameter to identify the resource being assigned to the project.

Given this analysis, let's consider the behaviors and information required to assign a project to a resource—basically the same process, but starting with a `Resource` instead of a `Project`.

Assigning a Project to a Resource

The use cases provide for the idea that a user could start by identifying a resource rather than a project. In this case, the user can still associate a project with the resource by selecting a project. This implies that the `Resource` object has a collection of projects to which the resource is assigned. The object model thus far represents this collection as `ResourceAssignments`.

Let's consider the behaviors and information for the `ResourceAssignments` collection and the items it would contain.

In this case, the user starts with a `Resource` and wishes to assign the resource to a project. So the `ResourceAssignments` object will have a couple of behaviors: listing the projects to which the resource is assigned, and assigning the resource to a new project. This can probably be handled by an `AssignTo()` method that accepts the `Id` property of a `Project`.

The items in `ResourceAssignments` have the behavior of returning information about the project assigned to the resource. The information of value to a user is likely the following:

- Project ID
- Project name
- Date assigned to the project
- Role of the resource on the project

Figure 3-6 shows the potential `ResourceAssignments` object and what its items might look like.

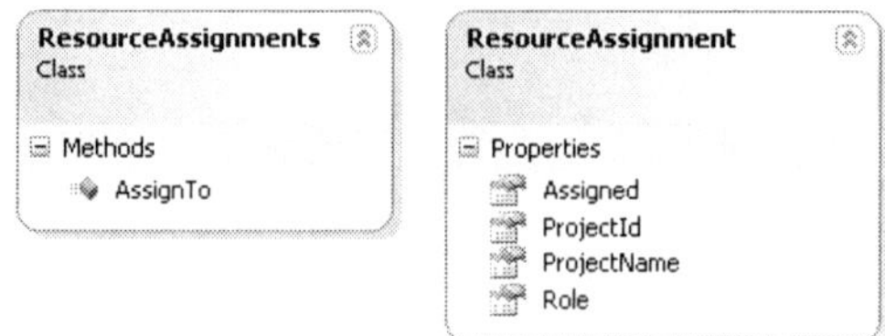

Figure 3-6. *The ResourceAssignments collection and the ResourceAssignment child object*

The AssignTo() method accepts a projectId parameter to identify the project to which the resource should be assigned.

Can the Classes Be Merged?

It is important to notice that the objects described by Figure 3-5 and Figure 3-6 are *similar*, but they are not the same. Yet they do share at least some common information, if not behavior. Both child classes contain Assigned and Role properties, implying that there's commonality between them.

Such commonality is not justification for combining the two classes into one, because their behaviors are distinctly different. The items in ProjectResources have one responsibility: managing information about a resource assigned to a project. The items in ResourceAssignments have a different responsibility: managing information about a project to which a resource is assigned. While this difference may seem subtle, it is a difference nonetheless.

It is tempting to consider that the two classes could be merged into one, as shown in Figure 3-7. Of course, ProjectName isn't valid if the user got to this object from a Project object, but it is valid if she got here through a Resource object. The same is true for several other properties.

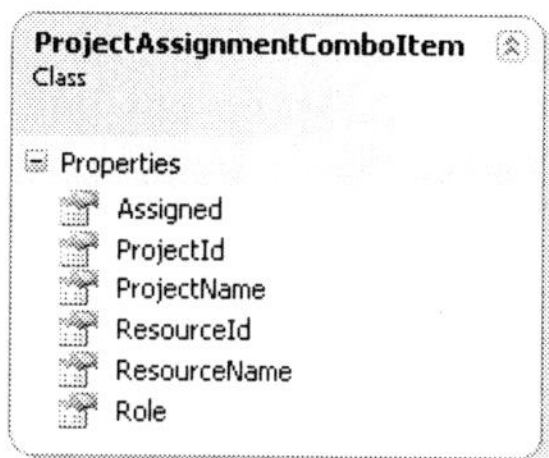

Figure 3-7. *Merged child items with assignment information*

Perhaps business logic could be added to properties to throw exceptions if they were called from an inappropriate context. But the obvious complexity of this sort of logic should give you pause. The problem is that one object is trying to handle more than one responsibility. Such a scenario means that the object model is flawed. Going down such a path will lead to complex, hard-to-maintain code.

Note Historically, this sort of complex code was referred to as *spaghetti code*. It turns out that with improper object design, it is *very* possible to end up with spaghetti code in business objects. The result is terrible, and is exactly what *good* object design is intended to prevent.

It should be quite clear at this point that merging the two collections or their child objects into a single set of objects isn't the right answer. They have different responsibilities, and so they should be separate objects.

But this leaves one glaring issue: what about the common properties and any common business logic they might require? How can two objects use the same data without causing duplication of business logic?

Dealing with Common Behaviors and Information

When designing relational databases, it is important to normalize the data. There are many aspects to normalization, but one of the most basic and critical is avoiding redundant data. A given data element should exist *exactly once* in the data model. And that's great for relational modeling.

Unfortunately, many people struggle with object design because they try to apply relational thinking to objects. But object design is *not the same* as relational design. Where the goal with relational design is to avoid duplication of data, the goal of object design is quite different.

There's no problem with a data field being used or exposed by different objects. I realize this may be hard to accept. We've all spent so many years being trained to think relationally that it is often hard to break away and think in terms of objects. Yet creating a good object model *requires* changing this mode of thought.

■ **Caution** Object design isn't about normalizing data. It is about normalizing *behavior*.

The goal in object design is to ensure that a given *behavior* exists only once within the object model. Simple examples of behavior include the idea of a string being required, or one value being larger than another. More complex behaviors might be the calculation of a tax or discount amount. Each behavior should exist only once in the object model, though it may be *used* from many different objects.

This is why collaboration is so critical to good object design. For example, one object—the `DiscountCalculator`—will implement the complex calculation for a discount. Many other objects may need to determine the discount, so they collaborate with `DiscountCalculator` to find that value. In this manner, the behavior exists exactly once in the model.

Dealing with Common Information

So the real question isn't whether the `Assigned` and `Role` *properties* can be put into a common object—that's relational thinking. Instead, the question is whether those properties have common *behaviors* (business rules or logic) that can be put into a common object.

As it turns out, the `Role` property must be validated to ensure any new value is a real role. Since the `Role` property can be set in both `ProjectResource` and `ResourceAssignment`, that behavior could be duplicated.

A better answer is to normalize that behavior, putting it into a central object. Let's call this new object `Assignment`, since it will be responsible for centralizing the code common to assignments of projects to resources, and resources to projects. Then both `ProjectResource` and `ResourceAssignment` can collaborate with `Assignment` to ensure that the `Role` property is validated.

This means that `Assignment` will contain the rule method that implements the role-validation behavior. In Chapter 6, you'll see how the CSLA .NET framework defines the `RuleHandler` delegate to support exactly this type of scenario.

Given a `ValidRole()` rule method in `Assignment`, both `ProjectResource` and `ResourceAssignment` merely have to associate that rule method with their `Role` properties to share the common behavior. Figure 3-8 illustrates this relationship.

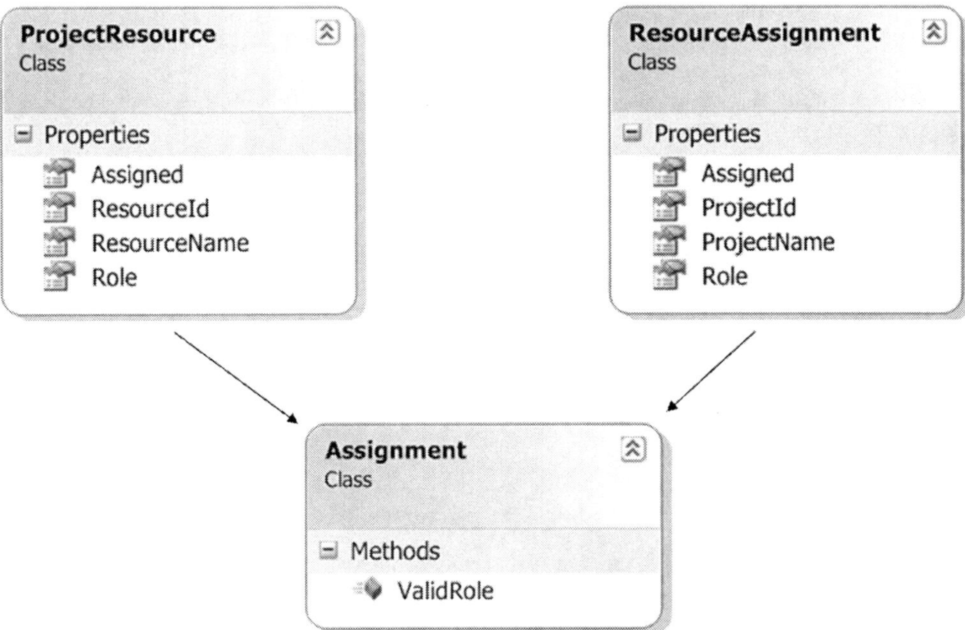

Figure 3-8. *ProjectResource and ResourceAssignment collaborating with Assignment*

In Chapter 17, I discuss the code to do exactly this.

Dealing with Common Behaviors

The responsibility of the `Assignment` object from Figure 3-8 is to manage the association between a project and a resource.

This means that the `Assignment` object's behavior could include the idea of associating a project with a resource. This is a broader behavior than that provided by `ProjectResources`, which assigns a resource to a project, or by `ResourceAssignments`, which assigns a project to a resource. In fact, the behavior of `Assignment` is more general and encompasses the needs of both other objects.

Of course, the `ProjectResource` and `ResourceAssignment` classes handle the real work of dealing with a resource assigned to a project, or a project associated with a resource. The collection classes really just add and remove these child objects, leaving it to the child objects to handle the details.

The end result is that `ProjectResource`, to fulfill its behavior, can ask `Assignment` to do the actual work, as shown in Figure 3-9. The same is true of `ResourceAssignment`. The implication is that `Assignment` could have a method such as `AddAssignment()` that accepts a project's `Id` property and a resource's `Id` property, along with the role the resource will play on the project.

■ **Tip** Object models should be simple and intuitive, even when underlying behaviors are complex. By centralizing common behaviors using objects internal to the business layer, a simpler and more tailored public interface can be exposed to the UI developer.

Similarly, `ProjectResource` and `ResourceAssignment` have behaviors that involve removing a resource from a project or removing a project from a resource. `Assignment`, then, will have a more general behavior to remove an association between a project and a resource.

Figure 3-9 shows the full extent of `Assignment`, including all the methods that implement behaviors common to both `ProjectResource` and `ResourceAssignment`.

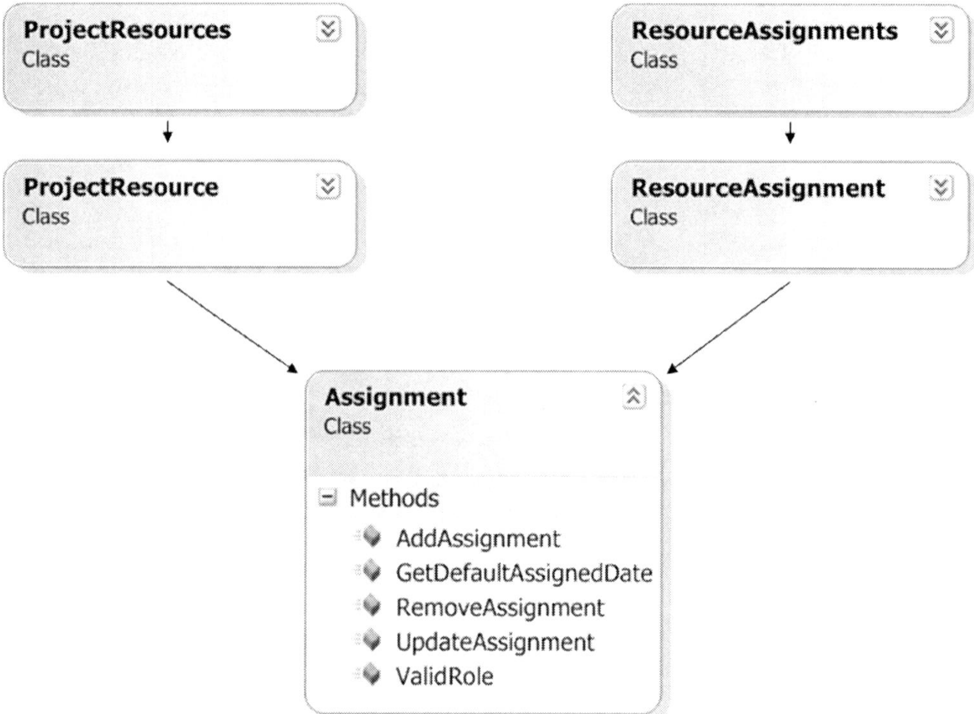

Figure 3-9. *Objects collaborating with Assignment*

At this point, all the common behaviors from `ProjectResource` and `ResourceAssignment` have been normalized into a single location in the object model.

Optimizing for Performance

Part of object design includes reviewing things to ensure that the model won't lead to poor performance. This isn't really a single step in the process, but rather something you should do on a continual basis during the whole process. However, once you think the object model is complete, you should always pause to review it for performance issues.

One primary performance issue with many object models deals with the use of relational thinking when designing the objects. Normalizing data within the object model is perhaps the most common flaw causing performance issues. Due to the design of `ProjectResource`, `ResourceAssignment`, and `Assignment`, the object model has already eliminated this issue by normalizing behavior instead of data. This helps avoid loading entire business objects just to display a couple of common data elements.

There is, however, another performance issue in the model. The `ProjectList` and `ResourceList` collection objects, as modeled, retrieve collections of `Project` and `Resource` business objects so that some of their data can be displayed in a list. Based on the use cases, the user then selects one of the objects and chooses to view, edit, or remove that object.

From a purely object-oriented perspective, it's attractive to think that you could just load a collection of `Project` objects and allow the user to pick the one he wants to edit. However, this could be very expensive, because it means loading all the data for *every* `Project` object, including each project's list of assigned resources, and so forth. As the user adds, edits, and removes `Project` objects, you would potentially have to maintain your collection in memory too.

Practical performance issues dictate that you're better off creating a read-only collection that contains only the information needed to create the user interface. (This is one of the primary reasons why CSLA .NET includes the `ReadOnlyListBase` class, which makes it easy to create such objects.)

This stems from behavioral design. The responsibility of a `Resource` object is to add and edit a valid resource. The responsibility of a `ResourceList` object is to get a read-only list of resources. It is clear that these responsibilities are in conflict. To use a `Resource` object as a child of `ResourceList`, it would need to be read-only—yet its whole purpose is to add and edit data!

Obviously, `ResourceList` and `ProjectList` must contain child objects other than `Resource` and `Project`. They should contain child objects that contain only the data to be displayed, in read-only format. These new child objects will have responsibilities appropriate to their purpose. `ResourceInfo`, for instance, will be responsible for returning read-only information about a resource.

■ **Tip** As discussed earlier, if there are common business rules or logic for properties exposed in such read-only objects, the common behaviors should be normalized into another object.

Figure 3-10 shows the two collection objects with their corresponding read-only child objects.

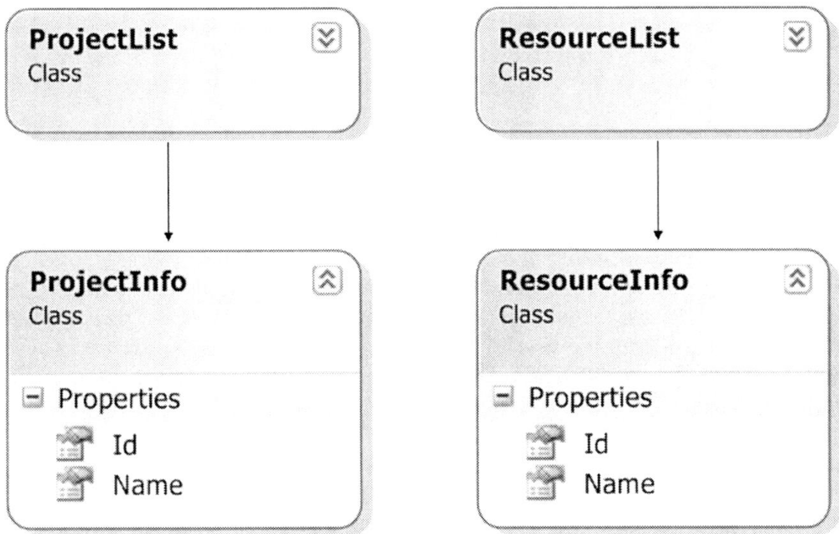

Figure 3-10. *The read-only collection objects, ProjectList and ResourceList*

The ProjectInfo object is responsible for providing read-only information about a project, while the ResourceInfo object provides read-only information about a resource. By loading the minimum amount of data required to meet these responsibilities, these objects provide a high-performance solution and follow good behavioral object design.

Inter-Object Collaboration

The object model has a RoleList object, responsible for providing a read-only list of role data. It also has a Roles object, responsible for editing the list of roles in the application. While these two objects have very distinct responsibilities, they do have a point of interaction that should be addressed.

Though not required by any use case from a user, the RoleList object can, and probably should, be cached. The list of roles won't change terribly often, yet the RoleList object will be used frequently to populate UI controls and to validate data from the user. There's no sense hitting the database every time to get the same data over and over.

You'll see how to easily implement the caching in Chapters 17 and 18, but first, there's a design issue to consider: what happens when the user edits the list of roles using the Roles object? In such a case, the RoleList object will be inaccurate.

■ **Note** There's a related issue too, which is when *another user* edits the list of roles. That issue is harder to solve, and requires either periodic cache expiration or some mechanism by which the database can notify the client that the roles have changed. Solving this problem is outside the scope of this discussion.

It is relatively trivial to have the Roles object notify RoleList to tell it that the data has changed. In such a case, RoleList can simply invalidate its cache so the data is reloaded on the next request. Again, the implementation of this behavior is shown in Chapter 18.

From an object model perspective, however, this means that there is interaction between Roles and RoleList. From a CRC perspective, this means that Roles collaborates with RoleList to expire the cache when appropriate.

Reviewing the Design

The final step in the object design process is to compare the new class diagram with the original use case descriptions to ensure that everything described in each use case can be accomplished through the use of these objects. Doing so helps to ensure that the object model covers all the user requirements. Figure 3-11 shows the complete object model, and Table 3-3 shows the updated CRC information.

The solid-lined arrows in Figure 3-11 indicate collaboration between objects, illustrating how many of them work together to provide the required functionality. The dashed lines show *navigation* between objects. For instance, if you have a ProjectInfo object, it is possible to navigate from there to a Project, typically by calling a GetProject() method.

While navigation between objects isn't strictly necessary, it is often of great benefit to UI developers. Consider that a UI developer will get access to a ProjectInfo object when the user selects a project from a control in the UI. In most cases, the next step is to load the associated Project so that the user can view or edit the data. Providing navigational support directly in the object model makes this trivial to implement within the UI.

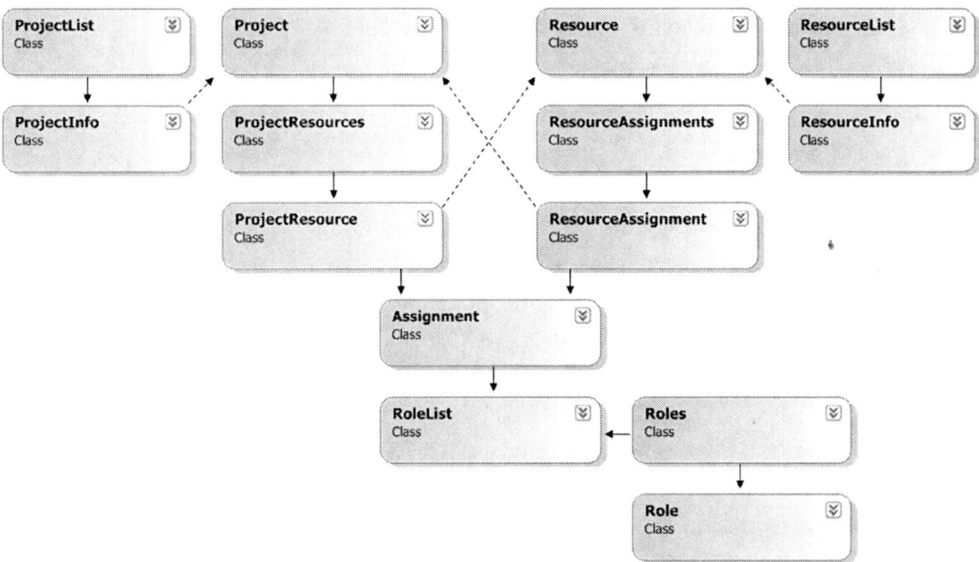

Figure 3-11. *Final Project Tracker object model*

Table 3-3. *Final List of Objects and Their Responsibilities*

Potential Class	Responsibility	Collaborators
`Project`	Adds and edits a valid project	`ProjectResources`, `CommonRules`
`ProjectResources`	Maintains a list of resources assigned to a project	`ProjectResource`
`ProjectResource`	Manages assignment of a resource to a project	`Assignment`, `CommonRules`, `Resource`
`Resource`	Adds and edits a valid resource	`ResourceAssignments`, `CommonRules`
`ResourceAssignments`	Maintains a list of projects to which a resource is assigned	`ResourceAssignment`
`ResourceAssignment`	Manages a project to which a resource is assigned	`Assignment`, `CommonRules`, `Project`
`Assignment`	Manages association of a project and a resource	`RoleList`
`ProjectList`	Gets a read-only list of projects	`ProjectInfo`
`ProjectInfo`	Provides read-only information for a project	`Project`
`ResourceList`	Gets a read-only list of resources	`ResourceInfo`

Table 3-3. *Final List of Objects and Their Responsibilities (Continued)*

Potential Class	Responsibility	Collaborators
`ResourceInfo`	Provides read-only information for a resource	`Resource`
`RoleList`	Gets a read-only list of roles	None
`Roles`	Maintains a list of roles in the system	`Role`, `RoleList`
`Role`	Adds and edits a valid role	None

If you review the use cases, you should find that the objects can be used to accomplish all of the tasks and processes described in the following list:

- Users can get a list of projects.
- Users can add a project.
- Users can edit a project.
- Users can remove a project.
- Users can get a list of resources.
- Users can add a resource.
- Users can edit a resource.
- Users can remove a resource.
- Users can assign a resource to a project (and vice versa).
- When a resource is assigned to a project, users can specify the role the resource will play on the project.

Custom Authentication

Though the objects required to service the business problem have been designed, there's one area left to address. For this application, I want to show how to use custom authentication. Perhaps this requirement became clear due to a user requirement to support users external to our organization: users that aren't in our corporate domain or Active Directory (AD).

The topic of authentication has been discussed several times in the book thus far, and you should remember that CSLA .NET supports Windows integrated (AD) authentication—in fact, that's the default. But it also supports custom authentication, allowing the business developer to create custom .NET principal and identity objects that authenticate the user using credentials stored in a database, LDAP server, or other location.

To this end, the object model will include two objects: `PTPrincipal` and `PTIdentity`. They are shown in Figure 3-12.

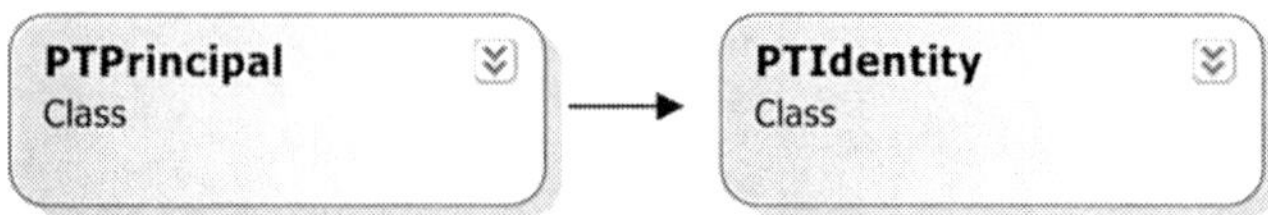

Figure 3-12. *The PTPrincipal and PTIdentity objects*

`PTPrincipal` is a .NET principal object and acts as the primary entry point for custom authentication and role-based authorization. `PTIdentity` is a .NET identity object and is responsible for representing the user's identity.

At this point, the object model can be considered complete.

Using CSLA .NET

The class diagrams created so far have focused entirely on the business domain—which is a good thing. Ideally, you should always start by focusing on business issues and deferring much of the technical design to a later stage in the process. Users typically don't understand (or care about) the technical issues behind the scenes, such as how you are going to implement the Cancel buttons or how to retrieve data from the database.

Of course, the business developer cares about these issues—but these issues can be dealt with after the basic object modeling is complete, once you have a good understanding of the business issues and confidence that your model can meet the requirements laid out in the use cases.

Going forward in this book, I'll be assuming the use of the CSLA .NET framework described in Chapter 2. Using this framework (or any comparable framework) means spending less time figuring out how to design or implement the features included in the framework. By relying on CSLA .NET, developers gain the benefits listed in Table 3-4.

Table 3-4. *Benefits Gained by Using CSLA .NET*

Feature	Description
Smart data	Business data is encapsulated in objects along with its associated business logic, so developers are never working with raw, unprotected data, and all business logic is centralized for easy maintenance.
Easy object creation	Developers use standard .NET object-oriented programming techniques to create business objects.
Flexible physical configuration	Data access runs locally or on an application server, without changing business code.
Object persistence	Clearly defined methods contain all data access code.
Optimized data access	Objects only persist themselves if their data has been changed. It's easy to select between various transaction technologies to balance between performance and features.
Optional n-level undo capabilities	Support for complex WPF or Windows Forms interfaces is easy, while also supporting high-performance web interfaces.
Business rule management	This reduces the code required to implement business and validation rules.
Authorization rule management	This reduces the code required to implement per-property authorization.
Simple UI creation	With full support for WPF, Windows Forms, and Web Forms data binding, minimal code is required to create sophisticated user interfaces (see Chapters 19 and 20).

Table 3-4. *Benefits Gained by Using CSLA .NET (Continued)*

Feature	Description
Web service support	Developers can readily create a web service interface for the application, so that other applications can tap into the application's functionality directly (see Chapter 21).
Custom authentication	This makes it easy to select between Windows integrated security and CSLA .NET custom security. It's also easy to customize CSLA .NET custom security to use preexisting security databases. In either case, standard .NET security objects are used, providing a standard way to access user security information.

To use CSLA .NET, developers merely need to determine which base classes to inherit from when creating each business class. For example, some business objects will be editable objects that can be loaded directly by the user. These need to inherit from `BusinessBase`, as shown in Figure 3-13.

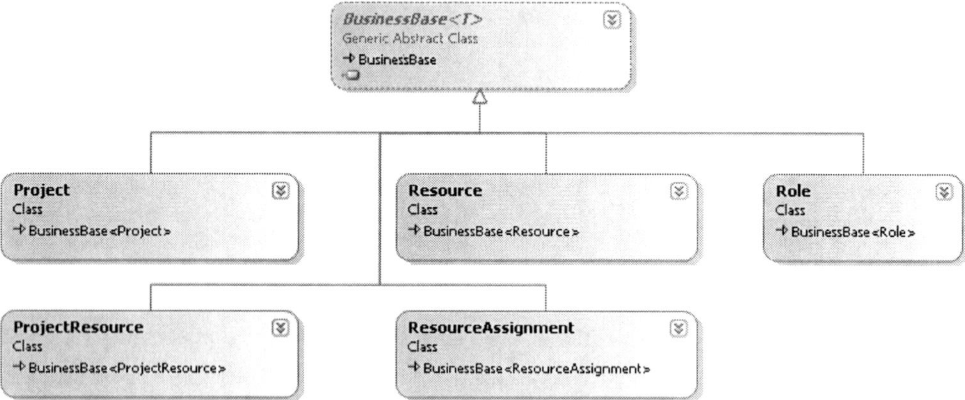

Figure 3-13. *Business objects subclassing BusinessBase*

By subclassing `BusinessBase`, all of these objects gain the full set of business object capabilities implemented in Chapters 6 through 16.

The model also includes objects that are *collections* of business objects, and they should inherit from `BusinessListBase`, as shown in Figure 3-14.

`BusinessListBase` supports the undo capabilities implemented for `BusinessBase`; the two base classes work hand in hand to provide this functionality.

As shown in Figure 3-15, the two objects that list read-only data for the user inherit from `ReadOnlyListBase`. This base class provides the support objects need for retrieving data from the database *without* the overhead of supporting undo or business rule tracking. Those features aren't required for read-only objects.

The `ProjectInfo` and `ResourceInfo` classes don't inherit from any CSLA .NET base classes. As you'll see in Chapters 17 and 18, they must be marked with the Serializable attribute, but they don't need to inherit from a special base class just to expose a set of read-only properties.

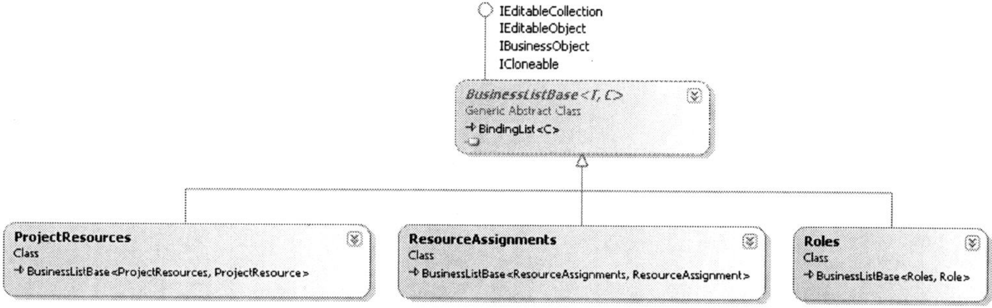

Figure 3-14. *Business objects subclassing BusinessListBase*

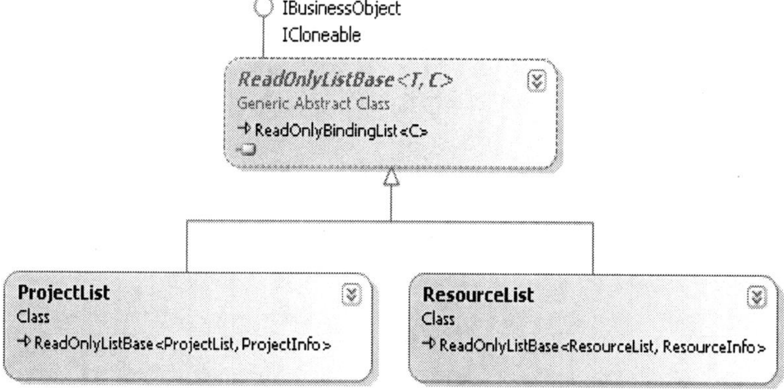

Figure 3-15. *Read-only list objects subclassing ReadOnlyListBase*

Next, there's the `RoleList` object, which is a read-only list of name/value data. Although this *could* be implemented using `ReadOnlyListBase`, Chapter 6 will describe the `NameValueListBase` class, as shown in Figure 3-16. This class provides a better alternative for building name/value lists and is designed to make it as easy as possible to create read-only lists of text values, so it's ideal for building the `RoleList` class.

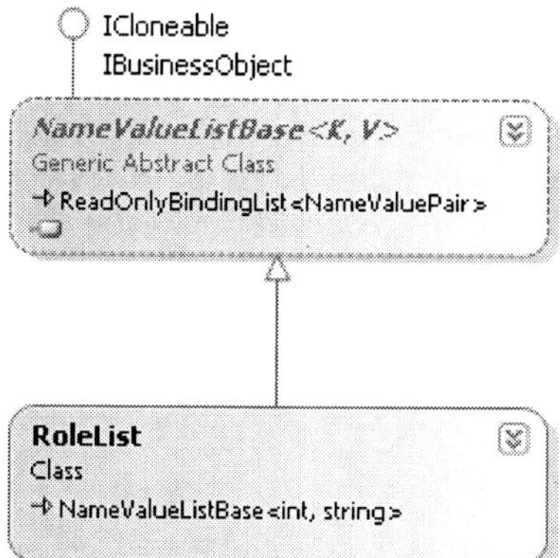

Figure 3-16. *RoleList subclassing NameValueListBase*

Finally, there are the two custom authentication objects: `PTPrincipal` and `PTIdentity`. Figure 3-17 shows these objects along with their CSLA .NET base classes.

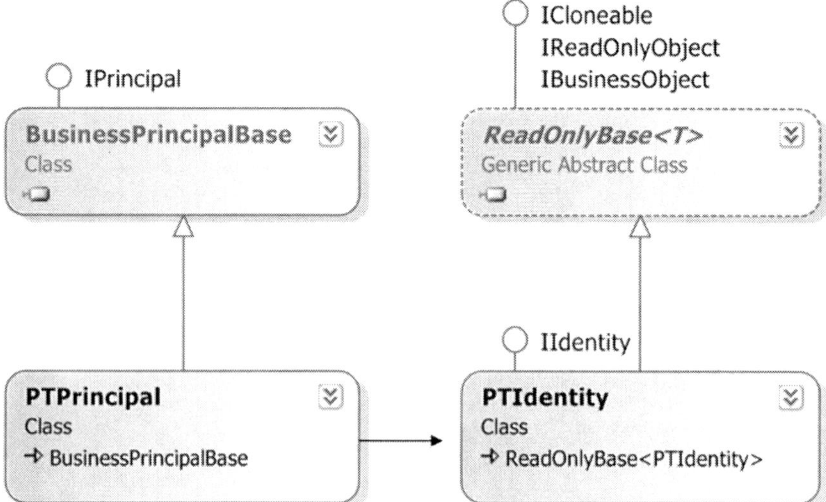

Figure 3-17. *Objects supporting custom authentication*

`PTPrincipal` inherits from `Csla.Security.BusinessPrincipalBase`, ensuring that it implements the `System.Security.Principal.IPrincipal` interface and also that it will work with the data portal, as implemented in Chapter 4. A required property from the `IPrincipal` interface is `Identity`, which provides a reference to a .NET identity object—in this case, `PTIdentity`. The `PTIdentity` object inherits from `ReadOnlyBase`. It exposes only read-only data, so this is a natural fit.

All of these classes will be implemented in Chapters 17 and 18. During that process, you'll see how to use the CSLA .NET framework to simplify the process of creating business objects.

Database Design

It's a rare thing to be able to design a database specifically for an application. More often than not, the database already exists, and developers must deal with its existing design. At best, you might be able to add some new tables or columns.

This is one reason why ORM is a key concept for object-oriented development. The object model designed earlier in the chapter matches the business requirements without giving any consideration to the database design. An important step in the development process is to create code that translates the data from the databases into the objects, and vice versa. That code will be included in Chapters 17 and 18 as the business objects are implemented.

In *this* chapter, let's create a database for use by the project-tracking application. One thing to note is that even though the database is created specifically for this application, the data model will not match the object model exactly. A good relational model and a good object model are almost never the same thing.

■ **Tip** Speaking of good relational models, I strongly recommend that database design be done by a professional DBA, not by software developers. While many software developers are reasonably competent at database design, DBAs are better at making the many optimizations and design choices. The database design shown here is that of a software developer, and I'm sure a DBA would see numerous ways to improve or tweak the results to work better in a production setting.

To make development and testing relatively easy, this will be a SQL Server 2008 Express database. As you'll see in Chapter 18, you write the data access code for each object, so neither CSLA .NET nor your business objects are required to use SQL Server 2008 Express or any other specific database. You can use any data storage technology you choose behind your objects. In most cases, your applications will use production database servers such as SQL Server 2008 Enterprise Edition, Oracle, or DB2, rather than the more limited Express Edition used here.

The database will include tables, along with some stored procedures to enable database access from code. Additionally, there will be a second database to contain security information for use by the `PTIdentity` object.

■ **Tip** If you're using a database other than SQL Server 2008 Express, you should translate the table creation and stored procedures to fit with your environment. You can find the database, table, and stored procedure scripts in the `PTData` project in the Source Code/Download area on the Apress website (`www.apress.com`) and from `www.lhotka.net/cslanet/download.aspx`.

While stored procedures may or may not offer any performance benefits, I believe they are a critical part of any business application. Stored procedures provide an abstract, logical interface to the database. They provide a level of indirection between the business objects and the underlying table structures, and thus they reduce coupling between the data management and business layers in your application. In short, stored procedures help make applications more maintainable over time.

That said, you'll notice that none of these stored procedures are complex, and every effort has been made to keep business logic out of the database and in the business objects. Putting the business logic in both the objects and the database is just another way to duplicate business logic, which increases maintenance costs for the application as a whole.

Creating the Databases

The `PTracker` database will contain tables and stored procedures to persist the data for the business objects in the object model designed earlier in the chapter. This is a SQL Server 2008 Express database, so you can think of it as being just another file in your project.

To create the database, open Visual Studio and create a new Class Library project named `PTDB`. I won't have you build this project at any point, so you can ignore the project settings and `Class1.cs` file. The purpose of this project is just so you can use Visual Studio to set up the database.

Choose Project ➤ Add New Item, and choose the Service-based Database option. As shown in Figure 3-18, name the file and click Add.

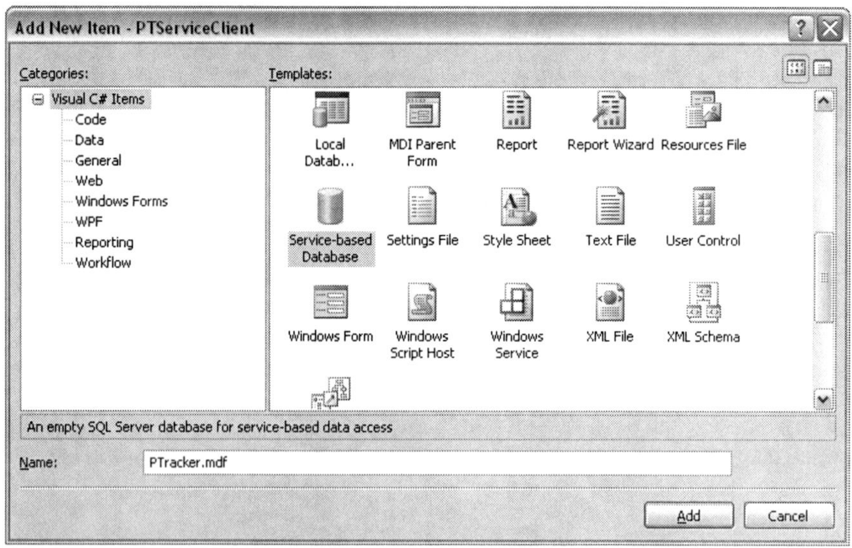

Figure 3-18. *Adding the PTracker database in Visual Studio*

Visual Studio will force you to walk through the process of creating a `DataSet` for the new database. You can walk through or cancel that wizard as you choose. It is not required for anything covered in this book.

Repeat the process to add a `Security.mdf` database as well. The end result is that you'll have two databases in the project—and more importantly, in the Server Explorer window, as shown in Figure 3-19.

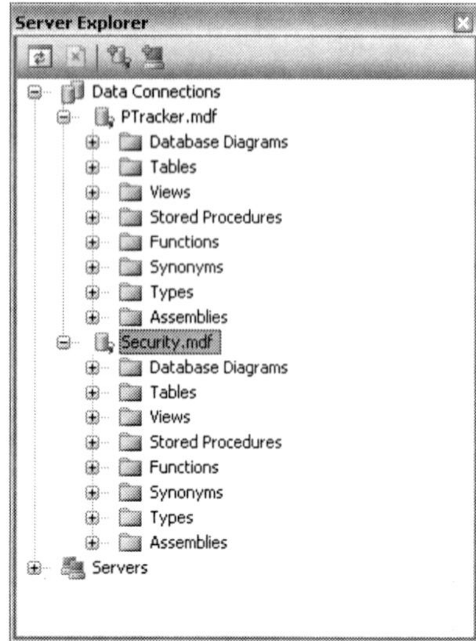

Figure 3-19. *The PTracker and Security databases in Server Explorer*

You can also create tables within Server Explorer: just right-click the Tables node under the database, and choose New Table. This will bring up a table designer in VS .NET, with which you can define the columns for the new table.

Once the columns, keys, and indexes have been set up, save the changes by closing the designer or clicking the Save button in the toolbar. At this point, you'll be prompted to provide a name for the table, and it will be added to the database.

PTracker Database

Follow this process to add each of the following four tables to the database.

Roles

The `Roles` table will store the list of possible roles a resource can fill when assigned to a project—it simply contains an `Id` value and the name of the role. Figure 3-20 shows the VS .NET designer with these columns added and the `Id` column configured as the primary key.

dbo.Roles: Table...CS\PTRACKER.MDF)

Column Name	Data Type	Allow Nulls
Id	int	☐
Name	varchar(50)	☐
LastChanged	timestamp	☐
		☐

Figure 3-20. *Design of the Roles table*

Notice that none of the columns allow `null` values. There's no business requirement to differentiate between an empty value and one that was never entered, so `null` values would make no sense.

The table also has a `LastChanged` column, which will be used to implement otimistic, first-write-wins concurrency in Chapter 18. It is of type `timestamp`, so it provides a unique, auto-incrementing value every time a row is inserted or updated. All the tables in the `PTracker` database will have this type of column.

Projects

The `Projects` table will contain the data for each project in the system. The columns for this table are shown in Figure 3-21.

dbo.Projects: T...CS\PTRACKER.MDF)

Column Name	Data Type	Allow Nulls
Id	uniqueidentifier	☐
Name	varchar(50)	☐
Started	datetime	☑
Ended	datetime	☑
Description	varchar(MAX)	☑
LastChanged	timestamp	☐
		☐

Figure 3-21. *Design of the Projects table*

The `Id` column is set up as the primary key, and it's of type `uniqueidentifier`, which is a `Guid` type in .NET.

There are many ways to create primary key columns in tables, including using auto-incrementing numeric values or user-assigned values. However, the use of a `uniqueidentifier` is particularly powerful when working with object-oriented designs. Other techniques don't assign the identifier until the data is added to the database, or they allow the user to provide the value, which means that you can't tell if it collides with an existing key value until the data is added to the database. With a `uniqueidentifier`, however, the business developer can write code to assign the primary key value to an object as the object is created. There's no need to wait until the object is inserted into the database to get or confirm the value. If the value isn't assigned ahead of time, the database will supply the value.

Notice that the two `datetime` fields allow `null` values. The `null` value is used here to indicate an empty value for a date. The `Description` column is also allowed to be `null`. This isn't because of any business requirement, but rather because it is quite common for database columns to allow `null` values in cases in which they're meaningless. Chapter 18 will illustrate how to easily ignore any `null` values in this column.

The `Description` column is of type `varchar(MAX)` so that it can hold a blob of text data. This field allows the user to enter a lengthy description of the project, if so desired.

Resources

The `Resources` table will hold the data for the various resources that can be assigned to a project. The columns for this table are shown in Figure 3-22.

Once again, the `Id` column is the primary key—it's an `int` that is configured as an identity column using the Column Properties window. This table has now been given an identity key; the code in Chapter 18 will demonstrate how to support this concept within your business objects.

As with the `Description` field in the `Projects` table, the `LastName` and `FirstName` columns allow `null` values even though they have no business meaning. Again, this is merely to illustrate how to build business objects to deal with real-world database designs and their intrinsic flaws.

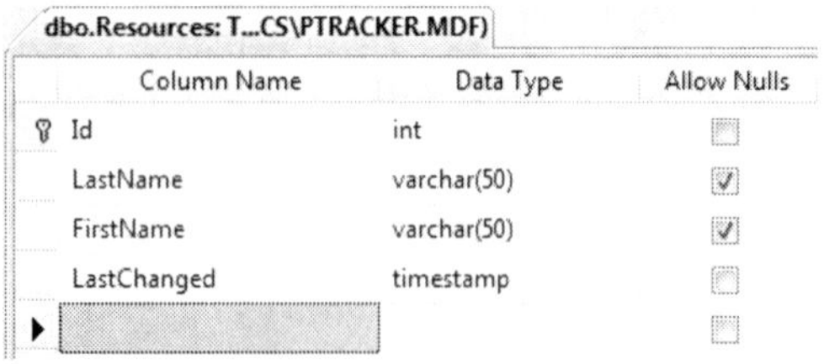

dbo.Resources: T...CS\PTRACKER.MDF)

Column Name	Data Type	Allow Nulls
Id	int	☐
LastName	varchar(50)	☑
FirstName	varchar(50)	☑
LastChanged	timestamp	☐
		☐

Figure 3-22. *Making the Id column an identity column*

Assignments

Finally, there's the `Assignments` table. A many-to-many relationship exists between projects and resources—a project can have a number of resources assigned to it, and a resource can be assigned to a number of projects.

The way you can represent this relationally is to create a *link table* that contains the primary keys of both tables. In this case, it will also include information about the relationship, including the date of the assignment and the role that the resource plays in the project, as shown in Figure 3-23.

The first two columns here are the primary keys from the `Projects` and `Resources` tables; when combined, they make up the primary key in the link table. Though the `Assigned` column is of `datetime` type, `null` values are not allowed. This is because this value can't be empty—a valid date is always required. The `Role` column is also a foreign key, linking back to the `Roles` table. The data in this table will be used to populate the `ProjectResource` and `ResourceAssignment` objects discussed earlier in the chapter.

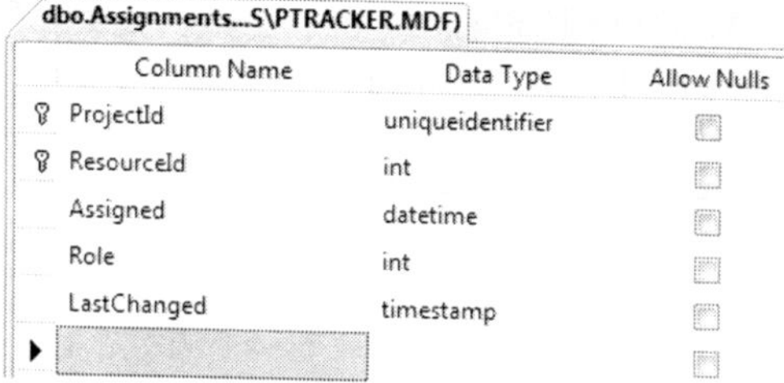

Figure 3-23. *Design for the Assignments table*

This really drives home the fact that a relational model isn't the same as an object-oriented model. The many-to-many relational design doesn't match up to the object model that represents much of the same data. The objects are designed around normalization of behavior, while the data model is designed around normalization of data.

Database Diagrams

Server Explorer in Visual Studio supports the creation of database diagrams, which are stored in the database. These diagrams not only illustrate the relationships between tables, but also tell SQL Server how to enforce and work with those relationships.

Under the `PTracker.mdf` node in Server Explorer, there's a node for Database Diagrams. Right-click this entry and choose New Diagram. Visual Studio will prompt you for the tables to be included in the diagram. Highlight all of them, and click Add and Close.

The result is a designer window in which the tables are shown as a diagram. You can drag and drop columns from tables to other tables in order to indicate relationships. For example, drag and drop the `Id` field from `Projects` to the `ProjectID` field in the `Assignments` table. This will bring up a Tables and Columns dialog box, in which you can specify the nature of this relationship, as shown in Figure 3-24. Click OK to create the relationship.

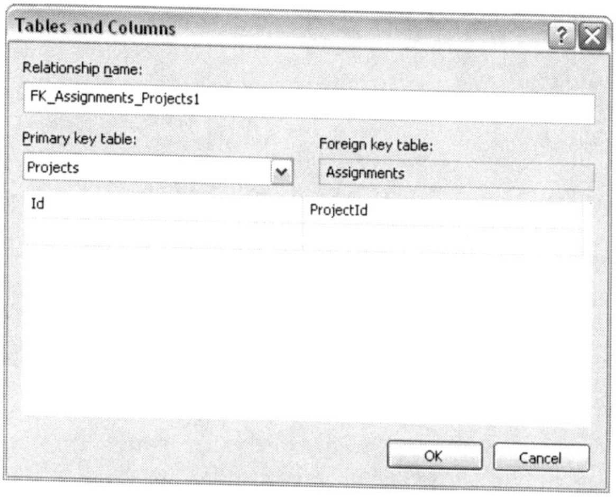

Figure 3-24. *Creating a relationship between Assignments and Projects*

Do the same to link the `Resources` table to `Assignments`. You can also link the `Roles` table's `Id` column to the `Role` column in `Assignments`, thereby allowing the database to ensure that only valid roles can be added to the table.

The resulting diagram should appear in a way that's similar to Figure 3-25.

Save the diagram to the database, naming it `PTrackerRelationships`. VS .NET will then ask whether to update the tables. Remember that these relationships are reflected as formal constraints within the database itself, so this diagram directly impacts the database design.

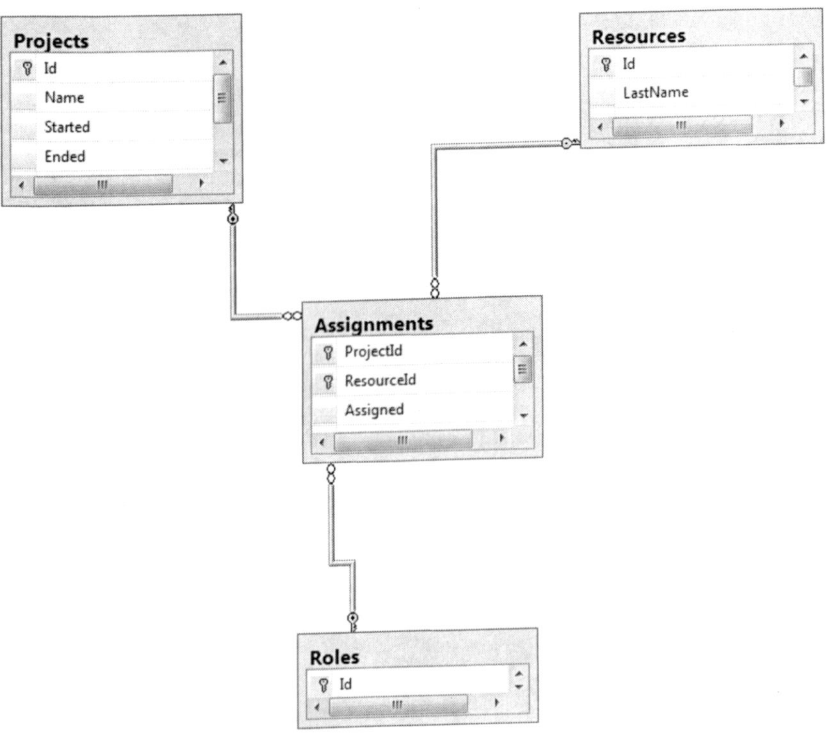

Figure 3-25. *Database diagram for the PTracker database*

Stored Procedures

Whenever possible, database access should be performed through stored procedures. Stored procedures offer powerful security control over the database and—perhaps most importantly—provide an abstraction layer between the physical structure of the database and the logical way in which it is used. The business objects created in Chapters 17 and 18 will make use of stored procedures for their database interaction.

I think this is true, even though you may use LINQ to SQL or other technologies to access the database. At the same time, technologies like LINQ to SQL offer flexible query capabilities that are nice to use. So I typically compromise, using LINQ to SQL to query for data, and using stored procedures (called through LINQ to SQL) for insert, update, and delete operations.

You can use Server Explorer to add the stored procedures to the database by right-clicking the Stored Procedures node under the database and choosing Add New Stored Procedure. This brings up a designer window in which you can write the stored procedure code. When you close the designer, the stored procedure will be added to the database.

Let's look at the stored procedures we'll need, starting with `addProject`.

addProject

The addProject procedure is called to add a record to the Projects table, as follows:

```
CREATE PROCEDURE addProject
  (
    @id uniqueidentifier,
    @name varchar(50),
    @started datetime,
    @ended datetime,
    @description varchar(MAX),
    @newLastChanged timestamp output
  )
AS
  INSERT INTO Projects
  (Id,Name,Started,Ended,Description)
  VALUES
  (@id,@name,@started,@ended,@description)

  SELECT @newLastChanged = LastChanged
  FROM Projects WHERE Id=@id
  RETURN
```

Note that this only adds the record to the Projects table; a separate stored procedure adds records to the Assignments table.

This stored procedure not only includes an INSERT statement, but also a SELECT statement that loads an output parameter value. This is required to support concurrency. Recall that all the tables in the database include a timestamp column, which is incremented automatically each time a row is inserted or updated. As you'll see in Chapter 18, the business object must keep track of this value. Since the value changes any time the row changes, the value is returned as the result of any INSERT or UPDATE operation.

updateProject

Not only are records added to the Projects table, but the application must allow them to be changed. The updateProject procedure provides this capability, as shown here:

```
CREATE PROCEDURE updateProject
  (
    @id uniqueidentifier,
    @name varchar(50),
    @started datetime,
    @ended datetime,
    @description varchar(MAX),
    @lastChanged timestamp,
    @newLastChanged timestamp output
  )
AS
  UPDATE Projects
  SET
    Name=@name,
    Started=@started,
    Ended=@ended,
    Description=@description
```

```
  WHERE Id=@id
    AND LastChanged=@lastChanged
  IF @@ROWCOUNT = 0
    BEGIN
      RAISERROR('Row has been edited by another user', 16, 1)
      RETURN
    END

  SELECT @newLastChanged = LastChanged
  FROM Projects WHERE Id=@id
  RETURN
```

Again, this procedure only updates the record in the Projects table; the related records in the Assignments table are updated separately.

Notice the @lastChanged parameter required by the procedure. This represents the last known timestamp value for the row. In Chapter 18, you'll see how this value is maintained by the business object.

When the object attempts to update the row, it provides the last known value for the LastChanged column. If that value hasn't changed in the database, then no other user has updated the row since the object read its data. But if the value *has* changed in the database, then some other user did change the data in the row since the object read the data. First-write-wins optimistic concurrency specifies that this second update can't be allowed, because it could overwrite changes made by that other user.

The UPDATE statement itself uses this parameter in the WHERE clause to ensure that the row is only updated if the value matches. The procedure then checks to see if the row was actually updated. If no rows were updated, it raises an error, which shows up as a database exception in the data access code of the business object.

On the other hand, if the update goes through and the row is changed, then a SELECT statement is executed to return the *new* value of the LastChanged column as an output parameter, so that the object can maintain the new value to allow possible future updates.

deleteProject

The deleteProject procedure deletes the appropriate record from the Projects table, and it removes any related records from the Assignments table. When creating the relationships between tables in the database diagram, the default is to *not* automatically cascade deletions to child tables.

```
CREATE PROCEDURE deleteProject
  (
    @id uniqueidentifier
  )
AS
  DELETE Assignments
  WHERE ProjectId=@id

  DELETE Projects
  WHERE Id=@id
  RETURN
```

If you set up your table relationships to cascade deletes automatically, then obviously the preceding stored procedure would only delete the data in the Projects table.

Though this procedure updates multiple tables, it does *not* include transactional code. Although you *could* manage the transaction at this level, you can gain flexibility by allowing the business object to manage the transaction.

Using the CSLA .NET framework, you have the option to run the data access code within a `System.Transactions` transactional context, to run it within an Enterprise Services distributed transaction, or to manage the transaction manually. When using either `System.Transactions` or Enterprise Services, transactional statements in the stored procedures will cause exceptions to occur. If you opt to handle the transactions manually, you can choose to put the transactional statements here in the stored procedure, or use an ADO.NET `Transaction` object within the business object's data access code.

addAssignment

When adding or editing a project or a resource, the user may also add or change the associated data in the `Assignments` table. The `addAssignment` procedure adds a new record as follows:

```
CREATE PROCEDURE addAssignment
  (
    @projectId uniqueidentifier,
    @resourceId int,
    @assigned datetime,
    @role int,
    @newLastChanged timestamp output
  )
AS
  INSERT INTO Assignments
  (ProjectId,ResourceId,Assigned,Role)
  VALUES
  (@projectId,@resourceId,@assigned,@role)

  SELECT @newLastChanged = LastChanged
  FROM Assignments
  WHERE ProjectId=@projectId AND ResourceId=@resourceId
  RETURN
```

This procedure may be called during the adding or editing of either a `Project` or a `Resource` object in the application.

Like `addProject`, this procedure ends with a `SELECT` statement that returns the new value of the `LastChanged` column for the row as an output parameter. The business object must maintain this value to allow for future updates of the row using the `updateAssignment` stored procedure.

updateAssignment

Likewise, there's a requirement to *update* records in the `Assignments` table:

```
CREATE PROCEDURE updateAssignment
  (
    @projectId uniqueidentifier,
    @resourceId int,
    @assigned datetime,
    @role int,
    @lastChanged timestamp,
    @newLastChanged timestamp output
  )
AS
  UPDATE Assignments
```

```
  SET
    Assigned=@assigned,
    Role=@role
  WHERE ProjectId=@projectId AND ResourceId=@resourceId
    AND LastChanged=@lastChanged
  IF @@ROWCOUNT = 0
    RAISERROR('Row has been edited by another user', 16, 1)

  SELECT @newLastChanged = LastChanged
  FROM Assignments
  WHERE ProjectId=@projectId AND ResourceId=@resourceId
  RETURN
```

As with addAssignment, this may be called when updating data from either a Project or a Resource object.

Notice the @lastChanged parameter. It is used in the same way the parameter was used in updateProject: to implement first-write-wins optimistic concurrency. If the UPDATE statement succeeds, the new value of the LastChanged column is returned as a result through an output parameter so the business object can maintain the new value.

deleteAssignment

As part of the process of updating a project or resource, it is possible that a specific record will be deleted from the Assignments table. An assignment is a child entity beneath a project or resource, and a user can remove a resource from a project, or a project from a resource. In either case, that specific assignment record must be removed from the database.

```
CREATE PROCEDURE deleteAssignment
  (
    @projectId uniqueidentifier,
    @resourceId int
  )
AS
  DELETE Ass ignments
  WHERE ProjectId=@projectId AND ResourceId=@resourceId
  RETURN
```

This completes the operations that can be performed on the Assignments data. Notice that there's no getAssignments procedure. This is because assignments are always children of a project and a resource. The business objects never retrieve just a list of assignments, except as part of retrieving a project or resource. The getProject procedure, for instance, also retrieves a list of assignments associated with the project.

addResource

When a new Resource object is created and saved, its data needs to be inserted into the Resources table.

```
CREATE PROCEDURE addResource
  (
    @lastName varchar(50),
    @firstName varchar(50),
    @newId int output,
    @newLastChanged timestamp output
  )
```

```
AS
  INSERT INTO Resources
  (LastName,FirstName)
  VALUES
  (@lastName,@firstName)

  SELECT @newId = Id, @newLastChanged = LastChanged
  FROM Resources WHERE Id=SCOPE_IDENTITY()
  RETURN
```

Remember that the Id column in the Resource table is an identity column. This means its value is automatically assigned by the database when a new row is inserted. The built-in SCOPE_IDENTITY() function is used to retrieve the generated key value, and that value is returned in an output parameter as a result of the stored procedure. In Chapter 18, you'll see how this value is retrieved by the Resource object so that the object becomes aware of the new value. Also, as in addProject, the new value for the LastChanged column is returned to the object.

The associated addAssignment procedure, which can be used to add related records to the Assignments table, was created earlier.

updateResource

Likewise, there's a need to update data in the Resources table, as shown here:

```
CREATE PROCEDURE updateResource
  (
    @id int,
    @lastName varchar(50),
    @firstName varchar(50),
    @lastChanged timestamp,
    @newLastChanged timestamp output
  )
AS
  UPDATE Resources
  SET
    LastName=@lastName,
    FirstName=@firstName
  WHERE Id=@id
    AND LastChanged=@lastChanged
  IF @@ROWCOUNT = 0
    RAISERROR('Row has been edited by another user', 16, 1)

  SELECT @newLastChanged = LastChanged
  FROM Resources WHERE Id=@id
  RETURN
```

This procedure will be called when an existing Resource object is edited and saved.

deleteResource

A Resource object can be removed from the system. This means removing not only the record from the Resources table, but also the associated records from the Assignments table, as shown here:

```
CREATE PROCEDURE deleteResource
  (
    @id int
  )
AS
  DELETE Assignments
  WHERE ResourceId=@id

  DELETE Resources
  WHERE Id=@id
  RETURN
```

This procedure works the same as deleteProject.

getRoles

The getRoles procedure will return the list of roles to populate the RoleList and Roles objects as follows:

```
CREATE PROCEDURE [dbo].[getRoles]
AS
  SELECT Id,Name,LastChanged
  FROM Roles
  RETURN
```

All the role data is returned as a result of this procedure. Though RoleList and Roles use the data differently, they both use the same set of values.

addRole

The addRole procedure adds a new entry to the Roles table.

```
CREATE PROCEDURE [dbo].[addRole]
  (
    @id int,
    @name varchar(50),
    @newLastChanged timestamp output
  )
AS
  INSERT INTO Roles
  (Id,Name)
  VALUES
  (@id,@name)

  SELECT @newLastChanged = LastChanged
  FROM Roles WHERE Id=@id
  RETURN
```

The Role object calls this stored procedure when it needs to insert its data into the database. As with the other add procedures, this one returns the new value of the LastChanged column for use by the business object.

updateRole

The updateRole procedure updates an existing entry in the Roles table.

```
CREATE PROCEDURE [dbo].[updateRole]
  (
    @id int,
    @name varchar(50),
    @lastChanged timestamp,
    @newLastChanged timestamp output
  )
AS
  UPDATE Roles
  SET
    Name=@name
  WHERE Id=@id
    AND LastChanged=@lastChanged
  IF @@ROWCOUNT = 0
    RAISERROR('Row has been edited by another user', 16, 1)

  SELECT @newLastChanged = LastChanged
  FROM Roles WHERE Id=@id
  RETURN
```

The Role object calls this stored procedure when it needs to update the data in the database.

deleteRole

The deleteRole procedure removes an entry from the Roles table.

```
CREATE PROCEDURE [dbo].[deleteRole]
  (
    @id int
  )
AS
  DELETE Roles
  WHERE Id=@id
  RETURN
```

The Role object calls this stored procedure when it needs to remove a row of data from the database.

At this point, stored procedures exist to do every bit of data access. In Chapter 18, the business objects will implement data access code using LINQ to SQL that makes use of these stored procedures.

Security Database

With the PTracker database complete, let's wrap up the chapter by creating the tables and stored procedures for the Security database. The PTIdentity object will use this database to perform custom authentication of a user's credentials. Assuming the user is valid, the user's roles will be loaded into the business object so they can be used for authorization as the application is used.

The PTPrincipal and PTIdentity objects will be implemented in Chapter 17. In most cases, you'll be creating similar custom security objects—but designed to use your preexisting security database tables. The database created in this chapter and the objects created in Chapters 17 and 18 exist primarily to demonstrate the basic process required for creating your own objects.

Figure 3-26 shows the two tables in the database, along with their relationship.

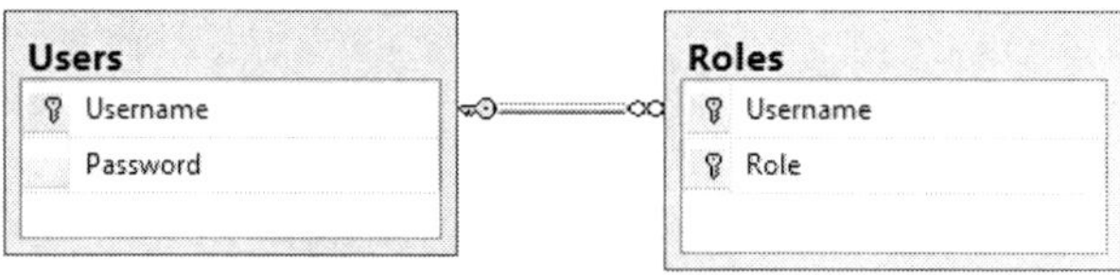

Figure 3-26. *Database diagram for the Security database*

In the Users table, Username and Password are both varchar(20) columns, as is the Role column in the Roles table. Only the Password column allows null values. All other values are required. Of course, a password should be required as well, but for this simple example, it is left as optional.

Finally, there's a Login stored procedure.

```
CREATE PROCEDURE Login
  (
    @user varchar(20),
    @pw varchar(20)
  )
AS
  SELECT Username
  FROM Users
  WHERE Username=@user AND Password=@pw;

  SELECT R.Role
  FROM Users AS U INNER JOIN Roles AS R ON
      R.UserName = U.UserName
  WHERE U.Username = @user and U.Password = @pw
  RETURN
```

PTIdentity calls this procedure to authenticate the user and retrieve the user's list of roles. As you'll see in Chapter 17, PTIdentity determines whether the user's credentials are valid or not by finding out whether any data is returned from this stored procedure. If no data is returned, then the user's credentials are assumed to be invalid and the user is not authenticated.

On the other hand, if the stored procedure does return data, then PTIdentity stores that data, especially the list of roles to which the user belongs. This list of security roles (not to be confused with the project roles from the PTracker database) is then used for authorization throughout the application. The CanReadProperty() and CanWriteProperty() methods on each business object rely on this data.

Conclusion

This chapter has started the process of building a sample application that will make use of the CSLA .NET framework. It's a simple project-tracking application that maintains a list of projects and a list of resources, and allows the resources to be assigned to the projects.

The application's design used an object-oriented analysis technique that involved creating use cases that described the various ways in which the users need to interact with the system. Based on the use cases, and by using elements of CRC-style design, a list of potential business objects was created and refined.

That object list was then used to create a preliminary class diagram that showed the classes, their key data fields, and their relationships. Based on the diagram, our understanding of the business domain, and the use cases, we were able to refine the design to arrive at a final class diagram that describes the business classes that will make up the application.

The next step was to determine the appropriate CSLA .NET base classes from which each business object should inherit. The editable business objects inherit from `BusinessBase`, and the collections of editable child objects inherit from `BusinessListBase`. The lists of read-only data inherit from `ReadOnlyListBase`, each of which contain simple child objects that don't inherit from a CSLA .NET base class at all. The list of simple name/value role data inherits from `NameValueListBase`.

Finally, a simple relational database was created to store the data for the application. In most applications, the database already exists, but in this case, we had the luxury of creating a database from scratch. Even so, it's interesting to note the differences between the object model and the relational model, thus highlighting the fact that a good object-oriented model and a good relational model are almost never the same.

Chapters 4 and 5 will discuss the basic structure of each type of business object directly supported by CSLA .NET. These chapters will also walk through a code template for each type. Later in the book, after walking through the implementation of CSLA .NET itself, Chapters 17 and 18 will implement the business objects designed in this chapter. Chapter 19 will show how to build a WPF UI based on those objects. In Chapter 20, a comparable Web Forms UI will be built, and Chapter 21 will walk through the construction of a WCF service interface that reuses the exact same objects.

CHAPTER 4

CSLA .NET Object Stereotypes

Chapters 6 through 16 cover the implementation of the CSLA .NET framework as described in Chapter 2. I think it is useful to get a good idea of the types of business objects the framework is designed to support before looking at the implementation itself. In this chapter and in Chapter 5, I discuss the primary types of objects supported by the framework and walk through the basic code structure of each object type.

In object-oriented design terms, objects that share a broad set of behavioral characteristics and play a similar role in the application architecture are said to belong to a *stereotype*. A stereotype is a way of categorizing or describing a broad set of similar objects. This chapter covers in detail the object stereotypes directly supported by CSLA .NET. You may extend or enhance CSLA .NET to support other stereotypes as required by your application but the stereotypes supported out of the box do cover the needs of most business applications.

This chapter covers the life cycle of each type of business object in general terms. Then in Chapter 5, I get into code, creating a basic template showing the structure of each stereotype:

- Editable root
- Editable child
- Editable, "switchable" (i.e., root or child) object
- Editable root collection
- Editable child collection
- Read-only root
- Read-only root collection
- Read-only child
- Read-only child collection
- Command object
- Name/value list
- Dynamic editable list
- Dynamic editable root
- Criteria

Though the templates are not complete business object implementations, each one illustrates the basic structure you need to follow when creating that type of business object. You can use this information to create class templates or code snippets for use in Visual Studio to make your development experience more productive.

Basic Terminology and Object Graph Structure

Most frameworks and application models have their own jargon and terminology, and CSLA .NET is no exception. To discuss the stereotypes supported by CSLA .NET, I think it is important to first define some common terms. These are listed in Table 4-1.

Table 4-1. *CSLA .NET Common Terms*

Term	Definition
Object graph	One or more objects that reference each other
Root object	An object that can be directly retrieved from the database; each object graph has exactly one root object
Child object	An object that is only retrieved from the database as part of another object (its parent)
Parent object	An object that contains child objects (a parent may also be a root)
Editable object	An object that implements public read-write properties, or methods that allow manipulation of data; editable objects can be retrieved and saved to the database; these may be root, parent, or child objects
Read-only object	An object that implements only read-only properties and does not expose methods that allow manipulation of data; read-only objects can be retrieved from the database but not saved; these may be root, parent, or child objects
Collection or list	An object that contains other objects; may be editable or read-only; may be a root or child, but is always a parent
Criteria object	An object that contains criteria or key information necessary to identify and create, retrieve, or delete another object

When working with CSLA .NET, there is always one object that is identified as the *root object*. This object may be a parent, in which case it contains other *child objects*, or it may simply be a single object, as shown in Figure 4-1.

Figure 4-1. *Simplest object graph*

Figure 4-2 illustrates a more complex object graph where the root object is also a parent containing two other objects.

Notice that the child list is also a parent containing other child objects. The important thing to remember is that an object graph can only have exactly one root object. That root object may contain many child or child list objects, and some of those child objects may also be parent objects. In other words, the CSLA .NET stereotypes have rich support for the concept of *containment*, where objects contain other objects.

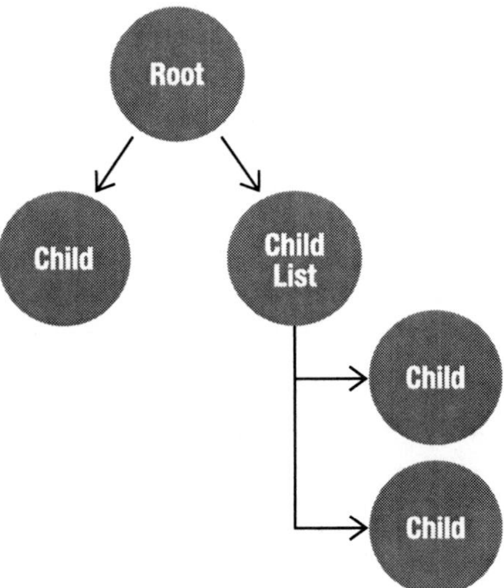

Figure 4-2. *Object graph illustrating containment*

A common example of containment is a sales order, which contains a list of line item objects. Typically the `SalesOrder` object is a root and a parent; the `LineItemList` object is a child and a parent; and each `LineItem` object is a child.

It is also possible for a list to be a root, as shown in Figure 4-3.

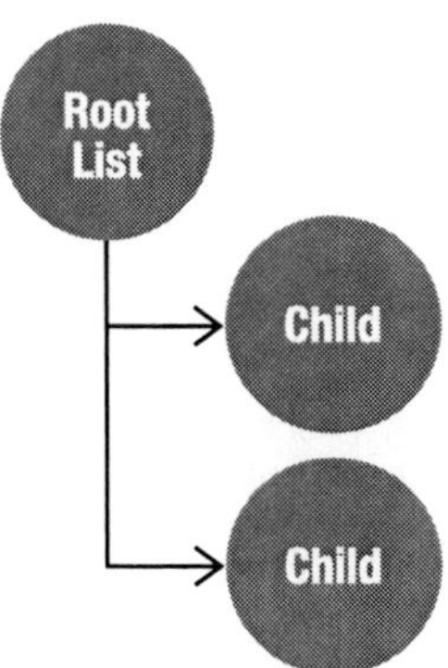

Figure 4-3. *Object graph with a root list object*

Another important object-oriented concept is the *using* relationship, where one object uses or interacts with another object but does *not* contain that object. This is a fundamentally different type of relationship, but it is quite common to accidentally confuse a using relationship with containment.

For example, the previously mentioned `SalesOrder` object might *use* a `CustomerInfo` object, but it makes no sense to think that a sales order contains or owns a customer, even though it may require information from a customer information object. Figure 4-4 illustrates how a *using* relationship can exist between two root objects.

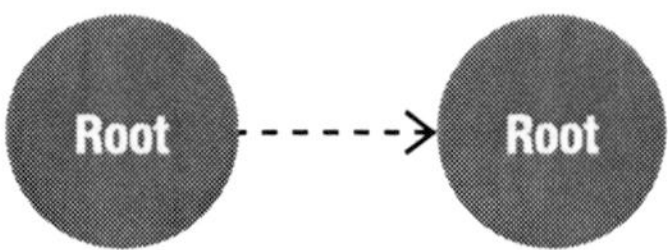

Figure 4-4. *A using relationship between two objects*

There are many variations on the *using* relationship, including a root using a child, a child using a root, or a child using another child. But the key to understanding the using relationship is to remember that neither object owns or contains or controls the other object. Editing or saving one object does not edit or save the other object.

This is fundamentally different from containment, where each parent owns its children and controls their lifetimes, and ultimately the root object owns all the objects in the object graph and their lifetimes are determined by the root object.

By combining these various concepts you can see how the stereotypes fit together. Table 4-2 lists the stereotypes and provides a definition for each. Additionally, the table lists the CSLA .NET base class you will inherit from to implement each stereotype.

Table 4-2. *CSLA .NET Object Stereotypes*

Stereotype	Acronym	Base Class	Definition
Editable root object	ER	`BusinessBase`	A root object with read-write properties
Editable child object	EC	`BusinessBase`	A child object with read-write properties
Switchable object	None	`BusinessBase`	A specialized editable object that can act as a root or child depending on how it is created
Editable root list	ERL	`BusinessListBase`	A root list containing editable child objects
Editable child list	ECL	`BusinessListBase`	A child list containing editable child objects
Read-only root object	ROR	`ReadOnlyBase`	A root object with read-only properties
Read-only child object	ROC	`ReadOnlyBase`	A child object with read-only properties
Read-only root list	RORL	`ReadOnlyListBase`	A root list containing read-only child objects
Read-only child list	ROCL	`ReadOnlyListBase`	A child list containing read-only child objects
Name/value list	NVL	`NameValueListBase`	A specialized read-only root list containing name/value read-only child objects
Command object	None	`CommandBase`	A root object capable of executing code on the client, then the application server, then the client

Table 4-2. *CSLA .NET Object Stereotypes*

Stereotype	Acronym	Base Class	Definition
Dynamic editable root	None	`BusinessBase`	A specialized editable root object that is retrieved as a "child" of a dynamic editable list but is saved individually
Dynamic editable list	ERLB	`EditableRootListBase`	A specialized root list containing editable dynamic editable *root* objects, which are retrieved as a group but are saved individually
Criteria	None	`CriteriaBase`	An object that contains criteria or key information necessary to identify and create, retrieve, or delete another object

By combining objects based on these stereotypes in various ways, it is possible to meet the needs of most business application use cases by using the object-oriented design techniques discussed in Chapter 3.

Business Object Life Cycle

Before getting into the code structure for the business objects, it's worth spending some time to understand the life cycle of those objects. By life cycle, I mean the sequence of methods and events that occur as the object is created and used. Although it isn't always possible to predict the business properties and methods that might exist on an object, there's a set of steps that occur during the lifetime of *every* business object.

Typically, an object is created by UI code, whether that's WPF, Windows Forms, Web Forms, a WCF service, or a Windows Workflow Foundation activity. Sometimes an object may be created by another object, which will happen when there's a *using* relationship between objects, for instance.

Object Creation

Whether editable or read-only, all root objects go through the same basic creation process. (Root objects are those that can be directly retrieved from the database, while child objects are retrieved within the context of a root object, though never directly.)

It's up to the root object to invoke methods on its child objects and child collections so that they can load their own data from the database. Usually, the root object actually calls the database and gets all the data back and then provides that data to the child objects and collections so that they can populate themselves. From a purely object-oriented perspective, it might be ideal to have each object encapsulate the logic to get its own data from the database, but in reality it's not practical to have each object independently contact the database to retrieve one row of data.

Root Object Creation

Root objects are created by calling a *factory method*, which is a method that's called in order to create an object. Factory methods will typically be `static` methods on the class. The factory method uses the CSLA .NET *data portal* to load the object with default values. The data portal is a CSLA .NET technology that abstracts communication with the application server (if there is one), enabling the mobile object concept described in Chapter 1.

I am often asked why you would need to communicate with the database to *create* a new object. Why not just use the constructor and be done with it? The reason is that business applications often need to load new objects with default values, and those values are often in database tables. While some simple objects can be directly created, it is quite common for an object to require data from the database as it is created.

The following steps outline the process of creating a new root object:

1. The factory method is called.
2. The factory method calls `DataPortal.Create()` to get the business object.
3. The data portal uses its channel adapter and message router functionality as described in Chapter 15; the result is that the data portal creates a new instance of the business object.
4. The data portal does one of the following:
   a. If no `ObjectFactory` attribute is specified, the `DataPortal_Create()` method is called and this is where the business object implements data access code to load its default values.
   b. If an `ObjectFactory` is specified, the data portal will create an instance of a factory object and will invoke a specified create method on that factory object. This method is responsible for creating an instance of the business object and implementing data access code to load its default values.
5. The business object is returned.

With no `ObjectFactory` attribute, from the business object's perspective, two methods are called, as follows:

- The default constructor
- `DataPortal_Create()`

This is illustrated in Figure 4-5.

If the object *doesn't* need to retrieve default values from the database, the `RunLocal` attribute can be used to short-circuit the data portal so the object initialization occurs in the same location as the calling code.

If an object doesn't require any initialization, the `DataPortal_Create()` method doesn't need to be overridden. The CSLA .NET base classes provide a default implementation decorated with `RunLocal`.

With an `ObjectFactory` attribute, the business developer will have defined two classes: the object factory class and the business class. From the object factory's perspective, two methods are called, as follows:

- The default constructor
- The create method specified by the `ObjectFactory` attribute

As illustrated in Figure 4-6, it is then entirely up to the object factory to create and initialize the business object.

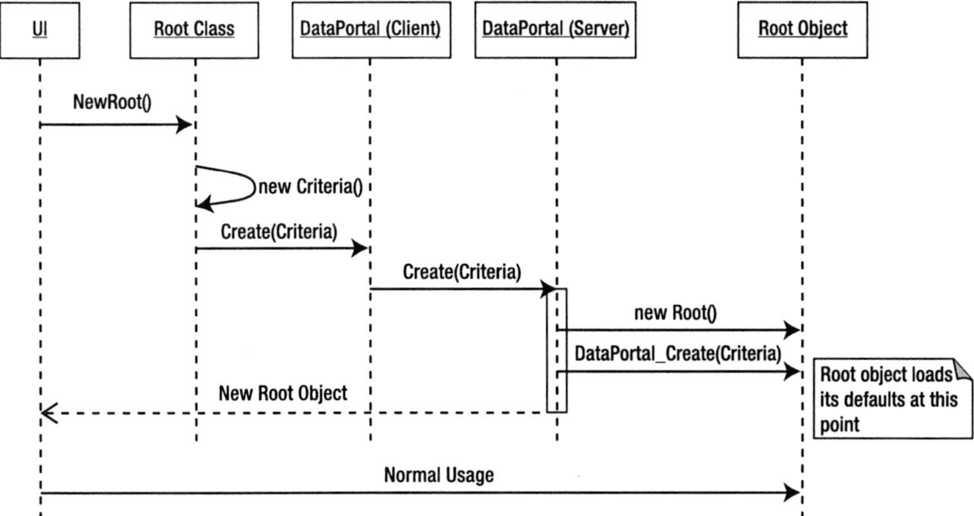

Figure 4-5. *Creating a root object*

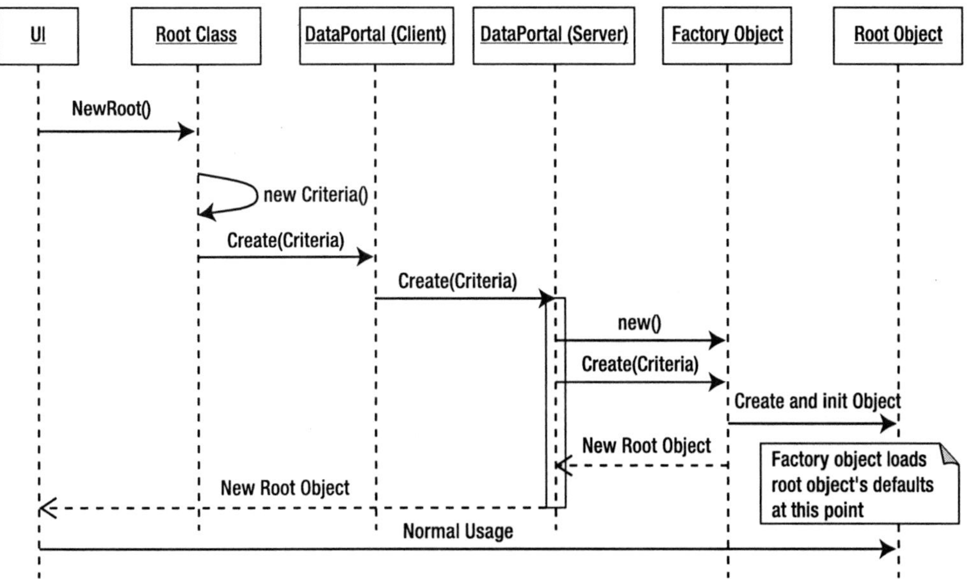

Figure 4-6. *Creating a root object with an object factory*

The `RunLocal` attribute can be applied to methods of an object factory and will have the same effect as it would on `DataPortal_Create()`, assuming the assembly containing the object factory class is deployed to the client workstation.

To the UI code, of course, there's no difference; that code just calls the factory method and gets an object back:

```
var root = Root.NewRoot();
```

For the business object, most of the work occurs in the DataPortal_Create() method, where the object's values are initialized.

The use of a criteria object is optional; the DataPortal.Create() method is overloaded to accept no parameter or criteria object parameter.

Child Object Creation

Child objects are usually created when the UI code calls an Add() method on the collection object that contains the child object. Ideally, the child class and the collection class will be in the same assembly, so the static factory methods on a child object can be scoped as internal, rather than public. This way, the UI can't directly create the object, but the collection object *can* create the child when the UI calls the collection's Add() method.

The CSLA .NET framework doesn't actually dictate this approach. Rather, it's a design choice on my part because I feel that it makes the use of the business objects more intuitive from the UI developer's perspective. It's quite possible to allow the UI code to create child objects directly by making the child factory methods public; the collection's Add() method would then accept a prebuilt child object as a parameter. I think that's less intuitive, but it's perfectly valid, and you can implement your objects that way if you choose.

■ **Note** Child objects can optionally be created through data binding, in which case the addition is handled by overriding the AddNewCore() method in the collection class.

Another way child objects are sometimes created is through *lazy loading*. In that case, the parent object creates the child object on demand, typically in the property get block for the child object. For example, the following code may be in the parent object:

```
public ChildType Child
{
  get
  {
    if (!FieldManager.FieldExists(ChildProperty))
      LoadProperty(ChildProperty, ChildType.NewChild());
    return GetProperty(ChildProperty);
  }
}
```

Notice how the NewChild() factory method is invoked to create an instance of the child object, but only if the UI code ever retrieves the value of the Child property.

As with the root objects, you may or may not need to load default values from the database when creating a child object.

■ **Tip** If you don't need to retrieve default values from the database, you could have the collection object create the child object directly, using the new keyword. For consistency, however, it's better to stick with the factory method approach so that all objects are created the same way.

The steps to create a child object that *doesn't* need to load itself with default values from the database are as follows:

1. The factory method (`internal` scope) is called.
2. The factory method calls `DataPortal.CreateChild()`, which creates an instance of the child object and marks it as a child.
3. The child object does any initialization in the `Child_Create()` method.
4. The child object is returned.
5. From the child object's perspective, two methods are called, as follows:
    - Default constructor
    - `Child_Create()`

This is illustrated in Figure 4-7.

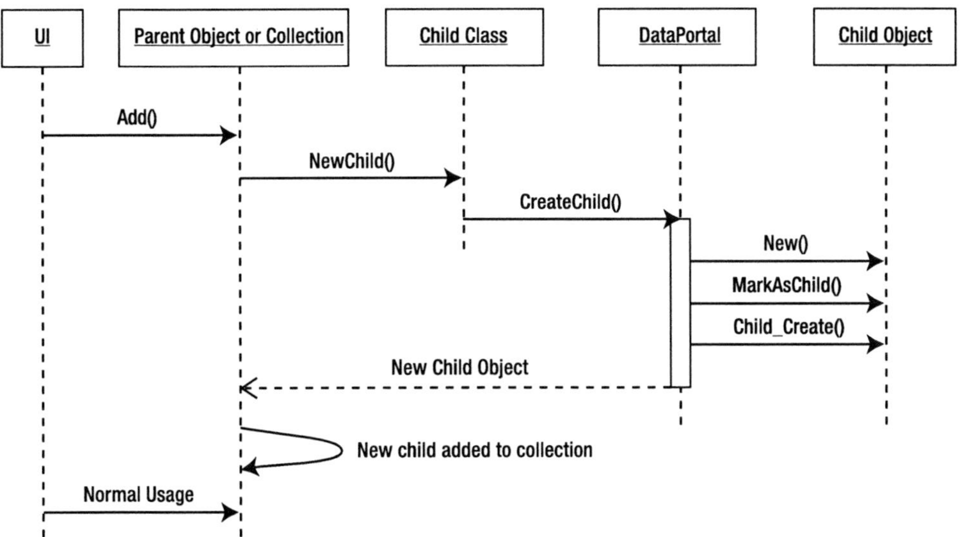

Figure 4-7. *Child object creation process with no data access*

Notice the use of the `CreateChild()` method on the data portal. This method tells the data portal to create an instance of the object, as a child, without making a call to a remote application server. This means the child object is created in the same location as the calling code, and the `Child_Create()` method runs in that location as well.

Once the child object is created and added to the parent, the UI code can access the child via the parent's interface. Typically, the parent provides an indexer that allows the UI to access child objects directly.

If the object needs to load itself with default values from the database, the process is a little different because the `Create()` method of the data portal must be invoked so the call is transferred to the application server (if there is one):

1. The factory method (`internal` scope) is called.
2. The factory method calls `DataPortal.Create()` to get the child business object.
3. The data portal uses its channel adapter and message router functionality as described in Chapter 15; the result is that the data portal creates a new instance of the business object.

4. The `DataPortal_Create()` method is called and this is where the child object implements data access code to load its default values.
5. The child object *must* call `MarkAsChild()` in the `DataPortal_Create()` implementation to mark the object as a child.
6. The child object is returned. Again, the factory method is called by the collection object rather than the UI, but the rest of the process is the same as with a root object.
7. From the child object's perspective, two methods are called, as follows:
   - The default constructor
   - `DataPortal_Create()`

This is illustrated in Figure 4-8.

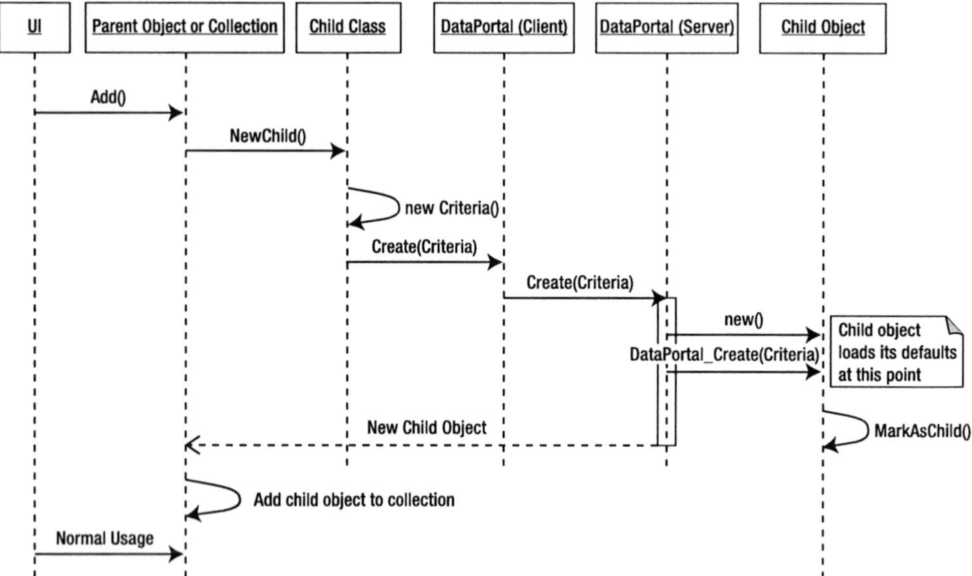

Figure 4-8. *Creating a child object using data access*

Note that in either of these cases, the UI code is the same: it calls the `Add()` method on the parent object and then interacts with the parent's interface to get access to the newly added child object. The UI is entirely unaware of how the child object is created (and possibly loaded with default values).

Also note that the *parent* object is unaware of the details. All it does is call the factory method on the child class and receive a new child object in return. All the details about *how* the child object got loaded with default values are encapsulated within the child class.

Finally, as with creating a root object, the use of a criteria object is optional.

Object Retrieval

Retrieving an existing object from the database is similar to the process of creating an object that requires default values from the database. Only a root object can be retrieved from the database directly by code in the user interface. Child objects are retrieved along with their parent root object, not independently.

Root Object Retrieval

To retrieve a root object, the UI code simply calls the `static` factory method on the class, providing the parameters that identify the object to be retrieved. The factory method calls `DataPortal.Fetch()`, which in turn creates the object and calls `DataPortal_Fetch()`, as follows:

1. The factory method is called.
2. The factory method calls `DataPortal.Fetch()` to get the business object.
3. The data portal uses its channel adapter and message router functionality as described in Chapter 15; the result is that the data portal creates a new instance of the business object.
4. The business object can do basic initialization in the constructor method.
5. The data portal does one of the following:
   a. If no `ObjectFactory` attribute is specified, the `DataPortal_Fetch()` method is called; this is where the business object implements data access code to retrieve the object's data from the database.
   b. If an `ObjectFactory` is specified, the data portal will create an instance of a factory object and will invoke a specified fetch method on that factory object. This method is responsible for creating an instance of the business object and implementing data access code to load it with data from the database.
6. The business object is returned.

If there is no `ObjectFactory` attribute on the business class, from the business object's perspective, two methods are called, as follows:

- The default constructor
- `DataPortal_Fetch()`

Figure 4-9 illustrates the process.

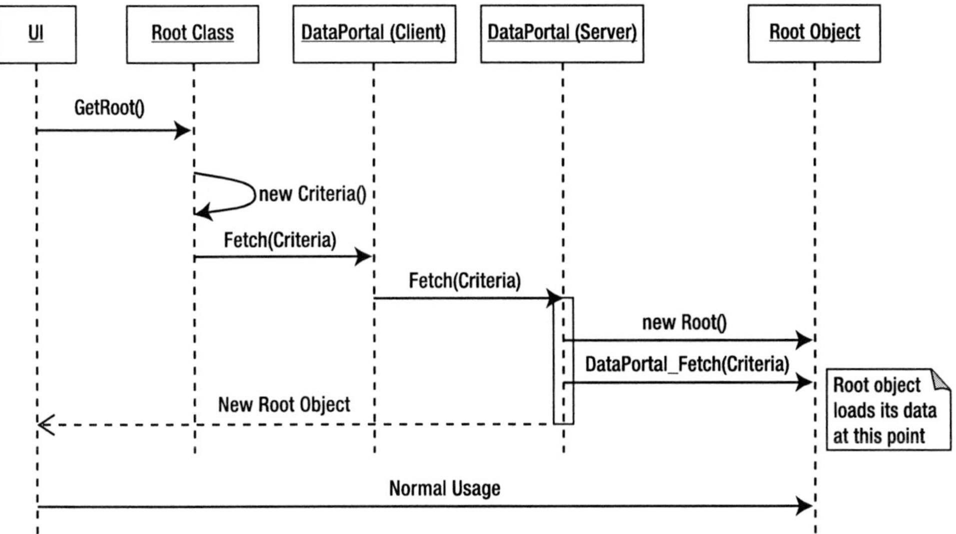

Figure 4-9. *Retrieving an existing root object*

With an ObjectFactory attribute, the business developer will have defined two classes: the object factory class and the business class. From the object factory's perspective, two methods are called, as follows:

- The default constructor
- The fetch method specified by the ObjectFactory attribute

As illustrated in Figure 4-10, it is then entirely up to the object factory to create an instance of the business class and to load it with data from the database.

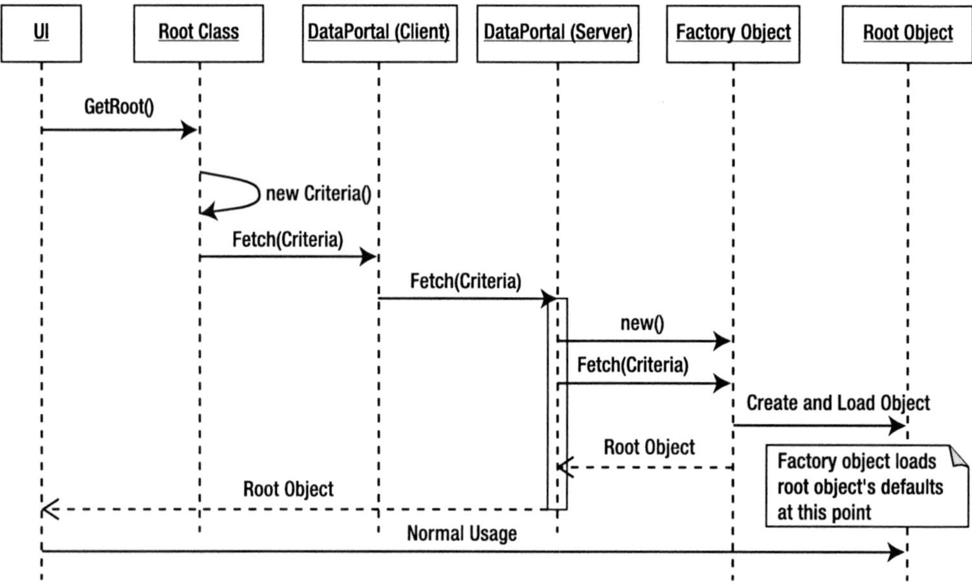

Figure 4-10. *Creating a root object with an object factory*

The RunLocal attribute can be applied to methods of an object factory and will have the same effect as it would on DataPortal_Fetch(), assuming the assembly containing the object factory class is deployed to the client workstation.

It's important to note that the root object's DataPortal_Fetch() or factory object's fetch method is responsible not only for loading the business object's data but also for starting the process of loading the data for its child objects.

The key thing to remember is that the data for the *entire* object, including its child objects, is retrieved when the root object is retrieved. This avoids having to go back across the network to retrieve each child object's data individually. Though the root object gets the *data,* it's up to each child object to populate itself based on that data.

The exception to this is if you choose to use lazy loading to load a child object or collection later in the root object's lifetime. In that case you would not load the child in the root object's DataPortal_Fetch() or factory object's fetch method. Instead you'd leave the child field with a null value at this point.

Let's dive one level deeper and discuss how child objects load their data.

Child Object Retrieval

The retrieval of a child object can be done in two different ways. You can use the data portal's support for loading child objects, or you can have your parent objects call methods on the child objects to create and load those objects however you choose.

The advantage to using the data portal to load the child objects is that it enables a simple and consistent approach for loading data into any object. However, there is some overhead to using the data portal in this manner, so it may not be appropriate in very performance-intensive scenarios.

The advantage to writing the code yourself is that you can design an optimized approach for your particular objects, and that may be very fast. However, you lose the benefits of standardization and simplicity provided by the data portal. Also, you must remember to have each child object manually call `MarkAsChild()` as it is created, typically in its constructor.

Note I believe it is important, when possible, to offer choices between performance and maintainability/simplicity. This allows individual application designers to make choices based on the needs of their specific organization and application. This type of choice, enabling you to trade off one cost/benefit for another, can be found in many places throughout CSLA .NET.

Either way the steps are basically the same. As stated earlier, the root object's `DataPortal_Fetch()` method or factory fetch method is responsible for loading not only the root object's data but also the data for all child objects. It then calls either the data portal or methods on the child objects themselves, passing the preloaded data as parameters so the child objects can load their fields with data. The sequence of events goes like this:

1. The root object's `DataPortal_Fetch()` creates the child *collection* using a factory method on the collection class (scoped as `internal`) and it passes an object containing the child data as a parameter.
2. The child collection's constructor loops through the list of child data provided by the parent, performing the following steps for each record:
   a. The child collection creates a child object by calling a factory method on the child class, passing the data for that particular child as a parameter.
   b. The collection object adds the child object to its collection.
3. At the end of the list of child data, the child collection and all child objects are fully populated.

Figure 4-11 is a sequence diagram that illustrates how this works using the data portal. Note that this diagram occurs *during the process of loading the root object's data.* This means that this diagram is really an expansion of Figure 4-8, the sequence diagram for retrieving a root object.

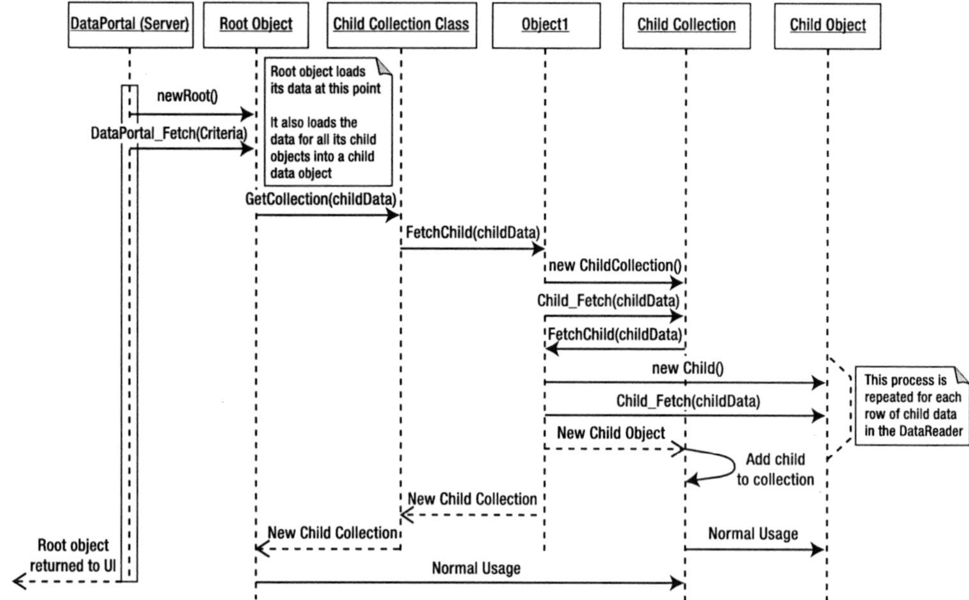

Figure 4-11. *Loading child objects with data*

Updating Editable Objects

For read-only objects, retrieval is the only data-access concept required. Editable business objects and editable collections (those deriving from `BusinessBase` and `BusinessListBase`) support update, insert, and delete operations as well.

Adding and Editing Root Objects

After an object is created or retrieved, the user will work with the object, changing its values by interacting with the user interface. At some point, the user may click the OK or Save button, thereby triggering the process of updating the object into the database. The sequence of events at that point is as follows:

1. The UI calls the `Save()` or `BeginSave()` method on the business object.
2. The `Save()` and `BeginSave()` methods call `DataPortal.Update()` to start the data portal process.
3. The data portal does one of the following:
    a. If no `ObjectFactory` attribute is specified, the data portal calls a `DataPortal.Update()`, `DataPortal_Insert()`, or `DataPortal_DeleteSelf()` method on the business object as appropriate; those methods contain the data access code needed to update, insert, or delete the data in the database.
    b. If an `ObjectFactory` attribute is specified, the data portal creates an instance of the specified factory class and calls the specified update method on the factory object. That update method is responsible for inserting, updating, or deleting the business object's data and returning an updated object as a result.

4. During the update process, the business object's data may change.
5. The updated business object is returned as a result of the Save() method.

If no ObjectFactory attribute is specified on the business class, from the business object's perspective, two methods are called:

- Save()
- One of DataPortal_Update(), DataPortal_Insert(), or DataPortal_DeleteSelf()

Figure 4-12 illustrates this process.

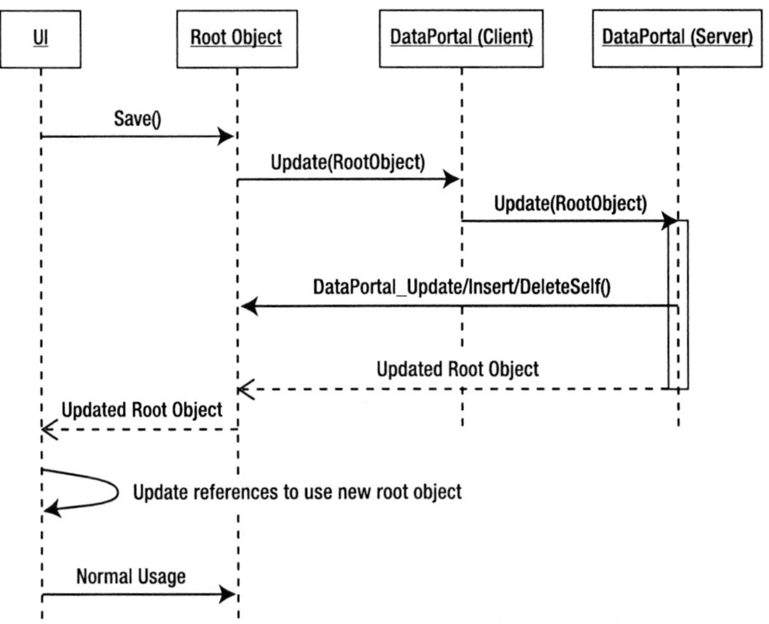

Figure 4-12. *Adding or updating a root object*

If an ObjectFactory attribute is specified on the business class, the business developer is responsible for creating two classes: the object factory class and the business class. Figure 4-13 illustrates that the object factory class must implement an update method that manages all insert, update, and delete operations for the business object type.

The Save() and BeginSave() methods are implemented in BusinessBase and BusinessListBase and typically require no change or customization. The framework's save methods include checks to ensure that objects can only be saved if the object is valid, has been changed, and isn't currently being edited and the user is authorized to do the update. This helps to optimize data access by preventing the update of an object that clearly can't be updated.

Tip If you don't like this behavior, your business class can override the framework's Save() and BeginSave() methods and replace that logic with other logic.

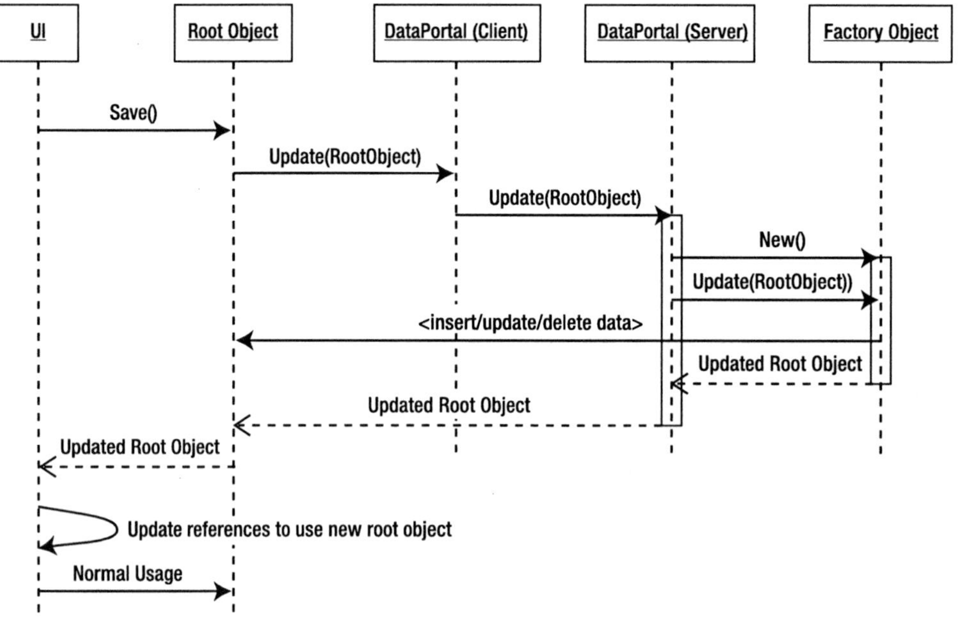

Figure 4-13. *Adding or updating a root object with an object factory class*

When not using `ObjectFactory`, all the data access code that handles the saving of the object is located in `DataPortal_Update()`, `DataPortal_Insert()`, and `DataPortal_DeleteSelf()`. All editable objects automatically maintain `IsNew` and `IsDeleted` properties, and the data portal includes logic to check these properties to route any save operation to the appropriate `DataPortal_XYZ` method.

■ **Note** It's important to understand that the updated root object returned to the UI is a *new* object. The UI *must* update its references to use this new object in lieu of the original root object.

The `DataPortal_XYZ` methods are responsible not only for saving the object's data but also for starting the process of saving all the *child object* data.

This is true when the `ObjectFactory` attribute is used as well. In that case the factory object is responsible for saving the business object's data and all child object data, as shown in Figure 4-13.

Adding, Editing, and Deleting Child Objects

Child objects are inserted, updated, or deleted as part of the process of updating a root parent object. As with retrieving child objects, you can use the data portal or your own custom methods to perform this task. Using the data portal incurs a certain amount of overhead but is simple and standardized, while implementing your own `internal` methods is often faster but harder to write and maintain.

When using the data portal, the parent object calls a CSLA .NET method to update its child objects, and the data portal automatically invokes `Child_Update()`, `Child_Insert()`, or `Child_DeleteSelf()` based on the child object's `IsNew` and `IsDeleted` properties. If you have a child collection, it will automatically cascade this call down to the objects contained in the collection. The basic process is the same as when you update a root object.

It is important to realize that all child object references are managed using a CSLA .NET feature called the *field manager*. The field manager helps manage child relationships and the state of child objects. It also simplifies the process of updating child objects when using the data portal.

If you want to manually write and call your own methods, your child collections will typically implement an `internal` method named `Update()`. This `Update()` method must loop through all the objects in the collection and in the `DeletedList` collection to tell each child object to update itself. Child objects within a collection typically implement `internal` methods, named `Insert()`, `Update()`, and `DeleteSelf()`, that can be called by the collection during the update process. It is helpful for related root, child, and child collection classes to be placed in the same project (assembly) so that they can use `internal` scope in this manner.

Because the manual approach is much more complex and bug-prone, I recommend using the data portal if at all possible. The sequence of events to add, edit, or delete a child object using the data portal is as follows:

1. The root object's `DataPortal_XYZ` method calls `FieldManager.UpdateChildren()`, which uses the data portal to update all child objects; typically the parent object is passed as a parameter so that child objects can use root object property values as needed (such as for foreign key values).
2. The data portal calls each child object's `Child_Update()`, `Child_Insert()`, or `Child_DeleleSelf()` method based on the child object's state.
3. At this point, all the child object data has been inserted, updated, or deleted as required.

Figure 4-14 illustrates this process. Remember that this diagram is connected with the previous diagram showing the update of a root object. The events depicted in this diagram occur as a result of the root object's `DataPortal_Insert()`, `DataPortal_Update()`, or `DataPortal_DeleteSelf()` being called, as shown earlier in Figure 4-12.

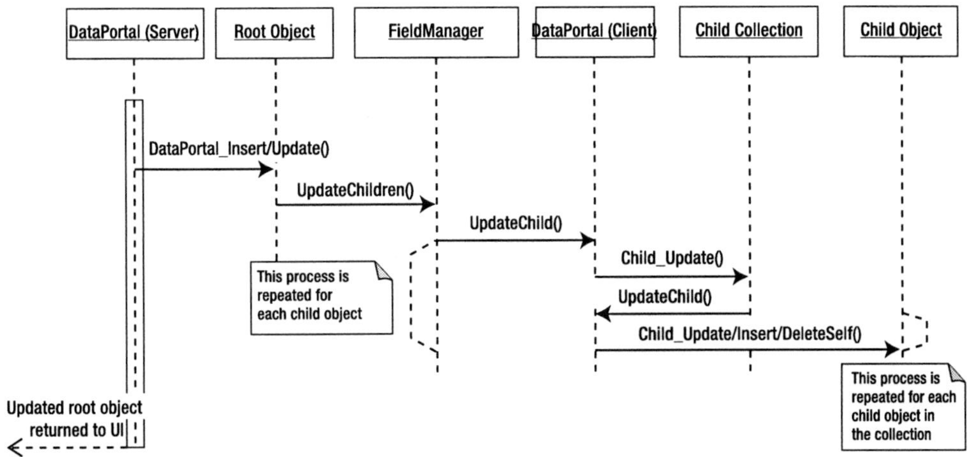

Figure 4-14. *Adding, updating, and deleting child objects in a collection*

Typically the business object author will only need to write the `Child_XYZ` methods in editable child objects. The field manager and data portal take care of most details, including a prebuilt implementation of `Child_Update()` for editable list objects.

The `Child_Insert()` and `Child_Update()` methods often accept parameters. The root object's primary key value is often a required piece of data when saving a child object (since it would be a foreign key in the table) and so a reference to the root object is usually passed as a parameter to the

FieldManager.UpdateChildren() method, and that value is automatically passed as a parameter to each child object's Child_Insert(), Child_Update(), or Child_DeleteSelf() method.

Passing a reference to the root object is better than passing any specific property value because it helps to decouple the root object from the child object. Using a reference means that the root object doesn't know or care what actual data is required by the child object during the update process; that behavior is encapsulated within the child class.

Deleting Root Objects

While child objects are deleted within the context of the root object that's being updated, deletion of root objects is a bit different. The data portal supports two ways of deleting objects: *immediate* and *deferred* deletion.

Immediate Deletion

Immediate deletion occurs when the UI code calls a static delete method on the business class, providing parameters that define the object to be deleted: typically, the same criteria that would be used to retrieve the object.

Most applications will use immediate deletion for root objects. The sequence of events flows like this:

1. The static delete method is called.
2. The static delete method calls DataPortal.Delete().
3. The data portal does one of the following:
    a. If no ObjectFactory attribute is specified, the data portal creates an instance of the business class and calls the DataPortal_Delete() method on the business object, which contains the code needed to delete the object's data (and any related child data, etc.).
    b. If an ObjectFactory attribute is specified, the data portal creates an instance of the specified object factory class and calls the specified delete method on the factory object, which contains the code needed to delete the business object's data (and any related child data, etc.).

When not using an ObjectFactory, from the business object's perspective, two methods are called, as follows:

- The default constructor
- DataPortal_Delete()

Figure 4-15 illustrates the process of immediate deletion.

Since this causes the deletion of a root object, the delete process must also remove any data for child objects. This can be done through LINQ to SQL, ADO.NET data access code, a stored procedure, or by the database (if cascading deletes are set up on the relationships). In the example application for this book, child data is deleted by the stored procedures created in Chapter 3.

When using the ObjectFactory attribute, the business developer is responsible for authoring two classes: the factory class and the business class. The factory class must implement a delete method that deletes the data for the business object and any child objects.

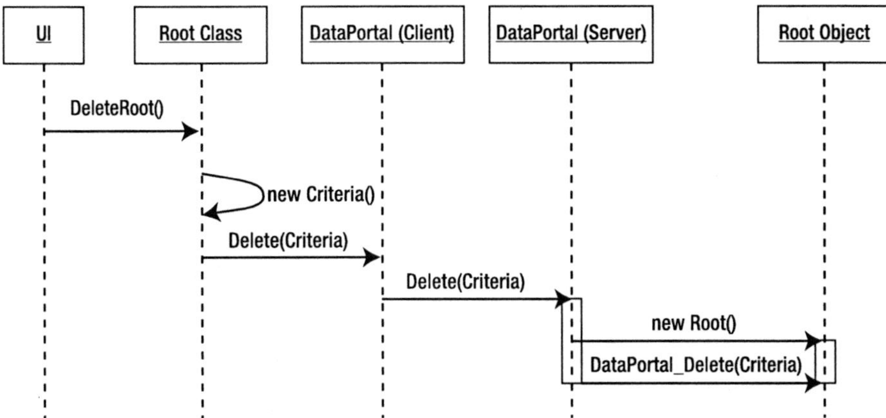

Figure 4-15. *Immediate deletion of a root object*

Deferred Deletion

Deferred deletion occurs when the business object is loaded into memory and the UI calls a method on the object to mark it for deletion. Then when the `Save()` method is called, the object is deleted rather than being inserted or updated.

The sequence of events flows like this:

1. The object is loaded by the UI.
2. The UI calls a method to mark the object for deletion (that method must call `MarkDeleted()`).
3. The UI calls the object's `Save()` or `BeginSave()` method.
4. The save method invokes the data portal just like it does when doing an insert or an update (as discussed earlier in this chapter).
5. The data portal does one of the following:
    a. When not using an `ObjectFactory` attribute, typically, the `DataPortal_DeleteSelf()` method calls the object's `DataPortal_Delete()` method, which contains the code needed to delete the object's data (and any related child data, etc.).
    b. When using an `ObjectFactory` attribute, the data portal creates an instance of the specified object factory class and invokes the specified delete method. This delete method contains the code needed to delete the business object's data, along with any related child data.

When not using an `ObjectFactory` attribute, from the business object's perspective, one method is called: `DataPortal_DeleteSelf()`.

Earlier in the chapter, Figure 4-12 showed the process of saving a root object; it also depicts deferred deletion.

When an `ObjectFactory` attribute is specified on the business class, the business developer must provide both a factory class and the business class. The factory class must implement a delete method that removes the business object's data, along with any child object data.

The CSLA .NET framework supports both deletion models to provide flexibility for the UI developer. It is up to the business object author to decide which model to support by implementing either a `static` or instance delete method on the object.

Disposing and Finalizing Objects

Most business objects contain moderate amounts of data in their fields. For these, the default .NET garbage collection behavior is fine. With that behavior, you don't know exactly when an object will be destroyed and its memory reclaimed. But that's almost always OK because it is exactly what garbage collection is designed to do.

However, the default garbage collection behavior may be insufficient when objects hold onto "expensive" or unmanaged resources until they're destroyed. These resources include things such as open database connections, open files on disk, synchronization objects, handles, and any other objects that already implement IDisposable. These are things that need to be released as soon as possible in order to prevent the application from wasting memory or blocking other users who might need to access a file or reuse a database connection. If business objects are written properly, most of these concerns should go away. Data access code should keep a database connection open for the shortest amount of time possible, and the same is true for any files the object might open on disk. However, there are cases in which business objects can legitimately contain an expensive resource—something like a multimegabyte image in a field, perhaps.

Implementing IDisposable

In such cases, the business object should implement the IDisposable interface, which will allow the UI code to tell the business object to release its resources. This interface requires that the object implement a Dispose() method to actually release those resources:

```
[Serializable]
public class MyBusinessClass :
  BusinessBase<MyBusinessClass>,
  IDisposable
{
  private bool _disposedValue;

  protected void Dispose(bool disposing)
  {
    if (!_disposedValue)
      if (disposing)
      {
        // free unmanaged resources
      }
    // free shared unmanaged resources
    _disposedValue = true;
  }

  public void Dispose()
  {
    Dispose(true);
    GC.SuppressFinalize(this);
  }

  ~MyBusinessClass()
  {
    Dispose(false);
  }
}
```

The UI code can now call the object's `Dispose()` method (or employ a `using` statement) when it has finished using the object, at which point the object will release its expensive resources.

Careful Object Disposal

If a business object is retrieved using a *remote* data portal configuration, the business object will be created and loaded on the server. It's then returned to the client. The result, however, is that there's a copy left in memory on the server. Because of this, there's no way to call the business object's `Dispose()` method on the server. To avoid this scenario, any time that the data portal may be configured to run outside of the client process, the business object designs *must* avoid any requirement for a `Dispose()` method.

■ **Note** If you're calling a remote data portal, you must avoid object designs that require `IDisposable`. Alternatively, you can modify the `SimpleDataPortal` class to explicitly call `Dispose()` on your business objects on the server.

Also, if a business object is retrieved using a *local* data portal configuration, the business object will be cloned, and the clone is what is actually saved and returned to the client. The result is that there's a copy left in memory on the client.

If you implement `IDisposable` in your business object and use a local data portal configuration, your UI code must call `Dispose()` on the original object if the `Save()` call is successful, and you'll have to modify the client-side `DataPortal` class to call `Dispose()` on the clone if an exception occurs during the update process. Happily, these are almost never issues you'll face with a properly designed business object because all database connections or open files should be closed in the same method from which they were opened.

Business Class Structure

As you've seen, business objects follow the same sequence of events for creation, retrieval, and updates. Because of this, there's a structure and a set of features that are common to all of them. Although the structure and features are common, the actual code varies for each business object. Due to the consistency in structure, however, there's great value in providing some foundations that make it easier for the business developer to know what needs to be done.

Also, there are differences between editable and read-only objects and between root and child objects. After discussing the features common to all business objects, which I do next, I'll create "templates" to illustrate the structure of each type of business object that you can create based on CSLA .NET.

There are some common features or conventions that should be followed when coding any business classes that will inherit from the CSLA .NET base classes. These are as follows:

- `Serializable` or `DataContract` attribute
- Common regions
- Non-`public` default constructor

Let's briefly discuss each of these requirements.

The Serializable or DataContract Attribute

All business objects must be unanchored so that they can move across the network as needed. This means that they must be marked as serializable by using the `Serializable` attribute, as shown here:

```
[Serializable]
public class MyBusinessClass
{
}
```

This is required for all business classes that inherit from any of the CSLA .NET base classes. It's also required for any objects that are referenced by business objects. If a business object references an object that isn't serializable, you must be sure to mark its field with the `NonSerialized` attribute to prevent the serialization process from attempting to serialize that object. If you don't do this, the result will be a runtime exception from the .NET Framework.

Alternately you can use the `DataContract` attribute, as shown here:

```
[DataContract]
public class MyBusinessClass
{
}
```

The `DataContract` attribute is part of WCF. WCF includes two serialization engines: `DataContractSerializer` and `NetDataContractSerializer` (NDCS). Both of these engines support two new attributes: `DataContract` and `DataMember`.

`DataContractSerializer` can be thought of as the replacement for the older `XmlSerializer`. This serializer is primarily designed to support service-oriented scenarios by creating and consuming SOAP-compliant XML blobs. Not all types or object graphs can be serialized using this component.

`NetDataContractSerializer` can be thought of as the replacement for the older `BinaryFormatter`. This serializer is primarily designed to support client/server or n-tier scenarios by providing full fidelity for even complex .NET data types. Any `Serializable` or `DataContract` type (or object graph of `Serializable` or `DataContract` types) can be serialized using this component. Only the NDCS is pertinent to this discussion because CSLA .NET uses the `BinaryFormatter` and only NDCS provides comparable functionality in WCF.

The `DataContract` attribute is somewhat like the `Serializable` attribute, in that it marks an object as being eligible for serialization by one of the new serializers. The `Serializable` attribute uses an *opt-out* model, where all fields are serialized unless you explicitly mark the field with the `NonSerialized` attribute. `DataContract`, on the other hand, uses an *opt-in* model, where fields (or properties) are only serialized if you explicitly mark them with the `DataMember` attribute.

The `BinaryFormatter`, of course, only understands the `Serializable` attribute. If you only mark a class with `DataContract`, the `BinaryFormatter` will throw an exception because it views the object as not being serializable.

The NDCS understands *both* the `DataContract` and `Serializable` attributes. This means that you can use NDCS to serialize objects that are `Serializable`, objects that are a `DataContract`, and even object graphs composed of both types of objects at once. This makes sense because all the core .NET types to date are `Serializable`, not `DataContract`. They can't be changed without massive repercussions throughout the existing .NET Framework itself. Any serializer intended to replace the `BinaryFormatter` must do what the `BinaryFormatter` does, and then do more.

When to Use DataContract

Given that DataContract and Serializable provide the same functionality, though with an opt-in or opt-out philosophy, the obvious question is when to use each option. Or to be blunt: when should anyone use DataContract?

In general, I don't recommend switching from Serializable to DataContract. For most business objects, the desired behavior is to include all fields when an object is serialized, and so the opt-out model used by Serializable is better.

If you use the opt-in model of DataContract, it is too easy to forget to put the DataMember attribute on a field, in which case that field is ignored when the object is serialized. The resulting bug can be difficult to discover and debug.

You should also be aware that WF uses the BinaryFormatter to serialize objects when a workflow is suspended. If you intend to use your business objects within a workflow, you should avoid using DataContract to ensure that your objects can be serialized if necessary.

The DataContract and DataMember attributes are designed to support service-oriented design. In Chapter 21, I show how you can build service-oriented WCF services. That is the appropriate place for using these attributes.

Serialization in CSLA .NET

CSLA .NET directly uses the BinaryFormatter in only a few places: when cloning an object graph, in the n-level undo implementation, and in some of the data portal channels.

CSLA .NET does support the optional use of DataContract when cloning an object graph and when using n-level undo. To do this, CSLA .NET must use the NDCS instead of the BinaryFormatter to do any explicit serialization.

Configuring CSLA .NET to Use NetDataContractSerializer

You must configure CSLA .NET to use NDCS rather than the BinaryFormatter. Because I believe the opt-out model is better for business object development, the default is to use the BinaryFormatter.

■ **Tip** I recommend that you only configure CSLA .NET to use the NDCS if you use the DataContract attribute instead of the Serializable attribute in your business classes.

To configure CSLA .NET to use the NDCS you must add an element to the appSettings of your app.config or web.config file:

```
<?xml version="1.0" encoding="utf-8" ?>
<configuration>
  <appSettings>
    <add key="CslaAuthentication" value="Csla" />
    <add key="CslaSerializationFormatter" value="NetDataContractSerializer"/>
```

This will cause both the clone and n-level undo implementations in CSLA .NET to use NDCS. The result is that you can use the DataContract attribute instead of or in combination with the Serializable attribute in your business classes.

Note that only the WCF data portal channel uses the NDCS, so if you use the `DataContract` attribute in your business objects you cannot use any of the older data portal channels.

Caution If you are using the `DataContract` and `DataMember` attributes in your business classes, you can only use the local or WCF data portal channels. The Remoting, Web Services, and Enterprise Services channels will all throw serialization exceptions if you attempt to use them.

The important thing to remember is that all business classes must use `Serializable` or `DataContract` to work with CSLA .NET. Throughout the rest of the book I assume the use of the `Serializable` attribute.

Common Regions

When writing code in VS .NET, the `#region` directive can be used to place code into collapsible regions. This helps organize the code and allows you to look only at the code pertaining to a specific type of functionality.

All business collection classes have a common set of regions, as follows:

- *Factory Methods*
- *Data Access*

And so classes derived from `BusinessListBase` and `ReadOnlyListBase` follow this basic structure:

```
[Serializable]
public class MyCollectionClass : Csla.baseclass<MyCollectionClass, MyChildType>
{
  #region Factory Methods

  #endregion

  #region Data Access

  #endregion
}
```

The one exception to this is when you use the `ObjectFactory` attribute on the business class, in which case there would be no *Data Access* region because that code would be in a separate object factory class.

All noncollection (editable and read-only) classes have the following set of regions:

- *Business Methods*
- *Business and Validation Rules*
- *Authorization Rules*
- *Factory Methods*
- *Data Access*

This means that the skeletal structure of a business object, with these regions, is as follows:

```
[Serializable]
public class MyBusinessClass : Csla.baseclass<MyBusinessClass>
{
  #region Business Methods

  #endregion

  #region Business and Validation Rules

  #endregion

  #region Authorization Rules

  #endregion

  #region Factory Methods

  #endregion

  #region Data Access

  #endregion
}
```

The one exception to this is when you use the `ObjectFactory` attribute on the business class, in which case there would be no *Data Access* region because that code would be in a separate object factory class.

Command objects that inherit from `CommandBase` have the following regions:

- *Authorization Rules*
- *Factory Methods*
- *Client-side Code*
- Server-side Code

```
[Serializable]
public class MyCommandClass : Csla.CommandBase
{
  #region Authorization Rules

  #endregion

  #region Factory Methods

  #endregion

  #region Client-side Code

  #endregion

  #region Server-side Code

  #endregion
}
```

The one exception to this is when you use the ObjectFactory attribute on the business class, in which case there would be no *Server-side Code* region because that code would be in the update method of a separate object factory class.

Name/value list objects that inherit from NameValueListBase will typically have the following regions:

- *Factory Methods*
- *Data Access*

```
[Serializable]
public class MyListClass : Csla.NameValueListBase<KeyType, ValueType>
{
  #region Factory Methods

  #endregion

  #region Data Access

  #endregion
}
```

The one exception to this is when you use the ObjectFactory attribute on the business class, in which case there would be no *Data Access* region because that code would be in a separate object factory class.

And objects that inherit from EditableRootListBase will typically have the following regions:

- *Factory Methods*
- *Data Access*

```
[Serializable]
public class MyListClass : Csla.EditableRootListBase<MyRootType>
{
  #region Factory Methods

  #endregion

  #region Data Access

  #endregion
}
```

Again, the one exception is when you use the ObjectFactory attribute on the business class; there would be no *Data Access* region in this case either.

The *Business Methods* region contains the methods that are used by UI code (or other client code) to interact with the business object. This includes any properties that allow retrieval or changing of values in the object as well as methods that operate on the object's data to perform business processing.

The *Business Rules* region contains the AddBusinessRules() method and any custom validation or business rule methods required by the object.

The *Authorization Rules* region contains the AddAuthorizationRules() and AddObjectAuthorizationRules() methods.

The *Factory Methods* region contains the static factory methods to create or retrieve the object, along with the static delete method (if the object is an editable root object). It also contains the default constructor for the class, which must be scoped as non-public (i.e., private or protected) to force the use of the factory methods when creating the business object.

The *Data Access* region contains the DataPortal_XYZ or Child_XYZ methods, unless you use the ObjectFactory attribute, in which case any code that would have been in the DataPortal_XYZ methods is in a separate object factory class.

Your business objects may require other code that doesn't fit neatly into these regions, and you should feel free to add extra regions if needed. But these regions cover the vast majority of code required by typical business objects, and in most cases they're all you'll need.

Object Factory Classes

Any root business object can specify an ObjectFactory attribute, which causes the data portal to change its behavior. Rather than directly interacting with the business object, the data portal creates an instance of an *object factory class* and it interacts with that factory object.

Applying the ObjectFactory attribute is straightforward:

```
[ObjectFactory("Factories.MyFactory,Factories")]
[Serializable]
public class MyBusinessClass : Csla.baseclass<MyBusinessClass>
```

The parameter passed to the attribute is an assembly-qualified type name for the object factory class. An instance of this class is created by the data portal.

■ **Note** It is possible to provide an *object factory loader*, which is a class you implement to create the factory object. If you do this, your object factory loader can interpret the string parameter to ObjectFactory in any way you choose. Use the CslaObjectFactoryLoader configuration setting in appSettings to specify the assembly-qualified type of your object factory loader, which must implement Csla.Server.IObjectFactoryLoader. The default object factory loader is Csla.Server.ObjectFactoryLoader.

You may also specify, as string values, the names of the create, fetch, update, and delete methods that should be invoked on the factory object. By default, the data portal invokes methods named Create(), Fetch(), Update() and Delete(), which must be implemented in the object factory class.

An object factory class looks like this:

```
public class MyFactory : Csla.Server.ObjectFactory
{
  public object Create()
  {
  }

  public object Fetch(SingleCriteria<MyBusinessClass, int> criteria)
  {
  }

  public object Update(object obj)
  {
  }

  public void Delete(SingleCriteria<MyBusinessClass, int> criteria)
  {
  }
}
```

As with the DataPortal_Create(), DataPortal_Fetch(), and DataPortal_Delete() methods, you may implement multiple overloads of the Create(), Fetch(), and Delete() methods, and the data portal will invoke the correct overload based on the parameters provided when the data portal is first called.

Inheriting from the `ObjectFactory` base class is optional but useful. The factory object is responsible for creating and manipulating the business object, including managing the business object's state values as I discuss in Chapter 18. The `ObjectFactory` base class provides the `protected` methods listed in Table 4-3 to assist in this process.

Table 4-3. *Protected Methods Supplied by ObjectFactory*

Method	Description
`MarkNew()`	Marks the business object as being a new object
`MarkOld()`	Marks the business object as being an old (preexisting) object
`MarkAsChild()`	Marks the business object as a child object

See Chapter 7 for a detailed discussion of these terms and concepts. For now you should understand that inheriting from `ObjectFactory` makes these methods available, and if you choose not to inherit from `ObjectFactory`, you'll have to develop your own mechanism for managing the states of your business objects.

Non-public Default Constructor

All business objects will be implemented to make use of the class-in-charge scheme discussed in Chapter 1. Factory methods are used in lieu of the `new` keyword, which means that it's best to prevent the use of `new`, thereby forcing the UI developer to use the factory methods instead.

The data portal mechanism requires business classes to include a default constructor. As I reviewed the create, fetch, update, and delete processes for each type of object earlier in this chapter, each sequence diagram showed how the server-side data portal created an instance of the business object. This is done using a technique that requires a default constructor.

By making the default constructor `private` or `protected` (and by not creating other `public` constructors), you ensure that UI code must use the factory methods to get an instance of any object:

```
// ...
#region Factory Methods

private MyBusinessClass()
{ /* require use of factory methods */ }

#endregion
// ...
```

This constructor both prevents the `new` keyword from being called by code outside this class and provides the data portal with the ability to create the object via reflection. Your classes might also include other non-`public` constructors, but this one is required for all objects.

Conclusion

This chapter discussed the basic concepts and requirements for all business classes based on CSLA .NET. I discussed the life cycle of business objects and walked through the creation, retrieval, update, and delete processes.

The basic structure of each type of business class was covered at a high level. There are common requirements, including making all the classes `Serializable`, implementing a common set of code regions for clarity of code, and including a non-`public` constructor. I continue that discussion in Chapter 5 by walking through the kind of code that goes into each code region for the different object stereotypes. Then Chapters 6 through 16 cover the implementation of the CSLA .NET framework that supports these stereotypes.

Finally, Chapters 17 through 21 show how to use these stereotypes and the framework to construct the Project Tracker application described in Chapter 3.

CHAPTER 5

CSLA .NET Object Templates

In Chapter 4, I discussed the common object stereotypes directly supported by CSLA .NET, as well as many of the high-level details about the structure and life cycle of the different types of business object.

In this chapter, I'll continue that discussion, but at a lower level of detail. This chapter will walk through each of the stereotypes, providing a generalized code template to show the detailed code structure of each one. As a refresher, these are the stereotypes that CSLA .NET supports directly:

- Editable root
- Editable child
- Editable, switchable (i.e., root or child) object
- Editable root collection
- Editable child collection
- Read-only root
- Read-only root collection
- Read-only child
- Read-only child collection
- Command object
- Name/value list
- Dynamic editable collection
- Dynamic editable root
- Criteria

If your application requires other stereotypes, you can usually extend CSLA .NET to accommodate those requirements, but these stereotypes are sufficient for the majority of business applications I've encountered in my career.

The templates I'll create in this chapter aren't complete business object implementations, but they do illustrate the basic structure you need to follow when creating that type of business object. This information will help you create class templates or code snippets for use in Visual Studio and will make your development experience more productive.

Business Class Structure

The flow of this chapter will be straightforward. I'll discuss each stereotype in turn, focusing on the coding template for each type of object.

Editable Root Business Objects

The most common type of object is the editable root business object, since any object-oriented system based on CSLA .NET typically has at least one root business object or root collection. (Examples of this type of object include the `Project` and `Resource` objects discussed in Chapter 3.) These objects often contain collections of child objects, as well as their own object-specific data.

In addition to being common, an editable object that's also a root object is the most complex object type, so its code template covers all the possible code regions discussed in Chapter 4. The basic structure for an editable root object, with example or template code in each region, is as follows:

```
[Serializable]
public class EditableRoot : BusinessBase<EditableRoot>
{
  #region Business Methods

  // TODO: add your own fields, properties and methods

  // example with private backing field
  private static PropertyInfo<int> IdProperty =
    RegisterProperty(typeof(EditableRoot), new PropertyInfo<int>("Id"));
  private int _Id = IdProperty.DefaultValue;
  public int Id
  {
    get { return GetProperty(IdProperty, _Id); }
    set { SetProperty(IdProperty, ref _Id, value); }
  }

  private static PropertyInfo<string> NameProperty =
    RegisterProperty(typeof(EditableRoot), new PropertyInfo<string>("Name"));
  public string Name
  {
    get { return GetProperty(NameProperty); }
    set { SetProperty(NameProperty, value); }
  }

  #endregion

  #region Validation Rules

  protected override void AddBusinessRules()
  {
    // TODO: add validation rules
    //ValidationRules.AddRule(RuleMethod, NameProperty);
  }

  #endregion

  #region Authorization Rules
```

```
protected override void AddAuthorizationRules()
{
  // TODO: add authorization rules
  //AuthorizationRules.AllowWrite(NameProperty, "Role");
}

private static void AddObjectAuthorizationRules()
{
  // TODO: add authorization rules
  //AuthorizationRules.AllowEdit(typeof(EditableRoot), "Role");
}

#endregion

#region Factory Methods

public static EditableRoot NewEditableRoot()
{
  return DataPortal.Create<EditableRoot>();
}

public static EditableRoot GetEditableRoot(int id)
{
  return DataPortal.Fetch<EditableRoot>(
    new SingleCriteria<EditableRoot, int>(id));
}

public static void DeleteEditableRoot(int id)
{
  DataPortal.Delete(new SingleCriteria<EditableRoot, int>(id));
}

private EditableRoot()
{ /* Require use of factory methods */ }

#endregion

#region Data Access

[RunLocal]
protected override void DataPortal_Create()
{
  // TODO: load default values
  // omit this override if you have no defaults to set
  base.DataPortal_Create();
}

private void DataPortal_Fetch(SingleCriteria<EditableRoot, int> criteria)
{
  // TODO: load values
}
```

```
    [Transactional(TransactionalTypes.TransactionScope)]
    protected override void DataPortal_Insert()
    {
      // TODO: insert values
    }

    [Transactional(TransactionalTypes.TransactionScope)]
    protected override void DataPortal_Update()
    {
      // TODO: update values
    }

    [Transactional(TransactionalTypes.TransactionScope)]
    protected override void DataPortal_DeleteSelf()
    {
      DataPortal_Delete(new SingleCriteria<EditableRoot, int>(this.Id));
    }

    [Transactional(TransactionalTypes.TransactionScope)]
    private void DataPortal_Delete(SingleCriteria<EditableRoot, int> criteria)
    {
      // TODO: delete values
    }

    #endregion


}
```

You must define the class, which includes making it serializable, giving it a name, and having it inherit from `BusinessBase`.

The *Business Methods* region includes all member or instance field declarations, along with any business-specific properties and methods. These properties and methods typically interact with the instance fields, performing calculations and other manipulation of the data based on the business logic.

I have included examples for the two most common types of property declaration. The first example uses a private backing field, which you declare directly in code:

```
// example with private backing field
private static PropertyInfo<int> IdProperty =
  RegisterProperty(typeof(EditableRoot), new PropertyInfo<int>("Id"));
private int _Id = IdProperty.DefaultValue;
public int Id
{
  get { return GetProperty(IdProperty, _Id); }
  set { SetProperty(IdProperty, ref _Id, value); }
}
```

This approach performs better than the alternative, but does require slightly more complex code. Additionally, if you intend on using CSLA .NET for Silverlight to create a Silverlight version of your application, this approach will require extra coding to support that environment.

■ **Note** While this book does not explicitly cover CSLA .NET for Silverlight, I will comment, where appropriate, on choices you can make in CSLA .NET for Windows that could make it easier or harder to reuse your code in CSLA .NET for Silverlight.

The second example uses a managed backing field, meaning that CSLA .NET manages the field value, so you don't need to declare your own field:

```
private static PropertyInfo<string> NameProperty =
  RegisterProperty(typeof(EditableRoot), new PropertyInfo<string>("Name"));
public string Name
{
  get { return GetProperty(NameProperty); }
  set { SetProperty(NameProperty, value); }
}
```

This approach does incur a performance penalty, because the field value is stored in a data structure instead of a simple field. However, it requires less code and works automatically with CSLA .NET for Silverlight in the Silverlight environment.

The *Validation Rules* region, at a minimum, overrides the `AddBusinessRules()` method. In this method, you call `ValidationRules.AddRule()` to associate rule methods with properties. This region may also include custom rule methods for rules that aren't already available in `Csla.Validation.CommonRules` or in your own library of rule methods.

The *Authorization Rules* region overrides the `AddAuthorizationRules()` method and implements the `static AddObjectAuthorizationRules()` method.

The `AddAuthorizationRules()` method should include calls to methods on the `AuthorizationRules` object: `AllowRead()`, `AllowWrite()`, `DenyRead()`, `DenyWrite()`, `AllowExecute()`, and `DenyExecute()`. Each one associates a property or method with a list of roles that are to be allowed read and write access to that element.

The `AddObjectAuthorization()` method allows you to specify the roles that can interact with the object itself. You can specify the roles that area allowed to create, get, edit, and delete the object. You do this by calling the `AllowCreate()`, `AllowGet()`, `AllowEdit()`, and `AllowDelete()` methods on the `Csla.Security.AuthorizationRules` type.

The purpose of this object-level authorization is to allow the UI developer to easily determine whether the current user can get, add, update, or delete this type of object. That way, the UI can enable, disable, or hide controls to provide appropriate visual cues to the end user. Additionally, the data portal uses these rules to ensure that only authorized users are able to perform a requested action.

In the *Factory Methods* region, `static` factory methods create, retrieve, and delete the object. Of course, these are just examples that you must change as appropriate. You must tailor the accepted parameters to match the identifying criteria for your particular business object.

The example code uses the CSLA .NET `SingleCriteria` class. As discussed in Chapter 4, if your object requires more complex criteria, you'll need to create your own criteria class. The criteria stereotype is discussed later in this chapter.

Finally, the *Data Access* region includes the `DataPortal_XYZ` methods. These methods must include the code to load defaults, retrieve object data, and insert, update, and delete object data, as appropriate. In most cases, you do this through ADO.NET, but you could just as easily implement this code to read or write to an XML file, call a web service, or use any other data store you can imagine.

You can safely omit the DataPortal_Create() method if your object doesn't require any initialization when you create it. If your object does require default values to be loaded into properties (hard-coded from a config file or from a database table), then you should implement the method to initialize those values.

Notice the RunLocal attribute on the DataPortal_Create() method.

```
[RunLocal]
protected override void DataPortal_Create()
```

This attribute is used to force the data portal to run the method locally. You use this attribute for methods that *do not* need to interact with server-side resources (like the database) when they are executed. Typically, you would only use this attribute on DataPortal_Create(), and only if you don't need to load default values from a database table into a new object. The use of the RunLocal attribute is optional, and when you use this attribute, the decorated DataPortal_XYZ method *must not access the database*, because it may not be running in a physical location where the database is available.

The Transactional attributes on the methods that insert, update, or delete data specify that those methods should run within a System.Transactions.TransactionScope transactional context.

```
[Transactional(TransactionalTypes.TransactionScope)]
protected override void DataPortal_Update()
```

You may opt instead to use the TransactionTypes.EnterpriseServices setting to run within a COM+ distributed transaction, or the TransactionTypes.Manual setting to handle your own transactions using ADO.NET or stored procedures.

■ **Tip** Many organizations use an abstract, metadata-driven Data Access layer. In environments like this, the business objects don't use ADO.NET directly. This works fine with CSLA .NET, since the data access code in the DataPortal_XYZ methods can interact with an abstract Data Access layer just as easily as it can interact with ADO.NET directly.

The key thing to note about this code template is that there's very little code in the class that's not related to the business requirements. Most of the code implements business properties, validation, and authorization rules or data access. The bulk of the nonbusiness code (code not specific to your business problem) is already implemented in the CSLA .NET framework.

Immediate or Deferred Deletion

As implemented in the template, the UI developer can delete the object by calling the static delete method and providing the criteria to identify the object to be deleted. Another option is to implement *deferred* deletion, whereby the object must be retrieved, marked as deleted, and then updated in order for it to be deleted. The object's data is then deleted as part of the update process.

To support deferred deletion, simply remove the static delete method.

```
//  public static void DeleteEditableRoot(int id)
//  {
//    DataPortal.Delete(new Criteria(id));
//  }
```

Then, the only way to delete the object is by calling the Delete() method on an instance of the object and updating that object to the database by calling Save(). You would use this UI code:

```
var root = EditableRoot.GetEditableRoot(123);
root.Delete();
root.Save();
```

Because immediate deletion is the more common model, that is what I chose to show in the template.

Object State Management

The data portal automatically manages the state of the business object. Table 5-1 shows the state of the object after each `DataPortal_XYZ` method.

Table 5-1. *Object State After Data Portal Methods Complete*

Method	Object State After Method Completes
`DataPortal_Create()`	`IsNew` is `true`; `IsDirty` is `true`; `IsDeleted` is `false`
`DataPortal_Fetch()`	`IsNew` is `false`; `IsDirty` is `false`; `IsDeleted` is `false`
`DataPortal_Insert()`	`IsNew` is `false`; `IsDirty` is `false`; `IsDeleted` is `false`
`DataPortal_Update()`	`IsNew` is `false`; `IsDirty` is `false`; `IsDeleted` is `false`
`DataPortal_DeleteSelf()`	`IsNew` is `true`; `IsDirty` is `true`; `IsDeleted` is `false`
`DataPortal_Delete()`	Not applicable; object not returned

Because the data portal takes care of these details, you can simply use the state properties without worrying about maintaining them yourself.

Using an Object Factory

You can also choose to use the `ObjectFactory` attribute on the business class to indicate that the data portal should use an object factory rather than interact with the business object directly.

In that case, you need to make some slight alterations to the template. You need to add the `ObjectFactory` attribute to the class.

```
[ObjectFactory("MyFactories.MyFactory, MyFactories")]
[Serializable]
public class EditableRoot : BusinessBase<EditableRoot>
```

You also need to eliminate the entire *Data Access* region from the template. The data portal will not invoke any `DataPortal_XYZ` methods if the class has an `ObjectFactory` attribute. Instead, the data portal will create an instance of the specified object factory type and will invoke methods on that object.

The following illustrates the basic structure of an object factory class:

```
public class MyFactory : Csla.Server.ObjectFactory
{
  public object Create()
  {
    EditableRoot result = new EditableRoot();
    // initialize the new object with default data
    MarkNew(result);
    return result;
  }
```

```
    public object Fetch(SingleCriteria<EditableRoot, int> criteria)
    {
      EditableRoot result = new EditableRoot();
      // load the new object with data based on the criteria
      MarkOld(result);
      return result;
    }

    public object Update(object obj)
    {
      // insert, update or delete the data for obj
      MarkOld(obj);
      return obj;
    }

    public void Delete(SingleCriteria<EditableRoot, int> criteria)
    {
      // delete data based on the criteria
    }
  }
```

The object factory assumes complete responsibility for creating and interacting with the business object, including setting the object's state by calling the protected methods from the `ObjectFactory` base class: `MarkNew()` and `MarkOld()`.

While the object factory model requires more code and effort, it does provide more flexibility, and it can provide better separation between the business and data access logic.

Editable Child Business Objects

Most applications will have some editable child objects, or even grandchild objects. Examples of these include the `ProjectResource` and `ResourceAssignment` objects from the Project Tracker reference application. In many cases, the child objects are contained within a child collection object, which I'll discuss later. In other cases, the child object might be referenced directly by the parent object. Either way, the basic structure of a child object is the same; in some ways, this template is similar to the editable root:

```
  [Serializable]
  public class EditableChild : BusinessBase<EditableChild>
  {
    #region Business Methods

    // TODO: add your own fields, properties, and methods

    // example with private backing field
    private static PropertyInfo<int> IdProperty =
      RegisterProperty(typeof(EditableChild), new PropertyInfo<int>("Id"));
    private int _Id = IdProperty.DefaultValue;
    public int Id
    {
      get { return GetProperty(IdProperty, _Id); }
      set { SetProperty(IdProperty, ref _Id, value); }
    }
```

```
// example with managed backing field
private static PropertyInfo<string> NameProperty =
  RegisterProperty(typeof(EditableChild), new PropertyInfo<string>("Name"));
public string Name
{
  get { return GetProperty(NameProperty); }
  set { SetProperty(NameProperty, value); }
}

#endregion

#region Validation Rules

protected override void AddBusinessRules()
{
  // TODO: add validation rules
  //ValidationRules.AddRule(RuleMethod, NameProperty);
}

#endregion

#region Authorization Rules

protected override void AddAuthorizationRules()
{
  // TODO: add authorization rules
  //AuthorizationRules.AllowWrite(NameProperty, "Role");
}

private static void AddObjectAuthorizationRules()
{
  // TODO: add authorization rules
  //AuthorizationRules.AllowEdit(typeof(EditableChild), "Role");
}

#endregion

#region Factory Methods

internal static EditableChild NewEditableChild()
{
  return DataPortal.CreateChild<EditableChild>();
}

internal static EditableChild GetEditableChild(object childData)
{
  return DataPortal.FetchChild<EditableChild>(childData);
}

private EditableChild()
{ /* Require use of factory methods */ }

#endregion
```

```
    #region Data Access

    protected override void Child_Create()
    {
      // TODO: load default values
      // omit this override if you have no defaults to set
      base.Child_Create();
    }

    private void Child_Fetch(object childData)
    {
      // TODO: load values
    }

    private void Child_Insert(object parent)
    {
      // TODO: insert values
    }

    private void Child_Update(object parent)
    {
      // TODO: update values
    }

    private void Child_DeleteSelf(object parent)
    {
      // TODO: delete values
    }

    #endregion
}
```

As with all business classes, this one is serializable and inherits from a CSLA .NET base class. The fact that it is a child object is specified by the data portal calls to `CreateChild()` and `FetchChild()` in the factory methods. Behind the scenes, the data portal calls the `MarkAsChild()` method so the object is explicitly marked as a child, and if you choose not to use the data portal to create your child objects, you'll need to ensure manually that `MarkAsChild()` is called.

The *Business Methods* region is the same as with a root object: it simply implements the properties and methods required by the business rules. Similarly, the *Validation Rules* and *Authorization Rules* regions are the same as with a root object.

The *Factory Methods* region is a bit different. The factory methods are `internal` rather than `public`, as they should be called only by the parent object, not by the UI code. Also, there's no need for a `static` delete method, because `BusinessBase` implements a `DeleteChild()` method that `BusinessListBase` calls automatically when the child is removed from a collection. Perhaps most importantly, notice the data portal calls to `CreateChild()` and `FetchChild()` (rather than to `Create()` and `Fetch()`) in the factory methods.

Also, notice how the `GetEditableChild()` method accepts a parameter containing *child data*. This parameter is passed from the parent and includes the data necessary to load this child object's field values. Normally this value will be a LINQ to SQL or ADO.NET Entity Framework entity object, an ADO.NET `DataReader` that is already pointing to the correct row of data, or something similar. And normally the parameter won't be of type `object`, but will be strongly typed.

The biggest difference from a root object comes in the *Data Access* region. Instead of `DataPortal_XYZ` methods, a child object implements `Child_XYZ` methods. The `Child_Create()` method is implemented to support the loading of default values on the creation of a new child object. Please note that *this method doesn't run on the application server*, so `Child_Create()` cannot talk to the database. It is only useful for loading default values that are hard-coded, from some other object, or from a client-side configuration file.

The `Child_Fetch()` method typically accepts a parameter containing the data that should be used to load the object's field values. Normally the parent object loads all the data for its children and provides that data through a parameter. A less efficient approach is to have each child object contact the database independently to load its data.

The `Child_Insert()`, `Child_Update()`, and `Child_Delete()` methods typically accept a reference to the parent object as a parameter. The assumption is that any child object will need data from the parent while being inserted or updated into the database. Most often, the parent contains a foreign key value required by the child object during data access.

■ **Note** Typically, the `parent` parameter will be strongly typed based on the class of the parent object itself.

In Project Tracker, for example, the `ProjectResource` child object needs the `Id` property from its parent `Project` object so that it can store it as a foreign key in the database. By getting a reference to its parent `Project` object, the `ProjectResource` gains access to that value as needed.

Loading Default Values from a Data Store

If you need to load default values from the database into a child object, the `NewEditableChild()` factory method must call `DataPortal.Create()`, and the object must implement a `DataPortal_Create()` method just like an editable root object. Because this is a child object, the `DataPortal_Create()` method would need to call `MarkAsChild()`, as shown here:

```
protected override void DataPortal_Create()
{
  MarkAsChild();
  // TODO: load default values here
  base.DataPortal_Create();
}
```

The rest of the `Child_XYZ` methods (`Fetch`, `Insert`, `Update`, and `DeleteSelf`) will all run on the application server and can assume they have access to the database.

You can choose to use the `ObjectFactory` with a child object as well, if you want to supply an object factory class. In this case, you would *not* implement a `DataPortal_Create()` method in the business class, but instead would implement a `Create()` method in the object factory class.

The object factory class would look like this:

```
public class MyChildFactory : Csla.Server.ObjectFactory
{
  public object Create()
  {
    EditableChild result = new EditableChild();
    // initialize the new object with default data
    MarkNew(result);
    MarkAsChild(result);
    return result;
  }
}
```

This is mostly the same as the code I described earlier for an editable root. The differences here are that only the `Create()` method is implemented, and the `MarkAsChild()` method is called to mark the new business object as a child object.

Object State Management

The data portal manages the state of the business object automatically. Table 5-2 shows the state of the object after each `Child_XYZ` method.

The only exception is that if you use the `ObjectFactory` attribute to initialize a new child object with values from the database, then the object factory will be responsible for setting the business object's state as it is created. Even in that case, the data portal will still manage the child object's state for fetch, insert, update, and delete operations.

Table 5-2. *Object State After Data Portal Methods Complete*

Method	Object State After Method Completes
`Child_Create()`	`IsNew` is `true`; `IsDirty` is `true`; `IsDeleted` is `false`
`Child_Fetch()`	`IsNew` is `false`; `IsDirty` is `false`; `IsDeleted` is `false`
`Child_Insert()`	`IsNew` is `false`; `IsDirty` is `false`; `IsDeleted` is `false`
`Child_Update()`	`IsNew` is `false`; `IsDirty` is `false`; `IsDeleted` is `false`
`Child_DeleteSelf()`	`IsNew` is `true`; `IsDirty` is `true`; `IsDeleted` is `false`

Because the data portal takes care of these details, you can simply use the state properties without worrying about maintaining them yourself.

Switchable Objects

It's possible that some classes must be instantiated as root objects on some occasions and as child objects on others. You can handle this by implementing a set of `static` factory methods for the root model, and another set for the child model. You also need to implement both the `DataPortal_XYZ` and `Child_XYZ` methods in the *Data Access* region.

■ **Tip** In most cases, the need for a switchable object indicates a flawed object model. Although there are exceptions for this that make sense, you should examine your object model carefully to see if there's a simpler solution before implementing a switchable object.

The template for creating a switchable object is the same as the editable root template, with the following exceptions:

- Dual factory methods
- Dual data access methods

Let's discuss each change in turn.

Dual Factory Methods

Instead of single factory methods to create and retrieve the object, you will need two methods for each operation: one public, the other internal. To keep this organized, you may consider creating separate code regions for each. For example, one region may have the root factories.

```
#region Root Factory Methods

public static SwitchableObject NewSwitchableObject()
{
  return DataPortal.Create<SwitchableObject>();
}

public static SwitchableObject GetSwitchableObject(int id)
{
  return DataPortal.Fetch<SwitchableObject>(
    new SingleCriteria<SwitchableObject, int>(id));
}

public static void DeleteSwitchableObject(int id)
{
  DataPortal.Delete(new SingleCriteria<SwitchableObject, int>(id));
}

#endregion
```

Notice that this region is no different from the factory region in an editable root. Then there's a whole other set of factory methods to support the object's use as a child.

```
#region Child Factory Methods

internal static SwitchableObject NewSwitchableChild()
{
  return DataPortal.CreateChild<SwitchableObject>();
}

internal static SwitchableObject GetSwitchableChild(object childData)
{
  return DataPortal.FetchChild<SwitchableObject>(childData);
}

private SwitchableObject()
{ /* Require use of factory methods */ }

#endregion
```

This set of factory methods is the same as what you'd see in an editable child.

The key here is that the UI can call the public factory methods directly to interact with the object as a root, while only a parent object can call the internal factory methods to use the object as a child.

Dual Data Access Methods

Because the public factory methods call the Create() and Fetch() methods on the data portal, those calls are routed to DataPortal_XYZ methods. In those cases, the object is a root, so you can call the Save() method, which also routes to the DataPortal_XYZ methods.

At the same time, the internal factory methods call CreateChild() and FetchChild() on the data portal, which route to Child_XYZ methods. In those cases, the object would be a child, so its parent would be responsible for saving the child object; that is also handled through Child_XYZ methods.

The end result is that the object must implement both sets of data access code to handle both the root and child scenarios. It is often simpler to create two data access regions—one for each set of methods. For example, here's the region for the root methods:

```
#region Root Data Access

[RunLocal]
protected override void DataPortal_Create()
{
  // TODO: load default values
  // omit this override if you have no defaults to set
  base.DataPortal_Create();
}

private void DataPortal_Fetch(SingleCriteria<SwitchableObject, int> criteria)
{
  // TODO: load values
}

[Transactional(TransactionalTypes.TransactionScope)]
protected override void DataPortal_Insert()
{
  // TODO: insert values
}

[Transactional(TransactionalTypes.TransactionScope)]
protected override void DataPortal_Update()
{
  // TODO: update values
}

[Transactional(TransactionalTypes.TransactionScope)]
protected override void DataPortal_DeleteSelf()
{
  DataPortal_Delete(new SingleCriteria<SwitchableObject, int>(this.Id));
}

[Transactional(TransactionalTypes.TransactionScope)]
private void DataPortal_Delete(SingleCriteria<SwitchableObject, int> criteria)
{
  // TODO: delete values
}

#endregion
```

This is the same code you'd see in an editable root object. You'll also need a region for the child scenario.

```
#region Child Data Access

protected override void Child_Create()
{
  // TODO: load default values
  // omit this override if you have no defaults to set
  base.Child_Create();
}

private void Child_Fetch(object childData)
{
  // TODO: load values
}

private void Child_Insert(object parent)
{
  // TODO: insert values
}

private void Child_Update(object parent)
{
  // TODO: update values
}

private void Child_DeleteSelf(object parent)
{
  // TODO: delete values
}

#endregion
```

Again, this is the same code you'd see in an editable child.

The result is that the object is treated as a root object when the `public` factory methods are called, and as a child when the `internal` factory methods are called. The data portal takes care of calling `MarkAsChild()` and managing the object's state, as shown previously in Tables 5-1 and 5-2.

Editable Root Collection

At times, applications need to retrieve a collection of child objects directly. To do this, you need to create a root collection object. For instance, the application may have a WPF UI consisting of a `ListBox` control that displays a collection of `Contact` objects. If the root object is a collection of child `Contact` objects, the UI developer can simply bind the collection to the `ListBox` (with an appropriate data template), and the user can edit all the objects in the list.

This approach means that all the child objects are handled as a single unit in terms of data access. They are loaded into the collection to start with, so the user can interact with all of them and then save them as a batch when all edits are complete. This is only subtly different from having a regular root object that has a collection of child objects. Figure 5-1 shows the regular root object approach on the left, and the collection root object approach on the right.

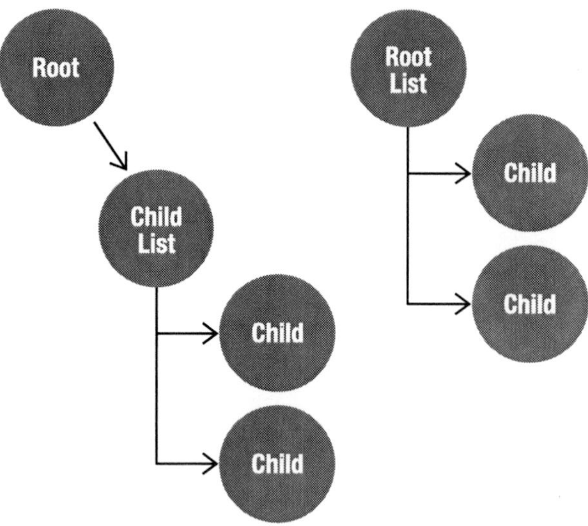

Figure 5-1. *Comparing simple root objects (left) and collection root objects (right)*

This approach isn't recommended when there are large numbers of potential child objects, because the retrieval process can become too slow. However, it can be useful in cases where you can specify criteria to limit the number of objects returned. To create an editable root collection object, use a template like this:

```
[Serializable]
public class EditableRootList :
  BusinessListBase<EditableRootList, EditableChild>
{
  #region Authorization Rules

  private static void AddObjectAuthorizationRules()
  {
    // TODO: add authorization rules
    //AuthorizationRules.AllowGet(typeof(EditableRootList), "Role");
  }

  #endregion

  #region Factory Methods

  public static EditableRootList NewEditableRootList()
  {
    return DataPortal.Create<EditableRootList>();
  }

  public static EditableRootList GetEditableRootList(int id)
  {
    return DataPortal.Fetch<EditableRootList>(
      new SingleCriteria<EditableRootList, int>(id));
  }
```

```
    private EditableRootList()
    { /* Require use of factory methods */ }

    #endregion

    #region Data Access

    private void DataPortal_Fetch(
      SingleCriteria<EditableRootList, int> criteria)
    {
      RaiseListChangedEvents = false;
      // TODO: load values into memory
      object childData = null;
      foreach (var item in (List<object>)childData)
        this.Add(EditableChild.GetEditableChild(childData));
      RaiseListChangedEvents = true;
    }

    #endregion
  }
```

The *Authorization Rules* region implements the `AddObjectAuthorizationRules()` method to define the roles that can interact with the object. This is the same as with an editable root object, and the UI developer can use this information to enable and disable UI elements accordingly. Also, the data portal uses these rules to ensure only authorized users are able to create, get, edit, or delete the collection object. The one difference is that this `AddObjectAuthorizationRules()` method only needs to define the roles allowed to get the object.

The *Factory Methods* region implements factory methods to create, retrieve, and (optionally) delete the collection. The methods rely on the data portal to do much of the work, ultimately delegating the call to the appropriate `DataPortal_XYZ` method.

In the *Data Access* region, the `DataPortal_Fetch()` method is responsible for getting the data from the database using whatever data access technology you choose. This is often LINQ to SQL, the ADO.NET Entity Framework, or raw ADO.NET. In any case, the Data Access layer must return the child data as a result so it can use it to load each individual child object with data.

You load each child object by calling the child object's factory method, passing the object's data as a parameter. The resulting child object is added to the collection. The `DataPortal_Fetch()` method sets the `RaiseListChanged Events` property to `false` before changing the collection, and then restores it to `true` once the operation is complete. Setting this property to `false` tells the base `BindingList<T>` class to stop raising the `ListChanged` event. When doing batches of updates or changes to a collection, this can increase performance.

The `BusinessListBase` class includes a default implementation of the `DataPortal_Update()` method, which loops through all child objects (and deleted child objects) to ensure the appropriate `Child_XYZ` method is called on each when the collection is being saved. Normally this is the desired behavior, but you can override `DataPortal_Update()` if you need to take control of the update process for some unusual scenario.

As with the editable root stereotype, you can use the `ObjectFactory` attribute to have the data portal invoke an object factory rather than invoke the `DataPortal_XYZ` methods directly in the business class.

Collection objects that inherit from `BusinessListBase` automatically support data binding in WPF, Windows Forms, and Web Forms. However, if you bind a collection to a Windows Forms `DataGrid` control, you may be surprised to find that the user can't just add new items by going to the bottom of the grid. You need to write a bit of extra code in your collection to enable this behavior.

In the constructor, you need to give data binding permission to add new items to the collection by setting the AllowNew property.

```
private EditableRootList()
{
  /* Require use of factory methods */
  AllowNew = true;
}
```

When you do this, you also *must override the* AddNewCore() *method.* This method is defined by the .NET collection base class from which BusinessListBase inherits, and it is this method that is responsible for creating a new child object and adding it to the collection when requested by data binding.

The override looks like this:

```
protected override EditableChild AddNewCore()
{
  var item = EditableChild.NewEditableChild();
  Add(item);
  return item;
}
```

The method must perform three tasks: create the object, add it to the collection, and return the object as a result. Notice that no parameter is provided to AddNewCore(). This means that you must be able to create new child objects without providing any criteria or other information. Usually this is not a problem, but if the only way to create your new child object is with some criteria information, then you won't be able to enable this feature of data binding.

Editable Child Collection

The most common type of collection is one that is contained within a parent object to manage a collection of child objects for that parent—for example, ProjectResources and ResourceAssignments in the sample application.

■ **Tip** Note that the parent object here might be a root object, or it might be a child itself. Child objects can be nested, if that's what the business object model requires. In other words, this concept supports not only root-to-child, but also child-to-grandchild and grandchild-to-great-grandchild relationships.

A child collection class inherits from BusinessListBase and has factory methods that use the CreateChild() and FetchChild() data portal methods, so the object is marked as a child when it is created. If you choose to avoid the data portal for creating the child object, you must make sure MarkAsChild() is called during the object's creation process to indicate that it's operating in child mode.

Remember that child objects are not retrieved or updated directly by the UI, but instead are retrieved or updated by the child object's parent object.

```
[Serializable]
public class EditableChildList :
  BusinessListBase<EditableChildList, EditableChild>
{
  #region Factory Methods
```

```
    internal static EditableChildList NewEditableChildList()
    {
      return DataPortal.CreateChild<EditableChildList>();
    }

    internal static EditableChildList GetEditableChildList(
      object childData)
    {
      return DataPortal.FetchChild<EditableChildList>(childData);
    }

    private EditableChildList()
    { }

    #endregion

    #region Data Access

    private void Child_Fetch(object childData)
    {
      RaiseListChangedEvents = false;
      foreach (var child in (IList<object>)childData)
        this.Add(EditableChild.GetEditableChild(child));
      RaiseListChangedEvents = true;
    }

    #endregion
  }
```

As you can see, this code is similar to a root collection in structure, though there is no *Authorization Rules* region.

The factory methods are somewhat different, because they are scoped as `internal` and call the child data portal methods. Notice that the `GetEditableChildList()` method requires that the parent provide a preloaded object containing the data for the list's child objects. It is less efficient, but possible, for the child list to go directly to the database in its `Child_Fetch()` method and load its own data, but typically the parent object provides this data, as mocked up here.

The *Data Access* region contains a `Child_Fetch()` method, which is responsible for creating all child objects by calling their factory methods, and adding those objects to the collection. As with any collection, the `RaiseListChangedEvents` property is set to `false` first, and to `true` when complete to prevent a flood of unnecessary `ListChanged` events during the data-retrieval process.

The `BusinessListBase` class contains a default implementation for `Child_Update()` that automatically calls the right `Child_XYZ` method on all child objects of the list when the list is saved. Normally this implementation is sufficient, but you can override `Child_Update()` to customize that behavior if required for some unusual edge case.

As with an editable root collection, you can set `AllowNew` to `true` and override `AddNewCore()` if you want data binding to add new items to the collection automatically.

Read-Only Business Objects

Sometimes, an application may need an object that provides data in a read-only fashion. For a read-only list of data, there's `ReadOnlyListBase`; however, if the requirement is for a single object containing read-only data, it should inherit from `ReadOnlyBase`. This is one of the simplest types of objects to create, since it does nothing more than retrieve and return data, as shown here:

```
[Serializable]
public class ReadOnlyRoot : ReadOnlyBase<ReadOnlyRoot>
{
  #region Business Methods

  // TODO: add your own fields, properties and methods

  // example with managed backing field
  private static PropertyInfo<int> IdProperty =
    RegisterProperty(typeof(ReadOnlyRoot), new PropertyInfo<int>("Id", "Id"));
  public int Id
  {
    get { return GetProperty(IdProperty); }
  }

  // example with private backing field
  private static PropertyInfo<string> NameProperty =
    RegisterProperty(typeof(ReadOnlyRoot),
    new PropertyInfo<string>("Name", "Name"));
  private string _name = NameProperty.DefaultValue;
  public string Name
  {
    get { return GetProperty(NameProperty, _name); }
  }

  #endregion

  #region Authorization Rules

  protected override void AddAuthorizationRules()
  {
    // TODO: add authorization rules
    //AuthorizationRules.AllowRead("Name", "Role");
  }

  private static void AddObjectAuthorizationRules()
  {
    // TODO: add authorization rules
    //AuthorizationRules.AllowGet(typeof(ReadOnlyRoot), "Role");
  }

  #endregion

  #region Factory Methods

  public static ReadOnlyRoot GetReadOnlyRoot(int id)
  {
    return DataPortal.Fetch<ReadOnlyRoot>(
      new SingleCriteria<ReadOnlyRoot, int>(id));
  }

  private ReadOnlyRoot()
  { /* require use of factory methods */ }
```

```
    #endregion

    #region Data Access

    private void DataPortal_Fetch(SingleCriteria<ReadOnlyRoot, int> criteria)
    {
      // TODO: load values
    }

    #endregion
  }
```

Like other business objects, a read-only object will have either managed or private fields that contain its data. Typically, it will also have read-only properties or methods that allow client code to retrieve values. As long as they don't change the state of the object, these may even be calculated values.

The `AddAuthorizationRules()` method only needs to add roles for read access, since no properties should be implemented to allow altering of data. Similarly, the `AddObjectAuthorizationRules()` method only needs to define the roles allowed to get the object.

In the *Factory Methods* region, there's just one factory method that retrieves the object by calling `DataPortal.Fetch()`. The *Data Access* region just contains `DataPortal_Fetch()`. Of course, there's no need to support updating or deleting a read-only object.

As with the editable root stereotype, you can use the `ObjectFactory` attribute to have the data portal invoke a `Fetch()` method from an object factory rather than invoke the `DataPortal_Fetch()` method in the business class directly.

Read-Only Child Objects

You create a read-only child object using the same code as that for a read-only root object. The only difference is how you handle the data portal and data access.

```
[Serializable]
public class ReadOnlyChild : ReadOnlyBase<ReadOnlyChild>
{
  #region Business Methods

  // TODO: add your own fields, properties, and methods

  // example with managed backing field
  private static PropertyInfo<int> IdProperty =
    RegisterProperty(typeof(ReadOnlyRoot),
    new PropertyInfo<int>("Id", "Id"));
  public int Id
  {
    get { return GetProperty(IdProperty); }
  }

  // example with private backing field
  private static PropertyInfo<string> NameProperty =
    RegisterProperty(typeof(ReadOnlyRoot),
    new PropertyInfo<string>("Name", "Name"));
  private string _name = NameProperty.DefaultValue;
```

```
    public string Name
    {
      get { return GetProperty(NameProperty, _name); }
    }

    #endregion

    #region Factory Methods

    internal static ReadOnlyChild GetReadOnlyChild(object childData)
    {
      return DataPortal.FetchChild<ReadOnlyChild>(childData);
    }

    private ReadOnlyChild()
    { /* require use of factory methods */ }

    #endregion

    #region Data Access

    private void Child_Fetch(object childData)
    {
      // TODO: load values from childData
    }

    #endregion
  }
```

As with a root object, a read-only child object should only have read-only properties. And as with an editable child, the factory method and data access method assume the parent object will be providing the pre-retrieved data needed to load the object's fields.

Read-Only Collection

Applications commonly retrieve read-only collections of objects. The CSLA .NET framework includes the `ReadOnlyListBase` class to help create read-only collections. It throws an exception any time there's an attempt to change which items are in the collection by adding or removing objects.

■ **Note** The template shown here is for the most common scenario: a read-only root collection. You can adapt this to provide a read-only child collection if desired.

However, there's no way for the collection object to stop client code from interacting with the child objects themselves. Typically, the items in the collection expose only read-only properties and methods. If read-write objects are put into the collection, the client code will be able to alter their data. A read-only collection only guarantees that objects can't be added or removed from the collection.

The child objects may be derived from `ReadOnlyBase`, but they could just as easily be simple objects that don't inherit from any CSLA .NET base class. The only requirements for these child objects are that they are implemented with read-only properties and that they are marked as `Serializable`.

The code for a typical read-only collection object looks like this:

```
[Serializable]
public class ReadOnlyList :
  ReadOnlyListBase<ReadOnlyList, ReadOnlyChild>
{
  #region Authorization Rules

  private static void AddObjectAuthorizationRules()
  {
    // TODO: add authorization rules
    //AuthorizationRules.AllowGet(typeof(ReadOnlyList), "Role");
  }

  #endregion

  #region Factory Methods

  public static ReadOnlyList GetReadOnlyList(string filter)
  {
    return DataPortal.Fetch<ReadOnlyList>(
      new SingleCriteria<ReadOnlyList, string>(filter));
  }

  private ReadOnlyList()
  { /* require use of factory methods */ }

  #endregion

  #region Data Access

  private void DataPortal_Fetch(
    SingleCriteria<ReadOnlyList, string> criteria)
  {
    RaiseListChangedEvents = false;
    IsReadOnly = false;
    // TODO: load values
    object objectData = null;
    foreach (var child in (List<object>)objectData)
      Add(ReadOnlyChild.GetReadOnlyChild(child));
    IsReadOnly = true;
    RaiseListChangedEvents = true;
  }

  #endregion
}
```

The *Authorization Rules* region contains only the `AddObjectAuthorizationRules()` method, which only needs to define the roles allowed to get the object.

The *Factory Methods* region has a factory method to return a collection loaded with data. It calls `DataPortal.Fetch()` and often passes in some criteria or filter value to restrict the results of the list.

Finally, the `DataPortal_Fetch()` method loads the object with data from the database. To do this, the `IsReadOnly` flag is set to `false`, the data is loaded from the database, and then `IsReadOnly` is set to `true`. When `IsReadOnly` is set to `true`, any attempt to add or remove items from the collection results in an exception being thrown. Temporarily setting it to `false` allows the code to insert all the appropriate child objects into the collection.

Also note that RaiseListChangedEvents is set to false and then true in a similar manner. To improve performance, this suppresses the raising of ListChanged events while the data is being loaded.

Read-Only Child Collection

A read-only child collection is virtually identical to a read-only root collection. The differences are in the factory methods and data access.

```
[Serializable]
public class ReadOnlyChildList :
  ReadOnlyListBase<ReadOnlyChildList, ReadOnlyChild>
{
  #region Authorization Rules

  private static void AddObjectAuthorizationRules()
  {
    // TODO: add authorization rules
    //AuthorizationRules.AllowGet(typeof(ReadOnlyChildList), "Role");
  }

  #endregion

  #region Factory Methods

  internal static ReadOnlyChildList GetReadOnlyChildList(object childData)
  {
    return DataPortal.FetchChild<ReadOnlyChildList>(childData);
  }

  private ReadOnlyChildList()
  { /* require use of factory methods */ }

  #endregion

  #region Data Access

  private void Child_Fetch(object childData)
  {
    RaiseListChangedEvents = false;
    IsReadOnly = false;
    // TODO: load values
    foreach (var child in (List<object>)childData)
      Add(ReadOnlyChild.GetReadOnlyChild(child));
    IsReadOnly = true;
    RaiseListChangedEvents = true;
  }

  #endregion
}
```

The internal factory method calls the FetchChild() data portal method, which in turn calls Child_Fetch(). Notice that the parent object is assumed to be providing some object containing all the data necessary to load the collection's child objects.

Command Objects

Command objects can be used in many ways. They may be called directly by UI code to execute arbitrary code on the application server, but even more often they are used *within* other business objects to execute code on the application server. A primary example is when a normal editable business object wants to implement an `Exists()` command. You'll see an example of this concept in the `Project` and `Resource` objects in the Project Tracker reference application.

If the UI is to use the object directly, the class will be `public`. On the other hand, if the UI is to use the object within the context of another business object, the class will be a `private` nested class within that business object. Either way, the structure of a command object is the same, as shown here:

```
[Serializable]
public class CommandObject : CommandBase
{
  #region Factory Methods

  public static bool Execute()
  {
    CommandObject cmd = new CommandObject();
    cmd.BeforeServer();
    cmd = DataPortal.Execute<CommandObject>(cmd);
    cmd.AfterServer();
    return cmd.Result;
  }

  private CommandObject()
  { /* require use of factory methods */ }

  #endregion

  #region Client-side Code

  // TODO: add your own fields and properties
  bool _result;

  public bool Result
  {
    get { return _result; }
  }

  private void BeforeServer()
  {
    // TODO: implement code to run on client
    // before server is called
  }

  private void AfterServer()
  {
    // TODO: implement code to run on client
    // after server is called
  }

  #endregion
```

```
    #region Server-side Code

    protected override void DataPortal_Execute()
    {
      // TODO: implement code to run on server
      // and set result value(s)
      _result = true;
    }

    #endregion
  }
```

This class structure is quite a bit different from anything you've seen so far.

The *Factory Methods* region is similar to many of the other templates thus far in structure, but its implementation is different. Rather than passing a criteria object to the server, the Execute() method creates and initializes an instance of the command object itself. That instance is then sent to the server through the data portal, which invokes the DataPortal_Execute() method on the server.

The Execute() method also calls BeforeServer() and AfterServer() methods, which are found in the *Client-side Code* region. The idea behind this is that the command object can be initialized on the client with any data required to perform the server-side processing. In fact, the object could do some processing or data gathering on the client before or after it is transferred to the server through the data portal. The client-side code may be as complex as needed to prepare to run the server-side code.

Then the data portal moves the object to the application server and calls the DataPortal_Execute() method in the *Server-side Code* region. The code in this method runs on the server and can do any server-side work. This might be something as simple as doing a quick database lookup, or it might be a complex server-side workflow. The code in this method can create and interact with other business objects (all on the server, of course). It can interact directly with the database or any other server-side resources, such as the server's file system or third-party software installed on the server.

As with the editable root stereotype, you can use the ObjectFactory attribute to have the data portal invoke an Update() method from an object factory rather than invoke the DataPortal_Execute() method in the command object directly.

Command objects are powerful because they provide high levels of flexibility for running both client and server code in a coordinated manner.

Name/Value List Objects

Perhaps the simplest business object to create is a name/value list that inherits from the NameValueListBase class in the CSLA .NET framework. The base class provides almost all the functionality needed, except the actual data access and factory method.

Because name/value list data is often static and changes rarely, it is often desirable to cache the data. You can do this in the factory method, as shown in this template:

```
[Serializable]
public class NameValueList : NameValueListBase<int, string>
{
  #region Factory Methods

  private static NameValueList _list;

  public static NameValueList GetNameValueList()
  {
    if (_list == null)
      _list = DataPortal.Fetch<NameValueList>();
```

```
      return _list;
    }

    public static void InvalidateCache()
    {
      _list = null;
    }

    private NameValueList()
    { /* require use of factory methods */ }

    #endregion

    #region Data Access

    private void DataPortal_Fetch()
    {
      RaiseListChangedEvents = false;
      IsReadOnly = false;
      // TODO: load values
      //object listData = null;
      //foreach (var item in listData)
      //  Add(new NameValueListBase<int, string>.
      //    NameValuePair(item.Key, item.Value));
      IsReadOnly = true;
      RaiseListChangedEvents = true;
    }

    #endregion
  }
```

The *Factory Methods* region declares a static field to hold the list once it is retrieved. Notice how the factory method returns the cached list if it is present; it only calls the data portal to retrieve the data if the list is `null`. You can also call an `InvalidateCache()` method to force a reload of the data if needed.

This caching behavior is optional—if it doesn't fit your need, then use a factory method, like this:

```
public static NameValueList GetNameValueList()
{
  return DataPortal.Fetch<NameValueList>();
}
```

The *Data Access* region contains only a `DataPortal_Fetch()` method, which calls the Data Access layer to retrieve the name/value data. The `NameValueListBase` class defines a strongly typed `NameValuePair` class, which is used to store each element of data. For each row of data from the database, a `NameValuePair` object is created and added to the collection.

Notice the use of the `IsReadOnly` property to temporarily unlock the collection and then relock it so it becomes read-only once the data has been loaded. The `RoleList` class in the Project Tracker reference application illustrates a complete implementation of a name/value list.

Dynamic Editable Collection

The dynamic editable collection stereotype is designed to support a narrow and focused scenario in which the UI is a Windows Forms grid control that is data bound to the collection, and in which the user wants his changes to each row saved as soon as he moves off each row.

This behavior is conceptually similar to some old Visual Basic behavior when using a DAO dynaset. In that case, changes made by the user to a row of data were automatically committed when the user navigated off that row in the UI.

The CSLA .NET base class used in this stereotype is the `EditableRootListBase` (ERLB). A collection that inherits from ERLB contains *editable root* objects (though with a twist), so each object can be saved individually rather than in a batch. While a collection that inherits from `BusinessListBase` saves all its child objects at once, a collection inheriting from ERLB saves each "child" one at a time.

At a high level, the collection is responsible for containing a list of editable root objects. It is also responsible for retrieving all those objects at once, but then saving them individually as the user inserts, updates, or deletes items in the list.

The ERLB base class handles most of the hard work itself, so the template code is focused primarily on retrieving the objects and adding them to the collection. When looking at this code, remember that the child objects are a modified editable root stereotype called dynamic editable root objects.

```
[Serializable]
public class DynamicRootList :
  EditableRootListBase<DynamicRoot>
{
  #region Business Methods

  protected override object AddNewCore()
  {
    DynamicRoot item = DynamicRoot.NewDynamicRoot();
    Add(item);
    return item;
  }

  #endregion

  #region  Authorization Rules

  private static void AddObjectAuthorizationRules()
  {
    // TODO: add authorization rules
    //AuthorizationRules.AllowGet(typeof(DynamicRootList), "Role");
    //AuthorizationRules.AllowEdit(typeof(DynamicRootList), "Role");
  }

  #endregion

  #region  Factory Methods

  public static DynamicRootList NewDynamicRootList()
  {
    return DataPortal.Create<DynamicRootList>();
  }

  public static DynamicRootList GetDynamicRootList()
  {
    return DataPortal.Fetch<DynamicRootList>();
  }
```

```
    private DynamicRootList()
    {
      // require use of factory methods
      AllowNew = true;
    }

    #endregion

    #region  Data Access

    private void DataPortal_Fetch()
    {
      // TODO: load values
      RaiseListChangedEvents = false;
      object listData = null;
      foreach (var item in (List<object>)listData)
        Add(DynamicRoot.GetDynamicRoot(item));
      RaiseListChangedEvents = true;
    }

    #endregion
  }
```

As with an editable root collection, you can set `AllowNew` to `true` and override `AddNewCore()` if you want data binding to automatically add new items to the collection. This template includes that functionality, because the typical use of a dynamic collection is to allow the user to add, edit, and remove objects.

The *Authorization Rules* region is the same as you've seen in the other root templates. The *Factory Methods* region allows creation of an empty collection, or retrieval of existing data through two different factories. The *Data Access* region includes the `DataPortal_Fetch()` method, which is responsible for calling the Data Access layer to get all the data for the objects that will be in the collection. This is the same kind of code you saw for the editable root collection stereotype.

What is interesting here is that the "child" objects being loaded are actually editable root objects. In the next section, I'll discuss the dynamic editable root stereotype. You'll be able to see how the `GetDynamicRoot()` factory method is implemented.

Dynamic Editable Root Objects

The dynamic editable root stereotype is virtually identical to the editable root stereotype, with one slight twist. Remember that this stereotype is designed to create the "child" objects contained within a dynamic editable collection. While these editable objects are saved individually, they are loaded all at once by the parent collection.

Note In this section, I assume you are familiar with the editable root template, and I only discuss the few changes required to meet the dynamic editable root stereotype.

This means that the objects must implement an `internal` factory for use by the parent collection. This factory usually replaces the normal `public` factory that calls `DataPortal.Fetch()`. The factory looks like this:

```
internal static DynamicRoot GetDynamicRoot(object rootData)
{
  return new DynamicRoot(rootData);
}
```

Unlike most factories, this one doesn't call the data portal. This code is being invoked from within the DataPortal_Fetch() of the parent collection object, so there's no need to call the data portal again. And since this is going to be a root object, you can't call the FetchChild() method like you would for a normal child object.

Instead, a constructor is called, and the object's data is passed as a parameter. Notice that the object's data is assumed to have been loaded by the parent collection and passed into this factory method as a parameter. That object may be an entity object from LINQ to SQL or the ADO.NET Entity Framework, or it may be an ADO.NET DataReader or other data object. Normally the parameter value would be strongly typed to match your particular data access mechanism.

This new constructor is *in addition* to the non-public default constructor that exists in all the templates. It looks like this:

```
private DynamicRoot(object rootData)
{
  Fetch(rootData);
}
```

All it does is call a private method named Fetch(), which does the real work of loading the object with data.

```
private void Fetch(object rootData)
{
  // TODO: load values from rootData
  MarkOld();
}
```

This Fetch() method is much the same as a Child_Fetch() method for a child object. It gets the data necessary to load the object's fields as a parameter, and it simply sets the field values.

However, because the data portal didn't call this Fetch() method, the object isn't automatically marked as a child. This is good, because it is a *root* object, not a child.

The call to MarkOld() is necessary because the object isn't automatically marked as "old" either. In Chapter 7, I'll discuss how business objects manage state such as being "new" or "old." For now, it is enough to know that when an object is retrieved from the database, it is marked as old by the data portal. Since the data portal didn't create this object directly, the business object must do this manually.

Because the object is a root object, at least in terms of being saved, you do need to implement the DataPortal_Insert(), DataPortal_Update(), and DataPortal_DeleteSelf() methods. This object will be saved individually as a root object.

You do not need to implement DataPortal_Delete(), because the ERLB base class does not use immediate deletion to delete its objects, so that method would never be invoked.

Criteria Objects

The root object templates shown in this chapter have all used the SingleCriteria class provided by CSLA .NET. Most objects can be identified by a single criteria value, and that type makes it easy to send any single criteria value through the data portal.

Some objects are more complex, however, and may require more complex criteria. For example, some tables use compound keys, so multiple criteria values are required to match the parts of the database key. As another example, many collections have complex and optional criteria. The user might specify a Name value sometimes, a Region value at other times, and both values at yet other times.

If your object has multiple criteria values, you'll need to create a custom criteria class. Your custom criteria class must simply contain the data that's required to identify the specific object to be retrieved or the default data to be loaded. Since it's passed by value to the data portal, this class must be marked as Serializable.

Criteria classes can be nested classes within the business class, or they can inherit from Csla.CriteriaBase. In most cases, it is simplest to nest the class within the business class. The Csla.CriteriaBase approach is intended primarily for use with code-generation tools.

■ **Tip** Technically, the criteria class can have *any* name, as long as it's Serializable and is either nested in the business class, implements ICriteria, or inherits from CriteriaBase. Some objects may have more than one criteria class, each one defining a different set of criteria that can be used to retrieve the object.

Since a criteria class is no more than a way to ferry data to the data portal, it doesn't need to be fancy. Typically, it's implemented with a constructor to make it easier to create and populate the object all at once. For example, here's a nested criteria class that includes an EmployeeID field:

```
[Serializable]
public class MyBusinessClass : Csla.baseclass<MyBusinessClass>
{
  // ...
  #region Data Access

  [Serializable]
  private class Criteria
  {
    private string _employeeId;
    public string EmployeId
    {
      get { return _employeeId; }
    }

    public Criteria(string employeeId)
    { _employeeId = employeeId; }
  }
  // ...
```

You can create an equivalent criteria class by subclassing CriteriaBase.

```
[Serializable]
Internal class MyBusinessClassCriteria : Csla.CriteriaBase
{
  private string _employeeId;
  public string EmployeId
  {
    get { return _employeeId; }
  }

  public MyBusinessClassCriteria(string employeeId)
    : base(typeof(MyBusinessClass))
  { _employeeId = employeeId; }
}
```

All criteria classes are constructed by using one of these two schemes or by creating a class that implements the ICriteria interface directly.

Nested criteria classes are scoped as private, because they are only needed within the context of the business class. The ICriteria interface and CriteriaBase class are typically used by code-generation tools, in which case the class is typically scoped more broadly so that it is available either project-wide or even to the UI.

■ **Note** Code generation is outside the scope of this book. For good information on code generation, including the rationale behind CriteriaBase, please refer to *Code Generation in Microsoft .NET* by Kathleen Dollard (Apress, 2004), and the index of CSLA .NET–compliant code-generation tools at www.lhotka.net/cslanet/codegen.aspx.

The criteria classes shown thus far include a constructor that accepts the criteria data value. This is done to simplify the code that will go into the business object's factory methods. Rather than forcing the business developer to create a criteria object and then load its values, this constructor allows the criteria object to be created and initialized in a single statement. In many cases, this means that a factory method will contain just one line of code—for instance:

```
public static Project GetProject(Guid id, Date start)
{
  return DataPortal.Fetch<Project>(new Criteria(id, start));
}
```

Many criteria classes contain a set of simple values (as in the examples here), but they can also be more complex, providing for more control over the selection of the object to be retrieved. If you have a root collection in which you're directly retrieving a collection of child objects, the criteria class may not define a single object, but rather may act as a search filter that returns the collection populated with all matching child objects.

Another interesting variation is to use BusinessBase as the base class for a public criteria class. In this case, the class must also implement the ICriteria interface so it can act as a proper criteria object. The value of this approach is that you can easily use data binding to create a UI so the user can enter values into the criteria object. The object can even have validation and authorization rules. Here's an example of such a class:

```
[Serializable]
public class MyCriteria : BusinessBase<MyCriteria>, ICriteria
{
  #region Business Methods

  private static PropertyInfo<int> IdProperty =
    RegisterProperty<int>(typeof(Project), new PropertyInfo<int>("Id"));
  public int id
  {
    get { return GetProperty(NameProperty); }
    set { SetProperty(NameProperty, value); }
  }

  #endregion

  #region ICriteria Members
```

```
    public Type ObjectType
    {
      get { return typeof(MyBusinessClass); }
    }

    #endregion
  }
```

This use of BusinessBase doesn't follow all the same rules as an editable root or child. For example, there's no need for the *Factory Methods* or *Data Access* regions and related code, because this object is never persisted like a normal editable object. It is just a fancy container for criteria values that supports data binding, validation, and authorization.

Conclusion

This chapter provides detailed code templates for each of the object stereotypes directly supported by CSLA .NET. These templates include the outline for the code necessary to implement properties, methods, validation rules, business rules, authorization, and data access.

These templates illustrate the implementation of the concepts discussed in Chapter 3, such as the life cycle of business objects and the process of creating, retrieving, updating, and deleting objects. Additionally, these templates are the basis on which the business objects for the Project Tracker reference application are built, so you can look at the templates and compare them to the fully operational objects in Project Tracker to see the evolution from high-level coding structure to actual implementation.

In Chapters 6–16, you'll learn how to implement the CSLA .NET framework that supports these stereotypes. In Chapters 17–21, you'll see how to use these stereotypes and the framework to create the Project Tracker application described in Chapter 3.

CHAPTER 6

Business Framework Implementation

In Chapter 1, I discuss the concepts behind the use of business objects and distributed objects. In Chapter 2, I explored the design of the business framework. Chapters 3 through 5 cover object-oriented design in general and then focus more around the specific stereotypes directly supported by CSLA .NET. In this chapter, I start walking through the implementation of the CSLA .NET framework by providing an overview of the namespaces and project structure of the framework. Then in Chapters 7 through 16, I provide detail about the implementation of each of the major features of the framework as discussed in Chapter 2.

The focus in this chapter is on the overall project structure and namespaces used to organize all the framework code and a walkthrough of the structure of the major types in the `Csla` and `Csla.Core` namespaces.

CSLA .NET has existed since around the year 2001 and has been steadily evolving since then, based on feedback from the user community and to keep up with the many changes Microsoft has made to the Microsoft .NET Framework. The result is that CSLA .NET is now a large and complex framework.

My goal, however, is to take complexity out of the application and place it into CSLA .NET so developers who use the framework don't need to deal with the complexity. In other words, CSLA .NET solves some pretty complicated issues and tries to expose its solutions in an easy-to-use manner.

As discussed in Chapters 4 and 5, business developers primarily interact with a limited set of base classes provided by CSLA .NET:

- `Csla.BusinessBase<T>`
- `Csla.BusinessListBase<T,C>`
- `Csla.ReadOnlyBase<T>`
- `Csla.ReadOnlyListBase<T,C>`
- `Csla.NameValueListBase<K,V>`
- `Csla.CommandBase`
- `Csla.EditableRootListBase<T>`
- `Csla.CriteriaBase`

These base classes are the primary classes from which most business objects inherit. Almost all the other classes in CSLA .NET exist to support the functionality provided by these base classes. In particular, `BusinessBase<T>` relies on quite a number of other classes. For instance, `Csla.BusinessBase<T>` inherits from `Csla.Core.BusinessBase`, which inherits from `Csla.Core.UndoableBase`. It also makes use of the `ValidationRules` and `AuthorizationRules` classes, among others.

I'll start by describing the overall structure of the `Csla` project and then discuss each of the namespaces and the functionality each contains, with some extra emphasis on the `Csla` and `Csla.Core` namespaces. Most of the namespaces contain implementations of major CSLA .NET features that are covered in detail in subsequent chapters.

Obviously, there is a lot to cover, and this book will only include the critical code from each class. You'll want to download the code for the book at `www.apress.com/book/view/1430210192` or `www.lhotka.net/cslanet/download.aspx` so you can see each complete class or type as it is discussed.

CSLA .NET Project Structure

The current version of CSLA .NET requires the use of Visual Studio 2008 and the Microsoft .NET Framework version 3.5 SP1. Earlier versions of CSLA .NET exist that support Microsoft .NET 1.0 through 3.0 and are also available from the download website.

CSLA .NET is implemented as a Class Library project named `Csla`. This means it builds as a DLL, which can be referenced by your business application projects.

Project Directory Structure

To keep all the source files in the project orderly, the project's code is organized into a set of folders. Table 6-1 lists the folders in the project.

Table 6-1. *Folders in the CSLA Project*

Folder	Purpose
\	These are the types most commonly used by developers as they build business objects based on CSLA .NET.
\Core	These types are used by other framework classes and often extend the .NET Framework or enable extension of CSLA .NET.
\Data	These types provide functionality to simplify writing data access code.
\DataPortalClient	These types are part of the data portal functionality (see Chapter 15).
\Linq	These types are required by the LINQ to CSLA functionality.
\Reflection	These are a set of helper types that abstract the use of reflection.
\Security	These are the types that implement authorization and help implement custom authentication.
\Serialization	These are a set of helper types that abstract the serialization of objects.
\Server	These types implement the server-side data portal functionality (see Chapter 15).
\Silverlight	These types enable interaction with CSLA .NET for Silverlight.
\Validation	These are the types that implement the business and validation rules support for editable business objects.
\Web	These are types and controls used to assist in the creation of Web Forms user interfaces.
\Windows	These are types and controls used to assist in the creation of Windows Forms user interfaces.

Table 6-1. *Folders in the CSLA Project*

Folder	Purpose
\Workflow	These are types used to assist in the creation of Windows Workflow Foundation workflows.
\Wpf	These contain types and controls used to assist in the creation of WPF user interfaces.

By organizing the various files into folders and related namespaces, the project is far easier to understand. There's an additional Diagrams folder in the code download, containing many of the diagrams (or pieces of them at least) used to create the figures in this book.

Project Settings

The `Csla` project is a Class Library and it targets the .NET Framework 3.5 SP1. You can see these settings in Visual Studio by double-clicking the Properties node under the `Csla` project in Solution Explorer and looking at the Application tab as shown in Figure 6-1.

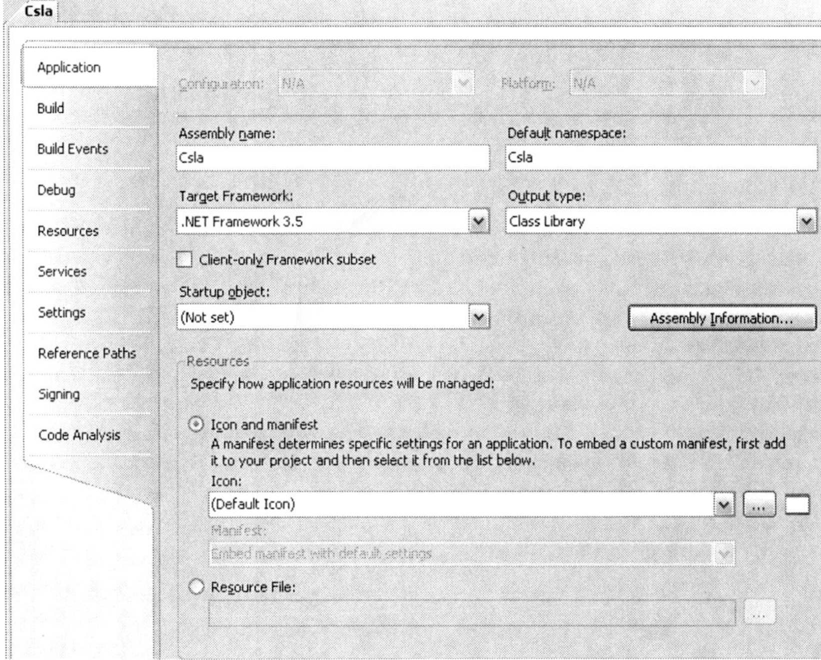

Figure 6-1. *Visual Studio Application tab*

You can also see the assembly information shown in Figure 6-2 by clicking the Assembly Information button.

Figure 6-2. *Assembly Information dialog*

■ **Note** The copyright information here must be preserved based on the license agreement. The license is available in the code download at `www.apress.com/book/view/1430210192` or `www.lhotka.net/cslanet/license.aspx`.

Project Signing

The `Csla.dll` file is a signed assembly. This means that the assembly has a strong name and so can be identified uniquely. This is required because CSLA .NET optionally can use Enterprise Services, which requires that assemblies be signed. Additionally, there are many scenarios where applications desire strongly named assemblies so they can ensure that they are really interacting with the assembly they referenced at development time.

Figure 6-3 shows the Signing tab in the project's properties window, where you can see that the `CslaKey.snk` file is being used to sign the assembly.

The `CslaKey.snk` file is included as a file in the project and contains a public/private key pair. The public key is available to any code consuming the assembly and can be used to ensure that the private key (which should be kept private) was used to sign the DLL.

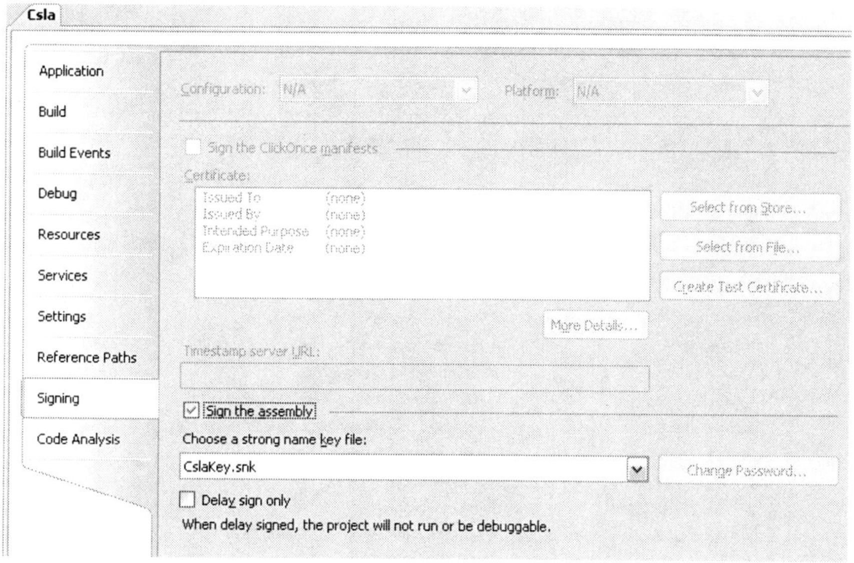

Figure 6-3. *Visual Studio Signing tab*

Normally, when you sign your assemblies you would want to protect your key file to ensure that the private key remains private. The CslaKey.snk file included in the download is there for convenience so you can easily build the project. You may wish to replace this with your own key file if you want your application to only use the Csla.dll assembly you built.

Supporting Localization

The CSLA .NET framework supports localization. For a framework, the key to supporting localization is to avoid using any string literal values that might be displayed to the end user. The .NET Framework and Visual Studio 2008 offer features to assist in this area through the use of resources.

To see the resource editor in Visual Studio, double-click the Properties node under the Csla project in Solution Explorer to bring up the project's properties window. Click the Resources tab to navigate to the built-in resource editor. Figure 6-4 shows this editor with several of the string resources from Resources.resx.

The complete set of resources is available in the Resources.resx file in the download. Additionally, a number of people around the world have been kind enough to translate the resources to various languages. As this is an ongoing process, refer to www.lhotka.net/cslanet/download.aspx for updates to the framework and resource files.

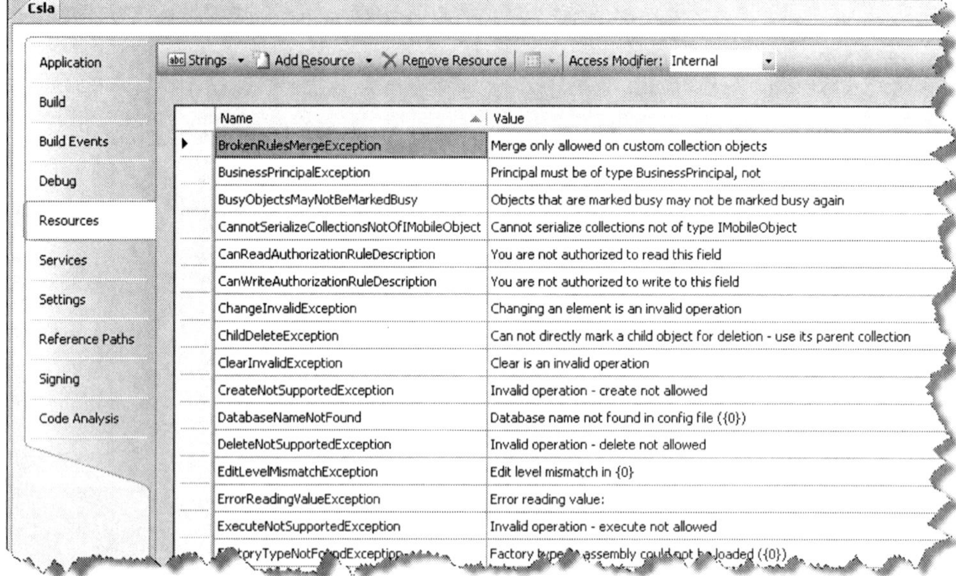

Figure 6-4. *Visual Studio resource editor*

Now that you understand the basic project structure, let's walk through each folder (and thus each namespace) in turn, so you have a high-level picture of the functionality contained in each one.

Csla Namespace

The `Csla` namespace contains the types that are most commonly used by business developers as they create business objects using CSLA .NET. The files in this namespace are in the top-level folder in the project: \.

The primary classes in this namespace are the base classes used to support the stereotypes discussed in Chapters 4 and 5. Figure 6-5 illustrates these classes.

As you can see, these base classes implement a great many interfaces. Some of the interfaces are standard .NET interfaces, such as `ICloneable`, but most of them are defined in the `Csla.Core` namespace and are part of CSLA .NET.

CSLA .NET is an *inheritance-based framework*, which means that the primary way developers use the framework is by inheriting from one of the framework's base classes. That is a powerful model because it allows a developer to tap into predefined functionality with very little effort. Much like inheriting from `Form` instantly gives you a fully functional window in Windows, inheriting from `BusinessBase` instantly gives you a fully functional business object that supports data binding, validation, authorization, and so forth.

However, inheritance is not terribly flexible. A class can only inherit from one thing, while it can implement many interfaces. So for the normal scenarios, the base classes are ideal, but for advanced scenarios such as building a UI framework on top of CSLA business objects, these interfaces are invaluable. I discuss these more in the section on the `Csla.Core` namespace later in the chapter.

Figure 6-5. *Primary classes in the Csla namespace*

Table 6-2 lists primary classes in the `Csla` namespace.

Table 6-2. *Primary Classes in the Csla Namespace*

Type	Description
`ApplicationContext`	Class that provides access to important application context information; used by the framework, business classes, and UI code
`BusinessBase`	Base class from which editable root, child, and switchable objects inherit
`BusinessListBase`	Base class from which editable root and child list objects inherit
`CommandBase`	Base class from which command objects inherit
`CriteriaBase`	Base class from which custom criteria objects inherit
`DataPortal`	Class that exposes the data portal functionality to the client
`EditableRootListBase`	Base class from which dynamic list objects inherit
`NameValueListBase`	Base class from which name/value list objects inherit
`PropertyInfo`	Class that defines metadata for each business object property
`ReadOnlyBase`	Base class from which read-only root and child objects inherit
`ReadOnlyListBase`	Base class from which read-only root and child list objects inherit
`SingleCriteria`	Class that provides a single value criteria for any object

Table 6-2. *Primary Classes in the Csla Namespace (Continued)*

Type	Description
SmartDate	Type that extends DateTime to add the concept of an empty date and other features
Utilities	Type that includes utility methods used by other classes

I'll discuss each of these types at a high level.

ApplicationContext

The ApplicationContext class is a central location from which application context information can be accessed. Some of this context comes from the application's configuration file, some from in-memory settings, and some from ambient environmental values in .NET.

Table 6-3 lists the context information available through ApplicationContext.

Table 6-3. *Context Data Contained Within ApplicationContext*

Context Data	Description
GlobalContext	Collection of context data that flows from client to server and then from server back to client; changes on either end are carried across the network
ClientContext	Collection of context data that flows from client to server; changes on the server are *not* carried back to the client
LocalContext	Collection of context data that exists only in the current location (client or server)
User	Current .NET security (principal) object; safely accesses this value independent of runtime (ASP.NET, WPF, etc.)
AuthenticationType	Authentication setting from CslaAuthentication config value
DataPortalProxy	Data portal proxy provider setting from CslaDataPortalProxy config value
DataPortalUrl	Data portal URL value for Remoting proxy from CslaDataPortalUrl config value
IsInRoleProvider	IsInRole provider type name from CslaIsInRoleProvider config value
AutoCloneOnUpdate	Setting indicating whether objects are cloned before update through local data portal, setting from CslaAutoCloneOnUpdate config value
SerializationFormatter	Serialization provider type name from CslaSerializationFormatter config value
PropertyChangedMode	Setting indicating how the PropertyChanged event should be raised (different for Windows Forms or WPF), setting from CslaPropertyChangedMode config value
ExecutionLocation	Value indicting whether the code is currently executing on the client or server side of the data portal

These context values can be grouped into three areas: configuration settings, ambient values, and context dictionaries.

Configuration Settings

The configuration settings include items read from the config file. This is done using the standard .NET `System.Configuration.ConfigurationManager` class. In this case `ApplicationContext` is simply wrapping existing functionality to provide a more abstract way to access the config values.

Ambient Values

The ambient values include the `User` and `ExecutionLocation` properties. Each one is different and is worth discussing.

User Property

When code is running outside ASP.NET, it relies on `System.Threading.Thread.CurrentPrincipal` to maintain the user's principal object. On the other hand, when code is running inside ASP.NET, the only reliable way to find the user's principal object is through `HttpContext.Current.User`. Normally, this would mean that you would have to write code to detect whether `HttpContext.Current` is `null`, and only use `System.Threading` if `HttpContext` isn't available. The `User` property automates this process on your behalf:

```
public static IPrincipal User
{
  get
  {
    if (HttpContext.Current == null)
      return Thread.CurrentPrincipal;
    else
      return HttpContext.Current.User;
  }
  set
  {
    if (HttpContext.Current != null)
      HttpContext.Current.User = value;
    Thread.CurrentPrincipal = value;
  }
}
```

In general, `Csla.ApplicationContext.User` should be used in favor of either `System.Threading` or `HttpContext` directly because it automatically adjusts to the environment in which your code is running. With CSLA .NET–based applications, this is particularly important because your client code could be a Windows Forms application but your server code could be running within ASP.NET. Remember that your business objects run in *both locations* and so must behave properly both inside and outside ASP.NET.

ExecutionLocation Property

The `ExecutionLocation` property can be used by business code to determine whether it is currently executing on the client or on the server. This is particularly useful when writing data access code because that code could run on either the client or the server, depending on whether the channel adapter uses `LocalProxy` or one of the remote proxies. Remember that `LocalProxy` is designed such that the "server-side" code runs on the client.

The property value is of type ExecutionLocations, defined by the following enumerated type:

```
public enum ExecutionLocations
{
  Client,
  Server
}
```

The ExecutionLocation value is global to both the client and server, so it is stored in a static field. This is shared by all threads on the server, but that's OK because it will always return the Server value when on the server, and Client when on the client:

```
private static ExecutionLocations _executionLocation =
  ExecutionLocations.Client;

public static ExecutionLocations ExecutionLocation
{
  get { return _executionLocation; }
}
```

The value defaults to Client. This is fine, as it should only be set to Server in the case that the Csla.Server.DataPortal class explicitly sets it to Server. Recall that in that DataPortal class there's a SetContext() method that only runs when the server-side components really are running on the server. In that case, it calls the SetExecutionLocation() method on ApplicationContext:

```
internal static void SetExecutionLocation(ExecutionLocations location)
{
  _executionLocation = location;
}
```

This way, the value is set to Server only when the code is known to physically be executing in a separate AppDomain, process, and probably computer from the client.

Context Dictionaries

Finally, let's discuss the three context dictionaries: LocalContext, ClientContext, and GlobalContext. On the surface, it seems like maintaining a set of globally available information is easy—just use a static field and be done with it. Unfortunately, things are quite a bit more complex when building a framework that must operate in a multithreaded server environment.

CSLA .NET supports client/server architectures through the data portal. The server-side components of the data portal may run in ASP.NET on an IIS server or within the Windows Activation Service (WAS) under Windows Server 2008.

In these cases, the server may be supporting many clients at the same time. All the client requests are handled by the *same Windows process* and by the *same .NET* AppDomain. It turns out that static fields exist at the AppDomain level: meaning that a given static field is shared across all threads in an AppDomain. This is problematic because multiple client requests are handled within the *same* AppDomain but on different threads. So static fields aren't the answer.

The solution is different in ASP.NET and in any other .NET code. Either way, the .NET Framework illustrates the right answer. Look at CurrentPrincipal; it is associated with the current Thread object, which provides an answer for any code running outside of ASP.NET. Within ASP.NET, there's the HttpContext object, which is automatically maintained by ASP.NET itself.

So, when outside ASP.NET, the answer is to associate the context data directly with the current Thread object, and when inside ASP.NET, the context data can be stored using the HttpContext.

Let's discuss the Thread option first. While the .NET Thread object already has a property for CurrentPrincipal, it doesn't have a property for the concept of LocalContext. But it does have a concept called *named slots*. Every Thread object has a collection associated with it. Each entry in this collection is referred to as a *slot*. Slots can be referred to by a key, or a *name*—hence the term *named slot*. The GetNameDataSlot() method on the Thread object returns access to a specific slot as an object of type LocalDataStoreSlot. You can then use the Thread object's GetData() and SetData() methods to get and set data in that slot.

While this is a bit more complex than dealing with a conventional collection, you can think of named slots as being like a collection of arbitrary values associated with a Thread object.

When running in ASP.NET, things are a bit simpler because HttpContext has an Items collection. This is a dictionary of name/value pairs that is automatically maintained by ASP.NET and is available to your code. Within ASP.NET, this is the only safe place to put shared data such as context data because ASP.NET may switch your code to run on different threads in certain advanced scenarios. This gets interesting when the application needs to know if it is running under ASP.NET or some other environment so it can store the values in the right location. When running under ASP.NET, thread-local storage isn't safe and HttpContext must be used. When running outside of ASP.NET, HttpContext isn't even available and thread-local storage is the right answer.

The reason thread-local storage isn't safe under ASP.NET is that under some circumstances with custom HttpModule types, ASP.NET may change the thread on which your code is executing. If that happens, any values attached to thread-local storage will be lost (because they are on the old thread, not the one your code is switched to by ASP.NET). So in ASP.NET, the HttpContext is the only safe location to store context values.

■ **Note** The context dictionaries I discuss here do not replace Session in ASP.NET. These context values are only available for the lifetime of a single server call. If you want to store values across pages or server calls, you should use Session.

I'll use the ClientContext to illustrate the solution. The context dictionary will be stored in either HttpContext or thread-local storage, based on the environment within which the code is running. And because this code may run in a multithreaded environment, it must employ locking to ensure thread safety.

First, there's the public property that exposes the value:

```
private static object _syncClientContext = new object();
private const string _clientContextName = "Csla.ClientContext";

public static ContextDictionary ClientContext
{
  get
  {
    lock (_syncClientContext)
    {
      ContextDictionary ctx = GetClientContext();
      if (ctx == null)
      {
        ctx = new ContextDictionary();
        SetClientContext(ctx);
      }
      return ctx;
    }
  }
}
```

When ClientContext is accessed, a lock is used to ensure thread safety. Within that lock, the GetClientContext() method is called to retrieve the context dictionary from its storage location:

```
internal static ContextDictionary GetClientContext()
{
  if (HttpContext.Current == null)
  {
    if (ApplicationContext.ExecutionLocation == ExecutionLocations.Client)
      lock (_syncClientContext)
        return (ContextDictionary)
          AppDomain.CurrentDomain.GetData(_clientContextName);
    else
    {
      LocalDataStoreSlot slot =
        Thread.GetNamedDataSlot(_clientContextName);
      return (ContextDictionary)Thread.GetData(slot);
    }
  }
  else
    return (ContextDictionary)
      HttpContext.Current.Items[_clientContextName];
}
```

This method detects whether the code is running in ASP.NET and retrieves the dictionary from HttpContext or thread-local storage as appropriate.

If the dictionary does not yet exist, it is created, then stored using the SetClientContext() method:

```
private static void SetClientContext(ContextDictionary clientContext)
{
  if (HttpContext.Current == null)
  {
    if (ApplicationContext.ExecutionLocation == ExecutionLocations.Client)
      lock (_syncClientContext)
        AppDomain.CurrentDomain.SetData(
          _clientContextName, clientContext);
    else
    {
      LocalDataStoreSlot slot =
        Thread.GetNamedDataSlot(_clientContextName);
      Thread.SetData(slot, clientContext);
    }
  }
  else
    HttpContext.Current.Items[_clientContextName] = clientContext;
}
```

This method works much the same way, checking to see if the code is running in ASP.NET and storing the value in the correct location.

Notice that both of these methods use `internal` scope. This is because they are invoked not only from the `LocalContext` property but also from the data portal. The `ClientContext` and `GlobalContext` values flow to and from the client and server through the data portal. Chapter 15 provides more details about the data portal.

At this point you should have an understanding about how the `ApplicationContext` class provides access to application context values to the rest of the application.

BusinessBase

The `BusinessBase<T>` class exposes most of the functionality for a single editable object and combines support for data binding, validation rules, authorization rules, and n-level undo. I discuss each of these feature areas in Chapters 7 through 16.

Like all base classes, this class must be `Serializable` and `abstract`. Much of its behavior flows from its base classes, or from other objects it contains. Here is the declaration of the class:

```
namespace Csla
{
  [Serializable]
  public abstract class BusinessBase<T> :
    Core.BusinessBase, Core.ISavable where T : BusinessBase<T>
```

The generic type `T` is constrained to be the type of business object being created, so a business class is declared like this:

```
[Serializable]
public class CustomerEdit : BusinessBase<CustomerEdit>
{
}
```

The `BusinessBase<T>` class inherits from `Csla.Core.BusinessBase`, where most of the implementation resides. The reason for this is that `BusinessBase<T>` is generic and thus doesn't support polymorphism. The `BusinessBase` base class is not generic and so provides a common base class for all editable objects that is polymorphic:

```
  [Serializable]
  public abstract class BusinessBase :
    Csla.Core.UndoableBase, IEditableBusinessObject,
    System.ComponentModel.IEditableObject,
    System.ComponentModel.IDataErrorInfo,
    ICloneable, Csla.Security.IAuthorizeReadWrite,
    IParent, Server.IDataPortalTarget,
    IManageProperties
```

As you can see, `BusinessBase` inherits from `UndoableBase` and then implements a lot of different interfaces. Some of these are standard .NET interfaces to support things such as data binding, while others are defined by CSLA .NET and are used within the framework itself or as extensibility points for users of the framework.

This class pulls together a lot of functionality. The goal is to abstract all this functionality into a set of easily understood behaviors that simplify the creation of business objects. Table 6-4 lists the functional areas.

Table 6-4. *Functional Areas Implemented in BusinessBase*

Functional Area	Description
Data binding	Provides support for Windows Forms, WPF, and Web Forms data binding against editable business objects
Business rules	Provide abstract access to the business and validation rules behavior and implement the `IDataErrorInfo` interface
Authorization rules	Provide abstract access to the authorization rules behavior
Object status tracking	Keeps track of whether the object is new, old, dirty, clean, or marked for deletion
Root, parent, and child behaviors	Implement behaviors so the object can function as a root object, a parent object, or a child of another object or collection
N-level undo	Provides access to the underlying n-level undo functionality implemented in `UndoableBase` and implements the `IEditableObject` interface
Cloning	Implements the `ICloneable` interface
Persistence	Provides access to the data portal and supports necessary data portal interaction for object persistence

Figure 6-6 shows the inheritance hierarchy of `BusinessBase<T>`, illustrating the base classes that work together to provide some of this functionality.

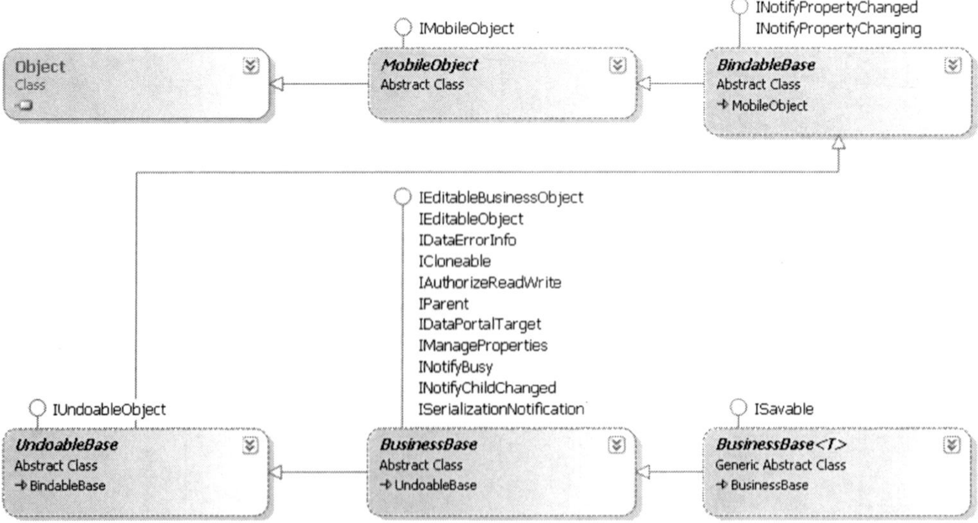

Figure 6-6. *Inheritance hierarchy for BusinessBase<T>*

These base classes are covered in Chapters 7 through 14 as each functional area is discussed.

■ **Note** `MobileObject` exists to support serialization through the `MobileFormatter`, which is part of CSLA .NET for Silverlight. CSLA .NET for Silverlight is outside the scope of this book, and `MobileObject` has no impact on how CSLA .NET works within the .NET runtime.

`BusinessBase<T>` also contains objects that it relies on to implement various behaviors, as illustrated in Figure 6-7.

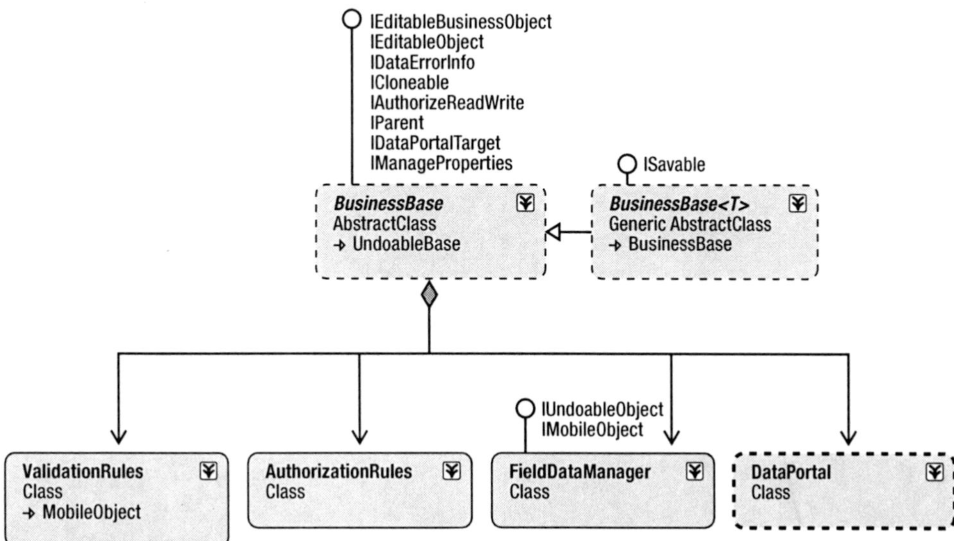

Figure 6-7. *Objects contained by BusinessBase<T>*

By combining inheritance, containment, and collaboration, `BusinessBase<T>` consolidates a great deal of functionality without becoming overly complex itself.

Editable objects are perhaps the most common business object used in most applications, and `BusinessBase<T>` combines a great deal of functionality. Because of this, the majority of Chapters 7 through 14 provide detail around this class and its behaviors.

BusinessListBase

The `BusinessListBase<T, C>` class provides the functionality to support editable root and child collections. It works closely with `BusinessBase<T>` to support data binding, parent-child relationships, n-level undo, and object persistence.

The class is `Serializable` and `abstract`:

```
namespace Csla
{
  [Serializable]
  public abstract class BusinessListBase<T, C> :
      Core.ExtendedBindingList<C>,
      Core.IEditableCollection, Core.IUndoableObject, ICloneable,
      Core.ISavable, Core.IParent, Server.IDataPortalTarget,
      IQueryable<C>, Linq.IIndexSearchable<C>, Core.IPositionMappable<C>
    where T : BusinessListBase<T, C>
    where C : Core.IEditableBusinessObject
```

Like `BusinessBase`, `BusinessListBase` inherits from a base class and implements quite a number of interfaces. It also collaborates with other framework objects to implement the behaviors listed in Table 6-4.

Figure 6-8 shows the inheritance hierarchy of `BusinessListBase`:

Figure 6-8. *Inheritance hierarchy for BusinessListBase<T>*

■ **Note** `MobileList<T>` exists to support serialization through the `MobileFormatter`, which is part of CSLA .NET for Silverlight. CSLA .NET for Silverlight is outside the scope of this book, and `MobileList<T>` has no impact on how CSLA .NET works within the .NET runtime.

Ultimately, the `BusinessListBase` inherits from `BindingList<T>` in the `System.ComponentModel` namespace. This is the .NET base class that provides support for collections that support data binding in Windows Forms and WPF.

■ **Note** WPF does include `ObservableCollection<T>` as a base class to support data binding. While that base class is useful in WPF, it is not recognized by Windows Forms or Web Forms data binding. Fortunately, `BindingList<T>` is recognized by all current UI technologies, including WPF, so is the best choice for any collection that needs to support any UI.

`ExtendedBindingList<T>` extends `BindingList<T>` by adding a `RemovingItem` event and an `AddRange()` method to all collections.

Editable collections are very common in most business applications. Chapters 7 through 14 expand on the implementation of the various features supported by `BusinessListBase`.

CommandBase

The `CommandBase` class supports the creation of command objects. As discussed in Chapter 5, command objects allow you to write code that runs on the client, the application server, and again on the client. This is the simplest of the base classes because all it needs to do is provide basic support for use of the data portal.

The class is defined like this:

```
[Serializable]
public abstract class CommandBase : Core.MobileObject,
  Core.ICommandObject, Server.IDataPortalTarget
```

As with all base classes, it is `Serializable` and `abstract`. It implements several interfaces, most notably `IDataPortalTarget` so the data portal can interact with the object as needed.

■ **Note** `MobileObject` exists to support serialization through the `MobileFormatter`, which is part of CSLA .NET for Silverlight. CSLA .NET for Silverlight is outside the scope of this book, and `MobileObject` has no impact on how CSLA .NET works within the .NET runtime.

Chapter 15 provides detail about how the data portal interacts with command objects.

CriteriaBase

The `CriteriaBase` class supports the creation of custom criteria objects as described in Chapter 5. Custom criteria classes must implement the `ICriteria` interface, and `CriteriaBase` merely simplifies that process. The `ICriteria` interface ensures that a custom criteria object can provide the data portal with the `Type` object representing the type of business object to be created, retrieved, or deleted.

`SingleCriteria` is a subclass of `CriteriaBase`. I discuss it later in this chapter.

The `Criteria` class is defined like this:

```
[Serializable]
public class CriteriaBase : Csla.Core.MobileObject, ICriteria
```

■ **Note** `MobileObject` exists to support serialization through the `MobileFormatter`, which is part of CSLA .NET for Silverlight. CSLA .NET for Silverlight is outside the scope of this book, and `MobileObject` has no impact on how CSLA .NET works within the .NET runtime.

The primary job of CriteriaBase is to provide a default implementation of ICriteria, making it easy to create a custom criteria class by simply subclassing CriteriaBase:

```
[Serializable]
public class MyCriteria : CriteriaBase
{
  public string Value1 { get; set; }
  public string Value2 { get; set; }

  public MyCriteria(string value1, string value2)
    : base(typeof(MyBusinessClass))
  {
    this.Value1 = value1;
    this.Value2 = value2;
  }
}
```

The highlighted line of code indicates the key point of interaction between this subclass and the base class. The CriteriaBase class needs to know the type of business object being created, retrieved, or deleted. It gets this Type object as a parameter to its constructor, and that value is typically provided directly by the subclass.

DataPortal

The data portal is covered in Chapter 15. One part of the data portal is the DataPortal classes in the Csla namespace. There are two classes: DataPortal and DataPortal<T>.

The DataPortal class is a static class, and it exposes a set of public methods that can be used for synchronous interaction with the data portal. It is declared like this:

```
public static class DataPortal
```

The most common way to use the data portal is through these synchronous static methods, and most business classes use the DataPortal class.

In WPF you can use the CslaDataProvider control from the Csla.Wpf namespace to asynchronously retrieve business objects. In other types of application, such as Windows Forms, you can use the .NET BackgroundWorker component to do the same thing, but that requires extra work on the part of the UI developer.

To minimize that effort, you can use the DataPortal<T> class, which provides asynchronous access to the data portal. This class is defined like this:

```
public class DataPortal<T>
```

Notice that this is not a static class, and in fact you must create an instance of the class to call its methods.

The data portal is a large and relatively complex part of CSLA .NET and is covered in Chapter 15.

EditableRootListBase

The EditableRootListBase class supports the creation of dynamic collections. As discussed in Chapter 5, these collections are designed specifically to support in-place editing of data in a Windows Forms DataGrid-style interface, where changes to each row of data should be saved immediately as the user moves off that row.

This base class exists primarily to support data binding and to abstract the interaction with the editable root objects it contains. It is declared like this:

```
[Serializable]
public abstract class EditableRootListBase<T> :
  Core.ExtendedBindingList<T>, Core.IParent, Server.IDataPortalTarget
  where T : Core.IEditableBusinessObject, Core.IUndoableObject, Core.ISavable
```

Like `BusinessListBase`, this class inherits from `ExtendedBindingList` and thus `BindingList<T>`. It gains support for data binding in WPF and Windows Forms from `BindingList<T>`. You can get an idea of the inheritance hierarchy for this class by looking at Figure 6-8.

It also implements numerous interfaces, enabling it to act as a parent object, interact with the data portal, and so forth. Chapters 7 through 14 detail the implementation of the various major subsystems used by `EditableRootListBase`.

NameValueListBase

The `NameValueListBase` class supports a specific type of read-only collection, where the items in the collection are simple name/value pairs. The class is defined like this:

```
[Serializable]
public abstract class NameValueListBase<K, V> :
  Core.ReadOnlyBindingList<NameValueListBase<K, V>.NameValuePair>,
  ICloneable, Core.IBusinessObject, Server.IDataPortalTarget
```

Notice how there are two type parameters: `K` and `V`. These are used to specify the types of the key and value elements in each item contained in the collection.

Also notice that the collection inherits from `ReadOnlyBindingList` in the `Csla.Core` namespace. Figure 6-9 illustrates the inheritance hierarchy for `NameValueListBase`.

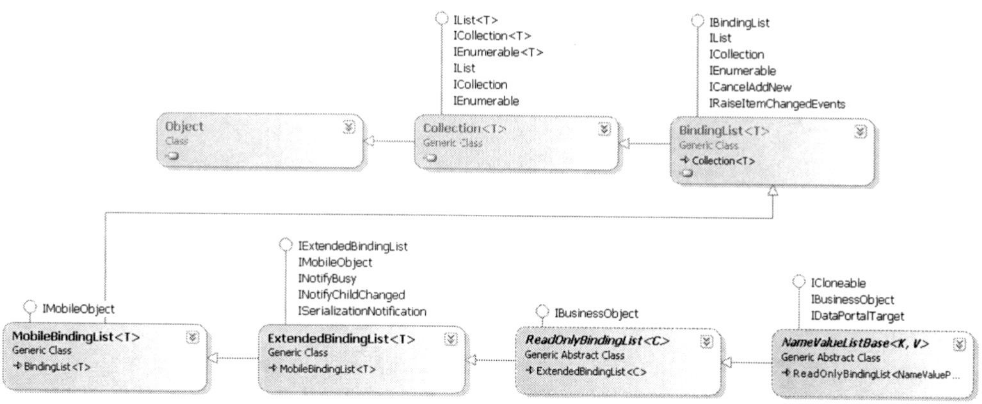

Figure 6-9. *Inheritance hierarchy for NameValueListBase<K, V>*

The `ReadOnlyBindingList` class extends `BindingList<T>`, adding the ability to have a read-only collection that fully supports data binding in WPF, Windows Forms, and Web Forms.

■ **Note** `MobileList<T>` exists to support serialization through the `MobileFormatter`, which is part of CSLA .NET for Silverlight. CSLA .NET for Silverlight is outside the scope of this book, and `MobileList<T>` has no impact on how CSLA .NET works within the .NET runtime.

The most interesting thing about NameValueListBase is that it contains a nested class called NameValuePair. NameValuePair is a simple class that exposes Key and Value properties, of types K and V respectively. It is declared like this:

```
[Serializable]
public class NameValuePair
```

This class uses a clever side effect of generics, because while NameValuePair itself isn't generic, it is able to use the generic type parameters of NameValueListBase because it is a nested class.

Combined, NameValueListBase and NameValuePair make it very easy to create read-only name/value collections that support data binding. These collections are often used to populate combo box or list controls and to implement validation logic where a value is required to exist in a list of known values.

PropertyInfo

The PropertyInfo<T> class supports the storage of metadata about the properties declared in a business class. When you declare a normal property in a business class it looks something like this:

```
public string Name
{
  get { return _name; }
  set { _name = value; }
}
```

In an editable business object, you'll typically also need to have the property check authorization, run business rules, and do other work. To help simplify this process, CSLA .NET allows you to declare the property using GetProperty() and SetProperty() helper methods:

```
public string Name
{
  get { return GetProperty("Name"); }
  set { SetProperty("Name", _value) }
}
```

The problem with this code is that the GetProperty() and SetProperty() methods need to know what property is being accessed or set so the correct authorization and business rules can be applied. Passing the property name in as a string literal is a maintenance issue. If someone refactors the property name to something like FirstName, the string literals won't be automatically updated. In fact, a detailed manual search through a lot of code might be required to find all the places where that string literal is used.

PropertyInfo objects help consolidate this string literal into one location, where the PropertyInfo object is created. Throughout CSLA .NET, any place where a property name is required, you can provide a PropertyInfo object instead:

```
private static PropertyInfo<string> NameProperty =
  RegisterProperty(new PropertyInfo<string>("Name"));
public string Name
{
  get { return GetProperty(NameProperty); }
  set { SetProperty(NameProperty, _value) }
}
```

Unfortunately, there's no way to entirely eliminate the string literal, but this technique allows the literal value to exist exactly one time in your entire class, minimizing the maintenance issue.

■ **Note** This technique is very similar to the DependencyProperty concept used by WPF and WF.

The PropertyInfo class is declared like this:

```
public class PropertyInfo<T> : Core.IPropertyInfo, IComparable
```

Notice that it implements an IPropertyInfo interface from the Csla.Core namespace. Technically, CSLA .NET accepts IPropertyInfo parameters everywhere, and this PropertyInfo class is just one possible implementation. This is an intentional extensibility point for CSLA .NET, allowing you to create other IPropertyInfo implementations (or subclasses of PropertyInfo) that store other metadata about each property.

One scenario where you might do this is if you want to store data access metadata, such as the database, table, and column name where the property value is stored.

ReadOnlyBase

The BusinessBase and BusinessListBase classes provide the tools needed to build editable objects and collections. However, most applications also include a number of read-only objects and collections. An application might have a read-only object that contains system configuration data, or a read-only collection of ProductType objects that are used just for lookup purposes.

The ReadOnlyBase class provides a base on which business developers can build read-only root and child objects. By definition, a read-only object is quite simple: it's just a container for data, possibly with authorization or formatting logic to control how that data is accessed. It doesn't support editing of the data, so there's no need for n-level undo, change events, or much of the other complexity built into BusinessBase.

ReadOnlyBase supports read-only properties, authorization, and persistence.

Like all base classes, this one is Serializable and abstract. It also implements Csla.Core.IBusinessObject to provide some level of polymorphic behavior even though this is a generic class:

```
[Serializable]
public abstract class ReadOnlyBase<T> : Core.MobileObject,
  ICloneable, Core.IReadOnlyObject,
  Csla.Security.IAuthorizeReadWrite, Server.IDataPortalTarget,
  Core.IManageProperties
  where T : ReadOnlyBase<T>
```

Like BusinessBase, the generic type T is constrained to be the type of business object being created, so a business class is declared like this:

```
[Serializable]
public class DefaultCustomerData : ReadOnlyBase<DefaultCustomerData>
{
}
```

Presumably, any business object based on this class would consist entirely of read-only properties or methods that just return values. ReadOnlyBase supports data binding, authorization, and persistence. Figure 6-10 illustrates the inheritance hierarchy for ReadOnlyBase.

■ **Note** MobileObject exists to support serialization through the MobileFormatter, which is part of CSLA .NET for Silverlight. CSLA .NET for Silverlight is outside the scope of this book, and MobileObject has no impact on how CSLA .NET works within the .NET runtime.

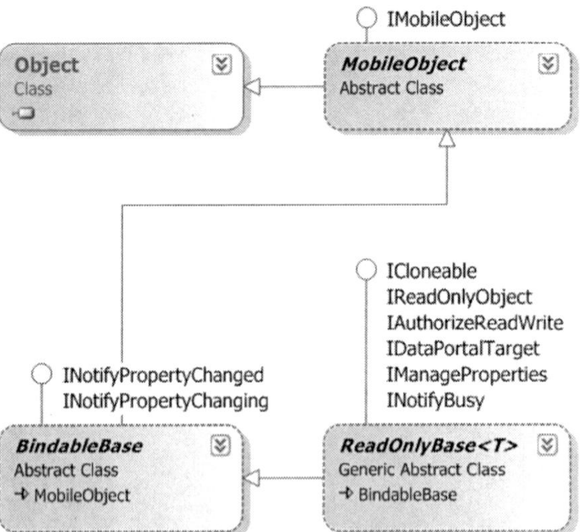

Figure 6-10. *Inheritance hierarchy for ReadOnlyBase<T>*

Because `ReadOnlyBase` provides such little functionality, it doesn't need a complex base class. It contains an `AuthorizationRules` object like `BusinessBase` and interacts with the `DataPortal` class, but otherwise it doesn't need most of the advanced features of CSLA .NET required by `BusinessBase`.

Read-only objects are common in most business applications, and the features supported by `ReadOnlyBase` are fully explored in Chapters 7 through 14.

ReadOnlyListBase

Like the `ReadOnlyBase` class, `ReadOnlyListBase` is quite simple. It is designed to make it easy for a business developer to create a business collection that doesn't allow items to be added or removed. Presumably, it will be used to contain read-only child objects, but any type of child object is allowed. Read-only collections do support data binding, authorization, and persistence.

The `ReadOnlyListBase` class is defined like this:

```
[Serializable]
public abstract class ReadOnlyListBase<T, C> :
  Core.ReadOnlyBindingList<C>, Csla.Core.IReadOnlyCollection,
  ICloneable, Server.IDataPortalTarget
  where T : ReadOnlyListBase<T, C>
```

Like `BusinessListBase`, it accepts two generic type parameters. Type `T` is constrained to be a subclass of this base class and refers to the type of the collection being created. Type `C` is the type of the child object to be contained within the collection, and it can be any type. Again, it would make the most sense for the child type to be some form of read-only object, but that's not required by the collection class. A business collection would be declared like this:

```
[Serializable]
public class CustomerList : Csla.ReadOnlyListBase<CustomerList, CustomerInfo>
{
}
```

This indicates that the collection contains child objects of type `CustomerInfo`.

Like NameValueListBase, this class inherits from ReadOnlyBindingList in the Csla.Core namespace. Look at Figure 6-9 to see how the inheritance hierarchy works for this class.

Read-only collections are very common in most business applications, and ReadOnlyListBase supports the root and child collection stereotypes discussed in Chapter 5.

SingleCriteria

The SingleCriteria<B, C> class is a subclass of CriteriaBase and provides an implementation of the most common criteria class, where a business object can be identified by a single criteria value.

The SingleCriteria class is defined like this:

```
[Serializable()]
public class SingleCriteria<B, C> : CriteriaBase
```

The B type parameter is the type of business object to create, retrieve, or delete. The C type parameter is the type of the criteria value being passed through the data portal.

Of course the interesting part about inheriting from CriteriaBase is that it requires the type of business object to be retrieved, so the constructor in SingleCriteria uses the B type parameter:

```
public SingleCriteria(C value)
  : base(typeof(B))
{
  _value = value;
}
```

The end result is that most business objects can be created, retrieved, or deleted using SingleCriteria by writing code like this:

```
return DataPortal.Fetch<CustomerEdit>(new SingleCriteria<CustomerEdit, int>(id));
```

If you need more extensive criteria objects, you can create your own subclasses of CriteriaBase, as discussed in Chapter 5.

SmartDate

The SmartDate type is a struct that contains and extends a DateTime value. It is discussed in Chapter 2 from a design perspective. The type is declared like this:

```
[Serializable]
[System.ComponentModel.TypeConverter(
    typeof(Csla.Core.TypeConverters.SmartDateConverter))]
public struct SmartDate : Csla.Core.ISmartField,
  IComparable, IConvertible, IFormattable,
  Csla.Serialization.Mobile.IMobileObject
```

■ **Note** The IMobileObject interface exists to support serialization through the MobileFormatter, which is part of CSLA .NET for Silverlight. CSLA .NET for Silverlight is outside the scope of this book, and IMobileObject has no impact on how CSLA .NET works within the .NET runtime.

Not only is this type Serializable but it has a custom type converter, specified by the TypeConverter attribute. In fact, SmartDate is a very complex type because it implements operators, type converters, and various other .NET features to act as closely as possible to the DateTime type.

Note The ISmartField interface, defined in Csla.Core, is used to allow the rest of the CSLA .NET framework to interact with any "smart" data types such as this that add string parsing and the concept of being "empty" to a type. You can implement ISmartField to create your own "smart" types such as SmartInt or SmartDouble, but be aware that your type will also need to override many operators and provide type converters much like SmartDate in order to act as a first-class type in .NET.

The implementation of SmartDate is covered in more detail in Chapter 16.

Utilities

The Utilities class contains utility methods that are used by other parts of the CSLA .NET framework. Many of these methods abstract the use of the .NET type system and reflection. Table 6-5 lists the methods in this class.

Table 6-5. *Public Methods in the Utilities Class*

Method	Description
IsNumeric	Provides functionality comparable to the VB runtime IsNumeric() function; determines whether a value can be converted to a number
CallByName	Provides functionality comparable to the VB runtime CallByName() function; calls a property or method by name, using reflection
GetPropertyType	Gets the type returned by a property, returning the primitive type even if the value is Nullable<T>
GetChildItemType	Gets the type of the items contained in a list or collection
CoerceValue	Coerces a value from one type into another type; somewhat like doing a cast but far more aggressive and powerful

While these methods exist primarily to support the CSLA .NET framework itself, they are public and can be used by business or UI code as well. In particular, IsNumeric(), CallByName(), and CoerceValue() can be useful in many scenarios.

The Csla namespace includes other types beyond those discussed in this chapter. The classes discussed here, and all the rest of the classes, exist to support important features such as data binding, business and validation rules, authorization rules, the data portal, LINQ to CSLA, and so forth. As I discuss each subsystem in Chapters 7 through 14, you'll get a full understanding of all the types.

Csla.Core Namespace

The Csla.Core namespace contains types that are not intended for daily use by business developers. Rather, these types are intended for use by the CSLA .NET framework itself and to enable advanced scenarios such as extending or customizing CSLA .NET. This is a primary motivation for putting them into their own namespace—to help keep them out of sight of business developers during normal development.

One primary use for the types in `Csla.Core` is to allow people to extend the framework. For instance, `Core.BusinessBase` could easily act as a starting point for creating some different or more advanced `BusinessBase`-style class. Likewise, `Core.ReadOnlyBindingList` is useful as a base for creating any type of read-only collection that supports data binding.

There are also numerous interfaces in `Csla.Core`, which are very useful if you are building a UI framework that interacts with business objects. The base classes exposed by CSLA .NET are generic types, such as `BusinessBase<T>`. While generics are a powerful tool, they have a major drawback in that generic types are not polymorphic. For example, a `List<string>` and `List<int>` are two different types that *do not* inherit from `List<T>`. In fact, their common base type is `IList`, which is *not* a generic type.

The same thing is true for `BusinessBase<Customer>` and `BusinessBase<Product>`. If you want to write code that can work with either type, you need to fall back to `Csla.Core.BusinessBase`, which is not a generic type. But if you want more focused behavior, such as the ability to save any editable object, you'd want to use the `Csla.Core.ISavable` interface. That interface is implemented by both `BusinessBase` and `BusinessListBase` because both support editable objects that can be saved. Table 6-6 lists the most commonly used classes and interfaces in `Csla.Core`.

Table 6-6. *Commonly Used Classes and Interfaces in Csla.Core*

Interface	Purpose
`BusinessBase`	Used to create code that can interact with any editable root or child object; base class for `BusinessBase<T>`
`ExtendedBindingList`	Used to add a `RemovingItem` event and an `AddRange()` method to `BindingList<T>`; base class for most collection types
`IBusinessObject`	Implemented by all base classes to provide one common type for all business objects
`ISavable`	Implemented by all editable base classes; used to create code that can polymorphically save any editable object
`ISmartField`	Implemented by all "smart" types such as `SmartDate`; can be used to create other "smart" types such as `SmartInt`, `SmartDouble`, etc.
`ISupportUndo`	Implemented by all undoable base classes; used to create UI frameworks that polymorphically implement form-level cancel buttons
`ITrackStatus`	Implemented by base classes that maintain object status such as `IsDirty`, `IsValid`, etc.; used to write code that polymorphically monitors or reacts to business object status
`ObjectCloner`	Contains code to clone any object decorated with the `Serializable` attribute (or `DataContract` attribute if CSLA is configured to use WCF serialization)
`ReadOnlyBindingList`	Can be used as a base class to create your own read-only collections that support data binding; base class for all read-only collection types

There are many more types in the `Csla.Core` namespace, but they are designed for internal use by CSLA .NET and are not intended for use by code outside the framework. However, several of these types are important to understanding the structure of other framework classes, and so I'll walk through them.

BusinessBase

Earlier in the chapter I discuss `BusinessBase<T>` and its base class, `BusinessBase`. The `BusinessBase` class is the non-generic base class for all editable root and child objects.

ExtendedBindingList

Most collection types in CSLA .NET inherit from `ExtendedBindingList`, including `BusinessListBase`, `ReadOnlyBindingList`, and `ReadOnlyListBase`.

`ExtendedBindingList` extends the `BindingList<T>` class from the `System.ComponentModel` namespace by adding a `RemovingItem` event and an `AddRange()` method.

The `BindingList<T>` already raises a `ListChanged` event, but that occurs after an item has been removed from the collection and doesn't provide a reference to the item that is removed. The new `RemovingItem` event occurs while the item is being removed from the list and provides a reference to the item that is being removed.

The `AddRange()` method allows you to add a range of items to the collection. It accepts an `IEnumerable<T>` and adds the items in that list to the end of the collection. This method can be used to merge two collections or to add more data to a collection over time.

Finally, `ExtendedBindingList` implements the `IsSelfBusy` and `IsBusy` properties and other functionality that is required for asynchronous object persistence, as I discuss in Chapter 15.

IBusinessObject Interface

Generic types such as `BindingList<T>` are very powerful because they allow a developer to easily create a strongly typed instance of the generic type. The following defines a strongly typed collection of type `string`:

```
BindingList<string> myStringList;
```

Similarly, the following defines a strongly typed collection of type `int`:

```
BindingList<int> myIntList;
```

Since both `myStringList` and `myIntList` are "of type" `BindingList<T>`, you might think they are polymorphic—that you could write one method that could act on both fields. But you can't. Generic types are *not* inherited and thus do not come from the same type. This is highly counterintuitive at first glance but nonetheless is a fact of life when working with generic types.

Since CSLA .NET makes use of generic types (`BusinessBase<T>`, `BusinessListBase<T,C>`, etc.), this is a problem. There are cases in which a UI developer will want to treat all business objects the same—or at least be able to use the .NET type system to determine whether an object is a business object.

In order to treat instances of a generic type polymorphically, or to do type checks to see if those instances come from the same type, the generic type must inherit from a non-generic base class or implement a non-generic interface. In the case of `BindingList<T>`, the generic type implements `IBindingList`. So both `myStringList` and `myIntList` can be treated as `IBindingList` types.

To provide this type of polymorphic behavior to CSLA .NET business objects, all business base classes implement `Csla.Core.IBusinessObject`. This, then, is the ultimate base type for all business objects. Here's the code for `IBusinessObject`:

```
namespace Csla.Core
{
  public interface IBusinessObject
  {
  }
}
```

Notice that this interface has no members (methods, properties, etc). This is because there are no common behaviors across both read-only and editable business objects. The interface remains useful, however, because it allows code to easily detect whether an object is a business object, through code like this:

```
if (theObject is Csla.Core.IBusinessObject)
{
  // theObject is a business object
}
```

The next couple of interfaces will have more members.

ICommandObject Interface

The final common interface is `ICommandObject`. Like `IBusinessObject`, this is an empty interface:

```
interface ICommandObject : IBusinessObject
{
}
```

Again, you can use this interface to easily determine whether a business object inherits from `CommandBase` within your business or UI code.

IEditableBusinessObject Interface

Editable business objects must provide a set of basic behaviors so the parts of CSLA .NET can interact with each other properly. These behaviors are defined by the `IEditableBusinessObject` interface. This interface is designed for internal use within CSLA .NET and should not be used by code outside the framework:

```
public interface IEditableBusinessObject :
  IBusinessObject, ISupportUndo, IUndoableObject, ITrackStatus
```

This interface is implemented by `BusinessBase` and ensures that behaviors related to n-level undo and parent-child relationships exist in that class. These features are discussed in more detail in Chapter 13.

IEditableCollection Interface

While a `BusinessListBase<T,C>` is both a business object and an editable object, it is also a collection. It turns out that collections need one extra behavior beyond a simple editable object, so the `IEditableCollection` interface adds that extra method:

```
public interface IEditableCollection : IUndoableObject
{
  void RemoveChild(Core.BusinessBase child);
}
```

The `RemoveChild()` method will be important later in the chapter during the implementation of `BusinessBase` and `BusinessListBase`, and specifically for the implementation of the `System.ComponentModel.IEditableObject` interface. This interface has some tricky requirements for interaction between a child object in a collection and the collection itself.

IReadOnlyObject Interface

In the same way that IBusinessObject provides a form of polymorphism and commonality across all business objects, IReadOnlyObject does the same thing for read-only business objects—specifically those that inherit from ReadOnlyBase<T>.

It turns out that all read-only objects support a method for authorization: CanReadProperty(). This method is defined in the interface as follows:

```
public interface IReadOnlyObject : IBusinessObject
{
  bool CanReadProperty(string propertyName);
}
```

The CanReadProperty() method is discussed in Chapter 12 when I discuss authorization.

IReadOnlyCollection Interface

The IReadOnlyCollection interface exists purely to support polymorphism for read-only collection objects that inherit from ReadOnlyListBase<T, C>. As such, it is an empty interface:

```
 interface IReadOnlyCollection : IBusinessObject
{
}
```

You can use this interface to easily determine whether a business object is a read-only collection as needed within your business or UI code.

ISavable Interface

Editable root objects in CSLA .NET implement a Save() method. This includes objects that inherit from both BusinessBase and BusinessListBase. The ISavable interface formalizes the concept of a savable object, which really means an editable root object. You can use this interface to create a UI framework that can save any editable root object:

```
public interface ISavable
{
  object Save();
  void SaveComplete(object newObject);
  event EventHandler<SavedEventArgs> Saved;
}
```

■ **Caution** The SaveComplete() method exists for internal use by CSLA .NET only and should never be used by business or UI code.

The ISavable interface defines a common Save() method and a Saved event. The Saved event is raised after an object has successfully saved itself by calling the data portal. This event follows the standard EventHandler pattern, passing two parameters to the event handler: a reference to the sender and a SavedEventArgs parameter. This SavedEventArgs parameter contains a reference to the new object that is returned as a result of the Save() method call.

The Saved event is intended to address the complexity that occurs when your business object is referenced in numerous locations throughout your application, by multiple forms in the UI, for instance. If you call Save() on the object in one location, all the other places where that object is referenced must be updated to use the new object returned as a result of Save().

The Saved event provides a solution because it is a standard, centralized, event that provides this notification. Any code holding a reference to a business object can handle the Saved event. That code will be notified when that object has been saved. The code can then update its reference to use the new object returned as a result of the Save() call.

ISmartField Interface

The SmartDate type extends DateTime to provide the concept of an empty date. It also adds the ability to convert the value into and out of a string representation to simplify binding the value to a TextBox type control in the UI.

■ **Note** SmartDate is discussed in depth in Chapter 16.

Members of the community have created other "smart" data types such as SmartInt or SmartDouble that provide the same concepts to those other data types. To standardize and simplify the creation of those types, CSLA .NET defines the ISmartField interface.

This interface allows CSLA .NET to interact with any "smart" data type in a consistent manner:

```
public interface ISmartField
{
  string Text { get; set; }
  bool IsEmpty { get; }
}
```

As you can see, the interface enables both the concept of an empty value and the ability to convert the value into and out of a text representation.

Creating a new data type, especially one that extends an existing type such as DateTime or int requires a lot of work. The goal is to have the new type work as much like the original as possible, which means overriding many (if not all) operators and providing support for type conversion and cast operations. I discuss some of these challenges in Chapter 16 when I cover the implementation of SmartDate.

ISupportUndo Interface

Many smart client UI frameworks enable cancel buttons or similar concepts and thus interact with the n-level undo support provided by CSLA .NET objects. The ISupportUndo interface is designed to make creating these UI frameworks easier, by providing a polymorphic interface the UI can use to interact with the objects:

```
public interface ISupportUndo
{
  void BeginEdit();
  void CancelEdit();
  void ApplyEdit();
}
```

I discuss n-level undo in detail in Chapter 13, but you can infer from the method names that the UI can call BeginEdit() before allowing the user to interact with the object, and then can call either CancelEdit() or ApplyEdit() to roll back or accept any changes the user has made to the object.

■ **Caution** When building a Windows Forms UI, it is *critical* that these methods be called only when the object is *not data bound to the UI.*

Using these methods, a UI developer or UI framework can allow users to edit an object and then click a cancel button to completely undo any changes they've made to the object.

ITrackStatus Interface

Editable objects maintain several status values about the state of the object. These status values are discussed in detail in Chapter 8, which covers their implementation in `BusinessBase` and `BusinessListBase`. The `ITrackStatus` interface allows a UI framework to get these status values in a polymorphic manner, regardless of the type of the editable object:

```
public interface ITrackStatus
{
  bool IsValid { get; }
  bool IsSelfValid { get; }
  bool IsDirty { get; }
  bool IsSelfDirty { get; }
  bool IsDeleted { get; }
  bool IsNew { get; }
  bool IsSavable { get; }
}
```

A UI framework often uses these status values to enable or disable various UI elements to give the user cues about what actions are possible at any point in time. As you'll see in Chapter 10, the `CslaDataProvider` automatically handles these details in a WPF interface.

IUndoableObject Interface

In the same way that `IBusinessObject` provides a form of polymorphism and commonality across all business objects, `IUndoableObject` does the same thing for any object that supports n-level undo. This includes those that inherit from `BusinessBase<T>` and `BusinessListBase<T,C>`, among others.

This polymorphic ability is of critical importance in the implementation of `UndoableBase`, as discussed in Chapter 13. `UndoableBase` needs to be able to treat all editable objects the same in order to implement the n-level undo functionality.

Here's the code for `IUndoableObject`:

```
public interface IUndoableObject
{
  int EditLevel { get; }
  void CopyState(int parentEditLevel, bool parentBindingEdit);
  void UndoChanges(int parentEditLevel, bool parentBindingEdit);
  void AcceptChanges(int parentEditLevel, bool parentBindingEdit);
}
```

The n-level undo support implemented by `UndoableBase` requires that every object implements the property and three methods listed in this interface.

Putting these methods in an interface is a double-edged sword. On one hand it clearly defines the methods and will make it easier to implement `UndoableBase`. On the other hand, these methods are now potentially available to any code using a business object. In other words, a UI developer could write code to call these methods—almost certainly causing nasty bugs and side-effects because these methods aren't designed for public use.

This is a difficult design decision when building frameworks. In this case the benefits of having a common interface for use by UndoableBase appears to outweigh the potential risk of a UI developer doing something foolish by calling the methods directly.

To help minimize this risk, the actual implementation methods in the base classes will keep these methods private. That way, they can only be called by directly casting the object to the IUndoableObject type.

ObjectCloner Class

All read-only and editable objects implement the System.ICloneable interface. This interface defines a Clone() method that returns an exact copy of the original object. Also remember that all business objects are mobile objects: marked with the Serializable attribute.

Creating a clone of a Serializable object is easily accomplished through the use of the BinaryFormatter object in the System.Runtime.Serialization.Formatters.Binary namespace.

Alternately you can configure CSLA .NET to use the NDCS provided as part of WCF. In that case, ObjectCloner can clone both Serializable and DataContract objects. I discuss the pros and cons of using the NDCS in Chapter 4, and as stated there, I recommend using the BinaryFormatter in most cases.

The implementation of cloning is a few lines of code. Rather than replicating this code in every base class, it can be centralized in a single object. All the base classes can then collaborate with this object to perform the clone operation.

The class contains the following code:

```
namespace Csla.Core
{
  public static class ObjectCloner
  {
    public static object Clone(object obj)
    {
      using (MemoryStream buffer = new MemoryStream())
      {
        ISerializationFormatter formatter =
          SerializationFormatterFactory.GetFormatter();
        formatter.Serialize(buffer, obj);
        buffer.Position = 0;
        object temp = formatter.Deserialize(buffer);
        return temp;
      }
    }
  }
}
```

This class is static, as there is no reason to create an instance of the class.

The Clone() method itself uses a .NET formatter to serialize the object's state into an in-memory buffer. All objects referenced by the business object are also automatically serialized into the same buffer. The combination of an object and all the objects it references, directly or indirectly, is called an *object graph*.

The SerializationFormatterFactory.GetFormatter() method returns an object that invokes either a BinaryFormatter or NDCS based on how CSLA .NET is configured. The default is to use the BinaryFormatter, but you can use the CslaSerializationFormatter configuration setting in the application's config file to use the NDCS if desired.

The in-memory buffer is immediately deserialized to create a copy of the original object graph. The buffer is then disposed, as it could consume a fair amount of memory, depending on the size of the fields in your objects.

The resulting copy is returned to the calling code.

ReadOnlyBindingList

The `ReadOnlyBindingList<C>` class implements a read-only collection based on `System.ComponentModel.BindingList<T>`. The standard `BindingList<T>` class implements a read-write collection that supports data binding, but there are numerous cases in which a read-only collection is useful. For example, `ReadOnlyBindingList` is the base class for `Csla.ReadOnlyListBase`, `Csla.NameValueListBase` and `Csla.Validation.BrokenRulesCollection`.

This class inherits from `BindingList<T>`. It is also `Serializable` and `abstract`, like all the framework base classes:

```
[Serializable]
public abstract class ReadOnlyBindingList<C> :
  System.ComponentModel.BindingList<C>, Core.IBusinessObject
{
}
```

All the basic collection and data binding behaviors are already implemented by `BindingList`. Making the collection read-only is a matter of overriding a few methods to prevent alteration of the collection. Of course, the collection has to be read-write at *some* point in order to get data into the collection at all. To control whether the collection is read-only, there's a field and a property:

```
private bool _isReadOnly = true;

public bool IsReadOnly
{
  get { return _isReadOnly; }
  protected set { _isReadOnly = value; }
}
```

Notice that while the `IsReadOnly` property is `public` for reading, it is `protected` for changing. This way, any code can determine whether the collection is read-only or read-write, but only a subclass can lock or unlock the collection.

The class contains a constructor that turns off the options to edit, remove, or create items in the collection by setting some properties in the `BindingList` base class:

```
protected ReadOnlyBindingList()
{
  AllowEdit = false;
  AllowRemove = false;
  AllowNew = false;
}
```

The rest of the class overrides the methods in `BindingList` that control alteration of the collection. Each override checks the `IsReadOnly` property and throws an exception when an attempt is made to change the collection when it is in read-only mode.

The only complicated overrides are `ClearItems()` and `RemoveItem()`. This is because `AllowRemove` is typically set to `false` and must be temporarily changed to `true` to allow the operation (when the collection is not in read-only mode). For instance, here's the `ClearItems()` method:

```
protected override void ClearItems()
{
  if (!IsReadOnly)
  {
    bool oldValue = AllowRemove;
    AllowRemove = true;
    base.ClearItems();
    DeferredLoadIndexIfNotLoaded();
    _indexSet.ClearIndexes();
    AllowRemove = oldValue;
  }
  else
    throw new NotSupportedException(Resources.ClearInvalidException);
}
```

The original `AllowRemove` value is restored after the operation is complete.

Notice the call to `DeferredLoadIndexIfNotLoaded()`, which triggers recreation of any indexes being maintained by LINQ to CSLA. LINQ to CSLA is discussed in Chapter 14.

This completes all the types in the `Csla.Core` namespace. You can look at the full implementation of each type by downloading the code from `www.apress.com/book/view/1430210192` or `www.lhotka.net/cslanet/download.aspx`. Also, Chapters 7 through 16 cover many of the concepts and code in more detail.

Conclusion

In this chapter I started discussing the implementation of the CSLA .NET framework. This chapter walked through the overall project structure, including the folders and namespaces used to organize the code and types in the framework. It also provided some detail around the types in the `Csla` and `Csla.Core` namespaces. You can start to see how the framework supports features such as the following:

- Data binding
- Business and validation rules
- Authorization rules
- Object status tracking
- Parent-child object relationships
- Editable and read-only objects
- N-level undo
- Object persistence and the data portal

Chapters 7 through 16 provide more detail about the implementation of each major framework feature. From Chapter 17 on, the focus is on building the simple business application designed in Chapter 3 to illustrate how the classes in the framework can be used to build applications based on business objects.

CHAPTER 7

Property Declarations

Chapter 6 introduced the idea of the PropertyInfo<T> class from the Csla namespace. This type allows a business object to declare metadata about the object's properties, and most importantly, it helps eliminate the use of a string literal to reference the property name throughout the business class.

While a business developer could use standard .NET property declaration syntax, it would require him to invoke the authorization, business, and validation rules; processing; and data binding behaviors of CSLA .NET manually in each property.

To simplify the code required to utilize all these behaviors, CSLA .NET supports a coding model that is more abstract, allowing the framework to do much of the work automatically. The syntax is similar to that of a *dependency property* in WPF or WF, but the implementation behind the scenes is quite different.

This chapter will focus on how CSLA .NET manages property metadata and helps a business object manage its property values to simplify and standardize business object code.

Declaring Properties

You have quite a few options for declaring a property in a CSLA .NET business object, and I'll walk you through all the details. You can choose to declare your own private backing fields, or you can allow CSLA .NET to manage the values of your properties. Before getting into those options in detail, I'll briefly walk through one common option so you get a feel for the overall structure.

Most properties are declared like this:

```
private static PropertyInfo<string> NameProperty =
  RegisterProperty(new PropertyInfo<string>("Name"));
public string Name
{
  get { return GetProperty(NameProperty); }
  set { SetProperty(NameProperty, value); }
}
```

The RegisterProperty() method registers the property's metadata with CSLA .NET, so the framework is aware of the property. Internally, CSLA .NET maintains a list of all the IPropertyInfo objects for each business object type. These values are static, so all instances of the type share one list.

The *field manager* subsystem in the Csla.Core.FieldManager namespace maintains the list of IPropertyInfo objects. I'll discuss the field manager later in the chapter.

The GetProperty() and SetProperty() methods help minimize the code you would otherwise have to write to trigger authorization, business, and validation rules; status tracking; and data binding.

Looking at BusinessBase in Csla.Core, you can see that GetProperty() has many overloads, but ultimately does the following:

```
protected P GetProperty<P>(
  PropertyInfo<P> propertyInfo, Security.NoAccessBehavior noAccess)
{
  P result = default(P);
  if (CanReadProperty(propertyInfo.Name, noAccess ==
                      Csla.Security.NoAccessBehavior.ThrowException))
    result = ReadProperty<P>(propertyInfo);
  else
    result = propertyInfo.DefaultValue;
  return result;
}
```

■ **Note** This technique is similar to the DependencyProperty concept that WPF and WF use.

The method calls CanReadProperty(), which is part of the authorization rules subsystem I'll discuss in Chapter 10. That method checks to see if the current user is allowed to read this property. If the user is not authorized, the method will either throw an exception or return false, depending on the value of the noAccess parameter.

Assuming no exception is thrown (which is the default), then either the value or a dummy default value will be returned. If the user is authorized to read the value, she gets the real value; otherwise, she gets a dummy value.

The ReadProperty() method is used to get the real value if appropriate. ReadProperty() is a protected method of BusinessBase, so it's available in your business class as well. You should use GetProperty() when you want authorization rules to apply, and ReadProperty() when you want to read the property regardless of authorization rules.

Normally, the UI disables the display of values that the user is not authorized to see, so even if a dummy value is returned here, the user will never see it. In fact, this is why the default behavior is to return a dummy value if the user isn't authorized to see the real value. Both Windows Forms and WPF data binding typically read the value, even if the control isn't visible to the user. If the property get throws an exception, then data binding will not work properly.

Looking at the SetProperty() method in BusinessBase, you can see that it is even more complex:

```
protected void SetProperty<P>(
  PropertyInfo<P> propertyInfo, P newValue,
  Security.NoAccessBehavior noAccess)
{
  if (CanWriteProperty(propertyInfo.Name, noAccess ==
                       Security.NoAccessBehavior.ThrowException))
  {
    try
    {
      P oldValue = default(P);
      var fieldData = FieldManager.GetFieldData(propertyInfo);
```

```
        if (fieldData == null)
        {
          oldValue = propertyInfo.DefaultValue;
          fieldData = FieldManager.LoadFieldData<P>(propertyInfo, oldValue);
        }
        else
        {
          var fd = fieldData as FieldManager.IFieldData<P>;
          if (fd != null)
            oldValue = fd.Value;
          else
            oldValue = (P)fieldData.Value;
        }
        LoadPropertyValue<P>(propertyInfo, oldValue, newValue, true);
      }
      catch (Exception ex)
      {
        throw
          new PropertyLoadException(
            string.Format(Properties.Resources.PropertyLoadException,
                                         propertyInfo.Name, ex.Message));
      }
    }
  }
```

While there's a lot of code here, the process flow can be distilled down to what you see in Figure 7-1.

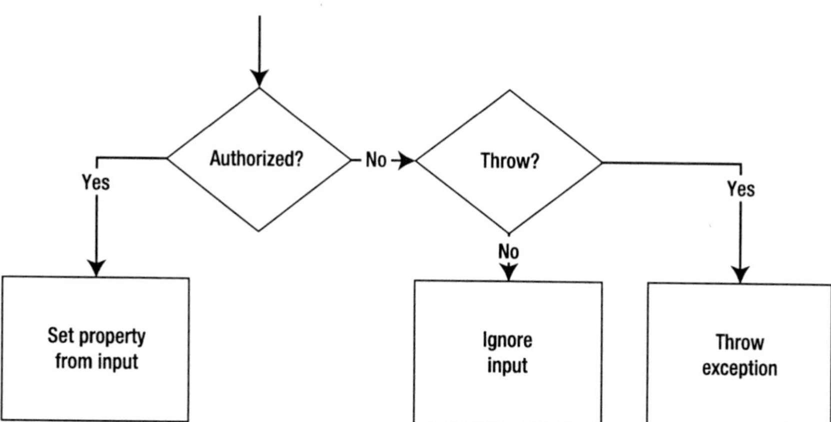

Figure 7-1. *SetProperty() process flow*

The `CanWriteProperty()` method takes care of the authorization; I'll discuss this in Chapter 10.

The `LoadPropertyValue()` method is a `private` helper method that takes care of actually setting the property value. It also does a lot of work, as shown in Figure 7-2.

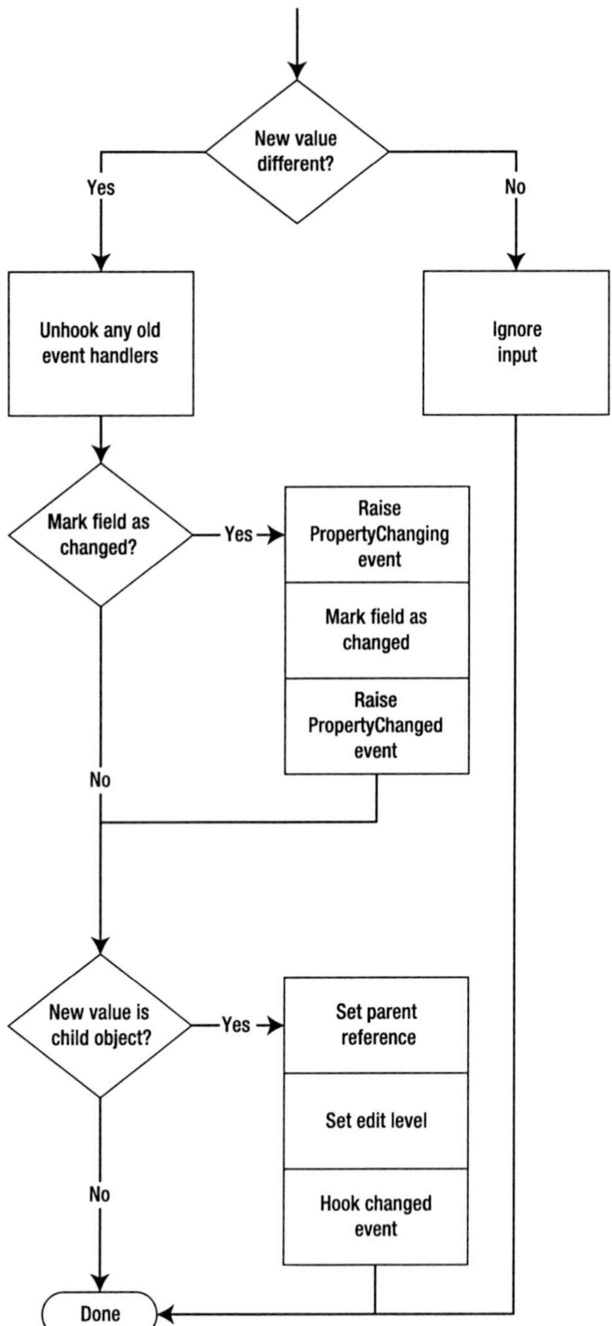

Figure 7-2. *LoadPropertyValue() process flow*

The `LoadProperty()` method sets a property's value by ultimately calling `LoadPropertyValue()`. It is `protected`, and your business code can use it. You should use `SetProperty()` when you want to trigger authorization, business, and validation rules, and you should use `LoadProperty()` when you want to simply set a property value without triggering any of those behaviors.

Table 7-1 lists the methods you can use to get and set property values in your business code.

Table 7-1. *Methods That Get and Set Property Values*

Method	Description
`GetProperty()`	Gets a property value after checking authorization
`ReadProperty()`	Gets a property value without checking authorization
`SetProperty()`	Sets a property value after checking authorization, then triggers business and validation rules and data binding behaviors
`LoadProperty()`	Sets a property value without checking authorization or triggering business or validation rules or data binding behaviors

Now that you have a high-level understanding of the way properties work, I'll dig into the specific options.

Property Declaration Options

Property values must be stored somewhere. In a typical object property, values are stored in *backing fields*, which are simply `private` fields declared in the class—for example:

```
private string _name = string.Empty;
private int _id;
```

If you use the compact property declaration syntax, the compiler will create a hidden `private` backing field on your behalf.

```
public string Name { get; set; }
```

In this case, you don't know or care about the field name, but the field is there nonetheless.

CSLA .NET allows you to use `private` backing fields if you would like, or you can allow CSLA .NET to manage the field values automatically.

Using `private` backing fields offers better performance, but it does require that you declare and initialize the backing field in your code. Managed backing fields incur a performance penalty, because CSLA .NET is actually storing the field values in a collection on your behalf, but they require less code in your business class.

■ **Note** When using CSLA .NET for Silverlight, managed backing fields are serialized automatically. However, you must write extra code to coordinate the serialization of all `private` backing fields.

You can use `private` backing fields for any field value required by your object. However, when it comes to storing references to child objects, I strongly recommend using managed backing fields. I'll discuss storing child references later in the chapter, as they are relatively complex. If you choose to store child references in `private` backing fields, then you'll have to deal with all that complexity yourself. On the other hand, a managed backing field takes care of everything automatically.

As with many features of CSLA .NET, you can choose which technique suits your needs best. In general, I typically use managed backing fields and only switch to private backing fields when dealing with large collections of objects where performance is a bigger issue.

Private Backing Fields

The four property helper methods have overloads that accept private backing fields as parameters. For example, you can call GetProperty() like this:

```
private static PropertyInfo<string> NameProperty =
  RegisterProperty(new PropertyInfo<string>("Name"));
private string _name = NameProperty.DefaultValue;
public string Name
{
  get { return GetProperty(NameProperty, _name); }
  set { SetProperty(NameProperty, ref _name, value); }
}
```

The bold lines indicate the differences with the previous example code. Notice that a field is now declared explicitly and is initialized to a default value.

Caution You must initialize string fields to a non-null value. Other fields may be optionally initialized, but I recommend initializing all fields as shown.

Also notice how the field is passed as a parameter to GetProperty(). As you can imagine, GetProperty() simply returns the value as a result, but only after checking authorization rules.

The SetProperty() method is more interesting, because the field is passed as a parameter using the ref qualifier. This means the field is passed by reference, so any changes you make to the field inside the SetProperty() method will actually change the value of the field itself.

In this case, SetProperty() still performs the steps shown in Figures 7-1 and 7-2, but if the property's value is ultimately changed, the new value will be put directly into that field, which is passed by reference.

Private Backing Fields with Type Conversion

There are variations on the four property helper methods that can be used to help convert a field from one type to another. For example, you may maintain the field value as an enum or SmartDate type, but declare the property itself to be of type string. This is useful when the user wants to see a friendly name, but the object wants a more computer-friendly data type for the property.

```
private static PropertyInfo<SmartDate> BirthDateProperty =
  RegisterProperty(new PropertyInfo<SmartDate>("BirthDate"));
private SmartDate _birthDate = BirthDateProperty.DefaultValue;
public string BirthDate
{
  get { return GetPropertyConvert<SmartDate, string>(
    BirthDateProperty, _birthDate); }
  set { SetProperty<SmartDate, string>(
    BirthDateProperty, ref _birthDate, value); }
}
```

Rather than calling GetProperty(), this code calls GetPropertyConvert(), which takes two type parameters. The first is the type of the backing field, and the second is the type of the property. The GetPropertyConvert() method is implemented in BusinessBase like this:

```
protected P GetPropertyConvert<F, P>(PropertyInfo<F> propertyInfo, F field)
{
  return Utilities.CoerceValue<P>(
    typeof(F), null,
    GetProperty<F>(
       propertyInfo.Name, field, propertyInfo.DefaultValue,
      Security.NoAccessBehavior.SuppressException));
}
```

This method delegates the task of getting the field value to the GetProperty() method you've already seen. However, it then uses Utilities.CoerceValue() to coerce the value to the specified property type.

You might wonder how this differs from just using a cast to change the value type. The CoerceValue() method attempts to perform a cast, but it's more aggressive and attempts other techniques of type conversion as well, including using .NET type converters. It also includes functionality to convert enum types into and out of text representations.

The end result is that these versions of the four property helper methods can save you a lot of code and complexity in cases where the property type and backing field type do not match.

Managed Backing Fields

My first property example illustrated how to declare a property that uses a managed backing field.

```
private static PropertyInfo<string> NameProperty =
  RegisterProperty(new PropertyInfo<string>("Name"));
public string Name
{
  get { return GetProperty(NameProperty); }
  set { SetProperty(NameProperty, value); }
}
```

Notice that no private field is declared, so there's no field to pass to the GetProperty() or SetProperty() method. Behind the scenes, the field manager stores and retrieves the value from a data structure. I'll discuss the field manager in more detail later.

Managed Backing Fields with Type Conversion

As with private backing fields, four methods get and set managed property values while converting the value to different types. The syntax is similar to what you've already seen.

```
private static PropertyInfo<CategoryEnum> CategoryProperty =
  RegisterProperty(new PropertyInfo<CategoryEnum>("Category"));
public string Category
{
  get { return GetPropertyConvert<CategoryEnum, string>(CategoryProperty); }
  set { SetPropertyConvert<CategoryEnum, string>(CategoryProperty, value); }
}
```

Again, rather than calling GetProperty() or SetProperty(), similar methods are called such as GetPropertyConvert(). These methods take two type parameters; the first is the type of the field value, and the second is the type of the property. The GetPropertyConvert() overload looks like this:

```
protected P GetPropertyConvert<F, P>(
  PropertyInfo<F> propertyInfo, Security.NoAccessBehavior noAccess)
{
  return Utilities.CoerceValue<P>(
    typeof(F), null, GetProperty<F>(propertyInfo, noAccess));
}
```

As with the earlier overload, this one gets the value and then passes it to `Utilities.CoerceValue()` to coerce the value to a different type.

Child Object Reference Fields

Business objects can contain other business objects. As discussed in Chapter 4, the containing object is a *parent object*, and the contained object is a *child object*. In this case, the parent object maintains a reference to the child object.

I'll discuss the issues around parent-child relationships in Chapter 9. For now, you should know that the normal way to create a property that references a child object is to write code like this in your parent object:

```
private static PropertyInfo<ChildType> ChildProperty =
  RegisterProperty(new PropertyInfo<ChildType>("Child"));
public ChildType Child
{
  get
  {
    if (!FieldManager.FieldExists(ChildProperty))
      LoadProperty(ChildProperty, ChildType.NewChild());
    return GetProperty(ChildProperty);
  }
}
```

This stores the child reference in a managed backing field, which allows the field manager to automatically take care of all the housekeeping details involved with a child reference.

The `RegisterProperty()` and `GetProperty()` calls should be familiar by this point. But these two lines are new:

```
if (!FieldManager.FieldExists(ChildProperty))
  LoadProperty(ChildProperty, ChildType.NewChild());
```

The first line uses the `FieldManager` to determine if this child object has been created. If it has not, then the second line uses `LoadProperty()` to add a new instance of the object as a child. The call to `ChildType.NewChild()` is invoking the child object's factory method, which is a concept I discussed in Chapters 4 and 5.

This relatively simple-looking code is hiding some fairly complex object interactions, and I'll discuss them later in Chapter 9 when I cover parent-child relationships.

RegisterProperty and Inheritance

If you look closely at the way `RegisterProperty()` is called in the example code in this chapter, you'll see that it is called while initializing a `static` field.

```
private static PropertyInfo<string> NameProperty =
  RegisterProperty(new PropertyInfo<string>("Name"));
```

It makes sense that your properties need to be registered with CSLA .NET before they can be used, and if your business class inherits directly from `BusinessBase` or `ReadOnlyBase`, then this will happen automatically. The reason is that any attempt to get or set a property will call the GetProperty() or SetProperty() method, which accepts the PropertyInfo field as a parameter—for example:

```
return GetProperty(NameProperty);
```

Any attempt to access a static field forces .NET to initialize all the static fields declared in that class.

However, if you use inheritance such that your business class inherits from a class that, in turn, inherits from BusinessBase or ReadOnlyBase, then things will get more complex. This is because of the way .NET initializes static fields, which turns out to be complex and counterintuitive.

The .NET runtime only initializes the static fields for a class when one of the static fields on that class is accessed (read or changed), or if the class has a static constructor. To be very clear, this means that instance methods and properties can be called *before the* static *fields are initialized.*

Unless you are *absolutely sure* that a static field from *every class in the inheritance hierarchy* has been accessed, you can't be sure that all the static fields have been initialized. The end result is that your properties might be accessed before they have all been registered, which will ultimately cause the field manager to throw an exception.

Note Remember that this is only an issue if your business classes don't inherit directly from a CSLA .NET base class.

You can use one of two techniques to prevent this issue. You can add a static constructor to each of your custom base classes, or you can ensure that some static field is initialized as each object instance is created.

Adding a static Constructor

Adding a static constructor is easy—for example:

```
[Serializable]
public abstract class CustomBase<T> : BusinessBase<T>
  where T : CustomBase<T>
{
  static CustomBase()
  { }
}
```

All static fields are initialized before the static constructor executes, so adding this bit of code ensures that the static fields in this class will be initialized before an instance of this class, or a subclass, can be created.

The downside to this is a performance impact. When you declare a static constructor in a class, the compiler injects code everywhere any method of this class is accessed, checking to ensure that the static constructor has been run before any other code. Obviously, all this extra checking can have a negative impact on performance.

It is actually slightly worse than this, because the compiler also injects code to ensure that the static constructor is only called exactly once, even in a multithreaded environment. So the code it injects is relatively complex and involves potential locking.

Initializing a Dummy static Field

An alternative to declaring a static constructor is to ensure that at least one static field is accessed in each class before an instance of that class, or a subclass, is created. You can do this by declaring a static field in every class and initializing it any time an instance of the object is created.

The trick is to remember that the .NET Framework creates instances two ways. Normal creation of an instance invokes the constructor of each class in the inheritance hierarchy, but deserialization (when using the BinaryFormatter or NetDataContractSerializer) doesn't invoke any constructors.

Fortunately, the BusinessBase and ReadOnlyBase classes include code, so they are notified when they are deserialized. In that case, they invoke a protected method called OnDeserialized(), which a business class can override to be notified that it has been deserialized.

Using this capability, you can force initialization of the static fields in a class by adding the following code to all your business and base classes when using a custom base class:

```
[Serializable]
public abstract class CustomBase<T> : BusinessBase<T>
  where T : CustomBase<T>
{
  private static int _forceInit;

  public CustomBase()
  {
    _forceInit = 1;
  }

  protected override void OnDeserialized(StreamingContext context)
  {
    _forceInit = 1;
  }
}
```

When an instance of this class, or a subclass, is created normally, the constructor is invoked. The constructor accesses the static field and ensures that all static fields are initialized. When an instance is created through deserialization, OnDeserialized() is invoked, which again accesses the static field and ensures that all static fields are initialized.

This technique requires a bit more code, but it doesn't incur the performance penalty of implementing a static constructor.

Regardless of which technique you use, the end result is that the static fields declared in each class are initialized before any properties can be accessed. This ensures that all the RegisterProperty() calls occur and that all properties are registered early in the process.

PropertyInfoManager

The PropertyInfoManager is responsible for managing all the properties that have been registered for each business object type using the RegisterProperty() method. This type is found in the Csla.Core.FieldManager namespace. Each time RegisterProperty() is called, it is associating an IPropertyInfo object with a specific business object type.

For each business object type, PropertyInfoManager maintains a list of IPropertyInfo objects that describe the properties registered for that type. This means that it also has a list of all the business object types, which is maintained in a Dictionary, as you can see in the PropertyInfoManager code:

```
private static Dictionary<Type, List<IPropertyInfo>> _propertyInfoCache;
```

This Dictionary is indexed by a Type object, representing the type of each business object with registered properties. The value is a List of IPropertyInfo objects, each containing metadata about a property registered to that type.

The hard part about this class is that its methods need to be thread-safe. In many cases, it will be used in a multithreaded environment, such as in ASP.NET, so access to this Dictionary and to each individual List object must be wrapped with locking code.

The PropertyInfoCache property does this for the Dictionary itself:

```
private static object _cacheLock = new object();

private static Dictionary<Type, List<IPropertyInfo>> PropertyInfoCache
{
  get
  {
    if (_propertyInfoCache == null)
    {
      lock (_cacheLock)
      {
        if (_propertyInfoCache == null)
          _propertyInfoCache = new Dictionary<Type, List<IPropertyInfo>>();
      }
    }
    return _propertyInfoCache;
  }
}
```

The private field _cacheLock is used to lock the region of code that creates the Dictionary if it doesn't already exist. Notice how the code checks the existence of the Dictionary both before and after the lock statement. This avoids a race condition, where multiple threads could wait on the lock and run the code inside the lock, even though the first thread to reach that point would have already created the Dictionary.

Similarly, the GetPropertyListCache() method protects both the use of the Dictionary and the creation of individual List objects for each business object type.

```
public static List<IPropertyInfo> GetPropertyListCache(Type objectType)
{
  var cache = PropertyInfoCache;
  List<IPropertyInfo> list = null;
  if (!(cache.TryGetValue(objectType, out list)))
  {
    lock (cache)
    {
      if (!(cache.TryGetValue(objectType, out list)))
      {
        list = new List<IPropertyInfo>();
        cache.Add(objectType, list);
      }
    }
  }
  return list;
}
```

This method uses the PropertyInfoCache property to safely get a reference to the Dictionary. It then uses the TryGetValue() method to attempt to retrieve the specific List<IPropertyInfo> for the business object type. If that is unsuccessful, a lock statement is used to ensure that only one thread can run the code that creates and adds the new List object to the Dictionary. Notice how the TryGetValue() is called *inside* the lock statement to prevent multiple threads from getting that far and creating duplicate List objects.

The RegisterProperty() method is used to register properties for a business object type by adding an IPropertyInfo object to the correct List. This method also employs locking to avoid threading issues.

```
public static PropertyInfo<T> RegisterProperty<T>(
  Type objectType, PropertyInfo<T> info)
{
  var list = GetPropertyListCache(objectType);
  lock (list)
  {
    list.Add(info);
    list.Sort();
  }
  return info;
}
```

In this case, the GetPropertyListCache() method is used to safely get a reference to the List object, then a lock statement is used to block access to that specific List object so only one property can be registered at a time.

Notice that the list is sorted as each item is added. This ensures that the list is sorted when all properties have been registered and guarantees that the values are in the same order each time. Later in the chapter, I'll discuss how these values provide a numeric index into the list of managed field values for each business object. The order of the properties is very important.

Of course, the RegisterProperty() methods are called when .NET does its initialization of the static fields on each class. You might expect that those method calls would occur in the same order all the time, thanks to .NET. Unfortunately, I don't trust that to be the case across C# and VB, or between the 32- and 64-bit .NET runtimes. As you'll see later, these values must be in the same order in a client/server situation, even if the client is 32-bit .NET in VB and the server is 64-bit .NET in C#. Sorting the property objects ensures that they're in the same order in the list, regardless of the programming language or the .NET runtime version.

Finally, the GetRegisteredProperties() method returns a list of properties registered for a business object type. Since this method is public, there's no way to know what the calling code will do with the result, so this method doesn't return the actual List. Instead, it returns a copy of the data in a new List.

```
public static List<IPropertyInfo> GetRegisteredProperties(Type objectType)
{
  var list = GetPropertyListCache(objectType);
  lock (list)
    return new List<IPropertyInfo>(list);
}
```

The original List object is locked to block any RegisterProperty() calls from changing the list while the items are being copied to the result.

BusinessBase and ReadOnlyBase use the PropertyInfoManager to manage all the details around tracking the properties registered for each business type.

Field Manager

The field manager is responsible for storing the values of all managed fields for each object instance. Each BusinessBase and ReadOnlyBase object contains an instance of FieldDataManager, which is the object responsible for storing the managed field values. These two base classes expose the FieldDataManager object as a protected property named FieldManager.

FieldManager Property

The BusinessBase and ReadOnlyBase classes expose a protected property named FieldManager to make the FieldDataManager available to the business object's code. For example, this code is in BusinessBase:

```
protected FieldManager.FieldDataManager FieldManager
{
  get
  {
    if (_fieldManager == null)
    {
      _fieldManager = new FieldManager.FieldDataManager(this.GetType());
      UndoableBase.ResetChildEditLevel(
        _fieldManager, this.EditLevel, this.BindingEdit);
    }
    return _fieldManager;
  }
}
```

This property is designed to only create an instance of the FieldDataManager on demand. The idea is that if your business class never uses any managed backing fields, no FieldDataManager object will be created. I chose to do this to minimize the overhead involved in creating a business object when managed fields aren't used.

This does complicate the use of the FieldManager property throughout the rest of BusinessBase and ReadOnlyBase. For example, BusinessBase includes this code:

```
public virtual bool IsDirty
{
  get {
    return IsSelfDirty || (_fieldManager != null && FieldManager.IsDirty());
  }
}
```

A parent object is considered dirty, or changed, if it or any of its child objects have been changed. To know if the object has been changed, the IsDirty property checks the FieldManager to find out if any managed fields or child objects have been changed. But before accessing the FieldManager property, it checks to see if the _fieldManager field is null. This prevents accidental creation of a FieldDataManager instance when there are no managed fields in the business object.

Getting back to the FieldManager property, you should see that a method called UndoableBase.ResetChildEditLevel() is called after the FieldDataManager instance is created. Technically, the FieldDataManager is a child object contained within the business object. Because it is a child object, its edit level for n-level undo must be kept in sync with the business object itself.

I'll discuss the concept of edit levels in Chapter 11. For now, it is enough to know that the ResetChildEditLevel() call ensures that the new child object is in sync with its parent.

FieldDataManager Class

The FieldDataManager class itself is relatively complex. Each instance of this class is a child of a business object. Also, because the field manager is responsible for storing the values of the business object's properties, it must participate in the n-level undo process discussed in Chapter 11. Here's the declaration of the class:

```
[Serializable()]
public class FieldDataManager : IUndoableObject, IMobileObject
```

The class is Serializable, because the data it contains may be serialized when the business object is cloned or moved across the network between a client and application server. It implements the IUndoableObject interface because it must participate in the n-level undo behaviors covered in Chapter 11.

■ **Note** The IMobileObject interface exists to support serialization through the MobileFormatter, which is part of CSLA .NET for Silverlight. CSLA .NET for Silverlight is outside the scope of this book, and IMobileObject has no impact on how CSLA .NET works within the .NET runtime.

The field manager's primary job is to maintain the values of all properties that use managed backing fields. Simplistically, it might seem that you could store these values in a Dictionary, keyed off the property name. That would work technically, but accessing elements in a Dictionary turns out to be a relatively slow operation.

■ **Note** My first implementation of the field manager did use a Dictionary, but the performance was too poor, so I shifted to the implementation I'm discussing here to address the issue.

Instead, the field values are maintained in an array of IFieldData objects.

```
private IFieldData[] _fieldData;
```

I'll discuss the IFieldData interface later. For now, I want to discuss how the property values are indexed into this array.

Generating a Consolidated Property List

What algorithm is used to set and get property values from this array in a meaningful manner? In short, each property is assigned a numeric index value between 0 and the number of properties registered for the business object type. Assigning these index values is the challenge, and it is complicated by inheritance.

Earlier in the chapter, I discussed the PropertyInfoManager and how it maintains a list of IPropertyInfo objects for each business object type. Remember that a business object type might be a subclass of some other type. It turns out that any level in the inheritance hierarchy might declare a property and register it by calling RegisterProperty().

This means that to get a consolidated list of all properties declared by a business object, it is necessary to walk through all the types in the inheritance hierarchy, getting the list of IPropertyInfo objects for each of the types. Obviously, that process could be relatively expensive, so it is done only once and the result is cached. FieldDataManager includes a GetConsolidatedList() method that retrieves the consolidated list of properties if it has already been generated, or calls CreateConsolidatedList() to create the list.

The CreateConsolidatedList() method is the interesting part of this process, because it assembles the consolidated list and assigns the numeric index values. Here is the method from the FieldDataManager class:

```
private static List<IPropertyInfo> CreateConsolidatedList(Type type)
{
  List<IPropertyInfo> result = new List<IPropertyInfo>();
  // get inheritance hierarchy
  Type current = type;
  List<Type> hierarchy = new List<Type>();
  do
  {
    hierarchy.Add(current);
    current = current.BaseType;
  } while (current != null && !current.Equals(typeof(BusinessBase)));
  // walk from top to bottom to build consolidated list
  for (int index = hierarchy.Count - 1; index >= 0; index--)
    result.AddRange(
      PropertyInfoManager.GetPropertyListCache(hierarchy[index]));
  // set Index properties on all unindexed PropertyInfo objects
  int max = -1;
  foreach (var item in result)
  {
    if (item.Index == -1)
    {
      max++;
      item.Index = max;
    }
    else
    {
      max = item.Index;
    }
  }
  // return consolidated list
  return result;
}
```

There's a lot going on here, so let's break it down. The first step is to get a list of all the types in this object's inheritance hierarchy.

```
Type current = type;
List<Type> hierarchy = new List<Type>();
do
{
  hierarchy.Add(current);
  current = current.BaseType;
} while (current != null && !current.Equals(typeof(BusinessBase)));
```

Since the `FieldDataManager` and the `RegisterProperty()` methods are declared in the `BusinessBase` class, there's no sense going any higher than that class. The result of this code is that the `hierarchy` field has a list of the types in this inheritance hierarchy, with the top-most base class being the last item in the list.

The next step is to loop through all those types, getting the list of any registered properties for each type. This is done from top to bottom, so the deepest base class is processed first.

```
for (int index = hierarchy.Count - 1; index >= 0; index--)
  result.AddRange(
    PropertyInfoManager.GetPropertyListCache(hierarchy[index]));
```

Remember that the registered properties for each type are stored in sorted order, so this algorithm guarantees that you end up with a consolidated list in the `result` field, where the `IPropertyInfo` objects are sorted within each type, and where the list starts with the deepest base type and moves out to end with the actual business object type.

Since the order is known and consistent in all cases, it is then possible to loop through all the `IPropertyInfo` objects and assign them a numeric index value, starting at `0` and counting up.

```
int max = -1;
foreach (var item in result)
{
  if (item.Index == -1)
  {
    max++;
    item.Index = max;
  }
  else
  {
    max = item.Index;
  }
}
```

Of course, the value is only set if it hasn't been set to start with. In the `PropertyInfo` class, the index value is initialized to `-1`, and this loop only changes the value if it is still set to that initial default. This is important, because a given base class could be the base class for numerous business classes, and the index values for that base class should only be set once.

The end result of this work is that there's a consolidated list of all registered properties for the business object type, that those properties are in a consistent order, and that each `IPropertyInfo` object has a unique numeric index value that you can use to index into the array of `IFieldData` objects where the actual object's field data is stored.

IFieldData and IFieldData<T> Interfaces

Each field value is stored in an object that implements the `IFieldData` interface. In other words, each field value is stored in an object that maintains the field value, along with some metadata about the field value.

That interface is declared like this:

```
public interface IFieldData : ITrackStatus
{
  string Name { get; }
  object Value { get; set; }
  void MarkClean();
}
```

This interface ensures that each field is stored in an object that exposes the name of the field and the field's value and allows the field to be marked as being unchanged.

This interface inherits from `ITrackStatus`, which I'll discuss in Chapter 6 and will cover in depth in Chapter 8. The result is that any `IFieldData` is guaranteed to expose status tracking properties such as `IsDirty` and `IsValid`.

There's also a generic version of the interface.

```
public interface IFieldData<T> : IFieldData
{
  new T Value { get; set; }
}
```

This generic interface simply extends the interface with a strongly typed `Value` property that replaces the loosely typed one.

The reason for the generic interface is performance. Most field values are value types, such as `int`, `float`, and `DateTime`. If you store such values in a field of type `object`, .NET will do what is called *boxing* and *unboxing*, meaning that the value will be converted into and out of being an `object` rather than being a simple value type.

The field manager always attempts to store values in an `IFieldData<T>` first, only falling back to an `IFieldData` if necessary. This helps avoid the cost of boxing and unboxing value types.

FieldData<T> Class

Now that you've seen the `IFieldData` and `IFieldData<T>` interfaces, it should come as no surprise that the framework includes a default implementation. Only `IFieldData<T>` is implemented in the framework, because the field manager always stores values using a strongly typed approach.

The primary purpose of the `FieldData` class is to store a field value, along with important metadata about that field. In particular, it also stores the field's name, type, and a flag indicating whether the field has been changed.

The implementation provided by `FieldData` is designed for performance over advanced functionality. For example, it determines whether a field has been changed by maintaining a simple flag that is set to `true` any time the value is changed.

```
public virtual T Value
{
  get
  {
    return _data;
  }
  set
  {
    _data = value;
    _isDirty = true;
  }
}
```

Even if the field is reset later to its original value, it is considered to have changed. While this is somewhat simplistic, it is also fast and minimizes resource overhead. The primary alternative would be for the object to maintain a copy of the field's original value so it can compare any new value to that original value to decide whether `IsDirty` should return `true` or `false`. Obviously, that would double the amount of memory required by each `FieldData` object and would double the amount of data transferred across the network in client/server scenarios.

■ **Note** As an extensibility point, it is possible to create your own implementations of `IFieldData` or `IFieldData<T>` to replace the default behaviors shown here. For example, you might do this if you want to store the original value of a field and replace the default `IsDirty` behavior to compare against that value.

You should now understand that the `FieldDataManager` maintains a list of field values in an array of `IFieldData`, where the objects are of type `FieldData<T>`. To conclude this topic, I want to discuss how framework classes retrieve and set the field values.

Getting Field Values

The FieldDataManager class exposes a GetFieldData() method that other framework classes can use to retrieve field values.

```
internal IFieldData GetFieldData(IPropertyInfo prop)
{
  try
  {
    return _fieldData[prop.Index];
  }
  catch (IndexOutOfRangeException ex)
  {
    throw new InvalidOperationException(Resources.PropertyNotRegistered, ex);
  }
}
```

This method simply uses the index from the IPropertyInfo parameter to find and return the IFieldData object from the array.

The interesting part of this method is the exception handling. Notice how any IndexOutOfRangeException is converted into the more useful InvalidOperationException, with the default message text of "One or more properties are not registered for this type." The most common issue people face when using managed fields is that they register the property incorrectly. The normal result would be an unintuitive IndexOutOfRangeException, so this code ensures that the business developer will get a more useful exception and message.

A field value is retrieved because BusinessBase or ReadOnlyBase needs the value. This means that GetFieldData() is invoked from a GetProperty() or ReadProperty() method in one of those classes. For example, here's the ReadProperty() method in BusinessBase, with the call to GetFieldData() and related code highlighted:

```
protected P ReadProperty<P>(PropertyInfo<P> propertyInfo)
{
  P result = default(P);
  FieldManager.IFieldData data = FieldManager.GetFieldData(propertyInfo);
  if (data != null)
  {
    FieldManager.IFieldData<P> fd = data as FieldManager.IFieldData<P>;
    if (fd != null)
      result = fd.Value;
    else
      result = (P)data.Value;
  }
  else
  {
    result = propertyInfo.DefaultValue;
    FieldManager.LoadFieldData<P>(propertyInfo, result);
  }
  return result;
}
```

The GetFieldData() method is called to get the IFieldData object from the field manager. Assuming there is a corresponding field, the code then attempts to cast the result to an IFieldData<P> to use the strongly typed interface.

```
    FieldManager.IFieldData<P> fd = data as FieldManager.IFieldData<P>;
    if (fd != null)
      result = fd.Value;
```

This is always the case when using the default `FieldData<T>` type provided by CSLA .NET, so the field value will be returned without boxing or unboxing.

If a person has implemented his own `IFieldData` that doesn't use the generic interface, then the boxed value must be converted to the right type and returned.

```
    else
      result = (P)data.Value;
```

`BusinessBase` and `ReadOnlyBase` use this technique when they need to retrieve managed field values.

Setting Field Values

`FieldDataManager` has two `SetFieldData()` methods: one generic and one not. The default is to use the generic overload, which looks like this:

```
internal void SetFieldData<P>(IPropertyInfo prop, P value)
{
  var field = GetOrCreateFieldData(prop);
  var fd = field as IFieldData<P>;
  if (fd != null)
    fd.Value = value;
  else
    field.Value = value;
}
```

This code retrieves (or creates) the `IFieldData` object from the array, then attempts to cast it to an `IFieldData<T>`. Normally this will succeed, because the storage object is a `FieldData<T>`. It's then possible to store the field value without boxing or unboxing.

The other overload is loosely typed, so it would incur boxing and unboxing costs. Even more, it will do type coercion if needed.

```
internal void SetFieldData(IPropertyInfo prop, object value)
{
  Type valueType;
  if (value != null)
    valueType = value.GetType();
  else
    valueType = prop.Type;
  value = Utilities.CoerceValue(prop.Type, valueType, null, value);
  var field = GetOrCreateFieldData(prop);
  field.Value = value;
}
```

This overload accepts the input value, then uses the `CoerceValue()` method to convert the value to the type expected by the field. Normally, you would expect that the inbound value is the same type (in which case `CoerceValue()` would do no work), but it is possible for a business object author to provide a value of some other type. This helps ensure that the value is converted to the right type before it is stored.

Only `BusinessBase` supports read-write properties, so only `BusinessBase` calls these methods. For example, here's the `LoadProperty()` method from `BusinessBase`:

```
protected void LoadProperty<P>(PropertyInfo<P> propertyInfo, P newValue)
{
  try
  {
    P oldValue = default(P);
    var fieldData = FieldManager.GetFieldData(propertyInfo);
    if (fieldData == null)
    {
      oldValue = propertyInfo.DefaultValue;
      fieldData = FieldManager.LoadFieldData<P>(propertyInfo, oldValue);
    }
    else
    {
      var fd = fieldData as FieldManager.IFieldData<P>;
      if (fd != null)
        oldValue = fd.Value;
      else
        oldValue = (P)fieldData.Value;
    }
    LoadPropertyValue<P>(propertyInfo, oldValue, newValue, false);
  }
  catch (Exception ex)
  {
    throw new PropertyLoadException(
      string.Format(Properties.Resources.PropertyLoadException,
                            propertyInfo.Name, ex.Message));
  }
}
```

The majority of this method is centered around *retrieving* the value from the field manager. It calls `GetFieldData()` to get the `IFieldData` object, and then it sets the `oldValue` field either to some default value or to the value retrieved from the field manager.

All that work is in preparation for a call to `LoadPropertyValue()`, which does the real work. The complex `LoadPropertyValue()` method implements the flowchart shown earlier in Figure 7-2. You can look at the full code from the Source Code/Download area of the Apress website (`www.apress.com`). The key thing to recognize is that it ultimately calls the `SetFieldData()` method from the field manager:

```
FieldManager.SetFieldData<P>(propertyInfo, newValue);
```

Throughout the entire process, the input value is strongly typed, including during the call to the field manager and storage in the `FieldData<T>` object.

You may be wondering, then, where that non-generic `SetFieldData()` overload is invoked. It is invoked from a non-generic overload of `SetProperty()` implemented in `BusinessBase`.

```
protected void SetProperty(IPropertyInfo propertyInfo, object newValue)
{
  FieldManager.SetFieldData(propertyInfo, newValue);
}
```

This overload of `SetProperty()` exists to support scenarios in which the business developer is loading the fields of the object from an external data source, such as an XML file or database. In that case, the developer might be looping through all the registered properties, loading the field data for each one, and would be unable to use a generic method in that case. Additionally, the input values may or may not be an exact match for the type of the field, which is why it is so important that the SetFieldData() method call CoerceValue() to convert the value to the right type.

At this point, you should have an understanding of how managed backing fields are implemented, including their storage in IFieldData objects, which are managed by the FieldDataManager and consumed in BusinessBase and ReadOnlyBase.

Conclusion

In this chapter, I discussed the options available for declaring and working with properties on your editable and read-only business objects. You should now understand how the framework handles both private backing fields and managed backing fields.

Chapters 8–16 will continue the implementation discussion by providing more detail about the implementation of each major framework feature. From Chapter 17 on, the focus will be on building the simple business application designed in Chapter 3, to illustrate how you can use the classes in the framework to build applications based on business objects.

CHAPTER 8

Object Status Management

The next topic I want to discuss in the implementation of CSLA .NET is how editable objects manage status information. Editable business objects maintain a set of consistent status information. Management of these values is mostly automated by `BusinessBase`, `BusinessListBase`, and the data portal.

Object Status Properties

All editable business objects should keep track of whether the object has just been created, whether its data has been changed, or whether it has been marked for deletion. Using the validation rules functionality, the object can also keep track of whether it's valid. Table 8-1 lists the object status properties in `BusinessBase` and `BusinessListBase`.

Table 8-1. *Object Status Properties*

Property	Description
`IsNew`	Indicates whether the object's primary identifying value in memory corresponds to a primary key in a database—if not, the object is new
`IsSelfDirty`	Indicates whether the object's data in memory is known to be different from data in the database—if different, the object is dirty
`IsDirty`	Indicates whether the object itself has been changed, or if any of its child objects have been changed
`IsSelfValid`	Indicates whether the object currently has any broken validation rules—if so, the object is not valid
`IsValid`	Indicates whether the object itself is valid, and whether all its child objects are also valid
`IsSavable`	Indicates whether the object can be saved by combining `IsValid`, `IsDirty`, authorization, and edit level, and whether there are any outstanding async validation rules running
`IsDeleted`	Indicates whether the object is marked for deletion

ITrackStatus Interface

In Chapter 6 I briefly discussed the ITrackStatus interface from the Csla.Core namespace. This interface is implemented by BusinessBase and BusinessListBase, allowing your code to gain access to the object status values without worrying about the specific object type:

```
public interface ITrackStatus
{
  bool IsValid { get; }
  bool IsSelfValid { get; }
  bool IsDirty { get; }
  bool IsSelfDirty { get; }
  bool IsDeleted { get; }
  bool IsNew { get; }
  bool IsSavable { get; }
}
```

This interface is used within CSLA .NET itself, but is also available to business object and UI framework authors.

I will now discuss the concepts behind an object being new, dirty, valid, and marked for deletion.

IsNew

When an object is "new," it means that the object exists in memory but not in the database or other persistent store. If the object's data resides in the database, the object is considered to be "old." I typically think of it this way: if the primary key value in the object corresponds to an existing primary key value in the database, the object is old; otherwise it is new.

The value behind the IsNew property is stored in an _isNew field. When an object is first created, this value defaults to the object being new:

```
private bool _isNew = true;
```

The IsNew property simply exposes this value:

```
[Browsable(false)]
public bool IsNew
{
  get { return _isNew; }
}
```

The property is adorned with the Browsable attribute from the System.ComponentModel namespace. This attribute tells data binding not to automatically bind this property. Without this attribute, data binding would automatically display this property in grids and on forms, and typically, this property shouldn't be displayed. This attribute is used on other properties in BusinessBase as well.

MarkOld Method

If the object is then loaded with data from the database, the _isNew field is set to false, through a protected MarkOld() method:

```
protected virtual void MarkOld()
{
  _isNew = false;
  MarkClean();
}
```

Notice that this process also sets the object to a "clean" status—a concept discussed later in this chapter when we look at the IsDirty property. When an object's data has just been loaded from the database, it is safe to assume that the object's data matches the data in the database and has not been changed and thus is "clean."

MarkNew Method

There's also a corresponding MarkNew() method:

```
protected virtual void MarkNew()
{
  _isNew = true;
  _isDeleted = false;
  MarkDirty();
}
```

These methods are normally called automatically by the data portal through the IDataPortalTarget interface, but since they are protected they are available to the business object author as well. This allows the business object to change its own state to handle those rare cases where the default behavior is inappropriate.

Knowing whether an object is new or old allows for implementation of the data portal in Chapter 15. The IsNew property will control the choice of whether to insert or update data into the database.

Sometimes, the IsNew property can be useful to the UI developer as well. Some UI behaviors may be different for a new object than for an existing object. The ability to edit the object's primary key data is a good example; this is often editable only up to the point that the data has been stored in the database. When the object becomes "old," the primary key is fixed.

IsSelfDirty

An object is considered to be "dirty," or changed, when the values in the object's fields do not match the values in the database. If the values in the object's fields do match the values in the database, the object is not dirty. It is virtually impossible to always know whether the object's values match those in the database, so the implementation shown here acts on a "best guess." The implementation relies on the business developer to indicate when an object has been changed and thus has become dirty.

A similar but related concept is that an object is considered dirty if it or any of its child objects have been changed. That concept is reflected by the IsDirty property, which is different from IsSelfDirty that reflects the status of only this specific object (not counting its child objects).

The current status of the value is maintained in a field:

```
private bool _isDirty = true;
```

The value is then exposed as a property:

```
[Browsable(false)]
public virtual bool IsSelfDirty
{
  get { return _isDirty; }
}
```

Notice that this property is marked as virtual. This is important because sometimes a business object isn't simply dirty because its data has changed. In this case, the business developer will need to override the IsSelfDirty property to provide a more sophisticated implementation.

■ **Note** While changing the behavior of IsSelfDirty is a rare scenario, the feature was requested numerous times by the community and so the property was made virtual.

The IsSelfDirty property defaults to true because a new object's field values won't correspond to values in the database.

MarkClean Method

If the object's values are subsequently loaded from the database, the _isDirty value is changed to false when MarkOld() is called because MarkOld() calls a MarkClean() method:

```
[EditorBrowsable(EditorBrowsableState.Advanced)]
protected void MarkClean()
{
  _isDirty = false;
  if (_fieldManager != null)
    FieldManager.MarkClean();
  OnUnknownPropertyChanged();
}
```

This method not only sets the _isDirty value to false but also calls MarkClean() on the FieldManager to mark all the fields it contains as being unchanged. Once the object and its fields are marked as unchanged, this method calls the OnUnknownPropertyChanged() method implemented in Csla.Core.BindableBase to raise the PropertyChanged event for all object properties. This notifies data binding that the object has changed, so WPF and Windows Forms can refresh the display for the user. I discuss the BindableBase class and data binding in Chapter 10.

MarkDirty Method

There's a corresponding MarkDirty() method as well. This method is called from various points in an object's lifetime, including any time a property value is changed or when the MarkNew() method is called. When a property value is changed, a specific PropertyChanged event is raised for that property.

If MarkDirty() is called at other times, when a specific property value *isn't* changed, the PropertyChanged event for all object properties should be raised. That way, data binding is notified of the change if *any* object property is bound to a UI control.

To be clear, the goal is to ensure that at least one PropertyChanged event is raised any time the object's state changes. If a specific property is changed, the PropertyChanged event should be raised *for that property*. But if there's no way to tell which properties are changed (like when the object is persisted to the database), there's no real option but to raise PropertyChanged for every property.

Implementing this requires a couple of overloads of the MarkDirty() method:

```
protected void MarkDirty()
{
  MarkDirty(false);
}

[EditorBrowsable(EditorBrowsableState.Advanced)]
protected void MarkDirty(bool suppressEvent)
{
  _isDirty = true;
  if (!suppressEvent)
    OnUnknownPropertyChanged();
}
```

The first overload can be called by a business developer if she wants to manually mark the object as changed. This is intended for use when unknown properties may have changed.

PropertyHasChanged Method

The second overload is called by the PropertyHasChanged() method:

```
protected virtual void PropertyHasChanged(string propertyName)
{
  MarkDirty(true);
  var propertyNames = ValidationRules.CheckRules(propertyName);
  if (ApplicationContext.PropertyChangedMode ==
                  ApplicationContext.PropertyChangedModes.Windows)
    OnPropertyChanged(propertyName);
  else
    foreach (var name in propertyNames)
      OnPropertyChanged(name);
}
```

The PropertyHasChanged() method is called by the SetProperty() methods discussed in Chapter 7 to indicate that a specific property has changed. Notice that in this case, any validation rules for the property are checked (the details on this are discussed in Chapter 11).

■ **Tip** This method is virtual, allowing you to add extra steps to the process if needed. Additionally, this means you can override the behavior to implement field-level dirty tracking if desired.

Then the object is marked as being dirty by raising the PropertyChanged event for the specific property that is changed. This isn't as simple as I would like because the code needs to behave differently when used by WPF as opposed to any other UI technology such as Windows Forms or Web Forms. Since there's no way to automatically detect whether this object is being used by WPF, there's a configuration switch the business developer can set to indicate how this method should behave.

Configuring the PropertyChangedMode

The Csla.ApplicationContext.PropertyChangedMode setting can be configured through the application's config file or in code.

In code, the UI developer will typically set the value by running the following line of code exactly once as the application starts up:

```
Csla.ApplicationContext.PropertyChangedMode =
  Csla.ApplicationContext.PropertyChangedModes.Xaml;
```

This only needs to be done in a WPF application, as the default is Windows, which is the correct setting for any non-WPF application.

The value can also be set in the application's app.config file by adding the following element to the <appSettings> element:

```
<add key="CslaPropertyChangedMode" value="Xaml" />
```

Either way, the result is that the PropertyChanged events are raised as required by WPF rather than as needed for Windows Forms or Web Forms.

Raising Events for WPF

In WPF, when a PropertyChanged event is handled by data binding, only the control(s) bound to *that specific property* are refreshed in the UI. This makes a lot of sense but causes a bit of complexity.

When a property is changed it triggers the execution of the business and validation rules associated with that property (see Chapter 11 for details). It also triggers the execution of rules associated with *dependent properties*. This means that changing one property can execute rules for multiple properties.

When a validation rule fails, the UI will display something to the user indicating that the value is invalid. WPF data binding knows to change the display for a control because it handles the PropertyChanged event for the property to which the control is data bound.

If the only PropertyChanged event raised is for the property that is changed, any broken validation rules for *dependent properties* will be ignored by data binding and won't be visible to the user.

Notice that the CheckRules() method call returns an array containing the names of all the properties for which business or validation rules are executed. This allows the PropertyHasChanged() method to raise PropertyChanged events for all those property names, not just for the property that is actually changed. The result is that broken validation rules are reflected in the UI, even for properties other than the one that is actually changed.

Raising Events for Windows Forms

In Windows Forms, data binding works differently. When a PropertyChanged event is handled by Windows Forms data binding, all controls bound to this business object are refreshed in the UI. Any single PropertyChanged event refreshes all the controls in the UI. This means that the fewer PropertyChanged events raised the better because each one causes a refresh of the UI.

For other technologies, such as Web Forms, the PropertyChanged event isn't used by data binding at all. But it is still important to raise the event because custom UI code often listens for this event so it knows that the object has been changed. Since most of this custom UI code was written before WPF, it tends to expect the Windows Forms–friendly behavior rather than the WPF-friendly behavior.

To this end, the default behavior is to raise only one PropertyChanged event for the property that is actually changed. This is true even if multiple properties have their validation rules run as a result of the change.

The final result is that the property's validation rules are checked, the IsDirty property is set to true, and the appropriate PropertyChanged events are raised.

IsDirty

You've seen how each individual business object manages its own IsSelfDirty property. When an object is a parent, things are slightly more complex. This is because a parent is considered to be changed if its fields have changed or if any of its child objects have been changed.

This is important because the IsDirty property is used by the data portal to optimize which objects to update into the database. If an object hasn't been changed, there's no sense trying to update the database with the values it already has. But consider the case of something like a parent SalesOrder object that contains a list of child LineItem objects. Even if users do not change the SalesOrder itself, if they change the LineItem objects, the object graph as a whole must be considered to have changed. When the UI code calls _salesOrder.Save(), it is reasonable to expect that the changed LineItem object (a child of the SalesOrder object) will be saved.

The IsDirty property makes it easy for the data portal code to determine whether the object graph has been changed because it consolidates the object's IsSelfDirty value with the IsDirty values of all child objects:

```
[Browsable(false)]
public virtual bool IsDirty
{
  get { return IsSelfDirty || (_fieldManager != null && FieldManager.IsDirty()); }
}
```

As discussed in Chapter 7, the `FieldManager` is used to determine whether any child objects contained by this object have been changed.

■ **Note** If you do not use managed backing fields to store your child object references, you'll need to override this method to also check the `IsDirty` status of your child objects. I recommend always using managed backing fields for child references so you don't need to worry about this issue.

Where `IsSelfDirty` provides the status for one object, `IsDirty` is often more useful because it provides the status for the object and all its child objects.

IsSelfValid

An object is considered to be valid if it has no currently broken validation rules. The `Csla.Validation` namespace is covered in Chapter 11 and provides management of the business rules. The `IsSelfValid` property merely exposes a flag indicating whether the object currently has broken rules or not.

There's also an `IsValid` property that reflects whether the current object, *or any of its child objects*, are invalid.

Here's the `IsSelfValid` code, which returns a value for only this object, not counting its child objects:

```
[Browsable(false)]
public virtual bool IsSelfValid
{
  get { return ValidationRules.IsValid; }
}
```

As with `IsSelfDirty`, this property is marked with the `Browsable` attribute so data binding defaults to ignoring the property.

There are no methods to directly control whether an object is valid. The validity of an object is managed by the business and validation rules subsystem discussed in Chapter 11. However, this method is `virtual`, so it is possible to replace or extend the way CSLA .NET manages the concept of validity if you so desire.

IsValid

While `IsSelfValid` indicates the validity of a specific object, the true validity of an object must also include the validity of any child objects. Even if an object itself is valid, if it contains invalid child objects, the object graph as a whole must be considered invalid.

The `IsValid` property combines the `IsSelfValid` result with the `IsValid` results of any child objects contained by this object:

```
[Browsable(false)]
public virtual bool IsValid
{
  get
  {
    return IsSelfValid && (_fieldManager == null || FieldManager.IsValid());
  }
}
```

Again, the FieldManager is used to determine whether any child objects are invalid. The result is that a business object is considered valid only if it, and all its child objects, are valid.

IsSavable

An object should only be saved to the database if it is valid and its data has changed and there are no outstanding asynchronous validation rules executing and the current user is authorized to update the object.

The IsValid property indicates whether the object is valid, and the IsValidating property indicates whether there are any outstanding asynchronous validation rules executing. The IsDirty property indicates whether the object's data has changed. The authorization rules subsystem is discussed in Chapter 12.

The IsSavable property is a simple helper to combine these concepts into a single property:

```
[Browsable(false)]
public virtual bool IsSavable
{
  get
  {
    bool auth;
    if (IsDeleted)
      auth = Csla.Security.AuthorizationRules.CanDeleteObject(this.GetType());
    else if (IsNew)
      auth = Csla.Security.AuthorizationRules.CanCreateObject(this.GetType());
    else
      auth = Csla.Security.AuthorizationRules.CanEditObject(this.GetType());
    return (auth && IsDirty && IsValid && !ValidationRules.IsValidating);
  }
}
```

The authorization code is interesting because it relies on the state of the object to decide which type of authorization is required. For example, if the IsDeleted property returns true, the object is marked for deletion and so the delete authorization is checked.

Assuming the user is authorized, the code makes sure the object has been changed and is valid and that there are no outstanding asynchronous validation rules executing.

The primary purpose for this property is to allow a UI developer to enable or disable a Save button (or similar UI element) such that the button is only enabled if the object can be saved. For example, it is used by the CslaDataProvider control to automatically enable and disable controls in WPF, as discussed in Chapter 19.

IsDeleted

The CSLA .NET framework provides for deferred or immediate deletion of an object. The *immediate* approach directly deletes an object's data from the database without first loading the object into memory. It requires prior knowledge of the object's primary key value(s) and is discussed in Chapters 4 and 5.

The *deferred* approach requires that the object is loaded into memory. The user can then view and manipulate the object's data and may decide to delete the object, in which case the object is marked for deletion. The object is not immediately deleted but rather it is deleted if and when the object is saved to the database. At that time, instead of inserting or updating the object's data, it is deleted from the database.

This approach is particularly useful for child objects in a collection. In such a case, the user may be adding and updating some child objects at the same time as deleting others. All the insert, update, and delete operations occur in a batch when the collection is saved to the database.

Whether an object is marked for deletion is tracked by the `_isDeleted` field and exposed through an `IsDeleted` property:

```
private bool _isDeleted;

[Browsable(false)]
public bool IsDeleted
{
  get { return _isDeleted; }
}
```

Like the other status properties, this one cannot be data bound.

MarkDeleted Method

As with `IsSelfDirty`, there's a `protected` method to allow the object to be marked for deletion when necessary:

```
protected void MarkDeleted()
{
  _isDeleted = true;
  MarkDirty();
}
```

Of course, marking the object as deleted is another way of changing its data, so the `MarkDirty()` method is called to indicate that the object's state has been changed.

Delete and DeleteChild Methods

The `MarkDeleted()` method is called from the `Delete()` and `DeleteChild()` methods. The `Delete()` method is used to mark a non-child object for deferred deletion, while `DeleteChild()` is called by a parent object (such as a collection) to mark the child object for deferred deletion:

```
public void Delete()
{
  if (this.IsChild)
    throw new NotSupportedException(Resources.ChildDeleteException);

  MarkDeleted();
}
```

```
internal void DeleteChild()
{
  if (!this.IsChild)
    throw new NotSupportedException(Resources.NoDeleteRootException);

  MarkDeleted();
}
```

Both methods do the same thing: call `MarkDelete()`. But `Delete()` is scoped as `public` and can only be called if the object is *not* a child object (a topic covered in the discussion about parent and child object behaviors in Chapter 9). Conversely, `DeleteChild()` can only be called if the object *is* a child. Since it is intended for use by `BusinessListBase`, it is scoped as `internal`.

At this point, you should have a good understanding of the various object status values managed by `BusinessBase` and `BusinessListBase`.

Conclusion

In this chapter, I continued discussing the implementation of the CSLA .NET framework. This chapter covered the object status values maintained by editable objects, allowing the rest of CSLA .NET, your business code, and your UI code to interact with your objects in a standardized manner.

All editable objects maintain the following status values:

- `IsSelfDirty`
- `IsDirty`
- `IsSelfValid`
- `IsValid`
- `IsNew`
- `IsSavable`
- `IsDeleted`

Some of these values are important to parent-child relationships, as discussed in Chapter 9. Others rely on validation and authorization, as discussed in Chapters 11 and 12. And many of them are used by the data portal as discussed in Chapter 15.

CHAPTER 9

Parent-Child Relationships

In Chapter 6, I started walking through the framework implementation. Chapter 7 covers how to declare properties, including properties that reference child objects, and Chapter 8 focuses on how object status values are tracked, including some interaction with child objects.

The idea of *child objects* is introduced in Chapter 3. A child object is contained by a *parent object*. Conversely, a parent object is an object that contains one or more child objects. The top-most parent of a group of objects is the *root object*, and that is the object that can be directly retrieved or updated into the database. Any child objects contained by that root object are retrieved or updated at the same time, a topic I cover in Chapter 15.

While many of the details of parent and child objects are covered in other chapters, this chapter recaps the concepts, consolidating them into one location for easy reference. First I talk about child properties of an editable object, then I talk about how editable collections work because they contain an entire list of child objects.

Parent Editable Object

One common scenario is to have an editable object be a parent of other objects. In many cases, the root object is also an editable object, as shown in Figure 9-1.

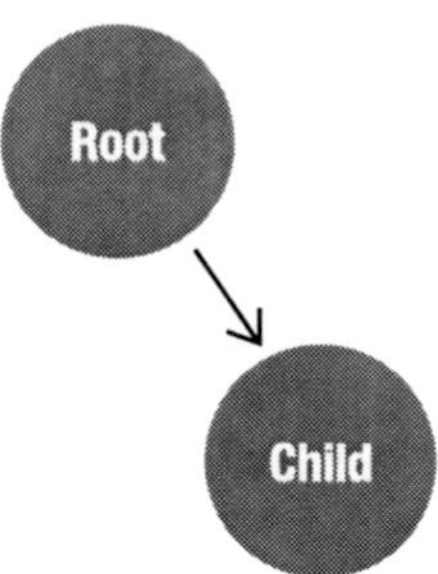

Figure 9-1. *Parent with single child*

A parent object may also contain a child collection, as shown in Figure 9-2.

In Figure 9-2 there are actually two parent objects. The `Root` object is the parent of `ChildList`, which is the parent of several `Child` objects. I discuss parent collections later in the chapter in the "Parent Editable Collection" section. For now let's focus on the editable object as a parent.

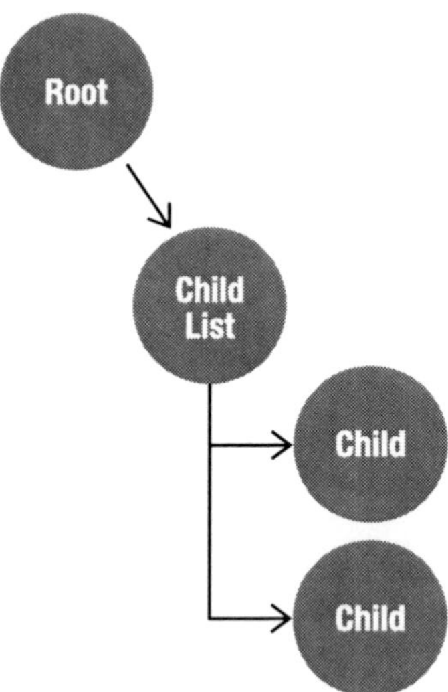

Figure 9-2. *Parent with single collection*

Parent-Child Interaction

In Chapter 7, I discuss the various options for declaring properties, including the use of `private` and managed backing fields. When declaring a property that contains a reference to a child object I strongly recommend always using a managed backing field, even if you are using `private` backing fields for your other properties. The reason for this is that using a managed backing field allows CSLA .NET to help you properly handle the child reference.

Table 9-1 lists the details managed for you by CSLA .NET.

Table 9-1. *Parent-Child Details Managed by CSLA .NET*

Method	Description
`IsValid`	A parent object is only valid if it and all its child objects are also valid.
`IsDirty`	A parent object is dirty (changed) if it or any of its child objects are dirty.
`IsBusy`	A parent object is busy (has an asynchronous operation running) if it or any of its child objects are busy.
Changed events	When a child object is changed, its changed event (`PropertyChanged` or `ListChanged`) results in the parent raising a `ChildChanged` event, which cascades up through the parent-child chain and is raised by every object, including the root object.
Parent reference	All child objects have a reference to their parent, which must be established when the child is attached to the parent and when the object graph is deserialized.
N-level undo	The edit levels of the parent and child interact with each other as discussed in Chapter 11.

If you don't use a managed backing field, you assume responsibility for handling all these details.

Note You can handle all these details manually. Prior to CSLA .NET 3.5, it was necessary to do this in all parent objects. Forgetting to do one of these steps (or doing one incorrectly) was one of the primary causes of bugs in pre-3.5 objects.

Each item in Table 9-1 deserves a little discussion.

IsValid and IsDirty Properties

In Chapter 8, I discussed object status values. One important concept is that a parent object is considered valid or changed based on a combination of its state and the state of its child object(s).

Each editable object has an IsSelfValid property that gets a value, indicating whether *that particular object* is valid. The concept of validity is discussed further in Chapter 11.

However, each editable object also has an IsValid property that gets a value indicating whether the object *and its child objects* are valid. For IsValid to return true, the object and *all* its child objects must be valid. This is handled through the implementation of IsValid and IsSelfValid in BusinessBase, combined with the FieldDataManager (discussed in Chapter 7), which interrogates all managed backing fields to find out if they are all valid.

Here's the IsValid implementation in FieldDataManager:

```
public bool IsValid()
{
  foreach (var item in _fieldData)
    if (item != null && !item.IsValid)
      return false;
  return true;
}
```

The validity of simple fields, such as a string or int value, is managed by the business object's validation rules, not the specific IsValid value for the field itself. The FieldData object simply returns true for IsValid at all times. But if the field is a reference to a child object, FieldData delegates the IsValid call to the actual child object, and so the child object's validity is what matters.

Here's the IsValid implementation in FieldData:

```
protected virtual bool IsValid
{
  get
  {
    ITrackStatus child = _data as ITrackStatus;
    if (child != null)
    {
      return child.IsValid;

    }
    else
    {
      return true;
    }
  }
}
```

Notice how the ITrackStatus interface is used to detect whether the field's value is an object capable of representing its own status values. If the field value can be cast to ITrackStatus, the child object's IsValid value is returned; otherwise, true is returned.

The IsDirty property of BusinessBase works exactly the same way, but the rule is slightly different. An object is considered to be changed, or dirty, if its data has changed or if any one of its child objects has been changed.

As with IsValid, the IsDirty property in BusinessBase works with FieldDataManager to determine whether any child objects have been changed. I won't walk through that code because it is essentially the same as the IsValid code shown here. You can look in the code from the download to see how IsDirty is implemented.

ChildChanged Event

When a property of an object is changed, a PropertyChanged event is raised. I discuss the PropertyChanged event and how it supports data binding in Chapter 10. For now it is enough to know that changing a property value in an object results in this event being raised.

If the child object is a collection or a list, inheriting from a BusinessListBase, a ListChanged event is raised when the list changes. This includes changes to properties of child objects contained in the list. In other words, when an object in the list changes, it raises a PropertyChanged event, which is handled by the list and results in a ListChanged event being raised. Again, I discuss ListChanged and data binding more in Chapter 10.

There are cases where the *parent* of an object needs to know that its child has been changed. For example, sometimes you'll have business or validation rules that must run in the parent when a child is changed.

To address this, BusinessBase includes code to handle the PropertyChanged or ListChanged events raised by any child objects. When such an event is handled, the result is a call to OnChildChanged(), which raises a ChildChanged event from the parent.

This means that the author of a parent business object can either override OnChildChanged() or handle the parent object's ChildChanged event. Either technique will result in notification that a child has changed.

The key is that BusinessBase includes code in the LoadPropertyValue() method (discussed in Chapter 7) to hook the PropertyChanged or ListChanged event of any child object when a reference to the child object is loaded into a managed backing field.

Also, when an object is serialized and deserialized (which occurs when it is cloned or flows through the data portal) all event hookups are lost. They must be reestablished when the object is deserialized, and that occurs in BusinessBase in the FieldDataDeserialized() method, which is called from the OnDeserializedHandler() method.

In both cases, the events are handled by these two methods in BusinessBase:

```
private void Child_PropertyChanged(
  object sender, PropertyChangedEventArgs e)
{
  OnChildChanged(sender, e, null);
}

private void Child_ListChanged(object sender, ListChangedEventArgs e)
{
  OnChildChanged(sender, null, e);
}
```

As you can see, they both call the OnChildChanged() method, which is protected and virtual:

```
[EditorBrowsable(EditorBrowsableState.Advanced)]
protected virtual void OnChildChanged(
  object source,
  PropertyChangedEventArgs propertyArgs,
  ListChangedEventArgs listArgs)
{
  Csla.Core.ChildChangedEventArgs args =
    new Csla.Core.ChildChangedEventArgs(source, propertyArgs, listArgs);
  if (_childChangedHandlers != null)
    _childChangedHandlers.Invoke(this, args);
}
```

This method uses the provided parameter values to create an instance of ChildChangedEventArgs, which is then used to raise the ChildChanged event.

The event itself is declared using the custom event declaration form:

```
[NonSerialized]
[NotUndoable]
private EventHandler<Csla.Core.ChildChangedEventArgs>
  _childChangedHandlers;

public event EventHandler<Csla.Core.ChildChangedEventArgs> ChildChanged
{
  add
  {
    _childChangedHandlers = (EventHandler<Csla.Core.ChildChangedEventArgs>)
      System.Delegate.Combine(_childChangedHandlers, value);
  }
  remove
  {
    _childChangedHandlers = (EventHandler<Csla.Core.ChildChangedEventArgs>)
      System.Delegate.Remove(_childChangedHandlers, value);
  }
}
```

This is substantially more code than a simple event declaration such as this:

```
public event EventHandler<Csla.Core.ChildChangedEventArgs> ChildChanged;
```

The reason for all the extra code is that the backing field for the event needs to be marked as NonSerialized and NotUndoable. All events on a Serializable object must be marked with NonSerialized. Failure to do this will result in serialization errors if the event is being handled by a nonserializable object such as a WPF Form or a Windows Forms Form or a Web Forms Page object. Similarly, any event declared in an undoable object (one that inherits from UndoableBase or implements IUndoableObject as discussed in Chapter 13) must mark the backing field as NotUndoable. Failure to do this will result in undo errors during data binding.

This long form for declaring events allows explicit declaration of the backing field (which is otherwise autogenerated by the compiler):

```
[NonSerialized]
[NotUndoable]
private EventHandler<Csla.Core.ChildChangedEventArgs>
  _childChangedHandlers;
```

This declares a delegate field to manage the event handler references and is normally done by the compiler. However, since this code is explicit, the declaration can be decorated with the NonSerialized and NotUndoable attributes. The result is that the ChildChanged event won't cause problems during serialization, n-level undo, or data binding.

You should now understand how BusinessBase handles all child PropertyChanged and ListChanged events and raises a ChildChanged event in response.

Parent Reference

All child objects maintain a reference to their immediate parent object. This reference is declared in BusinessBase as NonSerialized and NotUndoable:

```
[NotUndoable()]
[NonSerialized()]
private Core.IParent _parent;
```

The BinaryFormatter and NetDataContractSerializer can handle circular references in an object graph, so I could get away without the NonSerialized attribute. However, it has been observed that circular references in an object graph cause a *substantial* increase in the size of the byte stream that contains the serialized data. By using the NonSerialized attribute, I am reducing the size of the serialized data that is often transferred over the network in client/server scenarios.

The NotUndoable attribute is absolutely required. As you'll see in Chapter 13, the n-level undo support in CSLA .NET doesn't handle circular references, so if this attribute is missing, n-level undo would go into an infinite loop, resulting in a stack overflow exception.

Notice that the field type is IParent from the Csla.Core namespace. All parent objects are required to implement the IParent interface to enable interaction between the child and the parent. I discuss IParent later in this chapter.

The Parent property in BusinessBase is of this type as well:

```
[EditorBrowsable(EditorBrowsableState.Advanced)]
protected Core.IParent Parent
{
  get { return _parent; }
}
```

There's also a SetParent() method, which is invoked by the parent object to set the reference:

```
internal void SetParent(Core.IParent parent)
{
  _parent = parent;
}
```

This method is invoked by LoadPropertyValue() when the child object is set into a managed backing field. And it is invoked when the parent object is deserialized. Remember that the _parent field is NonSerialized, so when the child is deserialized the value is null. It must be restored to a meaningful value once deserialization is complete, and that occurs in the parent object's FieldDataDeserialized() method, which is invoked by the OnDeserializedHandler() method.

The result is that a child object can always get a reference to its immediate parent through its Parent property. This reference is used automatically in some cases, as I discuss later in the "Parent Editable Collection" section.

N-Level Undo

The n-level undo functionality of CSLA .NET is discussed in detail in Chapter 13. It is also discussed to some degree in Chapter 10 because n-level undo is used to provide important functionality for data binding.

There are several points in n-level undo and data binding, where parent and child objects must interact with each other. I won't discuss the details here; you can refer to Chapters 10 and 13.

IParent Interface

The `IParent` interface, declared in `Csla.Core`, allows a child object to interact with its parent:

```
public interface IParent
{
  void RemoveChild(Core.IEditableBusinessObject child);
  void ApplyEditChild(Core.IEditableBusinessObject child);
}
```

The `RemoveChild()` method is used by the data binding functionality discussed in Chapter 10. There are scenarios where data binding informs a child object that it has been removed or deleted and the child then must ask its parent to remove its reference to the child object.

The `ApplyEditChild()` method is used for interaction with the `EditableRootListBase` class, again triggered by data binding, so the parent collection can be notified that a child object's changes should be committed.

Perhaps more important than these two methods is the fact that the `IParent` interface provides a consistent type that is used by any child object when maintaining a reference to its immediate parent object.

At this point, you should have a high-level understanding of the features that CSLA .NET automatically provides when a child object reference is contained in a managed backing field. If you choose to use a private backing field to maintain a child object reference, you should make sure you replicate these behaviors as part of your implementation. Again, I recommend using managed backing fields to avoid having to do all that work.

Declaring Child Properties

There are several ways to use a managed backing field to reference a child object, depending on the specific features you desire. The variations center on how and when the child object is to be created.

You can create the child object as the parent object is created or retrieved from the database. Alternately you can create the child object on demand, meaning it is created the first time the UI (or other calling code) accesses the property that exposes the child object. Finally, you can use *lazy loading* to retrieve an existing child object in an on-demand manner.

Next I'll walk through each variation.

Create Child in DataPortal_XYZ Methods

The simplest property declaration is as follows:

```
private static PropertyInfo<ChildType> ChildProperty =
  RegisterProperty(new PropertyInfo<ChildType>("Child"));
public ChildType Child
{
  get { return GetProperty(ChildProperty); }
}
```

This stores the child reference in a managed backing field, which allows the field manager to automatically take care of all the housekeeping details involved with a child reference.

You should be wondering how the child object is actually created. This code simply returns a value, but that value must be initialized somewhere.

In Chapter 15 I discuss the data portal and object persistence. One feature of the data portal is that a root object is created or retrieved in methods you write, named `DataPortal_Create()` and `DataPortal_Fetch()`.

The `DataPortal_Create()` method is invoked by the data portal when your object should initialize itself with values appropriate for a new object. In many cases, this is where you'd also create a new, empty instance of your child object:

```
protected override void DataPortal_Create()
{
  LoadProperty(ChildProperty, Child.NewChild());
  base.DataPortal_Create();
}
```

The call to `ChildType.NewChild()` is invoking the child object's factory method, which is a concept I discuss in Chapters 4 and 5. It returns a new instance of the child object, which is then loaded into the property's managed backing field using the `LoadProperty()` method.

Similarly, the `DataPortal_Fetch()` method is invoked by the data portal when your object should load itself with data from the database. In most cases, this is where you'd also load any child objects with data from the database as well:

```
protected void DataPortal_Fetch(SingleCriteria<RootType, int> criteria)
{
  using (var ctx = ContextManager<DataContext>.GetManager("MyDatabase"))
  {
    // load root object with data here
    // get data for child here
    LoadProperty(ChildProperty, Child.GetChild(childData));
  }
}
```

There's a lot going on here, much of which is covered in Chapter 15. The important thing to realize is that the `Child.GetChild()` method is calling a factory method that creates an instance of the child object and loads that child object with data from the database. In many cases the data for the child object(s) is already loaded from the database by the code here in the parent, but that's not required.

Again, a `LoadProperty()` method is used to put the resulting child object into the managed backing field for the property.

The result is that when your root object is created or retrieved, `DataPortal_Create()` or `DataPortal_Fetch()` are invoked, and they both load a child object into the property using the `LoadProperty()` method. That value is then available to other business objects and the UI through the `public` property.

Additionally, any calls to the parent object's `IsValid` and `IsDirty` properties automatically take into account the `IsValid` and `IsDirty` status of your child object. And any change to the child object that results in a `PropertyChanged` or `ListChanged` will cause a `ChildChanged` event to be raised by the parent.

Create Child on Demand

It is very common to create a child object in the `DataPortal_Fetch()` method, so it can be efficiently loaded with data from the database as the parent object's data is also loaded. And that's a great approach. However, it seems unfortunate that you have to create a `DataPortal_Create()` method just to create an empty instance of a new child object. Many objects don't need to initialize values as they are created, and so you wouldn't need to implement DataPortal_Create() at all in that case (because there's a default implementation of DataPortal_Create() already provided by BusinessBase).

For the purpose of creating a new child object, you might choose to just create the child object *on demand*. In this case, you would not call LoadProperty() in the DataPortal_Create() method, as shown in the previous section. Instead, you'd enhance the property declaration itself like this:

```
private static PropertyInfo<ChildType> ChildProperty =
  RegisterProperty(new PropertyInfo<ChildType>("Child"));
public ChildType Child
{
  get
  {
    if (!FieldManager.FieldExists(ChildProperty))
      LoadProperty(ChildProperty, ChildType.NewChild());
    return GetProperty(ChildProperty);
  }
}
```

The FieldExists() method returns a value indicating whether this particular managed backing field exists yet. If it does not yet exist, the LoadProperty() method is called to load the backing field with a new child, created by the NewChild() factory method. On the other hand, if the managed backing field does already exist, the existing value is simply returned by the property.

The result of this approach is that a new child object is only created if and when this property is called the first time. It is created on demand.

This approach is also totally compatible with the idea of loading the child object in DataPortal_Fetch(). If the child object is created, initialized, and loaded in DataPortal_Fetch(), it will already exist by the time the property is invoked, and so that existing value is simply returned.

Lazy Load Child

There's one more variation you can use, which is on-demand *retrieval* of a child object. This is often called *lazy loading* of the child object. The idea here is that you would not create or load the child object in either DataPortal_Create() or DataPortal_Fetch(). Instead, you create or fetch the child object on demand in the property itself. There are wider implications here, especially in terms of how the child class is coded.

Before getting into the child class though, here's the property declaration in the parent:

```
private static PropertyInfo<ChildType> ChildProperty =
  RegisterProperty(new PropertyInfo<ChildType>("Child"));
public ChildType Child
{
  get
  {
    if (!FieldManager.FieldExists(ChildProperty))
      if (this.IsNew)
        LoadProperty(ChildProperty, ChildType.NewChild());
      else
        LoadProperty(ChildProperty, ChildType.GetChild(this));
    return GetProperty(ChildProperty);
  }
}
```

The basic concept is the same, in that the FieldExists() method is used to detect whether the child object already exists. If it does not already exist, the child object is created and loaded. But *that* process is a little different.

Notice that the parent object's IsNew property is used to determine whether the parent is a new object. If the parent is a new object, the child must be new as well, so the NewChild() factory method is invoked.

However, if the parent object is not new, it was loaded from the database, so it is reasonable to assume that there is child data in the database as well. So in this case the GetChild() factory method is called and the parent object is provided as a parameter to that factory.

■ **Caution** Remember that the child object is created the first time the property is accessed. It is easy to accidentally access a property, for example, by data binding the property to a UI. So if you want to use lazy loading, it is critical that you be very careful about how and when this property is accessed to avoid prematurely triggering lazy load process.

I won't fully discuss object persistence, factory methods, and the data portal until Chapter 15, so you may want to skip ahead and review those concepts, then return to the following discussion.

Enabling Lazy Loading in the Child Class

When using lazy loading, the code in a child class is different from normal. In fact, the child object will implement the same kind of factory and DataPortal_Fetch() as a root object. And you'll need to call MarkAsChild() manually because the data portal won't know to call it automatically on your behalf.

The child factory method will look like this:

```
internal ChildType GetChild(ParentType parent)
{
  return DataPortal.Fetch<ChildType>(
    new SingleCriteria<ChildType, int>(parent.Id));
}
```

The data portal is invoked to retrieve the child object, using properties from the parent object as criteria. In many cases a child object is loaded based on the parent object's unique ID value, which can be used as a foreign key, but the actual criteria values you use will depend on your specific object and data models.

■ **Tip** Notice that a reference to the parent object is provided as a parameter rather than specific parent properties. This provides good decoupling between the parent and child because this way the parent has no idea what data is required by the child's factory method.

As you'll see in Chapter 15, the data portal ultimately creates an instance of the object and invokes the DataPortal_Fetch() method. Normally, a child object wouldn't implement this method at all, but when using lazy loading you do implement this method. The method is responsible for loading the child object with data from the database:

```
private void DataPortal_Fetch(SingleCriteria<ChildType, int> criteria)
{
  MarkAsChild();
  // load child with data from database
}
```

The important thing to remember in this case is that you must call MarkAsChild() to indicate that this is a child object. You must do this manually because the data portal is being used to load the object here as though it were a *root* object. The data portal doesn't know to mark the object as a child automatically, so you must do it explicitly.

The end result is that the child object is created or retrieved on demand, using lazy loading.

At this point you should understand how an editable object can act as a parent or a child and how a parent object manages the references to its child objects. In the next section, I discuss how this works when the parent object is an editable collection.

Parent Editable Collection

Editable collections are created by inheriting from BusinessListBase, as discussed in Chapters 4 and 5. By definition, a collection is a parent because it contains the items in the collection.

To a large degree, the interactions between parent and child objects discussed already in this chapter also apply when the parent is a collection. For example, the BusinessListBase class implements the IParent interface. And BusinessListBase calls SetParent() as each child object is added to the collection or when the collection is deserialized. The same benefits and features I've already discussed apply to collections as well as editable objects.

However, editable collections provide some different behaviors as well, most notably around how items are deleted from the collection and how child events are cascaded up as ListChanged events from the collection (especially after deserialization of the collection).

Parent-Child Interaction

The BusinessListBase class provides the same set of behaviors in Table 9-1, earlier in the chapter. The primary difference in the implementation is that a collection has no intrinsic state of its own. Instead, its state comes from its child objects. In other words, the collection's IsValid and IsDirty properties simply reflect the underlying state of the child objects. For example, a collection is valid only if all the child objects it contains are valid.

The one big difference between an editable object and an editable collection is in terms of how ChildChanged events are handled.

ListChanged Event

Whereas an editable object handles any PropertyChanged or ListChanged events from its child objects and raises a ChildChanged event, an editable collection works a little differently.

An editable collection can only contain editable child objects so only needs to worry about those objects raising PropertyChanged and ChildChanged events. Any time a child object raises PropertyChanged, the collection raises a ListChanged event. This is automatic behavior provided by the BindingList<T> class from the System.ComponentModel namespace. Any time a child object raises a ChildChanged event, the collection raises its own ChildChanged event, effectively cascading the ChildChanged event up to each parent until it is raised by the editable root object.

Unfortunately, BindingList<T> doesn't automatically handle the case where the collection is serialized and deserialized, which happens when the object is cloned or transferred over the network in a client/server scenario. When a collection is deserialized, the ListChanged event is no longer automatically raised in response to a child object's PropertyChanged event.

To overcome this issue, BusinessListBase includes code to hook the PropertyChanged events from its child objects on deserialization and to raise the ListChanged event just like its base class did before serialization.

When the collection is deserialized, the formatter invokes OnDeserializedHandler(), which is implemented in ExtendedBindingList and includes code to hook the PropertyChanged events from all child objects in the list:

```
foreach (T item in this)
  OnAddEventHooksInternal(item);
```

The OnAddEventHooksInternal() method includes code to hook a number of child object events, most notably PropertyChanged:

```
INotifyPropertyChanged c = item as INotifyPropertyChanged;
if (c != null)
  c.PropertyChanged += Child_PropertyChanged;
```

The OnChildChangedInternal() method in BusinessListBase handles each child PropertyChanged event and raises a corresponding ListChanged event:

```
protected internal override void OnChildChangedInternal(
  object sender, ChildChangedEventArgs e)
{
  if (RaiseListChangedEvents && e.PropertyChangedArgs != null)
  {
    DeferredLoadIndexIfNotLoaded();
    if (_indexSet.HasIndexFor(e.PropertyChangedArgs.PropertyName))
      ReIndexItem((C)sender, e.PropertyChangedArgs.PropertyName);

    int index = IndexOf((C)sender);
    if (index >= 0)
    {
      PropertyDescriptor descriptor =
        GetPropertyDescriptor(e.PropertyChangedArgs.PropertyName);
      if (descriptor != null)
        OnListChanged(new ListChangedEventArgs(
          ListChangedType.ItemChanged,
          index, GetPropertyDescriptor(e.PropertyChangedArgs.PropertyName)));
      else
        OnListChanged(new ListChangedEventArgs(
          ListChangedType.ItemChanged, index));
      return;
    }
  }
}
```

There's code in here for LINQ to CSLA as well, which I discuss in Chapter 14. This method is invoked by the ExtendedBindingList base class, which contains the code to hook and unhook child object events as necessary.

I've highlighted the code relevant to the event discussion. You might expect that raising a ListChanged event would be easy, but it turns out to be quite complex. The reason is that the ListChanged event needs to provide both the index of the changed item and a PropertyDescriptor object for the child property that is changed.

Once the index value has been found, a GetPropertyDescriptor() method is called to find the PropertyDescriptor for the changed child property. Here's that method:

```
private static PropertyDescriptorCollection _propertyDescriptors;

private PropertyDescriptor GetPropertyDescriptor(string propertyName)
{
  if (_propertyDescriptors == null)
    _propertyDescriptors = TypeDescriptor.GetProperties(typeof(C));
  PropertyDescriptor result = null;
  foreach (PropertyDescriptor desc in _propertyDescriptors)
    if (desc.Name == propertyName)
    {
      result = desc;
      break;
    }
  return result;
}
```

The PropertyDescriptor concept comes from System.ComponentModel and is used extensively by Windows Forms data binding. This part of .NET is related to reflection but is a separate type system from reflection itself. Like reflection, however, the type descriptor functionality has a pretty high performance cost. To minimize the impact, the PropertyDescriptorCollection for the child object type is cached in a static field, so it is only retrieved once per AppDomain (typically once each time the application is run).

The PropertyChanged event only provides the name of the changed property, so it is necessary to loop through all the items in the PropertyDescriptorCollection to find the matching property name, at which point the resulting PropertyDescriptor can be returned. If no match is found, a null is returned.

While all this behavior is automatically handled by the BindingList<T> base class, this code is necessary because BindingList<T> doesn't handle the case where the collection has been serialized and deserialized.

Removing Child Objects from the Collection

It is possible to remove an item from the collection. The basic process is handled automatically by the BindingList<T> base class. However, there are some complications that must be handled by BusinessListBase. Specifically, any LINQ to CSLA index must be updated and there's interaction with the n-level undo behaviors, discussed in Chapter 13.

This last point about n-level undo is the most complex. If changes to a collection can be rolled back, any removed items must be restored and any newly added items removed.

I'll leave detailed discussions of LINQ to CSLA and n-level undo to their respective chapters. For now it is enough to know that the RemoveItem() method, which is a protected method provided by BindingList<T>, is invoked when a child item is to be removed. This method contains important code necessary for both LINQ to CSLA and n-level undo.

You should now have an understanding about how an editable collection provides not only the same parent functionality as an editable object but how it handles the child PropertyChanged events and must interact with the LINQ to CSLA and n-level undo functionality.

Conclusion

In this chapter I discussed how CSLA .NET supports important parent-child interactions, including the following:

- `IsValid`
- `IsDirty`
- Change events
- Parent reference
- N-level undo

Chapters 10 through 16 continue the coverage of the implementation of CSLA .NET. Then, from Chapter 17 on, the focus is on building the simple business application designed in Chapter 3 to illustrate how the classes in the framework can be used to build applications based on business objects.

CHAPTER 10

Data Binding

Data binding is a powerful concept that is supported by WPF, Windows Forms, and Web Forms. It is a Microsoft technology that provides an abstract and formal communication layer between the user interface and the business objects, or between the Interface Control layer and Business layer, to use the terms from Chapter 1.

It is important to maintain clear separation of concerns between the Interface Control and Business layers to avoid having business logic creep into the UI, or UI logic creep into the business objects. If either of those things occurs, the maintainability of your application will go down, and the cost of development and maintenance will go up. Having a prebuilt technology like data binding, which provides a powerful abstraction boundary between the two layers, can help a great deal.

At a very basic level, all .NET objects support data binding. However, to take full advantage of everything data binding has to offer, objects need to implement a set of interfaces and behaviors, some of which can be quite complex. I believe the end result is worth it, however, because this complex behavior can be implemented in a framework like CSLA .NET, so it doesn't impact your business objects directly. And with full support for data binding, you'll need to write a lot less code in the UI, and that increases the maintainability of any application.

I've been referring to data binding as though it were one technology. In reality, it is one *concept*, but the technology is somewhat different in WPF, Windows Forms, and Web Forms. Each type of UI has its own variation of data binding, though in each case the goal and end result are the same: to provide a clean, abstract way to connect the UI to the underlying business objects.

Of the three, Windows Forms data binding is the most mature and powerful. It turns out that if your objects support Windows Forms data binding, they automatically do almost everything required by WPF and Web Forms.

In this chapter, I'll discuss how the CSLA .NET framework supports data binding, first for Windows Forms and then for WPF. I'll wrap up with Web Forms, because it's the least demanding.

Windows Forms

Windows Forms data binding can interact with nearly any .NET object. However, there is a set of interfaces that an object can implement to *fully* support the data binding features. In fact, there's one set of interfaces for a simple object, and another set for a collection or list.

I'll discuss supporting data binding for a single object first, and then I'll discuss data binding support for collections and lists. I'll wrap up this section by discussing some custom controls provided by CSLA .NET to simplify the use of data binding in Windows Forms.

Object Data Binding

The .NET Framework defines three interfaces in support of data binding that an object should implement to fully support it. Table 10-1 lists the interfaces for a simple object.

Table 10-1. *Data Binding Interfaces for a Simple Object*

Interface	Description
`INotifyPropertyChanged`	Defines a `PropertyChanged` event that should be raised when a property of the object has changed
`IEditableObject`	Defines three methods that are used to undo or accept changes to the object
`IDataErrorInfo`	Defines properties that data binding can use to ask the object if it is valid and if each of its properties is valid

There's also an `INotifyPropertyChanging` interface, which is part of LINQ to SQL. It defines a `PropertyChanging` event that should be raised directly before a property is changed. Although data binding doesn't use this interface, CSLA .NET implements it, because the concept of an event that is raised before a property is changed can be useful in general.

Not all of these interfaces are implemented directly by `BusinessBase` itself. Figure 10-1 shows the inheritance hierarchy for `BusinessBase`.

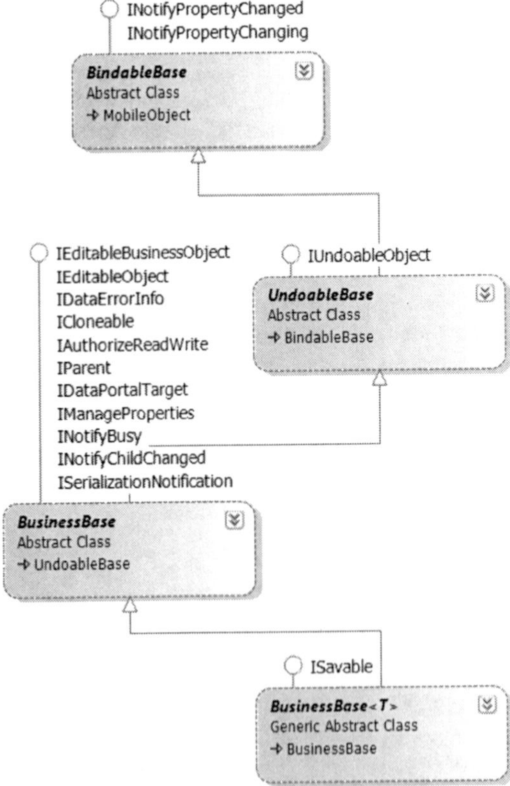

Figure 10-1. *Inheritance hierarchy for BusinessBase*

The `INotifyPropertyChanged` and `INotifyPropertyChanging` interfaces are implemented by `BindableBase`. The `IEditableObject` and `IDataErrorInfo` interfaces are implemented by `BusinessBase`.

I'll discuss each of the interfaces in turn.

The INotifyPropertyChanged Interface

The most basic interface, and the one that should be considered the least that any object author should implement, is INotifyPropertyChanged. This interface defines a PropertyChanged event that the business object should raise any time one of its properties is changed.

■ **Caution** The PropertyChanged event is handled differently in Windows Forms and WPF, and your object needs to implement the correct behaviors depending on the UI technology. I'll discuss the details later in this chapter.

This interface is implemented in BindableBase.

```
[Serializable()]
public abstract class BindableBase : MobileObject,
  System.ComponentModel.INotifyPropertyChanged,
  System.ComponentModel.INotifyPropertyChanging
```

This requires that the class declare the PropertyChanged event. This event is implemented using the longer custom event declaration syntax.

```
[NonSerialized]
private PropertyChangedEventHandler _nonSerializableChangedHandlers;
private PropertyChangedEventHandler _serializableChangedHandlers;

public event PropertyChangedEventHandler PropertyChanged
{
  add
  {
    if (value.Method.IsPublic &&
       (value.Method.DeclaringType.IsSerializable ||
        value.Method.IsStatic))
      _serializableChangedHandlers = (PropertyChangedEventHandler)
        System.Delegate.Combine(_serializableChangedHandlers, value);
    else
      _nonSerializableChangedHandlers = (PropertyChangedEventHandler)
        System.Delegate.Combine(_nonSerializableChangedHandlers, value);
  }
  remove
  {
    if (value.Method.IsPublic &&
       (value.Method.DeclaringType.IsSerializable ||
        value.Method.IsStatic))
      _serializableChangedHandlers = (PropertyChangedEventHandler)
        System.Delegate.Remove(_serializableChangedHandlers, value);
    else
      _nonSerializableChangedHandlers = (PropertyChangedEventHandler)
        System.Delegate.Remove(_nonSerializableChangedHandlers, value);
  }
}
```

Before declaring the event itself, the code declares two delegate fields. These fields will hold delegate references to all event handlers registered to receive the PropertyChanged event.

```
[NonSerialized()]
private PropertyChangedEventHandler _nonSerializableHandlers;
private PropertyChangedEventHandler _serializableHandlers;
```

Notice that one is declared with the NonSerialized attribute, while the other is not. The BinaryFormatter ignores the first one and all objects referenced by that delegate field. Objects referenced by the second field are serialized as normal.

The event declaration uses a block structure, including add and remove sections. Notice how the code in both sections checks to see if the event handler is contained within a serializable object.

```
if (value.Method.IsPublic && (value.Method.DeclaringType.IsSerializable ||
    value.Method.IsStatic))
```

If the event handler is contained in a serializable object, it will be added or removed from the serializable delegate; otherwise, it will be added or removed from the nonserialized delegate.

The thing about events and inheritance is that an event can only be raised by code in the class in which it is declared. This is because the event member can only be accessed directly from the class in which it is defined. It *can't* be raised by code in classes that inherit from this class. This means that business objects can't raise the PropertyChanged event directly, even though that is the goal. To solve this problem, the code follows a standard .NET design pattern by creating a protected method that in turn raises the event.

```
[EditorBrowsable(EditorBrowsableState.Advanced)]
protected virtual void OnPropertyChanged(string propertyName)
{
  if (_nonSerializableHandlers != null)
    _nonSerializableHandlers.Invoke(this,
      new PropertyChangedEventArgs(propertyName));
  if (_serializableHandlers != null)
    _serializableHandlers.Invoke(this,
      new PropertyChangedEventArgs(propertyName));
}
```

Any classes that inherit from the base class can call this method when they want to raise the event.

This method is marked with the EditorBrowsable attribute, indicating that this is an advanced method. In C#, this means that the method won't appear in IntelliSense unless the IDE is set to show advanced members. In VB, this means that the method appears in the All tab in IntelliSense, but won't appear in the Common tab.

The OnUnknownPropertyChanged() method covers a special case, different from the OnPropertyChanged() method. Where OnPropertyChanged() raises the PropertyChanged event for a single property, OnUnknownPropertyChanged() raises the event for a property with no name.

```
[EditorBrowsable(EditorBrowsableState.Advanced)]
protected virtual void OnUnknownPropertyChanged()
{
  OnPropertyChanged(string.Empty);
}
```

There are a number of cases in which the object's state will change in such a way that it isn't possible to know which properties actually changed. In that case, this blanket notification approach ensures that data binding is aware that *something* changed, so the UI updates as needed. Passing a property name of string.Empty or null is a "magic value" that tells data binding to refresh all bound property values.

The result is a base class that allows business objects to raise the PropertyChanged event, thereby supporting data binding and serialization.

The INotifyPropertyChanging Interface

The `INotifyPropertyChanging` interface is almost identical to `INotifyPropertyChanged`. The only real difference is the timing of when the `PropertyChanging` event is raised as opposed to the `PropertyChanged` event.

When a property value is about to be changed, the `PropertyChanging` event is raised first. Then the value is actually changed, and then the `PropertyChanged` event is raised. The methods in `BusinessBase`, such as the `LoadPropertyValue()` method, handle this. That method contains this code:

```
OnPropertyChanging(propertyInfo.Name);
FieldManager.SetFieldData<P>(propertyInfo, newValue);
PropertyHasChanged(propertyInfo.Name);
```

You can see the steps here clearly, including how both events are raised

I won't walk through the code for `INotifyPropertyChanging` here, because it is so similar to `INotifyPropertyChanged`. You can look at the code in `BindableBase` on your own.

The IEditableObject Interface

The `IEditableObject` interface allows data binding to tell your object to undo recent changes, or accept recent changes to the object's properties. It is used in many scenarios by Windows Forms data binding, including when an object is bound to a form using a `BindingSource` control, and when a collection of objects is bound to any grid control that supports in-place editing of the data.

The `IEditableObject` interface appears simple on the surface, but it's actually the most complex interface I'll discuss in this chapter. This is because there are a number of subtle idiosyncrasies in how this interface is called by data binding, and any object implementing the interface must deal with all the resulting edge cases.

The interface defines the three methods listed in Table 10-2.

Table 10-2. *Methods Defined by IEditableObject*

Method	Description
`BeginEdit`	Called by data binding to tell the object to take a snapshot of its property values
`CancelEdit`	Called by data binding to tell the object to undo any changes, restoring the property values to the snapshot taken when `BeginEdit()` was called
`EndEdit`	Called by data binding to tell the object to accept any changes, effectively discarding the snapshot taken when `BeginEdit()` was called

This doesn't sound that hard, until you read the fine print in the documentation and start using the interface and then discover the even *finer* print that isn't actually in the documentation at all.

■ **Note** Many of the lessons I've learned and the issues I've solved in the data binding implementation in CSLA .NET are due to a lot of hard work and research by the CSLA .NET community at `http://forums.lhotka.net`. Without the strong support and involvement by numerous people, many of the hard challenges would likely still be unsolved.

For example, it turns out that BeginEdit() may be called any number of times by data binding, but your implementation should only honor the first call. That first call to BeginEdit() must be balanced out by a subsequent call to either CancelEdit() or EndEdit(), at which point the *next* BeginEdit() call should be honored.

It is also the case that EndEdit() can be called multiple times, though only the first call should be honored. Worse yet, there are scenarios where neither CancelEdit() nor EndEdit() are called at all, leaving the object under the impression that it is still in the process of being edited.

This interface is implemented in BusinessBase. The implementation of this interface is related to the implementation of n-level undo, which I'll discuss in Chapter 13. The n-level undo feature already has the capability of taking a snapshot of the object's property values (actually its field values) and restoring them later if an undo is requested. The only difference is that IEditableObject is a *single level* of undo, while the n-level undo feature obviously supports multiple levels of undo.

The DisableIEditableObject Property

Some people have found the IEditableObject interface to be extremely challenging, especially if they are trying to create a UI that doesn't *want* to use all the data binding features. Windows Forms data binding uses this interface in numerous scenarios, and it can sometimes make life harder rather than easier.

To minimize this pain, it is possible to disable the interface by setting a DisableIEditableObject property on a specific business object.

■ **Caution** I don't recommend disabling the interface. If you disable it, data binding will not be able to interact with your object as it expects, and you may have to write extra UI code to compensate.

The BindingEdit Property

In addition to the DisableIEditableObject property, the BindingEdit property is used as a flag to indicate whether the n-level undo behavior was invoked through the BeginEdit() method from the IEditableObject interface. This flag allows the BeginEdit() method to only honor the first call.

The BindingEdit property is implemented in the UndoableBase class, because it is also used by some of the n-level undo behaviors I'll discuss in Chapter 13.

The BeginEdit Method

The BeginEdit() method uses the DisableIEditableObject and BindingEdit properties to determine whether to do any work. Here's the BeginEdit() code:

```
void System.ComponentModel.IEditableObject.BeginEdit()
{
  if (!_disableIEditableObject && !BindingEdit)
  {
    BindingEdit = true;
    BeginEdit();
  }
}
```

This method only performs real work if the interface is enabled (which it is by default) and if this is the first call to the method when BindingEdit is false. In that case, it sets BindingEdit to true to indicate that the object is reacting to the IEditableObject interface, and it calls the n-level undo

BeginEdit() method that I'll discuss in Chapter 13. For now, it is enough to know that this call to BeginEdit() takes a snapshot of the object's current state so it can be restored later if necessary.

The CancelEdit Method

The CancelEdit() implementation works in a similar manner, first checking the properties to determine whether it should do any work.

```
void System.ComponentModel.IEditableObject.CancelEdit()
{
  if (!_disableIEditableObject && BindingEdit)
  {
    CancelEdit();
    if (IsNew && _neverCommitted && EditLevel <= EditLevelAdded)
    {
      if (Parent != null)
        Parent.RemoveChild(this);
    }
  }
}
```

If this method does do work, it calls another CancelEdit() method, which is part of the n-level undo functionality I'll discuss in Chapter 13. That method restores the object's state to the most recent snapshot—the snapshot taken when BeginEdit() was called.

The next block of code is a bit complex and is necessary to support parent-child relationships. If this object is a child of some other object, then it is possible that it was just added as a child when BeginEdit() was called. If that's the case, then when CancelEdit() is called, this object should be removed as a child.

Consider this from the user's perspective. The user adds an item to a collection and starts editing that item. The user then realizes he doesn't really want to add it, so he presses Esc or performs some other UI gesture to cancel what he's doing. In this case, this new item's state isn't rolled back, because the user expects the new item to just go away entirely.

The call to Parent.RemoveChild() tells the parent object to remove this child entirely, which meets the user's expectation.

The best way to see this is to bind a collection to a DataGrid control, move to the last row so a new item is added, and then press Esc. Notice how the new item just disappears? This code enables that behavior.

Note In reality, this shouldn't be a common occurrence. Windows Forms 2.0 and higher uses a new interface, ICancelAddNew, that is implemented by BindingList<T>. This interface notifies the *collection* that the child should be removed, rather than notifying the child object itself. The code in the RemoveItem() method takes care of the ICancelAddNew case automatically, so this code is really here to support backward compatibility for anyone explicitly calling the IEditableObject interface on child objects.

The EndEdit Method

The final method is EndEdit(), which data binding calls when the changes to the object should be accepted. In other words, the snapshot taken by BeginEdit() can be discarded at this point, because there's no going back.

This is the simplest of the three methods:

```
void System.ComponentModel.IEditableObject.EndEdit()
{
  if (!_disableIEditableObject && BindingEdit)
  {
    ApplyEdit();
  }
}
```

It checks the two property values to see if it should do any work. If so, it calls the ApplyEdit() method from the n-level undo subsystem, telling n-level undo to discard the most recent snapshot of the object's state—the one taken when BeginEdit() was called.

At this point, you should understand how IEditableObject is implemented. This interface is used extensively by data binding, and it enables behaviors widely expected by end users of a Windows Forms application.

The IDataErrorInfo Interface

Windows Forms data binding uses the IDataErrorInfo interface to interrogate a data source for validation errors. This interface allows a data source, such as a business object, to provide human-readable descriptions of errors at the object and property levels. This information is used by grid controls and the ErrorProvider control to display error icons and tooltip descriptions.

The validation subsystem discussed in Chapter 11 provides a list of broken rules for each property on the object, making it relatively easy to implement IDataErrorInfo.

```
string IDataErrorInfo.Error
{
  get
  {
    if (!IsSelfValid)
      return ValidationRules.GetBrokenRules().ToString(
        Csla.Validation.RuleSeverity.Error);
    else
      return String.Empty;
  }
}

string IDataErrorInfo.this[string columnName]
{
  get
  {
    string result = string.Empty;
    if (!IsSelfValid)
    {
      Validation.BrokenRule rule =
        ValidationRules.GetBrokenRules().GetFirstBrokenRule(columnName);
      if (rule != null)
        result = rule.Description;
    }
    return result;
  }
}
```

The Error property returns a text value describing the validation errors for the object as a whole.

The indexer returns a text value describing any validation error for a specific property. In this implementation, only the first validation error in the list is returned. In either case, if there are no errors, an empty string value is returned—telling data binding that there are no broken rules to report.

It is important to realize that the rules are not *checked* when this interface is invoked. The rules are checked when a property changes or when the business developer explicitly runs the rules. When `IDataErrorInfo` is invoked, the rules have already been checked, so this implementation simply returns the precalculated results.

This is important because the `IDataErrorInfo` interface is invoked frequently. Each time data binding refreshes the UI or receives a `PropertyChanged` event from the object, it loops through all the bound properties to see if they're valid. You can expect `IDataErrorInfo` to be invoked dozens or hundreds of times during the lifetime of a single user interaction.

At this point, you should understand the four interfaces implemented by editable objects to support data binding. Some of these interfaces—`INotifyPropertyChanged` and `IEditableObject`, in particular—interact with any parent collection that might contain the object. I'll discuss data binding and collections next.

Collection Data Binding

Collections need to implement a set of interfaces to fully participate in data binding, and these interfaces are quite complex. Fortunately, Microsoft provides the `BindingList<T>` class in the `System.ComponentModel` namespace, which already implements all the interfaces. To help you fully understand the benefit provided by this class, Table 10-3 lists the interfaces you would otherwise have to implement by hand.

Table 10-3. *Data Binding Interfaces for Collections and Lists*

Interface	Description
`IBindingList`	Defines a `ListChanged` event that should be raised when the list changes, along with methods to support in-place editing in a grid, sorting, and other features
`ICancelAddNew`	Defines methods used for in-place editing in a grid
`IRaiseItemChangedEvents`	Indicates that the list will raise a `ListChanged` event when its child items raise `PropertyChanged` events

There's also an `IBindingListView` interface, which is optional. This interface extends `IBindingList` with extra features such as multicolumn sorting and filtering. By using LINQ, it is typically not necessary to rely on lists or collections to sort or filter themselves, as it is simpler to use a LINQ query to manipulate the data. Due to this, the `IBindingListView` interface is not as important as it was in older versions of the .NET Framework.

■ **Note** `IBindingListView` is not implemented in CSLA .NET, but you can find an implementation in the `CSLAcontrib` library at `www.codeplex.com/CSLAcontrib`.

Because `BusinessListBase` and the other CSLA .NET collection base classes ultimately inherit from `BindingList<T>`, they automatically provide full support for data binding.

It is important to realize, however, that `BindingList<T>` doesn't do *everything* necessary for a collection to work within the CSLA .NET framework. For example, `BusinessListBase` implements extra features to support n-level undo and abstract persistence, as discussed in Chapters 13 and 15.

Also, as I discussed in Chapter 9, `BusinessListBase` includes code to raise a `ListChanged` event when one of its child objects raises a `PropertyChanged` event. This is used after the deserialization of the collection, and is necessary because `BindingList<T>` doesn't handle the deserialization scenario.

By implementing the interfaces listed in Table 10-1 and inheriting from `BindingList<T>`, the CSLA .NET base classes provide full support for all the features of Windows Forms data binding. This includes the drag-and-drop concepts in the Visual Studio designer, along with the runtime behaviors for interacting with a `BindingSource` control and supporting in-place editing in grid controls.

Controls and Helper Objects

Though the interfaces and base classes I've discussed so far provide support for data binding, it turns out that the UI often still contains quite a bit of code to make data binding really work. Some of this code works around quirks in the behavior of data binding itself or in how it interacts with editable business objects. And some extends the UI to deal with the concept of per-property authorization—a feature I'll discuss in Chapter 12.

To minimize the code required in the UI, CSLA .NET includes three custom controls for Windows Forms that address the most common issues. These controls are a type of control called an *extender control*.

Extender controls are added to a form, and they in turn add properties and behaviors to other controls on the form, thus extending those other controls. A good example of this is the `ErrorProvider` control, which extends other controls by adding the ability to display an error icon with a tooltip describing the error.

The ReadWriteAuthorization Control

In Chapter 12, I will discuss the authorization feature supported by CSLA .NET business objects that makes them aware of whether each property can be read or changed. A key part of that implementation is the `IAuthorizeReadWrite` interface defined in `Csla.Core`. This interface defines `CanReadProperty()` and `CanWriteProperty()` to make it possible to determine whether the current user is allowed to get or set each property on the object.

One primary user of this functionality is the UI, which can decide to alter its appearance to give users clues as to whether they're able to view or alter each piece of data. While you could do this by hand for each control on every form, the `ReadWriteAuthorization` control helps automate the process of building a UI that enables or disables controls based on whether properties can be read or changed.

If a control is bound to a property, and the user does not have read access to that property due to authorization rules, the `ReadWriteAuthorization` control will disable that control. It also adds a handler for the control's `Format` event to intercept the value coming from the data source, substituting an empty value instead. The result is that data binding is prevented from displaying the data to the user.

Similarly, if the user doesn't have write access to a property, `ReadWriteAuthorization` will attempt to mark any controls bound to that property as being read-only (or failing that, disabled), ensuring that the user can't attempt to alter the property value.

Like all Windows Forms components, extender controls inherit from `System.ComponentModel.Component`. Additionally, to act as an extender control, the `ReadWriteAuthorization` control must implement the `IExtenderProvider` interface.

```
[DesignerCategory("")]
[ProvideProperty("ApplyAuthorization", typeof(Control))]
public class ReadWriteAuthorization : Component, IExtenderProvider
```

```
{
  public ReadWriteAuthorization(IContainer container)
  { container.Add(this); }
}
```

The ProvideProperty attribute is important. It specifies that ReadWriteAuthorization extends components of type Control by adding an ApplyAuthorization property to them. In other words, when a ReadWriteAuthorization control is on a form, all *other* controls on the form get a dynamically added ApplyAuthorization property. Figure 10-2 shows a text box control's Properties window with the dynamically added ApplyAuthorization property.

The UI developer can set this property to true or false to indicate whether the ReadWriteAuthorization control should apply authorization rules to that particular control. You'll see how this works as the control is implemented.

The DesignerCategory attribute is just used to help Visual Studio decide what kind of visual designer to use when editing the control. The value used here specifies that the default designer should be used.

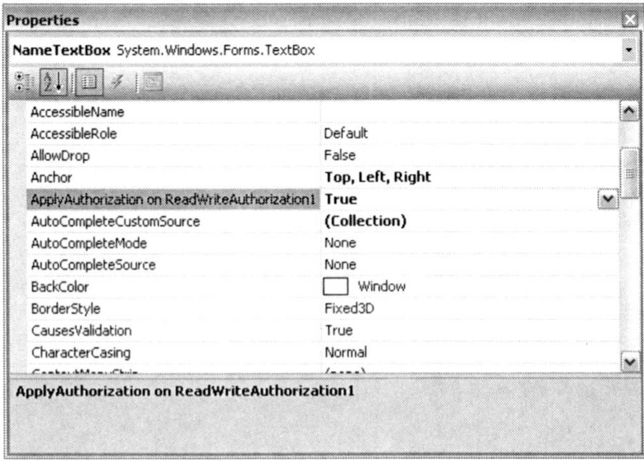

Figure 10-2. *ApplyAuthorization property added to NameTextBox*

The class also implements a constructor that accepts an IContainer parameter. This constructor is required for extender controls and is called by Windows Forms when the control is instantiated. Notice that the control adds itself to the container as required by the Windows Forms infrastructure.

The IExtenderProvider Interface

The IExtenderProvider interface defines just one method: CanExtend().Windows Forms calls this method to ask the extender control whether it wishes to extend any given control. Windows Forms calls CanExtend()automatically for every control on the form.

```
public bool CanExtend(object extendee)
{
  if (IsPropertyImplemented(extendee, "ReadOnly")
    || IsPropertyImplemented(extendee, "Enabled"))
    return true;
  else
    return false;
}
```

The ReadWriteAuthorization control can extend any control that implements either a ReadOnly or Enabled property. This covers most controls, making ReadWriteAuthorization broadly useful. If the potential target control implements either of these properties, a true result will be returned to indicate that the control will be extended.

The IsPropertyImplemented() method is a helper that uses reflection to check for the existence of the specified properties on the target control.

```
private static bool IsPropertyImplemented(
  object obj, string propertyName)
{
  if (obj.GetType().GetProperty(propertyName,
    BindingFlags.FlattenHierarchy |
    BindingFlags.Instance |
    BindingFlags.Public) != null)
    return true;
  else
    return false;
}
```

The ApplyAuthorization Property

The ProvideProperty attribute on ReadWriteAuthorization specified that an ApplyAuthorization property would be dynamically added to all controls extended by ReadWriteAuthorization. Of course, the controls being extended really have no knowledge of this new property or what to do with it. All the behavior associated with the property is contained within the extender control itself.

The extender control manages the ApplyAuthorization property by implementing both the GetApplyAuthorization() and SetApplyAuthorization() methods. Windows Forms calls these methods to get and set the property value for each control that has been extended. Windows Forms prepends Get and Set automatically to call these methods.

To manage a list of the controls that have been extended, a Dictionary object is used.

```
private Dictionary<Control, bool> _sources =
  new Dictionary<Control, bool>();

public bool GetApplyAuthorization(Control source)
{
  bool result;
  if (_sources.TryGetValue(source, out result))
    return result;
  else
    return false;
}

public void SetApplyAuthorization(Control source, bool value)
{
  if (_sources.ContainsKey(source))
    _sources[source] = value;
  else
    _sources.Add(source, value);
}
```

When Windows Forms indicates that the ApplyAuthorization property has been set for a particular extended control, the SetApplyAuthorization() method is called. This method records the value of the ApplyAuthorization property for that particular control, using the control itself as the key value within the Dictionary.

Conversely, when Windows Forms needs to know the property value of ApplyAuthorization for a particular control, it calls GetApplyAuthorization(). The value for that control is retrieved from the Dictionary object and returned. If the control can't be found in the Dictionary, then false is returned, since that control is obviously not being extended.

The end result here is that the ReadWriteAuthorization control maintains a list of all the controls it extends, along with their ApplyAuthorization property values. In short, it knows about all the controls it will affect, and whether it should be affecting them or not.

Applying Authorization Rules

At this point, the extender control's basic plumbing is complete. It gets to choose which controls to extend, and it maintains a list of all the controls it does extend, along with the ApplyAuthorization property value for each of those controls.

When the UI developer wants to enforce authorization rules for the whole form, she can do so by triggering the ReadWriteAuthorization control. To allow this, the control implements a ResetControlAuthorization() method. This method is public, so it can be called by code in the form itself. Typically, this method will be called immediately after a business object has been loaded and bound to the form, or immediately after the user has logged into or out of the application. It is also a good idea to call it after adding a new business object to the database, since some objects will change their authorization rules to be different for an old object than for a new object.

The ResetControlAuthorization() method loops through all the items in the list of extended controls. This list is the Dictionary object maintained by Get/SetApplyAuthorization, as discussed earlier. The ApplyAuthorization value for each control is checked, and if it is true, then the authorization rules are applied to that control.

```
public void ResetControlAuthorization()
{
  foreach (KeyValuePair<Control, bool> item in _sources)
  {
    if (item.Value)
    {
      // apply authorization rules
      ApplyAuthorizationRules(item.Key);
    }
  }
}
```

To apply the authorization rules, the code loops through the target control's list of data bindings. Each Binding object represents a connection between a property on the control and a data source, so it is possible to get a reference to the data source through the DataSource property.

```
private void ApplyAuthorizationRules(Control control)
{
  foreach (Binding binding in control.DataBindings)
  {
    // get the BindingSource if appropriate
    if (binding.DataSource is BindingSource)
    {
      BindingSource bs =
        (BindingSource)binding.DataSource;
      // get the BusinessObject if appropriate
      Csla.Security.IAuthorizeReadWrite ds =
        bs.Current as Csla.Security.IAuthorizeReadWrite;
```

```
          if (ds != null)
          {
            // get the object property name
            string propertyName =
              binding.BindingMemberInfo.BindingField;

            ApplyReadRules(
              control, binding,
              ds.CanReadProperty(propertyName));
            ApplyWriteRules(
              control, binding,
              ds.CanWriteProperty(propertyName));
          }
        }
      }
    }
```

If the data source implements `IAuthorizeReadWrite`, then both `ApplyReadRules()` and `ApplyWriteRules()` methods are called to change the target control's state based on whether the current user is authorized to read and write the property.

Notice that both `ApplyReadRules()` and `ApplyWriteRules()` accept the target control, the `Binding` object, and a Boolean indicating whether the user is authorized to perform the particular operation (read or write). This ensures that these methods have all the information they need to know to alter the target control's appearance.

The ApplyReadRules Method

Finally, we get to the heart of the matter: altering the target control. If the user is not allowed to read the property value, the target control must not display the value. To prevent display of the value, two things are done to the target control: it is disabled, and any values coming from the data source to the control are intercepted and replaced with an empty value.

Disabling the control is easily accomplished by setting its `Enabled` property to `false`. All controls have an `Enabled` property, so this is not an issue. Intercepting all values from the data source before they reach the control is more complex. Fortunately, data binding offers a solution through the `Format` event. All `Binding` objects have both `Format` and `Parse` events, which can be used to alter data as it moves from the data source to the control and then back to the data source.

The `Format` event is raised after the data value has been read from the data source, but *before* the value is provided to the control. The idea is that a UI developer can handle this event and use it to format the value for display. In this case, however, the value will simply be replaced with a default empty value instead, thus ensuring that the control never gets the real value that the user isn't authorized to see.

To handle the `Format` event, a method is required.

```
private void ReturnEmpty(
  object sender, ConvertEventArgs e)
{
  e.Value = GetEmptyValue(e.DesiredType);
}
```

```
private object GetEmptyValue(Type desiredType)
{
  object result = null;
  if (desiredType.IsValueType)
    result = Activator.CreateInstance(desiredType);
  return result;
}
```

The ReturnEmpty() method handles the Format event. It then calls GetEmptyValue() to get an empty value appropriate for the data type of the value read from the data source. That empty value is returned through e.Value. The result is that data binding puts this empty value into the control rather than the original value from the data source.

Within the ApplyReadRules() method, if the user is not authorized to read the property, the control will be disabled and the event handler will be set up.

```
ctl.Enabled = false;
binding.Format += new ConvertEventHandler(ReturnEmpty);

// clear the value displayed by the control
PropertyInfo propertyInfo =
  ctl.GetType().GetProperty(binding.PropertyName,
    BindingFlags.FlattenHierarchy |
    BindingFlags.Instance |
    BindingFlags.Public);
if (propertyInfo != null)
{
  propertyInfo.SetValue(ctl,
    GetEmptyValue(Utilities.GetPropertyType(propertyInfo.PropertyType)),
                                new object[] { });
}
```

Of course, the control might have already contained a value, and if so, that value must be removed. To do this, the type of the property value is retrieved using reflection, and the GetEmptyValue() method is called to get an appropriate empty value. This value is then placed into the control, overwriting any previous value the control may have had.

The reverse of the process occurs if the user *is* allowed to read the property. In that case, the control is enabled and the Format event handler is removed.

```
bool couldRead = ctl.Enabled;
ctl.Enabled = true;
binding.Format -=
  new ConvertEventHandler(ReturnEmpty);
if (!couldRead) binding.ReadValue();
```

Additionally, if the control was disabled before this code was run, it is assumed that the control doesn't contain a valid value. The ReadValue() method on the Binding object is called to force data binding to reload the control with the value from the data source.

The ApplyWriteRules Method

The ApplyWriteRules() method is similar to ApplyReadRules() but takes a slightly different approach. In this case, users may be able to view the data, but they certainly can't be allowed to edit the data. If the control implements a ReadOnly property, then it can be set to false; otherwise, the control must be entirely disabled through the use of its Enabled property.

As an optimization, if the control is a Label, the method will exit immediately. Because Label controls are so common, and they are read-only by definition, it is worth this special check.

The preference is to use the control's ReadOnly property if it is implemented by the control. Reflection is used to get a PropertyInfo object corresponding to the control's ReadOnly property.

```
// enable/disable writing of the value
PropertyInfo propertyInfo =
  ctl.GetType().GetProperty("ReadOnly",
    BindingFlags.FlattenHierarchy |
    BindingFlags.Instance |
    BindingFlags.Public);
if (propertyInfo != null)
{
  bool couldWrite = (!(bool)propertyInfo.GetValue(
    ctl, new object[] { }));
  propertyInfo.SetValue(ctl, !canWrite, new object[] { });
  if ((!couldWrite) && (canWrite))
    binding.ReadValue();
}
```

If a ReadOnly property is found, then it is set to true or false depending on whether the user is allowed or denied write access to the business object property.

```
propertyInfo.SetValue(ctl, !canWrite, new object[] { });
```

First, though, the value of the control's ReadOnly property is retrieved. If it is false, that means that the user was *already* able to edit the control—the user could write, so couldWrite is true. This is important, because if the user was *unable* to edit the control and now *is* able to edit the control, data binding needs to be told to reload the data from the data source into the control.

```
if ((!couldWrite) && (canWrite))
  binding.ReadValue();
```

Otherwise, it is possible for the user to be placed into an empty control even though there really is a value in the business object's property.

If the control doesn't have a ReadOnly property, then the Enabled property is used as a fallback. The same procedure is used, just with the Enabled property instead.

```
bool couldWrite = ctl.Enabled;
ctl.Enabled = canWrite;
if ((!couldWrite) && (canWrite))
  binding.ReadValue();
```

The end result is that when the user is denied write access to a business object's property, controls bound to that property are either set to ReadOnly or are disabled. And if the user is denied read access to a business object's property, controls bound to that property are disabled and empty values are placed in the control rather than any real values from the business object.

The BindingSourceRefresh Control

The BindingSourceRefresh control is also an extender control, but its purpose is quite different from the ReadWriteAuthorization control. It turns out that there's a quirk in the way Windows Forms data binding works. The BindingSourceRefresh control helps work around this quirk.

The quirk is that when data is changed in a business object, data binding doesn't always display the changes in the controls on the form. This occurs in the following sequence of events:

1. The user edits a value in a bound control.
2. Data binding puts the user's new value into the business object.
3. The business object alters the value in the property `set` block.
4. The business object raises its `PropertyChanged` event.

You would expect that data binding would handle the `PropertyChanged` event, realize that the property's data has changed, and then update the control with the new value. And that does happen for all controls *except the current control.* In other words, the `PropertyChanged` event causes data binding to refresh all *other* controls on the form except the control that initiated the change in the first place.

Obviously, this can be problematic. Consider a `TextBox` control that is bound to a business object property that uses a `SmartDate`. I'll discuss `SmartDate` in Chapter 16, but one of its features is to accept the + character as input and to replace it with tomorrow's date. Due to this data binding quirk, when the user enters a + character, that value is put into the business object, which translates it to tomorrow's date—but that new value is not displayed to the user. The user continues to see the + character.

What's even more confusing for users is that if they edit a *different* control, then the date text box control will be updated with tomorrow's date. Remember that data binding updates everything except the current control when it gets a `PropertyChanged` event.

This is the problem `BindingSourceRefresh` is intended to solve. It does so by interacting with the `BindingSource` control that manages the data binding for a given business object. While `ReadWriteAuthorization` extends controls like `TextBox` and `Label`, `BindingSourceRefresh` extends `BindingSource` controls.

The plumbing code in this control is virtually identical to `ReadWriteAuthorization`, so I won't walk through all the details of the control.

This control only extends `BindingSource` controls, and if it is enabled, it hooks the `BindingComplete` event raised by the `BindingSource` control. This event is raised by a `BindingSource` control after all controls have had their values updated through data binding—well, all controls except the current one, of course. The `Control_BindingComplete()` method takes the extra step of forcing the `BindingSource` control to refresh the value for the *current* binding as well.

```
private void Control_BindingComplete(
  object sender, BindingCompleteEventArgs e)
{
  switch (e.BindingCompleteState)
  {
    case BindingCompleteState.Exception:
      if (BindingError != null)
      {
        BindingError(this, new BindingErrorEventArgs(e.Binding, e.Exception));
      }
      break;
    default:
      if ((e.BindingCompleteContext ==
                BindingCompleteContext.DataSourceUpdate)
              && e.Binding.DataSource is BindingSource
              && GetReadValuesOnChange((BindingSource)e.Binding.DataSource))
      {
        e.Binding.ReadValue();
      }
      break;
  }
}
```

The BindingComplete event includes a BindingCompleteEventArgs parameter, and that parameter includes a property indicating whether the binding process completed with an exception or normally.

In the case of an exception, the BindingSourceRefresh control raises its *own* BindingError event, so the UI developer can be informed that an exception occurred and can take steps. By default, exceptions during binding are silently swallowed by data binding, and the only place you'll see them is in the output window of the debugger in Visual Studio. By raising this event when an error occurs, the control enables the UI developer to more easily detect and troubleshoot data binding issues.

The normal case, however, is that the binding succeeds. In that case, the e parameter includes a reference to the currently active Binding object. It is this Binding object that *isn't* refreshed automatically when data binding gets a PropertyChanged event from the underlying data source. By calling its ReadValue() method, this code forces data binding to read the value from the data source and update the current control's display as well.

The BindingSourceRefresh control should be used to force data refreshes for all BindingSource controls bound to detail forms. It isn't necessary when only complex controls such as a GridView or ListBox are bound to the object.

The CslaActionExtender Control and Associated Components

When an object is bound to a BindingSource control, the BindingSource control assumes it has full *and exclusive* control over the object. This means that when an object is data bound, the *only* interaction with the object should be through the BindingSource control. This includes doing things like saving the object, which is a concept the BindingSource doesn't understand. So how do you save an object? You must first unbind it; you need to disconnect it from the BindingSource.

This is also true for any explicit calls to BeginEdit(), CancelEdit(), or ApplyEdit(). I discuss these n-level undo methods in Chapter 13. The UI commonly calls these methods when it includes a top-level Cancel button on the form.

Unfortunately, unbinding an object from a BindingSource control is not as easy as setting the DataSource property to null. While that breaks the reference from the control to the object, it doesn't end any current edit session where the BindingSource has called BeginEdit() through the IEditableObject interface.

The next thing you might consider is simply calling EndEdit() or CancelEdit() on the BindingSource before setting the value to null.

```
bindingSource.EndEdit();
bindingSource.DataSource = null;
```

However, this won't work either, because as soon as you call EndEdit(), the BindingSource *immediately* calls BeginEdit(). You need to disconnect the object first, then end the edit session. This helper method demonstrates the process:

```
protected void UnbindBindingSource(
  BindingSource source, bool apply, bool isRoot)
{
  System.ComponentModel.IEditableObject current =
    source.Current as System.ComponentModel.IEditableObject;
  if (isRoot)
    source.DataSource = null;
  if (current != null)
    if (apply)
      current.EndEdit();
    else
      current.CancelEdit();
}
```

While you could include this code in each form or create a base form from which you inherit, that's complexity that would be nice to avoid.

The complexity is even worse if you have a master-detail display in your form. In that case, you must remember to unbind all child `BindingSource` controls first, and then unbind the root (master) `BindingSource` last.

To avoid all this complexity, CSLA .NET includes the `CslaActionExtender` control. This control extends any control that implements `IbuttonControl`, so the control automatically understands how to unbind the objects before interacting with them. Like the other controls I've discussed so far, this is an extender control, so it adds extra behaviors to existing controls—in this case, button-style controls.

Behind the scenes, `CslaActionExtender` uses `BindingSourceHelper` and `BindingSourceNode` objects to do the actual work. This is important, because you can use `BindingSourceHelper` and `BindingSourceNode` directly to get the same behavior if you're not using a button-style control. For example, if you implement your Save and Cancel buttons on a `ToolBar`, you'll be unable to use `CslaActionExtender`, but you'll still be able to use `BindingSourceHelper` and `BindingSourceNode` to simplify your UI code.

The BindingSourceNode Class

The `BindingSourceNode` class is designed to wrap a `BindingSource` component, which sits on your Windows form. The name of this class is due to the fact that it represents a node in what can be a tree of binding sources.

When binding a form to a business object that is a parent to one or more child objects or collections, the form requires a `BindingSource` component for each object or collection. This hierarchical set of `BindingSource` components is represented by a set of `BindingSourceNode` objects. The `BindingSourceNode` class has a recursive design. Not only does it contain a property to hold the corresponding `BindingSource` component, but it also contains a property that contains a list of other `BindingSourceNode` objects. Each instance also holds a reference to its parent.

It is through this design that a tree of `BindingSource` components can be represented like this:

```
private BindingSource _Source;
private List<BindingSourceNode> _Children;
private BindingSourceNode _Parent;
```

These member variables are exposed through public properties. The `BindingSourceNode` class also provides methods to assist you in any of the following tasks that involves binding or unbinding:

- `Bind`
- `Unbind`
- `SetEvents`
- `ResetBindings`

These methods wrap standard functionality that you need to perform in the case of saving a bound business object or invoking n-level undo functionality on a bound business object. As I mentioned earlier, when saving or undoing a business object that is participating in Windows Forms data binding, you must first properly unbind the object before acting upon it. The methods exposed by the `BindingSourceNode` class help you by performing this functionality for you and, more importantly, by taking into account any child `BindingSource` components that it may contain. Since the `BindingSourceNode` class uses a recursive design, the helper methods can be called from within any level of the tree, but more often than not, you will be addressing the top-level node. In fact, to avoid any potential n-level undo parent-to-child mismatches, this is the recommended practice.

Because the act of saving or invoking an undo operation involves more than one of the helper operations exposed by the BindingSourceNode object, additional methods are typically used from the Windows form.

```
public void Apply()
{
  SetEvents(false);
  Unbind(false);
}

public void Cancel(object businessObject)
{
  SetEvents(false);
  Unbind(true);
  Bind(businessObject);
}

public void Close()
{
  SetEvents(false);
  Unbind(true);
}
```

The BindingSourceHelper Class

The tree of BindingSourceNode objects is built using the BindingSourceHelper component. The BindingSourceHelper component exposes a static method called InitializeBindingSourceTree, which returns an instance of BindingSourceNode. This method builds the entire tree of BindingSource components on your form.

The InitializeBindingSourceTree() method accepts two arguments.

```
public static BindingSourceNode InitializeBindingSourceTree(
  IContainer container, BindingSource rootSource)
```

The two arguments correspond to the form's container property and the BindingSource object on your form that binds to your root object. You can find the form's container property in the designer partial class that gets created along with a form and modified dynamically every time you drop controls or components onto the form. The components you place on a form that sit in the component tray get added to the container property, so it is this property that the InitializeBindingSourceTree() method needs.

The functionality contained in BindingSourceHelper could have resided in BindingSourceNode as a static method, but it made more sense to separate these two classes out in the interest of maintaining a strict separation of the node class from the class that creates the actual tree. The design also allows for future enhancements to be added to the BindingSourceHelper class while maintaining a clean BindingSourceNode class.

Usage of these classes is quite simple and can save you lots of confusing code. In a conventional Windows Forms binding situation, you set up your BindingSource components declaratively and then set the DataSource property of the root BindingSource component to the top-level business object. This step is taken care of automatically if you're using the new components, in which case you obtain an instance of a BindingSourceNode class by calling the InitializeBindingSourceTree() method from the BindingSourceHelper component. After this, you simply call the Bind method of the new variable and send your top-level business object into its only argument.

```
BindingSourceNode _bindingTree = null;

private void BindUI()
{
     _bindingTree = BindingSourceHelper.InitializeBindingSourceTree(
        this.Container, orderBindingSource);
     _bindingTree.Bind(order);
}
```

You can now use the instance of the BindingSourceNode class, depicted in the previous code by the _bindingTree field, to unbind or rebind to assist you while performing save or undo operations. You use the BindingSourceNode class's Apply() method just before you save your business object. After this, you can incorporate the aid of the object's Bind() method. Use the Cancel method to invoke an undo operation; it rebinds the object afterwards automatically.

I should reiterate that the BindingSourceNode object contains the entire tree of BindingSource components as it corresponds to the parent-child object hierarchy you have designed into the business object that you will be binding. All actions performed on BindingSourceNode object propagate properly to the child nodes, and in fact do so in reverse order, so the lowest child gets hit first and the root gets hit last. Should you have two distinct object hierarchies represented on a Windows form, thus having two root BindingSource components, you would need two separate instances of the BindingSourceNode class. And remember, all interaction with your business object should now take place through these two classes.

The following is a sample of a form's code that uses all the functionality of these two components in a toolbar scenario, with a root object representing an order with some order detail children:

```
public partial class OrderMaint2 : Form
{
  public OrderMaint2()
  {
    InitializeComponent();
  }

  public OrderMaint2(Guid orderId)
  {
    InitializeComponent();
    _order = Order.GetOrderWithDetail(orderId);
    BindUI();
  }

  Order _order = null;
  BindingSourceNode _bindingTree = null;

  private void BindUI()
  {
    _bindingTree = BindingSourceHelper.InitializeBindingSourceTree(
    this.components, orderBindingSource);
    _bindingTree.Bind(_order);
  }

  private void toolSave_Click(object sender, EventArgs e)
  {
    if (Save())
      MessageBox.Show("Order saved.");
  }
```

```
    private void toolSaveNew_Click(object sender, EventArgs e)
    {
      if (Save())
      {
        _order = Order.NewOrder();
        BindUI();
      }
    }

    private void toolSaveClose_Click(object sender, EventArgs e)
    {
      if (Save())
        this.Close();
    }

    private void toolCancel_Click(object sender, EventArgs e)
    {
      _bindingTree.Cancel(_order);
    }

    private void toolClose_Click(object sender, EventArgs e)
    {
      _bindingTree.Close();
    }

    private bool Save()
    {
      bool ret = false;
      _bindingTree.Apply();

      try
      {
        _order = _order.Save();
        ret = true;
      }
      catch (Exception ex)
      {
        MessageBox.Show(ex.Message);
      }
      BindUI();
      return ret;
    }
  }
```

You can use the BindingSourceNode and BindingSourceHelper classes to save you a lot of code and complexity, but you're still responsible for code involving validation checking, broken rules reporting, exception handling, and, of course, the actual functionality to save or undo the object. You'll need to do this when you're using toolbars to allow users to interact with your forms, but if you're going to be using buttons or links, there is a better way.

Using the CslaActionExtender Control

As stated earlier, the CslaActionExtender component is an extender provider that adds functionality to any control that implements the IButtonControl interface. This means that you can use it with any Visual Studio button or link as well as with any third-party button control or link.

The CslaActionExtender makes use of both the BindingSourceNode and the BindingSourceHelper classes and provides an almost no-code approach to functionality for which you would normally have to write quite a bit of code. This functionality includes saving a business object, invoking undo functionality of a business object, and closing a form. Moreover, the saving functionality comes in three flavors, which I'll get to in a minute.

The CslaActionExtender component drags onto your form's component tray just like the ReadWriteAuthorization and BindingSourceRefresh components—and just like a BindingSource component, for that matter. You can hit the ground running on this control in just one step. Simply call the ResetActionBehaviors method of the component and pass your root business object into its one and only argument. This initializes the component and everything within it, just like the ResetControlAuthorization() method in the ReadWriteAuthorization component.

You'll then need some buttons on your form to represent certain actions. The mere presence of the CslaActionExtender component adds several properties to your buttons, all nicely organized in the Csla property browser category. The CslaActionExtender component can extend button or button-like controls to provide save, cancel, or close functionality automatically.

The CslaActionExtender component also includes properties and events of its own, the most important being the DataSource property, which you would point to a root BindingSource on the form. Table 10-4 lists other properties.

Table 10-4. *Properties of CslaActionExtender*

Property	Description
AutoShowBrokenRules	Allows the control to automatically display any broken rules found on the root object using a standard Windows Forms message box.
WarnIfCloseOnDirty	Allows the control to optionally warn you if you press a Close button while the bound business object is dirty.
DirtyWarningMessage	Used with WarnIfCloseOnDirty, this is the message that will display.
WarnOnCancel	Allows the control to warn you when you attempt to use a Cancel button for an undo operation when the bound business object is dirty.
WarnOnCancelMessage	Used with WarnOnCancel, this is the message that will display.

You can intercept all this functionality using the CslaActionExtender's event model, which I'll describe later.

Besides all these properties, which apply to the component as a whole, there are button-specific properties as well. The most important one is called ActionType and appears with the others in the Csla property browser category as ActionType on cslaActionExtender1. cslaActionExtender1 is the name of the CslaActionExtender component you dropped onto the form.

The default value for this property is None, which means this button provides no extended functionality at all. It also means that this button will not trigger any communication with the associated CslaActionExtender component. The other three values for this property are Save, Cancel, and Close. Setting this property to any one of these values assigns that functionality to the control.

When you set the property to Save, you have an additional option for a post-save action, configured by the PostSaveAction extended property. The possible values for this property are None, AndClose, and AndNew. As you can see, you can provide plenty of functionality for your form with virtually no code. Table 10-5 lists the other extended properties.

Table 10-5. *Extended Properties of CslaActionExtender*

Property	Description
`CommandName`	Uniquely identifies the control so that when an event is raised from the `CslaActionExtender` component, the subscriber can determine which control caused the event to fire
`DisableWhenClean`	Allows the monitoring of the underlying object graph's "dirty" state and provides automatic enabling and disabling of the button depending on the state
`RebindAfterSave`	Rebinds your object after a Save action has finished; this is set to `false` in the case of a Close button or a Save-AndNew button

■ **Note** When using the `DisableWhenClean` property, pay close attention to the Data Source Update mode for each individual entry control (`TextBox`, `CheckBox`, etc.). The default setting of `OnValidation` in combination with a `true` setting on the property causes the button to remain disabled until you tab out of the changed text field, which may not be a desired behavior. Alternatively, changing the mode to `OnPropertyChanged` produces a nice instant enabling effect on the button, but it also updates your `BindingSource` on every key press, thus setting your object's property on every key press and possibly running validation rules on every key press. This also may not be a desired behavior, depending on the weight of your business rules.

The `CslaActionExtender` control can keep track of almost everything having to do with your business object(s) except for how to create a new one. You determine how to create a new object when you write a factory method that makes a call to `DataPortal.Create`.

For this reason, if you configure one of your buttons with a `Save` value on the `ActionType` property and an `AddNew` value on the `PostSaveAction` property, you must trap the `SetForNew` event of the extender component. It is here where you need to reset your business object variable to a new instance and call your rebind method. This rebind method sets the `BindingSource` component's `DataSource` property, calls the `ResetControlAuthorization()` method on any `ReadWriteAuthorization` components you may be using, and calls `ResetActionBehaviors` on any `CslaActionExtender` components.

Table 10-6 lists other events of `CslaActionExtender`.

Table 10-6. *Events Raised by CslaActionExtender*

Event	Description
`BusinessObjectInvalid`	Raised when an attempt is made to save an invalid object. Remember that the validity check on the root object reads into all underlying child objects in the object graph. Also remember that information and warning rules do not invalidate an object.
`Clicking`	Raised immediately upon clicking the button, before any action takes place. The event allows the cancellation of any functionality that may follow.
`Clicked`	Raised at the very end of the determined action for the button.
`ErrorEncountered`	Raised when an exception is encountered while `CslaActionExtender` is executing some behavior.

Table 10-6. *Events Raised by CslaActionExtender*

Event	Description
`HasBrokenRules`	Raised when an attempt is made to save the object, and the object has one or more broken validation rules of any rule severity.
`ObjectSaving`	Raised after a successful validity check but before the object gets saved, allowing you to test for nonfatal rules and also for any broken rules down the object graph.
`ObjectSaved`	Raised immediately after a successful save operation.

Working with Multiple Root Objects

If your form requirements are to manage two (or more) distinct root business objects at the same time, you will require two (or more) `CslaActionExtender` components, each bound to a different root `BindingSource` component. It's important to note that this will cause every button or link on your form to display more than one of each of the extender properties. However, they will display along with the name of each `CslaActionExtender` component.

```
ActionType on cslaActionExtender1
ActionType on cslaActionExtender2
```

You can then assign specific buttons to interact with one `CslaActionExtender` component or the other, or even both.

■ **Note** CSLA .NET does not propagate broken rules in child objects or child collections up to the root object, so the interaction with broken rules from the `CslaActionExtender` only applies to the root object, and only when that root object is of type `BusinessBase`. However, the validity check aggregates the entire underlying object graph when you use managed backing fields for your child objects, or properly overrides the business object's `IsValid` and `IsDirty` properties.

The `CslaActionExtender` component will work with a `BindingSource` hierarchy where the root business object is either a type of `BusinessBase` or `BusinessListBase`, so it can indeed save you a lot of code and provide for an even cleaner UI.

The following is a sample of a form's code that uses the `CslaActionExtender` component to act upon an order object and its children:

```
public partial class OrderMaint : Form
{
  public OrderMaint()
  {
    InitializeComponent();
  }

  public OrderMaint(Guid orderId)
  {
    InitializeComponent();

    _order = Order.GetOrderWithDetail(orderId);
    BindUI();
  }
```

```
    Order _order = null;

    private void BindUI()
    {
      cslaActionExtender1.ResetActionBehaviors(_order);
    }

    private void cslaActionExtender1_SetForNew(
      object sender, CslaActionEventArgs e)
    {
      _order = Order.NewOrder();
      BindUI();
    }

    private void cslaActionExtender1_ErrorEncountered(
      object sender, ErrorEncounteredEventArgs e)
    {
      MessageBox.Show(e.Ex.Message);
    }
  }
```

At this point, you should have an understanding of the support provided for Windows Forms data binding within CSLA .NET. I chose to discuss Windows Forms first, because as a general rule, if you support Windows Forms data binding, you support everything else. That used to be true, but it's becoming less true as WPF matures, so I'll talk about WPF next.

WPF

WPF is the newest UI technology discussed in this chapter, and it is evolving rapidly. Even from .NET 3.0 to 3.5, and from 3.5 to 3.5 SP1, there have been substantial changes to the features provided by data binding in WPF. I expect the changes to continue as WPF rapidly matures toward parity with the features of Windows Forms data binding.

WPF data binding is similar in some ways to Windows Forms. Both technologies are rich and interactive, providing immediate, event-driven interaction between the UI and the business objects. WPF supports some of the same data binding interfaces used by Windows Forms, and it has some new ones of its own, most of which are optional or redundant.

I'll discuss supporting data binding for a single object first, and then I'll discuss data binding support for collections and lists. I'll wrap up this section by discussing some custom controls provided by CSLA .NET to simplify the use of data binding in WPF.

Object Data Binding

Binding to a single object in WPF is largely automatic. You can bind to nearly any object in .NET and it just works. As with Windows Forms, however, the data binding experience is enhanced if the object implements the same interfaces listed earlier in Table 10-1.

The `INotifyPropertyChanged` interface should be considered the bare minimum required to participate in data binding. It notifies data binding that a property of the object has changed. WPF handles the `PropertyChanged` event somewhat differently from Windows Forms—a topic I'll explore later in this section.

The WPF data grid control uses the `IEditableObject` interface to roll back changes to a row of data if the user presses Esc. The Windows Forms data grid relies on this same behavior.

■ **Note** At the time of this writing, the WPF data grid control is simply a project on CodePlex (`www.codeplex.com`) and is not an official part of the product. However, at present, it uses `IEditableObject`, as described here.

Data binding uses the `IDataErrorInfo` interface to change the display to visually indicate that the property to which a control is bound is invalid. Unlike Windows Forms, which uses an `ErrorProvider` control to do this, WPF data binding supports this concept natively, and you manage the appearance of a control with an invalid value by using an Extensible Application Markup Language (XAML) style.

Due to the differences between Windows Forms and WPF, the only interface needing further discussion is `INotifyPropertyChanged`.

PropertyChanged Event Handling

When WPF data binding handles a `PropertyChanged` event from an object, it assumes that only *that specific property* has changed. Because of that assumption, data binding only updates controls that are bound to that specific property. This is fundamentally different from Windows Forms, which updates all controls bound to the *same object* even if they are bound to different properties.

This means that when `BusinessBase` raises a `PropertyChanged` event, it needs to act differently for WPF than for Windows Forms. In the case of Windows Forms, even if multiple properties might have changed, it is most efficient to only raise `PropertyChanged` for one of the properties, since they'll all get refreshed anyway. However, in WPF, it is important to raise `PropertyChanged` for every property that changes. This includes properties changed directly by the user, as well as properties changed indirectly through business rules or processing. This also includes properties that didn't actually change, but may have become valid or invalid because some *other* property changed. For example, in an `Invoice` object, the `AmountDue` property might become invalid when the `CreditLimit` property is changed. If the object only raises `PropertyChanged` for `CreditLimit`, the UI won't display any visual cue to indicate that `AmountDue` is now invalid. Figure 10-3 illustrates this.

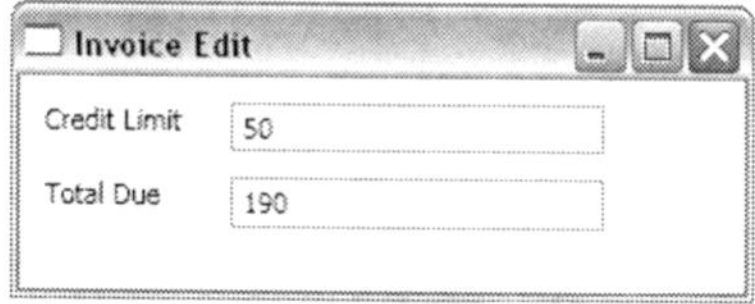

Figure 10-3. *Incorrect WPF display when using the Windows Forms model*

In Figure 10-3, the user sets the Total Due to 190 and then changes the Credit Limit from 5,000 to 50. Obviously, the Total Due now exceeds the credit limit and should be invalid, but no visual cue is provided for the user.

The object *also* needs to raise a `PropertyChanged` event for `AmountDue`, so data binding refreshes that property's display. If there's a `PropertyChanged` event for `CreditLimit` and `TotalDue`, the visual display will look like Figure 10-4.

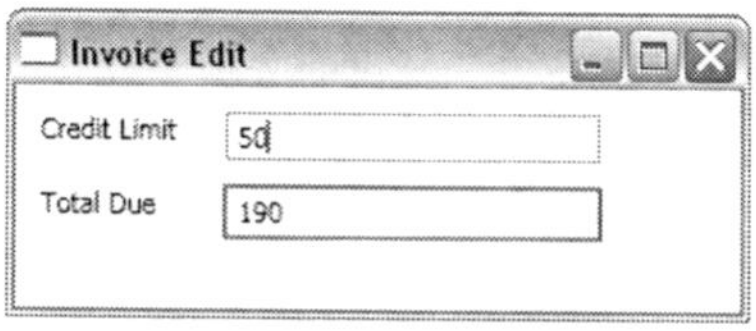

Figure 10-4. *Correct display when using the WPF data binding model*

In this case, the user did exactly the same thing, but when she reduced the Credit Limit and tabbed out of that control, the Total Due immediately showed that it was in error. You can implement this in BusinessBase, with a configuration setting in Csla.ApplicationContext.

Configuration

There's no universal way for a business object to know that it is data bound to a WPF form or a Windows Forms form, so you need to tell CSLA .NET which type of data binding is being used so the framework can adapt. You can do this by setting a config value in the app.config file in the appSettings section, as shown here:

```
<add key="CslaPropertyChangedMode" value="Xaml" />
```

or in code, as shown here:

```
Csla.ApplicationContext.PropertyChangedMode =
  Csla.ApplicationContext.PropertyChangedModes.Xaml;
```

If set in code, the value should be set exactly once, as the application starts up.

The default mode is Windows, which is necessary for backward compatibility with existing CSLA .NET code. This means that all WPF applications should set this property as shown, either in the config file or in code.

Raising PropertyChanged in BusinessBase

In the BusinessBase class, the code that raises the PropertyChanged event when a property is changed works differently depending on the PropertyChangedMode setting.

```
protected virtual void PropertyHasChanged(string propertyName)
{
  MarkDirty(true);
  var propertyNames = ValidationRules.CheckRules(propertyName);
  if (ApplicationContext.PropertyChangedMode ==
                  ApplicationContext.PropertyChangedModes.Windows)
    OnPropertyChanged(propertyName);
  else
    foreach (var name in propertyNames)
      OnPropertyChanged(name);
}
```

If the mode is Windows, then OnPropertyChanged() will be called to raise the event just one time, for the property that was just changed.

```
if (ApplicationContext.PropertyChangedMode ==
                ApplicationContext.PropertyChangedModes.Windows)
  OnPropertyChanged(propertyName);
```

If the mode is Xaml, then the code will loop through a list of all the properties for which validation rules were checked.

```
foreach (var name in propertyNames)
  OnPropertyChanged(name);
```

The CheckRules() method, which I'll discuss in Chapter 11, returns a string array containing the names of all the properties for which business or validation rules were invoked. This is effectively the list of all the properties that might need to be refreshed in the WPF interface.

The OnPropertyChanged() method is called for each property name, ensuring that the UI updates properly, even if changing one property affects the validation status of other properties.

Collection Data Binding

WPF supports two different interfaces for binding to collections: `INotifyCollectionChanged` and `IBindingList`. The `INotifyCollectionChanged` interface and the associated `ObservableCollection<T>` class were introduced with WPF. The `INotifyCollectionChanged` interface offers a simpler alternative to the relatively complex `IBindingList` interface.

It is important to realize that WPF supports both `IBindingList` and `INotifyCollectionChanged`. If a collection implements either interface, it will work fine with WPF data binding. However, for a collection to be useful in Windows Forms as well as WPF, then `IBindingList` is the only valid option.

A collection should never implement *both* interfaces. The `IBindingList` interface requires implementation of the `ListChanged` event, and `INotifyCollectionChanged` requires implementation of the `CollectionChanged` event. If a collection implements both, then it will raise both events, and WPF will *respond* to both events. Each action to a list affects data binding twice, so some very unexpected and undesired results would occur.

I've already discussed how the CSLA .NET collection classes inherit from `BindingList<T>` and thus implement `IBindingList`. This allows them to work properly with WPF, as well as Windows Forms and Web Forms.

Controls and Helper Objects

WPF data binding is powerful and fun to use. It minimizes the amount of code required in the UI, and it provides a clean layer of abstraction between the UI and your business layer. However, there are some areas where repetitive code can still be required in the UI, and to minimize this, CSLA .NET includes a set of custom WPF controls.

The CslaDataProvider Control

WPF has a data control concept similar to the data source control concept from ASP.NET 2.0. In WPF, these data controls are called data providers, and they allow declarative data access from your XAML code, or your code-behind.

Data provider controls are powerful, because they abstract the concept of data access within a WPF form, and they can support additional behaviors such as providing asynchronous access to data.

As with ASP.NET, WPF provides an `ObjectDataProvider` control that might, at first glance, appear to be a good way to work with CSLA .NET–style business objects. Unfortunately, the `ObjectDataProvider` has some of the same limitations as the ASP.NET `ObjectDataSource` control:

- It requires a `public` constructor.
- It has no way to call a `static` (or any other type of) factory method.

CSLA .NET–style business objects have non-`public` constructors, and factory methods are used to create or retrieve the object. Additionally, CSLA .NET objects intrinsically support n-level undo and persistence, and the `ObjectDataProvider` has no knowledge of those capabilities either.

What's needed is a data provider control that understands how to call `static` factory methods and how to manage the object's lifetime: interacting with n-level undo and CSLA .NET–style object persistence.

The `CslaDataProvider` is a WPF data provider control that understands how to interact with CSLA .NET business objects. This control can not only create or retrieve a business object, but it can also manage the object's entire lifetime through to saving (inserting, updating or deleting) the object into the database or canceling any changes made to the object by the user.

Finally, like many other data provider controls, `CslaDataProvider` supports asynchronous loading of the object by implementing an `IsAsynchronous` property. This can be a powerful feature in many cases, because it tells the control to create or retrieve the object on a background thread, and the UI updates automatically when the process is complete.

Declaring the Class

The .NET Framework includes a base class that makes it relatively easy to create a data provider control, and CslaDataProvider inherits from that class.

```
public class CslaDataProvider : DataSourceProvider
```

In the simplest case, a subclass of DataSourceProvider needs only to override the BeginQuery() method, where it creates or retrieves the object requested by data binding. The CslaDataProvider control does that, and quite a bit more.

The BeginQuery Method

A subclass of DataSourceProvider needs to override the BeginQuery() method, which data binding invokes when it needs the control to create or retrieve an object. This can happen in the following cases:

- When the WPF form is loaded and IsInitialLoadEnabled is true (the default)
- When a property of the data provider control is changed (via data binding or code)

The BeginQuery() method must honor some properties from the base class. First, it must support the concept of deferred refresh, which allows the UI code to set many properties of the data provider control and have the query run only once after they've all been set. The IsRefreshDeferred property on the base class controls this. Second, it also must support the IsInitialLoadEnabled property. If this property is false, then the first time BeginQuery() is invoked, it must return without doing any work. Finally, the CslaDataProvider control supports an IsAsynchronous property, and if that is true, then the query is run on a background thread.

Here's the code:

```
protected override void BeginQuery()
{
  if (this.IsRefreshDeferred)
    return;

  if (_firstRun)
  {
    _firstRun = false;
    if (!IsInitialLoadEnabled)
      return;
  }

  QueryRequest request = new QueryRequest();
  request.ObjectType = _objectType;
  request.FactoryMethod = _factoryMethod;
  request.FactoryParameters = _factoryParameters;
  request.ManageObjectLifetime = _manageLifetime;

  if (IsAsynchronous)
    System.Threading.ThreadPool.QueueUserWorkItem(DoQuery, request);
  else
    DoQuery(request);
}
```

You can see how the IsRefreshDeferred, IsInitialLoadEnabled, and IsAsynchronous properties are used to control the flow of the process.

Ultimately, the DoQuery() method handles the real work, either on a background thread or synchronously as appropriate.

The DoQuery Method

The DoQuery() method is relatively simple, because it just invokes the specified factory method and returns the resulting business object.

To invoke the factory method, it uses a bit of public reflection. This is necessary because the factory method name comes from XAML, so it's obviously just a string value. If you look at the code, you'll see how it first attempts to find a factory method with parameters that match those provided from the XAML.

```
BindingFlags flags = BindingFlags.Static |
                                   BindingFlags.Public |
                                   BindingFlags.FlattenHierarchy;
MethodInfo factory = request.ObjectType.GetMethod(
  request.FactoryMethod, flags,
  null,
  MethodCaller.GetParameterTypes(parameters), null);
```

Hopefully, that will succeed, and the factory can be invoked. However, if a strongly typed match can't be made, another attempt will be made to find any factory with the correct number of parameters.

```
if (factory == null)
{
  int parameterCount = parameters.Length;
  MethodInfo[] methods = request.ObjectType.GetMethods(flags);
  foreach (MethodInfo method in methods)
    if (method.Name == request.FactoryMethod &&
                         method.GetParameters().Length == parameterCount)
    {
      factory = method;
      break;
    }
}
```

This covers the case where a factory method is defined to accept parameters of type object, for example.

Assuming some matching factory method is found, it is invoked.

```
result = factory.Invoke(null, parameters);
```

If the ManageObjectLifetime property is true, then CslaDataProvider is expected to support the advanced save and cancel features. To do this, it must call the n-level undo BeginEdit() method on the object before returning it to data binding.

```
if (request.ManageObjectLifetime && result != null)
{
  Csla.Core.ISupportUndo undo = result as Csla.Core.ISupportUndo;
  if (undo != null)
    undo.BeginEdit();
}
```

Finally, the result is returned to data binding, along with any exception that may have occurred during the process.

```
base.OnQueryFinished(result, exceptionResult, null, null);
```

To be clear, if an exception occurs in DoQuery(), it is caught, and the Exception object is returned as part of this result. The exception isn't allowed to bubble up as normal. This is important, because this code could be running on a background thread. In that case, were the exception to simply bubble up, it would be unavailable to the UI developer, making debugging virtually impossible.

The `OnQueryFinished()` method returns the resulting object, if any, and the exception, if any, so they can be provided to the UI through data binding.

The CslaDataProviderCommandManager Class

Most data provider controls only create or retrieve data objects. They have no support for saving the object or for canceling changes, nor do they know how to add or remove items from a collection. However, these are common behaviors that are used in many forms, and if the control doesn't support them, then the UI developer must write code to do this work.

The `CslaDataProvider` control does implement these behaviors, which reduces the amount of code required to create a UI, sometimes even enabling a UI developer to create a fully interactive data editing form with *no code behind*.

The support for the save, cancel, add new item, and remove item behaviors is handled through the WPF concept of *commanding*. Some WPF controls can send a *command* to other controls, and this is often done instead of implementing an event handler. For example, a `Button` control can send a command rather than having a `Click` event handler.

The challenge, in this case, is that commands can only be routed to visual UI elements, and a data provider is not a visual element. To overcome this limitation and allow commands to be routed to `CslaDataProvider`, every instance of `CslaDataProvider` exposes an instance of `CslaDataProviderCommandManager`, which is a visual element (though it is never displayed to the user). Figure 10-5 shows this relationship.

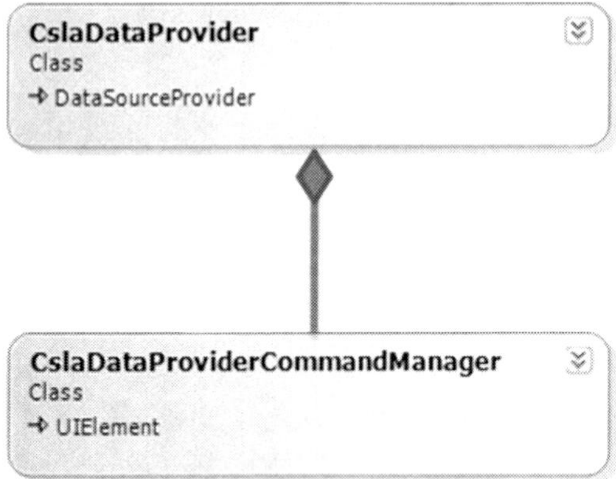

Figure 10-5. *CslaDataProvider and CslaDataProviderCommandManager*

This allows controls such as a button to route the appropriate command to the `CslaDataProviderCommandManager`, which invokes a method on the `CslaDataProvider` to do the actual work.

For example, this XAML defines a Save button:

```
<Button
  Command="ApplicationCommands.Save"
  CommandTarget="{Binding Source={StaticResource Project},
                          Path=CommandManager,
                          BindsDirectlyToSource=True}"
  HorizontalAlignment="Left" IsDefault="True">Save</Button>
```

Notice how the CommandTarget property is specified. The Source is a CslaDataProvider control, but the binding path indicates that the command should be routed to the data provider control's CommandManager property, which is an instance of CslaDataProviderCommandManager.

In CslaDataProviderCommandManager is a SaveCommand() method that is invoked by the WPF commanding infrastructure when the Button control is clicked:

```
private static void SaveCommand(object target, ExecutedRoutedEventArgs e)
{
  CslaDataProviderCommandManager ctl =
                          target as CslaDataProviderCommandManager;
  if (ctl != null && ctl.Provider != null)
    ctl.Provider.Save();
}
```

The CslaDataProviderCommandManager has a Provider property, which is a reference to its parent CslaDataProvider control. You can see how this code delegates the call to its parent:

```
ctl.Provider.Save();
```

Finally, in CslaDataProvider, the Save() method does the actual work of saving the business object by calling the object's Save() method.

```
result = savable.Save();
```

It is important to notice that the Save() method returns a new instance of the business object. I'll discuss the details in Chapter 15, but what this means here is that the new object must be provided to WPF data binding so the UI can update properly.

To do this, data binding must first be cleared and then provided with the new object.

```
// clear previous object
base.OnQueryFinished(null, exceptionResult, null, null);
// return result to base class
base.OnQueryFinished(result, null, null, null);
```

The first OnQueryFinished() call passes a null for the object value. This is necessary, because if the business object is returned before clearing the value, data binding will think it is the original object and it won't update the reference. This is much like the process of clearing and resetting a BindingSource in Windows Forms for the same reason.

The Undo (cancel), New (add new item), and Remove (remove item) commands are implemented using the same technique.

The CslaDataProvider control reduces the amount of UI code required to create a data-oriented WPF form. It can create or retrieve an object so the user can interact with the data. The control allows the UI developer to use commanding to add or remove items from a collection object. Finally, the control can be used to save or cancel the changes made by the user, all entirely through XAML.

The PropertyStatus Control

WPF doesn't have an exact equivalent to the Windows Forms ErrorProvider control or the Web Forms validation controls. As I discussed earlier and illustrated in Figures 10-3 and 10-4, some basic support for IDataErrorInfo is built into WPF data binding. It is possible to use XAML styling to display validation errors from the business object to the user using that technique.

However, that approach still doesn't allow you to easily display all three severities of validation errors that I will cover in Chapter 11: error, warning, and information. WPF also doesn't provide a simple way to indicate that an asynchronous validation rule is currently running for a property that is data bound to a UI control.

In Chapter 12, I'll discuss the authorization support built into CSLA .NET, which includes the ability to specify whether a user is allowed to read or write to specific properties. Ideally, a UI control bound to a property would enable or disable (or even become hidden) based on whether the user was allowed to edit or see the property value. There is no support for such a concept in WPF.

The PropertyStatus control in the Csla.Wpf namespace is designed to address these shortcomings. This control's default appearance is similar to the Windows Forms ErrorProvider control, although as shown in Figure 10-6, it displays all three rule severities. Of course, the control is fully stylable through XAML, so you can change the visual display as needed.

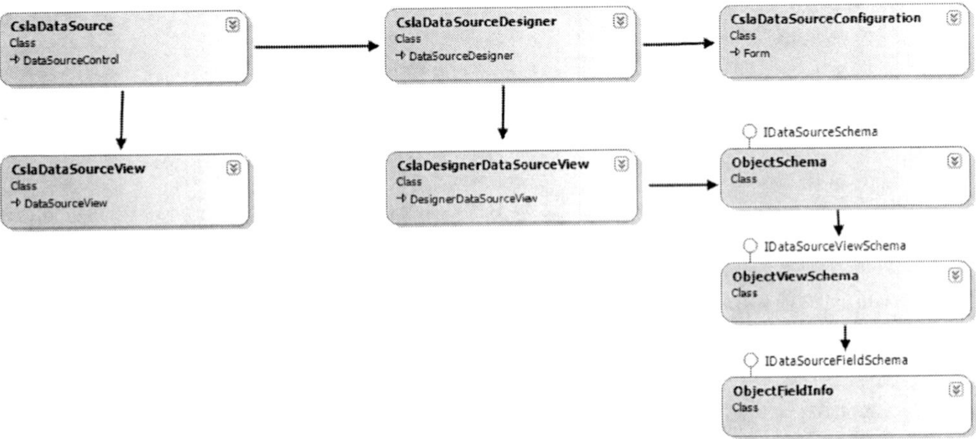

Figure 10-6. *PropertyStatus displaying broken validation rules*

The PropertyStatus control is typically used in a form along with a TextBox control or other data bound control. The PropertyStatus control not only has a display of its own for validation errors, but it can also control the display of the associated UI control for authorization purposes (disabling or hiding the control as necessary). Here's an example of using PropertyStatus:

```
<StackPanel Orientation="Horizontal">
  <TextBox x:Name="NameTextBox" Text="{Binding Path=Name}" />
  <csla:PropertyStatus Source="{Binding}"
                       Property="Name"
                       Target="{Binding ElementName=NameTextBox}"/>
</StackPanel>
```

The Source and Property properties must be set so the control has access to the business object property. The Target property must be set for the authorization support to work, and this is optional. If you don't want automatic disabling of the UI control based on the business object's authorization rules, then don't set the Target property.

Perhaps the most interesting part of the PropertyStatus control's implementation is the fact that it supports visual styling. Its default appearance is defined in the Generic.xaml file contained in the \Themes folder. WPF defines the name of the folder and file; you must use these names when building controls. In Generic.xaml, you'll find a Style element for the PropertyStatus control:

```
<Style TargetType="{x:Type csla:PropertyStatus}">
```

I won't go through all the XAML in the style, as it is quite extensive and key parts were created using Expression Blend. However, it's important to understand that this style references two ControlTemplate elements that are also defined in Generic.xaml: DefaultPopupTemplate and BrokenRuleTemplate. These are constituent parts of the overall control UI, and they allow a UI designer to override just parts of the visual display. For example, a designer could replace `DefaultPopupTemplate` to change the look and feel of the popup that is shown when the user hovers his mouse over an error icon.

The `PropertyStatus` style also uses a number of other named elements such as some `StoryBoard` elements and a `Grid` element. The names of these elements, as defined by `x:Key` properties, are important for linking the elements to the code that implements the control itself.

In the `PropertyStatus` control code, attributes are applied to the class to indicate that the control makes use of a series of control templates.

```
[TemplatePart(Name = "root", Type = typeof(FrameworkElement))]
[TemplatePart(Name = "popup", Type = typeof(Popup))]
[TemplatePart(Name = "errorImage", Type = typeof(FrameworkElement))]
[TemplatePart(Name = "warningImage", Type = typeof(FrameworkElement))]
[TemplatePart(Name = "informationImage", Type = typeof(FrameworkElement))]
[TemplatePart(Name = "busy", Type = typeof(BusyAnimation))]
[TemplatePart(Name = "Valid", Type = typeof(Storyboard))]
[TemplatePart(Name = "Error", Type = typeof(Storyboard))]
[TemplatePart(Name = "Warning", Type = typeof(Storyboard))]
[TemplatePart(Name = "Information", Type = typeof(Storyboard))]
public class PropertyStatus : ContentControl
```

The control also defines a set of dependency properties, such as the `Target` property discussed earlier. A dependency property is a special way of declaring properties so they are fully available to data binding in WPF and WF.

```
public static readonly DependencyProperty
  TargetProperty = DependencyProperty.Register(
    "Target",
    typeof(DependencyObject),
    typeof(PropertyStatus));

public DependencyObject Target
{
  get { return (DependencyObject)GetValue(TargetProperty); }
  set { SetValue(TargetProperty, value); }
}
```

As you can see, the declaration of a dependency property is not all that different from a CSLA .NET property with a managed backing field, as discussed in Chapter 7. In fact, I drew inspiration from the dependency property syntax when designing the managed backing field syntax for CSLA .NET.

WPF uses the `DependencyProperty` field to provide metadata about the dependency property, and it uses that metadata to support data binding. The use of dependency properties is required to create bindable properties in any WPF UI component such as a control. It is not required when creating data sources such as a business object.

The `Source` property is important, because it provides the control with access to the underlying data source object. When this property changes, the control must disconnect from any previous data source and connect to the new data source. This is required because the `PropertyStatus` control listens for events from the data source object. The `SetSource()` method coordinates this process.

```
private void SetSource(object oldSource, object newSource)
{
  DetachSource(oldSource);
  AttachSource(newSource);
```

```
    BusinessBase bb = newSource as BusinessBase;
    if (bb != null && !string.IsNullOrEmpty(Property))
      IsBusy = bb.IsPropertyBusy(Property);

    UpdateState();
  }
```

The UpdateState() method causes an immediate check of the validation status for the bound property from the data source object. This way, the UI is updated immediately to reflect the status of the new data source object. I'll cover the UpdateState() method later in this section of the chapter.

The DetachSource() and AttachSource() methods unhook and hook the event handlers for the data source object's BusyChanged and PropertyChanged events. For example, here's the AttachSource() method:

```
  private void AttachSource(object source)
  {
    INotifyBusy busy = source as INotifyBusy;
    if (busy != null)
      busy.BusyChanged += source_BusyChanged;

    INotifyPropertyChanged changed = source as INotifyPropertyChanged;
    if (changed != null)
      changed.PropertyChanged += source_PropertyChanged;
  }
```

The BusyChanged event is used to turn on and off a busy animation. The result is that the user has a visual indication that the business object property is currently executing an asynchronous validation rule. The default visual appearance in this case is to display a BusyAnimation control, which I'll discuss later in this chapter.

The PropertyChanged event is used to trigger a check of the source object's authorization and validation rules through a call to the UpdateState() method. The UpdateState() method uses the validation and authorization concepts discussed in Chapters 11 and 12 to ask the business object whether the property has any associated broken validation rules.

```
      List<BrokenRule> allRules = new List<BrokenRule>();
      foreach (var r in businessObject.BrokenRulesCollection)
        if (r.Property == Property)
          allRules.Add(r);
```

The allRules list is then used to update the icon display and populate the popup if the user hovers his mouse over the icon. This relies on the data source object being a BusinessBase object, and if it is not, then the broken rules processing will be skipped automatically.

There's similar functionality for authorization in the HandleTarget() method. This method is invoked when the control needs to check the authorization rules for the business object property. It does a cast to see if the object implements IAuthorizeReadWrite from the Csla.Security namespace. Since BusinessBase and ReadOnlyBase implement this interface, authorization works with both editable and read-only objects.

Here's the code that determines the read and write authorization for the business object property:

```
      var b = Source as Csla.Security.IAuthorizeReadWrite;
      if (b != null)
      {
        bool canRead = b.CanReadProperty(Property);
        bool canWrite = b.CanWriteProperty(Property);
```

The canRead and canWrite values are then used to change the display of the Target UI control to ensure that the user can't edit or see data if he isn't authorized.

The PropertyStatus control provides simple access to rich functionality around authorization, validation, and asynchronous rule processing for WPF applications.

The BusyAnimation Control

The data portal and validation rules subsystems in CSLA .NET both support asynchronous operations. These operations run in the background, and the user is able to interact with the application while they execute. In many cases, you'll want to give the user a visual cue that a background operation is executing; otherwise, the user may be unaware that the application is actually busy doing work.

The PropertyStatus control I discussed earlier in the chapter will automatically display a busy animation if an asynchronous validation rule is executing for the property that the PropertyStatus control is monitoring. To show this animation, the PropertyStatus control uses a BusyAnimation control from the Csla.Wpf namespace.

You can also directly use the BusyAnimation control to indicate other asynchronous operations. For example, you might bind this control to a CslaDataProvider control's IsBusy property so the user is aware that an asynchronous data retrieval operation is executing.

The BusyAnimation control is stylable, much like PropertyStatus. This means that its default appearance is defined by XAML in the Generic.xaml file from the \Themes folder in the Csla project. The XAML is quite long and is mostly composed of Storyboard elements to control the animation, but it does set some default values for properties as well.

```
<Style TargetType="{x:Type csla:BusyAnimation}">
    <Setter Property="Background" Value="Transparent" />
    <Setter Property="BorderBrush" Value="Black" />
    <Setter Property="BorderThickness" Value="1" />
    <Setter Property="Foreground" Value="Tan" />
    <Setter Property="StateDuration" Value="0:0:0.125" />
```

The animation of the storyboards is handled by a DispatchTimer, which is a special timer control designed to work with WPF UI elements.

```
  _timer = new DispatcherTimer();
  _timer.Interval = StateDuration;
  _timer.Tick += new EventHandler(timer_Tick);
```

The state of the storyboard is changed with each Tick event of the timer, moving from one frame of animation to the next.

```
private int _frame = 0;

void timer_Tick(object sender, EventArgs e)
{
  _isRunningStoryboard[_frame].Begin(_root);
  _frame = (_frame + 1) % NUM_STATES;
}
```

The BusyAnimation control is useful for giving the user an indication that a background task is executing, and you can use it with the asynchronous data portal and the CslaDataProvider control. The PropertyStatus control uses the BusyAnimation control automatically. I'll use this control in Chapter 19.

The DataDecoratorBase Control

WPF has the concept of a *decorator control*, which is a control that alters the appearance of the control it contains. In other words, a decorator control contains another control and "decorates" it by altering its appearance.

The Authorizer and ObjectStatus controls, which I'll discuss later, are both decorator controls. Their behavior requires that they be aware of when the current DataContext changes, and when the data object raises a changed event (PropertyChanged, ListChanged, or CollectionChanged). Rather than having those controls implement this behavior separately, the DataDecoratorBase control handles all those details.

I won't walk through the code for DataDecoratorBase in detail. It handles the DataContextChanged event so it is aware of when the data context changes.

```
public DataDecoratorBase()
{
  this.DataContextChanged +=
    new DependencyPropertyChangedEventHandler(Panel_DataContextChanged);
  this.Loaded += new RoutedEventHandler(Panel_Loaded);
}
```

When it detects that the context has changed, it unhooks any events from the old context object and hooks events on the new context object. The goal is to detect when the current data context object raises a changed event such as PropertyChanged.

When that happens, a virtual method named DataPropertyChanged() is called to notify any subclass.

```
private void DataObject_PropertyChanged(
  object sender, PropertyChangedEventArgs e)
{
  DataPropertyChanged(e);
}
```

The subclass can override DataPropertyChanged(), and can take any appropriate steps in response to the event. The DataDecoratorBase class exists to consolidate this event handling code so it isn't repeated in other controls. It also implements a helper method named FindChildBindings(). This method walks through all the controls contained within the DataDecoratorBase control, and each time it finds a control that is data bound it calls a virtual method named FoundBinding(). The subclass can override FoundBinding(), where it can do any processing necessary related to that binding.

The Authorizer Control

The ReadWriteAuthorization control from the Csla.Windows namespace helps Windows Forms developers build interfaces where the controls on the form alter their appearance based on whether the user is authorized to read or write to the underlying business object property.

The Authorizer control in the Csla.Wpf namespace provides similar functionality for WPF. The Authorizer control is a decorator control and is a subclass of DataDecoratorBase. If you want it to affect the appearance of multiple controls, you can nest those controls within a panel or other container control, then put that container control inside the Authorizer control.

In most cases, developers will probably prefer the PropertyStatus control instead of Authorizer, because it handles not only authorization but also validation and busy status notification. However, Authorizer does provide an alternative, making it easy to implement authorization for a group of data bound controls contained within the Authorizer control.

Authorizer uses the IAuthorizeReadWrite interface from the Csla.Security namespace to interact with the business object. I'll discuss this interface in more detail in Chapter 13. The control uses this interface to determine whether the user is authorized to read or write to each business object property that is data bound to a control contained within the Authorizer control.

Any time the underlying data object (DataContext) is changed or a Refresh() method is called, Authorizer scans all the controls it contains, checking each binding to see if the current user is authorized to read and write the associated property. DataDecoratorBase does much of the hard work.

Controlling Readability

If a property is not readable, Authorizer changes the UI control's Visibility to be Hidden or Collapsed. An attached property defined by Authorizer called NotVisibleModeProperty is used to choose which option should be used for each UI control.

```
private static readonly DependencyProperty NotVisibleModeProperty =
  DependencyProperty.RegisterAttached(
    "NotVisibleMode",
    typeof(VisibilityMode),
    typeof(Authorizer),
    new FrameworkPropertyMetadata(VisibilityMode.Collapsed),
    new ValidateValueCallback(IsValidVisibilityMode));
```

The SetRead() method determines whether the user is authorized to read a property, and it alters the bound control's Visibility accordingly.

```
private void SetRead(Binding bnd, UIElement ctl, IAuthorizeReadWrite source)
{
  bool canRead = source.CanReadProperty(bnd.Path.Path);
  VisibilityMode visibilityMode = GetNotVisibleMode(ctl);

  if (canRead)
    switch (visibilityMode)
    {
      case VisibilityMode.Collapsed:
        if (ctl.Visibility == Visibility.Collapsed)
          ctl.Visibility = Visibility.Visible;
        break;
      case VisibilityMode.Hidden:
        if (ctl.Visibility == Visibility.Hidden)
          ctl.Visibility = Visibility.Visible;
        break;
      default:
        break;
    }
  else
    switch (visibilityMode)
    {
      case VisibilityMode.Collapsed:
        ctl.Visibility = Visibility.Collapsed;
        break;
      case VisibilityMode.Hidden:
        ctl.Visibility = Visibility.Hidden;
        break;
      default:
        break;
    }
}
```

The Visibility property is set back to Visible if the user is authorized to read the value.

Controlling Updates

If a property is not updatable, Authorizer will check to see if the UI control has an IsReadOnly property; if it does, it will set the value to true. Otherwise, it will set the IsEnabled property to false, because all controls have that property. The SetWrite() method handles this.

```
private void SetWrite(Binding bnd, UIElement ctl, IAuthorizeReadWrite source)
{
  bool canWrite = source.CanWriteProperty(bnd.Path.Path);

  // enable/disable writing of the value
  PropertyInfo propertyInfo =
    ctl.GetType().GetProperty("IsReadOnly",
    BindingFlags.FlattenHierarchy |
    BindingFlags.Instance |
    BindingFlags.Public);
  if (propertyInfo != null)
  {
    propertyInfo.SetValue(
      ctl, !canWrite, new object[] { });
  }
  else
  {
    ctl.IsEnabled = canWrite;
  }
}
```

There is no standard interface you can use to find the IsReadOnly property, so reflection is used. If the property exists, it will be set; otherwise, the code will fall back to disabling the UI control entirely.

The Authorizer control can save a lot of UI code when building a form for editing details, because it manages the status of all data bound detail controls with little or no code required in the UI itself. You can see how this is used in Chapter 19.

The ObjectStatus Control

Editable CSLA .NET business objects that subclass BusinessBase have a set of valuable status properties. These properties are not available for data binding, because they are marked with the [Browsable(false)] attribute, and because they don't raise the PropertyChanged event when they change. These properties were discussed in Chapter 8 and are listed in Table 8-1.

Sometimes, you may need access to these properties within your XAML code. For example, you might want to enable or disable certain controls on the form based on whether the object's IsSavable property returns true or false.

The ObjectStatus control from the Csla.Wpf namespace exposes these properties as bindable properties from a WPF control. The ObjectStatus control takes the properties from its current DataContext and exposes them as dependency properties so they can be used in control-to-control data binding. Additionally, the ObjectStatus control includes code to detect when each of the status properties has changed, so it can raise appropriate PropertyChanged events for them.

This control is relatively simple. Any time the DataContext changes or the data object raises a changed event such as PropertyChanged, it re-reads the object's status values and updates its own bindable property values—for example:

```
if (IsDeleted != source.IsDeleted)
  IsDeleted = source.IsDeleted;
if (IsDirty != source.IsDirty)
  IsDirty = source.IsDirty;
```

```
if (IsNew != source.IsNew)
  IsNew = source.IsNew;
if (IsSavable != source.IsSavable)
  IsSavable = source.IsSavable;
if (IsValid != source.IsValid)
  IsValid = source.IsValid;
```

It only updates its own property value if that value differs from the business object's value. This is because setting the control's property value raises a PropertyChanged event from the control, and that will likely cause some other UI control to refresh based on a trigger or control-to-control data binding.

The end result is that you can create a control in the UI to display the status of the object. For example, here's a CheckBox control bound to the IsSavable property:

```
<CheckBox IsEnabled="False"
          IsChecked="{Binding
            RelativeSource={RelativeSource FindAncestor,
            AncestorType=csla:ObjectStatus,
            AncestorLevel=1},
            Path=IsSavable}">IsSavable</CheckBox>
```

The binding expression is quite complex, but the end result is that the control displays the current value of the IsSavable property for the business object referred to by the DataContext.

At this point, you should have an understanding of the support provided for WPF data binding within CSLA .NET. The last technology I'll cover is Web Forms, which is the simplest from a data binding perspective.

Web Forms

Of the three UI technologies discussed in this chapter, ASP.NET Web Forms has the fewest requirements on business objects. In fact, it imposes no specific requirements on your objects or collections at all.

Any object with properties can be bound to controls in a page. Any collection, list, or array that implements IEnumerable (the most basic of all collection interfaces) can be bound to list controls on a page. In short, it just works.

Controls and Helper Objects

However, there's one catch, and that is the way the Web Forms data source controls work—specifically, the ObjectDataSource control. This control imposes some restrictions on the objects it works with, and those restrictions mean it won't work with CSLA .NET objects.

To overcome this limitation, the CslaDataSource control is an ASP.NET data source control that is designed to work with objects containing business logic. This control allows the full use of Web Forms data binding with rich business objects.

The CslaDataSource Control

Data source controls in ASP.NET have two major areas of functionality: runtime and design time. Runtime functionality is the actual data binding implementation—it copies data from the data source to the controls and back again. Design time functionality exists to support Visual Studio 2005 and 2008, allowing developers to graphically create web pages using common controls like DataGridView and DetailsView when they are bound to the data source control.

The detailed design issues around building an ASP.NET data source control are outside the scope of this book. Nonetheless, I'll walk quickly through the code in these classes to call out the highlights of the implementation.

It turns out that implementing runtime functionality is relatively straightforward, but providing design time functionality is more complex. Table 10-7 lists the classes required to implement the `CslaDataSource` control's runtime and design time support.

Table 10-7. *Classes Required to Implement the CslaDataSource Control*

Class	Description
`CslaDataSource`	The data source control itself; the UI developer uses this directly
`CslaDataSourceView`	Provides the actual implementation of data binding for `CslaDataSource`
`CslaDataSourceConfiguration`	Provides a configuration UI form displayed in Visual Studio to configure the control
`CslaDataSourceDesigner`	The Visual Studio designer for `CslaDataSource`
`CslaDesignerDataSourceView`	Provides schema information and sample data for the designer
`ObjectSchema`	The schema object for a business object, responsible for returning an instance of ObjectViewSchema
`ObjectViewSchema`	Provides actual information about a business object—specifically, information about all the business object's bindable properties
`ObjectFieldInfo`	Maintains information about a specific field in the object schema

Figure 10-7 provides a helpful diagram that illustrates how these classes relate to each other.

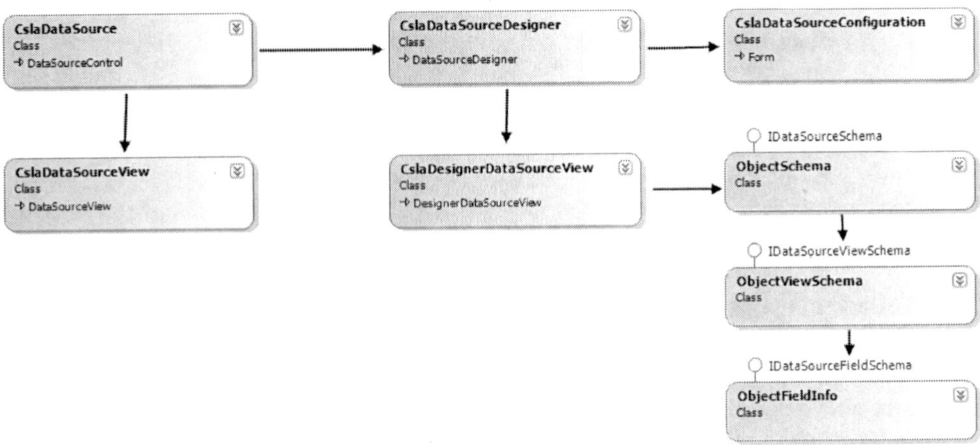

Figure 10-7. *Relationship between the classes in CslaDataSource*

The UI developer drags a CslaDataSource control onto a Web Form and interacts with it. While in Visual Studio, CslaDataSourceDesigner coordinates all that interaction, although in reality, all the hard work is done by CslaDesignerDataSourceView. The CslaDataSourceDesigner may open the CslaDataSourceConfiguration dialog to allow the user to configure some aspects of the control.

When a control such as GridView is bound to the CslaDataSource, it requests schema information about the data source. This schema information is created and returned by the ObjectSchema, ObjectViewSchema, and ObjectFieldInfo objects.

Finally, at runtime, the web form interacts with CslaDataSource to perform the actual data binding. All the hard work is actually handled by CslaDataSourceView, an instance of which is managed by the CslaDataSource control.

The only bit of functionality that a UI developer will see is that CslaDataSource declares and raises four events. The UI developer must respond to these events to provide the interaction with the business object. Table 10-8 lists the events.

Table 10-8. *Events Raised by the CslaDataSource Control*

Event	Description
SelectObject	Requests that the UI provide a reference to the business object that is the data source
InsertObject	Requests that the UI insert a new business object based on the data from the form
UpdateObject	Requests that the UI update a business object with the data from the form, based on the key value provided
DeleteObject	Requests that the UI delete the business object based on the key value provided

These four events are directly analogous to the four method names required by the ASP.NET ObjectDataSource. Rather than using reflection to invoke a set of methods, I opted to raise events, as I feel that this is an easier programming model. With the ObjectDataSource, the UI developer must implement four methods (or defer to those in an ADO.NET TableAdapter), while with CslaDataSource, the developer simply handles these four events.

There is a custom EventArgs class for each of the events: SelectObjectArgs, InsertObjectArgs, UpdateObjectArgs, and DeleteObjectArgs, respectively. Each one provides properties that are used within the event handler.

The end result is a fully functional data source control that understands CSLA .NET–style business objects. UI developers can use this control to leverage the data binding support of ASP.NET Web Forms when working with rich business objects.

Conclusion

In this chapter, I discussed how CSLA .NET supports data binding for the Windows Forms, WPF, and Web Forms user interface technologies. For simple objects, this involves the implementation of a number of interfaces, including

- INotifyPropertyChanging
- INotifyPropertyChanged
- IEditableObject
- IDataErrorInfo

For collections and lists, this involves the use of either `BindingList<T>` or `ObservableCollection<T>`. Since all three UI technologies support `BindingList<T>`, while only WPF supports `ObservableCollection<T>`, the CSLA .NET framework is based on the use of `BindingList<T>`.

By providing support for data binding in the framework, CSLA .NET ensures that all business objects created using the framework fully support the features of data binding in all major UI technologies. This helps reduce the complexity of the business objects as well as the amount of code required to create a UI that uses the objects.

Chapters 11 through 16 will continue the coverage of the implementation of CSLA .NET. Then, from Chapter 17 on, the focus will be on building the simple business application designed in Chapter 3 to illustrate how the classes in the framework can be used to build applications based on business objects.

CHAPTER 11

Business and Validation Rules

I've now walked through several aspects of the CSLA .NET implementation, including an overview of the framework, base classes, property declarations, object status management, parent-child relationships, and data binding.

This chapter will focus on how CSLA .NET supports business and validation rules in a standardized manner. In several previous chapters, I've made reference to the framework's support for business and validation rules. The rules are invoked when a property is set on an editable business object through the `SetProperty()` helper method. The business developer can also invoke the rules by explicitly calling the `CheckRules()` method of the `ValidationRules` object.

As validation rules are broken and unbroken, they are added to and removed from a list of broken rules. Each editable business object always has a list of the currently broken rules. If this list is empty, `IsSelfValid` is `true`; otherwise, it is `false`. Not only is the list used to drive the `IsSelfValid` property, but it is also used by the `IDataErrorInfo` implementation for data binding support. The list of broken rules is exposed as a property from the business object, so the list itself can be data bound and displayed to the end user if desired.

The CSLA .NET framework includes the infrastructure necessary to associate business and validation rules with properties, and to invoke those rules at appropriate points in the object's life cycle. That is the focus of this chapter.

Types of Rules

In the CSLA .NET model, business and validation rules are implemented as methods. Each rule is contained in its own method. Rules are then associated with properties of business objects. The `BusinessBase` class includes code to invoke these rules at appropriate points in the object's lifetime. For example, rules for a property are invoked when that property is changed, or when a dependent property is changed. They are also invoked when a new instance of the object is created, and they can be invoked explicitly by your code.

Normally, rules are associated with business objects on a *per-type* basis. This means that all instances of a specific business object type (such as `CustomerEdit`) will have the same rules associated with the same properties. This is a good thing, because it means that the work of associating the rules to properties is done once for that type, and the information is reused across all instances of the type. That saves both processing time and memory.

As an alternative, it is also possible to associate rules with a business object on a *per-instance* basis. This means that each instance of the business object has its own rules. The associations are set up as the object instance is created, and they are stored in memory for that specific object. Obviously, this can cause performance and memory-consumption issues if you have many instances of a type, so you should avoid this approach as a general rule. CSLA .NET supports this concept, because there are rare cases when rules must vary on a per-instance basis.

Per-type rules must be accessible to all instances of the business object type. Normally, per-type rule methods are static, so they are always available to any object instance. It is also possible to implement per-type rule methods as instance methods of a global singleton object, though this is a more complex technique and offers no clear benefit over the simpler static method approach. In this book, I implement static rule methods and recommend that approach.

Per-instance rule methods only need to be accessible to the specific object instance where they are used. Normally, they are implemented as private instance methods in the business class, although they can also be static methods. I won't use any per-instance rules in this book, and I recommend against their use.

Given this basic background on per-type and per-instance rule methods, I'll now move on to discuss the business and validation subsystem in CSLA .NET, starting with a deeper exploration of rule methods and how you implement them.

Csla.Validation Namespace

The Csla.Validation namespace contains types that assist the business developer in implementing and enforcing business rules. This includes managing a list of business rules for each of the object's properties and maintaining a list of currently broken business rules.

Obviously, the framework can't implement the actual business rules and validation code—that will vary from application to application. However, business rules follow a very specific pattern in that they are either broken or not. The result of a rule being checked is a Boolean value and a human-readable description of why the rule is broken. This makes it possible to check the rules and then maintain a list of broken rules—including human-readable descriptions of each rule.

RuleHandler Delegate

Given that rules follow a specific pattern, it is possible to define a method signature that covers virtually all business rules. In .NET, a method signature can be formally defined using a delegate; here's the definition for a rule method:

```
public delegate bool RuleHandler(object target, RuleArgs e);
```

Every rule is implemented as a method that returns a Boolean result: true if the rule is satisfied, false if the rule is broken. The object containing the data to be validated is passed as the first argument, and the second argument is a RuleArgs object that you can use to pass extra rule-specific information. This means that a business rule in a business class looks like this:

```
private static bool CustNameRequired(object target, RuleArgs e)
{
  if (string.IsNullOrEmpty(((Customer)target).Name))
  {
    e.Description = "Customer name required";
    return false;
  }
  else
    return true;
}
```

If the length of the target object's Name property is zero, then the rule is not satisfied, so it returns false. It also sets the Description property of the RuleArgs object to a human-readable description of why the rule is broken.

This illustrates a rule that you could implement within a single business class. By using reflection, you could write entirely reusable rule methods that any business class can use. You'll see some examples of this in the “Common Validation Rules” section later in this chapter, when I discuss the CommonRules class.

Rule methods can also be generic and, thus, strongly typed. In that case, they follow this signature:

```
public delegate bool RuleHandler<T, R>(T target, R e) where R : RuleArgs;
```

There are a couple of variations on how to use this delegate type to create a rule method. The most common is to provide only the type of T.

```
private static bool CustNameRequired<T>(T target, RuleArgs e)
  where T : Customer
{
  if (string.IsNullOrEmpty(target.Name))
  {
    e.Description = "Customer name required";
    return false;
  }
  else
    return true;
}
```

The highlighted lines show the differences from the previous implementation. Notice how the method is generic, and the generic type T is constrained to the type of the business object. This allows the compiler to realize that the target parameter is of type Customer (or a subclass), so you’re able to use all the properties of that class in the method implementation.

You can also supply both generic type parameters.

```
private static bool CustNameRequired<T, R>(T target, R e)
  where T : Customer, R : MyRuleArgsSubclass
{
  if (target.Name.Length > e.MaxLength)
  {
    e.Description = "Customer name too long";
    return false;
  }
  else
    return true;
}
```

This approach is less common, but it allows you to have strongly typed access to a custom subclass of RuleArgs that you’ve created for your rule method.

RuleArgs Class

The RuleHandler delegates specify the use of the RuleArgs object as a parameter to every rule method. This follows the general pattern used throughout .NET of passing an EventArgs parameter to all event handlers. Business rules aren’t event handlers, so RuleArgs doesn’t inherit from EventArgs, but it follows the same basic principle.

The goal is to be able to pass data into and out of the rule method in a clearly defined manner. At a minimum, RuleArgs passes the name of the property to be validated into the rule method, and it passes any broken rule description back out of the rule method. To do this, it simply contains a read-only PropertyName property and a read-write Description property.

More important is the fact that the author of a rule method can create a subclass of RuleArgs to provide *extra* information. For instance, implementing a maximum value rule implies that the maximum allowed value could be provided to the rule. To do this, the rule author would create a subclass of RuleArgs.

DecoratedRuleArgs Class

CSLA .NET includes one subclass of RuleArgs, called DecoratedRuleArgs. This class uses the decorator design pattern to attach an arbitrary list of name/value pairs to the RuleArgs class.

The intent of DecoratedRuleArgs is to make it possible to write rule methods that accept parameters, but without needing a custom RuleArgs subclass for each different rule method. To do this, DecoratedRuleArgs acts like a Dictionary, so it stores name/value pairs and allows them to be retrieved.

This simplifies the use of code generation for business classes, because all of your rule methods can accept exactly the same argument type, just with different name/value pairs in the list. For example, when associating a rule with a property where the rule needs a strongly typed argument, the code in the business object looks like this:

```
ValidationRules.AddRule(MyCustomRule,
  new MyCustomRuleArgs(NameProperty, "Arg1", "Arg2"));
```

To generate this code, a code generation tool would need to know the type of the custom RuleArgs subclass and the parameters needed for its constructor.

Using DecoratedRuleArgs, the code is more standardized.

```
var parameters = new Dictionary<string, object>();
parameters.Add("FirstArg", "Arg1");
parameters.Add("OtherArg", "Arg2");
ValidationRules.AddRule(MyCustomRule,
  new DecoratedRuleArgs(NameProperty, parameters));
```

The code generator still needs to know the names of the parameters required by the rule method, but it doesn't need to know the type of a custom RuleArgs subclass, nor does it need to worry about the order of the parameters in a constructor or other details that make code generation difficult.

RuleMethod Class

The ValidationRules class maintains a list of rules for each property. This implies that ValidationRules has information about each rule method. This is the purpose of the RuleMethod classes. There are three classes: RuleMethod, RuleMethod<T, R>, and AsyncRuleMethod.

They all work much the same way, with minor variations that I'll discuss. Here's the declaration of the most basic RuleMethod class:

```
internal class RuleMethod :
  IRuleMethod, IComparable, IComparable<IRuleMethod>
```

It stores information about each rule, including a delegate reference to the rule method itself, a unique name for the rule, and any custom RuleArgs object that should be passed to the rule method. This information is stored in a set of fields with associated properties. The fields are declared like this:

```
private RuleHandler _handler;
private string _ruleName = String.Empty;
private RuleArgs _args;
private int _priority;
```

The RuleMethod class is scoped as internal, as it is used by other classes in the Csla.Validation namespace, but shouldn't be used by code outside the framework.

The unique rule name associated with each rule is derived automatically by generating a URI with the rule:// prefix. The URI is created by combining the name of the rule method with the string representation of the RuleArgs object. The rule method is expressed as class/method to provide a unique value even if the same rule method name is used in different classes. The RuleArgs object, at a minimum, includes the target property name with which the rule is associated. It also includes any other argument values maintained by the RuleArgs object. For instance, a rule will appear as

```
rule://ruleClass/ruleMethod/targetProperty?arg1=value&arg2=value
```

When a RuleMethod object is created, it initializes its RuleName property value as follows:

```
_ruleName = string.Format(@"rule://{0}/{1}/{2}",
  Uri.EscapeDataString(_handler.Method.DeclaringType.FullName),
  _handler.Method.Name,
  _args.ToString());
```

The FullName property of the type includes the namespace and type name. Combining this with the name of the rule method provides unique identification of the specific rule method. Because the rule name must be unique, any custom subclasses of RuleArgs should be sure to override ToString() to return a value that includes any custom data that is part of the argument object in the form of

```
targetProperty?arg1=value&arg2=value&...
```

■ **Note** The RuleDescription class in the Csla.Validation namespace can be used to parse the rule:// URI string into its constituent parts, much like you'd use System.Uri to parse any other URI.

When the business developer associates a rule method with a property, ValidationRules creates a RuleMethod object to maintain all this information. This RuleMethod object is what's actually associated with the property, thus providing all the information needed to invoke the rule when appropriate.

One interesting bit of information is a priority value. Each rule association has a priority with a default value of 0. When rules are invoked by CSLA .NET, they are invoked in priority order, starting with the lowest value and counting up. So priority 0 rules run first, then priority 1, 2, and so forth. A business developer can use this priority scheme to gain some control over the order in which the rules are invoked.

The priority concept is important, because it works in concert with a *short-circuiting* feature. This feature allows CSLA .NET to stop invoking rules of a higher priority if any lower-priority rule has failed. By default, if any priority 0 rule fails, then no priority 1 or higher rules will be invoked. All priority 0 rules always run in any case.

There's also a generic version of RuleMethod, which is declared like this:

```
internal class RuleMethod<T, R>
  : IRuleMethod, IComparable, IComparable<IRuleMethod>
  where R : RuleArgs
```

It does the same thing as RuleMethod, but it stores strongly typed values based on the generic type parameters.

And there's the asynchronous version, which is declared like this:

```
internal class AsyncRuleMethod
  : IAsyncRuleMethod, IComparable, IComparable<IRuleMethod>
```

This is the same as RuleMethod, but it is designed to store a reference to an asynchronous rule method. That's a rule method that runs code on a background thread and calls back into ValidationRules when it is complete to report on whether the condition is met or the rule is broken.

All RuleMethod classes implement IRuleMethod, so CLSA .NET can treat them polymorphically. In particular, as rules are associated with properties of a business object, the IRuleMethod objects are maintained in a list for each property, and that list uses the IRuleMethod type to do this.

Any type of RuleMethod object handles the invocation of the rule method itself by exposing an Invoke() method.

```
public bool Invoke(object target)
{
  return _handler.Invoke(target, _args);
}
```

When ValidationRules is asked to check the business rules, it merely loops through its list of RuleMethod objects, asking each one to invoke the rule it represents. As you can see, the Invoke() method simply invokes the method via the delegate reference, passing in a reference to the object to be validated (the business object) and the RuleArgs object associated with the rule.

If you look at the declarations of RuleMethod and RuleMethod<T, R>, you'll see that they both implement IComparable<T>. This interface is a standard .NET interface that you can implement to control how your objects are compared for operations such as sorting.

This is important for these objects, because they will be sorted, and that sorting must be based on the value of the Priority property. To this end, here's the implementation of the interface:

```
int IComparable.CompareTo(object obj)
{
  return Priority.CompareTo(((IRuleMethod)obj).Priority);
}

int IComparable<IRuleMethod>.CompareTo(IRuleMethod other)
{
  return Priority.CompareTo(other.Priority);
}
```

This ensures that when the rules are sorted, they'll be sorted in ascending order by priority.

RuleDescription Class

As I discussed earlier, rules are described by use of a URI. A rule URI looks like this:

```
rule://ruleClass/ruleMethod/targetProperty?arg1=value&arg2=value
```

The RuleDescription class understands how to parse a rule:// URI for easier use. Rather than manually writing code to parse the URI, or using the more generic System.Uri class, you can use the RuleDescription class to easily get at the parts of the URI.

```
Csla.Validation.RuleDescription desc = new Csla.Validation.RuleDescription(
  "rule://typeName/methodName/propertyName?arg1=value&arg2=value");
string scheme = desc.Scheme;
string methodTypeName = desc.MethodTypeName;
string methodName = desc.MethodName;
string propertyName = desc.PropertyName;
List<string> args = new List<string>();
foreach (var item in desc.Arguments)
  args.Add(item.Key + ", " + item.Value);
```

Table 11-1 lists the properties available from RuleDescription.

This class is particularly useful to UI framework authors, as it allows a UI framework to easily parse the rules associated with a business object.

Table 11-1. *Properties Available from RuleDescription*

Property	Description
`Scheme`	Returns the URI scheme, which is always `rule://`
`MethodTypeName`	Returns the type that implements the rule method
`MethodName`	Returns the rule method name specified in the URI
`PropertyName`	Returns the name of the business object property with which this rule is associated
`Arguments`	Returns a `Dictionary` of name/value pairs representing the arguments passed to the rule method

ValidationRules Class

The `ValidationRules` class is the primary class in the `Csla.Validation` namespace. Every business object that uses the validation rules functionality will contain its own `ValidationRules` object. `ValidationRules` relies on the other classes in `Csla.Validation` to do its work. Together, these classes maintain the list of rules for each property and the list of currently broken rules.

ValidationRulesManager and SharedValidationRulesManager Classes

You've already seen how a business rule is defined based on the `RuleHandler` delegate. A key part of what `ValidationRules` does is to keep a list of such rule methods for each of the business object's properties. To do this, it relies on two other classes: `ValidationRulesManager` and `SharedValidationRulesManager`.

The `ValidationRulesManager` keeps a list of rules for each property. One way that `ValidationRulesManager` is used is to keep a list of rules that is unique for each instance of a business object. This means that each time a business object is created, a set of rules can be associated with the properties of *that particular instance*. This has a pretty big impact on performance and memory consumption, and it's usually not the right approach. However, sometimes objects really do need unique rules, and this class enables that scenario.

Another way `ValidationRulesManager` is used is by the `SharedValidationRulesManager`, as it keeps a list of rules for each business *type*. The `SharedValidationRulesManager` keeps a list of rules for each property that is common across all instances of a business object type. This means that the *first time* an instance of a given business class is created, the rules are associated with the properties of that type. The resulting associations are cached for the lifetime of the application and are shared by all instances of that business class. This has good performance and minimal memory consumption, and it's the recommended approach.

■ **Note** CLSA .NET version 2.1 introduced the shared rules concept in response to performance and memory issues caused by the original per-instance rule technique.

As you'll see in Chapter 17 when I create the example business library, I typically only use shared rules.

Shared Rules and Threading

The big challenge with sharing a list of validation rules across all instances of a business type is that those instances could be running in parallel on different threads. In particular, on a web or application server, many client requests may be running simultaneously, and they all need access to that same set of cached RuleMethod objects.

Within SharedValidationRules, a Dictionary is used to cache all the rules for all the business object types.

```
private static Dictionary<Type, ValidationRulesManager> _managers =
  new Dictionary<Type, ValidationRulesManager>();
```

It is indexed by Type, which is the type of the business objects used by the application. Each business object type has its own ValidationRulesManager, which stores the rules for that particular business type.

To safely gain access to the ValidationRulesManager object for a type, the GetManager() method is used.

```
internal static ValidationRulesManager GetManager(
  Type objectType, bool create)
{
  ValidationRulesManager result = null;
  if (!_managers.TryGetValue(objectType, out result) && create)
  {
    lock (_managers)
    {
      if (!_managers.TryGetValue(objectType, out result))
      {
        result = new ValidationRulesManager();
        _managers.Add(objectType, result);
      }
    }
  }
  return result;
}
```

This method implements a simple but effective locking scheme. Remember that multiple threads may be executing this code at exactly the same time, and those threads may all attempt to get a value from the Dictionary.

```
if (!_managers.TryGetValue(objectType, out result) && create)
```

If this succeeds, then there's no problem. Multiple threads can read from the Dictionary at once without causing an issue. Things get more complex if the result field comes back as null, because that means a new ValidationRulesManager must be added to the Dictionary. Only one thread can be allowed to do this, so the lock statement is used to ensure that only one thread can run the next bit of code at a time.

Note my careful choice of words: only one at a time. *Many* threads may run the code inside the lock statement, because many threads may have gotten a null value in result. So the code in the lock statement must ensure that only the *first* thread does any real work. It does this by rechecking to see if the value is in the Dictionary.

```
      if (!_managers.TryGetValue(objectType, out result))
      {
        result = new ValidationRulesManager();
        _managers.Add(objectType, result);
      }
```

Only the first thread gets a null value for result here, and then it add a new value to the Dictionary. Every subsequent thread gets a non-null value for result, which is the desired outcome.

Of course, the lock statement is hit only when the application is first run. Once this process completes for a business type, that first TryGetValue()always returns the requested value, so no locking occurs for the rest of the application's lifetime.

Associating Rules with Properties

The ValidationRulesManager stores the actual relationships between rules and properties for a specific business object type or instance. These values are stored in a Dictionary, which is indexed by the property name and contains a list of rules for each property.

```
private Dictionary<string, RulesList> _rulesList;
```

The RulesList object contains a list of IRuleMethod objects associated with the property, and a list of properties that are dependent on this property. A dependent property is one where its rules are checked any time *this* property's rules are checked. For example, if property B is dependent on property A, and you check the rules for property A, then the rules for property B are also checked automatically.

In RulesList then, there are two lists.

```
private List<IRuleMethod> _list = new List<IRuleMethod>();
private List<string> _dependentProperties;
```

When a rule is associated with a property, the IRuleMethod object for that association is added to _list. When a dependent property is added to this property, the name of the dependent property is added to _dependentProperties.

While the rules may be added in any order, you must sort them before you use them. This is important, because you must invoke them in priority order, from priority 0 to 1 to 2 and so forth. This allows the business developer to have some control over the order in which the rules execute, and it enables the concept of short-circuiting.

Short-circuiting is a feature that stops the processing of rules partway through. The result is that not all rules for a property are invoked. There are two ways to short-circuit rule processing for a property: a rule method can stop the processing explicitly, or CLSA .NET can be told to stop processing rules if any previous (higher-priority) rule has already returned false.

This feature is useful, because it allows the business developer to check all the inexpensive, easily checked rules first and only invoke expensive rules (such as those that might hit the database) if all previous rules were satisfied (returned true). The rule priority feature is a key part of this capability, because it allows the business developer to control the order in which rules are invoked.

When the list of rules is retrieved, a flag is checked to see if the list has been sorted. If it has not been sorted, the list is sorted and the flag is set to true. Since multiple threads could request the list at the same time, this code is protected with a lock scheme similar to the one I discussed earlier.

```
public List<IRuleMethod> GetList(bool applySort)
{
  if (applySort && !_sorted)
  {
    lock (_list)
    {
      if (applySort && !_sorted)
      {
        _list.Sort();
        _sorted = true;
      }
    }
  }
  return _list;
}
```

The result is that the ValidationRules object always gets a list of IRuleMethod objects for a property, sorted by priority.

The combination of the RuleMethod class, the Dictionary and List object combination, and the AddRule() methods covers the management of the rules associated with each property.

Checking Validation Rules

Once a set of rule methods has been associated with the properties of a business object, there needs to be a way to invoke those rules. Typically, when a single property is changed on a business object, only the rules for that property need to be checked. At other times, the rules for *all* the object's properties need to be checked. This is true when an object is first created, for instance, since multiple properties of the object could start out with invalid values.

To cover these two cases, ValidationRules implements two CheckRules() methods.

Checking Rules for One Property

The first checks the rules for a specific property.

```
public void CheckRules(Csla.Core.IPropertyInfo propertyInfo)
{
  CheckRules(propertyInfo.Name);
}

public string[] CheckRules(string propertyName)
{
  if (_suppressRuleChecking)
    return new string[] {};

  var result = new List<string>();
  result.Add(propertyName);

  // get the rules dictionary
  ValidationRulesManager rules = RulesToCheck;
  if (rules != null)
  {
    // get the rules list for this property
    RulesList rulesList = rules.GetRulesForProperty(propertyName, false);
    if (rulesList != null)
    {
      // get the actual list of rules (sorted by priority)
      List<IRuleMethod> list = rulesList.GetList(true);
      if (list != null)
        CheckRules(list);
      List<string> dependencies = rulesList.GetDependencyList(false);
      if (dependencies != null)
      {
        for (int i = 0; i < dependencies.Count; i++)
        {
          string dependentProperty = dependencies[i];
          result.Add(dependentProperty);
          CheckRules(rules, dependentProperty);
        }
```

```
        }
      }
    }
    return result.ToArray();
  }
```

There's a lot going on here, so I'll break it down.

There are two overloads: one takes an IPropertyInfo, and the other is a simple string. When a business object calls this method directly, the business developer will typically provide an IPropertyInfo, but internally all the work is done based on the property name as a string value.

Note The only reason the overload accepting a string parameter is public is for backward compatibility with older versions of CLSA .NET.

The first thing the method does is check to see if rule checking is suppressed:

```
if (_suppressRuleChecking)
  return new string[] {};
```

A business object can set ValidationRules.SuppressRuleChecking to true to prevent CheckRules() from doing any work. This is often useful when a lot of interdependent properties must be loaded all at once (such as behind a web page or XML service). In that case, an explicit call to CheckRules() is typically made after all property values have been loaded so the rules can be executed in a more efficient manner.

The methods return a string array. That array contains a list of the property names for which rules were checked. If a rule has dependent properties, then this call may check the rules for more than one property. The code in BusinessBase uses this string array to determine what PropertyChanged events should be raised, as I discussed in Chapter 10.

Of course, it is clear that at least the requested property's rules will be checked.

```
var result = new List<string>();
result.Add(propertyName);
```

This method gets the list of rules for this property by calling the RulesToCheck property.

```
ValidationRulesManager rules = RulesToCheck;
if (rules != null)
```

The RulesToCheck property is interesting, because it provides a consolidated list of the rules for this property. The list is a combination of the per-instance and per-type rules. Usually only per-type rules exist, but if there are per-instance rules, they are merged into the list as well, and the list is sorted by priority. Look at the property in the ValidationRules class to see how this is done.

Obviously, CheckRules() only continues to do work if the rules field is not null; if it is null, then no rules are associated with this property and the method can just exit. Assuming there are rules for this property, the list of rules is retrieved from the ValidationRulesManager, and the GetList() method is used to get the sorted list of IRuleMethod objects.

```
RulesList rulesList = rules.GetRulesForProperty(propertyName, false);
if (rulesList != null)
{
  // get the actual list of rules (sorted by priority)
  List<IRuleMethod> list = rulesList.GetList(true);
  if (list != null)
    CheckRules(list);
```

The sorted list is passed to another overload of CheckRules(). That overload is responsible for looping through the list and invoking each rule. It is also responsible for adding and removing items from the list of broken rules, which I'll discuss later in this chapter.

Finally, if there are any dependent properties associated with the current property, their rules are checked too.

```
for (int i = 0; i < dependencies.Count; i++)
{
  string dependentProperty = dependencies[i];
  result.Add(dependentProperty);
  CheckRules(rules, dependentProperty);
}
```

Another overload of CheckRules() is called here. It simply checks the rules for one specific property, without doing further checks for dependent properties. In other words, the dependent property concept isn't recursive. That's important because otherwise this code would have to check for circular dependency loops, and it would become too easy for a business developer to accidentally trigger checking too many properties when one property is changed.

Checking Rules for All Properties

The other public overload of CheckRules() allows the business developer to request that the rules for all properties be invoked. This method is commonly called when an object is first created and sometimes right after an object is loaded with data from the database. It is also commonly called when rule checking is suppressed, as a lot of properties are loaded. All rules are checked when the load process is complete.

This method is relatively short.

```
public void CheckRules()
{
  if (_suppressRuleChecking)
    return;

  ValidationRulesManager rules = RulesToCheck;
  if (rules != null)
  {
    foreach (KeyValuePair<string, RulesList> de in rules.RulesDictionary)
      CheckRules(de.Value.GetList(true));
  }
}
```

Like the property-specific overload, this one honors the SuppressRuleChecking property and immediately exits if rule checking is suppressed.

If rule checking is enabled, which is the default, then it retrieves all the rules for the entire object by calling RulesToCheck, and it loops through each entry in the Dictionary, executing the list of rules for each property.

At this point, it should be clear how ValidationRules associates rule methods with properties and is then able to check those rules for a specific property or for the business object as a whole.

Maintaining a List of Broken Rules

The ValidationRules object also maintains a list of currently broken validation rules for the object. This is used to implement IDataErrorInfo in BusinessBase, allowing each business object to easily indicate whether the object is valid. Because the broken rule objects in the list include the property name that is invalid, the broken rules list is also used to determine whether each individual property is valid or invalid.

The BrokenRulesCollection class maintains the list of broken rules for a business object, and is declared in ValidationRules like this:

```
private BrokenRulesCollection _brokenRules;

private BrokenRulesCollection BrokenRulesList
{
  get
  {
    if (_brokenRules == null)
      _brokenRules = new BrokenRulesCollection();
    return _brokenRules;
  }
}
```

Notice that the _brokenRules field is not adorned with either the NotUndoable or NonSerialized attributes. The list of currently broken rules is directly part of a business object's state, so it is subject to n-level undo operations and to being transferred across the network along with the business object.

This way, if a business developer transfers an invalid object across the network or makes a clone, the object will remain invalid, with its list of broken rules intact.

The BrokenRulesList value is also exposed via a public method on BusinessBase. To any external consumer, such as code in the UI, this is a read-only collection.

```
[Browsable(false)]
[EditorBrowsable(EditorBrowsableState.Advanced)]
public virtual Validation.BrokenRulesCollection BrokenRulesCollection
{
  get { return ValidationRules.GetBrokenRules(); }
}
```

The reason the collection is exposed publicly is to allow UI developers to use the list of broken rules as they see fit. Remember that a broken rule includes a human-readable description of the rule, so it is perfectly reasonable to display this list to the end user in some circumstances.

BrokenRule Class

When a rule method is invoked by the CheckRules() method, it returns true or false. If it returns false, the broken rule will be recorded into a BrokenRulesCollection. Here's the code from CheckRules() that implements this behavior:

```
        lock (BrokenRulesList)
        {
          if (ruleResult)
          {
            // the rule is not broken
            BrokenRulesList.Remove(rule);
          }
          else
          {
            // the rule is broken
            BrokenRulesList.Add(rule);
            if (rule.RuleArgs.Severity == RuleSeverity.Error)
              previousRuleBroken = true;
          }
        }
```

The BrokenRulesCollection object exposed by the BrokenRulesList property contains a list of BrokenRule objects, each representing a single broken business rule. The Add() and Remove() methods accept an IRuleMethod and create the BrokenRule object internally.

The BrokenRule object exposes read-only properties for the rule name, a human-readable description of the broken rule, and the name of the property that is broken. The class is available in the code download for the book, available at both www.apress.com/book/view/1430210192 and www.lhotka.net/cslanet/download.aspx.

BrokenRulesCollection Class

The BrokenRulesCollection class is used by ValidationRules to maintain the list of currently broken rules. Each broken rule is represented by a BrokenRule object. The collection inherits from Csla.Core.ReadOnlyBindingList and so is a read-only collection.

```
[Serializable()]
public class BrokenRulesCollection : Core.ReadOnlyBindingList<BrokenRule>
```

Though the collection is read-only, it does provide some internal methods to allow ValidationRules to add and remove items. These methods are used in the CheckRules() methods to ensure that broken rules are only in the list when appropriate.

The Add() methods are pretty straightforward.

```
internal void Add(IAsyncRuleMethod rule, AsyncRuleResult result)
{
  Remove(rule);
  IsReadOnly = false;
  BrokenRule item = new BrokenRule(rule, result);
  IncrementCount(item);
  Add(item);
  IsReadOnly = true;
}

internal void Add(IRuleMethod rule)
{
  Remove(rule);
  IsReadOnly = false;
  BrokenRule item = new BrokenRule(rule);
  IncrementCount(item);
  Add(item);
  IsReadOnly = true;
}
```

Both overloads do essentially the same thing, but for asynchronous and synchronous rule methods.

To avoid possible duplicate object issues, they first ensure that the broken rule isn't already in the list by calling the Remove() method. Then they change the collection to be read-write, add the rule to the collection, and set the collection back to be read-only.

While they could just see if the collection contains the broken rule, removing and re-adding the rule is better, because it ensures that the human-readable description for the rule is current. The rule method could have changed the description over time.

The IncrementCount() method is used to maintain counters for the number of Error, Warning, and Information severity rules that are broken. Each broken rule has one of these severities, and as an optimization, BrokenRulesCollection maintains a running count of the number of each severity that is broken at any point in time.

The Remove() method is a bit more complex.

```
internal void Remove(IRuleMethod rule)
{
  IsReadOnly = false;
  for (int index = 0; index < Count; index++)
    if (this[index].RuleName == rule.RuleName)
    {
      DecrementCount(this[index]);
      RemoveAt(index);
      break;
    }
  IsReadOnly = true;
}
```

It has to scan through the collection to find a rule with the same rule name. Notice that no exception is thrown if the item isn't in the collection. If it isn't there, that's fine—then there's just no need to remove it.

The DecrementCount() method is used to maintain counters for the number of Error, Warning, and Information severity rules that are broken. Each broken rule has one of these severities, and as an optimization, BrokenRulesCollection maintains a running count of the number of each severity that is broken at any point in time.

There are a few other methods in BrokenRulesCollection worth mentioning. They provide information about the contents of the collection and are listed in Table 11-2.

Table 11-2. *Methods and Properties Providing Information About Broken Rules*

Property/Method	Description
ErrorCount	Returns the current number of Error severity broken rules
WarningCount	Returns the current number of Warning severity broken rules
InformationCount	Returns the current number of Information severity broken rules
GetFirstMessage(string)	Scans the list and returns the first broken rule of any severity (if any) for a specified property
GetFirstMessage(string, RuleSeverity)	Scans the list and returns the first broken rule of the specified severity (if any) for a specified property
GetFirstBrokenRule(string)	Scans the list and returns the first broken rule of Error severity (if any) for a specified property; this method is used in BusinessBase to implement the IDataErrorInfo interface
ToArray()	Returns an array of broken rule descriptions for the business object
ToArray(RuleSeverity)	Returns an array of broken rule descriptions for a specific severity of broken rules in the business object

Table 11-2. *Methods and Properties Providing Information About Broken Rules (Continued)*

Property/Method	Description
`ToString()`	Concatenates the human-readable descriptions of all broken rules into a single `string` value, using `Environment.NewLine` as a separator; this too is used in the `IDataErrorInfo` implementation to return all the errors for the entire object
`ToString(string)`	Concatenates the human-readable descriptions of all broken rules into a `single` string value, using the `string` parameter as a separator; this is used in the `IDataErrorInfo` implementation to return all the errors for the entire object
`ToString(string, RuleSeverity)`	Concatenates the human-readable descriptions of all broken rules of the specified severity into a `single` string value, using the `string` parameter as a separator

All of these methods are available to the business and UI developer, and provide a great deal of flexibility for use of the broken rules information.

ValidationException

The `ValidationException` class allows CLSA .NET to throw a custom exception to indicate that a validation problem has occurred. This exception is thrown by the `Save()` method in `BusinessBase`.

This exception class doesn't add any new information to the base `Exception` class from the .NET Framework. Thus, its code is very simple, since it merely declares a set of constructors, each of which delegates to the `Exception` base class. You can look at the class in the code download for the book.

The reason `ValidationException` exists is to allow UI code to easily catch a `ValidationException` as being separate from other exceptions that might be thrown by the `Save()` method. For instance, UI code might look like this:

```
try
{
  customer = customer.Save();
}
catch (ValidationException ex)
{
  // handle validation exceptions
}
catch (Exception ex)
{
  // handle other exceptions
}
```

Even if they offer no extra information, custom exceptions are often valuable in this way.

You should now have a high-level understanding of how `ValidationRules` consolidates the association of rules with properties, and the tracking of broken rules. It provides a single entry point for use of the business and validation rule subsystem. You'll see this used in Chapter 17, and you'll see examples of some rule methods in the next section of this chapter.

Common Validation Rules

Most applications use a relatively small, common set of validation rules—such as that a `string` value is required or has a maximum length, or that a numeric value has a minimum or maximum value. Using reflection, it is possible to create highly reusable rule methods—which is the purpose behind the `Csla.Validation.CommonRules` class.

Obviously, using reflection incurs some performance cost, so these reusable rule methods may or may not be appropriate for every application. However, the code reuse offered by these methods is powerful, and most applications won't be adversely affected by this use of reflection. In the end, whether you decide to use these rule methods or not is up to you.

Tip If reflection-based rules are problematic for your application, you can implement hard-coded rule methods on a per-type basis.

If you find the idea of these reusable rules appealing and useful, you may opt to create your own library of reusable rules as part of your application. In that case, you can add a class to your project similar to `CommonRules`, and you can use the rule methods from `CommonRules` as a guide for building your own reusable rule methods.

CommonRules

The `RuleHandler` delegate specifies that every rule method accepts two parameters: a reference to the object containing the data, and a `RuleArgs` object that is used to pass extra information into and out of the rule method.

The base `RuleArgs` object has a `PropertyName` property that provides the rule method with the name of the property to be validated. It also includes a `Description` property that the rule method should set for a broken rule to describe why the rule was broken.

Table 11-3 lists the methods in the `CommonRules` class.

Table 11-3. *Methods in the CommonRules Class*

Method	Description
`StringRequired`	Ensures a `string` value is non-`null` and has a length greater than zero
`StringMinLength`	Ensures a `string` value has a minimum length
`StringMaxLength`	Ensures a `string` value doesn't exceed a maximum length
`IntegerMinValue`	Ensures an `int` value meets a minimum value
`IntegerMaxValue`	Ensures an `int` value doesn't exceed a maximum value
`MinValue`	Ensures any numeric value meets a minimum value
`MaxValue`	Ensures any numeric value doesn't exceed a maximum value
`RegEx`	Ensures a `string` value matches a regular expression

You can look at the code for each of these in the code download, but I do want to walk through a couple of them to explain how these methods work.

StringRequired

The simplest type of rule method is one that doesn't require any information beyond that provided by the basic RuleArgs parameter. For instance, the StringRequired() rule method only needs a reference to the object containing the value and the name of the property to be validated.

```
public static bool StringRequired(object target, RuleArgs e)
{
  string value = (string)Utilities.CallByName(
    target, e.PropertyName, CallType.Get);
  if (string.IsNullOrEmpty(value))
  {
    e.Description = string.Format(
      Resources.StringRequiredRule, RuleArgs.GetPropertyName(e));
    return false;
  }
  return true;
}
```

A CallByName() helper method is used to abstract the use of reflection to retrieve the property value based on the property name. It simply uses reflection to get a PropertyInfo object for the specified property, and then uses it to retrieve the property value.

If the property value is null or is an empty string, then the rule is broken, so the Description property of the RuleArgs object is set to describe the nature of the broken rule. Then false is returned from the rule method to indicate that the rule is broken. Otherwise, the rule method simply returns true to indicate that the rule is not broken.

Notice the use of the GetPropertyName() method on the RuleArgs class to retrieve the property name. While you can get the property name itself through e.PropertyName, the GetPropertyName() helper method will return the *friendly name* associated with the property if one exists, or the property name if there is no friendly name. In many cases, a friendly name such as *Product name* is a better value to show the user than the actual property name (like ProductName).

This rule is used within a business object by associating it with a property. A business object does this by overriding the AddBusinessRules() method defined by BusinessBase. Such code would look like this (assuming the developer adds a using statement for Csla.Validation to the top of the code):

```
[Serializable]
public class Customer : BusinessBase<Customer>
{
  protected override void AddBusinessRules()
  {
    ValidationRules.AddRule(CommonRules.StringRequired, NameProperty);
  }
  // rest of class...
}
```

This associates the rule method with the property defined by the NameProperty field (a PropertyInfo<string> value) so that the SetProperty() call within the property's set block will invoke the rule automatically. You'll see this and other rule methods used in Chapter 17 within the sample application's business objects.

StringMaxLength

A slightly more complex variation is where the rule method needs extra information beyond that provided by the basic RuleArgs parameter. In these cases, the RuleArgs class must be subclassed to create a new object that adds the extra information. A rule method to enforce a maximum length on a string, for instance, requires the maximum length value.

Custom RuleArgs Class

I recommend using DecoratedRuleArgs, which is a subclass of RuleArgs. I say this because DecoratedRuleArgs stores the custom argument values in a Dictionary, and thus provides a standardized way by which the code in AddBusinessRules() can create the RuleArgs parameter. This is particularly useful if you use code generation for your business classes, as standardization is critical when building code generation templates.

The custom RuleArgs classes in CommonRules are a hybrid approach. I do implement custom classes, but they subclass DecoratedRuleArgs. This means that the code in AddBusinessRules() can use either the strongly typed custom class, or DecoratedRuleArgs. Either approach works, so you can use StringMaxLength like this:

```
ValidationRules.AddRule(
  Csla.Validation.CommonRules.StringMaxLength,
  new Csla.Validation.CommonRules.MaxLengthRuleArgs(NameProperty, 5));
```

or like this:

```
var args = new Csla.Validation.DecoratedRuleArgs(NameProperty);
args["MaxLength"] = 5;
ValidationRules.AddRule(Csla.Validation.CommonRules.StringMaxLength, args);
```

You get the same end result. The first approach is better for hand-coding, because it is strongly typed. The second approach is better for code generation, because it is a standard approach that works with any rule method that accepts a DecoratedRuleArgs parameter. By implementing a custom subclass of DecoratedRuleArgs in CommonRules, I enable both scenarios.

■ **Tip** You don't need to create a custom subclass like this. It is possible to just use DecoratedRuleArgs directly and avoid all this work, though the code in AddBusinessRules() will then be loosely typed.

Here's a subclass of DecoratedRuleArgs that provides the maximum length value:

```
public class MaxLengthRuleArgs : DecoratedRuleArgs
{
  public int MaxLength
  {
    get { return (int)this["MaxLength"]; }
  }

  public MaxLengthRuleArgs(
    string propertyName, int maxLength)
    : base(propertyName)
  {
    this["MaxLength"] = maxLength;
    this["Format"] = string.Empty;
  }

  public MaxLengthRuleArgs(Core.IPropertyInfo propertyInfo, int maxLength)
    : base(propertyInfo)
  {
    this["MaxLength"] = maxLength;
    this["Format"] = string.Empty;
  }
```

```
    public MaxLengthRuleArgs(
      string propertyName, string friendlyName, int maxLength)
      : base(propertyName, friendlyName)
    {
      this["MaxLength"] = maxLength;
      this["Format"] = string.Empty;
    }

    public MaxLengthRuleArgs(
      string propertyName, int maxLength, string format)
      : base(propertyName)
    {
      this["MaxLength"] = maxLength;
      this["Format"] = format;
    }

    public MaxLengthRuleArgs(
      Core.IPropertyInfo propertyInfo, int maxLength, string format)
      : base(propertyInfo)
    {
      this["MaxLength"] = maxLength;
      this["Format"] = format;
    }

    public MaxLengthRuleArgs(
      string propertyName, string friendlyName, int maxLength, string format)
      : base(propertyName, friendlyName)
    {
      this["MaxLength"] = maxLength;
      this["Format"] = format;
    }
  }
```

All the custom `RuleArgs` subclasses in `CommonRules` follow this basic structure.

Rule Method

With the custom `RuleArgs` class defined, you can use it to implement a rule method. The `StringMaxLength()` rule method looks like this:

```
  public static bool StringMaxLength(
    object target, RuleArgs e)
  {
    DecoratedRuleArgs args = (DecoratedRuleArgs)e;
    int max = (int)args["MaxLength"];
    string value = (string)Utilities.CallByName(
      target, e.PropertyName, CallType.Get);
    if (!String.IsNullOrEmpty(value) && (value.Length > max))
    {
      string format = (string)args["Format"];
      string outValue;
      if (string.IsNullOrEmpty(format))
        outValue = max.ToString();
```

```
        else
          outValue = max.ToString(format);
        e.Description = String.Format(
          Resources.StringMaxLengthRule,
          RuleArgs.GetPropertyName(e), outValue);
        return false;
      }
      return true;
    }
```

This is similar to the StringRequired() rule method, except that it casts the RuleArgs parameter to the DecoratedRuleArgs type so that it can retrieve the MaxLength value. That value is then compared to the length of the specified property from the target object to see if the rule is broken or not.

■ **Note** It might seem like the RuleArgs parameter should just be of type DecoratedRuleArgs or MaxLengthRuleArgs, using the generic RuleHandler delegate. That would be ideal, but it would break backward compatibility with older versions of CLSA .NET, so I've chosen to take the approach shown here.

The CommonRules class includes other similar rule method implementations as listed in Table 11-3. You may choose to use them as they are, or as the basis for creating your own library of reusable rules for an application.

Conclusion

This chapter covered the business and validation rules subsystem of CLSA .NET. This is one of the most important parts of the framework, as it provides a standardized way by which you can implement business rules and have them execute as your object's properties are changed.

Chapter 12 will cover the important authorization subsystem, which provides similar capabilities for the authorization of property, method, and object access. Chapters 13 through 16 will continue discussing the implementation of CLSA .NET features, and then Chapters 17 through 21 will cover the implementation of the Project Tracker reference application.

CHAPTER 12

Authentication and Authorization

Most applications have some form of authorization, where they allow or disallow a user access to certain forms, pages, or application functions. Before any authorization can occur, the application must know the identity of the user, so most applications also use some type of authentication.

There are several types of authentication available to a .NET application, including the following:

- Integrated Windows domain or Active Directory
- ASP.NET membership provider
- Custom database tables or LDAP server

In every case, the user's identity and roles are maintained in a .NET principal object, which is available to all code in your application. The support for authorization provided by .NET is role-based. The current user has a set of roles and your code can determine whether the user is in a specified role by calling the `IsInRole()` method on the current principal object. This capability can be used by the UI developer to decide whether to allow a user access to each form or page in the application and is the underlying technology used by ASP.NET for this purpose.

CSLA .NET uses the standard .NET model as well, allowing a business developer to specify roles that are allowed to create, retrieve, update, and delete a business object. But CSLA .NET goes a step further and also allows the developer to specify which roles are allowed to read or write to a property and to call specific methods.

By default, CSLA .NET calls the standard `IsInRole()` method to check the user's roles, and so it automatically works with any .NET authentication model.

Authentication

CSLA .NET supports either integrated Windows authentication (Active Directory or AD) or custom authentication. Using the ASP.NET `MembershipProvider` is considered a form of custom authentication because CSLA .NET can be used totally outside of ASP.NET but you can still choose to authenticate using that model. In all cases, the current thread should have a valid principal object and associated identity object, allowing the authorization code discussed later in this chapter to verify the user's roles as appropriate.

You should also be aware that when using custom authentication, the data portal requires that the custom principal object inherit from the `Csla.Security.BusinessPrincipalBase` class. A business application implements its own principal and identity classes so it can authenticate the user and load the user's roles as appropriate for the application.

In the .NET security model used by CSLA .NET, the user is always identified by a *principal object*, which must implement the `IPrincipal` interface from the `System.Security.Principal` namespace. Every principal object contains exactly one *identity object*, which must implement the `IIdentity` interface from that same namespace.

If you are using integrated Windows authentication, the .NET environment automatically has WindowsPrincipal and WindowsIdentity objects initialized for you to use. They contain the user's identity and groups, based on the username entered when logging into the Windows workstation or website. In other words, your application has to do almost nothing in this case because Windows and .NET have done most of the work.

If you are using custom authentication (including using the ASP.NET MembershipProvider model), you must create your own custom principal and identity classes and you must get the username/password (or other credentials) from the user to create those objects. This is obviously more work but allows you the flexibility of authenticating the user in any way you choose.

The CSLA .NET framework includes the Csla.Security namespace, where you can find several classes to help in the implementation of custom authentication. Before I get into that namespace, however, you should understand how CSLA .NET manages and exposes the current .NET principal object in different environments.

I'll first discuss the Csla.ApplicationContext.User property, which manages and exposes the principal object in Windows, web, and WPF applications. Then I'll show you how to configure CSLA .NET to use either integrated Windows authentication or custom authentication. Once you understand those issues, I dig into the Csla.Security namespace.

Csla.ApplicationContext.User Property

When code is running outside ASP.NET, it relies on System.Threading.Thread.CurrentPrincipal to maintain the user's principal object. On the other hand, when code is running inside ASP.NET, the only reliable way to find the user's principal object is through HttpContext.Current.User. Normally, this would mean that you would have to write code to detect whether HttpContext.Current is null and only use System.Threading if HttpContext isn't available.

The User property of the Csla.ApplicationContext class automates this process on your behalf:

```
public static IPrincipal User
{
  get
  {
    if (HttpContext.Current == null)
      return Thread.CurrentPrincipal;
    else
      return HttpContext.Current.User;
  }
  set
  {
    if (HttpContext.Current != null)
      HttpContext.Current.User = value;
    Thread.CurrentPrincipal = value;
  }
}
```

In general, Csla.ApplicationContext.User should be used in favor of System.Threading or HttpContext because it automatically adjusts to the environment in which your code is running. With CSLA .NET–based applications, this is particularly important, because your client code could be a Windows Forms application but your server code could be running within ASP.NET. Remember that your business objects run in *both locations*, so must behave properly both inside and outside ASP.NET.

Windows Authentication

When using integrated Windows authentication, your application and .NET relies on the underlying Windows operating system to take care of the authentication and to provide information about the user. While most of the work is done for you by Windows and .NET, you do need to configure the environment, including both CSLA .NET and .NET itself.

Configuring CSLA .NET

CSLA .NET has one configuration option to control authentication and it is set in the application's `app.config` or `web.config` file in the `appSettings` block:

```
<add key="CslaAuthentication" value="Windows" />
```

This instructs CSLA .NET to rely on the .NET Framework and Windows to manage the current principal and identity objects. In other words, this tells CSLA .NET it doesn't have to deal with authentication and to just assume it has all been taken care of behind the scenes.

Configuring WPF and Windows Forms

If the application is running on a client workstation, the user who logged into the workstation defines the Windows identity of the user for all interactive applications. Within .NET, the default is to *not* use this value but rather to provide an unauthenticated `GenericPrincipal` from the `System.Security.Principal` namespace. You can change that by running this line of code as your application starts up:

```
AppDomain.CurrentDomain.SetPrincipalPolicy(
  System.Security.Principal.PrincipalPolicy.WindowsPrincipal);
```

This tells the .NET Framework to use the underlying `WindowsPrincipal` and `WindowsIdentity` objects as the current .NET principal and identity.

Configuring ASP.NET

In an ASP.NET environment, the process is controlled by `web.config` and your IIS virtual root settings. Your web server's virtual root must be configured to disallow anonymous access. The result is that the user must log into the website using his Windows credentials to access any pages. Obviously, this means the web server is authenticating the user's credentials.

You also need to configure ASP.NET to use Windows authentication and *impersonation*:

```
<authentication mode="Windows" />
<identity impersonate="true" />
```

If you only tell ASP.NET to use Windows authentication, it relies on the web server to do the work but doesn't change the current principal and identity to match that user on every page request. By setting both values, ASP.NET relies on the web server to handle authentication and then impersonates the identity of that user.

In many ways, integrated Windows authentication is the simplest approach. But it isn't always practical because many applications allow users that aren't in the Windows domain or Active Directory to log in, and so some form of custom authentication is required.

Custom Authentication

Custom authentication means that you are responsible for getting the user's credentials (often a username and password) and ensuring they are valid. The most common way to check the credentials is by comparing them to values in a database table. People also use the ASP.NET `MembershipProvider` model (which is also typically just a database table lookup), LDAP servers, Active Directory Application Mode (ADAM), and many other security data stores.

Configuring CSLA .NET

You must set the `CslaAuthentication` configuration option to `Csla` to instruct CSLA .NET to use custom authentication, relying on the developer to create a custom principal and identity and to make that custom principal the current principal on the client:

```
<add key="CslaAuthentication" value="Csla" />
```

The data portal, discussed in Chapter 15, is affected by this setting as well because when using custom authentication the data portal automatically serializes the current principal from the client to the application server on every data portal call. This means that the application server impersonates the client's custom identity.

Authentication Classes in Csla.Security

CSLA .NET is designed to support easier implementation of custom authentication with a set of classes. Table 12-1 lists these base classes.

Table 12-1. *Principal and Identity Classes in Csla.Security*

Class	Description
`BusinessPrincipalBase`	Base class for all custom principal objects
`CslaIdentity`	Base class for custom identity objects
`ICheckRoles`	Interface that a custom identity class can implement so `BusinessPrincipalBase` knows to delegate `IsInRole()` to that identity object
`IdentityFactory`	Data portal factory class containing methods to authenticate credentials against the ASP.NET `MembershipProvider`; used by `MembershipIdentity`
`MembershipIdentity`	Base class to assist in using the ASP.NET `MembershipProvider` to create a custom identity object
`UsernameCriteria`	Criteria class for passing a username and password to a custom identity object
`UnauthenticatedIdentity`	Simple subclass of `CslaIdentity` to provide a generic, unauthenticated identity object
`UnauthenticatedPrincipal`	Simple subclass of `BusinessPrincipalBase` to provide a generic, unauthenticated principal object

A developer can use these classes to implement custom authentication against almost any security store and to create custom principal and identity objects that can be used by .NET and CSLA .NET for authorization.

You can look at the code in these classes in the code download for this book (www.apress.com/book/view/1430210192 or www.lhotka.net/cslanet/download.aspx). Here, I focus on the issues they are designed to address.

Creating a Custom Principal Class

The data portal, which I discuss in Chapter 15, can only deal with Serializable objects. And when CSLA .NET is configured to use custom authentication, it automatically serializes the client principal and identity objects and copies them to the application server on each data portal call. The result is that the application server is able to impersonate the client's identity.

■ **Note** While CSLA .NET for Silverlight is not the topic of this book, it also has a data portal that serializes objects, and BusinessPrincipalBase is designed to work with CSLA .NET for Silverlight as well.

The BusinessPrincipalBase class is a very basic implementation of the IPrincipal interface from System.Security.Principal that is compatible with the data portal. The goal of this class is to make it easier for a business developer to create her own custom principal by subclassing BusinessPrincipalBase.

The simplest approach is a subclass like this:

```
[Serializable]
public class CustomPrincipal : BusinessPrincipalBase
{
  private CustomPrincipal(IIdentity identity)
    : base(identity)
  {   }

  public static void Login(string username, string password)
  {
    var identity = CustomIdentity.GetIdentity(username, password);
    Csla.ApplicationContext.User =
      new CustomPrincipal(identity);
  }

    public static void Logout()
    {
      var identity = new UnauthenticatedIdentity();
      Csla.ApplicationContext.User = new CustomPrincipal(identity);
    }
}
```

The Login() method calls the factory method on a CustomIdentity class (which I show in the next section) to get back an identity object. That identity object may or may not be authenticated, but it is a valid object either way. The identity object is passed as a parameter to the constructor of CustomPrincipal, which passes it to the BusinessPrincipalBase base class.

The important thing is that the resulting principal object, containing its identity object (either authenticated or not), is set as the current principal by setting the User property of Csla.ApplicationContext. This ensures that the principal is available to the current thread and/or the current HttpContext as appropriate.

As BusinessPrincipalBase implements IPrincipal, it has an Identity property that returns the identity object created in the Login() method. Its IsInRole() method calls the identity object contained by this principal, assuming that identity object is a subclass of CslaIdentity. Here's the IsInRole() implementation from BusinessPrincipalBase:

```
public virtual bool IsInRole(string role)
{
  var cslaIdentity = _identity as CslaIdentity;
  if (cslaIdentity != null)
    return cslaIdentity.IsInRole(role);
  else
    return false;
}
```

The method is virtual, so a subclass can replace the implementation, but if the identity object is a subclass of CslaIdentity, this implementation does the work automatically.

As you'll see in the next section of this chapter, I recommend having the identity object authenticate the user's credentials and (if successful) load the user's roles, all in one trip to the security store. Also, take a look at the Logout() method. Notice how it creates a CustomPrincipal object but with an UnauthenticatedIdentity as its identity. The UnauthenticatedIdentity object has no username and no roles and its IsAuthenticated property returns false.

You'll see a more complete example in Chapter 17 when I walk through the ProjectTracker reference application's business object implementation.

Creating a Custom Identity Class

Every principal object contains an identity object. In fact, the identity object is the object that contains information about the user, such as the username, how the user was authenticated, and so forth. Identity objects implement IIdentity from the System.Security.Principal namespace, and CslaIdentity is a base class that makes it easy to create custom identity classes that work with the data portal.

When a user logs in using custom authentication, the typical model is to authenticate his credentials using a read-only root object (see the stereotype discussion in Chapters 4 and 5). The CslaIdentity class inherits from ReadOnlyBase so it is not only an identity object but can handle the authentication process in its DataPortal_Fetch() method:

```
[Serializable]
public abstract partial class CslaIdentity :
  ReadOnlyBase<CslaIdentity>, IIdentity
```

By subclassing CslaIdentity, the developer can focus more directly on authenticating the user's credentials and (if successful) loading the user's list of roles. Here's a very simple subclass:

```
[Serializable]
public class CustomIdentity : CslaIdentity
{
  private CustomIdentity()
  { /* require use of factory method */ }

  public static void GetIdentity(string username, string password)
  {
    return DataPortal.Fetch<CustomIdentity>(
      new UsernameCriteria(username, password));
  }
```

```
    private void DataPortal_Fetch(UsernameCriteria criteria)
    {
      // authenticate credentials here
      if (authenticated)
      {
        base.Name = username;
        base.IsAuthenticated = true;
        base.Roles = roles; // list of roles from security store
      }
      else
      {
        base.Name = string.Empty;
        base.IsAuthenticated = false;
        base.Roles = null;
      }
    }
  }
```

This is just an example, and to make this work, the DataPortal_Fetch() method needs to be finished, so it talks to the security store to validate the user's credentials and loads the user's list of roles.

The UsernameCriteria class is used to easily pass the username and password credentials from the factory method through the data portal and to the DataPortal_Fetch() method. If an application uses credentials other than a username/password pair, the developer needs to create her own custom criteria class, as described in Chapter 5.

MembershipProvider Authentication

Creating a custom identity object that validates the user's credentials against the ASP.NET MembershipProvider component follows the same basic process I've discussed thus far. The developer needs to create a custom principal and custom identity class as shown previously.

However, CSLA .NET includes the MembershipIdentity class to simplify the process of validating the username and password against the ASP.NET security store. So instead of subclassing CslaIdentity, a developer can subclass MembershipIdentity because it already includes the code necessary to do the credential validation.

This means creating a subclass that looks like this:

```
[Serializable]
public class CustomIdentity : MembershipIdentity
{
  protected override void LoadCustomData()
  {
    // load roles and any custom properties here
  }
}
```

The MembershipIdentity base class takes care of validating the username and password but doesn't attempt to load any roles for the user. It does call the LoadCustomData() method shown here so the developer can override that method to load the user's roles and any other user-related data. By the time LoadCustomData() is invoked, the identity object is already loaded with the username, IsAuthenticated is true, and the identity object is essentially ready for use.

If the user's credentials are invalid, no exception is thrown. Instead, an unauthenticated instance of MembershipIdentity is returned, with an IsAuthenticated value of false. In this case, the LoadCustomData() method is not invoked because the identity doesn't represent a valid user.

You should now have an understanding of the difference between Windows and custom authentication. And you should understand how the `BusinessPrincipalBase` and various identity base classes can be used to create custom principal and identity objects that provide user and role information to .NET and CSLA .NET for authorization.

In the rest of the chapter I discuss how CSLA .NET supports authorization at the type and property levels.

Authorization

Authorization supports the idea that each business object property and method can have a list of roles that are allowed and denied access. I already touched on some of these concepts when I discussed how properties are declared in Chapter 7. Behind the scenes, those methods make use of an `AuthorizationRules` object from the `Csla.Security` namespace.

Every business object that uses authorization rules has an associated `AuthorizationRules` object that manages the list of roles associated with each property and method. The `AuthorizationRules` class also maintains a list of roles allowed to create, get, update, and delete each business object type.

To do this work, `AuthorizationRules` relies on a number of other classes. Table 12-2 lists the types required for authorization.

Table 12-2. *Types Used to Implement the Authorization Subsystem*

Type	Description
`AccessType`	Lists access types for properties and methods
`AuthorizationRules`	Coordinates the functionality of the authorization subsystem
`AuthorizationRulesManager`	Maintains list of roles for a business object or business object type
`IAuthorizeReadWrite`	Defines methods for use by UI components such as `Csla.Wpf.Authorizer`
`IsInRoleProvider`	Defines a delegate signature for the method that resolves whether the current user is in a specific role
`ObjectAuthorizationRules`	Maintains the cache of all object type level authorization roles for all business object types
`NoAccessBehavior`	Lists options describing what step should be taken when a user attempts an action but does not have access
`RolesForProperty`	Maintains a list of roles allowed and denied access to a property
`RolesForType`	Maintains a list of roles allowed and denied access to a business object type
`SharedAuthorizationRules`	Maintains the cache of all per-type property authorization roles defined for all business object types

I'll discuss how these types are used to implement authorization at the business object type level and at the property level.

Type Level Authorization

A business developer can specify what roles are allowed to create, get, update, and delete each business object type. This behavior is not at the *object instance* level but is at the *type* level. In other words, these roles are defined and can be accessed without ever creating an instance of a business object.

The intent of this functionality is to allow a UI developer to determine whether the user could create, retrieve, update, or delete an object. Ideally, the UI developer would do these checks before ever creating an instance of a business object, so the various buttons, menu items, and links the user would use to perform each action can be disabled if they don't work anyway.

The `AuthorizationRules` class uses the `ObjectAuthorizationRules` type to manage this behavior.

AddObjectAuthorizationRules Method

Inside a business class, a developer can write code like this to define these roles:

```
private static void AddObjectAuthorizationRules()
{
  Csla.Security.AuthorizationRules.AllowGet("Supervisor");
}
```

This indicates that the users in the Supervisor role should be allowed to retrieve instances of this business object type. Notice that the `AddObjectAuthorizationRules()` method is `static`, so it can be invoked without needing to first create an instance of the business object. Table 12-3 lists the `static` methods from the `AuthorizationRules` class available to the business object developer.

Table 12-3. *Per-Type Authentication Methods*

Method	Description
`AllowCreate()`	Specifies the roles allowed to create a new object
`AllowGet()`	Specifies the roles allowed to get an existing object
`AllowEdit()`	Specifies the roles allowed to edit and save (insert or update) an object
`AllowDelete()`	Specifies the roles allowed to delete an object

The `AddObjectAuthorizationRules()` method is invoked by `ObjectAuthorizationRules` the first time an attempt is made to get the list of roles for a business object type. Because all these values are maintained in a `static` cache, multithreading issues must be managed, just as I discuss in Chapter 11 in regard to validation.

Here's the `GetRoles()` method and the declaration of the `static` cache it uses:

```
private static Dictionary<Type, RolesForType> _managers =
  new Dictionary<Type, RolesForType>();

internal static RolesForType GetRoles(Type objectType)
{
  RolesForType result = null;
  if (!_managers.TryGetValue(objectType, out result))
  {
    lock (_managers)
    {
```

```
          if (!_managers.TryGetValue(objectType, out result))
          {
            result = new RolesForType();
            _managers.Add(objectType, result);
            // invoke method to add auth roles
            var flags = BindingFlags.Static |
                                  BindingFlags.Public |
                                  BindingFlags.NonPublic |
                                  BindingFlags.FlattenHierarchy;
            MethodInfo method = objectType.GetMethod(
              "AddObjectAuthorizationRules", flags);
            if (method != null)
              method.Invoke(null, null);
          }
        }
      }
      return result;
    }
```

The same kind of lock scheme I discuss in Chapter 11 is used here. The result is that the first thread to attempt to access this property and get through the lock statement will use reflection to invoke the AddObjectAuthorizationRules() method on the business class. This only happens once per AppDomain, and the roles are cached for use throughout the remainder of the application's lifetime.

The methods called by the business developer are defined in the AuthorizationRules class. For example, here's the AllowGet() method:

```
    public static void AllowGet(Type objectType, params string[] roles)
    {
      var typeRules = ObjectAuthorizationRules.GetRoles(objectType);
      typeRules.AllowGet(roles);
    }
```

There's no locking here because this method is intended for use only within the AddObjectBusinessRules() method, and that method is only invoked within the context of a lock statement, so it is already thread-safe.

Using Type Level Roles

Now that you understand how the type level roles are added and cached, it is important to understand how they are used. Any code in the business or UI layer can determine whether the current user is authorized to create, get, update, or delete a type of business object with code such as this:

```
  bool canGet = Csla.Security.AuthorizationRules.CanGetObject(typeof(MyObject));
```

There are CanCreateObject(), CanEditObject(), and CanDeleteObject() methods as well, and they work the same way. For example, here's the CanGetObject() method:

```
    public static bool CanGetObject(Type objectType)
    {
      bool result = true;
      var principal = ApplicationContext.User;
      var allow = Csla.Security.AuthorizationRules.GetAllowGetRoles(objectType);
      if (allow != null)
      {
```

```
    if (!Csla.Security.AuthorizationRulesManager.PrincipalRoleInList(
                    principal, allow))
      result = false;
  }
  else
  {
    var deny = Csla.Security.AuthorizationRules.GetDenyGetRoles(objectType);
    if (deny != null)
    {
      if (Csla.Security.AuthorizationRulesManager.PrincipalRoleInList(
                      principal, deny))
        result = false;
    }
  }
  return result;
}
```

The GetAllowGetRoles() and GetDenyGetRoles() methods are helper methods that retrieve the list of roles allowed and denied access to the get operation for the specified type:

```
internal static List<string> GetAllowGetRoles(Type objectType)
{
  var typeRules = ObjectAuthorizationRules.GetRoles(objectType);
  return typeRules.AllowGetRoles;
}
```

The PrincipalRoleInList() method loops through the list of roles to determine whether the current user is in any of the roles in the list. This method is just a simple loop, but it calls a private method named IsInRole() rather than calling the IsInRole() method on the current principal object.

Here's the IsInRole() method:

```
private static bool IsInRole(IPrincipal principal, string role)
{
  if (mIsInRoleProvider == null)
  {
    string provider = ApplicationContext.IsInRoleProvider;
    if (string.IsNullOrEmpty(provider))
      mIsInRoleProvider = IsInRoleDefault;
    else
    {
      string[] items = provider.Split(',');
      Type containingType = Type.GetType(items[0] + "," + items[1]);
      mIsInRoleProvider =
        (IsInRoleProvider)(Delegate.CreateDelegate(
          typeof(IsInRoleProvider),
          containingType, items[2]));
    }
  }
  return mIsInRoleProvider(principal, role);
}
```

This method abstracts the IsInRole() concept so it isn't necessarily tied to checking with the current principal object. If the application's config file contains an entry for an IsInRoleProvider() method, that method is used instead of the default. The config entry would go in the <appSettings> element and would look like this:

```
<add key="CslaIsInRoleProvider" value="Namespace.Class.Method,Assembly" />
```

The default IsInRoleProvider() exists in the AuthorizationRules class and looks like this:

```
private static bool IsInRoleDefault(IPrincipal principal, string role)
{
  return principal.IsInRole(role);
}
```

The reason for all this work is to allow an advanced business developer to replace how the IsInRole() operation is performed by substituting his own method for this one.

At this point you should understand how business type level authorization roles are stored in ObjectAuthorizationRules and how the AuthorizationRules class makes the behaviors available both to the business object developer and any other code that needs to check the rules.

Property and Method Level Authorization

It is quite common for a user to have access to a form or a page but not to all the data on that form. Or a user may be allowed to view some data but not change it, based on her role. CSLA .NET supports this concept by allowing a business developer to specify which roles are allowed or denied read and write access to each property on a business object. The developer can do the same thing for methods exposed by the object by specifying which roles are allowed to execute the method.

Per-property authorization is implemented by the GetProperty() and SetProperty() methods I discuss in Chapter 7. These two methods call CanReadProperty() and CanWriteProperty(), which actually perform the role checks with the help of the AuthorizationRules object.

Per-method authorization requires that the method implementation make an explicit call to CanExecuteMethod() before doing any actual work. The CanExecuteMethod() does the role check with the help of the AuthorizationRules object.

Table 12-4 lists the AuthorizationRules methods available to a business developer to specify roles that are allowed or denied access to properties and methods.

Table 12-4. *Property and Method Authorization Options*

Method	Description
AllowRead()	Specifies the roles allowed to read a property
DenyRead()	Specifies the roles not allowed to read a property
AllowWrite()	Specifies the roles allowed to write to a property
DenyWrite()	Specifies the roles not allowed to write to a property
AllowExecute()	Specifies the roles allowed to execute a method
DenyExecute()	Specifies the roles not allowed to execute a method

The default implementation provided by CSLA .NET is permissive. This means that by default, all users are allowed to read and write to all properties and to execute all methods. However, if one or more roles are allowed to read, write, or execute, all other roles are denied access. Alternately, you can choose to deny access to specific roles, in which case all other roles continue to have access.

Not only does each object enforce its rules but the rules are exposed publicly to the rest of the application. This is primarily so a UI developer can enable and disable UI controls to give the user visual cues about what she can and can't do. The IAuthorizeReadWrite interface in the Csla.Security namespace provides a standardized way to access this information, and it is used by the UI controls discussed in Chapter 10.

IAuthorizeReadWrite Interface

The `IAuthorizeReadWrite` interface defines a public interface for use by UI frameworks or other code that needs to determine what a user can do to an object's properties or methods. It looks like this:

```
public interface IAuthorizeReadWrite
{
  bool CanWriteProperty(string propertyName);
  bool CanReadProperty(string propertyName);
  bool CanExecuteMethod(string methodName);
}
```

This interface is implemented by `BusinessBase` and `ReadOnlyBase` and can be used against any business object with properties and methods.

Per-Type Authorization Rules

A business object developer must specify the roles that are allowed and denied access to each property and method. The `AuthorizationRules` class maintains two lists of the roles. One list is shared across all instances of each business object type and the other list is maintained for each individual object instance.

The list maintained across all instances of a type is far more efficient in terms of memory and performance and should be the preferred approach. A business object developer must override the `AddAuthorizationRules()` method to associate shared per-type roles with properties and methods. The code in the business object looks like this:

```
protected override void AddAuthorizationRules()
{
  AuthorizationRules.AllowRead(NameProperty, "Supervisor", "Guest");
  AuthorizationRules.DenyWrite(NameProperty, "Guest");
  AuthorizationRules.AllowExecute("DoWork", "Supervisor");
}
```

This specifies that the Supervisor and Guest roles are allowed to read the `Name` property, but the Guest role is specifically not allowed to alter the property. And the Supervisor role is allowed to execute the business object's `DoWork()` method.

The list of allowed and denied roles for each property and method is maintained within the `AuthorizationRules` object, which uses the types listed in Table 12-5 to store and retrieve the information.

Table 12-5. *Types Used to Maintain the Roles for an Object Type*

Type	Description
`SharedAuthorizationRules`	Maintains a cache with an `AuthorizationRulesManager` object for each business object type
`AuthorizationRulesManager`	Maintains a list of `RolesForProperty` objects, each one containing the roles for a specific property
`RolesForProperty`	Maintains the lists of allowed and denied roles for reading and writing a specific property

I'm not going to walk through the code for these classes. They use the same multithreaded locking scheme I discuss in Chapter 11 and earlier in this chapter. The roles are maintained in static fields and so are shared across each AppDomain and they are initialized once as the AppDomain starts up. This means they are initialized once for the lifetime of an application.

Per-Instance Authorization Rules

A business object can also have a list of roles for just that one instance. This is expensive in terms of memory and performance: memory because the lists of roles are maintained for *each instance of the business type*; performance because the lists of roles are initialized as each business object instance is created.

The reason for using this approach is if you have authorization rules that must vary on a per-instance basis. Such scenarios are fortunately rare because the overhead to associating the rules with each instance can be quite high.

If you want to use this model, the business developer must override AddInstanceAuthorizationRules() like this:

```
protected override void AddInstanceAuthorizationRules()
{
  AuthorizationRules.InstanceAllowRead(NameProperty, "Supervisor", "Guest");
  AuthorizationRules.InstanceDenyWrite(NameProperty, "Guest");
  AuthorizationRules.InstanceAllowExecute("DoWork", "Supervisor");
}
```

These roles are maintained in an AuthorizationRulesManager object that is created for each business object instance.

CanReadProperty, CanWriteProperty, and CanExecuteMethod Methods

The BusinessBase class implements three virtual methods that are used to determine whether the current user is allowed to read, write, or execute individual properties and methods. The ReadOnlyBase class implements only CanReadProperty() because it is designed to support read-only objects.

These methods are virtual so a business developer can override and extend their behavior. By default, these methods simply check the list of allowed and denied roles associated with each property or method.

To enhance performance, the result of a role check is cached and is only rechecked if the current principal object changes. This is particularly valuable in a WPF or Windows Forms application, where the principal will only change if the user logs in or out of the application (when using custom authentication). It has less value in web applications because the server is typically stateless and so the business object (and thus its cache) is destroyed at the end of each page or service request.

For example, here's the CanReadProperty() method from BusinessBase:

```
[EditorBrowsable(EditorBrowsableState.Advanced)]
public virtual bool CanReadProperty(string propertyName)
{
  bool result = true;

  VerifyAuthorizationCache();

  if (!_readResultCache.TryGetValue(propertyName, out result))
  {
    result = true;
```

```
      if (AuthorizationRules.HasReadAllowedRoles(propertyName))
      {
        // some users are explicitly granted read access
        // in which case all other users are denied
        if (!AuthorizationRules.IsReadAllowed(propertyName))
          result = false;
      }
      else if (AuthorizationRules.HasReadDeniedRoles(propertyName))
      {
        // some users are explicitly denied read access
        if (AuthorizationRules.IsReadDenied(propertyName))
          result = false;
      }
      // store value in cache
      _readResultCache.Add(propertyName, result);
    }

    return result;
  }
```

The `VerifyAuthorizationCache()` method does two things. First, it ensures that the cache of authorization values is initialized, and, second, it reinitializes the cache if the current principal has changed. In other words, this method makes sure the cache is ready for use and also that cached values for one user aren't used for a different user.

The `TryGetValue()` method is used to efficiently retrieve any cached value for a property from the cache. If there is no cached value for this property, the authorization rules are checked for this property.

The default authorization rules used by CSLA .NET are *permissive*. In other words, by default all users are allowed to read and write all properties (and to execute all methods). Table 12-6 lists the results of allowing or denying specific roles access.

Table 12-6. *Results of Allowing or Denying roles*

Allow	Deny	Result
None	None	All users have access.
Any	None	Only allowed roles have access.
None	Any	All roles except denied roles have access.
Any	Any	Only allowed roles have access.

Ultimately, the `IsReadAllowed()` and `IsReadDenied()` methods use the same `IsInRole()` provider scheme I discuss earlier in the chapter. This means that by default the current principal object's `IsInRole()` method is called but an advanced business developer could replace that behavior.

The `CanWriteProperty()` and `CanExecuteMethod()` methods follow the same approach and the same default behavior as described in Table 12-6. Together, these methods allow per-property and per-method authorization on all business objects.

Conclusion

This chapter covered the authorization subsystem provided by CSLA .NET. The authorization behaviors leverage the standard .NET principal and identity object model, which enables a role-based authorization scheme.

Using this scheme, a business developer can specify which roles are allowed to create, get, edit, and delete each type of business object. They can also control which roles are allowed or denied read and write access to each property on a business object. The same is true for methods implemented by a business object.

In Chapters 13 through 16 I discuss the rest of the major framework features. Then, starting with Chapter 17, I walk through the `ProjectTracker` reference application implementation.

CHAPTER 13

N-Level Undo

There are scenarios where an application requires the ability to undo changes made to an object. Data binding is one example because implementing the IEditableObject interface requires that an object be able to take a snapshot of its state, be edited, and then be able to return its state to that snapshot later. Another example is where the UI has a Cancel button that doesn't close the form or page, in which case the user expects that clicking Cancel will revert the form's data (and thus the business object) to a previous state.

Implementing an undo feature is challenging, especially when you consider parent-child object relationships. When undoing changes to an Invoice object, for example, it is necessary to remove all newly added line items, re-add all removed line items, and undo all edited line items—all that in addition to undoing changes to the Invoice object itself. It is important to remember that all child objects are part of the object's state.

Of course, it is also important to follow good object-oriented programming (OOP) practices, and a key tenet of OOP is to preserve *encapsulation*. This means one object can't directly manipulate the state (fields) of another object. So the Invoice object can't directly manipulate the state of its LineItemList collection or the LineItem objects it contains. Instead, it must ask each of those objects to manage its own state individually.

The undo functionality provided by CSLA .NET is *n-level undo*. This means that you can cause the object to take multiple snapshots of its state and then cancel or accept each level of changes:

```
_customer.BeginEdit();  // take a snapshot
_customer.Name = "ABC Corp";
_customer.BeginEdit();  // take a snapshot
_customer.Name = "RDL Corp";
_customer.BeginEdit();  // take a snapshot
_customer.Name = "XYZ Corp";
_customer.CancelEdit();  // undo to previous snapshot
_customer.CancelEdit();  // undo to second snapshot
_customer.ApplyEdit();  // keep first set of property changes
```

The end result is that the Name property has the value of ABC Corp because the second two sets of property changes were discarded by calls to CancelEdit().

Not all applications use n levels of undo. In fact, most web applications don't use undo at all, and the implementation in CSLA .NET is designed so no overhead is incurred if the feature isn't used.

Most WPF and Windows Forms applications use at least one level of undo because data binding uses the IEditableObject interface, which does take a snapshot of the object's state. If your WPF or Windows Forms interface also includes a Cancel button that doesn't close the form, you'll almost certainly use two levels of undo: one for IEditableObject and another for the form-level Cancel button.

Some WPF and Windows Forms UI designs may use modal windows to allow editing of child objects. If you don't use in-place editing in a grid control, it is quite common to pop up a modal window so the user can edit the details of each row in a grid. If those modal windows have a Cancel button, you'll almost certainly use n-level undo to implement the UI.

While the n-level undo functionality described in this chapter can't handle every type of UI, it does enable a wide range of UI styles, including the most widely used styles. If you don't use undo, no overhead is incurred. If you do use undo, it is designed to be relatively easy and as transparent as possible.

Using Undo

The undo functionality in CSLA .NET is designed to support two primary scenarios: data binding and manual invocation.

- Data binding uses the undo feature through the `IEditableObject` interface from the `System.ComponentModel` namespace. I discuss this interface in Chapter 10, but in this chapter I focus specifically on how it is supported through the undo functionality.
- Manual invocation of the undo functionality allows the developer to create various types of user experiences, including forms with Cancel buttons and nested modal forms for editing child or grandchild objects.

The behavior of the undo functionality is different for each of these scenarios. This is because data binding expects any `IEditableObject` implementation to work exactly the way it is implemented by the ADO.NET `DataSet` and `DataTable` objects. Those objects implement undo with some limitations:

- There is only one level of undo per object or row.
- Master-detail (parent-child) objects are independent.
- Only the first call to `BeginEdit()` is honored; subsequent calls are ignored.

The rules for manual invocation are the exact opposite of data binding:

- Any object can have any level of undo operations (n-level undo).
- Calling `BeginEdit()` on a parent also takes a snapshot of child object states.
- Each call to `BeginEdit()` takes another snapshot.

The implementation of undo provided by CSLA .NET supports both models and even allows them to be combined (within limits). For example, if you want to implement a form-level Cancel button, you can manually call `BeginEdit()` on an editable root object to take a snapshot of the entire object graph. Then you can bind the objects to the UI and allow data binding to interact with the objects following its rules. After unbinding the objects from the UI, you can then manually call `CancelEdit()` or `ApplyEdit()` to reject or accept all the changes done to any objects while they are bound to the UI.

The rest of the chapter focuses on the implementation of the undo functionality. Keep in mind that it supports both the data binding and manual invocation models.

Implementing Undo

The undo functionality provided by CSLA .NET preserves encapsulation, while providing powerful capabilities for objects and object graphs in a parent-child relationship. The `UndoableBase`, `BusinessBase`, and `BusinessListBase` classes work together to provide this functionality. The undo behaviors are exposed both through the implementation of `IEditableObject` and directly through `BeginEdit()`, `CancelEdit()`, and `ApplyEdit()` methods.

Figure 13-1 illustrates the relationship between the types that are used to implement the n-level undo functionality.

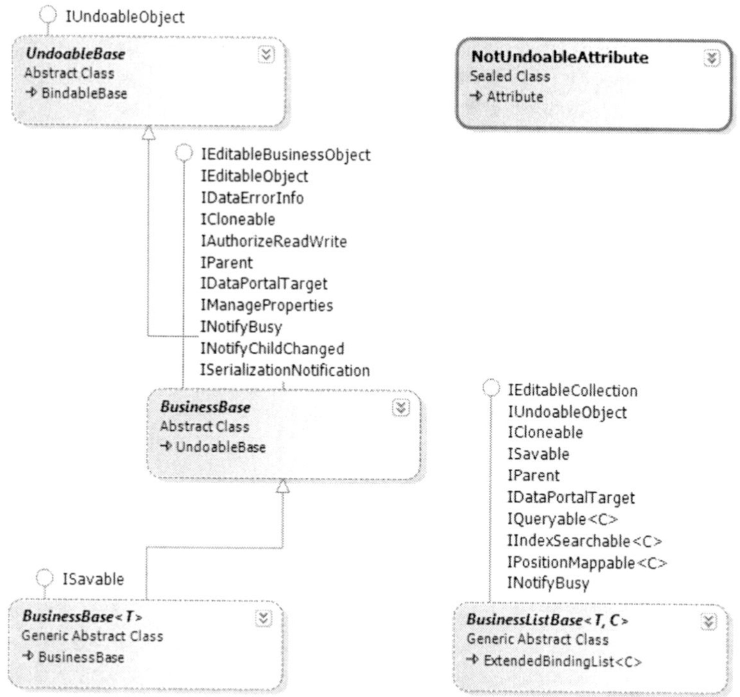

Figure 13-1. *Types used to implement undo functionality*

Most of the work occurs in UndoableBase, but BusinessBase and BusinessListBase also include important code for undo functionality.

Table 13-1 lists the key types involved in the process.

Table 13-1. *Key Types Required by N-Level Undo*

Type	Description
ISupportUndo	Provides public and polymorphic access to the n-level undo functionality; for use by UI developers and other framework authors
IUndoableObject	Allows UndoableBase to polymorphically interact with objects that support the undo functionality; not for use by code outside CSLA .NET
NotUndoableAttribute	Allows a business developer to specify that a field should be ignored by n-level undo
UndoableBase	Implements most undo functionality
UndoException	Is thrown when an undo-related exception occurs

In the rest of the chapter, I walk through the implementation of several of these types and the primary functionality they provide.

ISupportUndo Interface

When you need to manually invoke n-level undo methods, you'll often want to do so polymorphically, without worrying about the specific type of the business object. This is quite common when building reusable UI code or UI controls and enabling this scenario is the purpose behind the `ISupportUndo` interface. For example, the `CslaDataProvider` in the `Csla.Wpf` namespace uses `ISupportUndo` to call the n-level undo methods on any object that implements the interface.

The `ISupportUndo` interface defines the three n-level undo methods listed in Table 13-2.

Table 13-2. *N-Level Undo Methods Defined by ISupportUndo*

Method	Description
`BeginEdit()`	Takes a snapshot of the business object's state
`CancelEdit()`	Rolls the object's state back to the most recent snapshot taken by `BeginEdit()`
`ApplyEdit()`	Discards the most recent snapshot taken by `BeginEdit()`, leaving the object's state alone

These three methods encapsulate the functionality provided by n-level undo. The `ISupportUndo` interface is implemented by all editable objects, both single objects and collections.

NotUndoableAttribute Class

As discussed in Chapter 2, editable business objects and collections support n-level undo functionality. Sometimes, however, objects may have values that shouldn't be included in the snapshot that's taken before an object is edited. (These may be read-only values, or recalculated values, or values—large images, perhaps—that are simply so big you choose not to support undo for them.)

The custom attribute `NotUndoable` is used to allow a business developer to indicate that a field shouldn't be included in the undo operation.

The `UndoableBase` class, which implements the n-level undo operations, detects whether this attribute has been placed on any fields. If so, it will simply ignore that field within the undo process, neither taking a snapshot of its value nor restoring it in the case of a cancel operation.

■ **Note** Since the `NotUndoable` attribute is used by business developers as they write normal business code, it is in the `Csla` namespace along with all the other types intended for use by business developers.

The `NotUndoableAttribute` class contains the following code:

```
namespace Csla
{
  [AttributeUsage(AttributeTargets.Field)]
  public sealed class NotUndoableAttribute : Attribute
  {

  }
}
```

`AttributeUsage` specifies that this attribute can be applied only to fields. Beyond that, the `NotUndoable` attribute is merely a marker to indicate that certain actions should (or shouldn't) be taken by the n-level undo implementation, so there's no real code here at all.

UndoableBase Class

The `UndoableBase` class is where most of the work to handle n-level undo for an object takes place. This is pretty complex code that makes heavy use of reflection to find all the fields in each business object, take snapshots of their values, and then (potentially) restore their values later, in the case of an undo operation.

Remember, nothing *requires* the use of n-level undo. In many web scenarios there's no need to use these methods at all. A flat UI with no Cancel button has no requirement for undo functionality, so there's no reason to incur the overhead of taking a snapshot of the object's data. On the other hand, when creating a complex WPF or Windows Forms UI that involves modal dialog windows to allow editing of child objects (or even grandchild objects), it is often best to call these methods to provide support for OK and Cancel buttons on each of the dialog windows.

■ **Tip** Typically, a snapshot of a business object's fields is taken before the user or an application is allowed to interact with the object. That way, you can always undo back to that original state. The `BusinessBase` and `BusinessListBase` classes include a `BeginEdit()` method that triggers the snapshot process, a `CancelEdit()` method to restore the object's state to the last snapshot, and an `ApplyEdit()` method to commit any changes since the last snapshot.

The reason this snapshot process is so complex is that the values of *all* fields in each object must be copied, and each business object is essentially composed of several classes all merged together through inheritance and aggregation. This causes problems when classes have fields with the same names as fields in the classes they inherit from, and it causes particular problems if a class inherits from another class in a different assembly.

Since `UndoableBase` is a base class from which `BusinessBase` will ultimately derive, it must be marked as `Serializable`. It is also declared as `abstract`, so that no one can create an instance of this class directly. All business objects need to utilize the `INotifyPropertyChanged` interface implemented in `BindableBase` so they inherit from that, too. Finally, the n-level undo functionality relies on the `IUndoableObject` interface from the `Csla.Core` namespace, so that is implemented in this class (and in `BusinessListBase`, discussed later in its own section):

```
[Serializable]
public abstract class UndoableBase : Csla.Core.BindableBase,
  Csla.Core.IUndoableObject
{
}
```

With that base laid down, I can start to discuss how to implement the undo functionality. There are three operations involved: taking a snapshot of the object state, restoring the object state in case of an undo, and discarding the stored object state in case of an accept operation.

Additionally, if this object has child objects that implement `IUndoableObject`, those child objects must also perform the store, restore, and accept operations. To achieve this, any time the algorithm encounters a field that's derived from either of these types, it cascades the operation to that object so it can take appropriate action.

The three operations are implemented by a set of three methods:

- CopyState()
- UndoChanges()
- AcceptChanges()

CopyState

The CopyState() method takes a snapshot of the object's current data and stores it in a Stack object.

Stacking the Data

Since UndoableBase is an implementation of n-level undo capability, each object could end up storing a number of snapshots. As each undo or accept operation occurs, it gets rid of the most recently stored snapshot; this is the classic behavior of a "stack" data structure. Fortunately, the .NET Framework includes a prebuilt Stack<T> class that implements the required functionality. It is declared as follows:

```
[NotUndoable]
private Stack<byte[]> _stateStack = new Stack<byte[]>();
```

This field is marked as NotUndoable to prevent taking a snapshot of previous snapshots. CopyState() should just record the fields that contain actual business data. Once a snapshot has been taken of the object's data, the snapshot is serialized into a single byte stream. That byte stream is then put on the stack. From there, it can be retrieved and deserialized to perform an undo operation if needed.

Taking a Snapshot of the Data

The process of taking a snapshot of each field value in an object is a bit tricky. Reflection is used to walk through all the fields in the object. During this process, each field is checked to determine whether it has the NotUndoable attribute. If so, the field is ignored.

The big issue is that field names may not be unique within an object. To see what I mean, consider the following two classes:

```
namespace Test
{
  public class BaseClass
  {
    int _id;
  }

  public class SubClass : BaseClass
  {
    int _id;
  }
}
```

Here, each class has its own field named _id, and in most circumstances it's not a problem. However, when using reflection to walk through all the fields in a SubClass object, it will return *two* _id fields: one for each of the classes in the inheritance hierarchy.

To get an accurate snapshot of an object's data, CopyState() needs to accommodate this scenario. In practice, this means prefixing each field name with the full name of the class to which it belongs. Instead of two _id fields, the result is Test.BaseClass!_id and Test.SubClass!_id. The use of an exclamation point for a separator is arbitrary, but some character is necessary to separate the class name from the field name.

As if this weren't complex enough, reflection works differently with classes that are subclassed from other classes in the *same* assembly than with classes that are subclassed from classes in a *different* assembly. If in the previous example, BaseClass and SubClass are in the same assembly, one technique can be used; but if they're in different assemblies, a different technique is necessary. Of course, CopyState() should deal with both scenarios so the business developer doesn't have to worry about these details.

■ **Note** Not all the code for UndoableBase is listed in this book. I only cover the key parts of the algorithm. For the rest of the code, refer to the download at www.apress.com/book/view/1430210192 or www.lhotka.net/cslanet/download.aspx.

The following method deals with all of the preceding issues. I walk through how it works after the listing:

```
[EditorBrowsable(EditorBrowsableState.Never)]
protected void CopyState()
{
  CopyingState();

  Type currentType = this.GetType();
  HybridDictionary state = new HybridDictionary();
  FieldInfo[] fields;

  if (this.EditLevel + 1 > parentEditLevel)
    throw new UndoException(string.Format(
        Resources.EditLevelMismatchException, "CopyState"));

  do
  {
    // get the list of fields in this type
    fields = currentType.GetFields(
        BindingFlags.NonPublic |
        BindingFlags.Instance |
        BindingFlags.Public);

    foreach (FieldInfo field in fields)
    {
      // make sure we process only our variables
      if (field.DeclaringType == currentType)
      {
        // see if this field is marked as not undoable
        if (!NotUndoableField(field))
        {
          // the field is undoable, so it needs to be processed.
          object value = field.GetValue(this);

          if (typeof(Csla.Core.IUndoableObject).
              IsAssignableFrom(field.FieldType))
          {
            // make sure the variable has a value
```

```
              if (value == null)
              {
                // variable has no value - store that fact
                state.Add(GetFieldName(field), null);
              }
              else
              {
                // this is a child object, cascade the call
                ((Core.IUndoableObject)value).
                  CopyState(this.EditLevel + 1, BindingEdit);
              }
            }
            else
            {
              // this is a normal field, simply trap the value
              state.Add(GetFieldName(field), value);
            }
          }
        }
      }
      currentType = currentType.BaseType;
    } while (currentType != typeof(UndoableBase));

    // serialize the state and stack it
    using (MemoryStream buffer = new MemoryStream())
    {
      ISerializationFormatter formatter =
        SerializationFormatterFactory.GetFormatter();
      formatter.Serialize(buffer, state);
      _stateStack.Push(buffer.ToArray());
    }
    CopyStateComplete();
  }

  [EditorBrowsable(EditorBrowsableState.Advanced)]
  protected virtual void CopyingState()
  {
  }

  [EditorBrowsable(EditorBrowsableState.Advanced)]
  protected virtual void CopyStateComplete()
  {
  }
```

The CopyState() method is scoped as protected because BusinessBase subclasses UndoableBase, and the BeginEdit() method in BusinessBase will need to call CopyState().

To take a snapshot of data, there needs to be somewhere to store the various field values before they are pushed onto the stack. A HybridDictionary is ideal for this purpose, as it stores name-value pairs. It also provides high-speed access to values based on their names, which is important for the undo implementation. Finally, the HybridDictionary object supports .NET serialization, which means that it can be serialized and passed by value across the network as part of a business object.

The CopyState() routine is essentially a big loop that starts with the outermost class in the object's inheritance hierarchy and walks back up through the chain of classes until it gets to UndoableBase. At that point, it can stop—it knows that it has a snapshot of all the business data.

At the start and end of the process, methods are called so a subclass can do pre- and post-processing. Notice that `CopyingState()` and `CopyStateComplete()` are `virtual` methods with no implementation. The idea is that a subclass can override these methods if additional actions should be taken before or after the object's state is copied. They provide an extensibility point for advanced business developers.

Getting a List of Fields

It's inside the loop where the real work occurs. The first step is to get a list of all the fields corresponding to the current class:

```
// get the list of fields in this type
fields = currentType.GetFields(
  BindingFlags.NonPublic |
  BindingFlags.Instance |
  BindingFlags.Public);
```

It doesn't matter whether the fields are `public`—they all need to be recorded regardless of scope. What's more important is to only record instance fields, not those declared as `static`. The result of this call is an array of `FieldInfo` objects, each of which corresponds to a field in the business object.

Avoiding Double-Processing of Fields

As discussed earlier, the `FieldInfo` array could include fields from the base classes of the current class. Due to the way the JIT compiler optimizes code within the same assembly, if some base classes are in the same assembly as the actual business class, the same field name may be listed in multiple classes. As the code walks up the inheritance hierarchy, it could end up processing those fields twice. To avoid this, the code only looks at the fields that *directly* belong to the class currently being processed:

```
foreach(FieldInfo field in fields)
{
  // make sure we process only our variables
  if(field.DeclaringType == currentType)
```

Skipping NotUndoable Fields

At this point in the proceedings, it is established that the current `FieldInfo` object refers to a field within the object that's part of the current class in the inheritance hierarchy. However, a snapshot of the field should only be taken if it doesn't have the `NotUndoable` attribute:

```
// see if this field is marked as not undoable
if(!NotUndoableField(field))
```

Having reached this point, it is clear that the field value needs to be part of the snapshot, so there are two possibilities: this may be a regular field or it may be a reference to a child object that implements `Csla.Core.IUndoableObject`.

Cascading the Call to Child Objects or Collections

If the field is a reference to a `Csla.Core.IUndoableObject`, the `CopyState()` call must be cascaded to that object so that it can take its own snapshot:

```
if (typeof(Csla.Core.IUndoableObject).
    IsAssignableFrom(field.FieldType))
{
  // make sure the variable has a value
```

```
            if (value == null)
            {
              // variable has no value - store that fact
              state.Add(GetFieldName(field), null);
            }
            else
            {
              // this is a child object, cascade the call
              ((Core.IUndoableObject)value).
                CopyState(this.EditLevel + 1, BindingEdit);
            }
          }
```

If a field has a null value, a placeholder is put into the state dictionary so UndoChanges() can restore the value to null if needed.

Non-null values represent a child object, so the call is cascaded to that child. Notice that the parent object doesn't directly manipulate the state of its children because that would break encapsulation. Instead, it is up to the child object to manage its own state. Keep in mind that if the child object is derived from BusinessListBase, the call will automatically be cascaded down to each individual child object in the collection.

■ **Tip** Of course, the GetValue() method returns everything as type object, so the value is cast to IUndoableObject in order to call the CopyState() method.

I want to call your attention to the BindingEdit property that is passed as a parameter to the child's CopyState() method. The BindingEdit property indicates whether this object is currently data bound to a UI or not. If BindingEdit is true, the object is currently bound to the UI and data binding has called BeginEdit() through the IEditableObject interface.

Because this parameter is included, the code is calling the following overload of CopyState():

```
void IUndoableObject.CopyState(int parentEditLevel, bool parentBindingEdit)
{
  if (!parentBindingEdit)
    CopyState(parentEditLevel);
}
```

This overload is obviously not complex. It simply ensures that the child object only takes a snapshot of its own state when the parent is *not* using data binding. The idea is to provide the behaviors required by data binding *and* the behaviors for manual invocation, as I discussed earlier in the chapter.

You might wonder why the parent even tries to cascade the call to the child if BindingEdit is true. The reason is that it is the child object's decision whether it should take a snapshot of its state or not. This approach preserves encapsulation by letting the child object determine its own behavior. Some child objects, such as a BusinessBase child, will ignore the call. But other child objects such as FieldDataManager always take a snapshot of their state. In the case of FieldDataManager this is important, because it contains field values that are *directly part of the containing object*, so it isn't really a "child" in the same sense as an editable child that inherits from BusinessBase.

Later in this chapter you'll see that the methods to undo or accept any changes will work the same way—that is, they'll cascade the calls to any child objects. This way, all objects handle undo without breaking encapsulation.

Taking a Snapshot of a Regular Field

With a regular field, the code simply stores the field value into the HybridDictionary object, associating that value with the combined class name and field name:

```
// this is a normal field, simply trap the value
state.Add(GetFieldName(field), value);
```

Note that these "regular" fields might actually be complex types in and of themselves. All that is known is that the field doesn't reference an editable business object because the value didn't implement IUndoableObject. It could be a simple value such as an int or a string, or it could be a complex object (as long as that object is marked as Serializable).

Having gone through every field for every class in the object's inheritance hierarchy, the HybridDictionary contains a complete snapshot of all the data in the business object.

■ **Note** This snapshot includes some fields put into the BusinessBase class to keep track of the object's status (such as whether it's new, dirty, deleted, etc.). The snapshot also includes the collection of broken rules that will be implemented later. An undo operation restores the object to its previous state in every way.

Serializing and Stacking the HybridDictionary

At this point, the object's field values are recorded but the snapshot is in a complex data type: a HybridDictionary. To further complicate matters, some of the elements contained in the HybridDictionary might be references to more complex objects. In that case, the HybridDictionary just has a reference to the existing object, not a copy or a snapshot at all.

Fortunately, there's an easy answer to both issues. The BinaryFormatter or NetDataContractSerializer can be used to convert the HybridDictionary to a byte stream, reducing it from a complex data type to a very simple one for storage. Better yet, the very process of serializing the HybridDictionary automatically serializes any objects to which it has references.

This does require that all objects referenced by any business object must be marked as Serializable so that they can be included in the byte stream. If referenced objects aren't serializable, the serialization attempt results in a runtime error. Alternatively, any nonserializable object references can be marked as NotUndoable so that the undo process simply ignores them.

The code to do the serialization is fairly straightforward:

```
// serialize the state and stack it
using (MemoryStream buffer = new MemoryStream())
{
  ISerializationFormatter formatter =
    SerializationFormatterFactory.GetFormatter();
  formatter.Serialize(buffer, state);
  _stateStack.Push(buffer.ToArray());
}
```

The SerializationFormatterFactory uses the CslaSerializationFormatter config setting to determine whether to use the BinaryFormatter (the default) or the NetDataContractSerializer. This is set in the app.config or web.config file in the appSettings element:

```
<add key="CslaSerializationFormatter" value="NetDataContractSerializer" />
```

Either formatter works with Serializable objects, but only NetDataContractSerializer works with DataContract objects.

Regardless of which formatter is used, the formatter object serializes the HybridDictionary (and any objects to which it refers) into a stream of bytes in an in-memory buffer. The byte stream is simply extracted from the in-memory buffer and pushed onto the stack:

```
_stateStack.Push(buffer.ToArray());
```

Converting a MemoryStream to a byte array is not an issue because the MemoryStream is implemented to store its data in a byte array. The ToArray() method simply returns a reference to that existing array, so no data is copied.

The act of conversion to a byte array is important, however, because a byte array is serializable, while a MemoryStream object is not. If the business object is passed across the network by value while it is being edited, the stack of states needs to be serializable.

■ **Tip** Passing objects across the network while they're being edited is not anticipated, but since business objects are Serializable, you can't prevent the business developer from doing just that. If the stack were to reference a MemoryStream, the business application would get a runtime error as the serialization fails, and that's not acceptable. Converting the data to a byte array avoids accidentally crashing the application on the off chance that the business developer does decide to pass an object across the network as it's being edited.

At this point, we're a third of the way through implementing n-level undo support. It is now possible to create a stack of snapshots of an object's data. It is time to move on and discuss the undo and accept operations.

UndoChanges

The UndoChanges() method is the reverse of CopyState(). It takes a snapshot of data off the stack, deserializes it back into a HybridDictionary, and then takes each value from the HybridDictionary and restores it into the appropriate object field. Like CopyState(), there are virtual methods called before and after the process to allow subclasses to take additional actions.

The hard issues of walking through the types in the object's inheritance hierarchy and finding all the fields in the object are solved in the implementation of CopyState(). The structure of UndoChanges() is virtually identical, except that it restores field values rather than takes a snapshot of them.

Since the overall structure of UndoChanges() is essentially the reverse of CopyState(), I won't show the entire code here. Rather, I'll focus on the key functionality.

EditLevel

It is possible for a business developer to accidentally trigger a call to UndoChanges() when there is no state to restore. If this condition isn't caught, it will cause a runtime error. To avoid such a scenario, the first thing the UndoChanges() method does is to get the "edit level" of the object by retrieving the Count property from the stack object. If the edit level is 0, there's no state to restore, and UndoChanges() just exits without doing any work.

This edit level concept is even more important in the implementation of BusinessListBase, so you'll notice that the value is implemented as a property.

Also notice that the edit level is checked to make sure it is in sync with this object's parent object (if any):

```
if (this.EditLevel - 1 < parentEditLevel)
  throw
    new UndoException(string.Format(
      Resources.EditLevelMismatchException, "UndoChanges"));
```

All three of the undo methods do this check, and these exceptions help the business developer debug her code when using n-level undo.

The most common place where these exceptions occur is when using Windows Forms data binding because it is very easy for a UI developer to forget to properly unbind an object from the UI, leaving the object in a partially edited state. These exceptions help identify those situations so the developer can fix the UI code.

Re-Creating the HybridDictionary Object

Where CopyState() serializes the HybridDictionary into a byte array at the end of the process, the first thing UndoChanges() needs to do is pop the most recently added snapshot off the stack and deserialize it to re-create the HybridDictionary object containing the detailed values:

```
HybridDictionary state;
using (MemoryStream buffer = new MemoryStream(_stateStack.Pop()))
{
  buffer.Position = 0;
  ISerializationFormatter formatter =
    SerializationFormatterFactory.GetFormatter();
  state = (HybridDictionary)formatter.Deserialize(buffer);
}
```

This is the reverse of the process used to put the HybridDictionary onto the stack in the first place. The result of this process is a HybridDictionary containing all the data that was taken in the original snapshot.

Restoring the Object's State Data

With the HybridDictionary containing the original object values restored, it is possible to loop through the fields in the object in the same manner as CopyState().

When the code encounters a child business object that implements IUndoableObject, it cascades the UndoChanges() call to that child object so that it can do its own restore operation. Again, this is done to preserve encapsulation—only the code within a given object should manipulate that object's data.

With a "normal" field, its value is simply restored from the HybridDictionary:

```
// this is a regular field, restore its value
field.SetValue(this, state[GetFieldName(field)]);
```

At the end of this process, the object is reset to the state it was in when the most recent snapshot was taken. All that remains is to implement a method to *accept* changes, rather than to undo them.

AcceptChanges

AcceptChanges() is actually the simplest of the three methods. If changes are being accepted, it means that the current values in the object are the ones that should be kept, and the most recent snapshot is now meaningless and can be discarded. Like CopyState(), once this method is complete, a virtual AcceptChangesComplete() method is called to allow subclasses to take additional actions.

In concept, this means that all AcceptChanges() needs to do is discard the most recent snapshot:

```
_stateStack.Pop();
```

However, it is important to remember that the object may have child objects, and they need to know to accept changes as well. This requires looping through the object's fields to find any child objects that implement IUndoableObject. The AcceptChanges() method call must be cascaded to them, too.

The process of looping through the fields of the object is the same as in CopyState() and UndoChanges(). The only difference is where the method call is cascaded:

```
      // the field is undoable so see if it is a child object
        if (typeof(Csla.Core.IUndoableObject).
            IsAssignableFrom(field.FieldType))
        {
          object value = field.GetValue(this);
          // make sure the variable has a value
          if (value != null)
          {
            // it is a child object so cascade the call
            ((Core.IUndoableObject)value).AcceptChanges(
                this.EditLevel, BindingEdit);
          }
      }
```

Simple field values don't need any processing. Remember that the idea is that the current values have been accepted—so there's no need to change those current values at all.

You should now understand how the three undo methods in UndoableBase are able to take and restore a snapshot of an object's state, and how the calls are cascaded to child objects in a way that preserves encapsulation while supporting the needs of both data binding and manual invocation of the undo functionality.

BusinessBase Class

The UndoableBase class does the majority of the work to support the undo functionality. However, BusinessBase does include some methods that allow an editable object to participate in the undo process.

In particular, it is BusinessBase that implements ISupportUndo, and so it is BusinessBase that implements methods such as BeginEdit(). These methods are public to enable the manual invocation of the undo functionality.

BeginEdit Method

I'll start by discussing the simplest of the three methods. Here's the BeginEdit() method:

```
public void BeginEdit()
{
  CopyState(this.EditLevel + 1);
}
```

When the business or UI developer explicitly calls BeginEdit() the object takes a snapshot of its state and cascades that call to its child objects. You've already seen how this is done in the CopyState() method implemented in UndoableBase, and BeginEdit() relies on that preexisting behavior.

Remember that the undo methods in UndoableBase throw an exception if the object's edit level gets out of sync with its parent object. The parent's edit level is passed in as a parameter to each undo method, such as CopyState().

When manually invoking CopyState(), it is necessary to pass in a parameter indicating the future state of the edit level. When taking a snapshot, the future edit level is one higher than the current edit level.

In other words, this would cause an exception:

```
CopyState(this.EditLevel);
```

The reason is that CopyState() would see that it is about to raise the object's edit level above the value passed in as a parameter, so it would throw an exception. By passing in EditLevel + 1, the BeginEdit() method is effectively giving permission for the object to take a snapshot of its state.

CancelEdit Method

The CancelEdit() method is a little more complex. Actually, it isn't CancelEdit() that's more complex but the required post-processing implemented in an override of UndoChangesComplete() that is complex:

```
public void CancelEdit()
{
  UndoChanges(this.EditLevel - 1);
}

protected override void UndoChangesComplete()
{
  BindingEdit = false;
  ValidationRules.SetTarget(this);
  InitializeBusinessRules();
  OnUnknownPropertyChanged();
  base.UndoChangesComplete();
}
```

Like BeginEdit(), the CancelEdit() method lets UndoableBase do the hard work. But when the UndoChanges() method is complete, there is some housekeeping that must be done by BusinessBase, and that is handled by the UndoChangesComplete() override.

When either CancelEdit() or ApplyEdit() is called, that call ends any data binding edit currently in effect, so the BindingEdit property is set to false. If data binding calls BeginEdit() through IEditableObject, BindingEdit will be set to true again, but any cancel or accept operation ends that edit process.

An UndoChanges() operation effectively deserializes some data that is stored in the Stack object, as discussed earlier in the chapter. This means it is necessary to ensure that all the internal references between objects are correct. For example, the ValidationRules.SetTarget() method ensures that this object's ValidationRules object has the correct reference as the target for all business rules.

It is also the case that an undo operation probably changed one or more property values. Most likely, the user has changed some property values and the undo reset them to some previous values. The call to OnUnknownPropertyChanged() raises a PropertyChanged event so data binding knows that the UI needs to be refreshed to reflect the changes.

ApplyEdit Method

The ApplyEdit() method is also a little complex. It also does some processing beyond that provided by UndoableBase:

```
public void ApplyEdit()
{
  _neverCommitted = false;
  AcceptChanges(this.EditLevel - 1);
  BindingEdit = false;
}

protected override void AcceptChangesComplete()
{
  if (Parent != null)
    Parent.ApplyEditChild(this);
  base.AcceptChangesComplete();
}
```

Again, when either CancelEdit() or ApplyEdit() are called, that call ends any data binding edit currently in effect, so the BindingEdit property is set to false.

There's also a _neverCommitted flag that is used to track whether the ApplyEdit() method on this object has ever been called. This field is used in the IEditableObject implementation to support the automatic removal of child objects from a list but is only used for Windows Forms 1.0 style data binding (so is nearly obsolete at this point in time).

The most interesting bit of code here is in AcceptChangesComplete(), where a Parent.ApplyEditChild() method is called. This occurs if this object is a child of some other object and the ApplyEditChild() method is used to tell the parent object that its child's ApplyEdit() is invoked. The EditableRootListBase class uses this to determine that the user has completed editing a particular child object in the list, so it knows to trigger an immediate save of that child object's data. I discuss EditableRootListBase in more detail in Chapter 16.

At this point you've seen the code for the public methods that support the undo functionality. There are also three similar methods that support data binding through the IEditableObject interface.

IEditableObject Interface

The IEditableObject interface is used by data binding to interact with an object. As I discuss earlier in the chapter, data binding expects a *single* level of undo and that each object is independent of other objects (so no cascading of undo calls from parent to children).

The BeginEdit() method must detect whether the developer has disabled IEditableObject support and must also only honor the *first* call to BeginEdit() by data binding. It is important to realize that data binding may make many calls to BeginEdit() and only the first one should have any effect:

```
void System.ComponentModel.IEditableObject.BeginEdit()
{
  if (!_disableIEditableObject && !BindingEdit)
  {
    BindingEdit = true;
    BeginEdit();
  }
}
```

The BindingEdit property is set to true to indicate that the object is now bound to a UI. As you've already seen, this property is used to alter the behavior of other undo features and most importantly prevents cascading of method calls to child objects.

The CancelEdit() method is more complex because it supports the automatic removal of certain new objects when they are a child of a list:

```
void System.ComponentModel.IEditableObject.CancelEdit()
{
  if (!_disableIEditableObject && BindingEdit)
  {
    CancelEdit();
    if (IsNew && _neverCommitted && EditLevel <= EditLevelAdded)
    {
      // we're new and no EndEdit or ApplyEdit has ever been
      // called on us, and now we've been cancelled back to
      // where we were added so we should have ourselves
      // removed from the parent collection
      if (Parent != null)
        Parent.RemoveChild(this);
    }
  }
}
```

This call to Parent.RemoveChild() is only useful for Windows Forms 1.0 data binding when using the Windows Forms 1.0 grid control. When using modern data binding and grid controls, this code is unused because BindingList<T> handles the removal of child objects by itself.

The simplest of the three methods is ApplyEdit():

```
void System.ComponentModel.IEditableObject.EndEdit()
{
  if (!_disableIEditableObject && BindingEdit)
  {
    ApplyEdit();
  }
}
```

Assuming IEditableObject isn't disabled and that the object is currently data bound, this method simply delegates to the ApplyEdit() method I discussed earlier.

As you can see, the BusinessBase class exposes the undo functionality in three ways:

- Through public methods for manual invocation
- Through the ISupportUndo interface for manual invocation
- Through the IEditableObject interface for data binding

It also interacts with its UndoableBase base class to do most of the work, including interacting with child objects, such as editable collections. This means BusinessListBase must also participate in the undo functionality.

BusinessListBase Class

The BusinessListBase class combines some of what UndoableBase does and some of what you've seen in BusinessBase. Like UndoableBase, the BusinessListBase class implements IUndoableObject, and like BusinessBase it implements ISupportUndo and the three public undo methods.

The implementation of this functionality in a collection isn't as complex as it is for editable objects, however, because a collection is primarily responsible for cascading the method calls to all the child objects it contains.

Edit Level Tracking

The hardest part of implementing n-level undo functionality is that not only can child objects be added or deleted but they can be "undeleted" or "unadded" in the case of an undo operation. Csla.Core.BusinessBase and UndoableBase use the concept of an *edit level*. The edit level allows the object to keep track of how many BeginEdit() calls have been made to take a snapshot of its state without corresponding CancelEdit() or ApplyEdit() calls. More specifically, it tells the object how many states have been stacked up for undo operations.

BusinessListBase needs the same edit level tracking as in BusinessBase. However, a collection won't actually stack its states. Rather, it cascades the call to each of its child objects so that they can stack their *own* states. Because of this, the edit level can be tracked using a simple numeric counter. It merely counts how many unpaired BeginEdit() calls have been made:

```
// keep track of how many edit levels we have
private int _editLevel;
```

The implementations of CopyState(), UndoChanges(), and AcceptChanges() alter this value accordingly.

Reacting to Insert, Remove, or Clear Operations

Collection base classes don't implement `Add()` or `Remove()` methods directly because those are implemented by `Collection<T>`, which is the base class for `BindingList<T>`. However, they *do* need to perform certain operations any time that an insert or remove operation occurs. To accommodate this, `BindingList<T>` invokes certain `virtual` methods when these events occur. These methods can be overridden to respond to the events.

Child objects also must have the ability to remove themselves from the collection. Remember the implementation of `System.ComponentModel.IEditableObject` in `Clsa.Core.BusinessBase`—that code included a parent reference to the collection object and code to call a `RemoveChild()` method. This `RemoveChild()` method is part of the `IEditableCollection` interface implemented by `BusinessListBase`.

The important thing to realize is that `BusinessListBase` does extra processing in addition to the default behavior of the `BindingList` base class:

- It moves "deleted" items to and from a `DeletedList` so items can be "undeleted."
- It completely removes deleted items that are new (and thus not "undeleted" in an undo operation).
- It maintains any LINQ to CSLA indexes (as discussed in Chapter 14).
- It ensures that newly added child objects have an edit level corresponding to the collection's edit level.

To do this, the methods listed in Table 13-3 are implemented.

Table 13-3. *Methods Implemented for Insert, Remove, and Clear Operations*

Method	Source	Description
`RemoveChild()`	`IEditableCollection`	Removes a child object from the list
`RemoveItem()`	`base`	Removes an item (by index) from the list
`InsertItem()`	`base`	Inserts a new child into the list

The `RemoveChild()` method is called by a child object contained within the collection. This is called when a Windows Forms grid control requests that the child remove itself from the collection via the `System.ComponentModel.IEditableObject` interface.

■ **Note** In reality, this shouldn't be a common occurrence. Windows Forms 2.0 uses a new interface, `ICancelAddNew`, that is implemented by `BindingList<T>`. This interface notifies the *collection* that the child should be removed rather than notifying the child object itself. The code in the `RemoveItem()` method takes care of the `ICancelAddNew` case automatically, so this code is really here to support backward compatibility for anyone explicitly calling the `IEditableObject` interface on child objects.

The `RemoveItem()` method is called when an item is being removed from the collection. To support the concept of undo, the object isn't actually removed because it might need to be restored later. Rather, a `DeleteChild()` method is called, passing the object being removed as a parameter. You'll see the implementation of this method shortly. For now, it's enough to know that it keeps track of the object in case it must be restored later.

The `InsertItem()` method is called when an item is being added to the collection. The `EditLevelAdded` property is changed when a new child object is added to the collection, thus telling the child object the edit level at which it's being added. Recall that this property was implemented in BusinessBase to merely record the value so that it can be checked during undo operations. This value will be used in the collection's UndoChanges() and AcceptChanges() methods later on.

Also notice that the child object's SetParent() method is called to make sure its parent reference is correct. This way, if needed, it can call the collection's RemoveChild() method to remove itself from the collection.

Deleted Object Collection

To ensure that the collection can properly "undelete" objects in case of an undo operation, it needs to keep a list of the objects that have been "removed." The first step in accomplishing this goal is to maintain an internal list of deleted objects.

Along with implementing this list, there needs to be a ContainsDeleted() method so that the business or UI logic can find out whether the collection contains a specific deleted object.

BindingList already includes a Contains() method so that the UI code can ask the collection whether it contains a specific item. Since a BusinessListBase collection is unusual in that it contains two lists of objects, it's appropriate to allow client code to ask whether an object is contained in the deleted list as well as in the nondeleted list.

The list of deleted objects is kept as a List<C>—a strongly typed collection of child objects. That list is then exposed through a protected property so it is available to subclasses. Subclasses have access to the nondeleted items in the collection, so this just follows the same scoping model. The list object is created on demand to minimize overhead in the case that no items are ever removed from the collection.

Given the list for storing deleted child objects, it is possible to implement the methods to delete and undelete objects as needed.

Deleting a child object is really a matter of marking the object as deleted and moving it from the active list of child objects to DeletedList. Undeleting occurs when a child object has restored its state so that it's no longer marked as deleted. In that case, the child object must be moved from DeletedList back to the list of active objects in the collection.

The permutations here are vast. The ways in which combinations of calls to BeginEdit(), Add(), Remove(), CancelEdit(), and ApplyEdit() can be called are probably infinite. Let's look at some relatively common scenarios though to get a good understanding of what happens as child objects are deleted and undeleted.

First, consider a case in which the collection has been loaded with data from a database and the database includes one child object: A. Then, the UI calls BeginEdit() on the collection and adds a new object to the collection: B. Figure 13-2 shows what happens if these two objects are removed and then CancelEdit() is called on the collection object.

■ **Tip** In Figure 13-2, *EL* is the value of _editLevel in the collection; *ELA* is the _editLevelAdded value in each child object; and *DEL* is the IsDeleted value in each child object.

After both objects are removed from the collection, they're marked for deletion and moved to the DeletedList collection. This way they *appear* to be gone from the collection, but the collection still has access to them if needed.

After the CancelEdit() call, the collection's edit level goes back to 0. Since child A came from the database, it was "added" at edit level 0, so it sticks around. Child B on the other hand was added at edit level 1, so it goes away. Also, child A has its state reset as part of the CancelEdit() call (remember that CancelEdit() causes a cascade effect, so each child object restores its snapshot values). The result is that because of the undo operation, child A is no longer marked for deletion.

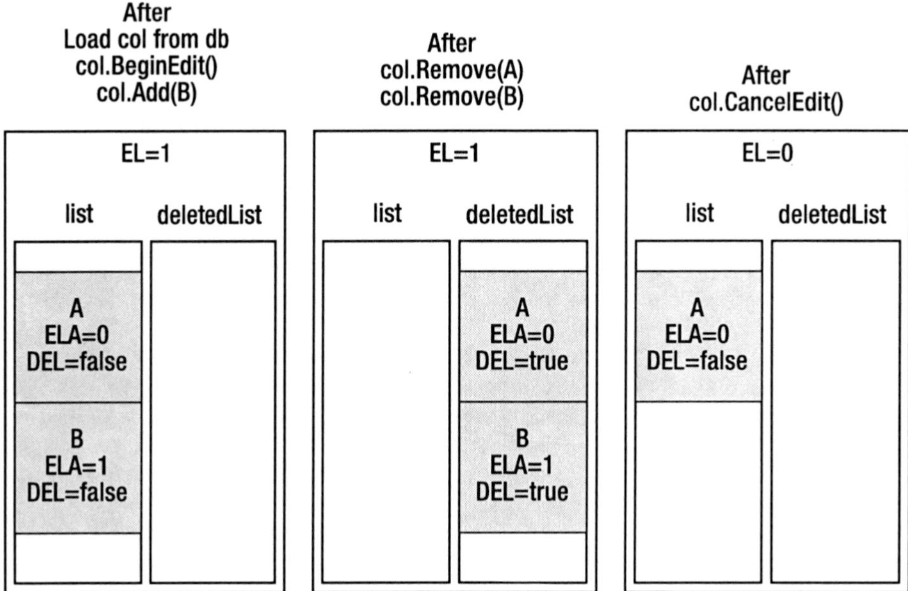

Figure 13-2. *Edit process in which objects are removed and CancelEdit is called*

Another common scenario follows the same process but with a call to `ApplyEdit()` at the end, as shown in Figure 13-3.

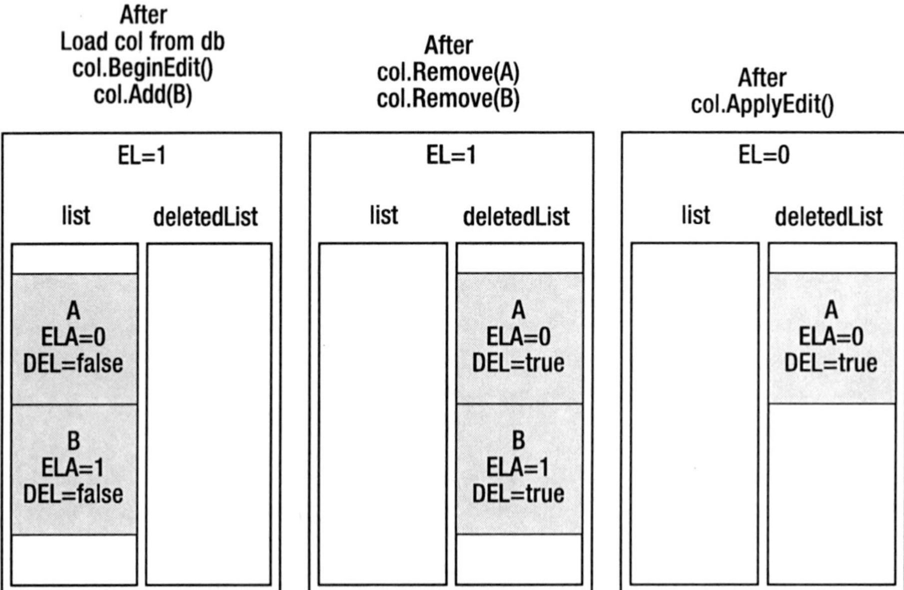

Figure 13-3. *Edit process in which objects are removed and ApplyEdit is called*

The first two steps are identical, of course, but after the call to ApplyEdit(), things are quite different. Since changes to the collection are accepted rather than rejected, the changes become permanent. Child A remains marked for deletion, and if the collection is saved back to the database, the data for child A is deleted from the database. Child B is totally gone at this point. It is a new object added *and deleted* at edit level 1, and all changes made at edit level 1 are accepted. Since the collection knows that B was never in the database (because it was *added* at edit level 1), it can simply discard the object entirely from memory.

Let's look at one last scenario. Just to illustrate how rough this gets, this will be more complex. It involves nested BeginEdit(), CancelEdit(), and ApplyEdit() calls on the collection. This can easily happen if the collection contains child or grandchild objects and they are displayed in a Windows Forms UI that uses modal dialog windows to edit each level (parent, child, grandchild, etc.).

Again, child A is loaded from the database and child B is added at edit level 1. Finally, C is added at edit level 2. Then all three child objects are removed, as shown in Figure 13-4.

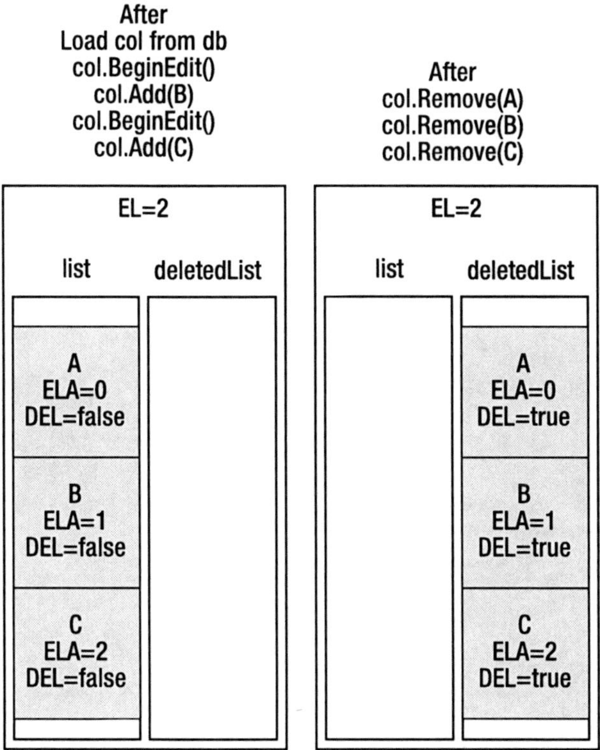

Figure 13-4. *The result after loading, adding, and removing objects*

Suppose ApplyEdit() is now called on the collection. This applies all edits made at edit level 2, putting the collection back to edit level 1. Since child C was added at edit level 2, it simply goes away, but child B sticks around because it was added at edit level 1, which is illustrated in Figure 13-5.

Both objects remain marked for deletion because the changes made at edit level 2 were *applied*. Were CancelEdit() called now, the collection would return to the same state as when the first BeginEdit() was called, meaning that only child A (not marked for deletion) would be left.

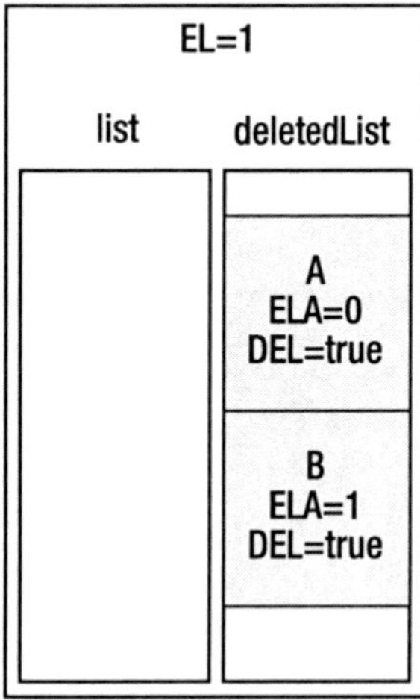

Figure 13-5. *Result after calling ApplyEdit*

Alternatively, a call to `ApplyEdit()` would commit all changes made at edit level 1: child `A` would continue to be marked for deletion, and child `B` would be totally discarded because it was added and deleted at edit level 1. Both of these possible outcomes are illustrated in Figure 13-6.

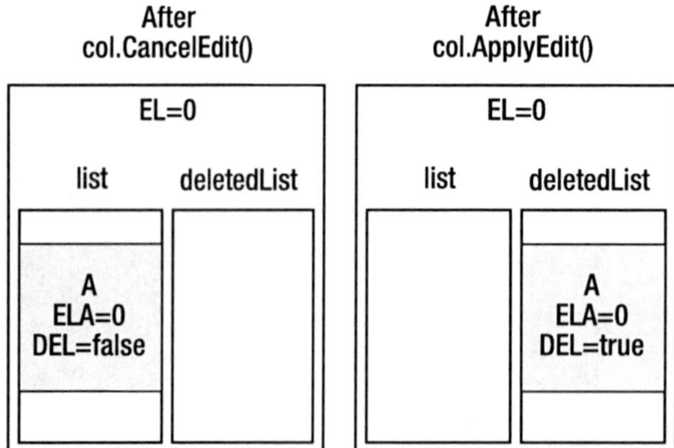

Figure 13-6. *Result after calling either CancelEdit or ApplyEdit*

Having gone through all that, let's take a look at the code that implements these behaviors. The `DeleteChild()` and `UnDeleteChild()` methods deal with marking the child objects as deleted and moving them between the active items in the collection and the `DeletedList` object:

```
private void DeleteChild(C child)
{
  // set child edit level
  Core.UndoableBase.ResetChildEditLevel(child, this.EditLevel, false);
  // remove from the index
  RemoveIndexItem(child);
  // remove from the position map
  RemoveFromMap(child);
  // mark the object as deleted
  child.DeleteChild();
  // and add it to the deleted collection for storage
  DeletedList.Add(child);
}

private void UnDeleteChild(C child)
{
  // since the object is no longer deleted, remove it from
  // the deleted collection
  DeletedList.Remove(child);

  // we are inserting an _existing_ object so
  // we need to preserve the object's editleveladded value
  // because it will be changed by the normal add process
  int saveLevel = child.EditLevelAdded;
  InsertIndexItem(child);
  Add(child);
  child.EditLevelAdded = saveLevel;
}
```

On the surface, this doesn't seem too complicated—but look at the code that deals with the child's `EditLevelAdded` property in the `UnDeleteChild()` method. In the `InsertItem()` method I discussed earlier, the assumption is that any child being added to the collection is a new object and therefore `InsertItem()` sets its edit level value to the collection's current value. However, the `InsertItem()` method is run when this *preexisting* object is reinserted into the collection, altering *its* edit level. That would leave the child object with an incorrect edit level value.

The problem is that in this case, the child object isn't a new object; it is a preexisting object that is just being restored to the collection. To solve this, the object's edit level value is stored in a temporary field, the child object is re-added to the collection, and then the child object's edit level value is reset to the original value, effectively leaving it unchanged.

CopyState

Everything has so far laid the groundwork for the n-level undo functionality. All the pieces now exist to make it possible to implement the `CopyState()`, `UndoChanges()`, and `AcceptChanges()` methods, and then the `BeginEdit()`, `CancelEdit()` and `ApplyEdit()` methods.

The `CopyState()` method needs to take a snapshot of the collection's current state. It is invoked when the `BeginEdit()` method is called on the root object (either the collection itself or the collection's parent object). At that time, the root object takes a snapshot of its own state and calls `CopyState()` on any child objects or collections so they can take snapshots of their states as well:

```
void Core.IUndoableObject.CopyState(
  int parentEditLevel, bool parentBindingEdit)
{
  if (!parentBindingEdit)
    CopyState(parentEditLevel);
}

private void CopyState(int parentEditLevel)
{
  if (this.EditLevel + 1 > parentEditLevel)
    throw new Core.UndoException(
      string.Format(Resources.EditLevelMismatchException, "CopyState"));

  // we are going a level deeper in editing
  _editLevel += 1;

  // cascade the call to all child objects
  foreach (C child in this)
    child.CopyState(_editLevel, false);

  // cascade the call to all deleted child objects
  foreach (C child in DeletedList)
    child.CopyState(_editLevel, false);
}
```

There are technically two CopyState() methods—one for the Csla.Core.IUndoableObject interface and the other a private implementation for use within BusinessListBase itself. The interface implementation merely delegates to the private implementation.

As CopyState() takes a snapshot of the collection's state, it increases the edit level by one. Remember that UndoableBase relies on the Stack object to track the edit level, but this code just uses a simple numeric counter. A collection has no state of its own, so there's nothing to add to a stack of states. Instead, a collection is only responsible for ensuring that all the objects it *contains* take snapshots of their states. All it needs to do is keep track of how many times CopyState() has been called, so the collection can properly implement the adding and removing of child objects, as described earlier.

Notice that the CopyState() call is also cascaded to the objects in DeletedList. This is important because those objects might at some point get restored as active objects in the collection. Even though they're not active at the moment (because they're marked for deletion), they need to be treated the same as regular nondeleted objects.

Overall, this process is *fairly* straightforward: the CopyState() call is just cascaded down to the child objects. The same can't be said for UndoChanges() or AcceptChanges().

UndoChanges

The UndoChanges() method is more complex than the CopyState() method. It too cascades the call down to the child objects, deleted or not, but it also needs to find any objects added since the latest snapshot. Those objects must be removed from the collection and discarded because an undo operation means that it must be as though they were never added. Furthermore, it needs to find any objects deleted since the latest snapshot. Those objects must be re-added to the collection.

Here's the complete method:

```
void Core.IUndoableObject.UndoChanges(
  int parentEditLevel, bool parentBindingEdit)
{
  if (!parentBindingEdit)
    UndoChanges(parentEditLevel);
}

private bool _completelyRemoveChild;

private void UndoChanges(int parentEditLevel)
{
  C child;

  if (this.EditLevel - 1 < parentEditLevel)
    throw new Core.UndoException(
      string.Format(Resources.EditLevelMismatchException, "UndoChanges"));

  // we are coming up one edit level
  _editLevel -= 1;
  if (_editLevel < 0) _editLevel = 0;

  bool oldRLCE = this.RaiseListChangedEvents;
  this.RaiseListChangedEvents = false;
  try
  {
    // Cancel edit on all current items
    for (int index = Count - 1; index >= 0; index--)
    {
      child = this[index];

      DeferredLoadIndexIfNotLoaded();
      _indexSet.RemoveItem(child);

      child.UndoChanges(_editLevel, false);

      _indexSet.InsertItem(child);

      // if item is below its point of addition, remove
      if (child.EditLevelAdded > _editLevel)
      {
        bool oldAllowRemove = this.AllowRemove;
        try
        {
          this.AllowRemove = true;
          _completelyRemoveChild = true;
          RemoveIndexItem(child);
          RemoveAt(index);
        }
```

```
          finally
          {
            _completelyRemoveChild = false;
            this.AllowRemove = oldAllowRemove;
          }
        }
      }

      // cancel edit on all deleted items
      for (int index = DeletedList.Count - 1; index >= 0; index--)
      {
        child = DeletedList[index];
        child.UndoChanges(_editLevel, false);
        if (child.EditLevelAdded > _editLevel)
        {
          // if item is below its point of addition, remove
          DeletedList.RemoveAt(index);
        }
        else
        {
          // if item is no longer deleted move back to main list
          if (!child.IsDeleted) UnDeleteChild(child);
        }
      }
    }
    finally
    {
      this.RaiseListChangedEvents = oldRLCE;
      OnListChanged(new ListChangedEventArgs(ListChangedType.Reset, -1));
    }
  }
```

First of all, `_editLevel` is decremented to indicate that one call to `CopyState()` has been countered.

Notice that the loops going through the collection itself and the `DeletedList` collections go from bottom to top, using a numeric index value. This is important because it allows safe removal of items from each collection. Neither a `foreach` loop nor a forward-moving numeric index would allow removal of items from the collections without causing a runtime error.

`UndoChanges()` is called on all child objects in the collection so that they can restore their individual states. After a child object's state is restored, the child object's edit level is checked to see when it was added to the collection. If the collection's new edit level is less than the edit level when the child object was added, it is a new child object that now must be discarded:

```
// if item is below its point of addition, remove
if (child.EditLevelAdded > _editLevel)
{
  bool oldAllowRemove = this.AllowRemove;
  try
  {
    this.AllowRemove = true;
    _completelyRemoveChild = true;
    RemoveIndexItem(child);
    RemoveAt(index);
  }
```

```
      finally
      {
        _completelyRemoveChild = false;
        this.AllowRemove = oldAllowRemove;
      }
    }
```

The same process occurs for the objects in DeletedList; again, UndoChanges() is called on each child object. Then there's a check to see if the child object is a newly added object that can now be discarded:

```
    if (child.EditLevelAdded > _editLevel)
    {
      // if item is below its point of addition, remove
      DeletedList.RemoveAt(index);
    }
```

A bit more work is required when dealing with the deleted child objects. It is possible that the undo operation needs to undelete an object. Remember that the IsDeleted flag is automatically maintained by UndoChanges(), so it is possible that the child object is no longer marked for deletion. In such a case, the object must be moved back into the active list:

```
    else
    {
      // if item is no longer deleted move back to main list
      if (!child.IsDeleted) UnDeleteChild(child);
    }
```

At the end of the process, the collection object and all its child objects will be in the state they were when CopyState() was last called. Any changes, additions, or deletions will have been undone.

AcceptChanges

The AcceptChanges() method isn't nearly as complicated as UndoChanges(). It also decrements the _editLevel field to counter one call to CopyState(). The method then cascades the AcceptChanges() call to each child object so that each child object can accept its own changes. The only complex bit of code is that the "edit level added" value of each child must also be altered:

```
void Core.IUndoableObject.AcceptChanges(
  int parentEditLevel, bool parentBindingEdit)
{
  if (!parentBindingEdit)
    AcceptChanges(parentEditLevel);
}

private void AcceptChanges(int parentEditLevel)
{
  if (this.EditLevel - 1 < parentEditLevel)
    throw new Core.UndoException(
      string.Format(Resources.EditLevelMismatchException, "AcceptChanges"));

  // we are coming up one edit level
  _editLevel -= 1;
  if (_editLevel < 0) _editLevel = 0;
```

```
    // cascade the call to all child objects
    foreach (C child in this)
    {
      child.AcceptChanges(_editLevel, false);
      // if item is below its point of addition, lower point of addition
      if (child.EditLevelAdded > _editLevel) child.EditLevelAdded = _editLevel;
    }

    // cascade the call to all deleted child objects
    for (int index = DeletedList.Count - 1; index >= 0; index--)
    {
      C child = DeletedList[index];
      child.AcceptChanges(_editLevel, false);
      // if item is below its point of addition, remove
      if (child.EditLevelAdded > _editLevel)
        DeletedList.RemoveAt(index);
    }
  }
```

While looping through the collection and `DeleteList`, the code makes sure that no child object maintains an `EditLevelAdded` value that's higher than the collection's new edit level.

Think back to the `LineItem` example and suppose the collection is at edit level 1 and the changes are accepted. In this case, the newly added `LineItem` object is to be kept—it's valid. Because of this, its `EditLevelAdded` property needs to be the same as the collection object, so it needs to be set to 0 as well.

This is important because there's nothing to stop the user from starting a *new* edit session and raising the collection's edit level to 1 again. If the user then cancels the operation, the collection shouldn't remove the previous `LineItem` object accidentally. It was already accepted once, and it should *stay* accepted.

This method won't remove any items from the collection as changes are accepted, so the simpler `foreach` looping structure can be used rather than the bottom-to-top numeric looping structure needed in the `UndoChanges()` method.

When looping through the `DeletedList` collection, however, the bottom-to-top approach is still required. This is because `DeletedList` may contain child items newly added to the collection and then marked for deletion. Since they are *new* objects, they have no corresponding data in the database, so they can simply be dropped from the collection in memory. In such a case, those child objects are removed from the list based on their edit level value.

This completes all the functionality needed to support n-level undo, allowing `BusinessListBase` to integrate with the code in the `UndoableBase` class.

BeginEdit, CancelEdit, and ApplyEdit

With the n-level undo methods complete, it is possible to implement the methods that the UI needs to control the edit process on a collection. Remember, though, that this control is only valid if the collection is a root object. If it's a child object, its edit process should be controlled by its parent object. This requires a check to ensure that the object isn't a child before allowing these methods to operate:

```
public void BeginEdit()
{
  if (this.IsChild)
    throw new NotSupportedException(Resources.NoBeginEditChildException);

  CopyState(this.EditLevel + 1);
}
```

```
public void CancelEdit()
{
  if (this.IsChild)
    throw new NotSupportedException(Resources.NoCancelEditChildException);

  UndoChanges(this.EditLevel - 1);
}

public void ApplyEdit()
{
  if (this.IsChild)
    throw new NotSupportedException(Resources.NoApplyEditChildException);

  AcceptChanges(this.EditLevel - 1);
}
```

All three methods are very straightforward and allow developers to create a UI that starts editing a collection with `BeginEdit()`, let the user interact with the collection, and then either cancel or accept the changes with `CancelEdit()` or `ApplyEdit()`.

These methods also provide the implementation for `ISupportUndo`, allowing a UI developer or other framework author to polymorphically interact with n-level undo on any editable object.

Conclusion

The n-level undo functionality provided by CSLA .NET is very flexible and powerful. It is also designed to incur no overhead if it isn't used. Many web applications or service-oriented applications don't need this feature so pay no cost in terms of performance.

Virtually all Windows Forms and WPF applications use at least the support provided for data binding and can choose to leverage the more powerful features for certain types of user interface.

Although the implementation of undo is quite complex and must deal with many edge cases, thanks to data binding and changes to the .NET Framework over the years, the complexity is encapsulated within CSLA .NET. Business object and UI developers can use the abstract API exposed by `ISupportUndo` or simply use data binding to interact with the undo functionality.

You may have noticed that there are numerous points in `BusinessListBase` where methods are called to maintain index maps. This is required for LINQ to CSLA, which is the topic of Chapter 14.

CHAPTER 14

LINQ to CSLA

With the introduction of LINQ, the entire language for how we interact with collections of objects, data, XML files, and any other IEnumerable<T> structure has been updated. LINQ provides a unified language—a single syntax for dealing with diverse structures. It opens many exciting possibilities for reducing the volume of source code.

In this chapter, I will show you how to take advantage of the features in LINQ to CSLA in order to reduce the amount of source code you write dealing with CSLA .NET collections. I will then explain the implementation of features in LINQ to CSLA, including indexing and making the results of LINQ queries bindable.

Reducing Code with LINQ

Consider the following code, written without using LINQ:

```
List<Project> lateProjects = new List<Project>();
foreach(Project project in allProjects)
{
  if (project.DueDate < DateTime.Now)
  {
    lateProjects.Add(project);
  }
}
```

LINQ replaces the previous eight lines of code with four lines of code that reveal the intent more clearly:

```
var lateProjects =
  from project in allProjects
  where project.DueDate < DateTime.Now
  select project;
```

Since a goal of CSLA .NET is to reduce the amount of code that you have to write, making CSLA .NET work well with LINQ is a requirement for CSLA .NET 3.5 and higher.

In the first example, not only are you stating what you want, but you're also writing exactly *how* those objects are going to be found. Using LINQ, by contrast, you're writing code at a higher level and specifying *what* you want (projects where the due date is earlier than now). However, you leave to the collection how you want the query to be handled. By having business code focus on the what rather than on the how, you can allow for further optimizations by the framework.

In fact, one optimization in CSLA .NET is a new Indexable attribute on properties of a child class. The Indexable attribute provides hints to the CSLA .NET collection classes about where they might create indexes. The collection classes, in turn, create and maintain indexes on properties in their child classes that are marked `Indexable`. Any code written the old way—because it specified not only *what* but *how*—would not be able to take advantage of that optimization without recoding. The latter example, by contrast, requires no updates when you decide to use indexes with your collection. I'll discuss indexes more in the next section.

Overview of LINQ to CSLA .NET

While LINQ provides some great opportunities, it also presents special challenges to the implementers of frameworks. One of the chief reasons for implementing a business object framework is the reduction of UI code you need to write to implement a solution. Therefore, the ability to bind collections that inherit from `BusinessListBase` is a critical component of a framework like CSLA .NET.

Binding to Results from LINQ to Objects

Just as collections that inherit from `BusinessListBase` should work properly with binding, so should the result of LINQ queries that are run over collections of `BusinessListBase` objects. Unfortunately, the result of a standard query from LINQ to Objects is a type called `Sequence<U>`. As shown in Figure 14-1, this new collection doesn't have awareness of the collection from which it is generated. This means that operations on the result of the query, such as change tracking and collection-level validation, will fail to work as expected, due to the fact that the new collection has no awareness of the old one.

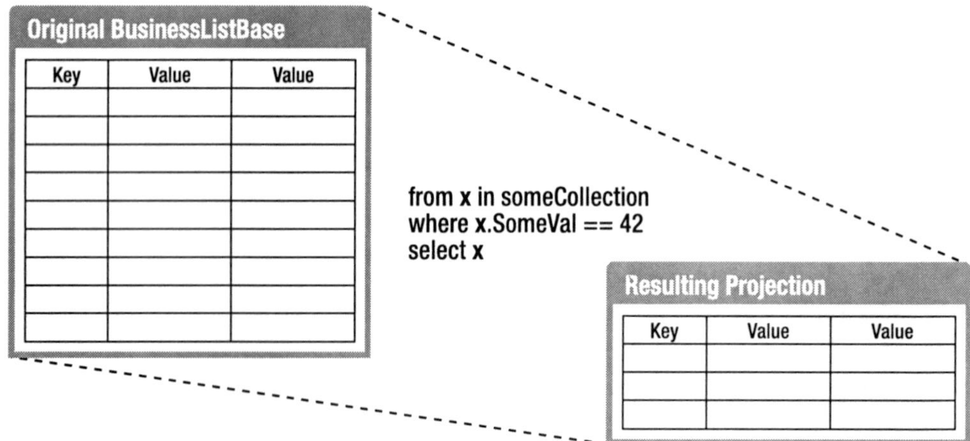

Figure 14-1. *Binding from a projection*

The overall goal in the development of LINQ to CSLA .NET is to make it possible to use LINQ with CSLA .NET collections and have data binding behavior work as expected. Namely, the goal is to make it so that you can bind to the result of a LINQ query performed against a CSLA .NET collection and have all the behavior you would expect when binding to the entire collection itself. Later in this chapter, I'll provide more detail about how this works.

Indexed LINQ Queries

Unlike most standard collections in the .NET Framework, such as `List<T>` and `Dictionary<K,V>`, collections in CSLA .NET are aware of changes that occur in the objects they contain. Because of this, my colleague Aaron Erickson and I have added the ability for business collections to optimize queries through the implementation of indexes. Let's say you're using LINQ to query against CSLA .NET collections under CSLA .NET 3.5 or higher. If you've marked fields as indexable using the `Indexable` attribute, then the implementation of `Where()`—the method that makes filtering work in the query—will take advantage of indices internal to the collection.

LINQ and Projection

Running a query against any `IEnumerable<T>` and generating a `Sequence<U>` of results using LINQ to Objects is called *projection*. The execution of a simple LINQ to Objects query has two main parts: a `where` clause, which applies criteria (in the form of an anonymous delegate or lambda) to find items, and a `select` clause, which transforms each result into something else. Let's start with a typical LINQ query, such as this one that selects numbers equal to 42 from an array of numbers and returns the square of the result:

```
var coolNumbers = from n in allNumbers where n == 42 select n * n;
```

The LINQ query syntax is merely syntactic sugar that you can rewrite in more traditional form as follows:

```
var coolNumbers = allNumbers.Where(n => n == 42).Select(n => n*n);
```

This core mechanism—filter and project—is at the heart of every LINQ query. The filter (`where`) determines which items from the collection matter, and the projection (`select`) transforms each result from one thing into another thing.

■ **Note** The term *projection* refers to the collection you can generate from the result of the `Select()` method.

Not all projections are equivalent. For example, let's say you call `Select()` like this: `.Select(n => n*0)`. In this case, it is impossible to determine how a change in the projected object should be reflected in the original. Since each result of `n*0` is always `0`, there is no information in the resulting object that would allow you to know which object it maps back to in the source collection. Because of the lack of a definitive mapping, synchronization of any individual item is impossible.

That said, in certain cases—such as the projection of the same object type you started with in the original collection (an *identity projection*) where you're operating on exactly the same object type you started with—you don't have to worry about trying to figure out how changes in the projection reflect back to changes in the original. You can map an object in the projected collection back to the source collection in a way that is deterministic. This fact makes it possible for CSLA .NET to allow for binding to this type of projection.

Identity Projections and LinqBindingList<T>

An identity projection is a query in which the result of the query contains items of the same type as the source collection. In CSLA .NET 3.5 and higher, identity projections are handled in a special way that allows for binding to the projection. CSLA .NET changes the behavior of queries such that if you run an identity projection over `BusinessListBase`, you will get a result known as a `LinqBindingList<T>`.

Understanding LinqBindingList

The best way to understand `LinqBindingList` is to think about it as a filter over `BusinessListBase`. When you remove an item from a `LinqBindingList`, it not only removes the item from the list, but it removes the item from the source list, and it removes any other `LinqBindingList` instances from queries generated earlier from the same source `BusinessListBase`, as shown in Figure 14-2. If you change a property in an item from within the `LinqBindingList`, the n-level undo mechanism in `BusinessListBase` will track the change.

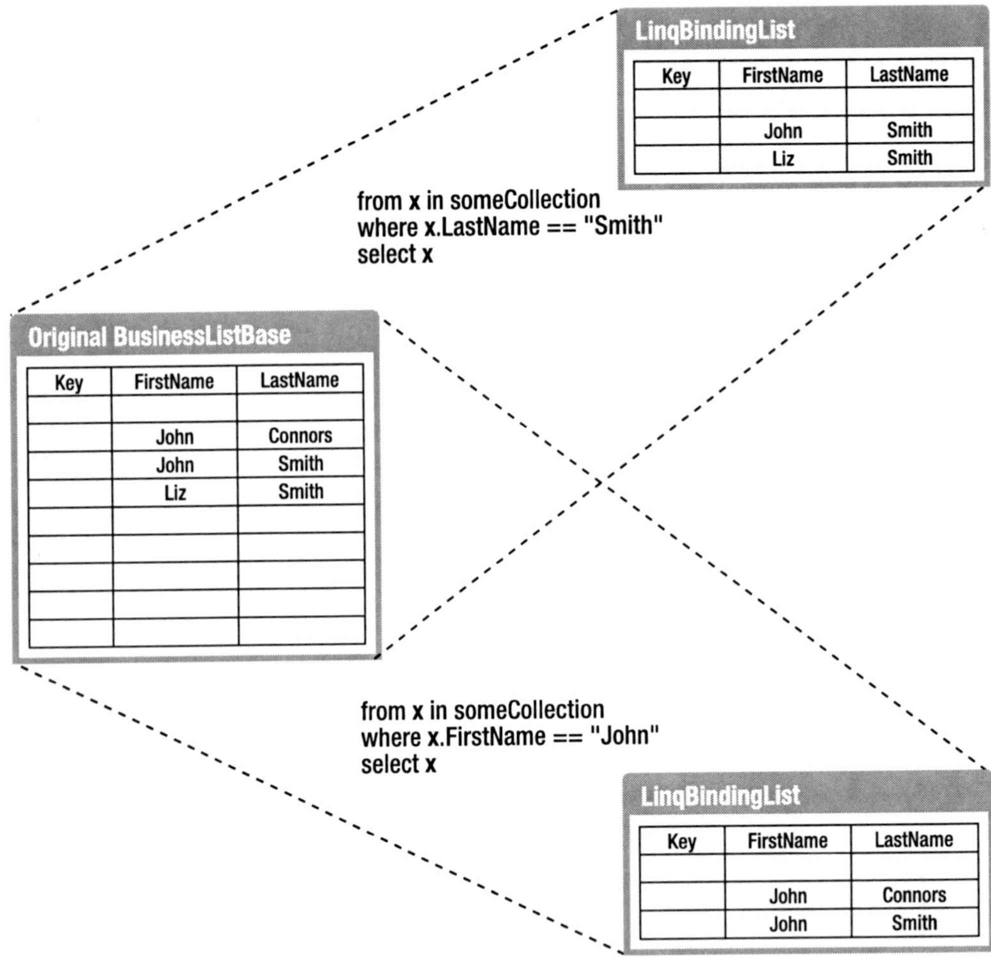

Figure 14-2. *Relationships between BusinessListBase and derived instances of LinqBindingList*

Adding an item to a `LinqBindingList` is possible, but only items that meet the criteria that were present upon creating the list using LINQ will appear in the `LinqBindingList`. On the other hand, adding an item to a `LinqBindingList` adds the item to the original list as well as any other `LinqBindingList` instances that resulted from queries against the original collection of business objects.

In the event that you decide to do a query from a `LinqBindingList`, another list of type `LinqBindingList` will be generated. It will act as though it were generated from the original list—not the sublist—and will exhibit all the behaviors described previously.

`LinqBindingList` is a class that is only ever meant to be produced from an identity projection performed over a class that derives from `BusinessListBase`. In this respect, it is similar to the `Sequence` class that LINQ to Objects provides, in that it is strictly the result of a LINQ query and not a structure that you would ever create outside of this context.

Overview of Indexed Search Using CSLA .NET

When searching for items in a BusinessListBase- or ReadOnlyListBase-based list, CSLA .NET is capable of doing an optimized search using an internal index if your child class marks the properties you are searching on as Indexable.

When either of the main collection classes in CSLA .NET encounters a child class with an Indexable attribute on a property, an internal index is built the first time a search using LINQ is conducted on that class. In cases where the property that is considered Indexable is IComparable, the indexing mechanism is a red-black tree. In cases where the property to be indexed is not IComparable (such as Color), the indexing mechanism is based on Dictionary<T>. Common IComparable property types that tend to be indexed are String, int, and DateTime, although others with custom IComparable implementations are possible.

Note CSLA .NET supports the ability to plug in your own indexing provider via the IndexingProvider property on BusinessListBase and ReadOnlyListBase. Note that doing so is not for the faint of heart. I provide more information about how to implement such a provider at the end of this chapter.

In either case, it is important to understand that all optimizations come at a cost. By implementing indexing on your objects, you are making add, remove, and update operations slower on your objects, and, in exchange, gaining tremendous benefits for optimization of searches. When you use indexing properly on large collections of business objects in memory on fields where comparison is a costly operation (such as strings), you can gain performance improvements that are several orders of magnitude faster. However, using indexing on fields that are not searched frequently and/or are updated frequently can actually cause performance to degrade. It is critical to have a sense for how you're going to use your child class when you start to use the Indexable attribute on properties within it, just like you would be careful about how you apply an index to a database table.

Serialization and Indexing

When a CSLA .NET collection is serialized, the indices within the collection do not pass the serialization boundary. This would be possible in theory, but the performance implications of having not only the objects themselves but all the indices on those objects get passed over the wire are not insignificant. In addition, the indexing mechanism depends on hash-code generation of objects that is only consistent at the scope of a physical machine—that is, hash codes are not guaranteed to be equivalent on, say, a 64-bit operating system and a 32-bit operating system—so it would be impractical to translate the index values during serialization in the absence of a generic hash code generator that could guarantee durability across machine boundaries.

While the index itself is not passed over the serialization boundary, the index is re-created according to the options specified on the child class. This typically happens upon the first instance of a query that utilizes the index on the other side of the serialization boundary.

Index Mode

When marking a child class using the Indexable attribute, you can further specify the behavior of the index. In some cases, you might think it is desirable to force the creation of an index for a child class. For example, if you know for sure that you are going to use the index and you don't want to take the performance hit the first time you use it, you would use the IndexModeAlways option on the attribute. This way, when items are added, they're indexed immediately rather than the first time a query needs it. On the other hand, if it is important to optimize for load time on the collection, and if it is acceptable to take the hit on index creation the first time you do a query that may take advantage of the index, you would use IndexModeOnDemand. The IndexModeNever option is provided to mark cases in which you want to ensure that indexes are never created on a field.

Table 14-1 summarizes the parameters of the Indexable attribute.

Table 14-1. *Index Modes*

Parameter	Description
IndexModeEnum.IndexModeOnDemand	Load an index only when needed.
IndexModeEnum.IndexModeAlways	Always load and maintain an index for this property.
IndexModeEnum.IndexModeNever	Never create an index for this property.

The following example illustrates the use of the Indexable attribute on a child class:

```
class Student : BusinessBase {
  [Indexable(IndexModeEnum.IndexModeNever)]
  public byte[] Photo {get; set; } //we never search by photo
  [Indexable(IndexModeEnum.IndexModeAlways)]
  public string SSN {get; set; } //we search by SSN all the time
  [Indexable(IndexModeEnum.IndexModeOnDemand)]
  public string FirstName {get; set; } //not as common of a search
  [Indexable]
  public string LastName {get; set; } // default is IndexModeOnDemand
}
```

The IQueryable Implementation for CSLA .NET

When fully implemented, the IQueryable interface is the mechanism by which anyone can provide his own implementation of LINQ. LINQ to XML, LINQ to SQL, and dozens of other LINQ providers all implement this interface. Thus, in order to provide the expected behavior when you run a LINQ query against BusinessListBase, IQueryable has been implemented for BusinessListBase.

The IQueryable interface mandates only three members be implemented. Table 14-2 shows which members are required for an IQueryable implementation.

Table 14-2. *IQueryable Members*

Member	Description
ElementType	Provides the source type for the implementation
Expression	The most recent expression tree associated with the collection
Provider	The IQueryProvider implementation used by IQueryable

ElementType and Expression both have reasonably simple implementations. In CSLA .NET, ElementType simply returns an instance of the child type as follows:

```
public Type ElementType
{
  get { return typeof(C); }
}
```

The Expression property is also fairly simple. It returns the expression tree associated with the collection (I'll cover expression trees in the next section). In BusinessListBase, this represents the entire collection, because you use LinqBindingList rather than BusinessListBase to represent the result of a query. In BusinessListBase, Expression returns a private backing field where the current expression is held.

```
public Expression Expression
{
  get {
      if (_expression == null)
          _expression = Expression.Constant(this);
      return _expression;
  }
}
```

The last member in any IQueryable implementation is the Provider property. The Provider is where the core of any IQueryable implementation really occurs. The property itself is fairly simple, returning a new instance of the CslaQueryProvider:

```
public IQueryProvider Provider
{
  get {
    return new Linq.CslaQueryProvider<T, C>(this);
  }
}
```

CslaQueryProvider is the CSLA .NET implementation of the IQueryProvider interface, which defines a custom implementation of LINQ. Of course, the devil is in the details, and understanding how an IQueryProvider works is key to understanding what LINQ to CSLA .NET is doing behind the scenes.

Understanding Expression Trees

The key to understanding LINQ is to understand the role of expression trees in the implementation of LINQ. Expression trees are representations of source code as data. Consider the following code passed to the Where() method in LINQ:

```
var result = someCollection.Where( x => x.SomeVal == 42);
```

The parameter provided to the Where() method is a lambda function—a more compact syntax for an anonymous method. However, when Where() is invoked, the lambda function is converted into a data structure in the form of an expression tree that looks like Figure 14-3.

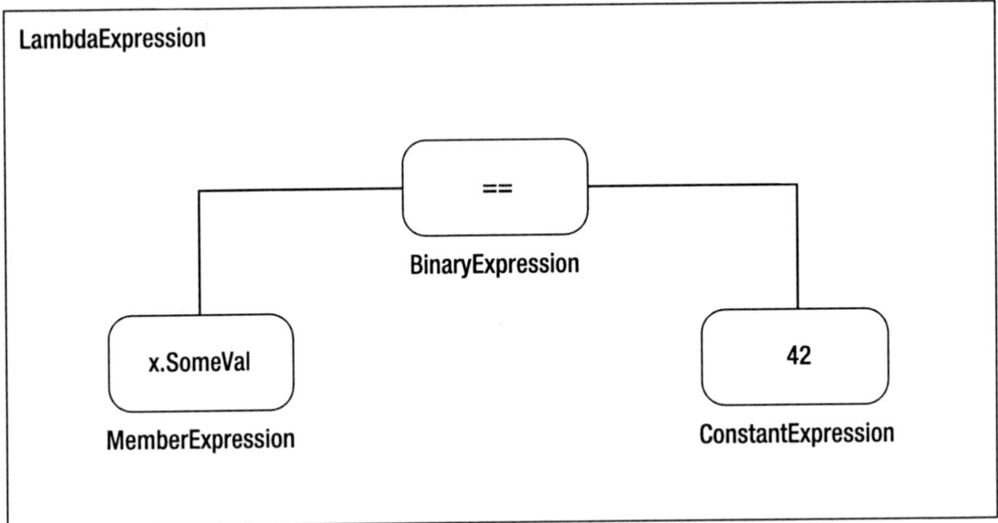

Figure 14-3. *A simple expression tree*

Expression trees allow for code to be executed by alternative means—that is, the code can be translated to other forms, such as SQL. For example, in LINQ to SQL, the previous expression will get converted into the following SQL query:

```
SELECT * FROM someCollection WHERE SomeVal = 42
```

What the expression gets converted to in other LINQ providers will vary according to the provider. For example, LINQ to XML could convert the expression to an XPath expression that ordinary code in the `System.Xml` namespace could execute.

In CSLA .NET, the key differences in how expressions are handled occur in two areas. First, the optimization of `Where` takes advantage of indexing (which I cover in detail later in this chapter). Second, CSLA .NET makes sure that LINQ queries against `BusinessListBase` return a `LinqBindingList` that synchronizes with the collection from which it was originally queried, rather than a `Sequence` that features no such synchronization. The indexing code analyzes the expression passed to the `Where` clause to determine if indexing is possible. The synchronization code analyzes the expression passed to the `Select` clause to determine if the projection is an identity projection, and thus, able to be synchronized.

Digging into IQueryProvider

The `IQueryProvider` interface contains, surprisingly, only four members, as shown in Table 14-3.

Table 14-3. *IQueryProvider Members*

Member	Description
`CreateQuery()`	Handles LINQ methods that return an `IQueryable` result
`CreateQuery<TResult>()`	`CreateQuery()`, but with a known return type
`Execute()`	Handles LINQ methods that return an `IQueryable` result
`Execute<TResult>()`	`Execute()`, but with a known return type

Of course, within this somewhat simple interface lies a great deal of complexity. The parameter provided to CreateQuery() or Execute() is an object of type Expression, which we must evaluate in a manner that returns an expected result. To further complicate this, when you choose to implement your own IQueryProvider, you give up the default LINQ to Objects implementation and are required to implement the entire range of possible Expression objects that might be passed in.

Evaluating Expression for Synchronization Support

To support synchronization, you must first determine whether you're handling an identity projection. That test, which is in CreateQuery(), is surprisingly simple. This only applies to the generic overload of CreateQuery() (CreateQuery<TResult>()), because in that version, it is known what type of IQueryable needs to be returned.

```
typeof(TElement) == typeof(C)
```

If this test passes, then you have an identity projection, because you'll be returning a collection that is of the same type as the source collection. In this case, you can return a LinqBindingList<C> object that will have all the appropriate information to allow for further query execution.

```
_filter = new LinqBindingList<C>(_parent, this, expression);
_filter.BuildFilterIndex();
return (IQueryable<TElement>)_filter;
```

Because there are corner cases in which the LinqBindingList needs to be referenced by the CslaQueryProvider object later on, you store it as a private field. The LinqBindingList needs to store three critical values, so the constructor takes three parameters: the original collection, the IQueryProvider instance, and the expression. The original collection is the _parent parameter. The IQueryProvider instance, which holds query execution state, is the this parameter. The expression, which allows the LinqBindingList to continue query execution when query results are requested, is the expression parameter.

Handling Non-Identity Projections

When the query does not return an identity projection, the CslaQueryProvider still needs to return the expected result. Also, non-identity projections still should be able to take advantage of the indexing features of CSLA .NET. In such cases, control of the query, outside of handling for the Where() method, is passed to the default implementation provided in LINQ to Objects.

Passing Control to the Default Handler

CreateQuery() and Execute() are called not only when a query is being established or filtered, but also when other LINQ extension methods are invoked, such as Count(), First(), and many others. To understand why the implementation of IQueryProvider works the way it does, you need to understand how LINQ to Objects injects itself into any IEnumerable.

All the methods in LINQ to Objects are implemented as static extension methods on the IEnumerable interface, defined in the Enumerable and Queryable classes in the System.Linq namespace. In fact, this is the reason why only upon including the System.Linq namespace do the LINQ extension methods come into scope. Implementation of IQueryable on a custom class changes this relationship. It is, by default, an all-or-nothing relationship, which means that once you implement your own IQueryProvider, you're expected to handle the entire set of extension methods defined on Enumerable (or at least, pass back a NonSupportedException).

However, in a case like CSLA .NET, a special problem is presented. Because you're overriding only part of LINQ, you have no desire to re-implement the other more than 100 members that constitute LINQ. To help with this, CSLA .NET matches the Expression passed to CreateQuery() or Execute()

against one of the static methods on the Enumerable class. The following snippet from the CreateQuery() implementation shows an example of this:

```
MethodCallExpression mex = (MethodCallExpression) expression;
Type listType = typeof(Enumerable);
MethodInfo[] listMethods = listType.GetMethods();
foreach (MethodInfo method in listMethods)
  if (MethodsEquivalent(mex,method))
  {
    Type[] genericArguments = mex.Method.GetGenericArguments();
    MethodInfo genericMethodInfo = method.MakeGenericMethod(genericArguments);
    var testObject = genericMethodInfo.Invoke(null, paramList.ToArray());
    IQueryable<TElement> objectQuery =
      ((IEnumerable<TElement>)testObject).AsQueryable<TElement>();
    return objectQuery;
  }
```

The code is fairly straightforward, with MethodsEquivalent() doing most of the work to determine whether a given MethodCallExpression (which all calls to CreateQuery() or Execute() pass) is logically equivalent to a given reflected method definition that comes from the Enumerable static class.

Once the correct MethodInfo from Enumerable is found, it is converted into a generic method call, which is then invoked dynamically via reflection and returned to the caller. The process is similar regardless of whether CreateQuery() or Execute() is being called.

This technique that CSLA .NET uses to match the Expression to the correct implementation using the MethodsEquivalent() function should continue to work even in the event that Microsoft adds more extension methods to IEnumerable<T> and implements them in the static Enumerable class. However, if Microsoft were to update the class name that holds the LINQ to Objects extension methods, a change to CSLA .NET would be required to support it.

LinqBindingList

The LinqBindingList<C> holds the details of the query generated by it (the expression and the IQueryProvider) and a reference to the parent list, so that changes, additions, and deletions in LinqBindingList<C> can be propagated to the parent list, and in turn, to other instances of LinqBindingList<C> that are derived from the same source.

LinqBindingList<C> itself implements the IQueryable<T> interface, allowing for subqueries against it that generate further LinqBindingList<C> instances. These subsequent LinqBindingList<C> instances are not children of the source LinqBindingList<C>. rather, they all have the same relationship to the original BusinessListBase<T, C>.

Indexed LINQ and CSLA .NET

Having the ability to analyze the expression tree that is passed to the Where() method in CSLA .NET provides an opportunity to optimize the query. Any indexing implementation is going to require

- Building and maintaining an index
- Intercepting the normal query operation such that the query can utilize the index

Managing the Index Set

Indices are maintained on fields that are marked with the Indexable property under circumstances described earlier in this chapter. These indices are managed through the _indexSet field, which is an object that conforms to the IIndexSet interface.

The index set hooks into the collection by being made aware of all changes, additions, and removals that can affect the index. Calls to methods on the _indexSet are made throughout BusinessListBase and ReadOnlyListBase, making it possible for the _indexSet to maintain itself.

Implementations of IIndex

Depending on the nature of your child object, there are several ways you can find items in a list quickly. As mentioned previously, you can organize those child objects that are comparable—that is, where someObj.SomeVal < x has meaning and is implemented—in a way that makes that query faster. CSLA .NET uses a balanced tree structure—a red-black tree—to perform this function. Other child objects that are not IComparable (such as Color) use a dictionary-based index instead.

One of the responsibilities of the index set is to choose an appropriate implementation of IIndex based on the type of object being indexed. An ideal indexing strategy allows not only for equality-based queries to use the index, but also for range-based queries to use the index.

Indices on IComparable Properties: Red-Black Tree

The red-black tree structure allows you to infer the order of the items. All items to the left of a given node in the tree are guaranteed to be lower. All items to the right of a given node in the tree are guaranteed to be higher. In the less-than operation, the key to making a ranged query work becomes enumerating through the left subtree of the node that either matches or is the lowest value that is higher than the value being compared. In a greater-than operation, it is the exact reverse: enumerating through the right subtree of the node that either matches or is the highest value that is lower than the value being compared.

The performance of lookup over balanced trees, such as red-black trees, is typically log(N) + 2, while retaining a good deal of memory efficiency and the ability to quickly find those items higher or lower than a given item. The performance characteristics of this lookup are good. Because CSLA .NET uses a red-black tree—a tree that guarantees that the depth is no deeper than log(N) + 2—you know that finding one item out of one million will take, at most, 22 comparison operations. Depending on where the item is, that same item without an index can take up to a million comparison operations, since without an index, each object has to be compared.

Indices on Other Properties: Dictionary

When the property you're building an index on does not implement IComparable, you can't use those structures in any kind of tree implementation, since placement of an item in a tree depends on item comparison. Therefore, to implement an index on a non-IComparable property, you need to use a Dictionary to enable fast lookup for equality-based queries.

The performance characteristics of the Dictionary are actually a little bit faster than a red-black tree most of the time, assuming that the GetHashCode() implementation generates a high probability that calls on different objects of your child type generate unique values. However, because there is a chance, however small, that two different objects can generate the same hash code, you may require more than the single compare operation that is typical with Dictionary. If you were to override GetHashCode() in a manner where you return the same number for all instances of your object, you would end up with zero benefit to using indexing at all.

■ **Caution** Implementation of `GetHashCode()` on your own is almost always a bad idea unless you really know what you're doing.

Expression Evaluation

The ability to evaluate the expression passed to the `Where()` extension method is the key that makes any indexing implementation in LINQ possible. LINQ to CSLA .NET evaluates the query to see if it can possibly use an index. If it is unable to use an index, it searches for the item using the same method that LINQ does by itself—namely, it compares each item and returns those items that match.

LINQ does not allow the `Where()` method to have a `LambdaExpression` parameter whose `Body` is anything other than a `BinaryExpression`—that is, something that eventually returns a `true` or `false` result. The nature of the `Where()` operation itself is the application of a test of an object for set inclusion. All `BinaryExpression` objects have `Left` and `Right` properties that represent either side of an expression. For example, consider the following expression:

```
x.MyProperty == 42
```

In this case, the `Left` of the `BinaryExpression` is `x.MyProperty`, and the `Right` of the `BinaryExpression` is `42`. You can also evaluate the `NodeType` of the `BinaryExpression` to learn that it is `ExpressionType.Equal`, indicating that this is an equality test.

Left Evaluation

The left side of the expression is evaluated to determine whether you're doing a query on a child property that has an index. Typically, this means that the `Left` expression is a property lookup, such as `x.MyProperty`. In other words, if the expression is a `MemberExpression`, CSLA .NET will know that you're possibly doing a property lookup on an indexed property. It can then check the `Name` of the `MemberExpression` and validate whether there is an index on a child property that matches the `Name` from the `MemberExpression`. If that test passes—that is, if there is a property lookup on the `Left` side—then you can continue doing an indexed query.

Right Evaluation

After CSLA .NET has determined that you're doing a query on an `Indexable` field, it evaluates the `Right` side to determine the value that you're comparing to. The contents of the right side can be much more variable, including everything from a `ConstantExpression` that represents a value (such as `42`) to something more complex, such as another method call.

In the case of a `ConstantExpression`, CSLA .NET simply casts it back to an object that is comparable to the property on the `Left` side. Other expressions require a dynamic invocation of the expression. You do this by calling the `Compile()` method on the expression, compiling the expression, and subsequently calling `DynamicInvoke()` and executing the expression. The result is an object that should at least be able to be tested for equality, and possibly other operations depending on the `IComparable` status of the property.

Indexed Search

Now that CSLA .NET knows it has an `Indexable` property and a value to compare, it proceeds to utilize the index and uses the `Dictionary` or red-black tree–based implementation of `IIndex` to search the index rather than the collection itself,. If the property is not `Indexable`, CSLA .NET will simply run the search in the default manner that a typical `IEnumerable` would use.

The Indexing Object Model

While the current implementation of indexing allows you to do a great deal of optimization, you can add even more optimization if you want to put forth the effort to do so. The model for indexing, as illustrated in Figure 14-4, is designed to support the provision of your own indexing mechanism, if you wish to extend the indexing capabilities of CSLA .NET.

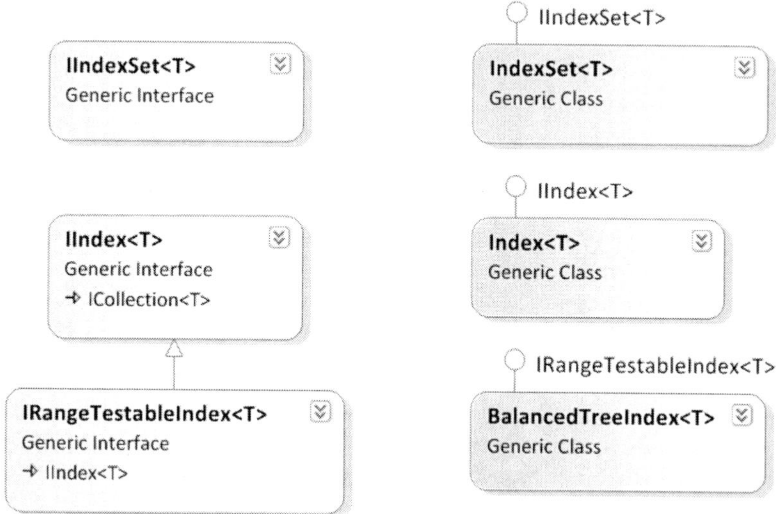

Figure 14-4. *The indexing object model*

In the next section, I'll cover the details of this interface and classes. Should you decide to implement your own indexing provider, you'll have an understanding of the default one provided with CSLA .NET.

IIndexSet

IIndexSet<T> is the initial interface you must implement if you wish to implement your own CSLA .NET indexing provider. Table 14-4 shows the required members for IIndexSet. CSLA .NET base collection classes such as BusinessListBase<C, T> and ReadOnlyListBase<C, T> know how to leverage this interface to take advantage of indexing.

Table 14-4. *IIndexSet Members*

Member	Description
InsertItem(T item)	The index item on all indexable properties
InsertItem(T item, string property)	The index item only on property if it is indexable
RemoveItem(T item)	Removes the item from all indices
RemoveItem(T item, string property)	Removes the item only from the index specified by property

Table 14-4. *IIndexSet Members (Continued)*

Member	Description
`ReindexItem(T item)`	Removes and adds the item from all indices
`ReindexItem(T item, string property)`	Removes and adds the item from a specific index
`ClearIndexes()`	Clears all the indices for all properties
`ClearIndex(string property)`	Clears a specific index
`Search(Expression expr)`	Performs a search, filtering by `expr`
`this [string property]`	Returns the `IIndex<T>` specified by `property`
`Load(string property)`	Creates an index on `property` over the source

`IIndexSet` needs to have a reference to the `IEnumerable` collection that it is indexing, such as `BusinessListBase` and other CSLA .NET collection classes. When you write a class that supports `IIndexSet`, you are typically managing the set of `IIndex` objects (individual indices, described in the following sections) that constitute the index set, and providing the logic for performing the search to determine whether the query can use an index.

You can think of the classes that implement this interface is coordinators for all indexing activity. Classes should evaluate the expression tree passed to `Search()`, determine the correct index to use (if applicable), and then either use the index (if it is an indexed property) or perform the search on the original collection (if there is no available index).

IndexSet

The `IndexSet` concrete class represents the default index provider implementation for CSLA .NET. The class maintains a set of indices appropriate for the property types that it is indexing. It provides an implementation of `Search()` that determines the `IComparable` status of the property being searched, determines the operation being used (such as equality and less-than operations), and assures that the appropriate operation is called on the index.

This class provides an example of most of the expression evaluation techniques I have talked about previously in this chapter. For example, the following method in the `IndexSet` class determines the value on the right side of the expression passed to `Search()`:

```
private object GetRightValue(Expression rightSide)
{
  //rightside is where I get the value...
  switch (rightSide.NodeType)
  {
    //shortcut constants, don't eval these, it will be faster
    case ExpressionType.Constant:
      ConstantExpression constExp = (ConstantExpression)rightSide;
      return (constExp.Value);
    // convert back to lambda and eval to get the value.
    default:
      //Lambdas can be created from expressions...
      LambdaExpression evalRight = Expression.Lambda(rightSide, null);
      //Compile it, invoke it, and get the resulting value
      return (evalRight.Compile().DynamicInvoke(null));
  }
}
```

The key to this code is looking at the type of node you're dealing with. All Expression objects implement the NodeType property, which gives you clues about the nature of the Expression you're dealing with. You now care about only two real cases: whether you have a ConstantExpression, allowing you to bypass a more expensive call to Compile() and DynamicInvoke(), or whether you do not have a constant, in which case you'll have to compile the expression, invoke it, and get the value that it will ultimately return. In either case, you get back an object that boxes the value you want to use in the Search() operation.

■ **Note** Compile() and DynamicInvoke() are expensive operations to conduct. You don't want to be doing these operations on a per-item basis as you search through a data structure.

Determining whether you have an index or not is much simpler.

```
bool IIndexSet<T>.HasIndexFor(string property)
{
  return _internalIndexSet.ContainsKey(property);
}
private bool HasIndexablePropertyOnLeft(Expression leftSide)
{
  if (leftSide.NodeType == ExpressionType.MemberAccess)
    return (
      this as IIndexSet<T>).HasIndexFor(((MemberExpression)leftSide).Member.Name
    );
  else
    return false;
}
```

Determining whether you have an index for a given property specified by a string is relatively simple, as you have an internal field _internalIndexSet that is really just a Dictionary of indices. You can call ContainsKey() on the _internalIndexSet to determine whether you have the index.

The examination of the expression that represents the left side of the total expression is slightly more complex. You need for this left-side expression to be a MemberExpression in order to make any sense of it. Thankfully, this is common, given that it rarely makes sense to have anything other than a MemberExpression on the left side. Note that this may be possible technically (i.e., x => 1 == 1 can be passed, which, in theory, would return all results).

The first thing you do is test the NodeType to ensure that it's a MemberAccess expression. If that is in fact the case, you know you can cast it to a MemberExpression, which then gives you access to the name of the property you're looking at (such as the name SomeProp on the left side, which is in an expression such as x => x.SomeProp == 42). With this information, you have everything you need to determine whether or not you have an index on the property.

Once you have established that you have a property that is Indexable and a value to check against the index, you can test the operation between both sides of the expression to determine which index operation to perform.

```
Func<T, bool> exprCompiled = expr.Compile();
BinaryExpression binExp = (BinaryExpression)expr.Body;
object val = GetRightValue(binExp.Right);
IRangeTestableIndex<T> rangedIndex;
if (_internalIndexSet[property] is IRangeTestableIndex<T>)
{
  rangedIndex = (IRangeTestableIndex<T>)_internalIndexSet[property];
```

```
switch (binExp.NodeType)
{
  case ExpressionType.Equal:

    foreach (T item in
              _internalIndexSet[property].WhereEqual(val, exprCompiled))
      yield return item;
    break;

  case ExpressionType.LessThan:

    foreach (T item in rangedIndex.WhereLessThan(val))
      yield return item;
    break;
    //and so forth, for other operations...
```

Based on the NodeType of the BinaryExpression object (shown as binExp), you can determine whether you have been passed an equality test, a less-than operation, or any other logical test. Of course, you have to make sure the index is IRangeTestableIndex before you try to use it in the context of a ranged logical operator such as less-than or greater-than. However, once you know that, you can handle each operation appropriately. If you can't handle the operation, pass it back to LINQ to Objects to handle in the default manner.

IIndex

IIndex represents the expected methods and behavior that an index should provide. Most implementations of IIndexSet contain one or more IIndex objects per property that is being indexed on T. IIndex derives from ICollection and adds the members shown in Table 14-5.

Table 14-5. *IIndex Members*

Member	Description
IndexField	Returns the PropertyInfo for the property that this index is indexing
WhereEqual()	Returns the items that match the value passed to it
ReIndex()	Removes and adds back the given item from the index
Loaded	Returns whether the index has been established
InvalidateIndex()	Sets the index as not loaded anymore
LoadComplete()	Sets the index as loaded

Writing an IIndex implementation involves implementing all the methods you typically would for ICollection and then adding implementation for the members shown in Table 14-5. A typical implementation wraps an appropriate data structure, such as a red-black tree or dictionary, or possibly even derives from it, and then adds the implementation of the methods, which make indexed operations able to work with an IIndexSet.

The only interesting part of building an IIndex implementation is the handling of WhereEqual(). Typically, WhereEqual() takes the object passed to it—which represents a value from a property of the child object—and uses some mechanism based on that value to find the item in a manner somehow faster than looking through every single one in the index. Exactly how this is done depends on the index structure. In a Dictionary-based structure, a hash code is generated from the property, and then the Where test is performed on each item with a matching hash code. On other structures, such as a red-black tree, the normal search mechanism for such a tree would be used to locate the appropriate key matches.

Index

The Index concrete class represents the default index implementation for child objects in CSLA .NET that don't implement IComparable. Like most IIndex implementations in CSLA .NET, the Index class implements ICollection methods, which then handle the collection operations that are ultimately handled by a private field where the actual index is kept. The following is typical for most ICollection methods in the Index implementation:

```
void ICollection<T>.Add(T item)
{
  DoAdd(item);
}

private void DoAdd(T item)
{
  //_theProp is the PropertyInfo this index is indexing
  if (_theProp != null)
  {
    int hashCode = _theProp.GetValue(item, null).GetHashCode();
    if (_index.ContainsKey(hashCode))
      _index[hashCode].Add(item);
    else
    {
      List<T> newList = new List<T>(1);
      newList.Add(item);
      _index.Add(hashCode, newList);
    }
  }
}
```

For the most part, this aspect of index design—the implementation of the ICollection members—is pretty straightforward. More interesting is the implementation of WhereEqual().

```
IEnumerable<T> IIndex<T>.WhereEqual(object pivotVal, Func<T, bool> expr)
{
  var hashCode = pivotVal.GetHashCode();
  LoadOnDemandIndex();
  if (_index.ContainsKey(hashCode))
    foreach (T item in _index[hashCode])
      if (expr(item))
        yield return item;
}
```

This method is a little more interesting. Because it uses a Dictionary to implement the index behind the scenes, it needs to determine the hash code of the value it is comparing against. Since the index may not be loaded, the method attempts to load the index on demand—a call that will do nothing if the index is already loaded. Once it knows the index is loaded, it can retrieve the list of items that match the hash code, which is returned by _index[hashCode]. Only within this list, which is almost always one or two items unless there is a serious problem with the hash code, does it need to test using expr to make sure that the test passes.

This works because of the relationship between the result of GetHashCode() and Equals(). As a rule, any two objects that are equal must generate the same hash code. The reverse, however, isn't true, as two different objects can generate the same hash code.

As you would expect with an index, the result is that the number of comparisons required to find an item using an index is vastly lower than it would be without an index. In fact, the larger the collection you're using an index on, the more benefit there is to using an index.

IRangeTestableIndex

IRangeTestableIndex<T> extends the IIndex<T> interface by adding support for indices that are capable of optimizing ranged query options, such as those backed by an ordered data structure like a red-black tree. Table 14-6 shows its members.

Table 14-6. *IRangeTestableIndex Members*

Member	Description
WhereLessThan()	Returns the items less than the value passed
WhereLessThanOrEqualTo()	Returns the items less than or equal to the value passed
WhereGreaterThan()	Returns the items greater than the value passed
WhereGreaterThanOrEqualTo()	Returns the items greater than or equal to the value passed

While it is not required to use this interface in any given indexing implementation, the built-in indexing provider, IndexSet<T>, utilizes this interface to specify behavior for those cases where T is IComparable.

BalancedTreeIndex

The BalancedTreeIndex<T> concrete class implementing IRangeTestableIndex represents the default index implementation for child objects in CSLA .NET that implement IComparable. It is fundamentally similar to Index in how it manages its internal collection, but it uses a red-black tree rather than a Dictionary for storage.

One of the methods that IRangeTestableIndex requires is the WhereGreaterThan() method. The implementation of the index passes control to the internal data structure as follows:

```
public IEnumerable<T> WhereGreaterThan(object pivotVal)
{
  var balancedIndex = (IBalancedSearch<T>)_index;
  return balancedIndex.ItemsGreaterThan(pivotVal);
}
```

The red-black tree implementation implements an interface called IBalancedSearch<T>, which takes advantage of the data structure of a balanced tree in order to efficiently iterate through those items greater than the value passed to it.

Understanding the internals of how a red-black tree works is best addressed through others who have written extensively on the subject, notably Robert Sedgewick in his classic, *Algorithms in C++* (Addison-Wesley Professional, 2002), which covers the implementation of red-black trees as well as numerous other useful low-level structures.

Conclusion

In this chapter, I covered how CSLA .NET works with LINQ to Objects. I showed you how to optimize the LINQ to Objects implementation to make sure it provides the expected behavior, and I explained how to use the capabilities of CSLA .NET to increase the performance of your in-memory queries. You should now understand the options for how you can index your collections in CSLA .NET, how projections work against CSLA .NET collections, and how CSLA .NET implements these features. Furthermore, you should have a reasonable idea of how you might get started to write your own indexing provider for CSLA .NET.

I'll provide information about how to use LINQ to SQL—or other LINQ providers in relation to data, for that matter—in Chapter 18, where I discuss the data portal and the various techniques you can use to implement it.

CHAPTER 15

Persistence and the Data Portal

This chapter will continue walking through the framework implementation by focusing on how CSLA .NET provides support for mobile objects. Chapter 1 introduced the concept of mobile objects, including the idea that in an ideal world, business logic would be available both on the client workstation (or web server) and on the application server. In this chapter, the implementation of data access is designed specifically to leverage the concept of mobile objects by enabling objects to move between client and server. When on the client, all the data binding and UI support from Chapters 7 to 13 is available to a UI developer; and when on the server, the objects can be persisted to a database or other data store.

Chapter 2 discussed the idea of a *data portal*. The data portal combines the channel adapter and message router design patterns to provide a simple, clearly defined point of entry to the server for all data access operations. In fact, the data portal entirely hides whether an application server is involved, allowing an application to switch between 2-tier and 3-tier physical deployments without changing any code.

A UI developer is entirely unaware of the use of a data portal. Instead, the UI developer will interact *only* with the business objects created by the business developer.

The business developer will make use of the `DataPortal` class from the `Csla` namespace to create, retrieve, update, and delete all business object data. This `DataPortal` class is the single entry point to the entire data portal infrastructure, which enables mobile objects and provides access to server-side resources such as distributed transaction support. The key features enabled by the data portal infrastructure include

- Enabling mobile objects
- Providing a consistent coding model for root and child objects
- Hiding the network transport (channel adapter)
- Exposing a single point of entry to the server (message router)
- Exposing server-side resources (database engine, distributed transactions, etc.)
- Allowing objects to persist themselves or to use an external persistence model
- Unifying context (passing context data to/from client and server)
- Using Windows integrated (AD) security
- Using CSLA .NET custom authentication (including impersonation)

Meeting all those needs means that the data portal is a complex entity. While to a business developer, it appears to consist only of the simple `DataPortal` class, there's actually a lot going on behind that class.

I've already discussed much of the authentication and authorization support in Chapter 12, but I will discuss some aspects of authentication in this chapter as well. Because the data portal is so complex, I'll spend some time discussing its design before walking through the implementation details.

Data Portal Design

One of the primary goals of object-oriented programming is to encapsulate all the functionality (data and implementation) for a domain object into a single class. This means, for instance, that all the business logic responsible for editing customer information should be in a `CustomerEdit` class.

In many cases, the business logic in an object directly supports a rich, interactive user experience. This is especially true for WPF or Windows Forms applications, in which the business object implements validation and calculation logic that should be run as the user enters values into each field on a form. To achieve this, the objects should be running on the client workstation or web server to be as close to the user as possible.

At the same time, most applications have back-end processing that is not interactive. In an n-tier deployment, this non-interactive business logic should run on an application server. Yet good object-oriented design dictates that all business logic should be encapsulated within objects rather than spread across the application. This can be challenging when an object needs to both interact with the user *and* perform back-end processing. Effectively, the object needs to be on the client sometimes and on the application server other times.

The idea of mobile objects solves this problem by allowing an object to physically move from one machine to another. This means it really is possible to have an object run on the client to interact with the user, then move to the application server to do back-end work like interacting with the database.

A key goal of the data portal is to enable the concept of mobile objects. In the end, not only will objects be able to go to the application server to persist their data to a database, but they will also be able to handle any other non-interactive back-end business behaviors that should run on the application server.

Separation of Business Logic and Data Access

At the same time, as discussed in Chapter 1, it is important to maintain clear logical layers in the application architecture. This means that the business logic and data access should be logically separated.

The term *logically separated* can mean many things. You might consider logical separation to include putting all your data access code into a limited set of predefined methods, and I think that is perfectly valid. Or you might consider logical separation to mean putting the data access code into a separate class or a separate assembly. To me, those are valid as well.

The data portal enables several techniques for logical separation:

- Data access code goes into a limited set of predefined methods.
- Data access code goes into a separate data access class (and optionally separate assembly), invoked by the business object.
- Data access code goes into a separate object factory class (and optionally separate assembly), invoked by the data portal.

All of these techniques provide logical separation of layers, though the latter two offer the psychological benefit of putting the code into a separate class for clarity.

Consistent Coding Model for Root and Child Objects

In Chapters 4 and 5, I walked through the coding model for the various stereotypes directly supported by CSLA .NET. As you can see from the code templates in Chapter 5, the data portal is used to create, retrieve, update, and delete both root and child objects, using a relatively consistent coding pattern for both.

A root object typically implements a set of `DataPortal_XYZ` methods such as `DataPortal_Create()` and `DataPortal_Fetch()`. These methods are invoked by the data portal in response to the business object's factory method calling `DataPortal.Create()` and `DataPortal.Fetch()`.

Similarly, a child object typically implements a set of `Child_XYZ` methods such as `Child_Create()` and `Child_Fetch()`. These methods are invoked by the data portal in response to the child object's factory method calling `DataPortal.CreateChild()` and `DataPortal.FetchChild()`.

Additionally, the field manager discussed in Chapter 7 plays a role in the process. In a parent business object's `DataPortal_Insert()` or `DataPortal_Update()` method, the object must update its child objects as well. This can be done in a single line of code.

```
FieldManager.UpdateChildren();
```

The field manager loops through all child references and has the data portal update each one by calling the appropriate `Child_XYZ` method based on the state of the child object.

`BusinessListBase` also participates by providing a prebuilt `Child_Update()` implementation that updates the collection's list of deleted items and active items. In fact, this method is useful even for a root collection, because the collection's `DataPortal_Update()` can look like this:

```
protected override void DataPortal_Update()
{
  // open database connection
  Child_Update();
  // close database connection
}
```

But what's even nicer is that for a *child collection*, the business developer typically has to write *no code at all* in the collection. The data portal handles updating a child collection automatically as long as the child objects implement `Child_XYZ` methods.

Channel Adapter and Message Router Patterns

The data portal combines two common design patterns: channel adapter and message router.

The channel adapter pattern provides a great deal of flexibility for n-tier applications by allowing the application to switch between 2-tier and 3-tier models, as well as between various network protocols.

The message router pattern helps to decouple the client and server by providing a clearly defined, single point of entry for all server interaction. Each call to the server is routed to an appropriate server-side object.

Channel Adapter

Chapter 1 discussed the costs and benefits of physical n-tier deployments. Ideally, an application will use as few physical tiers as possible. At the same time, it is good to have the flexibility to switch from a 2-tier to a 3-tier model, if needed, to meet future scalability or security requirements.

Switching to a 3-tier model means that there's now a network connection between the client (or web server) and the application server. The primary technology provided by .NET for such communication is WCF. However, this is just one (though the recommended one) of several options:

- WCF
- Remoting
- ASP.NET Web Services (ASMX)
- Enterprise Services (DCOM)

To avoid being locked into a single network communication technology, the data portal applies the channel adapter design pattern.

The channel adapter pattern allows the specific network technology to be changed through configuration rather than through code. A side effect of the implementation shown in this chapter is that *no network* is also an option. Thus, the data portal provides support for 2-tier or 3-tier deployment. In the 3-tier case, it supports various network technologies, all of which are configurable without changing any code.

Figure 15-1 illustrates the flow of a client call as it flows through the data portal.

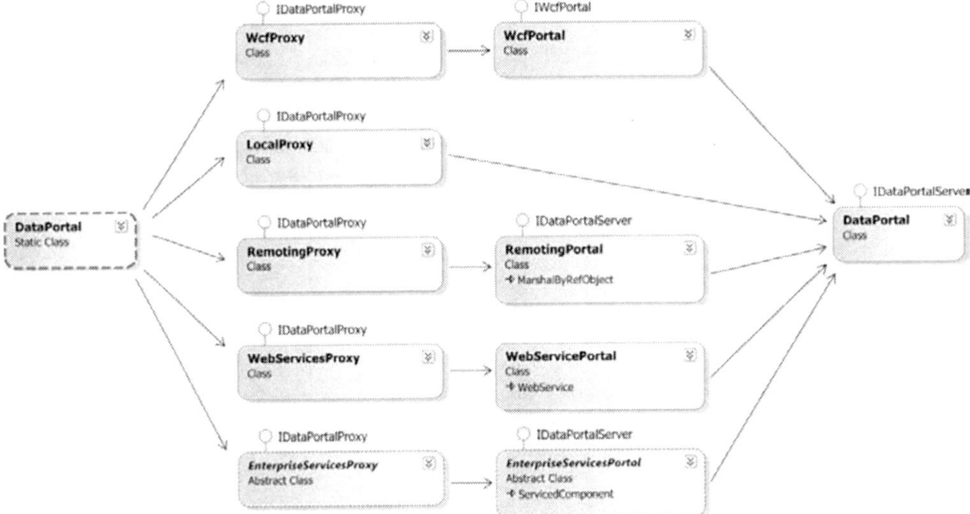

Figure 15-1. *Flow of a client call through the data portal*

Switching from one channel to another is done by changing a configuration file, not by changing code. Notice that the `LocalProxy` channel communicates directly with the `DataPortal` object (from the `Csla.Server` namespace) on the right. This is because it bypasses the network entirely, interacting with the object in memory on the client. All the other channel proxies use network communication to interact with the server-side object.

■ **Tip** The data portal also allows you to create your own proxy/host combination so you can support network channels other than those implemented in this chapter.

Table 15-1 lists the types required to implement the channel adapter portion of the data portal.

Table 15-1. *Types Required for the Channel Adapter Pattern*

Type	Namespace	Description
`MethodCaller`	`Csla.Reflection`	Utility class that encapsulates the use of reflection and dynamic method invocation to find method information and invoke methods
`CallMethodException`	`Csla.Reflection`	Exception thrown by the data portal when an exception occurs while calling a data access method
`RunLocalAttribute`	`Csla`	Attribute applied to a business object's data access methods to force the data portal to *always* run that method on the client, bypassing the configuration settings
`DataPortalEventArgs`	`Csla`	`EventArgs` subclass passed as a parameter for events raised by `Csla.DataPortal`
`DataPortal`	`Csla`	Primary entry point to the data portal infrastructure; used by business developers
`DataPortal<T>`	`Csla`	Primary entry point to the data portal for asynchronous behaviors; used by business developers
`DataPortal`	`Csla.Server`	Portal to the message router functionality on the server; acts as a single point of entry for all server communication
`IDataPortalServer`	`Csla.Server`	Interface defining the methods required for data portal host objects
`IDataPortalProxy`	`Csla.DataPortalClient`	Interface defining the methods required for client-side data portal proxy objects
`WcfProxy`	`Csla.DataPortalClient`	Uses WCF to communicate with a WCF server running in IIS, WAS, or a custom host (typically a Windows service)
`WcfPortal`	`Csla.Server.Hosts`	Exposed on the server by IIS, WAS, or a custom host; called by `WcfProxy`
`LocalProxy`	`Csla.DataPortalClient`	Loads the server-side data portal components directly into memory on the client and runs all "server-side" operations in the client process

Table 15-1. *Types Required for the Channel Adapter Pattern (Continued)*

Type	Namespace	Description
`RemotingProxy`	`Csla.DataPortalClient`	Uses .NET Remoting to communicate with a remoting server running in IIS or within a custom host (typically a Windows service)
`RemotingPortal`	`Csla.Server.Hosts`	Exposed on the server by IIS or a custom host; called by `RemotingProxy`
`EnterpriseServicesProxy`	`Csla.DataPortalClient`	Uses Enterprise Services (DCOM) to communicate with a server running in COM+
`EnterpriseServicesPortal`	`Csla.Server.Hosts`	Exposed on the server by Enterprise Services; called by `EnterpriseServicesProxy`
`WebServicesProxy`	`Csla.DataPortalClient`	Uses Web Services to communicate with a service hosted in IIS
`WebServicePortal`	`Csla.Server.Hosts`	Exposed on the server as a web service by IIS; called by `WebServicesProxy`

The .NET Remoting, Web Services, and Enterprise Services technologies are supported primarily for backward compatibility with older versions of CSLA .NET. I recommend using the WCF technology, and that is the technology I'll focus on in this chapter.

The point of the channel adapter is to allow a client to use the data portal without having to worry about how that call will be relayed to the `Csla.Server.DataPortal` object. Once the call makes it to the server-side `DataPortal` object, the message router pattern becomes important.

Message Router

One important lesson to be learned from the days of COM and MTS/COM+ is that it isn't wise to expose large numbers of classes and methods from a server. When a server exposes dozens or even hundreds of objects, the client must be aware of all of them in order to function.

Note Sadly, this lesson doesn't seem to have informed the designs of many service-oriented systems. Fortunately, the representational state transfer (REST) movement has picked up on the idea of limiting the entry points to a server and is helping to shape the industry in this direction.

If the client is aware of every server-side object, we get tight coupling and fragility. Any change to the server objects typically changes the server's public API, thus breaking all of the clients, often including those clients who aren't even using the object that was changed.

One way to avoid this fragility is to add a layer of abstraction. Specifically, you can implement the server to have a single point of entry that exposes a limited number of methods. This keeps the server's API clear and concise, minimizing the need for a server API change. The data portal will expose only the five methods listed in Table 15-2.

Table 15-2. *Methods Exposed by the Data Portal*

Method	Purpose
`Create()`	Creates a new object, loading it with default values from the database
`Fetch()`	Retrieves an existing object, first loading it with data from the database
`Update()`	Inserts, updates, or deletes data in the database corresponding to an existing object
`Delete()`	Deletes data in the database corresponding to an existing object
`Execute()`	Executes a command stereotype object on the server

Of course, the next question is, with a single point of entry, how do your clients get at the dozens or hundreds of objects on the server? It isn't like they aren't needed! That is the purpose of the message router.

The single point of entry to the server routes all client calls to the appropriate server-side object. If you think of each client call as a message, then this component routes messages to your server-side objects. In CSLA .NET, the message router is `Csla.Server.DataPortal`. Notice that it is also the endpoint for the channel adapter pattern discussed earlier; the data portal knits the two patterns together into a useful whole.

For `Csla.Server.DataPortal` to do its work, all server-side objects must conform to a standard design so the message router knows how to invoke them. Remember, the message router merely routes messages to objects—it is the object that actually does useful work in response to the message.

Figure 15-2 illustrates the flow of a call through the message router implementation. The `DataPortal` class (on the left of Figure 15-2) represents the `Csla.Server.DataPortal`—which was the rightmost entity in Figure 15-1. It relies on a `SimpleDataPortal` object to do the actual message routing—a fact that will become important shortly for support of distributed transactions.

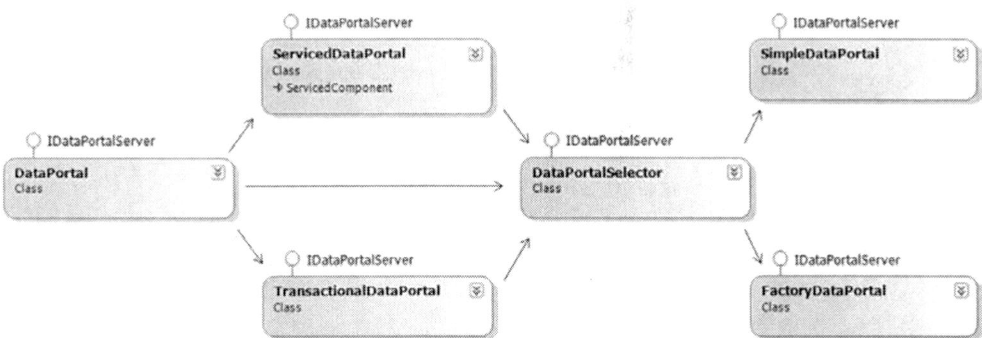

Figure 15-2. *Flow of a client call through the message router*

The `SimpleDataPortal` object routes each client call (message) to the actual business object that can handle the message. These are the same business classes and objects that make up the application's business logic layer.

In other words, the *same exact objects* used by the UI on the client are also called by the data portal on the server. This allows the objects to run on the client to interact with the user, and to run on the server to do back-end processing as needed.

The `FactoryDataPortal` object routes each client call (message) to an object factory that can handle the message. If a business developer chooses to use this object factory approach, he'll need to create an object factory for each root business object, so that factory object can create, retrieve, update, and delete the business object and its data.

Table 15-3 lists the classes needed, in addition to `Csla.DataPortal` and `Csla.Server.DataPortal`, to implement the message router behavior.

Table 15-3. *Types Required for the Message Router*

Type	Namespace	Description
`TransactionalDataPortal`	`Csla.Server`	Creates a `System.Transactions.TransactionScope` transaction and then delegates the call to `SimpleDataPortal`
`ServicedDataPortal`	`Csla.Server`	Creates a COM+ distributed transaction and then delegates the call to `SimpleDataPortal`
`DataPortalSelector`	`Csla.Server`	Determines whether to invoke the managed data portal (`SimpleDataPortal`) or object factory model (`FactoryDataPortal`)
`SimpleDataPortal`	`Csla.Server`	Entry point to the server, implementing the message router behavior and routing client calls to the appropriate business object on the server
`FactoryDataPortal`	`Csla.Server`	Entry point to the server, implementing the message router behavior and routing client calls to the appropriate object factory on the server
`ICriteria`	`Csla`	Interface that defines the required behavior for a non-nested criteria class
`CriteriaBase`	`Csla`	Optional base class for use when building criteria objects; criteria objects contain the criteria or key data needed to create, retrieve, or delete an object's data
`SingleCriteria`	`Csla`	Optional prebuilt criteria class that passes a single identifying value through the data portal for use in identifying the object to create, retrieve, or delete
`MethodCaller`	`Csla.Reflection`	Utility class that encapsulates the use of reflection and dynamic method invocation to find method information and to invoke methods

Notice that neither the channel adapter nor message router explicitly deal with moving objects between the client and server. This is because the .NET runtime typically handles object movement automatically as long as the objects are marked as `Serializable` or `DataContract`.

The ICriteria interface listed in Table 15-3 can be implemented by any criteria class, and *must* be implemented by any criteria class that is not nested inside its business class. For example, CriteriaBase and SingleCriteria implement this interface. During the implementation of SimpleDataPortal later in the chapter, you'll see how this interface is used.

Distributed Transaction Support

Several different technologies support database transactions, including transactions in the database itself, ADO.NET, Enterprise Services, and System.Transactions. When updating a single database (even multiple tables), any of them will work fine, and your decision will often be based on which is fastest or easiest to implement.

If your application needs to update multiple databases, however, the options are a bit more restrictive. Transactions that protect updates across multiple databases are referred to as *distributed transactions*. In SQL Server, you can implement distributed transactions within stored procedures. Outside the database, you can use Enterprise Services or System.Transactions.

Distributed transaction technologies use the Microsoft DTC to manage the transaction across multiple databases. There is a substantial performance cost to enlisting the DTC in a transaction. Your application, the DTC, and the database engine(s) all need to interact throughout the transactional process to ensure that a consistent commit or rollback occurs, and this interaction takes time.

Historically, you had to pick one transactional approach for your application. This often meant using distributed transactions even when they weren't required—and paying that performance cost.

The System.Transactions namespace offers a compromise through the TransactionScope object. It starts out using nondistributed transactions (like those used in ADO.NET), and thus offers high performance for most applications. However, as soon as your code uses a *second* database within a transaction, TransactionScope automatically enlists the DTC to protect the transaction. This means you get the benefits of distributed transactions when you need them, but you don't pay the price for them when they aren't needed.

■ **Caution** The TransactionScope object is a little tricky, because it will enlist the DTC if more than one database connection is opened, even to the same exact database. Later in the chapter, I'll discuss the ConnectionManager, ObjectContextManager, and ContextManager classes, which are designed to help you avoid this issue.

The data portal allows the developer to specify which transactional technology to use for each of a business object's data access methods. The TransactionalDataPortal and ServicedDataPortal classes in Figure 15-2 wrap the client's call in a TransactionScope or COM+ transactional context as requested.

The Csla.Server.DataPortal object uses the Transactional attribute to determine what type of transactional approach should be used for each call by the client. Ultimately, all calls end up being handled by SimpleDataPortal or FactoryDataPortal, which route the call to an appropriate object. The real question is whether that object will run within a preexisting transactional context or not.

The Transactional attribute is applied to the data access methods on the business object or factory object. The code in Csla.Server.DataPortal looks at the object's data access method that will ultimately be invoked by SimpleDataPortal or FactoryDataPortal, and it finds the value of the Transactional attribute (if any). Table 15-4 lists the options for this attribute.

Table 15-4. *Transactional Options Supported by the Data Portal*

Attribute	Result
None	The business object does not run within a preexisting transactional context and so must implement its own transactions using stored procedures or ADO.NET.
`TransactionalTypes.Manual`	Same as "none" in the previous entry.
`TransactionalTypes.EnterpriseServices`	The business object runs within a COM+ distributed transactional context.
`TransactionalTypes.TransactionScope`	The business object runs within a `TransactionScope` transaction.

By extending the message router concept to add transactional support, the data portal makes it easy for a business developer to leverage either Enterprise Services or `System.Transactions` as needed. At the same time, the complexity of both technologies is reduced by abstracting them within the data portal. If neither technology is appropriate for your needs, you can always choose to not use the `Transactional` attribute, and then you can manage the transactions yourself in your data access code.

Context and Location Transparency

A key goal for the data portal is to provide a consistent environment for the business objects. At a minimum, this means that both client and server should run under the same user identity (impersonation) and the same culture (localization). The business developer should be able to pass other arbitrary information between client and server as well.

In addition to context information, exception data from the server should flow back to the client with full fidelity. This is important both for debugging and at runtime. The UI often needs to know the specifics about any server-side exceptions in order to properly notify the user about what happened and then to take appropriate steps.

Figure 15-3 shows the objects used to flow data from the client to the server and back again to the client.

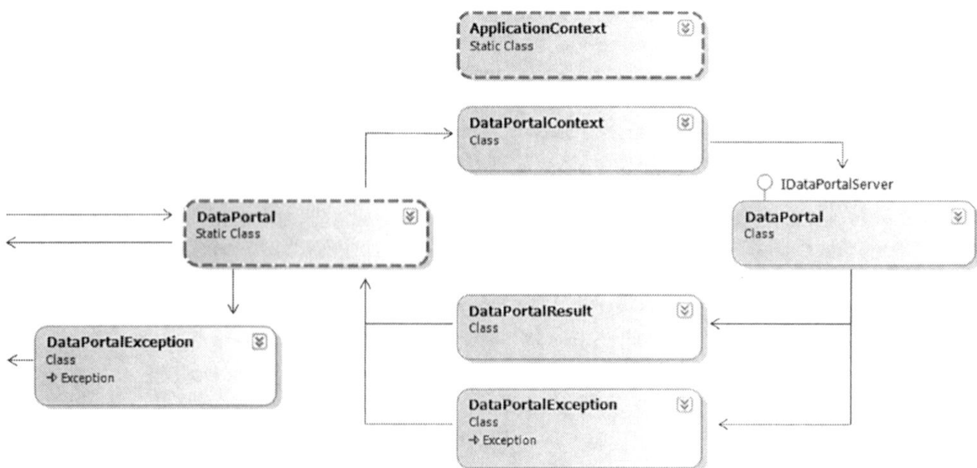

Figure 15-3. *Context and exception data flow to and from the server*

The arrows pointing off the left side of the diagram indicate communication with the calling code—typically the business object's factory methods. A business object calls `Csla.DataPortal` to invoke one of the data portal operations. `Csla.DataPortal` calls `Csla.Server.DataPortal` (using the channel adapter classes not shown here), passing a `DataPortalContext` object along with the actual client request.

The `DataPortalContext` object contains several types of context data, as listed in Table 15-5.

Table 15-5. *Context Data Contained Within DataPortalContext*

Context Data	Description
`GlobalContext`	Collection of context data that flows from client to server and then from server back to client; changes on either end are carried across the network
`ClientContext`	Collection of context data that flows from client to server; changes on the server are *not* carried back to the client
`Principal`	Client's `IPrincipal` object, which flows to the server if custom authentication is being used
`IsRemotePortal`	A flag indicating whether `Csla.Server.DataPortal` is actually running on a server or not
`ClientCulture`	Client thread's culture, which flows from the client to the server
`ClientUICulture`	Client thread's UI culture, which flows from the client to the server

The `GlobalContext` and `ClientContext` collections are exposed to both client and server code through `static` methods on the `Csla.ApplicationContext` class. All business object and UI code will use properties on the `ApplicationContext` class to access any context data. The `LocalContext` property of `ApplicationContext` is not transported through the data portal, because it is local to each individual machine.

When a call is made from the client to the server, the client's context data must flow to the server; the data portal does this by using the `DataPortalContext` object.

The `Csla.Server.DataPortal` object accepts the `DataPortalContext` object and uses its data to ensure that the server's context is set up properly before invoking the actual business object code. This means that by the time the business developer's code is running on the server, the server's `IPrincipal`, culture, and `ApplicationContext` are set to match those on the client.

■ **Caution** The exception to this is when using Windows integrated (AD) security. In that case, you must configure the server technology (such as IIS) to use Windows impersonation, or the server will not impersonate the user identity from the client.

There are two possible outcomes of the server-side processing: either it succeeds or it throws an exception.

If the call to the business object succeeds, `Csla.Server.DataPortal` returns a `DataPortalResult` object back to `Csla.DataPortal` on the client. The `DataPortalResult` object contains the information listed in Table 15-6.

`Csla.DataPortal` puts the `GlobalContext` data from `DataPortalResult` into the client's `Csla.ApplicationContext`, thus ensuring that any changes to that collection on the server are reflected on the client. It then returns the `ReturnObject` value as the result of the call itself.

Table 15-6. *Context Data Contained Within DataPortalResult*

Context Data	Description
`GlobalContext`	Collection of context data that flows from client to server and then from server back to client; changes on either end are carried across the network
`ReturnObject`	The business object being returned from the server to the client as a result of the data portal operation

You may use the bidirectional transfer of `GlobalContext` data to generate a consolidated list of debugging or logging information from the client, to the server, and back again to the client. On the other hand, if an exception occurs on the server—either within the data portal itself or, more likely, within the business object's code—that exception must be returned to the client. Either the business object or the UI on the client can use the exception information to deal with the exception in an appropriate manner.

In some cases, it can be useful to know the exact state of the business object graph on the server when the exception occurred. To this end, the object graph is also returned in the case of an exception. Keep in mind that it is returned *as it was at the time of the exception*, so the objects are often in an indeterminate state.

If an exception occurs on the server, `Csla.Server.DataPortal` catches the exception and wraps it as an `InnerException` within a `Csla.Server.DataPortalException` object. This `DataPortalException` object contains the information listed in Table 15-7.

Table 15-7. *Context Data Contained Within Csla.Server.DataPortalException*

Context Data	Description
`InnerException`	The actual server-side exception (which may also have `InnerException` objects of its own)
`StackTrace`	The stack trace information for the server-side exception
`DataPortalResult`	A `DataPortalResult` object (as discussed previously) containing both `GlobalContext` and the business object from the server

Again, `Csla.DataPortal` uses the information in the exception object to restore the `ApplicationContext` object's `GlobalContext`. Then it throws a `Csla.DataPortalException`, which is initialized with the data from the server.

The `Csla.DataPortalException` object is designed for use by business object or UI code. It provides access to the business object as it was on the server at the time of the exception. It also overrides the `StackTrace` property to append the server-side stack trace to the client-side stack trace, so the result shows the entire stack trace from where the exception occurred on the server all the way back to the client code.

■ **Note** `Csla.DataPortal` *always* throws a `Csla.DataPortalException` in case of failure. You must use either its `InnerException` or `BusinessException` properties, or the `GetBaseException()` method to retrieve the original exception that occurred.

In addition to `Csla.DataPortal` and `Csla.Server.DataPortal`, the types in Table 15-8 are required to implement the context behaviors discussed previously.

Table 15-8. *Types Required to Implement Context Passing and Location Transparency*

Type	Namespace	Description
`ApplicationContext`	`Csla`	Provides access to the `ClientContext` and `GlobalContext` collection objects, as well as other context information
`DataPortalException`	`Csla`	Exception thrown by the data portal in case of any server-side exceptions; the server-side exception is an `InnerException` within the `DataPortalException`
`DataPortalContext`	`Csla.Server`	Transfers context data from the client to the server on every data portal operation
`DataPortalResult`	`Csla.Server`	Transfers context and result data from the server to the client on every successful data portal operation
`DataPortalException`	`Csla.Server`	Transfers context and exception data from the server to the client on every unsuccessful data portal operation

This infrastructure ensures that business code running on the server will share the same key context data as the client. It also ensures that the client's `IPrincipal` object is transferred to the server when the application is using custom authentication. This is important information, not only for basic impersonation, but also for enabling authorization on the server.

Authorizing Server Calls

The data portal ensures that the application server will use the same principal object as the client when using custom authentication. And when using Windows AD authentication, you can configure your application server to use impersonation, so it runs under the same Windows identity as the client code.

Either way, because the client principal is available on the server, all the authorization features described in Chapter 12 are available to the business developer on both the client and the server. This means the per-property and object-level authorization rules associated with business objects are enforced whether the code is running on the client or server.

■ **Note** You should be aware that Windows integrated security has limits on how far it can impersonate a user. Normally, impersonation can only occur across one network hop, which would be from a client workstation to the application server. Using advanced Windows network configuration options, it may be possible to extend impersonation beyond one hop. Advanced Windows network configuration is outside the scope of this book.

However, some applications may require a higher-level authorization check to decide whether to allow a client request to be processed on the server *at all*. This check would occur before any attempt is made to invoke the data access methods in the business or factory object.

The data portal supports this concept by allowing a business developer to create an object that implements the `IAuthorizeDataPortal` interface from the `Csla.Server` namespace. If you want to use this feature, the application server's config file needs to include an entry in the appSettings element, specifying the assembly qualified name of this class—for example:

```
<add key="CslaAuthorizationProvider"
        value="NamespaceName.TypeName, AssemblyName" />
```

The IAuthorizeDataPortal interface requires that the class implement a single method: Authorize(). If the client call should not be allowed, this method should throw an exception; otherwise, the client call will be processed normally.

■ **Note** The data portal creates exactly one instance of the specified type. Because most application servers are multithreaded, you must ensure that the code you write in the Authorize() method is thread-safe.

This Authorize() method is invoked after the data portal has restored the client's principal (if using custom authentication), LocalContext, and GlobalContext onto the server's thread. The method is passed a request object containing the values listed in Table 15-9.

Table 15-9. *Values Provided to the Authorize Method*

Property	Description
ObjectType	Type of business object to be affected by the client request
RequestObject	Criteria object or business object provided by the client
Operation	Data portal operation requested by the client; member of the DataPortalOperations enumerated value

Your authorization class would look like this:

```
public class CustomAuthorizer : Csla.Server.IAuthorizeDataPortal
{
  public void Authorize(AuthorizationRequest clientRequest)
  {
    // perform authorization here
    // throw exception to stop processing
  }
}
```

This technique allows high-level control over client requests. If a request is allowed to continue processing, all the normal authorization behaviors described in Chapter 12 continue to apply. This is an optional feature, and by default, all data portal requests are allowed.

Asynchronous Behaviors

Thus far, I've been discussing the data portal in terms of synchronous behaviors. Each call to a static method of the Csla.DataPortal class is a synchronous operation.

However, the DataPortal<T> class provides asynchronous versions of the static methods on the non-generic DataPortal class. When performing asynchronous operations, it is necessary to have a consistent object through which the completion callback can arrive. This means that you must create an instance of DataPortal<T> to make asynchronous calls, and each instance can only have one outstanding asynchronous call running at a time.

Using DataPortal<T> is relatively straightforward.

```
var dp = new DataPortal<CustomerEdit>();
dp.BeginFetch(new SingleCriteria<CustomerEdit, int>(123),
                        (s, e) =>
  {
    // process result here
  });
```

You can use a lambda (as shown), an anonymous delegate, or a delegate reference to another method to implement the callback. Or you can set up an event handler for the FetchCompleted event on the DataPortal<T> object before starting the asynchronous call. The important thing is that the developer remembers that the callback will occur when the asynchronous operation is complete, and that BeginFetch() is a nonblocking call.

The DataPortal<T> class is really just a wrapper around the Csla.DataPortal class, designed to make normal synchronous data portal calls but from a background thread. To create the background threads, the DataPortal<T> methods use the standard .NET BackgroundWorker component.

By using the BackgroundWorker, the data portal gains some important benefits. All the background operations are executed on threads from the .NET thread pool, and all that work is abstracted by the BackgroundWorker component. More importantly, the BackgroundWorker component automatically marshals its asynchronous callback events onto the UI thread when running in WPF or Windows Forms.

This means that the event indicating that the background task is complete is running automatically on the UI thread in those environments, which dramatically simplifies related UI code. Even better, this reduces bugs that are commonly encountered where the UI developer forgets to marshal to the UI thread before interacting with visual controls.

Object Factories

Prior to CSLA .NET 3.6, all data portal calls were routed to methods implemented in the business class itself. These methods are called the DataPortal_XYZ methods—for example, DataPortal_Create().

In CSLA .NET 3.6, the concept of an *object factory* has been introduced as an option a business developer can use instead of the traditional data portal behavior. In this case, the developer puts an ObjectFactory attribute on the business class, which instructs the data portal to use the specified object factory to handle all persistence operations related to the business object type—for instance:

```
[ObjectFactory("MyProject.CustomerFactory, MyProject")]
public class CustomerEdit : BusinessBase<CustomerEdit>
```

This instructs the data portal to create an instance of a CustomerFactory class, using the string parameter as an assembly-qualified type name for the factory. The CustomerFactory object must implement methods to create, fetch, update, and delete CustomerEdit business objects. By default, these methods are named Create(), Fetch(), Update(), and Delete().

The factory object may choose to inherit from ObjectFactory in the Csla.Server namespace. The ObjectFactory class includes protected methods that make it easier to implement typical object factory behaviors. Here's the shell of an object factory:

```
public class CustomerFactory : ObjectFactory
{
  public object Create()
  {
    // create object and load with defaults
    MarkNew(result);
    return result;
  }
```

```
    public object Fetch(SingleCriteria<CustomerEdit, int> criteria)
    {
      // create object and load with data
      MarkOld(result);
      return result;
    }

    public object Update(object obj)
    {
      // insert/update/delete object and its child objects
      MarkOld(obj); // make sure to mark all child objects as old too
      return obj;
    }

    public void Delete(SingleCriteria<CustomerEdit, int> criteria)
    {
      // delete object data based on criteria
    }
  }
```

The `MarkNew()` and `MarkOld()` methods manipulate the status of the business object, as discussed in Chapter 8. When using the object factory model, the object factory assumes *all* responsibility for creating and managing the business object and its state. This includes not only the root object, but all child objects as well.

While factory objects require more work to implement than the traditional data portal technique, they enable the use of some external data access technologies that can't be invoked from inside an already existing business object instance. For example, you may use a data access tool that creates business object instances directly. Obviously, you can't use such a technology from inside an already existing business object, if that technology will be creating the business object instance!

At this point, you should have a good understanding of the various areas of functionality provided by the data portal, and the various classes and types used to implement that functionality. The rest of the chapter will walk through those classes. As with the previous chapters, not all code is shown in this chapter, so you'll want to get the code download for the book to follow along. You can download the code from the Source Code/Download area of the Apress website (`www.apress.com/book/view/1430210192`) or from `www.lhotka.net/cslanet/download.aspx`.

Base Class Support

In order to support persistence—the ability to save and restore from the database—objects need to implement methods that the UI can call. They also need to implement methods that can be called by the data portal on the server.

Figure 15-4 shows the basic process flow when the UI code wants to get a new business object or load a business object from the database.

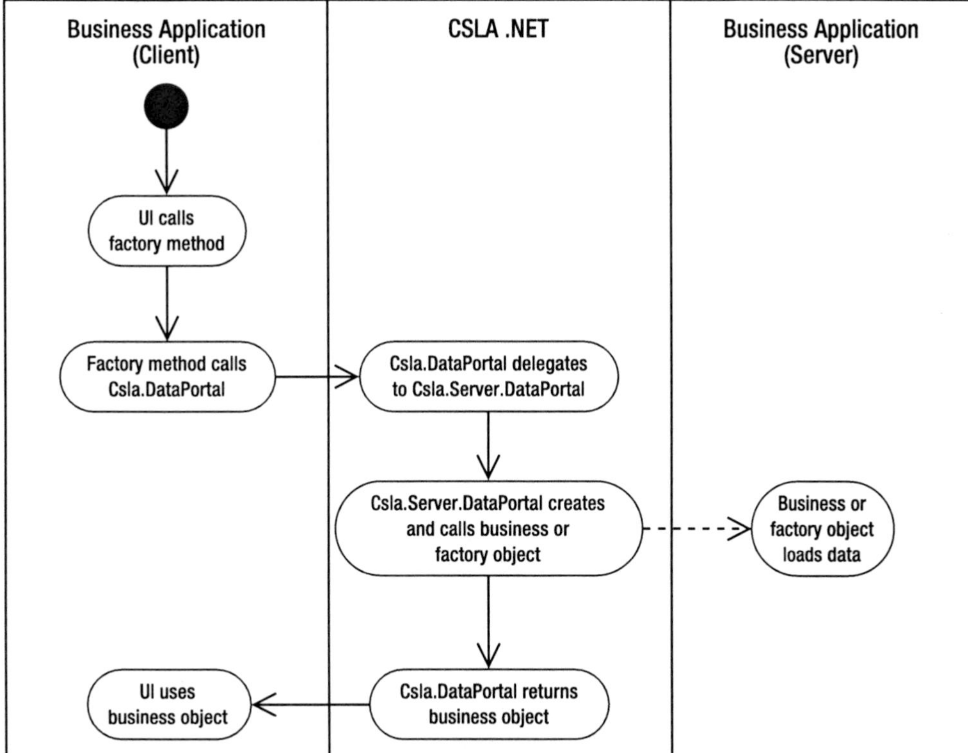

Figure 15-4. *Process flow to create or load a business object*

Following the class-in-charge model from Chapter 2, you can see that the UI code calls a factory method on the business class. The factory method then calls the appropriate method on the `Csla.DataPortal` class to create or retrieve the business object. The `Csla.Server.DataPortal` object then creates the object and invokes the appropriate data access method (`DataPortal_Create()` or `DataPortal_Fetch()`). The populated business object is returned to the UI, which the application can then use as needed.

Immediate deletion follows the same basic process, with the exception that no business object is returned to the UI as a result.

The `BusinessBase` and `BusinessListBase` classes implement a `Save()` method to make the update process work, as illustrated by Figure 15-5. The process is almost identical to creating or loading an object, except that the UI starts off by calling the `Save()` method *on the object to be saved*, rather than invoking a factory method on the business class.

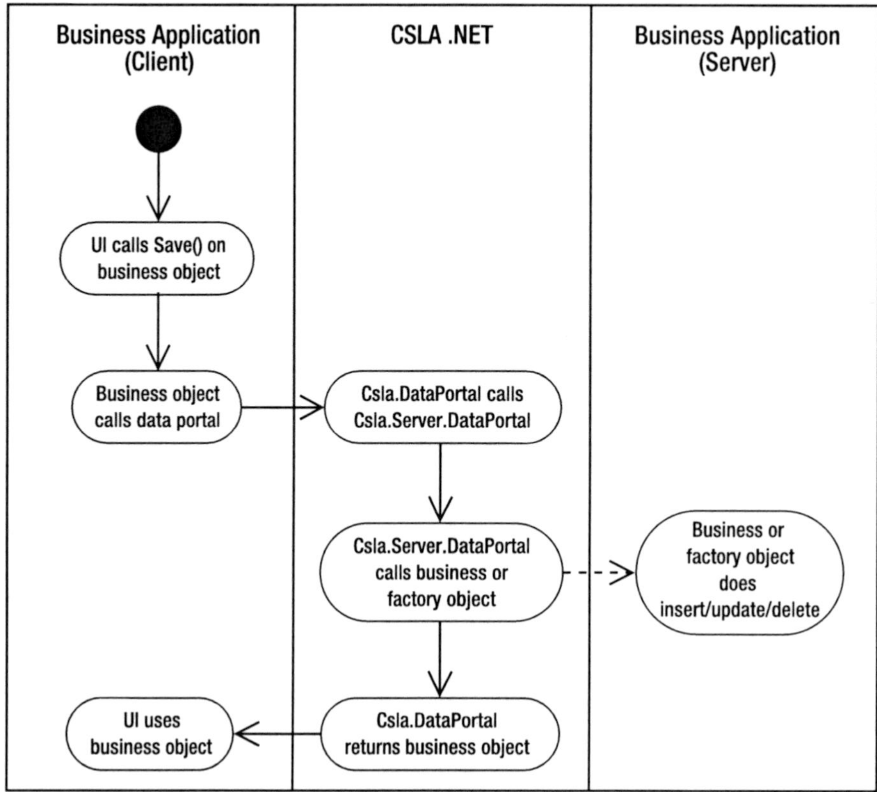

Figure 15-5. *Process flow for saving a business object*

Factory Methods and Criteria

Chapter 2 discussed the class-in-charge model and factory methods. When the UI needs to create or retrieve a business object, it will call a factory method that abstracts that behavior. You can implement factory methods in any class you choose as either instance or `static` methods. I prefer to implement them as `static` methods in the business class for the object they create or retrieve, as I think it makes them easier to find. Some people prefer to create a separate *factory class* with instance methods.

This means a `CustomerEdit` class will include `static` factory methods such as `GetCustomer()` and `NewCustomer()`, both of which return a `CustomerEdit` object as a result. It may also implement a `DeleteCustomer()` method, which would have no return value. The implementation of these methods would typically look like this:

```
public static CustomerEdit NewCustomer()
{
  return DataPortal.Create<CustomerEdit>();
}

public static CustomerEdit GetCustomer(int id)
{
  return DataPortal.
    Fetch<CustomerEdit>(new SingleCriteria<CustomerEdit, int>(id));
}
```

```
public static void DeleteCustomer(int id)
{
  DataPortal.Delete(new SingleCriteria<CustomerEdit, int>(id));
}
```

These are typical examples of factory methods implemented for most root objects.

Although I won't use the following technique in the rest of the book, you can create a factory class with instance methods if you prefer:

```
public class CustomerFactory
{
  public virtual CustomerEdit NewCustomer()
  {
    return DataPortal.Create<CustomerEdit>();
  }

  public virtual CustomerEdit GetCustomer(int id)
  {
    return DataPortal.
      Fetch<CustomerEdit>(new SingleCriteria<CustomerEdit, int>(id));
  }

  public virtual void DeleteCustomer(int id)
  {
    DataPortal.Delete(new SingleCriteria<CustomerEdit, int>(id));
  }
}
```

The methods are `virtual`, because the primary motivation for using a factory class like this is to allow subclassing of the factory to customize the behavior.

I'll be using `static` factory methods throughout the rest of the book.

Save Methods

The factory methods cover creating, retrieving, and deleting objects. This leaves inserting and updating (and deferred deletion). In both of these cases, the object already exists in memory, so the `Save()` and `BeginSave()` methods are instance methods on any editable object.

The `Save()` method allows synchronous save operations and is the simplest to use.

```
_customer = _customer.Save();
```

The `BeginSave()` method allows asynchronous save operations and is harder to use, because your code must work in an asynchronous manner, including providing a callback handler that is invoked when the operation is complete.

```
  // disable UI elements that can't be used during save
  _customer.BeginSave(SaveComplete);
  // ...

private void SaveComplete(object sender, SavedEventArgs e)
{
  if (e.Error != null)
  {
    // handle exception here
  }
```

```
    else
    {
      _customer = e.NewObject;
      // update the UI or other code to use the result
      // re-enable any disabled UI elements
    }
  }
```

Notice that the address to SaveComplete() is provided as a parameter to the BeginSave() method. This means SaveComplete() is invoked when the asynchronous operation completes. In WPF and Windows Forms, this callback occurs on the UI thread.

Both Save() and BeginSave() ultimately do the same thing in that they insert, update, or delete the editable root business object.

One Save() method can be used to support inserting and updating an object's data because all editable objects have an IsNew property. Recall that the definition of a "new" object is that the object's primary key value doesn't exist in the database. This means that if IsNew is true, then Save() causes an insert operation; otherwise, Save() causes an update operation.

BusinessBase and BusinessListBase are the base classes for all editable business objects, and both of these base classes implement Save() methods and BeginSave().

Synchronous Save Methods

Here are the two overloads for Save() in BusinessBase:

```
public virtual T Save()
{
  T result;
  if (this.IsChild)
    throw new NotSupportedException(
                                  Resources.NoSaveChildException);
  if (EditLevel > 0)
    throw new Validation.ValidationException(
                                  Resources.NoSaveEditingException);
  if (!IsValid && !IsDeleted)
    throw new Validation.ValidationException(
                                  Resources.NoSaveInvalidException);
  if (IsDirty)
    result = (T)DataPortal.Update(this);
  else
    result = (T)this;
  OnSaved(result, null);
  return result;
}

public T Save(bool forceUpdate)
{
  if (forceUpdate && IsNew)
  {
    // mark the object as old - which makes it
    // not dirty
    MarkOld();
    // now mark the object as dirty so it can save
    MarkDirty(true);
  }
  return this.Save();
}
```

The first `Save()` method is the primary one that does the real work. It implements a set of common rules that make sense for most objects. Specifically, it does the following:

- Ensures that the object is not a child (since child objects must be saved as part of their parent)
- Makes sure that the object isn't currently being edited (a check primarily intended to assist with debugging)
- Checks to see if the object is valid; invalid objects can't be saved
- Checks to make sure the object is dirty; there's no sense saving unchanged data into the database

Notice that the method is `virtual`, so if a business developer needs a different set of rules for an object, it is possible to override this method and implement something else.

The second `Save()` method exists to support stateless web applications and the scenario where business objects are used to implement XML services. It allows a service author to create a new instance of the object, load it with data, and then *force* the object to do an update (rather than an insert) operation. The reason for this is that when creating a stateless web page or service that updates data, the web page or application calling the server typically passes *all* the data needed to update the database; there's no need to retrieve the existing data just to overwrite it. This optional overload of `Save()` enables those scenarios.

This is done by first calling `MarkOld()` to set `IsNew` to `false`, and then calling `MarkDirty()` to set `IsDirty` to `true`.

In either case, it is the `DataPortal.Update()` call that ultimately triggers the data portal infrastructure to move the object to the application server so it can interact with the database.

It is important to notice that the `Save()` method returns an instance of the business object. Recall that .NET doesn't actually move objects across the network; rather, it makes *copies* of the objects. The `DataPortal.Update()` call causes .NET to copy this object to the server so the copy can update itself into the database. That process could change the state of the object (especially if you are using primary keys assigned by the database or timestamps for concurrency). The resulting object is then copied back to the client and returned as a result of the `Save()` method.

Note It is critical that the UI updates all its references to use the new object returned by `Save()`. Failure to do this means that the UI will be displaying and editing old data from the old version of the object. Do not call `Save()` like this:

```
_customer.Save();
```

Do call `Save()` like this:

```
_customer = _customer.Save();
```

The same basic code can be found in `BusinessListBase` as well.

Asynchronous BeginSave Methods

There are four overloads of `BeginSave()`, because it can optionally accept the `forceUpdate` parameter like `Save()`, and it can also optionally accept a delegate reference to a method that will be invoked when the asynchronous operation is complete.

All the overloads invoke the following method:

```
public virtual void BeginSave(EventHandler<SavedEventArgs> handler)
{
  if (this.IsChild)
  {
    NotSupportedException error = new NotSupportedException(
                                          Resources.NoSaveChildException);
    OnSaved(null, error);
    if (handler != null)
      handler(this, new SavedEventArgs(null, error));
  }
  else if (EditLevel > 0)
  {
    Validation.ValidationException error = new Validation.ValidationException(
                                          Resources.NoSaveEditingException);
    OnSaved(null, error);
    if (handler != null)
      handler(this, new SavedEventArgs(null, error));
  }
  else if (!IsValid && !IsDeleted)
  {
    Validation.ValidationException error = new Validation.ValidationException(
                                          Resources.NoSaveEditingException);
    OnSaved(null, error);
    if (handler != null)
      handler(this, new SavedEventArgs(null, error));
  }
  else
  {
    if (IsDirty)
    {
      DataPortal.BeginUpdate<T>(this, (o, e) =>
      {
        T result = e.Object;
        OnSaved(result, e.Error);
        if (handler != null)
          handler(result, new SavedEventArgs(result, e.Error));
      });
    }
    else
    {
      OnSaved((T)this, null);
      if (handler != null)
        handler(this, new SavedEventArgs(this, null));
    }
  }
}
```

Like the Save() method, BeginSave() performs a series of checks to see if the object should really be saved. However, rather than throwing exceptions immediately, the exceptions are routed to the callback handler and to any code that handles the business object's Saved event.

I chose to do this because it allows the business developer to put all her exception-handling code into the callback handler. If BeginSave() actually threw exceptions, the business or UI developer would need to handle exceptions when calling BeginSave() and also in the callback handler, because any asynchronous exceptions would always be handled in the callback handler. The approach taken by this implementation allows the business or UI developer to do all work in one location.

The overall structure and process of BeginSave() is the same as for Save(), except that the BeginUpdate() method is called on the data portal instead of Update(). A lambda expression is used to handle the asynchronous callback from the data portal method.

```
DataPortal.BeginUpdate<T>(this, (o, e) =>
{
  T result = e.Object;
  OnSaved(result, e.Error);
  if (handler != null)
    handler(result, new SavedEventArgs(result, e.Error));
});
```

When the asynchronous data portal method completes, the OnSaved() method is called to raise the Saved event on the business object, and the callback handler is also invoked if it isn't null.

Updating Child Objects with the Field Manager

Editable objects may contain child objects—either editable child objects or editable child collections (which in turn contain editable child objects). If managed backing fields are used (see Chapter 7) to maintain the child object references, then the field manager can be used to simplify the process of saving the child objects.

The FieldDataManager class implements an UpdateChildren() method that can be called by an editable object's insert or update data access method. The UpdateChildren() method loops through all the managed backing fields and uses the data portal to update all child objects. Here's the code:

```
public void UpdateChildren(params object[] parameters)
{
  foreach (var item in _fieldData)
  {
    if (item != null)
    {
      object obj = item.Value;
      if (obj is IEditableBusinessObject || obj is IEditableCollection)
        Csla.DataPortal.UpdateChild(obj, parameters);
    }
  }
}
```

The data portal's UpdateChild() method is invoked on each child object, which causes the data portal to invoke the appropriate Child_XYZ method on each child object. I'll discuss this feature of the data portal later in this chapter.

Updating Editable Collections

Editable collections contain editable child objects. Updating child objects in an editable collection must be done in a specific manner, because the collection contains a list of deleted items as well as a list of active (nondeleted) items.

The deleted item list must be updated first, so those items are deleted before any active items can be updated. This is because it is quite possible that an active item will replace one of the deleted items, so updating the active list first could result in primary key collisions in the database.

Rather than having the business developer write the code to update all the child objects in every collection, BusinessListBase implements a Child_Update() method that does the work. Here's that method:

```
[EditorBrowsable(EditorBrowsableState.Advanced)]
protected virtual void Child_Update(params object[] parameters)
{
  var oldRLCE = this.RaiseListChangedEvents;
  this.RaiseListChangedEvents = false;
  try
  {
    foreach (var child in DeletedList)
      DataPortal.UpdateChild(child, parameters);
    DeletedList.Clear();

    foreach (var child in this)
      DataPortal.UpdateChild(child, parameters);
  }
  finally
  {
    this.RaiseListChangedEvents = oldRLCE;
  }
}
```

The `RaiseListChangedEvents` property is set to `false` to prevent the collection from raising events during the update process. This helps avoid both performance issues and UI "flickering" as the update occurs (otherwise, these events may cause data binding to refresh the UI as each item is updated).

Then the items in `DeletedList` are updated, which really means they are all deleted. This is handled by the data portal's `UpdateChild()` method, which invokes each child object's `Child_DeleteSelf()` method. Because they've been deleted, `DeletedList` is then cleared so it reflects the state of the underlying data store.

Now the active items in the collection are updated, which means they are inserted or updated based on the state of each child object. The data portal's `UpdateChild()` method handles those details, calling the appropriate `Child_Insert()` or `Child_Update()` method.

Finally, the `RaiseListChangedEvents` property is restored to its previous value, so the collection can continue to be used normally.

A business developer may explicitly call `Child_Update()` in an editable root collection as I discussed earlier in this chapter. Normally, a business developer needs to write *no code* for an editable child collection, because the data portal will automatically call the `Child_Update()` method when the parent object calls `FieldManager.UpdateChildren()` to update its children (including the editable child collection).

This completes the features provided by the business object base classes that are required for the data portal to function. Before covering the data portal implementation in detail, I need to discuss how the data portal uses (and avoids) reflection.

Reflection and Dynamic Method Invocation

The data portal dynamically invokes methods on business and factory objects. Invoking methods dynamically requires the use of reflection, and that can cause performance issues when used frequently. Since the data portal can be used to create, retrieve, update, and delete child objects, it is quite possible for hundreds of methods to be invoked to save just one object graph.

The .NET Framework supports the concept of *dynamic method invocation*, where reflection is used just once to create a dynamic delegate reference to a method. That delegate is used to actually invoke the method, resulting in performance nearly as good as a strongly typed call to the method.

Of course, that dynamic delegate must be stored somewhere, so we need to cache the delegates and retrieve them from the cache. The end result is that using dynamic delegates is still slower than strongly typed method calls, but it's faster than using reflection on each call.

The `Csla.Reflection` namespace includes classes used by the data portal (and other parts of CSLA .NET) to dynamically invoke methods using dynamic delegates. Table 15-10 lists the types in that namespace.

Table 15-10. *Types in the Csla.Reflection Namespace*

Type	Description
`CallMethodException`	Thrown when a method can't be invoked dynamically
`DynamicMethodHandle`	Maintains a reference to a dynamic method delegate, along with related metadata
`DynamicMethodHandlerFactory`	Creates a dynamic method delegate
`LateBoundObject`	Provides a wrapper around any object to simplify the invocation of dynamic methods on that object
`MethodCacheKey`	Defines the key information for a dynamic method, so the `DynamicMethodHandle` can be stored and retrieved as necessary
`MethodCaller`	Provides an abstract API for use when dynamically calling methods on objects

Creating and using dynamic method delegates is complex and is outside the scope of this book. You should realize, however, that the `MethodCaller` and `LateBoundObject` classes are designed as the public entry points to this functionality, and they are used by the data portal implementation.

The MethodCaller Class

The heart of the subsystem is the `MethodCaller` class. This class exposes the methods listed in Table 15-11; these methods enable the dynamic invocation of methods.

Table 15-11. *Public Methods on MethodCaller*

Method	Description
`CreateInstance()`	Creates an instance of an object
`CallMethodIfImplemented()`	Invokes a method by name, if that method exists on the target object
`CallMethod()`	Invokes a method by name, throwing an exception if that method doesn't exist
`GetMethod()`	Gets a `MethodInfo` object for a method by name, matching any supplied parameters using standard overloading rules
`FindMethod()`	Gets a `MethodInfo` object for a method by name, matching any supplied parameters using standard overloading rules, with special behaviors to deal with generic parameters and `abstract` base classes

Table 15-11. *Public Methods on MethodCaller (Continued)*

Method	Description
GetParameterTypes()	Gets a list of Type objects corresponding to the type of parameter values provided to the method
GetObjectType()	Returns a business object type based on a supplied criteria object, taking into account the ICriteria interface and nested criteria classes

The MethodCaller class also includes the code to cache dynamic method delegates, and that technique is used automatically when CallMethod() and CallMethodIfImplemented() are used. In other words, MethodCaller uses reflection only to create dynamic method delegates, and it uses those delegates to make all method calls to the target objects. The method delegates are cached for the lifetime of the AppDomain, so they're typically created only once each time an application is run.

The GetObjectType Method

I do want to explore one method in a little more detail. The GetObjectType() method is designed specifically to support the data portal, and it's important to understand how it uses criteria objects to identify the business object type. Both Csla.DataPortal and Csla.Server.DataPortal use this method to determine the type of business object involved in the data portal request. This method uses the criteria object supplied by the factory method in the business class to find the type of the business object itself.

This method supports the two options discussed in Chapter 5: where the criteria class is nested within the business class, and where the criteria object inherits from Csla.CriteriaBase (and thus implements ICriteria).

```
public static Type GetObjectType(object criteria)
{
  var strong = criteria as ICriteria;
  if (strong != null)
  {
    // get the type of the actual business object
    // from the ICriteria
    return strong.ObjectType;
  }
  else if (criteria != null)
  {
    // get the type of the actual business object
    // based on the nested class scheme in the book
    return criteria.GetType().DeclaringType;
  }
  else return null;
}
```

If the criteria object implements ICriteria, then the code will simply cast the object to type ICriteria and retrieve the business object type by calling the ObjectType property.

With a nested criteria class, the code gets the type of the criteria object and then returns the DeclaringType value from the Type object. The DeclaringType property returns the type of the class within which the criteria class is nested.

The LateBoundObject Class

The LateBoundObject class is designed to act as a wrapper around any .NET object, making it easy to dynamically invoke methods on that object. It is used like this:

```
lateBound = new LateBoundObject<CustomerEdit>(_customer);
lateBound.CallMethod("SomeMethod", 123, "abc");
```

Behind the scenes, the wrapper object simply delegates all calls to MethodCaller, and you could choose to use MethodCaller directly. The reason for using LateBoundObject is to write code that is easier to read.

Now let's move on and implement the data portal itself, feature by feature. The data portal is designed to provide a set of core features, including

- Implementing a channel adapter
- Supporting distributed transactional technologies
- Implementing a message router
- Transferring context and providing location transparency

The remainder of the chapter will walk through each functional area in turn, discussing the implementation of the classes supporting the concept.

Channel Adapter

The data portal is exposed to the business developer through the Csla.DataPortal class. This class implements a set of static methods to make it as easy as possible for the business developer to create, retrieve, update, or delete objects. All the channel adapter behaviors are hidden behind the Csla.DataPortal class.

The RunLocal Attribute

The data portal routes client calls to the server based on the client application's configuration settings in its config file. If the configuration is set to use an actual application server, the client call is sent across the network using the channel adapter pattern. However, there are cases in which the business developer knows that there's no need to send the call across the network—even if the application is configured that way.

The most common example of this is in the creation of new business objects. The DataPortal.Create() method is called to create a new object, and it in turn triggers a call to the business object's DataPortal_Create() method or a factory object's Create() method. Either way, the target method loads the business object with default values from the database.

But what if an object doesn't need to load defaults from the database? In that case, there would be no reason to go across the network at all, and it would be nice to short-circuit the call so that particular object's create method would run on the client.

This is the purpose behind the RunLocal attribute. A business developer can mark a data access method with this attribute to tell the data portal to force the call to run on the client, regardless of how the application is configured in general. Such a business method would look like this:

```
[RunLocal]
private void DataPortal_Create(Criteria criteria)
{
  // set default values here
}
```

The data portal always invokes this DataPortal_Create() method without first crossing a network boundary. So if DataPortal.Create() were called on the client, this method would run on the client, and if DataPortal.Create() were called on the application server, the DataPortal_Create() method would run on the server.

When using a factory object, the attribute is applied to the factory method.

```
public class CustomerFactory : ObjectFactory
{
  [RunLocal]
  public void Create()
  {
    // create object and
    // set default values here
  }
}
```

If the assembly containing the factory has been deployed to the client, the data portal will find this attribute and will invoke the Create() method on the client. If you don't deploy your factory assembly to the client, obviously the code must run on the server, so the data portal would ignore the RunLocal attribute.

The DataPortal Class

The primary entry point for the entire data portal infrastructure is the Csla.DataPortal class. Business developers use the methods on this class to trigger all the data portal behaviors. This class is involved in both the channel adapter implementation and in handling context information. This section will focus on the channel adapter code in the class, while I'll discuss the context-handling code later in the chapter.

The Csla.DataPortal class exposes five primary methods, described in Table 15-12, that can be called by business logic to create, retrieve, update, or delete root objects, or to execute command objects.

Table 15-12. *Methods Exposed by the Data Portal for Root Objects*

Method	Description
Create()	Calls Csla.Server.DataPortal, which then invokes the DataPortal_Create() method (or the Create() method in an object factory)
Fetch()	Calls Csla.Server.DataPortal, which then invokes the DataPortal_Fetch() method (or the Fetch() method in an object factory)
Update()	Calls Csla.Server.DataPortal, which then invokes the DataPortal_Insert(), DataPortal_Update(), or DataPortal_DeleteSelf() methods, as appropriate (or the Update() method in an object factory)
Delete()	Calls Csla.Server.DataPortal, which then invokes the DataPortal_Delete() method (or the Delete() method in an object factory)
Execute()	Calls Csla.Server.DataPortal, which then invokes the DataPortal_Execute() method (or the Update() method in an object factory)

The data portal also includes methods used to create, retrieve, update, or delete child objects. Table 15-13 lists these methods.

Table 15-13. *Methods Exposed by the Data Portal for Child Objects*

Method	Description
`CreateChild()`	Calls `ChildDataPortal`, which then invokes the `Child_Create()` method on the child object
`FetchChild()`	Calls `ChildDataPortal`, which then invokes the `Child_Fetch()` method on the child object
`UpdateChild()`	Calls `ChildDataPortal`, which then invokes the `Child_Insert()`, `Child_Update()`, or `Child_DeleteSelf()` method on the child object

The class also raises two `static` events that the business developer or UI developer can handle. The `DataPortalInvoke` event is raised before the server is called, and the `DataPortalInvokeComplete` event is raised after the server call has returned.

Behind the scenes, each `DataPortal` method determines the network protocol to be used when contacting the server in order to delegate the call to `Csla.Server.DataPortal`. Of course, `Csla.Server.DataPortal` ultimately delegates the call to `Csla.Server.SimpleDataPortal` and then to the business object on the server.

The `Csla.DataPortal` class is designed to expose `static` methods. As such, it is a `static` class.

```
public static class DataPortal
{
}
```

This ensures that instances of the class won't be created.

Each of the five data portal methods works in a similar manner. I'm not going to walk through all five; instead, I'll discuss the `Fetch()` method in some detail, and I'll briefly cover the `Update()` method (because it is somewhat unique). First, though, you should be aware of the events raised by the `DataPortal` class on each call, and how the data portal connects with the server.

DataPortal Events

The `DataPortal` class defines two events: `DataPortalInvoke` and `DataPortalInvokeComplete`.

```
public static event Action<DataPortalEventArgs> DataPortalInvoke;
public static event Action<DataPortalEventArgs> DataPortalInvokeComplete;

private static void OnDataPortalInvoke(DataPortalEventArgs e)
{
  Action<DataPortalEventArgs> action = DataPortalInvoke;
  if (action != null)
    action(e);
}

private static void OnDataPortalInvokeComplete(DataPortalEventArgs e)
{
  Action<DataPortalEventArgs> action = DataPortalInvokeComplete;
  if (action != null)
    action(e);
}
```

These follow the standard approach by providing helper methods to raise the events.

Also notice the use of the Action<T> generic template. The .NET Framework provides this as a helper when declaring events that have a custom EventArgs subclass as a single parameter. A corresponding EventHandler<T> template helps when declaring the standard sender and EventArgs pattern for event methods.

A DataPortalEventArgs object is provided as a parameter to these events. This object includes information of value when handling the event as described in Table 15-14.

Table 15-14. *Properties of the DataPortalEventArgs Class*

Property	Description
DataPortalContext	The data portal context passed to the server
Operation	The data portal operation requested by the caller
Exception	Any exception that occurred during processing
ObjectType	The type of business object

This information can be used by code handling the event to better understand all the information being passed to the server as part of the client message.

Creating the Proxy Object

One of the most important functions of Csla.DataPortal is to determine the appropriate network protocol (if any) to be used when interacting with Csla.Server.DataPortal. Each protocol, or data portal channel, is managed by a proxy object that implements the IDataPortalProxy interface from the Csla.DataPortalClient namespace. This interface ensures that all proxy classes implement the methods required by Csla.DataPortal.

The proxy object to be used is defined in the application's configuration file. That's the web.config file for ASP.NET applications, and myprogram.exe.config for Windows applications (where myprogram is the name of your program). Within Visual Studio, a Windows configuration file is named app.config, so I'll refer to them as app.config files from here forward.

Config files can include an <appSettings> section to store application settings, and it is in this section that the CSLA .NET configuration settings are located. The following shows how this section would look for an application set to use WCF:

```
<appSettings>
  <add key="CslaDataPortalProxy"
       value="Csla.DataPortalClient.WcfProxy, Csla"/>
</appSettings>
```

The CslaDataPortalProxy key defines the proxy class that should be used by the data portal. Different proxy objects may require or support other configuration data. In this example, you must also configure WCF itself by including a top-level system.serviceModel element in your app.config file—for example:

```
<system.serviceModel>
  <client>
    <endpoint name="WcfDataPortal"
              address="http://serverName/virtualRoot/WcfPortal.svc"
              binding="wsHttpBinding"
              contract="Csla.Server.Hosts.IWcfPortal" />
  </client>
</system.serviceModel>
```

Normally only the highlighted line needs to be changed to properly specify the URL to the application server.

The `GetDataPortalProxy()` method uses this information to create an instance of the correct proxy object.

```
private static Type _proxyType;

private static DataPortalClient.IDataPortalProxy
  GetDataPortalProxy(bool forceLocal)
{
  if (forceLocal)
  {
    return new DataPortalClient.LocalProxy();
  }
  else
  {
    Csla.DataPortalClient.IDataPortalProxy portal;
    string proxyTypeName = ApplicationContext.DataPortalProxy;
    if (proxyTypeName == "Local")
      portal = new DataPortalClient.LocalProxy();
    else
    {
      if (_proxyType == null)
      {
        _proxyType = Type.GetType(proxyTypeName, true, true);
      }
      portal = (DataPortalClient.IDataPortalProxy)
        Activator.CreateInstance(_proxyType);
    }
    return portal;
  }
}
```

The proxy object is created on each call to avoid possible threading issues. Since the data portal can be used asynchronously, it is important to avoid the use of `static` fields because they'd be shared across multiple threads. The alternative is to use instance fields, but then locking code is required, and locking can lead to performance issues.

Notice that the `_proxyType` field is `static`, so it's shared across all threads. The data portal configuration comes from the config file and is the same for all threads in the application, so this value can be safely shared.

If the `forceLocal` parameter is `true`, then only a local proxy is returned. The `LocalProxy` object is a special proxy that doesn't use any network protocols at all, but rather runs the "server-side" data portal components directly within the client process. I'll cover this class later in the chapter.

When `forceLocal` is `false`, the real work begins. First, the proxy string is retrieved from the `CslaDataPortalProxy` key in the config file by calling the `ApplicationContext.DataPortalProxy` property. The property reads the config file and returns the value associated with the `CslaDataPortalProxy` key.

If that key value is `"Local"`, then again an instance of the `LocalProxy` class is created and returned. The `ApplicationContext.DataPortalProxy` method also returns a `LocalProxy` object if the key is not found in the config file. This makes `LocalProxy` the default proxy.

If some other config value is returned, then it is parsed and used to create an instance of the appropriate proxy class.

```
if (_proxyType == null)
{
  string typeName =
    proxyTypeName.Substring(0, proxyTypeName.IndexOf(",")).Trim();
  string assemblyName =
    proxyTypeName.Substring(proxyTypeName.IndexOf(",") + 1).Trim();
  _proxyType = Type.GetType(typeName + "," + assemblyName, true, true);
}
portal = (DataPortalClient.IDataPortalProxy)
  Activator.CreateInstance(_proxyType);
```

In the preceding `<appSettings>` example, notice that the value is a comma-separated value with the full class name on the left and the assembly name on the right. This follows the .NET standard for describing classes that are to be dynamically loaded.

The config value is parsed to pull out the full type name and assembly name. Then `Activator.CreateInstance()` is called to create an instance of the object. The .NET runtime automatically loads the assembly if needed.

The result is that the appropriate proxy object is returned for use by the data portal in communicating with the server-side components.

Root Object Data Access Methods

The five data portal methods listed in Table 15-12 are all relatively similar in that they follow the same basic process. I'll walk through the `Fetch()` method in some detail so you can see how it works. All five methods follow this basic flow:

1. Ensure the user is authorized to perform the action.
2. Get metadata for the business method to be ultimately invoked.
3. Get the data portal proxy object.
4. Create a `DataPortalContext` object.
5. Raise the `DataPortalInvoke` event.
6. Delegate the call to the proxy object (and thus to the server).
7. Handle and throw any exceptions.
8. Restore the `GlobalContext` returned from the server.
9. Raise the `DataPortalInvokeComplete` event.
10. Return the resulting business object (if appropriate).

Let's look at the `Fetch()` method in detail.

The Fetch Method

There are several `Fetch()` method overloads, all of which ultimately delegate to the actual implementation.

```
public static object Fetch(Type objectType, object criteria)
{
  Server.DataPortalResult result = null;
  Server.DataPortalContext dpContext = null;
  try
  {
    OnDataPortalInitInvoke(null);
```

```
    if (!Csla.Security.AuthorizationRules.CanGetObject(objectType))
      throw new System.Security.SecurityException(
            string.Format(Resources.UserNotAuthorizedException,
                                "get",
                                objectType.Name));

    var method =
      Server.DataPortalMethodCache.GetFetchMethod(objectType, criteria);

    DataPortalClient.IDataPortalProxy proxy;
    proxy = GetDataPortalProxy(method.RunLocal);

    dpContext =
      new Server.DataPortalContext(GetPrincipal(),
      proxy.IsServerRemote);

    OnDataPortalInvoke(new DataPortalEventArgs(
            dpContext, objectType, DataPortalOperations.Fetch));

    try
    {
      result = proxy.Fetch(objectType, criteria, dpContext);
    }
    catch (Server.DataPortalException ex)
    {
      result = ex.Result;
      if (proxy.IsServerRemote)
        ApplicationContext.SetGlobalContext(result.GlobalContext);
      string innerMessage = string.Empty;
      if (ex.InnerException is Csla.Reflection.CallMethodException)
      {
        if (ex.InnerException.InnerException != null)
          innerMessage = ex.InnerException.InnerException.Message;
      }
      else
      {
        innerMessage = ex.InnerException.Message;
      }
      throw new DataPortalException(
        String.
          Format("DataPortal.Fetch {0} ({1})", Resources.Failed, innerMessage),
          ex.InnerException, result.ReturnObject);
    }

    if (proxy.IsServerRemote)
      ApplicationContext.SetGlobalContext(result.GlobalContext);

    OnDataPortalInvokeComplete(new DataPortalEventArgs(
                dpContext, objectType, DataPortalOperations.Fetch));
  }
  catch (Exception ex)
  {
    OnDataPortalInvokeComplete(new DataPortalEventArgs(
                dpContext, objectType, DataPortalOperations.Fetch, ex));
```

```
    throw;
  }
  return result.ReturnObject;
}
```

The generic overloads simply cast the result so the calling code doesn't have to.

```
public static T Fetch<T>()
{
  return (T)Fetch(typeof(T), EmptyCriteria);
}
```

Remember that the data portal can return virtually any type of object, so the actual Fetch() method implementation must deal with results of type object.

Looking at the code, you should see all the steps listed in the preceding bulleted list. The first is to ensure the user is authorized.

```
if (!Csla.Security.AuthorizationRules.CanGetObject(objectType))
  throw new System.Security.SecurityException(
    string.Format(Resources.UserNotAuthorizedException,
                  "get",
                  objectType.Name));
```

Then the DataPortalMethodCache is used to retrieve (or create) the metadata for the business method that will ultimately be invoked on the server.

```
var method =
   Server.DataPortalMethodCache.GetFetchMethod(objectType, criteria);
```

The result is a DataPortalMethodInfo object that contains metadata for the business method. At this point, the most important bit of information is whether the RunLocal attribute has been applied to the method on the business class. This Boolean value is used as a parameter to the GetDataPortalProxy() method, which returns the appropriate proxy object for server communication.

```
DataPortalClient.IDataPortalProxy proxy;
proxy = GetDataPortalProxy(method.RunLocal);
```

Next, a DataPortalContext object is created and initialized. The details of this object and the means of dealing with context information are discussed later in the chapter.

```
dpContext =
  new Server.DataPortalContext(GetPrincipal(),
  proxy.IsServerRemote);
```

Then the DataPortalInvoke event is raised, notifying client-side business or UI logic that a data portal call is about to take place.

```
OnDataPortalInvoke(new DataPortalEventArgs(
  dpContext, objectType, DataPortalOperations.Fetch));
```

Finally, the Fetch() call itself is delegated to the proxy object.

```
result = proxy.Fetch(objectType, criteria, dpContext);
```

All a proxy object does is relay the method call across the network to Csla.Server.DataPortal, so you can almost think of this as delegating the call directly to Csla.Server.DataPortal, which in turn delegates to either FactoryDataPortal or SimpleDataPortal. The ultimate result is that a factory object's Fetch() method or the business object's DataPortal_Fetch() method is invoked on the server.

■ Note Remember that the default is that the "server-side" code actually runs in the client process on the client workstation (or web server). Even so, the full sequence of events described here occur—just much faster than if network communication were involved.

An exception could occur while calling the server. Most likely, the exception could occur in the business logic running on the server, though exceptions can also occur due to network issues or similar problems. When an exception does occur in business code on the server, it will be reflected here as a `Csla.Server.DataPortalException`, which is caught and handled.

```
result = ex.Result;
if (proxy.IsServerRemote)
  ApplicationContext.SetGlobalContext(result.GlobalContext);
string innerMessage = string.Empty;
if (ex.InnerException is Csla.Reflection.CallMethodException)
{
  if (ex.InnerException.InnerException != null)
    innerMessage = ex.InnerException.InnerException.Message;
}
else
{
  innerMessage = ex.InnerException.Message;
}
throw new DataPortalException(
  String.
    Format("DataPortal.Fetch {0} ({1})", Resources.Failed, innerMessage),
    ex.InnerException, result.ReturnObject);
```

The `Csla.Server.DataPortalException` returns the business object from the server—exactly as it was when the exception occurred. It also returns the `GlobalContext` information from the server so that it can be used to update the client's context data. Ultimately, the data from the server is used to create a `Csla.DataPortalException` that is thrown back to the business object. It can be handled by the business object or the UI code as appropriate.

Notice that the `Csla.DataPortalException` object contains not only all the exception details from the server, but also the business object from the server. This object can be useful when debugging server-side exceptions.

More commonly, an exception *won't* occur. In that case, the result returned from the server includes the `GlobalContext` data from the server, which is used to update the context on the client.

```
if (proxy.IsServerRemote)
  ApplicationContext.SetGlobalContext (result);
```

The details around context are discussed later in the chapter. With the server call complete, the `DataPortalInvokeComplete` event is raised.

```
OnDataPortalInvokeComplete(new DataPortalEventArgs(
   dpContext, objectType, DataPortalOperations.Fetch));
```

Finally, the business object created and loaded with data on the server is returned to the factory method that called `DataPortal.Fetch()` in the first place.

Remember that in a physical n-tier scenario, this is a copy of the object that was created on the server. .NET serialized the object on the server, transferred its data to the client, and deserialized it on the client. This object being returned as a result of the `Fetch()` method exists on the client workstation, so other client-side objects and UI components can use it in an efficient manner.

The Create() and Delete() methods are virtually identical. The only meaningful difference is that the Delete() method has no return value.

The Update Method

The Update() method is similar, but it doesn't get a criteria object as a parameter. Instead, it gets passed the business object itself.

```
public static object Update(object obj)
```

This way, it can pass the business object to Csla.Server.DataPortal, which ultimately calls the factory or business object's insert, update, or delete method, causing the object's data to be used to update the database. It also checks to see if the business object inherits from Csla.CommandBase, and if so, it invokes the object's execute method instead (or the factory object's update method).

The reason the Update() method is so different is because it has to use the business object's state to determine what method will be invoked. This information is necessary so the method can be checked for a RunLocal attribute. To do this, the method must first determine whether the ObjectFactory attribute has been applied to the business class.

```
var factoryInfo =
  ObjectFactoryAttribute.GetObjectFactoryAttribute(objectType);
if (factoryInfo != null)
```

When using a factory object, either an update or delete method will be invoked. The actual method names come from the ObjectFactory attribute as well.

```
var factoryType = FactoryDataPortal.FactoryLoader.GetFactoryType(
    factoryInfo.FactoryTypeName);
if (obj is Core.BusinessBase && ((Core.BusinessBase)obj).IsDeleted)
{
  if (!Csla.Security.AuthorizationRules.CanDeleteObject(objectType))
    throw new System.Security.SecurityException(
        string.Format(Resources.UserNotAuthorizedException,
        "delete",
        objectType.Name));
  method = Server.DataPortalMethodCache.GetMethodInfo(
      factoryType, factoryInfo.DeleteMethodName, new object[] { obj });
}
else
{
  if (!Csla.Security.AuthorizationRules.CanEditObject(objectType))
    throw new System.Security.SecurityException(
       string.Format(Resources.UserNotAuthorizedException,
       "save",
       objectType.Name));
  method = Server.DataPortalMethodCache.GetMethodInfo(
     factoryType, factoryInfo.UpdateMethodName, new object[] { obj });
}
```

Notice that the factory object type is retrieved using a FactoryLoader property from the FactoryDataPortal class. I'll discuss this later in the chapter. For now, it is enough to realize that this property returns an object that can provide the type of the factory that will be invoked.

If the business object is a subclass of BusinessBase, then its IsDeleted property is used to determine whether the delete or update method will be invoked. The appropriate authorization check is also made. The end result here is that the method field contains the metadata for the method to be invoked so the RunLocal attribute's presence can be determined.

If there's no ObjectFactory attribute, then the traditional DataPortal_XYZ methods will be invoked on the business object itself. In this case, the business object's state is again used to determine whether DataPortal_Insert(), DataPortal_Update(), DataPortal_DeleteSelf(), or DataPortal_Execute() will be invoked. And the method field is set to contain the metadata for that method.

The rest of the process is fundamentally the same as Fetch(). The proxy is created, the DataPortalInvoke event raised, the call is delegated to the proxy, and the result is processed.

Child Object Data Access Methods

The methods listed in Table 15-13 are used to create, retrieve, and update child objects. These methods are quite different from the methods I just discussed that deal with root objects.

When dealing with root objects, the data portal uses all the features I've discussed in this chapter, including the channel adapter, message router, distributed transaction support, and so forth. However, when dealing with child objects, the data portal assumes it is already in the process of working with a root object. So the assumption is that the code is already on the right physical computer and in the right transactional context. The data portal doesn't need to worry about any of those details when dealing with child objects.

This means that the data portal's only responsibility when dealing with child objects is to refer the call to the ChildDataPortal class in the Csla.Server namespace. I'll discuss this class later in the chapter, but for now it is enough to know that ChildDataPortal will invoke the child object's Child_XYZ methods.

Since all three methods listed in Table 15-13 are virtually identical, I'll show the code for just one here:

```
public static T FetchChild<T>(params object[] parameters)
{
  Server.ChildDataPortal portal = new Server.ChildDataPortal();
  return (T)(portal.Fetch(typeof(T), parameters));
}
```

The method simply creates an instance of ChildDataPortal and delegates the call to that object.

What is interesting about this code is that the FetchChild() method accepts a params parameter. This means the calling code can pass in virtually any value or list of parameter values, and those values are passed along to ChildDataPortal and ultimately to the Child_XYZ method.

The DataPortal<T> Class

The data portal supports asynchronous operations through the DataPortal<T> class in the Csla namespace. This class has the five *instance* methods shown in Table 15-15, which are similar to the static methods of Csla.DataPortal.

Table 15-15. *Methods on the DataPortal<T> Class*

Method	Description
BeginCreate()	Starts an asynchronous create operation
BeginFetch()	Starts an asynchronous fetch operation
BeginUpdate()	Starts an asynchronous update operation
BeginDelete()	Starts an asynchronous delete operation
BeginExecute()	Starts an asynchronous execute operation

Each of these methods delegates to `Csla.DataPortal` to do the real work, so you've already seen how the complex parts work. These asynchronous methods use the .NET `BackgroundWorker` component to take care of the threading details. This means the asynchronous work runs on a thread from the .NET thread pool, and that in WPF and Windows Forms applications, the asynchronous callbacks occur on the UI thread automatically.

Of course, the code calling `DataPortal<T>` needs to be notified when the asynchronous operation is complete. For each of the methods in Table 15-15, there is a corresponding event. For example, a `FetchCompleted` event corresponds to `BeginFetch()`.

```
public event EventHandler<DataPortalResult<T>> FetchCompleted;
```

Calling code can subscribe to this event and then call the data portal method.

```
var dp = new DataPortal<CustomerEdit>();
dp.FetchCompleted += GotCustomerEdit;
dp.BeginFetch();
```

In this case, when the async operation completes, the `GotCustomerEdit()` method is invoked automatically.

The `BeginFetch()` method has two overloads: one to accept a criteria parameter, and the other without. They both work the same way.

```
public void BeginFetch(object criteria)
{
  var bw = new System.ComponentModel.BackgroundWorker();
  bw.RunWorkerCompleted += Fetch_RunWorkerCompleted;
  bw.DoWork += Fetch_DoWork;
  bw.RunWorkerAsync(new DataPortalAsyncRequest(criteria));
}
```

The method creates a `BackgroundWorker` object, sets up handlers for the `RunWorkerCompleted` and `DoWork` events, and then starts the background task. It is important to realize that this method does not block; instead, it completes and returns immediately, while the data portal request is being processed on a background thread.

The `DoWork` handler executes the background task.

```
private void Fetch_DoWork(
    object sender, System.ComponentModel.DoWorkEventArgs e)
{
  var request = e.Argument as DataPortalAsyncRequest;
  SetThreadContext(request);

  object state = request.Argument;
  T result = default(T);
  if (state is int)
    result = (T)Csla.DataPortal.Fetch<T>();
  else
    result = (T)Csla.DataPortal.Fetch<T>(state);
  e.Result = new DataPortalAsyncResult(
    result, Csla.ApplicationContext.GlobalContext);
}
```

This method runs on the background thread and delegates the call to `Csla.DataPortal` to do the real work. However, it must deal with context information because `ApplicationContext` manages its data on a per-thread basis. In other words, the `ClientContext` and `GlobalContext` values must be set on the background thread before calling `Csla.DataPortal`, so the data portal can send them to the application server like normal.

Also notice that GlobalContext is included as part of the result returned through the DataPortalAsyncResult object. Again, this value must be taken from the background thread and made available to the calling thread.

The BackgroundWorker component's RunWorkerCompleted event handler is invoked when DoWork is complete, either successfully or due to an exception.

```
private void Fetch_RunWorkerCompleted(
  object sender, System.ComponentModel.RunWorkerCompletedEventArgs e)
{
  var result = e.Result as DataPortalAsyncResult;
  if (result != null)
  {
    _globalContext = result.GlobalContext;
    if (result.Result != null)
      OnFetchCompleted(new DataPortalResult<T>((T)result.Result, e.Error));
    else
      OnFetchCompleted(new DataPortalResult<T>(default(T), e.Error));
  }
  else
    OnFetchCompleted(new DataPortalResult<T>(default(T), e.Error));
}
```

In a WPF or Windows Forms application, this method will run on the UI thread. In other environments, such as ASP.NET, it will run on an indeterminate thread, so an ASP.NET developer must be aware that *her* callback will also occur on an indeterminate thread.

This method raises the FetchCompleted event from the DataPortal<T> object by calling OnFetchCompleted(). That event notifies the calling code that the async operation is complete.

Notice that the GlobalContext returned from the data portal call is placed into a _globalContext field, and is thus exposed through a GlobalContext property on the DataPortal<T> object. The value is *not* used to replace the GlobalContext on the calling thread, because numerous async operations could be running at once, and they'd each overwrite the GlobalContext values. By providing the resulting context through a property, it is up to the calling code to decide what to do with any returned context values.

The other four methods work the same way, essentially wrapping Csla.DataPortal calls so they occur on a background thread, with the results returned through an event.

At this point, the role of Csla.DataPortal and DataPortal<T> as gateways to the data portal overall should be clear. The other end of the channel adapter is the Csla.Server.DataPortal class, which is also the entry point to the message router pattern. I'll discuss the details of Csla.Server.DataPortal later in the chapter as part of the message router section.

First, though, I want to walk through the Local and WcfProxy classes, and corresponding host classes, used to implement the primary data portal channels supported by CSLA .NET.

The IDataPortalServer Interface

Each channel comes in two parts: a proxy on the client and a host on the server. Csla.DataPortal calls the proxy, which in turn transfers the call to the host by using its channel. The host then delegates the call to a Csla.Server.DataPortal object. To ensure that all the parts of this chain can reliably interact, there are two interfaces: Csla.Server.IDataPortalServer and Csla.DataPortalClient.IDataPortalProxy.

The IDataPortalServer interface defines the methods common across the entire process.

```
public interface IDataPortalServer
{
  DataPortalResult Create(
    Type objectType, object criteria, DataPortalContext context);
  DataPortalResult Fetch(
    Type objectType, object criteria, DataPortalContext context);
  DataPortalResult Update(object obj, DataPortalContext context);
  DataPortalResult Delete(
    Type objectType, object criteria, DataPortalContext context);
}
```

Notice that these are the same method signatures as implemented in the `static` methods on `Csla.DataPortal`, making it easy for that class to delegate its calls through a proxy and host all the way to `Csla.Server.DataPortal`.

The IDataPortalProxy Interface

All the proxy classes implement a common `Csla.DataPortalClient.IDataPortalProxy` interface so they can be used by `Csla.DataPortal`. This interface inherits from `Csla.Server.IDataPortalServer`, ensuring that all proxy classes will have the same methods as all server-side host classes.

```
public interface IDataPortalProxy : Server.IDataPortalServer
{
  bool IsServerRemote { get;}
}
```

In addition to the four data methods, proxy classes need to report whether they interact with an actual server-side host or not. As you'll see, the `LocalProxy` interacts with a *client-side* host, while `WcfProxy` interacts with a remote host. Recall that in `Csla.DataPortal`, the `IsServerRemote` property was used to control whether the context data was set and restored. If the "server-side" code is running inside the client process, then much of that work can be bypassed, improving performance.

The LocalProxy Class

The default option for a "network" channel is not to use the network at all, but rather to run the "server-side" code inside the client process. This option offers the best performance, though possibly at the cost of security or scalability. The various trade-offs of n-tier deployments were discussed in Chapter 1.

Even when running the "server-side" code in-process on the client, the data portal uses a proxy for the local "channel": `Csla.DataPortalClient.LocalProxy`. As with all proxy classes, this one implements the `Csla.DataPortalClient.IDataPortalProxy` interface, exposing a standard set of methods and properties for use by `Csla.DataPortal`.

Because this proxy doesn't actually use a network protocol, it is the simplest of all the proxies.

```
public class LocalProxy : DataPortalClient.IDataPortalProxy
{
  private Server.IDataPortalServer _portal =
    new Server.DataPortal();

  public DataPortalResult Create(
    Type objectType, object criteria, DataPortalContext context)
  {
    return _portal.Create(objectType, criteria, context);
  }
```

```
    public DataPortalResult Fetch(
      Type objectType, object criteria, DataPortalContext context)
    {
      return _portal.Fetch(objectType, criteria, context);
    }

    public DataPortalResult Update(object obj, DataPortalContext context)
    {
      return _portal.Update(obj, context);
    }

    public DataPortalResult Delete(
      Type objectType, object criteria, DataPortalContext context)
    {
      return _portal.Delete(objectType, criteria, context);
    }

    public bool IsServerRemote
    {
      get { return false; }
    }
  }
```

All this proxy does is directly create an instance of Csla.Server.DataPortal.

```
private Server.IDataPortalServer _portal =
  new Server.DataPortal();
```

Each of the data methods (Create(), Fetch(), etc.) simply delegates to this object. The result is that the client call is handled by a Csla.Server.DataPortal object running within the client AppDomain and on the client's thread. Due to this, the IsServerRemote property returns false.

The WcfProxy Class

More interesting is the WCF channel. This is implemented on the client by the WcfProxy class, and on the server by the WcfPortal class. When Csla.DataPortal delegates a call into WcfProxy, it uses WCF to pass that call to a WcfPortal object on the server. That object then delegates the call to a Csla.Server.DataPortal object.

Because WCF automatically serializes objects across the network, the WcfProxy class is not much more complex than LocalProxy. It relies on standard WCF configuration to determine how to communicate with the application server. WCF configuration is provided through a system.serviceModel element in the app.config file, and in this element the developer provides a client endpoint. That endpoint specifies the address, binding, and contract for the server component.

The client endpoint has a name, which WCF uses to locate the right endpoint in the config file. That name defaults to WcfDataPortal, but can be overridden by setting the static property named EndPoint in the WcfProxy class.

```
Csla.DataPortalClient.WcfProxy.EndPoint = "CustomDataPortalName";
```

The data portal methods use the name to retrieve the correct WCF configuration. All the methods work the same; here's the Fetch() method:

```
public DataPortalResult Fetch(
  Type objectType, object criteria, DataPortalContext context)
{
  ChannelFactory<IWcfPortal> cf = new ChannelFactory<IWcfPortal>(_endPoint);
  IWcfPortal svr = cf.CreateChannel();
  WcfResponse response =
    svr.Fetch(new FetchRequest(objectType, criteria, context));
  cf.Close();

  object result = response.Result;
  if (result is Exception)
    throw (Exception)result;
  return (DataPortalResult)result;
}
```

Each method gets a ChannelFactory corresponding to the specified endpoint, and uses that ChannelFactory to create a proxy reference to the server.

```
ChannelFactory<IWcfPortal> cf = new ChannelFactory<IWcfPortal>(_endPoint);
IWcfPortal svr = cf.CreateChannel();
```

The server is then called.

```
WcfResponse response =
  svr.Fetch(new FetchRequest(objectType, criteria, context));
```

Finally, the result (exception or not) is handled.

```
object result = response.Result;
if (result is Exception)
  throw (Exception)result;
return (DataPortalResult)result;
```

The reason this is so simple is that WCF handles virtually all the details. The only limitation on the use of WCF is that only synchronous bindings are supported. This means the most common bindings—HTTP and TCP—work fine, as do named pipes or any other synchronous network protocol.

The WcfPortal Class

You've seen the client proxy for the WCF channel. It requires that a WcfPortal object, implementing an IWcfPortal interface, be hosted by the application server.

The WcfPortal object's job is simple. It accepts a call from the client and delegates it to an instance of Csla.Server.DataPortal. Of course, it is a WCF service, so more important than the WcfPortal class is the IWcfPortal interface that defines the service contract.

```
[ServiceContract(Namespace="http://ws.lhotka.net/WcfDataPortal")]
public interface IWcfPortal
{
  [OperationContract]
  [UseNetDataContract]
  WcfResponse Create(CreateRequest request);
  [OperationContract]
  [UseNetDataContract]
  WcfResponse Fetch(FetchRequest request);
  [OperationContract]
  [UseNetDataContract]
```

```
    WcfResponse Update(UpdateRequest request);
    [OperationContract]
    [UseNetDataContract]
    WcfResponse Delete(DeleteRequest request);
  }
```

This interface defines the four methods supported by the IDataPortalServer interface, but it doesn't actually conform to that interface. The reason is that this is designed as a service-oriented interface, where each method accepts a request message and returns a response message.

Each message type, such as FetchRequest, is a data contract, described with the DataContract and DataMember attributes. You can look at the code in the download to see what property values are passed to and from the data portal through these request and response messages.

Notice the UseNetDataContract attribute on each operation in the interface. By default, WCF uses a serializer called the DataContractSerializer. Unfortunately, this serializer is not capable of serializing an object graph such that you can deserialize the byte stream to get an exact clone of the original graph. Luckily, WCF includes the NetDataContractSerializer that *does* provide the required functionality, working with objects marked as Serializable or DataContract.

The UseNetDataContract attribute is a custom attribute provided by CSLA .NET that tells WCF to use the NetDataContractSerializer instead of the DataContractSerializer when passing data to and from the server.

The WcfPortal class itself simply implements the IWcfPortal interface. It has a couple of WCF attributes on the class itself.

```
[ServiceBehavior(InstanceContextMode = InstanceContextMode.PerCall)]
[AspNetCompatibilityRequirements(RequirementsMode =
    AspNetCompatibilityRequirementsMode.Allowed)]
public class WcfPortal : IWcfPortal
```

The InstanceContextMode value is used to specify that each WCF call should be handled by an independent instance of the WcfPortal object. This helps ensure isolation between data portal calls.

The AspNetCompatibilityRequirements attribute is used to indicate that the service can run in ASP compatibility mode if requested. This is necessary to allow some Windows identity impersonation scenarios.

The WcfPortal class implements the four data portal methods. Each one works the same way. Here's the Fetch() method:

```
public WcfResponse Fetch(FetchRequest request)
{
  Csla.Server.DataPortal portal = new Csla.Server.DataPortal();
  object result;
  try
  {
    result =
      portal.Fetch(request.ObjectType, request.Criteria, request.Context);
  }
  catch (Exception ex)
  {
    result = ex;
  }
  return new WcfResponse(result);
}
```

The method simply accepts the client's call, creates an instance of Csla.Server.DataPortal, and delegates the call.

It catches all exceptions and returns any exception as part of the response message. This is important, because this technique allows the entire server-side stack trace and other exception data to flow back to the calling code on the client. That makes debugging much easier than if all that was returned were the exception message text.

The proxy and host classes for .NET Remoting, Web Services, and Enterprise Services all work in a similar manner. As these technologies are all effectively replaced by WCF, I won't discuss them in detail in this book.

At this point, you've seen the code that implements the channel adapter, including the `Csla.DataPortal` class used by business developers and the `LocalProxy` and `WcfProxy` implementations, along with the WCF host. Let's move on now to discuss the server-side portions of the data portal, starting with distributed transaction support, and then move on to the message router pattern.

Distributed Transaction Support

Though it may use different network channels to do its work, the primary job of `Csla.DataPortal` is to delegate the client's call to an object on the server. This object is of type `Csla.Server.DataPortal`, and its primary responsibility is to route the client's call to `Csla.Server.SimpleDataPortal`, which actually implements the message router behavior.

`Csla.Server.DataPortal` is involved in this process so it can establish a distributed transactional context if requested by the business object. The CSLA .NET framework allows a business developer to choose between handling transactions manually, using Enterprise Services (COM+) transactions, or using `System.Transactions`.

The Transactional Attribute

The business developer indicates his preference through the use of the custom `Csla.TransactionalAttribute`. Earlier in the chapter, Table 15-4 listed all the possible options when using this attribute on a `DataPortal_XYZ` or factory object method.

The `TransactionalTypes` enumerated list contains all the options that can be specified with the `Transactional` attribute when it is applied to a data access method.

```
public enum TransactionalTypes
{
  EnterpriseServices,
  TransactionScope,
  Manual
}
```

This type is used to define the parameter value for the constructor in the `TransactionalAttribute` class.

The Csla.Server.DataPortal Object

Ultimately, all client calls go through the channel adapter and are handled on the server by an instance of `Csla.Server.DataPortal`. This object uses the value of the `Transactional` attribute (if any) on the data access method to determine how to route the call to the `DataPortalSelector`. The call will go via one of the following three routes:

- The `Manual` option routes directly to `DataPortalSelector`.
- The `EnterpriseServices` option routes through `ServicedDataPortal`.
- The `TransactionScope` option routes through `TransactionalDataPortal`.

The Csla.Server.DataPortal object also takes care of establishing the correct context on the server based on the context provided by the client. I discuss the details of this process later in the chapter.

Csla.Server.DataPortal implements IDataPortalServer, and thus the four data methods. Each of these methods follows the same basic flow:

1. Set up the server's context.
2. Execute any attached IAuthorizeDataPortal object.
3. Get the metadata for the data access method to be invoked.
4. Check the Transactional attribute on that method metadata.
5. Route the call based on the Transactional attribute.
6. Clear the server's context.
7. Return the result provided by DataPortalSelector.

As with most of the data portal classes, all the methods operate in much the same way. I'll use Fetch() and Update() as examples.

The Fetch Method

The Fetch() method implements the steps listed previously.

```
public DataPortalResult Fetch(
  Type objectType, object criteria, DataPortalContext context)
{
  try
  {
    SetContext(context);

    Authorize(new AuthorizeRequest(
      objectType, criteria, DataPortalOperations.Fetch));

    DataPortalResult result;

    DataPortalMethodInfo method =
      DataPortalMethodCache.GetFetchMethod(objectType, criteria);

    IDataPortalServer portal;
    switch (method.TransactionalType)
    {
      case TransactionalTypes.EnterpriseServices:
        portal = new ServicedDataPortal();
        try
        {
          result = portal.Fetch(objectType, criteria, context);
        }
        finally
        {
          ((ServicedDataPortal)portal).Dispose();
        }
        break;
      case TransactionalTypes.TransactionScope:
        portal = new TransactionalDataPortal();
        result = portal.Fetch(objectType, criteria, context);
        break;
```

```
          default:
            portal = new DataPortalSelector();
            result = portal.Fetch(objectType, criteria, context);
            break;
        }
        return result;
      }
      catch (Csla.Server.DataPortalException ex)
      {
        Exception tmp = ex;
        throw;
      }
      catch (Exception ex)
      {
        throw new DataPortalException(
          "DataPortal.Fetch " + Resources.FailedOnServer,
          ex, new DataPortalResult());
      }
      finally
      {
        ClearContext(context);
      }
    }
```

After setting the server's context (a topic I discuss later in the chapter), the Authorize() method is called. This method uses the value of CslaAuthorizationProvider from the config file to create and call the Authorize() method on an IAuthorizeDataPortal implementation as discussed earlier in this chapter. If no value is provided in the config file, a default Authorize() implementation is invoked that allows all calls to execute.

The metadata for the data access method is then retrieved from the method cache (or loaded into the cache if this is the first time the method has been called).

```
DataPortalMethodInfo method =
  DataPortalMethodCache.GetFetchMethod(objectType, criteria);
```

This uses the same technique you saw in Csla.DataPortal earlier in the chapter. If the data portal is running in 2-tier or local mode, then the "client" and "server" code share the same cache. If the data portal is running in 3-tier or remote mode, then the client and server each maintain their own cache of method metadata.

The DataPortalMethodInfo object includes a property that returns the Transactional attribute value for the data access method. If there is no Transactional attribute on the method, then the Manual type is returned as a default. The resulting value is used in a switch statement to properly route the call. If EnterpriseServices was specified, then an instance of Csla.Server.ServicedDataPortal is created and the call is delegated to that object.

```
case TransactionalTypes.EnterpriseServices:
  portal = new ServicedDataPortal();
  try
  {
    result = portal.Fetch(objectType, criteria, context);
  }
  finally
  {
    ((ServicedDataPortal)portal).Dispose();
  }
  break;
```

As with all Enterprise Services objects, a try...finally block is used to ensure that the object is properly disposed when the call is complete. I'll cover the details of the ServicedDataPortal class shortly.

If TransactionScope was specified, then an instance of Csla.Server.TransactionalDataPortal is created and the call is delegated to that object.

```
case TransactionalTypes.TransactionScope:
  portal = new TransactionalDataPortal();
  result = portal.Fetch(objectType, criteria, context);
  break;
```

I'll cover details of the TransactionalDataPortal class shortly.

Finally, the default is to allow the business developer to handle any transactions manually. In that case, an instance of Csla.Server.DataPortalSelector is created directly, and the call is delegated to that object.

```
default:
  portal = new DataPortalSelector();
  result = portal.Fetch(objectType, criteria, context);
  break;
```

Both ServicedDataPortal and TransactionalDataPortal delegate their calls to DataPortalSelector too—so in the end, DataPortalSelector handles all client calls. By calling it directly, without involving any transactional technologies, this default approach allows the business developer to handle any transactions as she sees fit.

Once the Fetch() call is complete, the server's context is cleared (details discussed later), and the result is returned to the client.

```
return result;
```

If an exception occurs during the processing, it is caught, the server's context is cleared, and the exception is rethrown so it can be handled by Csla.DataPortal, as discussed earlier in the chapter.

The **Create()** and **Delete()** methods are virtually identical to **Fetch()**. However, the **Update()** method is a little different.

The Update Method

The Update() method is more complex. This is because Update() handles BusinessBase and CommandBase subclasses differently from other objects. The specific DataPortal_XYZ method to be invoked varies based on the base class of the business object. This complicates the process of retrieving the MethodInfo object.

```
DataPortalMethodInfo method;

// ...

  string methodName;
  if (obj is CommandBase)
    methodName = "DataPortal_Execute";
  else if (obj is Core.BusinessBase)
  {
    Core.BusinessBase tmp = (Core.BusinessBase)obj;
    if (tmp.IsDeleted)
      methodName = "DataPortal_DeleteSelf";
    else
      if (tmp.IsNew)
        methodName = "DataPortal_Insert";
```

```
            else
              methodName = "DataPortal_Update";
        }
        else
          methodName = "DataPortal_Update";

        method = DataPortalMethodCache.GetMethodInfo(
          obj.GetType(), methodName);
```

The same GetMethodInfo() call is used as in Fetch(), but the *name* of the method is determined based on the type and state of the business object itself. If the business object is a subclass of CommandBase, then the method name is DataPortal_Execute. For any other objects that don't inherit from BusinessBase, the method name is DataPortal_Update.

If the business object is a subclass of BusinessBase, however, the object's state becomes important. If the object is marked for deletion, then the method name is DataPortal_DeleteSelf. If the object is new, the name is DataPortal_Insert; otherwise, it is DataPortal_Update.

Once the MethodInfo object has been retrieved, the rest of the code is essentially the same as in the other three methods.

Now let's discuss the two remaining classes that set up an appropriate transaction context.

The ServicedDataPortal Class

The ServicedDataPortal class has one job: to create a distributed COM+ transactional context within which DataPortalSelector (and thus the business object) will run. When a call is routed through ServicedDataPortal, a distributed transactional context is created, ensuring that the business object's DataPortal_XYZ methods run within that context.

Normally, to run within a COM+ distributed transaction, an object must inherit from System.EnterpriseServices.ServicedComponent. This is a problem for typical business objects, since you don't *usually* want them to run within COM+, and no one likes all the deployment complexity that comes with a ServicedComponent.

ServicedDataPortal allows business objects to avoid this complexity. It does inherit from ServicedComponent, and it includes the appropriate Enterprise Services attributes to trigger the use of a distributed transaction. But it turns out that when a ServicedComponent running in a transactional context calls a normal .NET object, *that object also runs in the transaction*. This is true even when the normal .NET object doesn't inherit from ServicedComponent.

Figure 15-6 illustrates the use of this concept.

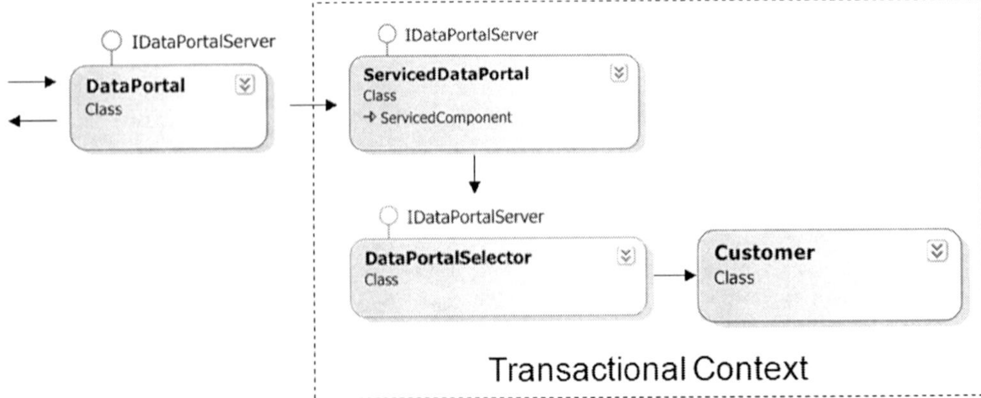

Figure 15-6. *Using ServicedDataPortal to wrap a business object in a transaction*

Once the transactional context is established by ServicedDataPortal, all normal .NET objects invoked from that point forward run within the same context.

ServicedDataPortal itself inherits from ServicedComponent in the System.EnterpriseServices namespace and includes some key attributes.

```
[Transaction(TransactionOption.Required)]
[EventTrackingEnabled(true)]
[ComVisible(true)]
public class ServicedDataPortal : ServicedComponent, IDataPortalServer
{
}
```

The Transaction attribute specifies that this object *must* run within a COM+ transactional context. If it is called by another object that already established such a context, this object will run within that context; otherwise, it will create a new context.

The EventTrackingEnabled attribute indicates that this object will interact with COM+ to enable the "spinning balls" in the component services management console. This is only important (or even visible) if the data portal is running within COM+ on the server—meaning that the EnterpriseServicesProxy is used by the client to interact with the server.

The ComVisible attribute makes this class visible to COM, which is a requirement for any class that is to be hosted in COM+.

Because ServicedDataPortal inherits from ServicedComponent, the Csla.dll assembly itself must be configured so it can be hosted in COM+. Specifically, the assembly must be signed with a key (CslaKey.snk in the project), and the project must have a reference to the System.EntepriseServices assembly.

The class also implements the IDataPortalServer interface, ensuring that it implements the four data methods. Each of these methods has another Enterprise Services attribute: AutoComplete.

```
[AutoComplete(true)]
public DataPortalResult Update(
  object obj, DataPortalContext context)
{
  var portal = new DataPortalSelector();
  return portal.Update(obj, context);
}
```

The AutoComplete attribute is used to tell COM+ that this method will vote to commit the transaction unless it throws an exception. In other words, if an exception is thrown, the method will vote to roll back the transaction; otherwise, it will vote to commit the transaction.

This fits with the overall model of the data portal, which relies on the business object to throw exceptions in case of failure. The data portal uses the exception to return important information about the failure back to the client. ServicedDataPortal also relies on the exception to tell COM+ to roll back the transaction.

Notice how the Fetch() method simply creates an instance of DataPortalSelector and delegates the call to that object. This is the same thing that Csla.Server.DataPortal did for manual transactions, except in this case, DataPortalSelector and the business object are wrapped in a distributed transactional context.

The other three data methods are implemented in the same manner.

The TransactionalDataPortal Class

The TransactionalDataPortal is designed in a manner similar to ServicedDataPortal. Rather than using Enterprise Services, however, this object uses the transactional capabilities provided by the System.Transactions namespace, and in particular the TransactionScope object.

This class simply implements IdataPortalServer.

```
public class TransactionalDataPortal : IDataPortalServer
{
}
```

This ensures that it implements the four data methods. Each of these methods follows the same structure: create a TransactionScope object and delegate the call to an instance of DataPortalSelector. For instance, here's the Update() method:

```
public DataPortalResult Update(
  object obj, DataPortalContext context)
{
  DataPortalResult result;
  using (TransactionScope tr = new TransactionScope())
  {
    var portal = new DataPortalSelector();
    result = portal.Update(obj, context);
    tr.Complete();
  }
  return result;
}
```

The first thing this method does is create a TransactionScope object from the System.Transactions namespace. Just the act of instantiating such an object creates a transactional context. It is not a *distributed* transactional context, but rather a lighter-weight context. If the business object interacts with more than one database, however, it will automatically become a distributed transaction.

The using block here ensures both that the TransactionScope object will be properly disposed, and perhaps more importantly, that the transaction will be committed or rolled back as appropriate. If the object is disposed before the Complete() method is called, then the transaction is rolled back. Again, this model relies on the underlying assumption that the business code will throw an exception to indicate failure. This is the same model that is used by ServicedDataPortal, and really by the data portal infrastructure overall.

Within the using block, the code creates an instance of DataPortalSelector and delegates the call to that object, which in turn calls the business object. Assuming no exception is thrown by the business object, the Complete() method is called to indicate that the transaction should be committed.

The other three methods are implemented in the same manner. Regardless of which transactional model is used, all calls end up being handled by a DataPortalSelector object, which implements the message router concept.

Message Router

The message router functionality picks up where the channel adapter leaves off. The channel adapter gets the client call from the client to the server, ultimately calling Csla.Server.DataPortal. Recall that every host class (LocalPortal, WcfPortal, etc.) ends up delegating every method call to an instance of Csla.Server.DataPortal. That object routes the call to a DataPortalSelector object, possibly first setting up a transactional context.

The focus in this section of the chapter will be on the DataPortalSelector, FactoryDataPortal, and SimplePortal classes, which route the client request to the appropriate object and method supplied by the business developer. Figure 15-7 shows the relationship between these three types.

The purpose of DataPortalSelector is to route the call to the appropriate object, so SimpleDataPortal or FactoryDataPortal can call the data access method implemented by the business developer.

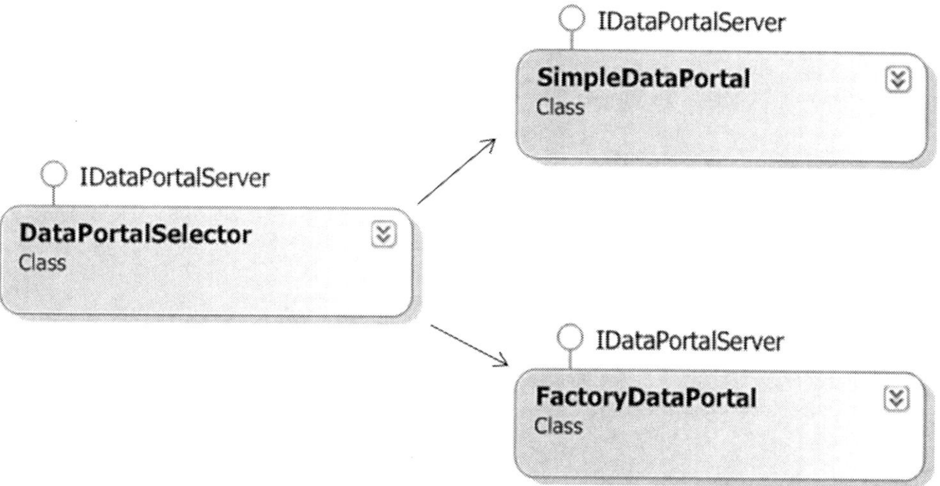

Figure 15-7. *DataPortalSelector routes to SimpleDataPortal or FactoryDataPortal*

The DataPortalSelector Class

The `DataPortalSelector` class determines if the business object has an `ObjectFactory` attribute and uses that information to route the call. It calls a `GetObjectFactoryAttribute()` helper method from the `ObjectFactoryAttribute` class.

```
internal static ObjectFactoryAttribute GetObjectFactoryAttribute(
  Type objectType)
{
  var result = objectType.GetCustomAttributes(
    typeof(ObjectFactoryAttribute), true);
  if (result != null && result.Length > 0)
    return result[0] as ObjectFactoryAttribute;
  else
    return null;
}
```

This is standard reflection code for retrieving an attribute from a type.

The result is used in `DataPortalSelector` to route the call to the correct object. For example, here's the `Fetch()` method:

```
public DataPortalResult Fetch(
  Type objectType, object criteria, DataPortalContext context)
{
  try
  {
    context.FactoryInfo =
      ObjectFactoryAttribute.GetObjectFactoryAttribute(objectType);
    if (context.FactoryInfo == null)
    {
      var dp = new SimpleDataPortal();
      return dp.Fetch(objectType, criteria, context);
    }
```

```
      else
      {
        var dp = new FactoryDataPortal();
        return dp.Fetch(objectType, criteria, context);
      }
    }
    catch (DataPortalException)
    {
      throw;
    }
    catch (Exception ex)
    {
      throw new DataPortalException(
        "DataPortal.Fetch " + Resources.FailedOnServer,
        ex, new DataPortalResult());
    }
  }
```

If an ObjectFactory attribute is present, the call is routed to a FactoryDataPortal; otherwise, it goes to a SimpleDataPortal.

The exception handling is perhaps the most interesting part of the code. It is possible for code right here in DataPortalSelector to fail, so that must be handled by wrapping such an exception in a DataPortalException. However, it is also possible that FactoryDataPortal or SimpleDataPortal could have already caught and wrapped an exception into a DataPortalException. To avoid double-wrapping of such exceptions, any DataPortalException is simply rethrown.

The SimpleDataPortal Class

If no ObjectFactory attribute is used, all client calls end up being handled on the server by an instance of SimpleDataPortal. This class is the counterpart to the client-side Csla.DataPortal, since it is this class that interacts directly with the business objects designed by the business developer.

SimpleDataPortal implements the four data methods defined by IDataPortalServer: Create(), Fetch(), Update(), and Delete(). Each of these methods follows the same basic processing flow:

1. Create or get an instance of the business object.
2. Call the object's DataPortal_OnDataPortalInvoke() method (if implemented).
3. Set the object's status (new, dirty, etc.) as appropriate.
4. Call the appropriate DataPortal_XYZ method on the object.
5. Call the object's DataPortal_OnDataPortalInvokeComplete() method (if implemented).
6. In case of exception, call the object's DataPortal_OnDataPortalException() method (if implemented) and throw a Csla.Server.DataPortalException.
7. Return the resulting business object (if appropriate).

As I've done previously in the chapter, I'll walk through the Fetch() method and also discuss the Update() method, as they are representative of the overall process.

The Fetch Method

The Fetch() method illustrates every step in the preceding list.

```
public DataPortalResult Fetch(
  Type objectType, object criteria, DataPortalContext context)
{
  LateBoundObject obj = null;
  IDataPortalTarget target = null;
  var eventArgs = new DataPortalEventArgs(
    context, objectType, DataPortalOperations.Fetch);
  try
  {
    // create an instance of the business object.
    obj = new LateBoundObject(objectType);

    target = obj.Instance as IDataPortalTarget;

    if (target != null)
    {
      target.DataPortal_OnDataPortalInvoke(eventArgs);
      target.MarkOld();
    }
    else
    {
      obj.CallMethodIfImplemented("DataPortal_OnDataPortalInvoke", eventArgs);
      obj.CallMethodIfImplemented("MarkOld");
    }

    // tell the business object to fetch its data
    if (criteria is int)
      obj.CallMethod("DataPortal_Fetch");
    else
      obj.CallMethod("DataPortal_Fetch", criteria);

    if (target != null)
      target.DataPortal_OnDataPortalInvokeComplete(eventArgs);
    else
      obj.CallMethodIfImplemented(
        "DataPortal_OnDataPortalInvokeComplete",
        eventArgs);

    // return the populated business object as a result
    return new DataPortalResult(obj.Instance);
  }
  catch (Exception ex)
  {
    try
    {
      if (target != null)
        target.DataPortal_OnDataPortalException(eventArgs, ex);
      else
        obj.CallMethodIfImplemented(
          "DataPortal_OnDataPortalException",
          eventArgs, ex);
    }
```

```
        catch
        {
          // ignore exceptions from the exception handler
        }
        object outval = null;
        if (obj != null) outval = obj.Instance;
        throw new DataPortalException(
          "DataPortal.Fetch " + Resources.FailedOnServer,
          ex, new DataPortalResult(outval));
      }
    }
```

The first step is to create an instance of the business object. This is done using a feature of the `LateBoundObject` type from the `Csla.Reflection` namespace. `LateBoundObject` uses dynamic method invocation to create an instance of the business object, even if the business class has a non-`public` default constructor.

```
obj = new LateBoundObject(objectType);
```

The constructors on business classes are not normally `public`. They are either `private` or `protected`, thus forcing the UI developer to use the factory methods to create or retrieve business objects.

If it is not already loaded into memory, the .NET runtime will automatically load the assembly containing the business object class.

■ **Tip** To ensure .NET can find your business assembly, the assembly must be in the same directory as the client application's `exe` file, in the `Bin` directory. Alternatively, you may install the assembly into the .NET GAC. A more advanced solution is to handle the current `AppDomain` object's `AssemblyResolve` event, where you would load the desired assembly and provide it to the .NET runtime.

The `objectType` parameter is passed from the client. Recall that in `Csla.DataPortal`, the type of the object to be created was determined and passed as a parameter to the `Fetch()` method.

The next step in the process is to tell the business object that it is about to be invoked by the data portal. To minimize the use of reflection, an attempt is made to cast the object to the `IDataPortalTarget` interface. Technically, the data portal can work with nearly any `Serializable` .NET object, even if the object isn't based on a CSLA .NET base class. In such a case, the object might not implement `IDataPortalTarget`, so the data portal doesn't assume that all objects will implement the interface.

If the cast succeeds, the interface is used to invoke the method; otherwise, `MethodCaller` is used to invoke the method by name.

```
target = obj.Instance as IDataPortalTarget;

if (target != null)
{
  target.DataPortal_OnDataPortalInvoke(eventArgs);
  target.MarkOld();
}
else
{
  obj.CallMethodIfImplemented("DataPortal_OnDataPortalInvoke", eventArgs);
  obj.CallMethodIfImplemented("MarkOld");
}
```

Note The `IDataPortalTarget` interface is scoped as internal to avoid exposing these methods to code outside the data portal. This interface is implemented by the CSLA .NET base classes, so reflection is not used when interacting with most business objects.

A business developer can override the `DataPortal_OnDataPortalInvoke()` method to do any preprocessing prior to an actual `DataPortal_XYZ` method being called.

Also notice that the object's status is updated with a call to `MarkOld()`. Because `Fetch()` is retrieving already existing data from the database, the object will meet the definition of being "old" when this method completes. Object status values were discussed in Chapter 8.

The next step is to call the actual `DataPortal_XYZ` method.

```
if (criteria is int)
  obj.CallMethod("DataPortal_Fetch");
else
  obj.CallMethod("DataPortal_Fetch", criteria);
```

Remember that the `obj` field is a `LateBoundObject` that wraps the business object. This means when `CallMethod()` is used, the business object's method is invoked using a dynamic delegate.

A criteria object must be some actual object, not a primitive type. But `Csla.DataPortal` has overloads for `Fetch()` that don't require *any* criteria parameter. No parameter at all is not the same as `null`, so the data portal uses a "magic value" to indicate whether no parameter was passed. If an `int` value is provided as the criteria, that indicates that *no value was supplied*, not even `null`.

Consider the following code:

```
result = DataPortal.Fetch();
result = DataPortal.Fetch(null);
result = DataPortal.Fetch(new SingleCriteria<CustomerEdit, int>(123));
```

The first call should route to

```
private void DataPortal_Fetch()
```

The second two expect a method that accepts one parameter. Perhaps this:

```
private void DataPortal_Fetch(SingleCriteria<CustomerEdit, int> criteria)
```

Behind the scenes, the data portal uses an `int` value to specify that no parameter was provided, so the parameterless call to `Fetch()` is routed correctly.

Now that the `DataPortal_Fetch()` method has been invoked, the object is notified that the data portal processing is complete.

```
if (target != null)
  target.DataPortal_OnDataPortalInvokeComplete(eventArgs);
else
  obj.CallMethodIfImplemented(
    "DataPortal_OnDataPortalInvokeComplete",
    eventArgs);
```

Finally, the newly created object is wrapped in a `Csla.Server.DataPortalResult` object and returned.

```
return new DataPortalResult(obj.Instance);
```

Again, remember that `obj` is a `LateBoundObject`, so its `Instance` property is used to retrieve the actual business object it contains.

That concludes the normal sequence of events in the method. Of course, it is possible that an exception occurred during the processing. In that case, the exception is caught and the object is notified that an exception occurred.

```
try
{
  if (target != null)
    target.DataPortal_OnDataPortalException(eventArgs, ex);
  else
    obj.CallMethodIfImplemented(
      "DataPortal_OnDataPortalException",
      eventArgs, ex);
}
catch
{
  // ignore exceptions from the exception handler
}
```

This optional call to `DataPortal_OnDataPortalException()` is wrapped in its own `try...catch` statement. Even if an exception occurs while calling *this* method, the code needs to continue. There's little that can be done if the exception-handling code has an exception, so such an exception is simply ignored.

In any case, the exception is wrapped in a `Csla.Server.DataPortalException`, which is thrown back to `Csla.DataPortal`.

```
object outval = null;
if (obj != null) outval = obj.Instance;
throw new DataPortalException(
  "DataPortal.Fetch " + Resources.FailedOnServer,
  ex, new DataPortalResult(outval));
```

Remember that `DataPortalException` contains the original exception as an `InnerException`, and also traps the stack trace from the server exception so it is available on the client. Also keep in mind that all the proxy/host channel implementations ensure that the exception is returned to the client with full fidelity, so `Csla.DataPortal` gets the full exception detail regardless of the network channel used.

At this point, you should understand how the flow of the data methods is implemented. The remaining methods the same flow with minor variations, with the `Update()` method being the most unique.

The Update Method

The `Update()` method is more complex. Remember that the `Update()` process adapts itself to the type of business object being updated, so it checks to see if the object is a subclass of `BusinessBase` or `CommandBase` and behaves appropriately. Also recall that the actual business object is passed as a parameter to `Update()`, so this method doesn't need to create an instance of the business object at all.

Processing a BusinessBase Object

It starts right out by attempting to cast the business object as `BusinessBase`. If the cast succeeds, the resulting `BusinessBase` field is used to check the object's status. Also notice the use of the `lb` field. This field is a `LateBoundObject` instance that wraps the business object, simplifying dynamic calls to properties and methods.

```
var busObj = obj as Core.BusinessBase;
if (busObj != null)
{
  if (busObj.IsDeleted)
  {
    if (!busObj.IsNew)
    {
      // tell the object to delete itself
      lb.CallMethod("DataPortal_DeleteSelf");
    }
    if (target != null)
      target.MarkNew();
    else
      lb.CallMethodIfImplemented("MarkNew");
  }
  else
  {
    if (busObj.IsNew)
    {
      // tell the object to insert itself
      lb.CallMethod("DataPortal_Insert");
    }
    else
    {
      // tell the object to update itself
      lb.CallMethod("DataPortal_Update");
    }
    if (target != null)
      target.MarkOld();
    else
      lb.CallMethodIfImplemented("MarkOld");
  }
}
```

If the object's `IsDeleted` property returns `true`, then the object should be deleted. It is possible that the object is also *new*, in which case there's actually nothing to delete; otherwise, the `DataPortal_DeleteSelf()` method is invoked.

In either case, the `MarkNew()` method is invoked to reset the object's state to new and dirty. From Chapter 8, the definition of a "new" object is that its primary key value isn't in the database, and since that data was just deleted, the object certainly meets that criteria. The definition of a "dirty" object is that its data values don't match values in the database, and again, the object now certainly meets that criteria as well.

If the object wasn't marked for deletion, then it will need to be either inserted or updated. If `IsNew` is `true`, then `DataPortal_Insert()` is invoked. Similarly, if the object isn't new, then `DataPortal_Update()` is invoked. In either case, the object's primary key and data values now reflect values in the database, so the object is clearly not new or dirty. The `MarkOld()` method is called to set the object's state accordingly.

Processing a CommandBase Object

If the business object inherits from `Csla.CommandBase`, things are simpler. In this case, only the object's `DataPortal_Execute()` method is invoked:

```
else if (obj is CommandBase)
{
  operation = DataPortalOperations.Execute;
  // tell the object to update itself
  lb.CallMethod("DataPortal_Execute");
}
```

A command object should implement all server-side code in its `DataPortal_Execute()` method.

Processing All Other Objects

For any other objects (most commonly subclasses of `BusinessListBase`), the `DataPortal_Update()` method is invoked, followed by an optional call to `MarkOld()`.

```
lb.CallMethod("DataPortal_Update");
if (target != null)
  target.MarkOld();
else
  lb.CallMethodIfImplemented("MarkOld");
```

As in `Fetch()`, the `DataPortal_OnDataPortalInvoke()` method is called before any of this other processing, and `DataPortal_OnDataPortalInvokeComplete()` is called once it is all done. The business object is returned as a result, wrapped in a `DataPortalResult` object. Any exceptions are handled in the same way as in `Fetch()`.

That completes the `SimpleDataPortal` class. Notice how all client calls are automatically routed to a dynamically created business object based on the type of business object required. `SimpleDataPortal` is entirely unaware of the particulars of any business application; it blindly routes client calls to the appropriate destinations.

The FactoryDataPortal Class

The `FactoryDataPortal` is invoked when the business object has an `ObjectFactory` attribute. In some ways, this is the simpler of the two classes, because it pushes more of the work on the author of the factory object. Though this means the business developer does more work, it also means the business developer has more flexibility.

The FactoryLoader Property

Earlier in the chapter, the `DataPortalSelector` code called a static property named `FactoryLoader`. The `FactoryLoader` property uses the `CslaObjectFactoryLoader` config setting from the `appSettings` element to create an object that can load factory objects.

```
public static IObjectFactoryLoader FactoryLoader
{
  get
  {
    if (_factoryLoader == null)
    {
      string setting =
        ConfigurationManager.AppSettings["CslaObjectFactoryLoader"];
      if (!string.IsNullOrEmpty(setting))
        _factoryLoader =
          (IObjectFactoryLoader)Activator.CreateInstance(
             Type.GetType(setting, true, true));
```

```
        else
          _factoryLoader = new ObjectFactoryLoader();
      }
      return _factoryLoader;
    }
    set
    {
      _factoryLoader = value;
    }
  }
```

This approach provides a level of indirection that can be useful for swapping out data access layer implementations. CSLA .NET provides a default factory loader, `ObjectFactoryLoader`, which interprets the `ObjectFactory` attribute's factory name parameter as an assembly qualified type name—for example:

```
[ObjectFactory("Namespace.TypeName, Assembly")]
```

The default `ObjectFactoryLoader` uses this text value to create an instance of the specified type. However, a business developer could create her own factory loader by implementing `IObjectFactoryLoader` from the `Csla.Server` namespace and telling CSLA .NET to use her factory loader by setting the `CslaObjectFactoryLoader` config value. Her custom factory loader could interpret the `ObjectFactory` parameter value in any way, such as looking up the type name from an XML file.

In any case, the `FactoryLoader` property returns an `IObjectFactoryLoader`, which must implement the two methods listed in Table 15-16.

Table 15-16. *Methods Defined by IObjectFactoryLoader*

Method	Description
`GetFactoryType()`	Returns a `Type` object corresponding to the type of factory object that will be used
`GetFactory()`	Returns an instance of the factory object to be used

The other data portal classes you've seen in this chapter use the `GetFactoryType()` method to get type information about the factory object when necessary. In the end, though, it is the `FactoryDataPortal` itself that calls `GetFactory()` to create an instance of the factory object. That occurs within the various data portal methods.

As with the other data portal types, `FactoryDataPortal` implements the `Create()`, `Fetch()`, `Update()`, and `Delete()` methods. These methods are all implemented using the same process:

1. Invoke the specified factory method.
2. Wrap any exceptions in a `DataPortalException`.
3. Return any result.

The Fetch Method

Since all the methods are the same, I'll only walk through the `Fetch()` method.

```
public DataPortalResult Fetch(
  Type objectType, object criteria, DataPortalContext context)
{
  try
  {
    DataPortalResult result = null;
    if (criteria is int)
      result = InvokeMethod(
        context.FactoryInfo.FactoryTypeName,
        context.FactoryInfo.FetchMethodName,
        context);
    else
      result = InvokeMethod(
        context.FactoryInfo.FactoryTypeName,
        context.FactoryInfo.FetchMethodName,
        criteria, context);
    return result;
  }
  catch (Exception ex)
  {
    throw new DataPortalException(
      context.FactoryInfo.FetchMethodName + " " + Resources.FailedOnServer,
      ex, new DataPortalResult());
  }
}
```

The `InvokeMethod()` helper is used to make the actual method call on the factory object. There are two overloads: one with a criteria parameter and one without. Again, the "magic type" of `int` is used to indicate that no criteria value was provided by the client code.

Any exception is wrapped into a `DataPortalException` and thrown back to the caller.

The InvokeMethod Method

The `InvokeMethod()` method follows these steps:

1. Create an instance of the factory object.
2. Call an `Invoke()` method (if present).
3. Call the data access method.
4. Call an `InvokeComplete()` method (if present).
5. If an exception occurs, call an `InvokeError()` method (if present).
6. Return the result.

The optional `Invoke()`, `InvokeComplete()`, and `InvokeError()` methods may be implemented by a factory object if the factory wants to do pre- or post-processing.

Here's the `InvokeMethod()` code:

```
private DataPortalResult InvokeMethod(
  string factoryTypeName, string methodName,
  object e, DataPortalContext context)
{
  object factory = FactoryLoader.GetFactory(factoryTypeName);
  Csla.Reflection.MethodCaller.CallMethodIfImplemented(
    factory, "Invoke", context);
```

```
    object result = null;
    try
    {
      result = Csla.Reflection.MethodCaller.CallMethod(
        factory, methodName, e);
      Csla.Reflection.MethodCaller.CallMethodIfImplemented(
        factory, "InvokeComplete", context);
    }
    catch (Exception ex)
    {
      Csla.Reflection.MethodCaller.CallMethodIfImplemented(
        factory, "InvokeError", ex);
      throw;
    }
    return new DataPortalResult(result);
  }
```

You can see how each step is implemented by using the MethodCaller component from Csla.Reflection to dynamically invoke the various methods. Because the names of the create, fetch, update, and delete methods can be specified as parameters to the ObjectFactory attribute, the actual method invocation uses the supplied name.

```
result = Csla.Reflection.MethodCaller.CallMethod(
  factory, methodName, e);
```

This particular overload of InvokeMethod() provides a criteria parameter to the method. The other overload does the same work, but doesn't provide a criteria parameter.

```
result = Csla.Reflection.MethodCaller.CallMethod(
  factory, methodName);
```

In both overloads, the steps are the same, and the result is that the appropriate data access method is invoked on the factory object.

Whether the business class has the ObjectFactory attribute or not, the result of a call to DataPortalSelector is that a business object is created, retrieved, updated, or deleted. The result, or resulting DataPortalException, is returned to Csla.Server.DataPortal and from there to the client's Csla.DataPortal and to the client code itself.

The ChildDataPortal Class

Earlier in the chapter, I discussed how the data portal supports creating, retrieving, and updating child objects. The Csla.DataPortal class exposes a set of methods that a business class can use to trigger these behaviors, but those methods ultimately delegate to the ChildDataPortal class where the real work occurs.

The ChildDataPortal class implements the methods listed in Table 15-17.

Table 15-17. *Methods Implemented by ChildDataPortal*

Method	Description
Create()	Creates an instance of the child object and invokes its Child_Create() method
Fetch()	Creates an instance of the child object and invokes its Child_Fetch() method
Update()	Invokes Child_Insert(), Child_Update(), or Child_DeleteSelf() on the child object based on the child object's state

The overall behavior of these methods is similar to how the SimpleDataPortal works with root objects, in that the ChildDataPortal is responsible for calling predefined methods on the child object. There are even pre- and post-processing methods so the business object developer can be notified before and after the data access method has been invoked.

The Create() and Fetch() methods are virtually identical. The Update() method does the same things, but as with the other Update() methods you've seen, it uses the child object's IsNew and IsDeleted properties to decide which Child_XYZ method to invoke.

Because these methods are so similar to those in SimpleDataPortal, I won't repeat the code here. You should understand that each method follows a set of steps:

1. Create or get an instance of the business object.
2. Call the object's Child_OnDataPortalInvoke() method (if implemented).
3. Set the object's status (new, dirty, etc.) as appropriate.
4. Call the appropriate Child_XYZ method on the object.
5. Call the object's Child_OnDataPortalInvokeComplete() method (if implemented).
6. In case of exception, call the object's Child_OnDataPortalException() method (if implemented) and throw a Csla.DataPortalException.
7. Return the resulting business object (if appropriate).

As you can see, these are the same steps followed by the SimpleDataPortal methods, except Child_XYZ methods are called instead of DataPortal_XYZ methods. The same dynamic delegate scheme is used, which means LateBoundObject and MethodCaller are leveraged to call the methods dynamically.

By supporting child objects, the data portal enables the same coding model for both root and child objects, which makes it easier to build and maintain business objects.

Context and Location Transparency

The final major area of functionality provided by the data portal is that it manages context information to provide a level of location transparency between the client and server. Specifically, it allows the business application to pass data from the client to the server and from the server to the client on each data portal call, in addition to the actual call itself. The data portal uses this capability itself to pass security and culture information from the client to the server.

You've already seen most of the code that implements the context-passing behaviors. Csla.DataPortal is responsible for passing the client context to the server and for updating the client's context with any changes from the server. Csla.Server.DataPortal is responsible for setting the server's context based on the data passed from the client, and for returning the global context from the server back to the client.

To maintain the context and pass it between client and server, several objects are used. Let's discuss them now.

The DataPortalContext Class

Earlier in the chapter, you saw how the Csla.DataPortal class implements static methods used by business developers to interact with the data portal. Each of those methods dealt with context data—creating a DataPortalContext object to pass to the server. On the server, Csla.Server.DataPortal uses the data in DataPortalContext to set up the server's context to match the client.

Of course, the phrase "on the server" is relative, since the data portal could be configured to use the LocalProxy. In that case, the "server-side" components actually run in the same process as your client code. Obviously, the context data is *already* present in that case, so there's no need to transfer it; and the data portal includes code to short-circuit the process when the server-side data portal components are running locally.

The DataPortalContext object is created and initialized in Csla.DataPortal within each data method.

```
dpContext =
  new Server.DataPortalContext(GetPrincipal(),
  proxy.IsServerRemote);
```

The DataPortalContext object is a container for the set of context data to be passed from the client to the server. The data it contains is defined by the fields declared in DataPortalContext.

```
private IPrincipal _principal;
private bool _remotePortal;
private string _clientCulture;
private string _clientUICulture;
private ContextDictionary _clientContext;
private ContextDictionary _globalContext;
```

■ **Note** The ContextDictionary type is a special dictionary type that is compatible with CSLA .NET for Silverlight. CSLA .NET for Silverlight is outside the scope of this book, but you should understand that ContextDictionary is a subclass of HybridDictionary, enhanced so it can be serialized to and from Silverlight.

These data elements were described in Table 15-5 earlier in the chapter. The key here is that DataPortalContext is marked as Serializable, and therefore when it is serialized, all the values in these fields are also serialized.

The values are loaded when the DataPortalContext object is created. The two culture values are pulled directly off the client's current Thread object. The _clientContext and _globalContext values are set based on the values in Csla.ApplicationContext.

Each of the values is exposed through a corresponding property so they can be used to set up the context data on the server.

Setting the Server Context

The server's context is set by Csla.Server.DataPortal as the first step in each of the four data methods. The work is handled by the SetContext() method in Csla.Server.DataPortal. This method follows this basic flow:

1. Do nothing if the "server" code is running on the client; otherwise, call ApplicationContext to set the client and global context collections.
2. Set the server Thread to use the client's culture settings.
3. If using Windows authentication, set the AppDomain to use the WindowsPrincipal.

4. If using custom authentication, set the server Thread to use the IPrincipal supplied from the client.

Let's walk through the code in SetContext() that implements these steps. First is the check to see if the "server" code is actually running locally in the client process (using the LocalProxy in the channel adapter).

```
if (!context.IsRemotePortal) return;
```

If the server code is running locally, then there's no sense setting any context data, because it is already set up. If the server code really is running remotely, though, the context data does need to be set up on the server, starting by restoring the client and global context data.

```
ApplicationContext.SetContext(
  context.ClientContext, context.GlobalContext);
```

Remember that the client context comes from the client to the server only, while the global context will ultimately be returned to the client, reflecting any changes made on the server. The ApplicationContext also has an ExecutionLocation property that business code can use to determine whether the code is currently executing on the client or the server. This value must be set to indicate that execution is on the server.

```
ApplicationContext.SetExecutionLocation(
  ApplicationContext.ExecutionLocations.Server);
```

Like the client context, the two culture values flow from the client to the server. They are used to set the current Thread object on the server to match the client settings.

```
System.Threading.Thread.CurrentThread.CurrentCulture =
  new System.Globalization.CultureInfo(context.ClientCulture);
System.Threading.Thread.CurrentThread.CurrentUICulture =
  new System.Globalization.CultureInfo(context.ClientUICulture);
```

Of the two, perhaps the most important is the CurrentUICulture, as this is the setting that dictates the language used when retrieving resource values such as those used throughout the CSLA .NET framework.

Finally, if custom authentication is being used, the IPrincipal object representing the user's identity is passed from the client to the server. It must be set on the current Thread or HttpContext as the CurrentPrincipal or User to effectively impersonate the user on the server. Csla.ApplicationContext handles this.

```
if (ApplicationContext.AuthenticationType == "Windows")
{
  // When using integrated security, Principal must be null
  if (context.Principal != null)
  {
    System.Security.SecurityException ex =
      new System.Security.SecurityException(
         Resources.NoPrincipalAllowedException);
    ex.Action = System.Security.Permissions.SecurityAction.Deny;
    throw ex;
  }
  // Set .NET to use integrated security
  AppDomain.CurrentDomain.SetPrincipalPolicy(
     PrincipalPolicy.WindowsPrincipal);
}
```

```
else
{
  // We expect some Principal object
  if (context.Principal == null)
  {
    System.Security.SecurityException ex =
      new System.Security.SecurityException(
        Resources.BusinessPrincipalException + " Nothing");
    ex.Action = System.Security.Permissions.SecurityAction.Deny;
    throw ex;
  }
  ApplicationContext.User = context.Principal;
```

There's a lot going on here, so let's break it down a bit. First, there's the check to ensure that custom authentication is being used. If Windows integrated (AD) security is being used, then Windows itself handles any impersonation, based on the configuration of the host (IIS, WAS, COM+, etc). In that case, the `IPrincipal` value passed from the client must be `null`; otherwise, it will be invalid, and the code will throw an exception.

■ **Tip** The check of the principal object's type is done to ensure that both the client and the server are using the same authentication scheme. If the client is using custom authentication and the server is using Windows integrated security, this exception will be thrown. Custom authentication was discussed in Chapter 12.

If the server is configured to use custom authentication, however, the rest of the code is executed. In that case, the first step is to make sure that the client did pass a valid `IPrincipal` object to the server. "Valid" in this case means that it isn't `null`. Given a valid `IPrincipal` object, the server's principal value is set to match that of the client. An invalid `IPrincipal` value results in an exception being thrown.

Remember that an `IAuthorizeDataPortal` implementation can be provided to further authorize each data portal request, as I discussed earlier in this chapter.

Clearing the Server Context

Once all the server-side processing is complete, the server clears the context values on its `Thread` object. This is done to prevent other code from accidentally gaining access to the client's context or security information. `Csla.Server.DataPortal` handles this in its `ClearContext()` method.

```
private static void ClearContext(DataPortalContext context)
{
  // if the dataportal is not remote then
  // do nothing
  if (!context.IsRemotePortal) return;
  ApplicationContext.Clear();
  if (ApplicationContext.AuthenticationType != "Windows")
    ApplicationContext.User = null;
}
```

This method is called at the end of each data method in `Csla.Server.DataPortal`. Notice that it calls `Csla.ApplicationContext` to clear the client and global context values. Then if custom authentication is being used, `Csla.ApplicationContext` is called to set the principal value to `null`, removing the `IPrincipal` value from the server thread.

The DataPortalResult Class

Using the DataPortalContext object, Csla.DataPortal and Csla.Server.DataPortal convey client context data to the server. That's great for the client context, client culture, and client IPrincipal, but the global context data needs to be returned to the client when the server is done. This is handled by Csla.Server.DataPortalResult on a successful call, and Csla.Server.DataPortalException in the case of a server-side exception.

The Csla.Server.DataPortalResult object is primarily responsible for returning the business object that was created, retrieved, or updated on the server back to the client. However, it also contains the global context collection from the server.

When the DataPortalResult object is created by FactoryDataPortal or SimpleDataPortal, it automatically pulls the global context data from ApplicationContext.

```
public DataPortalResult(object returnObject)
{
  _returnObject = returnObject;
  _globalContext = ApplicationContext.GetGlobalContext();
}
```

This way, the global context data is carried back to the client along with the business object.

Csla.Server.DataPortalException

Where Csla.Server.DataPortalResult returns the business object and context to the client for a successful server-side operation, Csla.Server.DataPortalException returns that data in the case of a server-side exception. Obviously, the primary responsibility of DataPortalException is to return the details about the exception, including the server-side stack trace, back to the client. This information is captured when the exception is created.

```
public DataPortalException(
  string message, Exception ex, DataPortalResult result)
  : base(message, ex)
{
  _innerStackTrace = ex.StackTrace;
  _result = result;
}
```

Notice that a DataPortalResult object is required as a parameter to the constructor. This DataPortalResult object is returned to the client as part of the exception, thus ensuring that both the business object (exactly as it was when the exception occurred) and the global context from the server are returned to the client as well.

At this point, you have walked through all the various types and classes used to implement the core mobile object and data access functionality in the framework.

Conclusion

This chapter has walked through the various types and classes in the framework that enable both mobile objects and data access. The details of mobile objects are managed by a concept called the data portal. You should understand that the data portal incorporates several areas of functionality:

- Logical separation of business and data access layers
- Consistent coding model for root and child objects
- Channel adapter design pattern
- Flexible distributed transactional support
- Message router design pattern
- Context and location transparency

The channel adapter provides for flexibility in terms of how (or if) the client communicates with an application server to run server-side code. The distributed transactional support abstracts the use of Enterprise Services or `System.Transactions`. The message router handles the routing of client calls to your business components on the server, minimizing the coupling between client and server by enabling a single point of entry to the server. Behind the scenes, the data portal provides transparent context flow from the client to the server and back to the client. This includes implementing impersonation when using custom authentication.

At this point, the discussion of the CSLA .NET framework implementation is nearly complete. Chapter 16 will cover various other features of the framework, and then Chapters 17 onward will discuss how to use the framework to build applications.

CHAPTER 16

Other Framework Features

This is the final chapter covering the implementation of the CSLA .NET framework. The framework is based on the concepts in Chapter 1 and the design in Chapter 2. Chapters 6 through 15 walked through the implementation of the major features of the framework, including the base classes, validation, authorization, LINQ to CSLA, data binding, and the concept of mobile objects and support for object persistence.

This chapter concludes the implementation of the framework by discussing several classes that are useful when building business applications. The following topic areas will be addressed:

- Date handling
- Data access
- Executing workflows

There are many views on what makes good UI design. One common view holds that the user should be free to enter arbitrary text and it is up to the application to try and make sense of the entry. Nowhere is this truer than with date values, and the `SmartDate` type is designed to simplify how a business developer uses dates and exposes them to the UI.

When it comes to data access, the .NET Framework provides powerful support through many technologies, including LINQ to SQL, the ADO.NET Entity Framework, and raw ADO.NET itself. Even with all these options, dealing with data remains somewhat complex.

It is quite common to use `TransactionScope` to manage transactions, but to avoid the overhead of the DTC, you must ensure that only one database connection is opened during the entire transaction. The `ConnectionManager`, `ObjectContextManager`, and `ContextManager` classes help make that easy to implement in your data access code.

Another common issue when using raw ADO.NET is that database columns often store `null` values, but the application requires simpler, empty values (e.g., an empty `string` instead of a `null`). The `SafeDataReader` eliminates `null` values from the data, transforming them into appropriate empty values instead.

Yet another issue when dealing with data, especially in Web Forms and XML services, is that data must be copied from business objects into and out of other types of objects. This is especially true when building web services because data coming into a web service is contained in a proxy object, and that data must be moved into or out of your business objects. The `DataMapper` class helps streamline this process, reducing the amount of code you must write and maintain.

You can use business objects with workflows. Workflows consist of activities, and each activity is a stand-alone piece of functionality that can be implemented using business objects. That doesn't require any extra support from CSLA .NET. But business objects, especially using the command object stereotype, can be used to execute workflows and CSLA .NET includes the `WorkflowManager` class to simplify that process.

As you can see, this chapter is a collection of topics that don't fit neatly into the categories covered in the chapters thus far. But the elements discussed here are often some of the most widely used parts of the CSLA .NET framework.

Date Handling with SmartDate

One common view of good UI design holds that the user should be free to enter arbitrary text and it is up to the application to make sense of the entry. Nowhere is this truer than with date values, and the `SmartDate` type is designed to simplify how a business developer uses dates and exposes them to the UI.

Examples of free-form date entry are easy to find. Just look at widely used applications such as Microsoft Money or Intuit's Quicken. In these applications, users are free to enter dates in whatever format is easiest for them. Additionally, various shortcuts are supported; for example, the plus character (+) means *tomorrow*, while the minus (-) means *yesterday*.

Most users find this approach more appealing than being forced to enter a date in a strict format through a masked edit control or having to always use the mouse for a graphical calendar control. Of course, being able to additionally support a calendar control is a great UI design choice.

Date handling is also quite challenging because the standard `DateTime` data type doesn't have any comprehension of an "empty" or "blank" date. Many applications have date values that may be empty for a time and are filled in later. Consider a sales order in which the shipment date is unknown when the order is entered. That date should remain blank or empty until an actual date is known. Without the concept of an empty date, an application will require the user to enter an invalid "placeholder" date until the real date is known; and that's just poor application design.

■ **Tip** In the early 1990s, I worked at a company where all "far-future" dates were entered as 12/31/99. Guess how much trouble the company had around Y2K, when all of its never-to-be-delivered orders started coming due.

It is true that the `Nullable<T>` type can be applied to a `DateTime` value like this: `Nullable<DateTime>`. This allows a date to be "empty" in a limited sense. Unfortunately, that isn't enough for many applications because an actual date value can't be meaningfully compared to a `null` value. Is the `null` value greater than or less than a given date? With `Nullable<T>`, the answer is an exception, which is not a very useful answer.

Additionally, data binding doesn't deal well with `null` values, so exposing a `null` value from a business object's property often complicates the UI code.

The `Csla.SmartDate` type is designed to augment the standard .NET `DateTime` type to make it easier to work with date values. In particular, it provides the following key features:

- Automatic translation between `string` and `DateTime` types
- Translation of shortcut values to valid dates
- Understanding of the concept of an "empty" date
- Meaningful comparison between a date and an empty date

Creating your own primitive data type turns out to be very complex, and all the details are outside the scope of this book. When you create a primitive data type you must provide operator overloads and type converters, support formatting, and implement other .NET concepts. The `SmartDate` type is even more complex because it is designed to be as similar as possible to the preexisting `DateTime` data type.

The DateTime data type is marked sealed, meaning that a new type can't inherit from it to create a different data type. However, it is possible to use containment and delegation to "wrap" a DateTime value with extra functionality. That's exactly how the SmartDate type is implemented. Like DateTime itself, SmartDate is a value type:

```
[Serializable]
[System.ComponentModel.TypeConverter(
  typeof(Csla.Core.TypeConverters.SmartDateConverter))]
public struct SmartDate : Csla.Core.ISmartField,
  IComparable, IConvertible, IFormattable, Csla.Serialization.Mobile.IMobileObject
{
  private DateTime _date;
  private bool _initialized;
  private EmptyValue _emptyValue;
  private string _format;
  private static string _defaultFormat;
```

The type has an associated TypeConverter so it can be converted to and from string, DateTime, DateTime?, and DateTimeOffset values. It also implements IConvertible and a set of implicit and explicit operator overloads to enable various type conversion and casting behaviors.

The IComparable interface allows SmartDate values to have meaningful comparisons to values of type SmartDate, DateTime, DateTime?, DateTimeOffset, and string. The IFormattable interface allows SmartDate values to be formatted using an IFormatProvider and is implemented to achieve similar functionality to DateTime. All these interfaces and type conversion concepts are standard parts of .NET and are things that any primitive type should implement.

The ISmartField interface is unique to CSLA .NET. It exists to allow other people to author similar primitive types, such that CSLA .NET uses them properly. The CSLA .NET community has created types such as SmartInt, SmartBool, and so forth, and this interface is designed to allow those types to integrate smoothly into CSLA .NET.

■ **Note** The IMobileObject interface is for compatibility with CSLA .NET for Silverlight. CSLA .NET for Silverlight is outside the scope of this book, but this interface allows SmartDate values to properly serialize to and from Silverlight clients when using CSLA .NET for Silverlight.

The most important field is the _date field, which is the underlying DateTime value of the SmartDate. Remember that in the end, SmartDate is just a wrapper around a DateTime value.

Supporting empty date values is more complex than it might appear. An empty date still has meaning and, in fact, it is possible to compare a regular date to an empty date and get a valid result.

Consider a sales order example. If the shipment date of a sales order is unknown, the date will be empty. But effectively, that empty date is infinitely far in the future. Were you to compare that empty shipment date to any other date, the shipment date would be the larger of the two. Conversely, there are cases in which an empty date should be considered to be smaller than the smallest possible date.

This concept is important, as it allows for meaningful comparisons between dates and empty dates. Such comparisons make implementation of validation rules and other business logic far simpler. You can, for instance, loop through a set of Order objects to find all the objects with a shipment date before today, without the need to worry about empty dates:

```
foreach (Order order in OrderList)
  if (order.ShipmentDate <= DateTime.Today)
```

Assuming ShipmentDate is a SmartDate, it will work great, and any empty dates will be considered to be larger than any actual date value.

The _emptyValue field keeps track of whether the SmartDate instance should consider an empty date to be the smallest or largest possible date value. If it is EmptyValue.MaxDate, an empty date is considered to be the largest possible value, while EmptyValue.MinDate indicates the reverse.

The _format field stores a .NET format string that provides the default format for converting a DateTime value into a string representation.

The _defaultFormat is a static field that provides a default value for _format if it hasn't been explicitly set on an instance of SmartDate.

The _initialized field keeps track of whether the SmartDate has been initialized. Remember that SmartDate is a struct not an object. This severely restricts how the type's fields can be initialized.

Initializing the Struct

As with any struct, SmartDate can be created with or without calling a constructor. This means a business object could declare SmartDate fields using any of the following:

```
private SmartDate _date1;
private SmartDate _date2 = new SmartDate(EmptyValue.MinDate);
private SmartDate _date3 = new SmartDate(DateTime.Today);
private SmartDate _date4 = new SmartDate(DateTime.Today, EmptyValue.MaxDate);
private SmartDate _date5 = new SmartDate("1/1/2008", EmptyValue.MaxDate);
private SmartDate _date6 = new SmartDate("",EmptyValue.MaxDate);
```

In the first two cases, the SmartDate starts out being empty, with *empty* meaning that it has a value smaller than any other date.

The _date3 value starts out containing the current date. If it is set to an empty value later, that empty value will correspond to a value smaller than any other date.

The next two values are initialized to either the current date or a fixed date based on a string value. In both cases, if the SmartDate is set to an empty value later, that empty value will correspond to a value larger than any other date.

Finally, _date6 is initialized to an empty date value, where that value is larger than any other date.

Handling this initialization is a bit tricky because the C# compiler requires that all instance fields in a struct be assigned a value in any constructor before any properties or methods can be called. Yet the _date5 and _date6 fields in particular require that a method be called to parse the string value into a date value. Due to this compiler limitation, each constructor sets all instance fields to values (sometimes dummy values) and then calls properties or methods as needed.

An additional complication is that a struct can't have a default constructor. Yet even in the previous case of _date1, some initialization is required. This is the purpose of the _initialized instance field. It, of course, defaults to a value of false so can be used in the properties of the struct to determine whether the struct has been initialized. As you'll see, this allows SmartDate to initialize itself the first time a property is called, assuming it hasn't been initialized previously.

All the constructors follow the same basic flow. Here's one of them:

```
public SmartDate(string value, EmptyValue emptyValue)
{
  _emptyValue = emptyValue;
  _format = null;
  _initialized = true;
  _date = DateTime.MinValue;
  this.Text = value;
}
```

Notice that all the instance fields are assigned values. Even the _date field is assigned a value, though as you'll see, the Text property immediately changes that value based on the value parameter passed into the constructor. This includes translation of an empty string value into the appropriate empty date value.

Supporting Empty Dates

SmartDate already has a field to control whether an empty date represents the largest or smallest possible date. This field is exposed as a property so that other code can determine how dates are handled:

```
public bool EmptyIsMin
{
  get { return (_emptyValue == EmptyValue.MinDate); }
}
```

SmartDate also implements an IsEmpty property so that code can ask if the SmartDate object represents an empty date:

```
public bool IsEmpty
{
  get
  {
    if (_emptyValue == EmptyValue.MinDate)
      return this.Date.Equals(DateTime.MinValue);
    else
      return this.Date.Equals(DateTime.MaxValue);
  }
}
```

Notice the use of the _emptyValue field to determine whether an empty date is to be considered the largest or smallest possible date for comparison purposes. If it is the smallest date, it is empty if the date value equals DateTime.MinValue; if it is the largest date, it is empty if the value equals DateTime.MaxValue.

Conversion Functions

Given this understanding of empty dates, it is possible to create a couple of functions to convert dates to text (or text to dates) intelligently. For consistency with other .NET types, SmartDate also includes a Parse() method to convert a string into a SmartDate. These are static methods so that they can be used even without creating an instance of SmartDate. Using these methods, a developer can write business logic such as this:

```
DateTime userDate = SmartDate.StringToDate(userDateString);
```

Table 16-1 shows the results of this function based on various user text inputs.

Table 16-1. *Results of the StringToDate Method Based on Various Inputs*

User Text Input	EmptyValue	Result of StringToDate
string.Empty	MinDate (default)	DateTime.MinValue
string.Empty	MaxDate	DateTime.MaxValue
Any text that can be parsed as a date	Ignored	A date value

StringToDate() converts a string value containing a date into a DateTime value. It knows that an empty string should be converted to either the smallest or the largest date, based on an optional parameter.

It also handles translation of shortcut values to valid date values. The characters ., +, and -, correspond to today, tomorrow, and yesterday, respectively. Additionally, the values t, today, tom, tomorrow, y, and yesterday work in a similar manner. These text values are defined in the project's Resource.resx file and are subject to localization for other languages.

Given a string of nonzero length, StringToDate() attempts to parse it directly to a DateTime field. If that fails, the various shortcut values are checked. If that fails as well, an exception is thrown to indicate that the string value can't be parsed into a date.

SmartDate also implements the Parse() and TryParse() methods, which provide a more standard API for translating a text value into a non-text type. These methods simply delegate the calls to the StringToDate() method.

SmartDate can translate dates the other way as well, such as converting a DateTime field into a string and retaining the concept of an empty date. Again, an optional parameter controls whether an empty date represents the smallest or the largest possible date. Another parameter controls the format of the date as it's converted to a string. Table 16-2 illustrates the results for various inputs.

Table 16-2. *Results of the DateToString Method Based on Various Inputs*

User Date Input	EmptyValue	Result of DateToString
DateTime.MinValue	MinDate (default)	string.Empty
DateTime.MinValue	MaxDate	DateTime.MinValue
DateTime.MaxValue	MinDate (default)	DateTime.MaxValue
DateTime.MaxValue	MaxDate	string.Empty
Any other valid date	Ignored	String representing the date value

The DateToString() method functions as a mirror to the StringToDate() method. This means it is possible to start with an empty string, convert it to a DateTime, and then convert that DateTime back into an empty string.

This method uses a format string, which defines how the DateTime value is to be formatted as a string. This is used to create a complete .NET format string such as {0:d}.

Text Functions

Next, let's implement functions in SmartDate that support both text and DateTime access to the underlying DateTime value. When business code needs to expose a date value to the UI, it will often prefer to expose it as a string. (Exposing it as a DateTime precludes the possibility of the user entering a blank value for an empty date; and while that's great if the date is required, it isn't good for optional date values.)

Exposing a date as text requires the ability to format the date properly. To make this manageable, the _format field is used to control the format used for outputting a date. The default value for _format is d for the short date format. SmartDate includes a FormatString property so that the business developer can alter this format value to override the default.

There's also a SetDefaultFormatString() method, which is static. This can be used to provide an application-wide change to the default format string, though the FormatString property can still override the default on a per-instance basis.

Given the FormatString property, the Text property can use the StringToDate() and DateToString() methods to translate between text and date values. This property can be used to retrieve or set values using string representations of dates, where an empty string is appropriately handled:

```
public string Text
{
  get { return DateToString(this.Date, FormatString, _emptyValue); }
  set { this.Date = StringToDate(value, _emptyValue); }
}
```

This property is used in the constructors as well, meaning that the same rules for dealing with an empty date apply during object initialization as when setting its value via the Text property.

There's one other text-oriented method to implement: ToString(). All objects in .NET have a ToString() method, which ideally returns a useful text representation of the object's contents. In this case, it should return the formatted date value:

```
public override string ToString()
{
  return this.Text;
}
```

Since the Text property already converts the SmartDate value to a string, this is easy to implement.

Date Functions

It should be possible to treat a SmartDate like a regular DateTime—as much as possible, anyway. Since it's not possible for it to inherit from DateTime, there's no way for it to be treated just like a regular DateTime. The best approximation is to implement a Date property that returns the internal value:

```
public DateTime Date
{
  get
  {
    if (!_initialized)
    {
      _date = DateTime.MinValue;
      _initialized = true;
    }
    return _date;
  }
  set
  {
    _date = value;
    _initialized = true;
  }
}
```

Notice the use of the _initialized field to determine whether the SmartDate has been initialized. If the SmartDate instance is declared without explicitly calling one of the constructors, it will not be initialized; so the _date field needs to be set before it can be returned. It is set to DateTime.MinValue because that is the empty date when _emptyValue is MinDate (which it is by default).

SmartDate also implements numerous conversion methods and operator overloads as well as the same set of date manipulation functions to add and subtract values as DateTime. The end result is that you can use a SmartDate instead of a DateTime value in almost any scenario, unless the consuming code directly expects a DateTime type.

Database Format

The final bit of code in SmartDate exists to help simplify data access. This is done by implementing a method that allows a SmartDate value to be converted to a format suitable for writing to the database. Though SmartDate already has methods to convert a date to text and text to a date, it doesn't have any good way of getting a date formatted properly to write to a database. Specifically, it needs a way to either write a valid date or write a null value if the date is empty.

In ADO.NET, a null value is usually expressed as DBNull.Value, so it is possible to implement a method that returns either a valid DateTime object or DBNull.Value:

```
public object DBValue
{
  get
  {
    if (this.IsEmpty)
      return DBNull.Value;
    else
      return this.Date;
  }
}
```

Since SmartDate already implements an IsEmpty() property, the code here is pretty straightforward. If the value is empty, DBNull.Value is returned, which can be used to put a null value into a database via ADO.NET. Otherwise, a valid date value is returned.

At this point, you've seen the implementation of the core SmartDate functionality. While using SmartDate is certainly optional, it does offer business developers an easy way to handle dates that must be represented as text and to support the concept of an empty date. Later, the section on the SafeDataReader discusses some data access functionality to make it easy to save and restore a SmartDate from a database.

This same approach can be used to make other data types "smart" if you so desire. Even with the Nullable<T> support from the .NET Framework, dealing with empty values often requires extra coding, which is often most efficiently placed in a framework class such as SmartDate.

Data Access

Almost all applications employ some data access. Obviously, the CSLA .NET framework puts heavy emphasis on enabling data access through the data portal, as described in Chapter 15. Beyond the basic requirement to create, read, update, and delete data, however, there are other needs.

One of the most common issues occurs when using the TransactionScope object from the System.Transactions namespace to provide transactional behaviors. While TransactionScope is very powerful, it has one big limitation in that it uses the DTC to manage any transaction where the code opens more than one database connection. If you are only working with a single database, it doesn't make sense to pay the performance cost of the DTC, and yet it can be difficult to ensure your code always reuses the same database connection.

■ **Note** There are other things that can trigger the use of the DTC when using TransactionScope. These include using a database other than SQL Server 2005 or 2008 or interacting with other resource managers (e.g., MSMQ). CSLA .NET doesn't help address these issues.

The ConnectionManager class helps you write consistent data access code, which automatically reuses the same database connection. Similarly, the ObjectContextManager and ContextManager classes do the same thing for ADO.NET Entity Framework and LINQ to SQL code, respectively.

During the process of reading data from a database, many application developers find themselves writing repetitive code to eliminate null database values. SafeDataReader is a wrapper around any ADO.NET DataReader object that automatically eliminates any null values that might come from the database.

When creating many web applications using either Web Forms or Web Services, data must be copied into and out of business objects. In the case of Web Forms data binding, data comes from the page in a dictionary of name/value pairs, which must be copied into the business object's properties. With Web Services, the data sent or received over the network often travels through simple DTOs. The properties of those DTOs must be copied into or out of a business object within the web service. The DataMapper class contains methods to simplify these tasks.

Managing Database Connections and Contexts

The TransactionScope object is a convenient and powerful way to manage transactions in .NET. It offers the performance of ADO.NET transactions with the coding simplicity of Enterprise Services. All you need to do is wrap your data access code in a using block:

```
using (var tr = new TransactionScope())
{
  // open database and do data access here
  tr.Commit();
}
```

You get the same behavior with the data portal by using the Transactional attribute on your data access method, as discussed in Chapter 15. The catch is that you can't open more than one database connection within that using block or TransactionScope will enlist the DTC to manage the transaction. That typically causes a 15 percent performance cost, which doesn't make sense if all you are doing is opening multiple connections to the same database with the same connection string. And that is quite common, especially when updating an object graph into the database. In many cases, the simplest way to write your data access code is to put the insert, update, and delete calls in a method for each business object so your code inserts a sales order, then each line item. And to keep things simple, each object opens its own connection to the database.

Of course, each object doesn't *really* open its own connection to the database because database connection pooling automatically causes reuse of the same connection. So this technique is simple and performs well and is very attractive—until you use TransactionScope.

So what's needed is some way by which the data access methods can *appear* to open a new connection each time but in reality use the same already open connection. This is the purpose behind the types listed in Table 16-3, which are found in the Csla.Data namespace.

Table 16-3. *Connection Manager Types*

Type	Description
ConnectionManager	Opens and manages an ADO.NET IDbConnection object
ObjectContextManager	Opens and manages an ADO.NET Entity Framework object context
ContextManager	Opens and manages a LINQ to SQL data context

All three of these classes use a similar technique and are used in data access code in a similar manner. If you are using TransactionScope and the ConnectionManager, for example, your root business object's data access method would look like this:

```
[Transactional(TransactionTypes.TransactionScope)]
private void DataPortal_Insert()
{
  using (var ctx = ConnectionManager<SqlConnection>.GetManager("MyDb"))
  {
    // insert object's data here using ctx.Connection
    // ...
    FieldManager.UpdateChildren(this);
  }
}
```

In this example, I'm letting the data portal put the code into a TransactionScope by using the Transactional attribute. The ConnectionManager creates and opens a SqlConnection object, using MyDb as the key to look up the connection string from the application's connectionStrings section in the config file.

All code inside the using block can use ctx.Connection to access the open connection object. When the using block exits, the connection is automatically closed.

Notice the UpdateChildren() call though. This causes all child objects contained by this object to be updated. Each child object needs to insert its own data, too. It is important to realize that UpdateChildren() is called *inside the using block* so the connection is open.

A child's data access method would look like this:

```
private void Child_Insert(object parent)
{
  using (var ctx = ConnectionManager<SqlConnection>.GetManager("MyDb"))
  {
    // insert object's data here using ctx.Connection
  }
}
```

The child code also uses the ConnectionManager. This time, however, ConnectionManager determines that there's already an open connection for MyDb and so it simply returns that already open connection. It also increases a *reference count* so it knows that it is nested within two using blocks. That way when this using block exists, it does not close the connection. Instead it just decrements the reference count. Only when the reference count reaches zero does the connection get closed.

The ObjectContextManager and ContextManager classes work in exactly the same way, except they manage ObjectContext and DataContext objects respectively. Of course each of those object types contains an open database connection, and the real goal is to reuse that already open database connection.

ConnectionManager

Because all three classes are so similar, I'll walk through ConnectionManager in detail and only briefly discuss the implementation of the other two.

The ConnectionManager class contains a database connection, which is a disposable object. This means that ConnectionManager must also be disposable, so it implements the IDisposable interface:

```
public class ConnectionManager<C> :
  IDisposable where C : IDbConnection, new()
```

ConnectionManager can decrement the reference count each time Dispose() is called and can close the connection when the reference count reaches zero. I discuss this later in this section.

Notice that this is a generic type. And moreover, the type parameter, C, is constrained to only accept types that implement IDbConnection and that have a public default constructor. This works fine with most connection types such as SqlConnection and is a requirement of the factory method that must create and open the connection:

```
public static ConnectionManager<C> GetManager(
  string database, bool isDatabaseName)
{
  if (isDatabaseName)
  {
    var conn =
      ConfigurationManager.ConnectionStrings[database].ConnectionString;
    if (string.IsNullOrEmpty(conn))
      throw new ConfigurationErrorsException(
        String.Format(Resources.DatabaseNameNotFound, database));
    database = conn;
  }

  lock (_lock)
  {
    ConnectionManager<C> mgr = null;
    if (ApplicationContext.LocalContext.Contains("__db:" + database))
    {
      mgr = (ConnectionManager<C>)(
        ApplicationContext.LocalContext["__db:" + database]);

    }
    else
    {
      mgr = new ConnectionManager<C>(database);
      ApplicationContext.LocalContext["__db:" + database] = mgr;
    }
    mgr.AddRef();
    return mgr;
  }
}
```

The first part of this method determines whether the database parameter is the connection string or the name of the database. By default it is the name of the database, and the code uses the .NET ConfigurationManager to retrieve a connection string from the application's config file.

Once the code has a connection string, it can create and open the database connection. It does this within a lock statement because this is a static method. By convention, static methods in .NET should be implemented in a thread-safe manner, and this lock statement ensures that only one thread at a time can attempt to create an open connection.

The first thing the code does is attempt to retrieve any existing ConnectionManager from a cache. I am using *thread local storage* for the cache because TLS is a globally available location for storing per-thread data:

```
if (ApplicationContext.LocalContext.Contains("__db:" + database))
{
  mgr = (ConnectionManager<C>)(
    ApplicationContext.LocalContext["__db:" + database]);
```

Not all database connection objects are thread-safe, so ConnectionManager manages its connection objects on a per-thread basis to avoid accidentally providing a connection object from one thread to some other thread.

Notice that the database name is used as a key value to store and retrieve the ConnectionManager object. This allows the ConnectionManager to have many open connections at once, each for a different database.

If a preexisting ConnectionManager is in TLS, it is retrieved. If there isn't one in TLS, a new one is created and put into TLS:

```
else
{
  mgr = new ConnectionManager<C>(database);
  ApplicationContext.LocalContext["__db:" + database] = mgr;
```

The ConnectionManager has a constructor that creates and opens the connection object:

```
private ConnectionManager(string connectionString)
{
  _connectionString = connectionString;

  // open connection
  _connection = new C();
  _connection.ConnectionString = connectionString;
  _connection.Open();
}
```

Here's where the constraints on C become important. The new constraint ensures that it is possible to create a new C(), and the IDbConnection constraint ensures the object has a ConnectionString property and an Open() method.

Back in the static method, either an existing object is retrieved from TLS or a new one is created. Either way, its AddRef() method is called to increment its reference count (because it is now inside a using block) and the CommandManager instance is returned to the caller.

In the Dispose() method, the reference count is decremented:

```
public void Dispose()
{
  DeRef();
}
```

And in the DeRef() method, when the reference count reaches zero, the connection is closed:

```
private void DeRef()
{
  lock (_lock)
  {
    _refCount -= 1;
    if (_refCount == 0)
    {
      _connection.Dispose();
      ApplicationContext.LocalContext.Remove("__db:" + _connectionString);
    }
  }
}
```

That is also the trigger for removing the CommandManager instance from TLS.

You should now understand how calling the GetManager() method creates or retrieves the manager object and the underlying connection, while incrementing the reference count. And how the Dispose() method decrements the reference count and cleans everything up when the count reaches zero.

The ObjectContextManager and ContextManager work in exactly the same way, but with different types of connection objects.

ObjectContextManager

The ObjectContextManager class manages an ADO.NET Entity Framework ObjectContext object in the same way CommandManager manages ADO.NET connection objects. Here's the class definition:

```
public class ObjectContextManager<C> :
  IDisposable where C : ObjectContext
```

The constraint on the generic type parameter, C, is that it must be an ObjectContext type. The new constraint can't be used because ObjectContext doesn't have a default public constructor.

In the constructor of ObjectContextManager, the code does create an instance of the ObjectContext object by using Activator.CreateInstance():

```
private ObjectContextManager(string connectionString)
{
  _connectionString = connectionString;
  _context = (C)(Activator.CreateInstance(typeof(C), connectionString));
}
```

There's a small amount of fragility here in that the code expects that the constructor will accept a single string parameter that contains the database connection. But this is pretty low-risk because if Microsoft changes that API, it would break virtually all code that uses the Entity Framework in any application.

Other than these differences, the ObjectContextManager works just like ConnectionManager, using reference counting to determine when it can close the context.

ContextManager

The ContextManager class manages a LINQ to SQL DataContext object in the same way CommandManager manages ADO.NET connection objects. Here's the class definition:

```
public class ContextManager<C> :
  IDisposable where C : DataContext
```

The constraint on the generic type parameter, C, is that it must be a DataContext type. The new constraint can't be used because DataContext doesn't have a default public constructor.

In the constructor of ContextManager, the code does create an instance of the DataContext object by using Activator.CreateInstance():

```
private ContextManager(string connectionString)
{
  _connectionString = connectionString;
  _context = (C)(Activator.CreateInstance(typeof(C), connectionString));
}
```

This is also a bit fragile because, like ObjectContextManager, the code expects that the constructor will accept a single string parameter that contains the database connection. There's a similar low risk because if Microsoft changes that API it would break almost everything that uses LINQ to SQL.

Apart from those differences, the ContextManager works just like ConnectionManager, counting references to determine when it can close the context.

SafeDataReader

There are only three reasons null values should be allowed in database columns. The first is to support foreign key relationships between tables. Ideally, in this case, your key values aren't real data values but are actual keys, so you can use null values to indicate that no data exists for a given foreign key relationship.

The second is when the business rules dictate that the application cares about the difference between a value that was never entered and a value that is zero (or an empty `string`). In other words, the end user actually cares about the difference between "" and `null` or between `0` and `null`. There are applications where this matters—where the business rules revolve around whether a field ever had a value (even an empty one) or never had a value at all.

The third reason for using a `null` value is when a data type doesn't intrinsically support the concept of an empty field. The most common example is the SQL `DateTime` data type, which has no way to represent an empty date value; it *always* contains a valid date. In such a case, `null` values in the database column are used specifically to indicate an empty date.

Of course, these last two reasons are mutually exclusive. When using `null` values to differentiate between an empty field and one that never had a value, you need to come up with some other scheme to indicate an empty `DateTime` field. The solution to this problem is outside the scope of this book—but thankfully the problem itself is quite rare.

The reality is that very few applications ever care about the difference between an empty value and one that was never entered, so the first scenario seldom applies. If it *does* apply to your application, dealing with `null` values at the database level isn't an issue because you'll use nullable types from the database all the way through to the UI. In this case, you can ignore `SafeDataReader` entirely, as it has no value for your application.

But for most applications, the only reason for using `null` values is the second scenario, and this one is quite common. Any application that uses date values, and for which an empty date is a valid entry, will likely use `null` to represent an empty date.

Unfortunately, a whole lot of poorly designed databases allow `null` values in columns where *neither* scenario applies, and we developers have to deal with them. These are databases that contain `null` values even if the application makes no distinction between a `0` and a `null`.

Writing defensive code to guard against tables in which `null` values are erroneously allowed can quickly bloat data access code and make it hard to read. To avoid this, the `SafeDataReader` class takes care of these details automatically by eliminating `null` values and converting them into a set of default values.

As a rule, DataReader objects are `sealed`, meaning that you can't simply subclass an existing DataReader class (such as `SqlDataReader`) and extend it. However, like the `SmartDate` class with `DateTime`, it is quite possible to encapsulate or "wrap" a DataReader object.

To ensure that `SafeDataReader` can wrap *any* DataReader object, it relies on the root `IDataReader` interface from the `System.Data` namespace that's implemented by all DataReader objects. Also, since `SafeDataReader` is to *be* a DataReader object, it must implement that interface as well:

```
public class SafeDataReader : IDataReader
{
  private IDataReader _dataReader;

  protected IDataReader DataReader
  {
    get { return _dataReader; }
  }

  public SafeDataReader(IDataReader dataReader)
  {
    _dataReader = dataReader;
  }
}
```

The class defines a field to store a reference to the *real* DataReader that it is encapsulating. That field is exposed as a protected property as well, allowing for subclasses of `SafeDataReader` in the future.

There's also a constructor that accepts the `IDataReader` object to be encapsulated as a parameter.

This means that ADO.NET code in a business object's DataPortal_Fetch() method might appear as follows:

```
var dr = new SafeDataReader(cm.ExecuteReader());
```

The ExecuteReader() method returns an object that implements IDataReader (such as SqlDataReader) that is used to initialize the SafeDataReader object. The rest of the code in the data access method can use the SafeDataReader object just like a regular DataReader object because it implements IDataReader. The benefit, though, is that the business object's data access code never has to worry about getting a null value from the database.

The implementation of IDataReader is a lengthy business—it contains a lot of methods—so I'm not going to go through all of it here. Instead I'll cover a few methods to illustrate how the overall class is implemented.

GetString

There are two overloads for each method that returns column data, one that takes an ordinal column position and the other that takes the string name of the property. This second overload is a convenience but makes the code in a business object much more readable. All the methods that return column data are "null protected" with code like this:

```
public string GetString(string name)
{
  return GetString(_dataReader.GetOrdinal(name));
}

public virtual string GetString(int i)
{
  if( _dataReader.IsDBNull(i))
    return string.Empty;
  else
    return _dataReader.GetString(i);
}
```

If the value in the database is null, the method returns some more palatable value—typically, whatever passes for "empty" for the specific data type. If the value isn't null, it simply returns the value from the underlying DataReader object.

For string values, the empty value is string.Empty; for numeric types, it is 0; and for Boolean types, it is false. You can look at the full code for SafeDataReader to see all the translations.

Notice that the GetString() method that actually does the translation of values is marked as virtual. This allows you to override the behavior of any of these methods by creating a subclass of SafeDataReader.

The GetOrdinal() method translates the column name into an ordinal (numeric) value, which can be used to actually retrieve the value from the underlying IDataReader object. GetOrdinal() looks like this:

```
public int GetOrdinal(string name)
{
  return _dataReader.GetOrdinal(name);
}
```

Every data type supported by IDataReader (and there are a lot of them) has a pair of methods that reads the data from the underlying IDataReader object, replacing null values with empty default values as appropriate.

GetDateTime and GetSmartDate

Most types have empty values that are obvious, but DateTime is problematic as it has no empty value. The minimum date value is arbitrarily used as the empty value. This isn't perfect, but it does avoid returning a null value or throwing an exception.

A better solution may be to use the SmartDate type instead of DateTime. To simplify retrieval of a date value from the database into a SmartDate, SafeDataReader implements two variations of a GetSmartDate() method:

```
public Csla.SmartDate GetSmartDate(string name)
{
  return GetSmartDate(_dataReader.GetOrdinal(name), true);
}

public virtual Csla.SmartDate GetSmartDate(int i)
{
  return GetSmartDate(i, true);
}

public Csla.SmartDate GetSmartDate(string name, bool minIsEmpty)
{
  return GetSmartDate(_dataReader.GetOrdinal(name), minIsEmpty);
}

public virtual Csla.SmartDate GetSmartDate(
  int i, bool minIsEmpty)
{
  if (_dataReader.IsDBNull(i))
    return new Csla.SmartDate(minIsEmpty);
  else
    return new Csla.SmartDate(
      _dataReader.GetDateTime(i), minIsEmpty);
}
```

Data access code in a business object can choose either to accept the minimum date value as being equivalent to empty or to retrieve a SmartDate that understands the concept of an empty date:

```
SmartDate myDate = dr.GetSmartDate(0);
```

or

```
SmartDate myDate = dr.GetSmartDate(0, false);
```

GetBoolean

Likewise, there is no empty value for the bool type. GetBoolean() arbitrarily returns a false value in this case.

Other Methods

The IDataReader interface also includes a number of methods that don't return column values, such as the Read() method:

```
public bool Read()
{
  return _dataReader.Read();
}
```

In these cases, it simply delegates the method call down to the underlying DataReader object for it to handle. Any return values are passed back to the calling code, so the fact that SafeDataReader is involved is entirely transparent.

The SafeDataReader class can be used to simplify data access code dramatically, any time an object is working with tables in which null values are allowed in columns where the application doesn't care about the difference between an empty and a null value. If your application *does* care about the use of null values, you can simply use the regular DataReader objects instead.

DataMapper

When Web Forms data binding needs to insert or update data, it provides the data elements to the ASP.NET data source control in the form of a dictionary object of name/value pairs. The CslaDataSource control discussed in Chapter 10 simply provides this dictionary object to the UI code as an event argument.

This means that in a typical Web Forms application that uses the CslaDataSource, the UI code must copy the values from the dictionary to the business object's properties. The name is the name of the property to be updated and the value is the value to be placed into the property of the business object. Copying the values isn't hard—the code looks something like this:

```
cust.FirstName = e.Values["FirstName"].ToString();
cust.LastName = e.Values["LastName"].ToString();
cust.City = e.Values["City"].ToString();
```

Unfortunately, this is tedious code to write and debug; and if your object has a lot of properties, this can add up to a lot of lines of code. An alternative is to use reflection to automate the process of copying the values.

Tip If you feel that reflection is too slow for this purpose, you can continue to write all the mapping code by hand. Keep in mind, however, that data binding uses reflection extensively anyway, so this little bit of additional reflection is not likely to cause any serious performance issues.

A similar problem exists when building web services. Business objects should not be returned directly as a result of a web service, as that would break encapsulation. In such a case, your business object interface would become part of the web service interface, preventing you from ever adding or changing properties on the object without running the risk of breaking any clients of the web service.

Instead, data should be copied from the business object into a DTO, which is then returned to the web service client. Conversely, data from the client often comes into the web service in the form of a DTO. These DTOs are often created based on WSDL or an XSD defining the contract for the data being passed over the web service. The end result is that the code in a web service has to map property values from business objects to and from DTOs. That code often looks like this:

```
cust.FirstName = dto.FirstName;
cust.LastName = dto.LastName;
cust.City = dto.City;
```

Again, this isn't hard code to write but it's tedious and could add up to many lines.

The DataMapper class uses reflection to help automate these data mapping operations, from either a collection implementing IDictionary or an object with public properties.

In both cases, it is possible or even likely that some properties can't be mapped. Business objects often have read-only properties, and obviously it isn't possible to set those values. Yet the IDictionary or DTO may have a value for that property. It is up to the business developer to deal on a case-by-case basis with properties that can't be automatically mapped.

The DataMapper class will accept a list of property names to be ignored. Properties matching those names simply won't be mapped during the process. Additionally, DataMapper will accept a Boolean flag that can be used to suppress exceptions during the mapping process. This can be used simply to ignore any failures.

An alternative is to provide DataMapper with a DataMap object that explicitly describes the source and target properties for the mapping.

Setting Values

The core of the DataMapper class is the SetValue() method. This method is ultimately responsible for putting a value into a specified property of a target object:

```
public static void SetValue(
  object target, MemberInfo memberInfo, object value)
{
  if (value != null)
  {
    object oldValue;
    Type pType;
    if (memberInfo.MemberType == MemberTypes.Property)
    {
      PropertyInfo pInfo = (PropertyInfo)memberInfo;
      pType = pInfo.PropertyType;
      oldValue = pInfo.GetValue(target, null);
    }
    else
    {
      FieldInfo fInfo = (FieldInfo)memberInfo;
      pType = fInfo.FieldType;
      oldValue = fInfo.GetValue(target);
    }
    Type vType =
      Utilities.GetPropertyType(value.GetType());
    value = Utilities.CoerceValue(pType, vType, oldValue, value);
  }
  if (memberInfo.MemberType == MemberTypes.Property)
    ((PropertyInfo)memberInfo).SetValue(target, value, null);
  else
    ((FieldInfo)memberInfo).SetValue(target, value);
}
```

A MemberInfo object is passed in as a parameter. This is a reflection object that can describe a property or a field of the target object that is to receive the new value.

The type of the property or field is retrieved using reflection. But it is important to realize that this type may be imprecise thanks to generics and the Nullable<T> concept. So the specific type of the property's return value is retrieved using a GetPropertyType() helper method in the Utilities class. That helper method exists to deal with the possibility that the property could return a value of type Nullable<T>. If that happens, the real underlying data type (behind the Nullable<T> type) must be returned. Here's the GetPropertyType() method from the Utilities class:

```
public static Type GetPropertyType(Type propertyType)
{
  Type type = propertyType;
  if (type.IsGenericType &&
    (type.GetGenericTypeDefinition() == typeof(Nullable<>)))
    return Nullable.GetUnderlyingType(type);
  return type;
}
```

If `Nullable<T>` isn't involved, the original type passed as a parameter is simply returned. But if `Nullable<T>` is involved, the underlying type is returned instead:

```
return Nullable.GetUnderlyingType(type);
```

This ensures that the actual data type of the property is used rather than `Nullable<T>`.

Back in the `SetValue()` method, the `PropertyInfo` object has a `SetValue()` method that sets the value of the property, but it requires that the new value have the same data type as the property itself. The `CoerceValue()` method from the `Utilities` class is used to coerce the new value to the required type:

```
value = Utilities.CoerceValue(pType, vType, oldValue, value);
```

The `CoerceValue()` method uses a number of techniques in an attempt to coerce a value to the new type:

- If the value is already the right type, do nothing.
- If the target type is `Nullable<T>`, try to convert to `T`.
- If the target type is an `enum`, try to parse the value.
- If the target type is a `SmartDate`, try to cast the value.
- If the target type is a primitive type or `decimal` and the value is an empty `string`, set the value to `0`.
- If nothing has worked yet, call `Convert.ChangeType()` to convert the type.
- If `ChangeType()` fails, see if there's a `TypeConverter` for the target type and if so use the `TypeConverter`.
- If nothing has worked yet, throw an exception.

The `CoerceValue()` method is used in numerous places in CSLA .NET, and it is public so a business developer can use it as well.

Back in the `SetValue()` method, the value has been coerced to the correct type so it can be used to set the property or field value:

```
if (memberInfo.MemberType == MemberTypes.Property)
  ((PropertyInfo)memberInfo).SetValue(target, value, null);
else
  ((FieldInfo)memberInfo).SetValue(target, value);
```

The end result is that the specified property or field is set to the new value.

Mapping from IDictionary

A collection that implements `IDictionary` is effectively a name/value list. The `DataMapper.Map()` method assumes that the names in the list correspond directly to the names of properties on the business object to be loaded with data. It simply loops through all the keys in the dictionary, attempting to set the value of each entry into the target object.

While looping through the key values in the dictionary, the ignoreList is checked on each entry. If the key from the dictionary is in the ignore list, that value is ignored.

Otherwise, the SetValue() method is called to assign the new value to the specified property of the target object.

Note A DataMap cannot be used when mapping from an IDictionary to an object. This feature is designed specifically to support Web Forms data binding, and in that model the names of the UI elements and the object properties must match.

If an exception occurs while a property is being set, it is caught. If suppressExceptions is true, the exception is ignored; otherwise, it is wrapped in an ArgumentException. The reason for wrapping it in a new exception object is so the property name can be included in the message returned to the calling code. That bit of information is invaluable when using the Map() method.

Mapping from an Object

Mapping from one object to another is done in a similar manner. The primary exception is that the list of source property names doesn't come from the keys in a dictionary but rather the list must be retrieved from the source object.

Note The Map() method can be used to map to or from a business object.

The GetSourceProperties() method retrieves the list of properties from the source object:

```
private static PropertyInfo[] GetSourceProperties(Type sourceType)
{
  List<PropertyInfo> result = new List<PropertyInfo>();
  PropertyDescriptorCollection props =
    TypeDescriptor.GetProperties(sourceType);
  foreach (PropertyDescriptor item in props)
    if (item.IsBrowsable)
      result.Add(sourceType.GetProperty(item.Name));
  return result.ToArray();
}
```

This method filters out methods that are marked as [Browsable(false)]. This is useful when the source object is a CSLA .NET–style business object, as the IsDirty, IsNew, and similar properties from BusinessBase are automatically filtered out. The result is that GetSourceProperties() returns a list of properties that are subject to data binding.

First, reflection is invoked by calling the GetProperties() method to retrieve a collection of PropertyDescriptor objects. These are similar to the more commonly used PropertyInfo objects, but they are designed to help support data binding. This means they include an IsBrowsable property that can be used to filter out those properties that aren't browsable.

A PropertyInfo object is added to the result list for all browsable properties and then that result list is converted to an array and returned to the calling code.

The calling code is an overload of the Map() method that accepts two objects rather than an IDictionary and an object:

```
public static void Map(
  object source, object target,
  bool suppressExceptions,
  params string[] ignoreList)
{
  List<string> ignore = new List<string>(ignoreList);
  PropertyInfo[] sourceProperties =
    GetSourceProperties(source.GetType());
  foreach (PropertyInfo sourceProperty in sourceProperties)
  {
    string propertyName = sourceProperty.Name;
    if (!ignore.Contains(propertyName))
    {
      try
      {
        SetValue(
          target, propertyName,
          sourceProperty.GetValue(source, null));
      }
      catch (Exception ex)
      {
        if (!suppressExceptions)
          throw new ArgumentException(
            String.Format("{0} ({1})",
            Resources.PropertyCopyFailed, propertyName), ex);
      }
    }
  }
}
```

The source object's properties are retrieved into an array of `PropertyInfo` objects:

```
PropertyInfo[] sourceProperties =
  GetSourceProperties(source.GetType());
```

Then the method loops through each element in that array, checking each one against the list of properties to be ignored. If the property isn't in the ignore list, the `SetValue()` method is called to set the property on the target object. The `GetValue()` method on the `PropertyInfo` object is used to retrieve the value from the source object:

```
SetValue(
  target, propertyName,
  sourceProperty.GetValue(source, null));
```

Exceptions are handled (or ignored) just like they are when copying from an `IDictionary`.

While the `DataMapper` functionality may not be useful in all cases, it is useful in *many* cases and can dramatically reduce the amount of tedious data-copying code a business developer needs to write to use data binding in Web Forms or to implement XML services.

Mapping from an Object with a DataMap

You can also create a `DataMap` to describe the mapping of properties or fields from one object to another. This `DataMap` can be passed to the `DataMapper` object's `Map()` method, and in that case the `DataMap` is used to determine the source and target properties or fields.

A DataMap is created using code like this:

```
var map = new DataMap(typeof(CustomerData), typeof(CustomerEdit));
map.AddPropertyMapping("Name", "ShortName");
```

The DataMap constructor requires that the types of the source and target objects be provided. This is required because it does use reflection behind the scenes to get PropertyInfo or FieldInfo objects for each property or field you specify. Table 16-4 lists the methods used to load a DataMap with mappings.

Table 16-4. *Methods on DataMap*

Method	Description
AddPropertyMapping()	Sets up a mapping from one property to another property
AddFieldMapping()	Sets up a mapping from one field to another field (even if the fields are non-public)
AddFieldToPropertyMapping()	Sets up a mapping from a field to a property
AddPropertyToFieldMapping()	Sets up a mapping from a property to a field

These methods give you the flexibility to map most values from one object to another in a very flexible manner.

■ **Caution** Reflection against public members is much faster than against non-public members. If you set up a DataMap that copies to or from non-public properties or fields, you should do careful performance testing to ensure you are comfortable with the results.

The Map() method works the same as described earlier except that it uses the information in the DataMap object to determine the source and target properties or fields. Because you are specifying the map explicitly, no ignoreList parameter is used.

At this point you've seen the major classes in the Csla.Data namespace. Most applications use at least some of these types in their data access code.

Windows Workflow Foundation

WF has been a pillar of the .NET Framework since version 3.0. WF is a basic workflow engine, but it also comes with a designer that integrates into Visual Studio.

It is important to realize that workflow, in general, is a procedural programming model. You might think that there's little need for object-oriented concepts in the workflow world because procedural programming and object-oriented programming are quite different. But that isn't entirely the case.

Certainly, the workflow itself is procedural: workflows are basically animated flowcharts after all. But an object-oriented application can invoke a workflow, and workflow activities can be constructed using objects behind the scenes.

A workflow activity is by definition a self-contained unit of functionality with defined inputs and outputs. This is also the basic definition of a *use case*. As a result, you can view a workflow activity as a use case. This is exciting because creating workflow activities using object-oriented design concepts is as close as most of us will ever get to doing pure object design without all the complexities of user interaction and so forth.

Figure 16-1 illustrates at a high level one architectural view of using both objects and workflows.

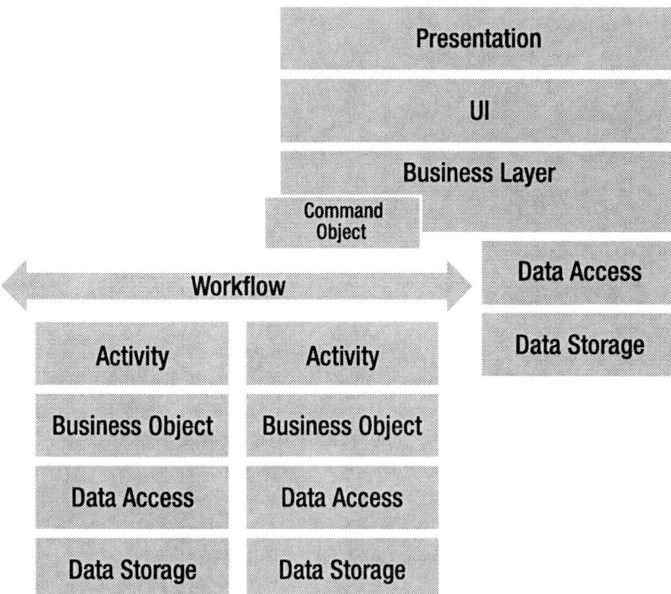

Figure 16-1. *Architectural view of using workflows and objects*

At the top of the diagram is your normal application, with its presentation, UI, business data access, and data storage layers. In this case, however, the business layer invokes a workflow through a command object. The workflow itself (in the lower left of the diagram) executes a series of activities. Each activity is implemented using business objects, which in turn invoke data access and data storage layers.

The important thing to keep in mind with Figure 16-1 is the level of encapsulation involved. To the application's business layer, the workflow is a black box that performs some useful operation. To the workflow, each activity is a black box and performs a specific task. Each activity relies on business objects to implement its task, and the activity should view these objects as black boxes.

Maintaining this level of encapsulation is important, as it provides maximum flexibility and reuse. It allows you to change the workflow without having an impact (directly at least) on the calling application. It allows you to change the implementation of an activity without having an impact (directly) on the workflow or the calling application. Finally, it allows you to change the implementation of the business objects used by an activity without having an impact on the activity, the workflow, or the calling application.

Pragmatically, most applications have two general types of functionality. There's the part that interacts with the user, displaying and collecting data. Then there's the part that performs non-interactive back-end processing, typically once the user is done entering his data.

Generally speaking, workflow can be very useful in implementing that non-interactive back-end processing. You can use WF to run a workflow on a background thread, and sometimes it is easier to visualize complex processing using the flowchart-style designer than directly through code.

Starting a Workflow from an Object

Executing a workflow from a business object is not much different from executing a workflow in any other context. If you add a workflow console application in Visual Studio, the code will include the basic template for executing your workflow. Any time you execute a workflow, you'll follow this basic pattern:

1. Create a thread synchronization object.
2. Create a workflow runtime instance.
3. Set up some event handlers (at least for `Completed` and `Terminated`) where you `Set()` the synchronization object.
4. Create the workflow instance.
5. Start the workflow instance.
6. Wait on the thread synchronization object until it is `Set()` by one of the event handlers.

However, there is one important difference when using business objects both to start the workflow and to build workflow activities. To use business objects when creating workflow activities, the workflow project references the business layer. To execute a workflow, you need access to a `Type` object for that workflow, which implies that the business layer would have a reference to the workflow project. This sort of circular reference between assemblies is not allowed by .NET.

If you look back at Figure 16-1, the workflow is architecturally treated as just another interface to the business layer. And that's a good way to think about the workflow. That means that having the workflow reference the assembly containing the business objects is a good thing, so I don't recommend changing that.

To avoid a circular reference, the business layer must not reference the workflow assembly. You can avoid the circular reference by dynamically loading the workflow type. This is done with code like this:

```
Type workflowType = Type.GetType("Namespace.WorkflowClass, Assembly");
WorkflowInstance instance =
  workflowRuntime.CreateWorkflow(workflowType);
```

The `Namespace.WorkflowClass` part of the text is the fully qualified type name of the workflow class, including namespace. The `Assembly` part of the text is the name of the assembly containing the workflow class. Notice how the `CreateWorkflow()` method then accepts the `Type` object. This allows the workflow runtime to properly create an instance of the workflow, without this code needing a reference to the assembly that contains the workflow.

WorkflowManager Class

CSLA .NET provides a `WorkflowManager` class in the `Csla.Workflow` namespace to help abstract the process of executing a workflow. The primary purpose of this class is to help manage the use of thread synchronization, while maintaining the flexibility provided by the workflow runtime model.

Table 16-5 lists the methods provided by the `WorkflowManager` object.

Several of these methods allow you to execute a workflow or to resume a suspended workflow. In both cases, control won't return to your code until the workflow is completed, terminated, or suspended.

Other methods allow you to start execution of a workflow on a background thread or to resume execution of a workflow on a background thread. Your thread remains active and can be used to perform other tasks while the workflow is running.

Table 16-5. *Methods Provided by WorkflowManager*

Method	Description
`ExecuteWorkflow`	Synchronously executes a workflow, blocking the calling thread until the workflow stops
`BeginWorkflow`	Asynchronously starts executing a workflow; the calling thread is not blocked but must call `EndWorkflow()` at some point
`WaitForEnd`	Synchronously waits for the workflow to stop; returns immediately if the workflow has already stopped; this method can optionally dispose the WF runtime instance
`ResumeWorkflow`	Synchronously resumes execution of a workflow, blocking the calling thread until the workflow stops
`BeginResumeWorkflow`	Asynchronously resumes execution of a workflow; the calling thread is not blocked but must call `EndWorkflow()` at some point
`InitializeRuntime`	Synchronously initializes the WF runtime, allowing the calling code to manipulate the runtime before calling one of the methods to execute or resume a workflow
`DisposeRuntime`	Synchronously disposes the workflow runtime

Synchronous Execution of a Workflow

In its simplest usage, the `WorkflowManager` can execute a workflow, by `Type` or type name, in two lines of code:

```
WorkflowManager mgr = new WorkflowManager();
mgr.ExecuteWorkflow("PTWorkflow.ProjectWorkflow, PTWorkflow");
```

In this case, the `ExecuteWorkflow()` method creates a `Type` object for the workflow based on the assembly qualified name of the workflow, such as `PTWorkflow.ProjectWorkflow, PTWorkflow`. Alternatively, you can just pass a `Type` object as a parameter rather than the type name:

```
WorkflowManager mgr = new WorkflowManager();
mgr.ExecuteWorkflow(typeof(ProjectWorkflow));
```

Either way, this synchronously executes the workflow. When `ExecuteWorkflow()` returns, the workflow is complete or terminated and the workflow runtime is disposed.

You can examine `mgr.Status` to determine the final state of the workflow. The possible values are listed in Table 16-6.

Table 16-6. *WorkflowManager Status Property Values*

Status	Description
`Initializing`	The workflow is being initialized and has not yet started executing.
`Executing`	The workflow is being executed.
`Completed`	The workflow completed properly.
`Terminated`	The workflow was abnormally terminated. Use the `Error` property to get the exception.
`Suspended`	The workflow was suspended.

Table 16-6. *WorkflowManager Status Property Values (Continued)*

Status	Description
`Idled`	The workflow is idled.
`Aborted`	The workflow was aborted.

For simple workflows, you can expect `Completed` or `Terminated` results once the `ExecuteWorkflow()` method has returned.

Dealing with Idled or Suspended Workflows

More complex workflows might use a persistence service to store an idled or suspended workflow to a database so it can be resumed later. That complicates the code slightly because you need to associate a persistence service with the workflow runtime and be more detailed in checking the status of the workflow when `ExecuteWorkflow()` returns.

This code shows the basic structure required to execute a workflow that might be idled or suspended and that will be persisted to a database in both those cases:

```
Csla.Workflow.WorkflowManager mgr = new Csla.Workflow.WorkflowManager();
mgr.InitializeRuntime();

// associate your persistence service with mgr.RuntimeInstance here

mgr.ExecuteWorkflow("WorkflowApp.Workflow1, WorkflowApp", false);
if (mgr.Status == Csla.Workflow.WorkflowStatus.Suspended)
{
  Guid instanceId = mgr.WorkflowInstance.InstanceId;
  mgr.WorkflowInstance.Unload();
  // store instanceId so you can resume the workflow later
}
mgr.DisposeRuntime();
```

If you expect your workflow might become idled or suspended and you want to store that workflow instance in a database to resume later, you need to provide a persistence service to the workflow runtime.

Associating a Persistence Service with the Runtime

By explicitly calling `InitializeRuntime()`, the previous code creates and initializes the workflow runtime, allowing you to then associate a persistence service (or other services) with that runtime. This is done with code similar to the following:

```
Csla.Workflow.WorkflowManager mgr = new Csla.Workflow.WorkflowManager();
mgr.InitializeRuntime();

string connectionString =
  @"Data Source=ineroth;Initial Catalog=WorkflowPersistenceStore;
    Persist Security Info=True;User ID=test;Password=test";
bool unloadOnIdle = true;
TimeSpan instanceOwnershipDuration = TimeSpan.MaxValue;
TimeSpan loadingInterval = new TimeSpan(0, 2, 0);
```

```
// Add the SqlWorkflowPersistenceService to the runtime engine.
SqlWorkflowPersistenceService persistService =
  new SqlWorkflowPersistenceService(
    connectionString, unloadOnIdle,
    instanceOwnershipDuration, loadingInterval);
mgr.RuntimeInstance.AddService(persistService);
```

This code creates and configures an instance of SqlWorkflowPersistenceService, a built-in persistence service provided with WF. This persistence service stores the serialized workflow state in the SQL Server database specified by the connection string. Before using that database, you need to run a prebuilt SQL script to set up the required tables and do some other administrative tasks. This MSDN article describes the required steps: http://msdn2.microsoft.com/en-US/library/aa349366.aspx.

The unloadOnIdle parameter also specifies that an Idled workflow should be automatically persisted.

Notice the last line of code:

```
mgr.RuntimeInstance.AddService(persistService);
```

This line of code adds the service to the workflow runtime instance being used by the WorkflowManager.

Unloading a Suspended Workflow

Returning to the original code that executes the workflow, notice that ExecuteWorkflow() is called with an extra parameter of false. This parameter indicates that the workflow runtime should not be disposed before ExecuteWorkflow() returns. This is important because if the workflow is suspended, you need to use the runtime to persist the workflow by calling the workflow's Unload() method:

```
if (mgr.Status == Csla.Workflow.WorkflowStatus.Suspended)
{
  Guid instanceId = mgr.WorkflowInstance.InstanceId;
  mgr.WorkflowInstance.Unload();
  // store instanceId so you can resume the workflow later
}
```

Once this is done, the DisposeRuntime() method of the WorkflowManager is called to dispose the workflow runtime.

Make special note of the comment in the previous code. If you unload a workflow, you need the workflow's InstanceId value, a Guid, to reload and resume the workflow later. Without this value the workflow can't be reloaded.

Loading and Resuming a Workflow

The following code reloads and resumes the workflow, assuming the instanceId field contains a valid workflow ID:

```
Csla.Workflow.WorkflowManager mgr = new Csla.Workflow.WorkflowManager();
mgr.InitializeRuntime();

// associate your persistence service with mgr.RuntimeInstance here

mgr.ResumeWorkflow(instanceId);
```

The ResumeWorkflow() method uses the instanceId value to load the workflow instance from the persistence service and then resumes the workflow execution.

At this point, you should understand how to execute, unload, and resume a workflow that could become idle or suspended as it runs.

Resuming a Suspended Workflow Without Unloading

You don't have to unload a suspended workflow. You could keep the workflow instance in memory and simply resume it. This is often valuable if the workflow requires that the application or user do something immediately to allow the workflow to continue.

The following code shows how to resume a suspended workflow without unloading it:

```
Csla.Workflow.WorkflowManager mgr = new Csla.Workflow.WorkflowManager();

mgr.ExecuteWorkflow("WorkflowApp.Workflow1, WorkflowApp", false);
if (mgr.Status == Csla.Workflow.WorkflowStatus.Suspended)
{
  // perform any actions required before resuming the workflow
  mgr.ResumeWorkflow(false);
}
mgr.DisposeRuntime();
```

Notice that no persistence service is required because the workflow is never unloaded. However, the `ExecuteWorkflow()` method is still called such that the workflow runtime is not disposed when it completes. The `Status` property is then checked, and if the workflow is suspended, the application needs to do any work that is required before the workflow is resumed. This is represented by the first highlighted line of code.

The second highlighted line of code shows how to resume the current workflow. Since the workflow wasn't unloaded, it is still in memory, just suspended. The `ResumeWorkflow()` method call resumes the workflow and allows it to run to completion.

Executing a Workflow from a Business Object

You can use the `WorkflowManager` class to simplify execution of a workflow from within a business object or you can directly invoke the WF objects yourself. Either way, a workflow is typically executed from one of the `DataPortal_XYZ` methods in a business object or the data access method in a factory object.

Execution of a workflow should fit naturally into your object model. Remember that the UI layer always interacts with your business objects, never with the database or any other services directly. If your application makes use of a workflow to perform some back-end processing, that processing should be represented somehow within your object model.

In many cases, this situation means that the workflow will be represented by a command object, which is a subclass of `CommandBase`. For example, you could execute a workflow from a `ProjectCloser` object. From the UI perspective, this object is clearly responsible for closing a project, and the fact that it uses a workflow to do the work is an implementation detail:

```
[Serializable]
public class ProjectCloser : CommandBase
{
  public static void CloseProject(Guid id)
  {
    ProjectCloser cmd = new ProjectCloser(id);
    cmd = DataPortal.Execute<ProjectCloser>(cmd);
  }
```

```
    private Guid _projectId;

    private ProjectCloser()
    { /* require use of factory methods */ }

    private ProjectCloser(Guid projectId)
    {
      _projectId = projectId;
    }

    protected override void DataPortal_Execute()
    {
      Dictionary<string, object> parameters = new Dictionary<string, object>();
      parameters.Add("ProjectId", _projectId);

      WorkflowManager mgr = new WorkflowManager();
      mgr.ExecuteWorkflow(
        "PTWorkflow.ProjectWorkflow, PTWorkflow", parameters);

      if (mgr.Status == WorkflowStatus.Terminated)
        throw mgr.Error;
    }
  }
```

The code in DataPortal_Execute() is highlighted, as this is the code that executes the workflow.

Notice the use of a Dictionary to pass in name/value parameters to the workflow. The parameter sets the ProjectId dependency property of the workflow. The assumption is that the workflow will have defined one or more dependency properties, such as ProjectId, that accept inbound parameter values.

It is also important to note that ExecuteWorkflow() is called using the type name of the workflow. This avoids any circular reference that might be caused if activities within the workflow make use of the same business assembly that contains the ProjectCloser class.

When ExecuteWorkflow() completes, the Status property is checked to see whether the workflow terminated abnormally. The exception from the workflow is then thrown, indicating to the original caller of the object that the command failed.

With ProjectCloser implemented this way, any code using the business layer can close a project like this:

```
ProjectCloser.CloseProject(projectId);
```

The calling code doesn't need to be concerned with workflows, threading, or any of the details. Everything is abstracted behind the business object.

Better yet, ProjectCloser is a standard CSLA .NET business object, which means that its call to DataPortal.Execute() uses the data portal. If the application is configured properly, it means that the workflow would run on the application server, or if the application is configured to use a local data portal, the workflow would run on the client machine.

The WorkflowManager is a useful tool when mixing business objects and workflows in the same application. But it can be useful in any scenario where workflows are used because it abstracts away many of the more complex aspects involved in executing a workflow.

Conclusion

This chapter concludes creation of the CSLA .NET framework. Over the past several chapters, you have learned how CSLA .NET delivers a wide variety of functionality to support the development of business objects. This chapter combined a range of capabilities, including the following:

- Date handling
- Data access
- Executing WF workflows

The remainder of the book focuses on how to use this framework to create business objects, a data access layer, and a variety of UIs for those objects, including WPF, Web Forms, and XML services.

CHAPTER 17

Business Object Implementation

This chapter will implement the business objects designed in Chapter 3 by following the business object coding structures from Chapters 4 and 5. This chapter will illustrate how to write code to create business objects that enjoy all the features and capabilities built into the CSLA .NET framework. The great thing is that almost all the code in the business objects will be focused on business. Each business class will largely consist of four areas:

- Class declaration
- Property declarations
- Business and validation rules
- Per-type and per-property authorization rules

I'll discuss object persistence and data access in Chapter 18. The focus in this chapter is on how business objects support the UI and other business consumers by providing a rich set of properties that automatically leverage business, validation, and authorization rules.

The example object model created in Chapter 3 includes editable objects and collections, parent-child collection relationships, read-only lists, a name/value list, and command objects. It also makes use of custom authentication, requiring the creation of custom principal and identity objects. The custom identity object will be a read-only object. In the end, the sample application makes use of every CSLA .NET base class available.

In this chapter, I won't walk through all the code in the `ProjectTracker` business object library. Instead, I'll focus on providing examples of how to implement common types of business objects and how to establish various object relationships. For the complete code, please refer to the code download for CSLA .NET 3.6, available at `www.lhotka.net/cslanet/download.aspx`.

ProjectTracker Objects

Chapter 3 covered the creation of an object model for the sample project-tracking application. This object model, shown in Figure 17-1, includes some editable root business objects (`Project` and `Resource`), some editable child objects (`ProjectResource` and `ResourceAssignment`), some collections of child objects (`ProjectResources` and `ResourceAssignments`), and a name/value list (`RoleList`). It also includes two read-only collections (`ProjectList` and `ResourceList`) and an editable root collection (`Roles`).

The solid arrows indicate using relationships, where one object uses another for some purpose—either as a parent-child relationship or for collaboration. The dashed lines indicate navigation, where a method exists so the UI developer can easily get a reference to the target object. Of course, Chapter 3 has complete details on the object model.

By implementing these objects, you should get a good feel for the practical process of taking the class templates from Chapters 4 and 5 and applying them to the creation of real business classes.

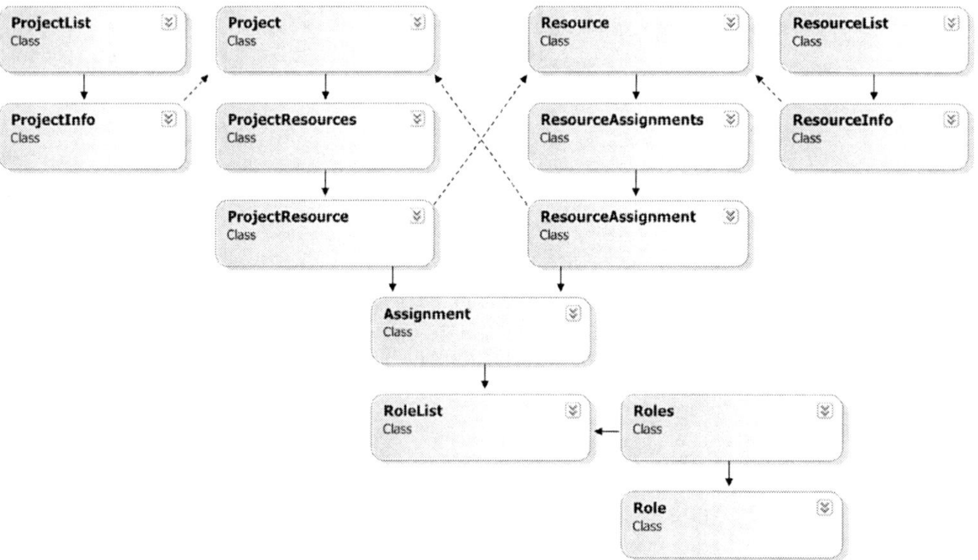

Figure 17-1. *ProjectTracker application classes*

Setting Up the Project

Technically, business classes can be placed in a Class Library, Windows Application, or website-type project in Visual Studio. But to get the full advantages of mobile objects and the CSLA .NET framework, they really must be placed in a Class Library project.

By putting the business classes in a DLL, it becomes possible for the business objects to be used by different *front ends*. This is important, because Chapters 19 through 21 will use the exact same business DLL to create WPF, Web Forms, and WCF service interfaces. It's equally important in real-world applications, since they too often have multiple interfaces. Even if an application starts with a single interface, the odds are good that at some time in the future, it will need a new one.

I prefer to collect all my projects under a single Visual Studio solution, including the business library, the WPF and web UI projects, and the WCF service project. To this end, you'll find all the code in a `ProjectTrackercs` solution in the code download, with each project and website contained inside.

The `ProjectTracker.Library` Class Library project is a library of business classes based on the design from Chapter 3. This library contains all the business logic for the Project Tracker application.

The code in `ProjectTracker.Library` uses the CSLA .NET framework, so the project references `Csla.dll`. This is a file reference that is set up through the Add Reference dialog box, as shown in Figure 17-2. This makes the CSLA .NET framework available for use within the project, and is typically all that is required.

However, remember that `Csla.dll` includes code that might run in Enterprise Services (COM+). In particular, this includes both the `ServicedDataPortal` and `EnterpriseServicesPortal` components of the data portal, as discussed in Chapter 15. If you choose to use the Enterprise Services features, then you might need to reference `System.EnterpriseServices.dll` as well.

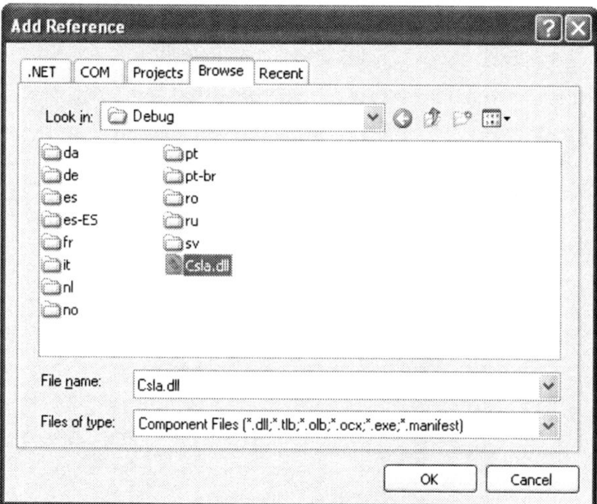

Figure 17-2. *Referencing the Csla.dll assembly*

The specific case in which this is required is if you configure the data portal to run locally in the client process *and* you mark your `DataPortal_XYZ` methods with `[Transactional(TransactionTypes.EnterpriseServices)]`. This combination causes the direct use of a `ServicedComponent` within the client process, so it requires a reference to `System.EnterpriseServices.dll`. It also has the side effect of requiring that `Csla.dll` be registered with COM+, which is handled automatically if the user is an administrator on the client workstation, but otherwise must be done manually by an administrator using the `regsvcs.exe` command line utility (or as part of a standard `msi` setup process).

■ **Caution** By default, COM+ is not enabled on Windows XP SP2 or later, or Windows Vista. If you attempt to run your data access code on the client, and you use Enterprise Services, then you will need to enable COM+ on the client workstations where the application is deployed. This configuration typically has poor performance characteristics and is not recommended.

If you don't use the `[Transactional(TransactionTypes.EnterpriseServices)]` attribute on your `DataPortal_XYZ` methods, no code will use Enterprise Services in the client process, so you won't have to worry about these details.

Business Class Implementation

The business classes implemented here follow the object-oriented design created in Chapter 3. That chapter identified not only the classes to be created, but also which CSLA .NET base classes each one will subclass.

I'll walk through the first few classes in detail. The other classes will be very similar, so for those I'll discuss only the key features. Of course, the complete code for all classes is available in the code download for the book.

Project

The `Project` class is an editable root class that represents a single project in the application. It will follow the `EditableRoot` template, as discussed in Chapter 5. This means that it inherits from `BusinessBase`, as shown in Figure 17-3.

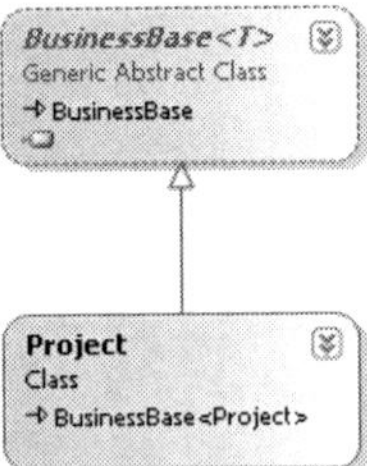

Figure 17-3. *The Project class is a subclass of BusinessBase.*

Since this is the first business class to be created, I'll walk through the code in detail. You can assume that subsequent classes follow a similar structure overall.

The `Project` class uses a number of CSLA .NET features. To make this easier, it imports a couple of CSLA .NET namespaces in addition to the standard items in the C# class template.

```
using System;
using System.Linq;
using Csla;
using Csla.Data;
using Csla.Security;
```

The class itself is contained within the `ProjectTracker.Library` namespace and is declared as follows:

```
namespace ProjectTracker.Library
{
  [Serializable]
  public class Project : BusinessBase<Project>
```

The `BusinessBase` class requires one generic type parameter. This is the type of the business object itself, and is used to provide strongly typed `Save()` and `Clone()` methods for the object as discussed in Chapter 6.

The class will contain the standard code regions discussed in Chapter 4:

- *Business Methods*
- *Business and Validation Rules*
- *Authorization Rules*
- *Factory Methods*
- *Data Access*

In this chapter, I'll discuss the first three regions, leaving the last two for Chapter 18.

The class also has a region named *Exists*. This region implements an `Exists()` method that can be used to determine if a specific project's data exists in the database. I'll discuss the code in the *Exists* region in Chapter 18, because it deals mostly with database interaction.

Let's walk through each region in turn.

Business Methods

The *Business Methods* region includes the declaration of all instance fields, along with the properties and methods that implement business logic around those fields. Since Project is a parent class, it also includes some special code designed to work well with its child objects.

In this class, I am using managed backing fields, as discussed in Chapter 7. If you would like to look at an example of private backing fields, look at the Resource class. That class is very similar to the Project class; the only real difference is that it uses private backing fields instead of managed backing fields as shown momentarily.

■ **Note** The ProjectTracker application intentionally uses different coding models in different classes. The purpose of this inconsistent coding is to illustrate various concepts within this one application, to meet the needs of this book. A real-world application should choose one model and use it consistently.

Read-Only Properties

The bulk of the code in the *Business Methods* region for most objects will be the properties. Some objects may include complex methods implementing business logic, but virtually all objects include properties to allow the UI to view or update the object's values.

The Id property of the Project is read-only. It also represents the object's unique primary key value in the database.

```
private static PropertyInfo<Guid> IdProperty =
  RegisterProperty(new PropertyInfo<Guid>("Id"));
[System.ComponentModel.DataObjectField(true, true)]
public Guid Id
{
  get { return GetProperty(IdProperty); }
}
```

Since this is the primary key for the data in the database, the value can also be considered to be a unique identifier for the object itself. The DataObjectField attribute is used to specify that the property is both a primary key and identity value. This attribute is used by data binding, and in particular by the CslaDataSource ASP.NET control discussed in Chapter 10. The attribute is optional, but is useful for helping to identify the nature of primary key properties.

Notice the use of the GetProperty() method in the get block. This helper method was discussed in Chapter 7, and it automatically checks the authorization rules before returning the value. If the user is not authorized to read the property, a default value is returned.

The Id property illustrates several things: a read-only property, a primary identity key value, and the use of the GetProperty() helper method.

Read-Write Properties

Now let's try something a bit more interesting by creating a read-write property: Name.

```
private static PropertyInfo<string> NameProperty =
  RegisterProperty(
    new PropertyInfo<string>("Name", "Project name"));
public string Name
{
  get { return GetProperty(NameProperty); }
  set { SetProperty(NameProperty, value); }
}
```

Since this is neither a primary key nor an identity value, there's no immediate need to use the DataObjectField attribute. You may still opt to use this attribute on your properties to provide this extra information for other purposes such as automated unit testing.

Notice that the PropertyInfo() object is passed the property name, along with a human-readable friendly name for the property. That friendly name is provided to all business and validation rule methods, and is automatically used by the rules in Csla.Validation.CommonRules when generating broken rule descriptions.

The get block is virtually identical to that in the Id property. In fact, the get block for properties will always be the same—the only difference is the name of the property.

The set block is similar in that it uses the SetProperty() helper method. As discussed in Chapter 7, this method does the following:

- Ensures the user is authorized to set the property; if not, it throws an exception
- Ensures the new value is different from the existing value; if not, it exits silently
- Raises the PropertyChanging event
- Replaces the existing value with the new value
- Marks the object as having been changed
- Executes all business and validation rules
- Raises the PropertyChanged event for data binding

Assuming the user is authorized to change the property value, the code checks to see if the provided value is actually new. If it's the same as the value already in the object, then there's no sense in any work being done.

Additionally, since this is a string value, it is possible to receive a null as the new value. The SetProperty() method ensures that any null values are converted to empty strings before further processing.

So, if the user is authorized to change the value, and the value is different from what is already in the object, then the new value is stored in the object. It is important to realize that this occurs *before* any validation code runs. This means that the object could end up storing *invalid values*. That's OK, though, because the object has an IsValid property that can be used to determine whether any validation rules are currently being violated by values in the object.

Prior to the property value being changed, a PropertyChanging event is raised. This event is only used by LINQ to SQL and isn't used by any other part of the .NET Framework. I have chosen to raise this event from CSLA .NET because it may be useful for business or UI code to be notified that the property is about to be changed.

The business and validation rules to be checked are associated with the property in the AddBusinessRules() method, which is implemented later in the chapter. Most rule methods assume that the value to be validated is already in the object's property, which is why it is important that the property be set to the new value before the validation rules are invoked.

The IsDirty property indicates whether the object's data has been changed. Since a new value has been put into the object, this property will now return true.

Finally, since the object's data has changed, any UI bound to the object through data binding must update its display. This is done by raising a PropertyChanged event, as discussed in Chapter 10.

Most read-write properties look just like the preceding Name property. For instance, here's the Description property:

```
private static PropertyInfo<string> DescriptionProperty =
  RegisterProperty(new PropertyInfo<string>("Description"));
public string Description
{
```

```
    get
    {
      return GetProperty(DescriptionProperty);
    }
    set
    {
      SetProperty(DescriptionProperty, value);
    }
  }
```

Notice that other than having a different property name, it is identical to the Name property. The vast majority of property methods will look exactly like this. In fact, you can find a code snippet for both read-only and read-write properties in the Snippets subdirectory in the CSLA .NET code download.

■ **Tip** You can manually install the snippet files for use in Visual Studio 2008. By default, you should copy them to the Visual C#\My Code Snippets directory under My Documents\Visual Studio 2008\Code Snippets. I typically put them in a Csla directory beneath My Code Snippets.

SmartDate Properties

So far, you've seen how to implement properties for type Guid and string. Most types follow this same approach, with obvious small variation for formatting of values and so forth. But dates are a tougher issue.

One way to deal with dates is to expose them as DateTime values directly. This works well for date values that are required, for which an empty date isn't an option. And of course, it only works well if you are binding the property to a date-aware control. Unfortunately, most of the date-aware controls don't allow the user to just type a free-form date value, so they aren't good for any sort of heads-down data entry scenarios.

The SmartDate class from Chapter 16 is intended to help solve this dilemma by making it easy for a business class to expose a date value as a string, yet also be able to treat it like a date. Additionally, SmartDate allows for empty date values—it gives you the option of treating an empty date as the smallest or largest possible date for the purposes of comparison.

The Started and Ended properties utilize the SmartDate data type. Here's the Started property:

```
private static PropertyInfo<SmartDate> StartedProperty =
  RegisterProperty(
    new PropertyInfo<SmartDate>("Started"));
public string Started
{
  get
  {
    return GetPropertyConvert<SmartDate, string>(StartedProperty);
  }
  set
  {
    SetPropertyConvert<SmartDate, string>(StartedProperty, value);
  }
}
```

Notice that this is a string property, so it can be data bound to any text input control. This means the user can enter the date value in any format that can be parsed, including the shortcuts added to SmartDate in Chapter 16 (like + for tomorrow).

The get block uses the GetPropertyConvert() helper method to return the SmartDate value but convert it into a string value. The SmartDate type automatically converts its value to a string that is formatted based on the format string in the SmartDate instance (by default it is d, the short date format).

The set block uses the SetPropertyConvert() helper to set the SmartDate with the string value provided by the user. The type conversion code in SmartDate automatically uses the parsing algorithm built into SmartDate. That way, the value is stored as a date internal to SmartDate itself. This is important because it allows SmartDate values to be compared to each other, as well as to DateTime values. This comparison capability will be used later when the validation rules are implemented in Project.

The end result is that the UI sees a string property, but all the features and functionality of a date type are available inside the business class. The Ended property is declared the same way.

You should be aware that this technique can be used to create properties of one type where the value is stored as another type, as long as the two types can be converted into each other by the CoerceValue() method in Csla.Utilities. For example, you can create a string property where the value is stored in an enum, or any other type that can be converted into and out of a string value.

Child Collection Properties

The final business property in this region provides client code with access to the collection of child objects.

```
private static PropertyInfo<ProjectResources> ResourcesProperty =
  RegisterProperty(
    new PropertyInfo<ProjectResources>("Resources"));
public ProjectResources Resources
{
  get
  {
    if (!(FieldManager.FieldExists(ResourcesProperty)))
      LoadProperty(
        ResourcesProperty,
        ProjectResources.NewProjectResources());
    return GetProperty(ResourcesProperty);
  }
}
```

The collection itself is exposed as a read-only property, but since it is an editable collection derived from BusinessListBase, the UI code will be able to add and remove child items as needed.

This property is declared using a *lazy creation* scheme, so the child collection is only created when it is used. In Chapter 18, you'll see how it is created when the object is being loaded from a database, but for a new Project object, the child collection is created on demand the first time this property is invoked. I discussed lazy creation and lazy loading in Chapter 7.

Because CSLA .NET does a lot of work to simplify the use of child objects, I recommend always using managed backing fields for child object references, even if you use private backing fields for your other property values.

Overriding GetIdValue

The BusinessBase class defines a GetIdValue() method. This method was marked as abstract in earlier versions of CSLA .NET, but is no longer required or recommended. It exists now for backward compatibility only.

The purpose behind the GetIdValue() method was to allow BusinessBase to automatically implement the standard System.Object overrides: Equals(), GetHashCode(), and ToString(). It is still used to provide an override of ToString(), but not Equals() or GetHashCode(). I find it easier to simply override ToString() than to override GetIdValue(), and that is what I recommend.

```
public override string ToString()
{
  return Id.ToString();
}
```

The reason for essentially removing GetIdValue() and the Equals() implementation is that WPF has a strict interpretation of how Equals() should work, and that implementation does not include the concept of *logical equality*.

Logical equality is the idea that one object is equal to another based on some logical comparison that has meaning for your business logic. For example, you might decide two objects with the same Id property value are equal, even if other property values are different.

WPF, however, only works properly if Equals() uses one of the following models:

- Two objects are the same if they are the exact same instance; Equals() is effectively the same as ReferenceEquals().
- Two objects are the same if they have the exact same property values for all properties.

Neither of these definitions is compatible with the idea of logical equality, so CSLA .NET no longer supports that concept either. If your application requires logical equality, you'll have to implement your own Equals() overload in your code, and you won't be able to data bind your objects to a WPF interface.

Business and Validation Rules

The *Business and Validation Rules* region implements the AddBusinessRules() method to associate validation rules to properties of the business object. As discussed in Chapter 11, validation rules are implemented as rule methods that conform to the Csla.Validation.RuleHandler delegate.

This region also implements any custom rule methods for the object. The rule methods provided in Csla.Validation.CommonRules are designed to handle most common validation requirements, but some objects have rules that aren't implemented in the CommonRules class.

AddBusinessRules

Let's look first at the AddBusinessRules() implementation.

```
protected override void AddBusinessRules()
{
  ValidationRules.AddRule(
    Csla.Validation.CommonRules.StringRequired,
    new Csla.Validation.RuleArgs(NameProperty));
  ValidationRules.AddRule(
    Csla.Validation.CommonRules.StringMaxLength,
    new Csla.Validation.CommonRules.MaxLengthRuleArgs(
      NameProperty, 50));

  ValidationRules.AddRule<Project>(
    StartDateGTEndDate<Project>,
    StartedProperty);
  ValidationRules.AddRule<Project>(
    StartDateGTEndDate<Project>,
    EndedProperty);
  ValidationRules.AddDependentProperty(
    StartedProperty, EndedProperty, true);
}
```

This method is automatically invoked by the CSLA .NET framework any time validation rules need to be associated with the object's properties. It is invoked just once for the lifetime of the application's AppDomain. For a smart client, this occurs once each time the application is run. On a server, it occurs once each time the server's AppDomain is created, often only when the server is rebooted.

The method should contain a series of ValidationRules.AddRule() method calls as shown here. Each call to AddRule() associates a validation rule with a property. In the simplest case, this means associating a rule method like StringRequired to a property like Name.

```
ValidationRules.AddRule(
  Csla.Validation.CommonRules.StringRequired, NameProperty);
```

With this done, any time the Name property is changed, the rule will be run by executing the StringRequired method. The implementation for this method was covered in Chapter 11.

■ **Note** The rule will also be applied if ValidationRules.CheckRules() is called with no parameters, as that causes the validation rules for *all* properties to be checked. Or you can force the rules for a specific property to be run with a call such as ValidationRules.CheckRules(NameProperty).

Other rules are a bit more complex, requiring extra parameter values to operate. This is the case with the StringMaxLength rule, for instance.

```
ValidationRules.AddRule(
  Csla.Validation.CommonRules.StringMaxLength,
  new Csla.Validation.CommonRules.MaxLengthRuleArgs(
    NameProperty, 50));
```

Notice that in this case, a MaxLengthRuleArgs object is created, supplying both the PropertyInfo<T> representing the property against which the rule is to be run and the maximum length for a valid string.

Because MaxLengthArgs is a subclass of DecoratedRuleArgs, you could also accomplish the same thing with code like this:

```
var args = new Csla.Validation.DecoratedRuleArgs(NameProperty);
args["MaxLength"] = 50;
ValidationRules.AddRule(
  Csla.Validation.CommonRules.StringMaxLength,
  args);
```

This second approach requires more code, but is friendlier to code generation. I recommend writing all rule methods to accept their parameter as a DecoratedRuleArgs, because it simplifies the creation of code generation templates that create this code.

Both of the rules so far have been in the CommonRules class. But Project has a custom rule method as well: StartDateGTEndDate. This rule is associated with both the Started and Ended properties.

```
ValidationRules.AddRule(
  StartDateGTEndDate, StartedProperty);
ValidationRules.AddRule(
  StartDateGTEndDate, EndedProperty);
```

As you'll see, this custom rule compares the two date values to ensure that the project doesn't end before it begins.

Interdependent Properties

Sometimes an object will have properties that are interdependent or at least have interdependent validation logic. The Started and Ended properties are good examples of this case. Later on, you'll see how to implement a business validation rule saying that the value of Ended must not be earlier than the value of Started—a project can't end before it begins.

This complicates matters slightly, because a change to either property can affect the validity of the other value. Suppose that Started and Ended begin with valid dates, but then Ended is changed to a date earlier than Started. At that point, the Ended property is invalid, but so is the Started property. Because the properties are interdependent, *both* should become invalid when the interdependent rule is violated. Similarly, if the interdependent rule later becomes unbroken, both properties should become valid.

This is the purpose behind the AddDependentProperty() method used in AddBusinessRules().

```
ValidationRules.AddDependentProperty(StartedProperty, EndedProperty, true);
```

This call to the AddDependentProperty() method tells the business rules subsystem in CSLA .NET that any time the rules for the Started property are checked, the rules for Ended should be checked too, because the last parameter is true.

The result is that any interdependent business rules are run on both properties, so both properties will become invalid or valid as appropriate.

Custom Rule Methods

Chapter 11 discussed the CommonRules class and the rule methods it contains. The basic concepts behind implementing a rule method were discussed at that time. The core requirement for all rule methods is that they conform to the Csla.Validation.RuleHandler delegate signature. They also must return true if the rule is unbroken and false if it is broken. Additionally, if the rule is broken, e.Description should be set to provide a human-readable description of the problem.

None of the rules in CommonRules are designed to ensure that one SmartDate value is greater than another, so Project implements this as a custom rule.

```
private static bool StartDateGTEndDate<T>(
  T target, Csla.Validation.RuleArgs e) where T : Project
{
  if (target.ReadProperty(StartedProperty) >
      target.ReadProperty(EndedProperty))
  {
    e.Description = "Start date can't be after end date";
    return false;
  }
  else
  {
    return true;
  }
}
```

This rule method is comparable to those in the CommonRules class, but it doesn't use reflection to do its work. It doesn't need to because it is *inside* the Project class and thus has direct access to all the private and protected members of the object.

Also notice that this is a generic method, and the target parameter is of type T. More importantly, T is constrained to be of type Project. This means the method can use the target parameter in a strongly typed manner to access the private or protected members of the object. It is the combination of being implemented in the business class and of using a constrained generic type for the target parameter that allows the rule method to be strongly typed like this.

The code accesses the ReadProperty() helper method directly to get the values of each property. It then uses those values to do the comparison. If the project start date is greater than the project end date, then the rule is broken and the method returns false; otherwise, it returns true.

This method is invoked any time either the `Started` or `Ended` properties are changed, or by an explicit call to `ValidationRules.CheckRules()` in the code.

Authorization Rules

The *Authorization Rules* region implements the `AddAuthorizationRules()` method to define per-property authorization rules. It also includes the `AddObjectAuthorizationRules()` to define per-type authorization rules.

AddAuthorizationRules

Like `AddBusinessRules()`, the `AddAuthorizationRules()` method is called automatically by the CSLA .NET framework any time the authorization rules for the object need to be configured. This method contains only a series of calls to `AuthorizationRules`, specifying which security roles are allowed or denied read and write access to each property.

```
protected override void AddAuthorizationRules()
{
  AuthorizationRules.AllowWrite(
    NameProperty, "ProjectManager");
  AuthorizationRules.AllowWrite(
    StartedProperty, "ProjectManager");
  AuthorizationRules.AllowWrite(
    EndedProperty, "ProjectManager");
  AuthorizationRules.AllowWrite(
    DescriptionProperty, "ProjectManager");
}
```

In this example, there are no restrictions on who can read properties, so there are no calls to `AllowRead()` or `DenyRead()`. Recall from Chapter 12 that if no roles are specified for allow or deny, then *all* users are allowed access.

Similarly, there are no restrictions on methods, so `AllowExecute()` and `DenyExecute()` are not used here.

■ **Tip** If the default implementation for authorization as implemented in Chapter 12 doesn't meet your needs, the business object can override the `CanReadProperty()` and `CanWriteProperty()` methods from `BusinessBase` and you can implement your own algorithm.

However, there are restrictions on who can change property values. In particular, only users in the `ProjectManager` role are allowed to change any properties on the object, so each property is associated with this role—for instance:

```
AuthorizationRules.AllowWrite(NameProperty, "ProjectManager");
```

Remember, the `ProjectManager` role is a security role, so it is either a Windows domain or Active Directory group, or a custom security role loaded when the user is authenticated. This sample application uses custom authentication, so the user's roles come from a SQL Server database.

The `AllowWrite()` method, like all the methods on `AuthorizationRules`, accepts the property's `PropertyInfo<T>` identifier, followed by a comma-separated list of the roles allowed to alter this property. The list of roles is a `params` parameter, making it easy to specify several roles on one line.

AddObjectAuthorizationRules

The business developer can also specify the roles that are allowed to create, retrieve, edit, and delete Project objects. The data portal uses this information to automatically ensure only authorized users perform each action. This information is available to the UI developer so he can enable, disable, or hide UI elements based on the user's permissions.

The roles are defined by implementing the AddObjectAuthorizationRules() method in the business object.

```
protected static void AddObjectAuthorizationRules()
{
  AuthorizationRules.AllowCreate(
    typeof(Project), "ProjectManager");
  AuthorizationRules.AllowEdit(
    typeof(Project), "ProjectManager");
  AuthorizationRules.AllowDelete(
    typeof(Project), "ProjectManager");
  AuthorizationRules.AllowDelete(
    typeof(Project), "Administrator");
}
```

The AllowCreate(), AllowGet(), AllowEdit(), and AllowDelete() methods are used to specify the roles that are allowed to perform each action. If no roles are specified (for example, there's no call to AllowGet() here), then all users are allowed to perform that action.

The AddObjectAuthorizationRules() method is a static method. CSLA .NET invokes it automatically the first time any code attempts to call one of the methods that checks authorization. Table 17-1 lists the static methods of interest to a UI developer implemented by Csla.AuthorizationRules.

Table 17-1. *Methods to Check Per-Type Authorization*

Method	Description
CanCreate()	Returns true if the current user is authorized to create an instance of the specified object type
CanGet()	Returns true if the current user is authorized to retrieve an instance of the specified object type
CanEdit()	Returns true if the current user is authorized to edit (insert or update) an instance of the specified object type
CanDelete()	Returns true if the current user is authorized to delete an instance of the specified object type

To use this functionality, each business object can implement AddObjectAuthorizationRules() to specify the roles allowed to perform each operation.

At this point, you should understand how to define read-only and read-write properties that utilize the authorization and business rules defined for each property. The Project class also includes *Factory Methods* and *Data Access* regions, which I'll discuss in Chapter 18. For now, I'll consider our discussion of the Project class complete.

ProjectResources

A Project object contains a collection of child objects, each one representing a resource assigned to the project. The collection is maintained by a ProjectResources collection object, which is created by inheriting from Csla.BusinessListBase. The ProjectResources class has three regions:

- *Business Methods*
- *Factory Methods*
- *Data Access*

The *Business Methods* region contains the Assign() method, which assigns a resource to the project. It also contains some helpful overloads of common methods, such as a Contains() method that accepts the Id value of a Resource. This is useful because the Contains() method provided by BusinessListBase() only accepts a ProjectResource object; however, as you'll see in Chapters 19 and 20, the UI code needs to see if the collection contains a ProjectResource object based on its Id value.

The *Factory Methods* region contains a set of internal-scoped factory methods for use by the Project object in creating and loading the collection with data. Finally, the *Data Access* region implements code to load the collection with data and to save the child objects in the collection into the database.

Before getting into the *Business Methods* region, let's take a look at the class declaration.

```
[Serializable]
public class ProjectResources :
  BusinessListBase<ProjectResources, ProjectResource>
```

Like all business classes, this one is Serializable. It also inherits from a CSLA .NET base class—in this case, BusinessListBase. The BusinessListBase class requires two generic type parameters.

The first one is the type of the collection itself. That value is used to provide strongly typed methods such as Clone() and Save().

The second one is the type of the child objects contained within the collection. That value is used to make the collection itself strongly typed and affects many methods on the collection, including the indexer, Remove(), Contains(), and others.

Business Methods

The *Business Methods* region contains a set of methods that provide business functionality for use by UI code. In many cases, these methods are overloads of methods common to all collections, but they accept parameters that provide much simpler use for the UI developer. The methods are listed in Table 17-2.

Table 17-2. *Business Methods in ProjectResources*

Method	Description
Assign	Assigns a resource to the project
GetItem	Returns a child object based on a resource Id value
Remove	Removes a child object based on a resource Id value
Contains	Searches for a child object based on a resource Id value
ContainsDeleted	Searches for a deleted child object based on a resource Id value

Of all these methods, only Assign() is truly required. All the other methods merely provide simpler access to the collection's functionality. Still, that simpler access translates into much less code in the UI, so it is well worth implementing in the object.

Assign

The Assign() method assigns a resource to the project. It accepts a resource Id value as a parameter, and adds a new ProjectResource object to the collection representing the assignment of the resource.

```
public void Assign(int resourceId)
{
  if (!Contains(resourceId))
  {
    ProjectResource resource =
      ProjectResource.NewProjectResource(resourceId);
    this.Add(resource);
  }
  else
    throw new InvalidOperationException(
      "Resource already assigned to project");
}
```

A resource can only be assigned to a project one time, so the collection is first checked to see if it contains an entry with that same resource Id value. Notice that the simpler Contains() overload is useful already—I'll get to its implementation shortly.

Assuming the resource isn't already assigned, a new ProjectResource child object is created and initialized by calling the NewProjectResource() factory method. Notice that the resource Id value is passed to the new child object, establishing the proper connection between the project and resource. The child object is then added to the collection, completing the process.

This means the UI code to add a resource to a project looks like this:

```
project.Resources.Assign(resourceId);
```

where resourceId is the primary key of the resource to be assigned.

GetItem

Collections have an indexer that provides access to individual items in the collection based on a numeric index value. It is also useful to be able to get a specific child object based on other data in the child objects themselves. In this case, it will be necessary to retrieve a child item based on the Id property of the resource that was assigned to the project, and this requires a method that accepts the Id property and returns the corresponding child object.

```
public ProjectResource GetItem(int resourceId)
{
  return this.SingleOrDefault((r) =>
    r.ResourceId == resourceId);
}
```

In principle, this method operates much like an indexer—but the default indexer's parameter is a positional index, while the GetItem() method's parameter indicates the Id value of the resource. Simply overloading the indexer would be a cleaner solution, but this isn't possible because the default indexer accepts an int, and so does this new "overload." The result would be a duplicate method signature, so this must be a method rather than an overload of the indexer.

Remove, Contains, and ContainsDeleted

Collections that inherit from BusinessListBase automatically have Remove(), Contains(), and ContainsDeleted() methods. Each of these accepts a reference to a child object as a parameter, and often that is sufficient.

For this collection, however, it turns out that the UI code in Chapters 19 and 20 is much simpler if it is possible to remove or check for a child object based on a resource Id property value rather than a child object reference. To provide this capability, each of these three methods is overloaded with a different implementation. For instance, here's the Remove() method:

```
public void Remove(int resourceId)
{
  foreach (ProjectResource res in this)
  {
    if (res.ResourceId == resourceId)
    {
      Remove(res);
      break;
    }
  }
}
```

This method accepts the resourceId value as a parameter, and that value is used to locate the child object (if any) in the collection. The Contains() and ContainsDeleted() overloads follow the same basic approach.

Not all collections will need overloads of this type, but such overloads are often useful to simplify the use of the collection and reduce code in the UI.

This completes the ProjectResources collection code, though I'll revisit this class in Chapter 18 to discuss the *Factory Methods* and *Data Access* regions.

ProjectResource

A Project contains a child collection: ProjectResources. The ProjectResources collection contains ProjectResource objects. As designed in Chapter 3, each ProjectResource object represents a resource that has been assigned to the project.

Also remember from Chapter 3 that ProjectResource shares some behaviors with ResourceAssignment, and those common behaviors were factored out into an Assignment object. As you look through the code in ProjectResource, you'll see calls to the behaviors in Assignment, as ProjectResource collaborates with that other object to implement its own behaviors. I'll discuss the Assignment class after ProjectResource.

ProjectResource is an editable child object, so that is the template (from Chapter 5) that I'll follow here. Editable child objects have the following code regions:

- *Business Methods*
- *Business and Validation Rules*
- *Authorization Rules*
- *Factory Methods*
- *Data Access*

The class is declared as follows:

```
[Serializable]
public class ProjectResource :
  BusinessBase<ProjectResource>, IHoldRoles
```

As with Project, the class inherits from BusinessBase, providing the type of the business object itself as the type parameter.

The class also implements an interface: IHoldRoles. This interface will be defined in the Assignments class later in the chapter, and it defines a Role property. This interface will be used by code that validates the Role property value.

I'll cover the *Factory Methods* and *Data Access* regions in Chapter 18, and I'll cover the *Business Methods, Business and Validation Rules,* and *Authorization Rules* regions now.

Business Methods

The *Business Methods* region is constructed in the same manner as Project. It contains read-only and read-write property declarations that are implemented using managed backing fields. If you want to see an example of an editable child using private backing fields, you can look at the ResourceAssignment class.

Because the property declarations are so consistent, I won't include any code here. As discussed in Chapter 7, one goal of CSLA .NET is to make property declarations standardized, which means they all look the same.

The ProjectResource class does include a GetResource() method.

```
public Resource GetResource()
{
  CanExecuteMethod("GetResource", true);
  return Resource.GetResource(GetProperty(ResourceIdProperty));
}
```

At first glance, through the use cases in Chapter 3, someone might think that a Project contains a list of Resource objects that are assigned to the project. That's a common mistake when doing object design, because both Project and Resource are clearly root objects. In reality, a Project contains a list of *assigned resources,* which are represented by the ProjectResource class.

But a ProjectResource does have a logical relationship with Resource. This is a sort of navigable using relationship, where you can envision navigating from a ProjectResource child object to a Resource root object. This is the purpose behind the GetResource() method: to implement this navigation relationship explicitly. A UI developer might use this method to show a modal dialog, so the user can edit the Resource data associated with a resource assigned to a project.

Notice the use of CanExecuteMethod() at the top of the implementation. This method checks the current user's authorization to make sure she's allowed to execute this method. If the user is not authorized, CanExecuteMethod() will throw an exception.

Business and Validation Rules

The *Business and Validation Rules* region is much like that in Project, in that it implements the AddBusinessRules() method and could include custom rule methods. In this case, however, the one custom rule required by ProjectResource is also required by ResourceAssignment. Since the rule is a form of common behavior, its implementation is located in the Assignment class.

```
protected override void AddBusinessRules()
{
  ValidationRules.AddRule<ProjectResource>(
    Assignment.ValidRole, RoleProperty);
}
```

The ValidRole rule from the Assignment class is associated with the Role property. That rule is designed to ensure that the Role property is set to a value corresponding to a role in the RoleList collection (which I'll discuss later in the chapter). The IHoldRoles interface will be used to allow the ValidRule method to access the Role property.

Authorization Rules

The *Authorization Rules* region implements the `AddAuthorizationRules()` method, establishing the roles authorized to read and write each property. For this object, the only restrictions are that the `Role` property can only be changed by a `ProjectManager`, and the `Guest` role isn't allowed to invoke the `GetResource()` method.

```
protected override void AddAuthorizationRules()
{
  AuthorizationRules.AllowWrite(RoleProperty, "ProjectManager");
  AuthorizationRules.DenyExecute("GetResource", "Guest");
}
```

These roles are checked by each property and by the `CanExecuteMethod()` method.

This completes the `ProjectResource` class, and really the whole `Project` object family. Of course, you don't quite have the whole picture yet, because `ProjectResource` collaborates with both `Assignment` and `RoleList` to do its work. I'll discuss those classes next.

Assignment

The `Assignment` class contains the behaviors common to both `ProjectResource` and `ResourceAssignment` as designed in Chapter 3. Figure 17-4 shows the collaboration relationship between these objects.

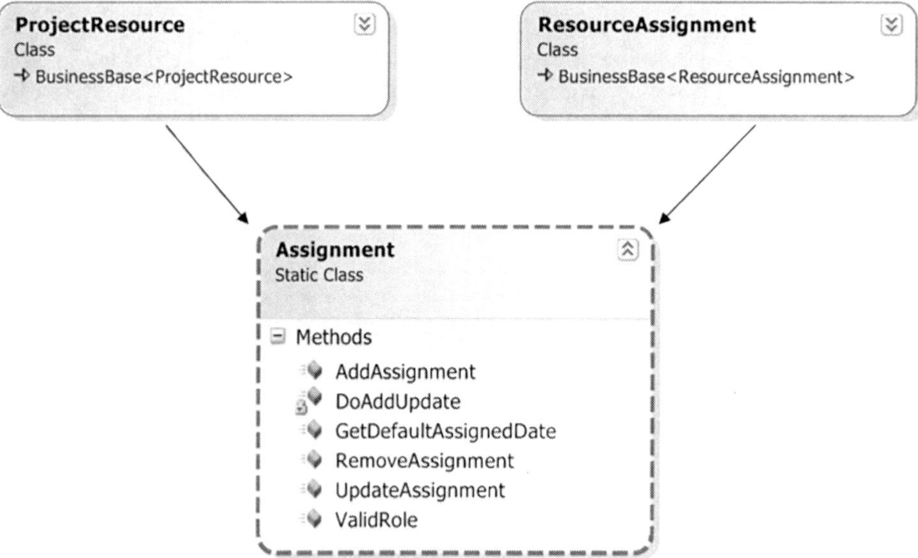

Figure 17-4. *Objects collaborating with Assignment*

Since `Assignment` only implements behaviors and contains no data, it is declared as a `static` class.

```
internal static class Assignment
```

Notice that it doesn't inherit from any CSLA .NET base classes. It has no need, since it is merely a collection of common behaviors. Specifically, it contains a business method, a custom validation rule, and a set of data access methods.

Business Methods

When a resource is associated with a project, the date of that association is recorded. Though it may seem somewhat trivial, the code to determine that date value is a common behavior between `ProjectResource` and `ResourceAssignment`, so it is implemented in the `Assignment` class.

```
public static DateTime GetDefaultAssignedDate()
{
  return DateTime.Today;
}
```

This is an example of the concept of normalization of behavior I discussed in Chapter 3.

Business and Validation Rules

Similarly, both `ProjectResource` and `ResourceAssignment` have a `Role` property, allowing the role of the resource on the project to be changed. When that value is changed, it must be validated. Of course, this is handled by implementing a rule method conforming to the `RuleHandler` delegate defined by CSLA .NET. This is common behavior, so it is implemented in `Assignment`.

```
public static bool ValidRole<T>(T target, RuleArgs e)
  where T : IHoldRoles
{
  int role = target.Role;

  if (RoleList.GetList().ContainsKey(role))
  {
    return true;
  }
  else
  {
    e.Description = "Role must be in RoleList";
    return false;
  }
}
```

This method uses the `IHoldRoles` interface to retrieve the value of the `Role` property from the specified target object. This interface is defined like this:

```
internal interface IHoldRoles
{
  int Role { get; set;}
}
```

Notice that the interface is `internal` in scope. It is only used within this assembly by the `ValidRole()` method, so there's no need to expose it as a public interface. Since both `ProjectResource` and `ResourceAssignment` implement this interface, the `ValidRole()` method has strongly typed access to the `Role` property on both objects.

Using the retrieved role value, the `RoleList` collection is asked whether it contains an entry with that value as a key. If it does, then the role is valid; otherwise, it is not valid, so `e.Description` is set to indicate the nature of the problem and `false` is returned as a result.

The `RoleList` object automatically caches the list of roles, so only the first call to `GetList()` by the application goes to the database, and subsequent calls are handled from the in-memory cache.

The `Assignment` class illustrates how to normalize behavior through collaboration, helping to ensure that a given behavior is only implemented once within the business layer.

RoleList

The final object used by Project, ProjectResources, ProjectResource, and Assignment is the RoleList collection. This is a name/value list based on the Roles table from Chapter 3. The name (key) values are of type int, while the values are the string names of each role.

The CSLA .NET framework includes the NameValueListBase class to help simplify the creation of name/value list objects. Such objects are so common in business applications that it is worth having a base class to support this one specialized scenario.

Chapter 5 includes a template for name/value list classes, and RoleList will follow that template. It includes the *Business Methods, Factory Methods,* and *Data Access* regions. The class is declared like this:

```
[Serializable]
public class RoleList : NameValueListBase<int, string>
```

Notice the generic type parameters. The first specifies the data type of the name or key, while the second specifies the data type of the value. These data types are used to define the name and value types of the NameValuePair child objects contained in the collection.

Business Methods

The only business method in this class is DefaultRole(), which returns the default role for a resource newly assigned to a project. Not all name/value collections will provide a method to specify the default role, but it is often helpful. Recall that this method is used by ProjectResource as a new ProjectResource object is created. Here's the method:

```
public static int DefaultRole()
{
  RoleList list = GetList();
  if (list.Count > 0)
    return list.Items[0].Key;
  else
    throw new NullReferenceException(
      "No roles available; default role can not be returned");
}
```

The implementation in this application is very simplistic, as it just returns the first item in the collection. In a more complex application, the default value might be specified in the database.

The rest of the code in this class deals with loading the list from the database, and will be discussed in Chapter 18.

This completes the Project object family, including all collaboration objects. Next, I'll walk briefly through the Resource object family.

Resource and Related Objects

The other primary root object in the object model is Resource. Like Project, a Resource object can be directly created, retrieved, or updated. It also contains a list of child objects.

Since I've already walked through the creation of an editable root business object in detail, there's no need to do the same for the Resource class. However, the Resource and ResourceAssignment classes use private backing fields for their properties, rather than the managed backing fields I've shown thus far.

For example, here's the Id property from the Resource class:

```
private static PropertyInfo<int> IdProperty =
  RegisterProperty(new PropertyInfo<int>("Id"));
private int _id = IdProperty.DefaultValue;
[System.ComponentModel.DataObjectField(true, true)]
public int Id
{
  get { return GetProperty(IdProperty, _id); }
}
```

In this case, a `private` field is declared to store the property value:

```
private int _id = IdProperty.DefaultValue;
```

The value is initialized to a default value from the `ResourceInfo<T>` object. This is *absolutely required* for `string` values, and is optional for other types. This is important for a `string` value, because the default for a `string` is `null`, but if your property provides a `null` value to data binding, an exception may result, as not all UI technologies support `null` values.

Also notice how the field is passed to the `GetProperty()` method.

```
  get { return GetProperty(IdProperty, _id); }
```

In this case, `GetProperty()` checks the user's authorization and returns either a default value (if the user isn't authorized) or the value of `_id`.

The `FirstName` property is an example of a read-write property.

```
private static PropertyInfo<string> FirstNameProperty =
  RegisterProperty(
    new PropertyInfo<string>("FirstName", "First name"));
private string _firstName = FirstNameProperty.DefaultValue;
public string FirstName
{
  get
  {
    return GetProperty(FirstNameProperty, _firstName);
  }
  set
  {
    SetProperty(FirstNameProperty, ref _firstName, value);
  }
}
```

Again, the field is declared and initialized.

```
private string _firstName = FirstNameProperty.DefaultValue;
```

The field is provided to `GetProperty()` just like in the previous example. However, notice how it is passed to `SetProperty()`.

```
  set { SetProperty(FirstNameProperty, ref _firstName, value); }
```

The field is passed by reference, using the `ref` keyword. This means the `SetProperty()` method has a reference to the actual field, so it can set the field with the new value. This overload of `SetProperty()` follows the exact same steps I discussed earlier in the chapter for the `Name` property in the `Project` class, but this overload sets the `private` field value.

The Resource, ResourceAssignments, and ResourceAssignment objects are otherwise totally comparable to Project, ProjectResources, and ProjectResource, so I won't cover their code in detail here. You can look at the code for these classes by downloading the code for the book.

ProjectList and ResourceList

The ProjectList and ResourceList classes are both read-only collections of read-only data. They exist to provide the UI with an efficient way to get a list of projects and resources for display to the user.

On the surface, it might seem that you could simply retrieve a collection of Project or Resource objects and display their data. But that would mean retrieving a lot of data that the user may never use. Instead, it's more efficient to retrieve a small set of read-only objects for display purposes, and then retrieve an actual Project or Resource object once the user has chosen which one to use.

The CSLA .NET framework includes the ReadOnlyListBase class, which is designed specifically to support this type of read-only list. Such a collection typically contains objects that inherit from ReadOnlyBase.

Because these two read-only collections are so similar in implementation, I'm only going to walk through the ResourceList class in this chapter. You can look at the code for ProjectList in the code download.

The ResourceList class inherits from Csla.ReadOnlyListBase.

```
[Serializable]
public class ResourceList :
  ReadOnlyListBase<ResourceList, ResourceInfo>
```

ReadOnlyListBase requires two generic type parameters. The first is the type of the collection object itself and is used to create the strongly typed Clone() method.

The only code in ResourceList deals with data access, and I'll discuss that in Chapter 18. There's no other code, because ReadOnlyListBase handles all the details required for a normal read-only list, which makes the business object developer's job easy.

The list contains read-only child objects of type ResourceInfo. This is a separate class that implements simple read-only properties to expose the resource data.

ResourceInfo

The ResourceList class is a collection of ResourceInfo objects. Each ResourceInfo object provides read-only access to a subset of data from the Resources table. The class is defined like this:

```
[Serializable]
public class ResourceInfo :
  ReadOnlyBase<ResourceInfo>
```

It inherits from ReadOnlyBase, which requires one generic type parameter: the type of the business object. This type parameter is used to implement the strongly typed Clone() method.

Business Methods

The ResourceInfo object exposes two properties: Id and Name.

```
private int _id;
public int Id
{
  get { return _id; }
}
```

```
private string _name;
public string Name
{
  get { return _name; }
}

public override string ToString()
{
  return _name;
}
```

I'm not using the field manager for this object, and I often don't use it for simple read-only objects. While ReadOnlyBase supports the field manager, if your read-only object has no authorization rules, then the field manager will provide no real value and you can write code similar to that shown here.

■ **Note** If you intend to use CSLA .NET for Silverlight, then you should base all your objects off CSLA .NET base classes, and you should strongly consider using managed backing fields. While CSLA .NET for Silverlight is outside the scope of this book, it is designed to work best with objects that use the field manager and managed backing fields.

I've also chosen to override ToString() so it returns the _name field value. This is important, because when the collection is data bound to a list control like a ListBox, it is the ToString() value that will be displayed to the user.

As you can see, creating a read-only list is usually a very simple process.

Roles

The RoleList object provides a read-only, cached list of roles that a resource can hold when assigned to a project. But that list of roles needs to be maintained, and that is the purpose behind the Roles collection. This is an editable root collection that contains a list of editable child Role objects.

The Roles class illustrates how to create an editable root collection based on the template code from Chapter 5. The class inherits from BusinessListBase.

```
[Serializable]
public class Roles :
  BusinessListBase<Roles, Role>
```

The first generic type parameter specifies the type of the collection itself, while the second provides the type of the child objects contained in the collection.

An editable root collection has *Business Methods*, *Authorization Rules*, *Factory Methods*, and *Data Access* regions. By this point, you've seen good examples of each region, so I'll just focus on the parts that are unique for a root collection. For instance, the *Authorization Rules* region includes only the static authorization rules discussed earlier in the chapter, so I'll bypass talking about that code here.

Business Methods

The Roles class implements an overloaded Remove() method that accepts a role's Id value rather than a Role object. This simplifies removal of child objects, especially in the Web Forms UI that will be created in Chapter 20.

```
public void Remove(int id)
{
  foreach (Role item in this)
  {
    if (item.Id == id)
    {
      Remove(item);
      break;
    }
  }
}
```

It also implements a GetRoleById() method to retrieve a child Role object based on the role Id value.

```
public Role GetRoleById(int id)
{
  foreach (Role item in this)
  {
    if (item.Id == id)
    {
      return item;
    }
  }
  return null;
}
```

Again, this exists to simplify the creation of the Web Forms UI.

Finally, and probably of most interest, is the AddNewCore() override.

```
protected override object AddNewCore()
{
  Role item = Role.NewRole();
  Add(item);
  return item;
}
```

When using WPF or Windows Forms data binding, it is possible to allow grid controls to automatically add new items to a collection when the user moves to the last row of the grid. The collection object itself controls whether this option is available, and the Roles collection supports the concept. Turning the option on is done in the collection's constructor.

```
private Roles()
{
  this.Saved +=
    new EventHandler<Csla.Core.SavedEventArgs>(Roles_Saved);
  this.AllowNew = true;
}
```

If AllowNew is set to true, then the object *must* override AddNewCore(), as shown here. I'll discuss the rest of the constructor code in Chapter 18 as part of the data access code.

■ **Note** This option is not enabled for ProjectResources or ResourceAssignments because it isn't possible to add a new ProjectResource or ResourceAssignment child object to those collections without first gathering extra information from the user (specifically the resource or project to be assigned). You can only allow a grid control to add new child objects if you can implement AddNewCore() to create a new child object with no user interaction.

The AddNewCore() method is called by data binding when a new item needs to be added to the collection. The method is responsible for creating a new child object, adding it to the collection, and returning it as a result.

It is important to realize that this puts a serious constraint on the child objects, since it must be possible to create them without user input. In other words, it must be possible to create a child object based purely on default values provided by your code or from the database. If your child object has a parameterless factory method (like the NewRole() method in the preceding AddNewCore() method) for creating a new object, then you are ready to go.

Role

The Roles object is an editable root collection that contains a list of editable child Role objects. Each Role object is an editable child, so it is similar in structure to ProjectResource and ResourceAssignment.

The design decision that makes this object unique and interesting is that its key value, Id, is a user-entered value. Unlike Project (in which the value is generated automatically by the object) or Resource (in which the value is generated by the database), this object's key value must be entered directly by the user.

From a data access perspective, this isn't overly complex. The Roles table views the Id column as a primary key, so it already ensures that duplicate values aren't allowed in the database. Of course, sending the object all the way to the database to find out about a validation rule being violated is wasteful. It is far better to detect the condition as soon as a duplicate key value is entered.

Additionally, the user shouldn't have to guess to find an appropriate value when adding a new role to the application. When a new Role object is created, it can set its Id property to an appropriate default value.

Setting a Default Value

The Id property contains code to find a default value if the Id property has never been set to a value:

```
private static PropertyInfo<int> IdProperty =
  RegisterProperty(new PropertyInfo<int>("Id"));
private bool _idSet;
public int Id
{
  get
  {
    if (!_idSet)
    {
     _idSet = true;
      SetProperty(IdProperty, GetMax() + 1);1);
    }
    return GetProperty(IdProperty);
  }
  set
  {
   _idSet = true;
    SetProperty(IdProperty, value);
  }
}
```

If the Id property is read, and it hasn't been set prior to this point, the code calls a GetMax() method to determine the current maximum Id value in the list.

```
private int GetMax()
{
  Roles parent = (Roles)this.Parent;
  return parent.Max(r => r.Id);
}
```

This method loops through the objects in the parent `Roles` collection to find the maximum value for any existing `Id` property, and then it returns that value. Back in the `Id` property's `get` code, the property is set to that value plus one.

```
if (!_idSet)
{
  _idSet = true;
  SetProperty(IdProperty, GetMax() + 1);
}
```

Your first thought might be that this should be done in the object's constructor. The problem with that is that the `Parent` property in the base class isn't set to a valid value when the constructor runs.

■ **Note** Both the data portal and .NET serialization create the object using constructors that can't provide parameters such as the parent object reference. To overcome this limitation, `BusinessListBase` includes code to call a `SetParent()` method on its child objects at key points in the object's life cycle.

Since the default value can't be set in the constructor, it is set in the `Id` property on the first request for the value—unless the value has been set previously, either through the property `set` block or when the data was loaded from the database.

Preventing Duplicate Values

The requirement to have no duplicate `Id` property values is simply a validation rule, so it is implemented as a rule method in the `Role` object's *Business and Validation Rules* region.

```
private static bool NoDuplicates<T>(
  T target, Csla.Validation.RuleArgs e) where T : Role
{
  Roles parent = (Roles)target.Parent;
  if (parent != null)
  {
    foreach (Role item in parent)
    {
      if (item.Id == target.ReadProperty(IdProperty) &&
        !(ReferenceEquals(item, target)))
      {
        e.Description = "Role Id must be unique";
        return false;
      }
    }
  }
  return true;
}
```

When this rule is run, it loops through the list of Role objects in the parent Roles collection to see if any other child object has the same Id value. If there's a match, the method returns false; otherwise, it returns true.

The rule method is associated with the Id property in the AddBusinessRules() method.

```
protected override void AddBusinessRules()
{
  ValidationRules.AddRule<Role>(NoDuplicates, IdProperty);
  ValidationRules.AddRule(
    Csla.Validation.CommonRules.StringRequired, NameProperty);
}
```

This custom rule ensures that duplicate Id values are caught as they are entered, so that the data doesn't have to be sent to the database to find out about the problem. As you'll see in Chapter 19, this is particularly nice in a WPF (or Windows Forms) UI, since the user gets instant and automatic feedback about what is wrong.

Implementing Exists Methods

The first object discussed in the chapter was Project, and I covered all the code in that class except for the Exists() command implementation. Many objects can benefit from the implementation of an Exists() command, as it allows the UI to quickly and easily determine if a given object's data is in the database without having to fully instantiate the object itself. Ideally, a UI developer could write conditional code like this:

```
if (Project.Exists(productId))
```

Implementing an Exists() command also provides an opportunity to make use of Csla.CommandBase to create a command object. This makes sense, since all an Exists() command needs to do is run a stored procedure in the database and report on the result. Because the Exists() command is so data-focused, I'll cover it in Chapter 18.

At this point, you should understand how the business objects in ProjectTracker.Library are implemented. The only classes yet to be discussed are the ones supporting custom authentication.

Custom Authentication

Applications may use either Windows integrated (AD) or custom authentication.

Using Windows integrated security requires no extra coding in the business layer, and the only code required in the UI is to tell .NET to use Windows authentication, by calling AppDomain.CurrentDomain.SetPrincipalPolicy() in WPF, Windows Forms, or in the web.config file for Web Forms or a WCF service.

Custom authentication requires some extra code in the business layer, however, because custom principal and identity classes must be created. The details of the design were discussed in Chapter 3, so I'll focus on the implementation here.

PTPrincipal

PTPrincipal is a custom principal object that can be assigned as the current principal on the Thread object and in the HttpContext. You set the current principal by setting the value of Csla.ApplicationContext.User, as I discussed in Chapter 12.

Within .NET, the principal object is the centerpiece for authorization. The object must implement System.Security.Principal.IPrincipal, which defines an Identity property and an IsInRole()

method. CSLA .NET provides a helpful base class you can use when creating a custom principal, `Csla.Security.BusinessPrincipalBase`, so `PTPrincipal` inherits from that class.

```
[Serializable]
public class PTPrincipal : Csla.Security.BusinessPrincipalBase
```

Principal objects typically have a constructor that accepts the identity object that represents the user's identity, and `PTPrincipal` is no exception.

```
private PTPrincipal(IIdentity identity)
  : base(identity)
{ }
```

The `BusinessPrincipalBase` class also has a constructor that requires an identity object. This object is used to implement the `Identity` property in that base class, so it doesn't need to be implemented in `PTPrincipal`.

`BusinessPrincipalBase` also includes a default `IsInRole()` implementation that automatically delegates the `IsInRole()` request to its identity object, assuming the identity object implements the `ICheckRoles` interface defined in `Csla.Security`. The `CslaIdentity` class implements this interface, so it's an ideal base class to use when creating your own custom identity class.

The identity object actually represents the user's identity and profile, so it contains the list of roles for the user as well.

Login and Logout

The UI will need to collect the user's credentials and initiate any login or logout process. However, the actual login and logout process can be encapsulated within `PTPrincipal` to help simplify the code in the UI. To do this, `static` methods named `Login()` and `Logout()` are implemented in the class. This allows the UI to write code like this:

```
if (PTPrincipal.Login(username, password))
{
}
```

and this:

```
PTPrincipal.Logout();
```

As you'll see in Chapter 21, there are times when building XML services (and sometimes when building web applications) when you need to reload a principal object *without authenticating the credentials*. In some scenarios, you do the authentication on the initial call, but then just reload the principal and identity objects from the database on each subsequent call.

Using ASP.NET or WCF features, the application knows that the user was authenticated, but thanks to the stateless nature of some web architectures, the principal and identity objects must be re-created on each service or page request.

In this case, it is important to be able to reload the principal with code like this:

```
PTPrincipal.LoadPrincipal(username);
```

The `LoadPrincipal()` method works much like `Login()`, but it doesn't require the password because it doesn't authenticate the credentials.

Login and LoadPrincipal

The `Login()` and `LoadPrincipal()` methods call a `SetPrincipal()` helper method. This method creates an instance of `PTIdentity` and uses that identity object to create a new `PTPrincipal` object.

```
public static bool Login(string username, string password)
{
  return SetPrincipal(
    PTIdentity.GetIdentity(username, password));
}

public static void LoadPrincipal(string username)
{
  SetPrincipal(PTIdentity.GetIdentity(username));
}

private static bool SetPrincipal(PTIdentity identity)
{
  if (identity.IsAuthenticated)
  {
    PTPrincipal principal = new PTPrincipal(identity);
    Csla.ApplicationContext.User = principal;
  }
  return identity.IsAuthenticated;
}
```

Notice that PTIdentity has a GetIdentity() factory method with two overloads. The first accepts a username and password and performs authentication. The second accepts only a username and simply reloads the identity object with data.

With a PTIdentity object created, its IsAuthenticated property can be checked to see if the user's credentials were valid. If they were valid, the identity object is used to create a new PTPrincipal object, and that object is set to be the current principal by using the ApplicationContext object's User property, as discussed in Chapter 12.

```
PTPrincipal principal = new PTPrincipal(identity);
Csla.ApplicationContext.User = principal;
```

If the credentials weren't valid, then the current principal value is left unchanged.

In any case, the IsAuthenticated value is returned as a result so the UI code can take appropriate steps based on whether the user was successfully logged in or not.

Logout

The Logout() method is much simpler. All it needs to do is ensure that the current principal value is set to an unauthenticated principal object—that means a principal object whose identity object has an IsAuthenticated property that returns false.

```
public static void Logout()
{
  Csla.ApplicationContext.User = new UnauthenticatedPrincipal();
}
```

To achieve this result, the User property is set to an instance of UnauthenticatedPrincipal() from the Csla.Security namespace. This class is designed to provide a simple unauthenticated principal and identity.

PTIdentity

As you've seen, PTPrincipal isn't overly complex. It leaves most of the work to PTIdentity, including verification of the user's credentials and retrieval of the user's roles.

`PTIdentity` inherits from `CslaIdentity` from the `Csla.Security` namespace. `CslaIdentity` is designed to simplify the creation of a custom identity object.

```
[Serializable]
public class PTIdentity : CslaIdentity
```

Because `CslaIdentity` handles most of the details, the only code in `PTIdentity` is the data access code required to authenticate the username and password against the database, and to load the list of roles for the user (assuming the credentials are valid). I'll discuss that code in Chapter 18.

Conclusion

This chapter implemented the property declarations, business and validation rules, and authorization rules for the business objects designed in Chapter 3, using the templates and concepts discussed in Chapters 4 and 5. The result is `ProjectTracker.Library`, the business layer for the sample `ProjectTracker` application, including the following:

- `Project`
- `ProjectResources`
- `ProjectResource`
- `Resource`
- `ResourceAssignments`
- `ResourceAssignment`
- `Assignment`
- `RoleList`
- `Roles`
- `Role`

The library also includes classes to support custom authentication:

- `PTPrincipal`
- `PTIdentity`

This business library will be used to create WPF, Web Forms, and XML services interfaces in Chapters 19 through 21. First, though, in Chapter 18, I'll finish the implementation of these classes by walking through their factory methods and persistence code.

CHAPTER 18

Example Data Access

In Chapter 17, I walked through the business objects for the ProjectTracker application from Chapter 3. The focus in Chapter 17 is on how the objects implement properties, along with business, validation, and authorization rules. In this chapter, I discuss how those same objects implement persistence and data access, focusing on how their factory methods use the CSLA .NET data portal and how data is retrieved and updated into the database.

In this chapter, I don't walk through all the code in the ProjectTracker business object library. Instead, I focus on providing examples of how to implement common types of business objects and how to establish various object relationships. For the complete code, refer to the code download for this book, available at www.lhotka.net/cslanet or www.apress.com/book/view/1430210192.

Before digging into the ProjectTracker code, I will spend some time discussing some of the options available in terms of designing a data access layer and how your business objects and the data portal can interact with that layer. The ProjectTracker application uses just one technique, but there are several techniques to choose from.

Data Access Layer Design

As I discuss in Chapter 1, it is very important that any application use logical layering to organize its code. The most important area to avoid is mixing UI and business logic, keeping UI code out of the business layer and business logic out of the UI layer. A close second, in terms of importance, is to avoid mixing business and data access logic.

Business logic should exist independently of the data storage or data access concepts. In other words, your application's business logic should be the same regardless of whether the data is stored in SQL Server or an XML file. The logic should not change just because you use ADO.NET or LINQ to SQL to interact with the data store.

Similarly, your choice of data storage technology or data access technique shouldn't be affected when you change your business logic. Changing the way you calculate, validate, or authorize your object properties shouldn't require a switch from using a DataSet to using the ADO.NET Entity Framework.

Achieving this level of separation is best done by logically layering your application so you have a formal business layer that is separate from your data access layer. This allows either layer to change (within reason) without affecting the other layer.

CSLA .NET supports several different models, each with good and bad points. I'll discuss the models first and then the reasoning you might use to choose between them.

Data Access Models

The CSLA .NET data portal supports two models for business object persistence, which means there are two basic approaches for interacting with a data access layer:

- The data portal calls the business object's `DataPortal_XYZ` methods, which call the data access layer.
- The data portal calls an object factory object, which is either the data access layer or which calls the data access layer.

Each technique can be used in several different ways. Table 18-1 lists the most common designs for the data access layer.

Table 18-1. *Common Data Access Layer Designs*

Data Portal Mode	Data Access Model	Description
`DataPortal_XYZ`	Embedded in object	The data access code is embedded directly in the `DataPortal_XYZ` methods in the business object.
`DataPortal_XYZ`	In separate assembly	The data access code is in a separate assembly, which is invoked by code in the `DataPortal_XYZ` methods.
`ObjectFactory`	Data access in factory	The data portal invokes a factory object, which is the data access layer.
`ObjectFactory`	Data access in separate assembly	The data portal invokes a factory object, which then invokes the data access layer which is in a separate assembly.

I'll give a brief description of each technique and then follow up with a discussion around the good and bad points of each.

Using the DataPortal_XYZ Methods

The traditional way to use the data portal is to allow the data portal to invoke `DataPortal_XYZ` methods on the business object. This means the business object is in charge of its own persistence. It can directly encapsulate the data access code or it can invoke some external data access object, but the business object is in control.

This is a simple, powerful model that typically results in the simplest code. The technique works with nearly any data access technology, including the following:

- ADO.NET `Connection`, `Command`, `DataReader` objects
- LINQ to SQL
- ADO.NET Entity Framework
- Remote XML services
- XML data files (or other text files)

Because the data portal helps manage the state of the business objects, the code in the `DataPortal_XYZ` and `Child_XYZ` methods can be very focused on interacting with the data source or data access layer and getting or setting the business object's fields.

Data Access in DataPortal_XYZ Methods

The simplest model is to put the data access code directly into the DataPortal_XYZ methods. When coupled with direct use of ADO.NET Command and DataReader objects this model also offers superior performance. However, this model does put the data access code directly in the business class, which somewhat blurs the separation of business and data access layers. I think there's still pretty good logical separation because the data access code is encapsulated in clearly defined DataPortal_XYZ methods, but the separation isn't as clean as having the data access code in totally separate objects or assemblies.

An example of this model could look like this DataPortal_Fetch() method:

```
private void DataPortal_Fetch(SingleCriteria<CustomerEdit, int> criteria)
{
  using (var ctx = ConnectionManager<SqlConnection>.GetManager("MyDb"))
  {
    using (var cm = ctx.Connection.CreateCommand())
    {
      cm.CommandType = CommandTypes.Text;
      cm.CommandText = "SELECT Id, Name FROM Customer WHERE id=@id";
      using (var dr = new SafeDataReader(cm.ExecuteReader()))
      {
        dr.Read();
        LoadProperty(IdProperty, dr.GetInt32("Id"));
        LoadProperty(NameProperty, dr.GetString("Name"));
      }
    }
  }
}
```

The code is clean and concise, and performance is about as good as you can get because the DataReader is the lowest level object used to retrieve data from a database.

It is important to realize that this technique can be used with LINQ to SQL, the ADO.NET Entity Framework, or virtually any other data access technology. The basic approach is the same in all cases: get the data from the database and put it into the object's fields, or take the data from the object's fields and put it into the database.

DataPortal_XYZ Methods Invoke Separate Data Access

A slightly more complex model is to separate the data access code into an external object, which might be in a separate assembly that is referenced by the business assembly. This approach provides slightly better separation between layers, though it does add some complexity.

In this case, you must give careful thought to the interface that will be exposed by your data access layer because that is the interface that will be invoked by the business object. The way you design your data access layer's interface is often dictated by several factors:

- The data access technology being used (ADO.NET, LINQ to SQL, etc.)
- The need to change from one data access technology to another (e.g., from LINQ to SQL to the ADO.NET Entity Framework)
- The need to change from one data storage technology to another (e.g., from Oracle to SQL Server)

Detailed exploration of all these design factors is outside the scope of this book, but you should employ standard concepts such as loose coupling, interfaces, polymorphism, and abstraction to accomplish these goals.

A DataPortal_Fetch() method, where the data access layer is external but still uses ADO.NET, might look like this:

```
private void DataPortal_Fetch(SingleCriteria<CustomerEdit, int> criteria)
{
  using (var dal = new CustomerDal())
  {
    using (SafeDataReader dr = dal.GetCustomer(criteria.Value))
    {
        dr.Read();
        LoadProperty(IdProperty, dr.GetInt32("Id"));
        LoadProperty(NameProperty, dr.GetString("Name"));
    }
  }
}
```

Notice that the LoadProperty() method calls are the same as in the previous example. The primary difference is that this code doesn't open the database nor does it set up or call the Command object. The interaction with the database is abstracted away into the CustomerDal object and its GetCustomer() method.

The CustomerDal object is very likely in a separate assembly that is referenced by the business assembly. That data access assembly only needs to be deployed to the application server (if the data portal is configured to use a remote application server), so the code that interacts with the database is not deployed to the client. Arguably, this increases the security of the application to some degree.

The CustomerDal class might look like this:

```
public class CustomerDal : IDisposable
{
  private SqlConnection _cn;
  private SqlCommand _cm;

  public CustomerDal()
  {
    var conn = System.Configuration.ConfigurationManager.
                     ConnectionStrings["MyDb"].ConnectionString;
    _cn = new SqlConnection(conn);
    _cn.Open();
  }

  public SafeDataReader GetCustomer(int id)
  {
    _cm = _cn.CreateCommand();
    _cm.CommandType = CommandTypes.Text;
    _cm.CommandText = "SELECT Id, Name FROM Customer WHERE id=@id";
    return new SafeDataReader(_cm.ExecuteReader());
  }

  public void Dispose()
  {
    if (_cm != null)
      _cm.Dispose();
    if (_cn != null)
      _cn.Dispose();
  }
}
```

There are many ways you might choose to design your data access objects; this is just one example. But this example illustrates some important ideas. Your data access objects must encapsulate database interaction and must safely dispose of or close all connection, command, context, or other data access objects. They must define a set of public methods that can be invoked by the business object, accepting parameters and returning types that are available to both the business and data access assemblies.

As you'll see in the `ProjectTracker` code later in this chapter, LINQ to SQL is a very nice technology for creating this sort of data access assembly without having to write any code by hand. The ADO.NET Entity Framework offers the same simplicity but with more powerful mapping between the entity objects and the database schema.

However, both technologies incur some overhead when compared to the use of raw ADO.NET shown here, so you need to choose whether you value simplicity and autogenerated code or maximum performance.

Using an Object Factory

A business object can be decorated with an `ObjectFactory` attribute, which causes the data portal to create an instance of the factory object and to invoke methods on the factory object rather than on the business object. I discuss this capability in Chapter 15.

Using the `ObjectFactory` technique essentially reverses the responsibility of the objects, when compared to the `DataPortal_XYZ` approach. If you use an `ObjectFactory` attribute, the factory object assumes full responsibility for creating the business object, getting or setting it with data, and managing the object's state (such as `IsNew` and `IsDirty`). The data portal abdicates all these responsibilities to the factory object.

Typically, the factory objects are in a different assembly, separate from the business assembly. In some cases, the factory assembly directly contains the data access code, while in other cases it may just coordinate the process, invoking yet another assembly that contains the data access code.

The factory assembly can reference the business assembly and can have access to the business object types. This is the direct opposite of the `DataPortal_XYZ` model, where the business assembly references the data access assembly.

This means that you need to come up with some way for the factory object to load the business object's fields with data, ideally without breaking encapsulation. Such a requirement is very challenging to say the least. Usually factory objects do break encapsulation, using reflection or dynamic method invocation to cheat and interact with the business object's internal state directly.

It is better in terms of performance and object-oriented design to avoid cheating, which means that your business objects need to expose some public interface that can be used by the factory object. Sadly, such a public interface can be used by the UI or other objects as well, and that can be a problem. A compromise is to have the factory class in the same assembly as the business classes so you can use `internal` methods. And this can work well as long as the data access code is in another assembly.

Data Access in Object Factory

When using a factory object, you may choose to put the data access code directly into the factory object itself. The data portal will invoke this factory object, and the factory object must manage all interaction with the business object itself.

This approach is the simplest way to use the object factory model but does restrict flexibility. In particular, if you want the data access layer to be in its own assembly, the factory classes must be in that separate assembly. That prevents use of `internal` scoped methods on the business object to manage interaction between the factory and business objects.

Assuming the factory object is in a separate assembly, here's an example of a factory class with a `Fetch()` method:

```
public class CustomerFactory : ObjectFactory
{
  public object Fetch(SingleCriteria<Customer, int> criteria)
  {
    using (var ctx = ConnectionManager<SqlConnection>.GetManager("MyDb"))
    {
      using (var cm = ctx.Connection.CreateCommand())
      {
        cm.CommandType = CommandTypes.Text;
        cm.CommandText = "SELECT Id, Name FROM Customer WHERE id=@id";
        cm.Parameters.AddWithValue("@id", criteria.Value);
        using (var dr = new SafeDataReader(cm.ExecuteReader()))
        {
          dr.Read();
          var result = (BusinessLibrary.CustomerEdit)Activator.CreateInstance(
            typeof(BusinessLibrary.CustomerEdit), true);
          MarkNew(result);
          result.LoadData(dr);
          return result;
        }
      }
    }
  }
}
```

Inheriting from `ObjectFactory` (in the `Csla.Server` namespace) is strictly optional but does provide access to the `MarkNew()`, `MarkOld()`, and `MarkAsChild()` methods. If you don't inherit from `ObjectFactory`, you'll need to come up with your own way to invoke these methods on the business objects.

Notice that this implementation requires that `CustomerEdit` implement a `LoadData()` method. That method may look like this:

```
public void LoadData(SafeDataReader dr)
{
  LoadProperty(IdProperty, dr.GetInt32("Id"));
  LoadProperty(NameProperty, dr.GetString("Name"));
}
```

The important points are that all the data access code (opening the database, executing any queries, etc.) are all in the factory class, which is in an assembly that is only deployed to the application server (assuming the data portal is configured to use a remote app server). And encapsulation is preserved because the business object is managing its own internal fields within the `LoadData()` method.

This is not really ideal though because the business object is tightly coupled to the `DataReader` provided by the factory object. And this only works because the `DataReader` type is shared by both the business and factory assemblies. If the factory assembly used LINQ to SQL or the ADO.NET Entity Framework, this model wouldn't work because the business assembly would not have access to the entity types defined in the factory assembly, so it would be impossible to write a `LoadData()` method. In these cases, you must either use reflection to load the business object with data or switch to the more complex but flexible model where the factories and data access are in separate assemblies.

Object Factory Invokes Separate Data Access

The more flexible and powerful way to use an object factory is to design the factory objects to interact with a separate data access layer. In this case, you have three logical elements:

- Business object
- Factory object
- Data access object

The factory object may be in the business assembly, in its own assembly or in the data access assembly. There's a strong advantage to having it in the business assembly, however, because then it can use `internal` methods of the business object to get and set the business object's data. This is the approach I'll show here.

In the following code, I assume that the factory object is in the business assembly and the data access code is in a separate assembly. I also assume the use of the ADO.NET Entity Framework to create the data access assembly. The factory object could look like this:

```
public class CustomerFactory : ObjectFactory
{
  public object Fetch(SingleCriteria<CustomerEdit, int> criteria)
  {
    using (var ctx = ObjectContextManager<MyDbEntities>.GetManager("MyDb"))
    {
      var data = from r in ctx.ObjectContext.Customer
                 where r.Id == criteria.Value
                 select r;
      var result = (BusinessLibrary.CustomerEdit)Activator.CreateInstance(
        typeof(BusinessLibrary.CustomerEdit), true);
      MarkNew(result);
      result.LoadData(data.Single());
      return result;
    }
  }
}
```

This code uses an entity model defined using ADO.NET Entity Framework in another assembly to interact with the database. To do this, the business assembly must reference the data access assembly so the factory object (and the business object) has access to the entity types.

The business object's `LoadData()` method can be internal and can use the entity types:

```
internal void LoadData(Customer data)
{
  LoadProperty(IdProperty, data.Id);
  LoadProperty(NameProperty, data.Name);
}
```

Having the factory class in the same assembly as the business class allows the use of the `internal` scope, so `LoadData()` isn't visible to UI or other code. However, having the factory class in the business assembly does reduce the physical separation of the two layers slightly.

You could move the factory class into its own assembly, separate from the data access assembly. Both the factory and business assemblies would reference the data access assembly, and the code shown here would work the same way; except the `LoadData()` method would be `public` in that case.

As you can see, there are many options for building and using a data access layer with business objects. The `DataPortal_XYZ` model puts the business object in charge of the process, while the `ObjectFactory` model puts all responsibility on the factory object. Either way, you can choose to put the data access code into a separate assembly, at the cost of increased complexity.

In fact, these choices are all a matter of balancing competing concerns. I discuss some of these issues next.

Balancing Design Issues

There are several important concepts that must be balanced when designing a data access layer for business objects, including the following:

- Performance
- Encapsulation
- Layering
- Complexity

Obviously, performance is an important consideration, and the decisions you make concerning data access can have a major impact on overall application performance.

A primary goal of CSLA .NET is to enable object-oriented principles in design and programming of the business layer, so those principles should be honored.

As I discuss in Chapter 1 and earlier in this chapter, it is important to maintain clear separation between the business and data access layers. This increases maintainability and reduces the cost of the application over its lifetime.

Even layering can't solve all problems. Sadly, it is quite easy to come up with overly complex solutions to many problems. Trying to balance performance with layering can lead to some very complex solutions, and that reduces maintainability and drives up the cost of software. You must be alert for complexity and try to avoid it when possible.

The core challenge in design is to preserve encapsulation, while not harming performance (overmuch) or increasing complexity too badly.

Business objects contain their own data, which follows the basic object-oriented principle of encapsulation. Objects encapsulate behaviors and the data required to implement those behaviors. Other objects should never be allowed to directly manipulate the data encapsulated within an object because that would break encapsulation.

However, the data access layer needs access to the data in each business object. The data access layer needs to get data from the database and put it into the business object and get data from the object to put into the database. The question of how to do this without breaking encapsulation and without causing serious performance issues is perhaps the single biggest challenge you'll face when designing a data access layer for your business objects.

■ **Note** In this discussion, I assume you are not putting the data access code directly into the `DataPortal_XYZ` methods. This approach is the simplest model and avoids most of the trade-offs discussed here but it does have the drawback of potentially blurring the boundary between the business and data access layers, which is why many people choose to accept the complexity of having an external data access object and/or assembly.

This issue occurs whether you use private or managed backing fields, as discussed in Chapter 7. Either way, the management of the object's field values is private to the business object, and other objects can't (and shouldn't) directly manipulate the business object's state.

You are left with two primary options:

- Have the business object manipulate its own state data.
- Break encapsulation by having other objects manipulate the business object's state data.

Preserving Encapsulation

If you choose to preserve encapsulation, your data access layer must accept or provide data to the business object without manipulating the business object directly. For example, consider this `DataPortal_Fetch()` method from a business object:

```
private void DataPortal_Fetch(SingleCriteria<CustomerEdit, int> criteria)
{
  using (var dal = new CustomerDal())
  {
    CustomerData data = dal.GetCustomer(criteria.Value);
    LoadProperty(IdProperty, data.Id);
    LoadProperty(NameProperty, data.Name);
  }
}
```

In this example, the data access layer is implemented in an object called `CustomerDal`, which exposes a `GetCustomer()` method. That method doesn't set the fields of the business object directly but instead returns some DTO of type `CustomerData`. The DTO might look like this:

```
public class CustomerData
{
  public int Id { get; set; }
  public string Name { get; set; }
}
```

The business object can then load its own field data from that DTO. Each `LoadProperty()` method call copies a value from the DTO to the business object's field. This preserves encapsulation because no object directly manipulates the internal state of another object.

This technique provides a high level of flexibility and decoupling so is very powerful. It does incur some overhead, however, because the `CustomerDal` object copies the data from the database into a `CustomerData` object (the DTO) and the data is copied from there into the fields of the business object.

Earlier in the chapter, I discussed some code where the data access layer returns an open `DataReader` and that avoids this double copy of the data. The drawback of that technique is that it couples the data access and business objects to raw ADO.NET, so while it is faster it is less flexible.

There are numerous variations on this theme, for example, using an `ObjectFactory` and `LoadData()` method as shown earlier in the chapter. And you might use LINQ to SQL or the ADO.NET Entity Framework to create your DTO or entity objects rather than coding them by hand. But the overall design concept remains consistent and provides good separation of concerns but with some overhead in terms of performance and complexity.

Breaking Encapsulation

You may choose to break encapsulation, allowing the data access layer to directly manipulate the data inside each business object. Generally speaking, breaking encapsulation is a bad thing because it increases coupling and reduces maintainability. However, many ORM technologies are designed specifically to manipulate the internal states of objects. This is somewhat more acceptable than writing such code yourself because it is a framework or tool that is breaking encapsulation, not user code.

If you choose to use a preexisting ORM tool that is capable of creating your business object instances and loading the objects with data, you will probably want to use the `ObjectFactory` model discussed earlier in the chapter. In this case, the `ObjectFactory` acts as a coordinator, invoking the ORM tool so it can create your business objects and load them with data. When that's done, the factory object can return the business object to the data portal.

There are many ORM tools available in the .NET ecosystem, and a detailed discussion of using them is outside the scope of this book. You should know that the primary motivation for adding the `ObjectFactory` concept to CSLA .NET is to open the possibility of using ORM tools in this manner. Whether any specific ORM tool can or can't create CSLA .NET business objects will depend on that tool.

You may choose to break encapsulation yourself by writing your own data access component that directly loads business objects with data. There are several techniques you can use in this case, including the following:

- Use reflection to set the `private` fields of the business object or to call the `protected` `LoadProperty()` methods.
- Use dynamic method invocation to set the `private` fields of the business object or to call the `protected` `LoadProperty()` methods.
- Create an interface that exposes a duplicate set of the business object properties and implement this interface to call `ReadProperty()` and `LoadProperty()`, thus bypassing authorization and validation logic.

In all cases, the point is to allow an external object (the data access object) to directly manipulate the data of the business object without invoking the normal authorization, business, or validation rules of the business object.

Ideally, this will be done in a way that doesn't allow *other code*, such as UI code, to also break encapsulation. Breaking encapsulation is a form of cheating, and if it becomes widespread, it can be the source of many bugs, which will reduce the maintainability and increase the cost of your application.

Unfortunately, the "safe" solutions such as reflection do have negative implications for performance, while the "unsafe" solutions such as a `public` interface can be quite fast but open the door to abuse by UI code or other application code.

Overall, I recommend that you preserve encapsulation if at all possible. While it may take a little extra work to do so, the result is a more maintainable application that preserves the core tenets of object-oriented programming and design.

At this point, you should have an understanding of the flexibility offered by CSLA .NET in terms of object persistence. The rest of this chapter focuses on the implementation of a data access layer for the example `ProjectTracker` objects I discuss in Chapter 17.

Data Access Objects

In Chapter 17, I walk through the implementation of the example `ProjectTracker` business objects, following the design from Chapter 3. The focus in Chapter 17 is on property declarations as well as business, validation, and authorization rules.

The rest of this chapter focuses on those same objects but in terms of persistence. I discuss the factory and data access methods and how they are implemented.

For this application I have chosen to use LINQ to SQL to create a data access layer in a project named `ProjectTracker.DalLinq`. You'll find this project in the `ProjectTracker` solution as part of the code download.

Using LINQ to SQL

LINQ to SQL and the ADO.NET Entity Framework are the newest data access technologies available in .NET. Many people using the ADO.NET Entity Framework also use LINQ to Entities, which results in data access code that is very similar to LINQ to SQL code. In other words, you can use LINQ to SQL or the ADO.NET Entity Framework to accomplish the same task, using almost the same code shown here.

I chose to use LINQ to SQL because it was released several months ahead of the ADO.NET Entity Framework, so I have had more experience with this particular technology. Also, I like the way LINQ to SQL supports the use of stored procedures. The Visual Studio LINQ to SQL designer automatically wraps stored procedures with a set of strongly typed .NET methods, making them very easy to use.

I like stored procedures a great deal because they offer clean separation between the physical database structure and the logical interactions I want to have with the database from my application. This separation maintains a good boundary between the data access and data storage layers discussed in Chapter 1.

■ Note As time goes on, I fully expect to enhance `ProjectTracker` to use the ADO.NET Entity Framework. If you download the latest version of CSLA .NET and the `ProjectTracker` reference application, you will likely find examples of this technology, alongside LINQ to SQL.

Previous versions of the `ProjectTracker` reference application (for CSLA .NET 3.0 and older) used raw ADO.NET `Connection`, `Command`, and `DataReader` objects. Those techniques continue to work as in the past, and you should feel free to download and examine older versions of the `ProjectTracker` code for examples of using that approach. All code is available from `www.lhotka.net/cslanet`.

The data access code in `ProjectTracker` is designed following the `DataPortal_XYZ` model discussed earlier in this chapter. This means the data portal invokes a `DataPortal_XYZ` method, which uses the LINQ to SQL data access objects to interact with the database. The data access objects are in a separate assembly, which only needs to be deployed to the server (assuming the data portal is configured to use a remote application server).

The ProjectTracker.DalLinq Project

The data access code is in a project named `ProjectTracker.DalLinq`. I use the Visual Studio LINQ to SQL designer to create the data access layer, only writing one simple class manually.

I added a LINQ to SQL class, shown in Figure 18-1, by adding a new item to the project.

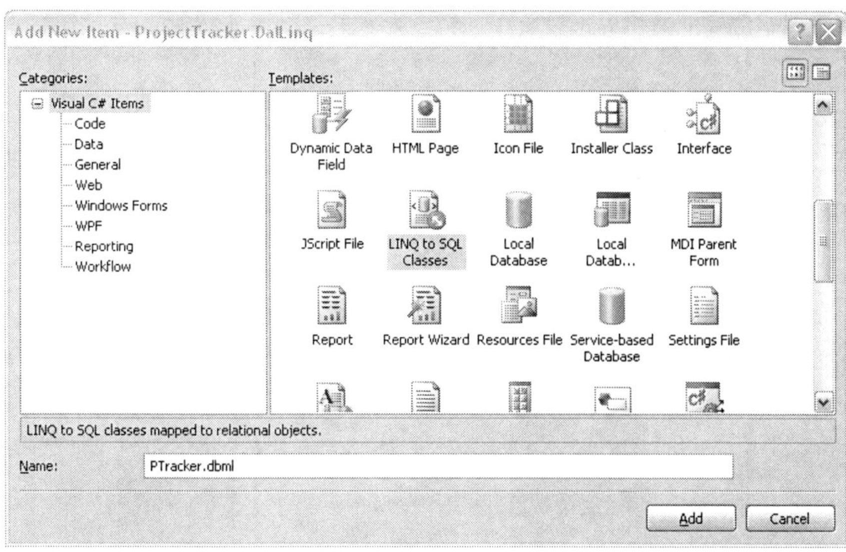

Figure 18-1. *Adding a LINQ to SQL class*

The result is a blank designer surface. You can drag and drop items onto this surface from the Data Connections node in the Server Explorer window in Visual Studio. I chose to drag all the tables and stored procedures from the `PTracker.mdf` database onto the designer. The tables go on the left, the stored procedures on the right. Figure 18-2 shows the resulting designer surface.

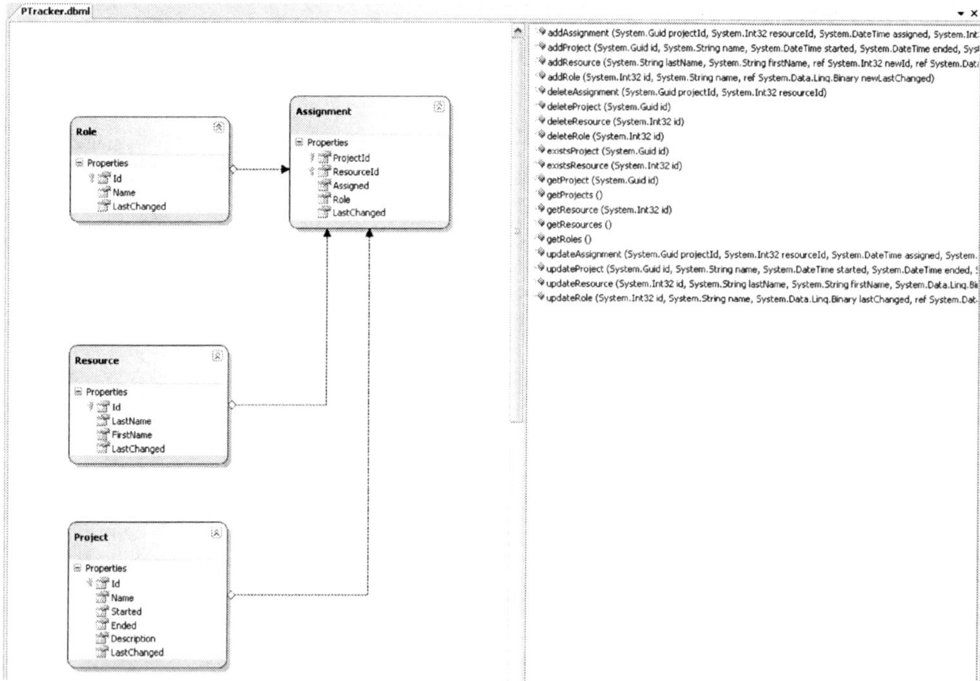

Figure 18-2. *Populated LINQ to SQL designer surface*

It is important to realize that the Visual Studio LINQ to SQL designer does not generate the right code for stored procedures that return multiple result sets. The `getProject` and `getResource` stored procedures do return multiple result sets but the wrapper code created by LINQ to SQL will only return the first result set.

Note This is not a limitation of LINQ to SQL itself but rather of the Visual Studio designer. If you don't use the designer, you can create LINQ to SQL wrapper code that does return multiple result sets.

The reason these stored procedures return multiple result sets is because they already exist in the database from previous versions of `ProjectTracker`. The older version of `ProjectTracker` used direct ADO.NET calls to get a `DataReader` containing both the parent and child data in a single call to the database.

While I could have rewritten the stored procedures, splitting each one into two separate stored procedures, I chose to use this as an opportunity to illustrate how you might deal with similar preexisting situations. There are limited options:

- Rework the stored procedures and all existing code that uses them.
- Create new, stored procedures (keeping the old ones) and maintain both sets into the future.
- Use the dynamic query features of LINQ to SQL to directly query the database.

Neither of the first two options is attractive, as they require either changes to existing code or duplication of code into the future. So I have decided, for this example, to use the third option and avoid those particular stored procedures altogether.

This has the benefit of allowing `ProjectTracker` to illustrate how to use LINQ to SQL with and without stored procedures, and you can see examples of both techniques as you look through the code.

The `ProjectTracker.DalLinq` project also includes `Security.dbml`, which contains the LINQ to SQL objects for the security database.

These `dbml` files represent the LINQ to SQL objects corresponding to the underlying database. When the project is built, this information is used to generate .NET classes in the shape of each table and .NET methods that wrap each stored procedure. Effectively, the `dbml` files define the data access layer for the application.

Other than dragging and dropping items from the Server Explorer onto the LINQ to SQL designer surfaces, I wrote absolutely no code to create the data access layer.

The one class I did manually add to the project simply contains the names of the databases, corresponding to the connection string entries expected in the application's config file:

```
public class Database
{
  public const string PTracker = "PTracker";
  public const string Security = "Security";
}
```

These values are used by the `DataPortal_XYZ` code so that code doesn't need to hard-code the database names. The result is that the code in the `ProjectTracker.Library` assembly (which is deployed to the client) doesn't even know the name of the key needed to find the connection string for the database. That information is contained in the data access assembly.

Next, I walk through the code for some of the business objects to illustrate how they interact with these data access objects.

Business Class Implementation

With all the data access logic encapsulated by the LINQ to SQL objects in the `ProjectTracker.DalLinq` project, the business objects in `ProjectTracker.Library` can implement their persistence code.

The `ProjectTracker.Library` assembly does need a reference to the data access library, as shown in Figure 18-3.

With this set up, I'll walk through the first few classes in detail. The other classes are very similar, so for those I'll discuss only the key features. Of course, the complete code for all classes is available in the code download for the book.

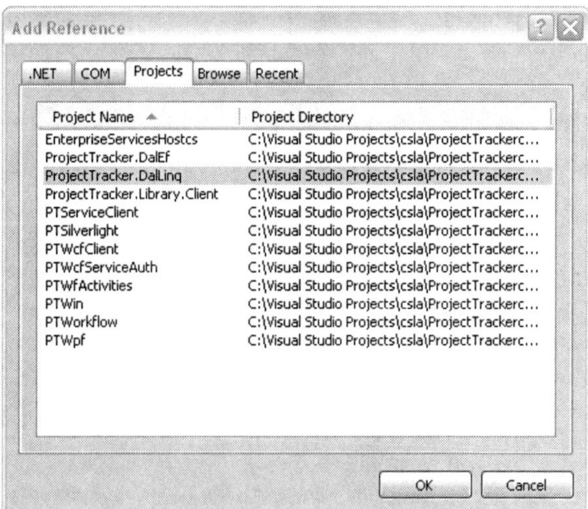

Figure 18-3. *ProjectTracker.Library references ProjectTracker.DalLinq*

Project

The `Project` class is an editable root class that represents a single project in the application. Root objects are the only objects that can be directly retrieved or updated through the data portal, so this is a good place to start.

Also, a `Project` contains a child list named `ProjectResources`, which contains `ProjectResource` child objects. I'll walk through each of these classes so you can see how a parent-child, or one-to-many, relationship is handled.

Factory Methods

Creating and retrieving an object is managed by *factory methods* as discussed in Chapter 1. The factory design pattern is powerful because it abstracts the creation or retrieval process from both the caller (typically the UI) and the business object itself.

In a typical CSLA-style business object, the default constructor is declared with non-`public` scope (either `private` or `protected`) to force the use of the factory methods for creating or retrieving the object. While this is not strictly necessary, it is a good thing to do. Without making the constructor `private`, it is far too easy for a UI developer to forget to use the factory method and to instead use the `new` keyword to create the object, leading to bugs in the UI code.

I'll start by looking at the factory methods:

```
public static Project NewProject()
{
  return DataPortal.Create<Project>();
}

public static Project GetProject(Guid id)
{
  return DataPortal.Fetch<Project>(new SingleCriteria<Project, Guid>(id));
}
```

```
public static void DeleteProject(Guid id)
{
  DataPortal.Delete(new SingleCriteria<Project, Guid>(id));
}
```

The `NewProject()` method creates a new instance of `Project`, which loads default values from the database if required. To do this, it simply calls `DataPortal.Create()` to trigger the data portal process, as discussed in Chapter 15. The data portal automatically checks the per-type authorization, as discussed in Chapter 12, to determine whether the user is authorized to add a new `Project` to the system. If the user isn't authorized, there's no sense even creating a new instance of the object so an exception is thrown.

■ **Note** Ideally, this authorization exception would never be thrown. Good UI design dictates that the UI should hide or disable the options that would allow users to add a new object if they aren't authorized to do so. If that is done properly, the user should never be able to even attempt to create a new object if they aren't authorized. The UI developer can call `Csla.Security.AuthorizationRules.CanCreateObject()` to determine whether to disable or hide UI elements.

The `GetProject()` factory method retrieves an existing `Project` object, which is populated with data from the database. This method accepts the primary key value for the data as a parameter and passes it to `DataPortal.Fetch()` through a new `SingleCriteria` object.

The data portal ultimately creates a new `Project` object and calls its `DataPortal_Fetch()` method to do the actual data access. The criteria object is passed through this process, so the `DataPortal_Fetch()` method will have access to the `Guid` key value.

Again, the data portal checks the per-type authorization rules to determine whether the user is allowed to get an existing object. If not, an exception is thrown.

There's also a `static` method to allow immediate deletion of a `Project`. Authorization is checked first to ensure that the user is allowed to delete the data. `DeleteProject()` accepts the primary key value for the data and uses it to create a `SingleCriteria` object. It then calls `DataPortal.Delete()` to trigger the deletion process, ultimately resulting in the object's `DataPortal_Delete()` method being invoked to do the actual deletion of the data.

Non-Public Constructor

As noted earlier, all business objects should include a default constructor, as shown here:

```
private Project()
{ /* require use of factory methods */ }
```

This is straight out of the template from Chapter 5. It ensures that client code must use the factory methods to create or retrieve a `Project` object, and it provides the data portal with a constructor that it can call via reflection.

Overriding Save

The default implementation for `Save()` is good—it checks to ensure the object is valid and dirty before saving. It also checks the per-type authorization rules in Chapter 12 to ensure the user is allowed to update or delete the object.

In some advanced scenarios, you may need to override `Save()` to customize its behavior, but that should not normally be required. If you do override `Save()`, you should also override the asynchronous `BeginSave()` equivalent:

```
public override void Save()
{
  // do custom work here
  return base.Save();
}

public override void BeginSave(
  EventHandler<Csla.Core.SavedEventArgs> handler,
  object userState)
{
  // do custom work here
  base.BeginSave(handler, userState);
}
```

Like most classes, the `Project` class has no reason to override these methods. I'm showing this code here as an example of what you might do if necessary.

The factory methods and `Save()` method ultimately invoke either `DataPortal_XYZ` methods on the business object or methods on a factory object. Since the `Project` class doesn't have an `ObjectFactory` attribute, the data portal invokes `DataPortal_XYZ` methods.

Data Access

The *Data Access* region implements the `DataPortal_XYZ` methods that support the creation, retrieval, addition, updating, and deletion of a `Project` object's data. Because this is an editable root object, it implements all the possible methods:

- `DataPortal_Create()`
- `DataPortal_Fetch()`
- `DataPortal_Insert()`
- `DataPortal_Update()`
- `DataPortal_DeleteSelf()`
- `DataPortal_Delete()`

The fetch and delete factory methods pass a `SingleCriteria` object to the data portal. `SingleCriteria` is a CSLA .NET type that contains a single criteria value. As discussed in Chapters 4 and 5, if you need more complex criteria you need to create your own criteria class.

In this sample application, the `DataPortal_XYZ` methods are relatively straightforward, simply calling the LINQ to SQL data access objects. Keep in mind, however, that these routines could be much more complex, interacting with multiple databases, merging data from various sources, and doing whatever is required to retrieve and update data in your business environment.

Handling Transactions

As discussed in Chapters 2 and 15, the data portal supports three transactional models: manual, Enterprise Services, and `System.Transactions`. The preferred model for performance and simplicity is `System.Transactions`, and so that is the model used in the sample application.

This means that each method that updates data is decorated with the `Transactional (TransactionTypes.TransactionScope)` attribute. Since this tells the data portal to wrap the code in a `TransactionScope` object, there's no need to write any LINQ to SQL, ADO.NET, or stored procedure transactional code. All the transaction details are handled by the `TransactionScope` object from `System.Transactions`.

As you look at the data access code, notice that it never actually *catches* any exceptions. The code leverages `using` blocks to ensure that the LINQ to SQL context object (and thus any database connection, command, and DataReader objects) is disposed properly, but no exceptions are caught. The reasons for this are twofold:

- First, the code uses the `Transactional` attribute, which causes it to run within a `System.Transactions` transactional context. An exception automatically causes the transaction to be rolled back, which is exactly the desired result. If the exceptions are caught, the transaction won't be rolled back and the application would misbehave.
- Second, if an exception occurs, normal processing shouldn't continue. Instead, the client code needs to be notified that the operation failed and why. Returning the exception to the client code allows the client code to know that there was a problem during data access. The client code can then choose how to handle that the object couldn't be created, retrieved, updated, or deleted. Remember that the original exception is wrapped in a `DataPortalException`, which includes extra information that can be used by the client when handling the exception.

DataPortal_Create

The `DataPortal_Create()` method is called by the data portal when it is asked to create a new `Project` object. In some cases, this method loads the new object with default values from the database, and in simpler cases it may load hard-coded defaults or set no defaults at all.

The `Project` object has no need for loading default values, so the `DataPortal_Create()` method simply loads some default, hard-coded values rather than talking to the database:

```
[RunLocal]
protected override void DataPortal_Create()
{
  LoadProperty(IdProperty, Guid.NewGuid());
  Started = System.Convert.ToString(System.DateTime.Today);
  ValidationRules.CheckRules();
}
```

The method is decorated with the `RunLocal` attribute because it doesn't do any data access but rather sets hard-coded or calculated default values. If the method did load default values from the database, the `RunLocal` attribute would not be applied, causing the data portal to run the code on the application server. With the `RunLocal` attribute on the method, the data portal short-circuits its processing and runs this method locally.

■ **Note** In a more complex object, in which default values come from the database, this method would call data access code to retrieve those values and use them to initialize the object's fields. In that case, the `RunLocal` attribute would not be used.

Notice how the code directly alters the state of the object. For instance, the `Id` property value is set to a new `Guid` value by calling `LoadProperty()`. If your object uses private backing fields, as discussed in Chapter 7, it would directly set the field values.

Since not all properties can be set, it is best to be consistent and always set fields directly. Setting a property causes the authorization, business, and validation rules for that property to be checked. That's a lot of overhead for data you are simply loading from the database. And it is possible that values from the database won't meet the business or validation rules or that the user isn't allowed to change the property (even though you want to load it from the database).

In short, you shouldn't set the properties; you must set the backing field (managed or private).

Of course, the default values set in a new object might not conform to the object's validation rules. In fact, the Name property starts out as an empty string value, which means it is invalid, since that is a required property. This is specified in the AddBusinessRules() method in Chapter 17 by associating this property with the StringRequired rule method.

To ensure that all validation rules are run against the newly created object's data, ValidationRules.CheckRules() is called. Calling this method with no parameters causes it to run all the validation rules associated with all properties of the object, as defined in the object's AddBusinessRules() method.

■ **Tip** BusinessBase includes a default DataPortal_Create() implementation that is marked as RunLocal and calls ValidationRules.CheckRules(). For many simple objects, you do not need to override DataPortal_Create() at all.

The end result is that the new object is loaded with default values and those values are validated. The new object is then returned by the data portal to the factory method (NewProject(), in this case), which typically returns it to the UI code.

DataPortal_Fetch

More interesting and complex is the DataPortal_Fetch() method, which is called by the data portal to tell the object that it should load its data from the database (or other data source). The sample method accepts a SingleCriteria object as a parameter, which contains the criteria data needed to identify the data to load:

```
private void DataPortal_Fetch(SingleCriteria<Project, Guid> criteria)
{
  using (var ctx =
    ContextManager<ProjectTracker.DalLinq.PTrackerDataContext>.
    GetManager(ProjectTracker.DalLinq.Database.PTracker))
  {
    // get project data
    var data = (from p in ctx.DataContext.Projects
                where p.Id == criteria.Value
                select p).Single();
    LoadProperty(IdProperty, data.Id);
    LoadProperty(NameProperty, data.Name);
    LoadPropertyConvert<SmartDate, System.DateTime?>(
      StartedProperty, data.Started);
    LoadPropertyConvert<SmartDate, System.DateTime?>(
      EndedProperty, data.Ended);
    LoadProperty(DescriptionProperty, data.Description);
    _timestamp = data.LastChanged.ToArray();

    // get child data
    LoadProperty(
      ResourcesProperty,
      ProjectResources.GetProjectResources(
        data.Assignments.ToArray()));
  }
}
```

This method is not marked with either the RunLocal or Transactional attributes. Since it does interact with the database, RunLocal is inappropriate. That attribute could prevent the data portal from running this code on the application server, causing runtime errors when the database is inaccessible. Also, since this method doesn't update any data, it doesn't need transactional protection, and so there's no need for the Transactional attribute.

Remember that the data portal, as discussed in Chapter 15, will invoke the appropriate DataPortal_Fetch() overload based on the type of criteria parameter value. It is possible to have multiple DataPortal_Fetch() overloads with different criteria parameter types.

You should also notice that no exceptions are caught by this code. If the requested Id value doesn't exist in the database, the result will be a SQL exception, which will automatically flow back through the data portal to the UI code contained within a DataPortalException. This is intentional, as it allows the UI to have full access to the exception's details so the UI can decide how to notify the user that the data doesn't exist in the database.

The first thing the method does is use the ContextManager to open a LINQ to SQL context object and connection to the database:

```
using (var ctx =
  ContextManager<ProjectTracker.DalLinq.PTrackerDataContext>.
  GetManager(ProjectTracker.DalLinq.Database.PTracker))
```

The ContextManager, ConnectionManager, and ObjectContextManager classes are in the Csla.Data namespace and provide an abstract way to work with LINQ to SQL context objects, ADO.NET connection objects, and ADO.NET Entity Framework context objects, respectively. These are discussed in Chapter 16.

Then, within the using block, a LINQ query is used to retrieve the project data:

```
var data = (from p in ctx.DataContext.Projects
            where p.Id == criteria.Value
            select p).Single();
```

Note the use of the criteria.Value parameter. This is the value that is provided by the code that calls the factory method. Since this query returns only one row of data, the Single() method is used to return just the one value rather than a list of values. This means that the data field contains a value of type ProjectTracker.DalLinq.Project, a type defined by the data access layer.

The data field is then used to populate the object like this:

```
LoadProperty(IdProperty, data.Id);
LoadProperty(NameProperty, data.Name);
LoadPropertyConvert<SmartDate, System.DateTime?>(
  StartedProperty, data.Started);
LoadPropertyConvert<SmartDate, System.DateTime?>(
  EndedProperty, data.Ended);
LoadProperty(DescriptionProperty, data.Description);
_timestamp = data.LastChanged.ToArray();
```

There is no need to cast the values, as they are already in .NET types thanks to LINQ to SQL. The only exceptions are the DateTime? values, which must be converted to a SmartDate. This is handled by using the LoadPropertyConvert() method instead of LoadProperty(). These helper methods are discussed in Chapter 7.

Also, notice that the LastChanged column is retrieved and placed into the _timestamp byte array. This value is never exposed outside the object but is maintained for later use if the object is updated. LastChanged is a timestamp value in the database table and is used by the updateProject stored procedure to implement first-write-wins optimistic concurrency. The object must be able to provide updateProject with the original timestamp value that is in the table when the data is first loaded.

Since the _timestamp value is never exposed as a property of the object, it isn't managed by the field manager. Instead, I'm storing it using a simple private field.

At this point, the Project object's fields have been loaded. But Project contains a collection of child objects and they need to be loaded as well. LINQ to SQL is helpful here because it understands the relationships between the database tables (see Figure 18-2) that it inferred from the database schema. This means the data field has an Assignments property which returns a list of Assignment entity objects from the data access layer. This list is passed to the factory method for the ProjectResources object, an editable child list:

```
LoadProperty(
  ResourcesProperty,
  ProjectResources.GetProjectResources(
    data.Assignments.ToArray()));
```

It is important to realize that the data.Assignments.ToArray() call causes LINQ to SQL to make a second query to the database to retrieve the list of assignments. LINQ to SQL uses a lazy loading scheme and only retrieves data when necessary.

You can force LINQ to SQL to eager load the Assignments data by adding this line of code before executing the first LINQ query:

```
ctx.DataContext.LoadOptions.
  LoadWith<ProjectTracker.DalLinq.Project>(c => c.Assignments);
```

The LoadWith() method specifies that any time a Project is retrieved, the Assignments data should be retrieved immediately.

Now that the object contains data loaded directly from the database, it is an "old" object. The definition of an old object is that the primary key value in the object matches a primary key value in the database. In Chapter 15, the data portal is implemented to automatically call the object's MarkOld() method before DataPortal_Fetch() is invoked. That ensures that the object's IsNew and IsDirty properties will return false and that your code in DataPortal_Fetch() can use those properties if desired.

DataPortal_Insert

The DataPortal_Insert() method handles the case in which a new object needs to insert its data into the database. It is invoked by the data portal as a result of the UI calling the object's Save() method when the object's IsNew property is true.

As with all the methods that change the database, this one is marked with the Transactional attribute to ensure that the code is transactionally protected:

```
[Transactional(TransactionalTypes.TransactionScope)]
protected override void DataPortal_Insert()
{
  using (var ctx =
    ContextManager<ProjectTracker.DalLinq.PTrackerDataContext>.
    GetManager(ProjectTracker.DalLinq.Database.PTracker))
  {
    // insert project data
    System.Data.Linq.Binary lastChanged = null;
    ctx.DataContext.addProject(
      ReadProperty(IdProperty),
      ReadProperty(NameProperty),
      ReadProperty(StartedProperty),
      ReadProperty(EndedProperty),
      ReadProperty(DescriptionProperty),
      ref lastChanged);
    _timestamp = lastChanged.ToArray();
```

```
      // update child objects
      FieldManager.UpdateChildren(this);
    }
  }
```

Like DataPortal_Fetch(), the DataPortal_Insert() method opens a LINQ to SQL context and thus a connection to the database. It then invokes the addProject stored procedure, using the strongly typed .NET wrapper created by the LINQ to SQL designer:

```
ctx.DataContext.addProject(
  ReadProperty(IdProperty),
  ReadProperty(NameProperty),
  ReadProperty(StartedProperty),
  ReadProperty(EndedProperty),
  ReadProperty(DescriptionProperty),
  ref lastChanged);
```

Again, there is no need to cast the values because the addProject() method is strongly typed using .NET types. Any conversion to database types is handled by LINQ to SQL automatically. Even the SmartDate types work here because the SmartDate type can be cast to DateTime? and the compiler handles that automatically.

The lastChanged parameter is passed by ref because the stored procedure returns the timestamp value generated as the data is inserted into the table. This value is then set into the _timestamp field:

```
_timestamp = lastChanged.ToArray();
```

Other stored procedures may return values as well. For example, in the Resource class the addResource stored procedure not only returns a timestamp but also a database-generated int ID value:

```
ctx.DataContext.addResource(
  _lastName, _firstName, ref newId, ref newLastChanged);
_id = System.Convert.ToInt32(newId);
_timestamp = newLastChanged.ToArray();
```

Notice how both parameters are passed by ref.

Back in the Project class, once the call to addProject() is complete, the Project object's data is in the database. However, a Project contains child objects, and their data must be added to the database as well. The field manager is helpful here because it has an UpdateChildren() method that automatically updates all child objects contained by the current object:

```
FieldManager.UpdateChildren(this);
```

The UpdateChildren() method calls DataPortal.UpdateChild() to update each child object contained in the Project. In this case, that means the ProjectResources collection is updated. I show the code for the collection later in the "ProjectResources" section.

The fact that this is passed as a parameter is important because the child objects contained in the collection have a foreign key relationship to the project. By passing this as a parameter, the child objects have access to the Project object's Id property and thus to the foreign key value they require.

■ **Note** You could just pass the Id property value but that would cause tighter coupling between the parent and its children. By passing a reference to the Project object, the parent doesn't know or care what information is required by its children because it has made all the information available. The less one object knows about the needs of another, the better.

Once DataPortal_Insert() is complete, the data portal automatically invokes the MarkOld() method on the object, ensuring that the IsNew and IsDirty properties are both false. Since the object's primary key value in memory now matches a primary key value in the database, it is not new; and since the rest of the object's data values match those in the database, it is not dirty.

Once all the objects have inserted their data, the database transaction completes. Recall that the DataPortal_Insert() method is decorated with the Transactional attribute and the data portal automatically commits the transaction and disposes the TransactionScope object. However, if the object's code throws an exception, the transaction is automatically rolled back, so no changes are made to the database.

DataPortal_Update

The DataPortal_Update() method is almost identical to DataPortal_Insert() but it is called by the data portal in the case that IsNew is false. It calls the updateProject() method from the data access layer, which invokes the updateProject stored procedure in the database:

```
ctx.DataContext.updateProject(
  ReadProperty(IdProperty),
  ReadProperty(NameProperty),
  ReadProperty(StartedProperty),
  ReadProperty(EndedProperty),
  ReadProperty(DescriptionProperty),
  _timestamp,
  ref lastChanged);
_timestamp = lastChanged.ToArray();
```

However, the updateProject stored procedure requires one extra parameter not required by addProject: the timestamp value for the LastChanged column. This is required for the first-write-wins optimistic concurrency implemented by the stored procedure. The goal is to ensure that multiple users can't overwrite each other's changes to the data. Other than this one extra parameter, the DataPortal_Update() method is very similar to DataPortal_Insert().

DataPortal_DeleteSelf

The final method that the data portal may invoke when the UI calls the object's Save() method is DataPortal_DeleteSelf(). This method is invoked if the object's IsDeleted property is true and its IsNew property is false. In this case, the object needs to delete itself from the database.

Remember that there are two ways objects can be deleted: through immediate or deferred deletion. Deferred deletion is when the object is loaded into memory, its IsDeleted property is set to true, and Save() is called. Immediate deletion is when a factory method is called and passes criteria identifying the object to the DataPortal.Delete() method.

In the case of immediate deletion, the data portal ultimately calls DataPortal_Delete(), passing the criteria object to that method so it knows which data to delete. Deferred deletion calls DataPortal_DeleteSelf(), passing no criteria object because the object is fully populated with data already.

■ Note Implementing the DataPortal_DeleteSelf() method is only required if your object supports deferred deletion. In the Project object, deferred deletion is not supported, but I am implementing the method anyway to illustrate how it is done.

The simplest way to implement DataPortal_DeleteSelf() is to create a criteria object and delegate the call to DataPortal_Delete():

```
[Transactional(TransactionalTypes.TransactionScope)]
protected override void DataPortal_DeleteSelf()
{
  DataPortal_Delete(
    new SingleCriteria<Project, Guid>(ReadProperty(IdProperty)));
}
```

You might wonder why the data portal couldn't do this for you automatically. But remember that the data portal has no idea what values are required to identify your business object's data. Thus, you must create the criteria object and pass it to `DataPortal_Delete()`.

DataPortal_Delete

The final data portal method is `DataPortal_Delete()`. This method is called from two possible sources; if immediate deletion is used, the UI will call the `static` deletion method, which will call `DataPortal_Delete()`; and if deferred deletion is used, `DataPortal_Delete()` is called by `DataPortal_DeleteSelf()`. A `SingleCriteria` object is passed as a parameter, identifying the data to be deleted. Then it's just a matter of calling the `deleteProject` stored procedure as follows:

```
[Transactional(TransactionalTypes.TransactionScope)]
private void DataPortal_Delete(SingleCriteria<Project, Guid> criteria)
{
  using (var ctx =
    ContextManager<ProjectTracker.DalLinq.PTrackerDataContext>.
    GetManager(ProjectTracker.DalLinq.Database.PTracker))
  {
    // delete project data
    ctx.DataContext.deleteProject(criteria.Value);
    // reset child list field
    LoadProperty(ResourcesProperty, ProjectResources.NewProjectResources());
  }
}
```

The method just opens a LINQ to SQL context and calls the `deleteProject` stored procedure. That stored procedure deletes the project data and any assignment data related to the project.

The `ProjectResources` child collection is replaced with an empty collection. Since the stored procedure just removed the data in the database, the collection should be empty as well.

In the downloaded code for this book, you'll also see a code region for an `Exists` command, which I discuss later in the "Implementing Exists Methods" section.

ProjectResources

A `Project` object contains a collection of child objects, each one representing a resource assigned to the project.

Child objects follow the same basic structure as a root object, in that they have factory methods that call the data portal, and the data portal invokes methods to do the data access. Those are called the `Child_XYZ` methods.

Factory Methods

The *Factory Methods* region contains two factory methods and a `private` constructor, much like the `Project` class.

The two factory methods are declared as `internal` scope since they are not for use by the UI code. Rather, they are intended for use by the `Project` object that contains the collection:

```
internal static ProjectResources NewProjectResources()
{
  return DataPortal.CreateChild<ProjectResources>();
}

internal static ProjectResources GetProjectResources(
  ProjectTracker.DalLinq.Assignment[] data)
{
  return DataPortal.FetchChild<ProjectResources>(data);
}

private ProjectResources()
{ /* require use of factory methods */ }
```

In both cases, the factory methods simply call the data portal to create or retrieve the collection object. The CreateChild() method causes the data portal to invoke a Child_Create() method, while FetchChild() causes invocation of Child_Fetch(). The advantage of using the data portal in this manner is that it automatically manages the object state, setting IsChild, IsNew, and IsDirty automatically.

Data Access

The *Data Access* region in a child collection object is very similar to that of a root object such as Project. Instead of containing DataPortal_XYZ methods, it contains Child_XYZ methods. These are somewhat different but are intended to do the same things: create, retrieve, insert, update, and delete the object's data.

In the DataPortal_Fetch() method of Project, a call is made to the GetProjectResources() factory method in ProjectResources. That factory method calls the data portal's ChildFetch() method, passing the data access object from the Project object as a parameter:

```
private void Child_Fetch(
  ProjectTracker.DalLinq.Assignment[] data)
{
  this.RaiseListChangedEvents = false;
  foreach (var value in data)
    this.Add(ProjectResource.GetResource(value));
  this.RaiseListChangedEvents = true;
}
```

Remember that it is an array of Assignment objects from the data access assembly that is passed as a parameter. This code loops through the items in that array, adding a child object to the collection for each item. Each child object is created by calling a GetResource() factory method, which I discuss later in the chapter.

The RaiseListChangedEvents property is set to false and then true to suppress the ListChanged events that would otherwise be raised as each item is added. The DataPortal_Insert() and DataPortal_Update() methods of Project call the field manager's UpdateChildren() method. That method finds each child object and calls DataPortal.UpdateChild() on that child object. The data portal calls Child_Update() on a child collection object, and that method is responsible for updating all the objects contained in the collection.

The BusinessListBase class already has an implementation of Child_Update() that does all the work. This means that a normal business collection doesn't have to be affected; it just works.

You can override Child_Update() if you need to do some extra processing in addition to updating the items in the collection.

I've now shown all the ProjectResources collection code.

ProjectResource

A Project contains a child collection: ProjectResources. The ProjectResources collection contains ProjectResource objects. As designed in Chapter 3, each ProjectResource object represents a resource that has been assigned to the project.

Also remember from Chapter 3 that ProjectResource shares some behaviors with ResourceAssignment and those common behaviors are factored out into an Assignment object. As you look through the code in ProjectResource, you'll see calls to the behaviors in Assignment, as ProjectResource collaborates with that other object to implement its own behaviors.

Factory Methods

Like ProjectResources, this object has two factory methods scoped as internal. These methods are intended for use only by the parent object, ProjectResources:

```
internal static ProjectResource NewProjectResource(int resourceId)
{
  return DataPortal.CreateChild<ProjectResource>(
    resourceId, RoleList.DefaultRole());
}

internal static ProjectResource GetResource(
  ProjectTracker.DalLinq.Assignment data)
{
  return DataPortal.FetchChild<ProjectResource>(data);
}

private ProjectResource()
{ /* require use of factory methods */ }
```

The NewProjectResource() factory method accepts a resourceId value as a parameter. That value is used to retrieve the corresponding Resource object from the database with a call to CreateChild() that results in invocation of Child_Create().

Two parameters are passed to the CreateChild() method, the resourceId parameter (the ID of the resource being assigned to the project), and the role the resource will fill on the project. This second value is provided by calling the DefaultRole() method on the RoleList class from Chapter 17.

The GetResource() factory method is called by ProjectResources as it is being loaded with data from the database. Recall that ProjectResources gets an array of Assignment data access objects and loops through all the rows in that array, creating a new ProjectResource for each item. To do this, it calls the GetResource() factory method, passing the item as a parameter. This parameter is passed to the FetchChild() method of the data portal, which invokes Child_Fetch().

Using the data portal's CreateChild() and FetchChild() methods allows the data portal to automatically set the child object's IsChild, IsNew, and IsDirty properties.

Data Access

The *Data Access* region contains the code to initialize a new instance of the class when created as a new object or loaded from the database. It also contains methods to insert, update, and delete the object's data in the database.

Creating a New Object

When a Resource is assigned to a Project, a new ProjectResource object must be added to the ProjectResources collection. This process starts with the Assign() method of the ProjectResources collection, which invokes the NewProjectResource() factory method in the ProjectResource class, passing the Resource object's Id value as a parameter.

The NewProjectResource() factory method calls the data portal's CreateChild() method, which causes the data portal to create a new object and invoke the Child_Create() method:

```
private void Child_Create(int resourceId, int role)
{
  var res = Resource.GetResource(resourceId);
  LoadProperty(ResourceIdProperty, res.Id);
  LoadProperty(LastNameProperty, res.LastName);
  LoadProperty(FirstNameProperty, res.FirstName);
  LoadProperty(AssignedProperty, Assignment.GetDefaultAssignedDate());
  LoadProperty(RoleProperty, role);
}
```

This method is a bit different than the other methods so far because it has to initialize the new object with existing data, specifically with details about the resource being assigned to the project. To get these details, it retrieves a Resource object by calling the GetResource() factory method.

■ **Note** Technically, this approach is a misuse of the Resource object. The responsibility of the Resource object is to edit resource data, and here I'm using it just to retrieve data. In this particular case, I know that there's no extra cost to using the existing Resource class because I'm using all its fields. However, if I were just using three out of dozens of properties, I'd create a read-only root object to retrieve only the data I needed.

The values from the Resource object are used to populate the new ProjectResource object so it represents the fact that a resource has been assigned to the project.

Loading an Existing Object

When a Project is being loaded from the database, it calls ProjectResources to load all the child objects. ProjectResources loops through all the items in the Assignment data access object array supplied by Project, creating a ProjectResource child object for each item. That item is ultimately passed into the Child_Fetch() method where the object's fields are set:

```
private void Child_Fetch(ProjectTracker.DalLinq.Assignment data)
{
  LoadProperty(ResourceIdProperty, data.ResourceId);
  LoadProperty(LastNameProperty, data.Resource.LastName);
  LoadProperty(FirstNameProperty, data.Resource.FirstName);
  LoadProperty(AssignedProperty, data.Assigned);
  LoadProperty(RoleProperty, data.Role);
  _timestamp = data.LastChanged.ToArray();
}
```

This code is very similar to the code in Project to load the object's fields from the data access object. Each property's value is loaded, along with the timestamp value for this row in the database, thus enabling implementation of first-write-wins optimistic concurrency for the child objects as well as the Project object itself.

Once the object has been populated with data directly from the database, it is not new or dirty. The data portal automatically calls the object's MarkOld() method to set the IsNew and IsDirty property values to false before invoking the Child_Fetch() method to ensure these values are correct and to allow your object to use the properties if desired.

Inserting Data

When ProjectResources is asked to update its data into the database, it's Child_Update() method loops through all the child objects. Any child objects with IsDeleted set to false and IsNew set to true have their Insert() method called. The child object is responsible for inserting its own data into the database:

```
private void Child_Insert(Project project)
{
  _timestamp = Assignment.AddAssignment(
    project.Id,
    ReadProperty(ResourceIdProperty),
    ReadProperty(AssignedProperty),
    ReadProperty(RoleProperty));
}
```

In Chapter 3, the object design process reveals that ProjectResource and ResourceAssignment both create a relationship between a project and a resource using the same data in the same way. Due to this, the Insert() method delegates most of its work to an AddAssignment() method in the Assignment class.

Looking at the Assignment class, you can see the AddAssignment() method:

```
public static byte[] AddAssignment(
  Guid projectId,
  int resourceId,
  SmartDate assigned,
  int role)
{
  using (var ctx =
    ContextManager<ProjectTracker.DalLinq.PTrackerDataContext>.
    GetManager(ProjectTracker.DalLinq.Database.PTracker))
  {
    System.Data.Linq.Binary lastChanged = null;
    ctx.DataContext.addAssignment(
      projectId,
      resourceId,
      assigned,
      role,
      ref lastChanged);
    return lastChanged.ToArray();
  }
}
```

This method simply calls the addAssignment stored procedure by using LINQ to SQL. It is centralized in the Assignment class because this same code is required by both ProjectResource and ResourceAssignment, so I've normalized the behavior into this one location.

I want to call your attention to an important fact: this method uses the ContextManager to get access to the LINQ to SQL context object. Remember that this method is called because the root Project object is being inserted or updated and that the field manager's UpdateChildren() method is invoked *inside* the using block for the ContextManager in the Project class.

This is important because this call to the ContextManager returns the preexisting context object, not a new one. That first call, in the Project class, creates and opens a new context and database connection. That one context is reused by any other objects until that top-level using block exits and the context object is disposed.

Because the Project object's DataPortal_Insert() and DataPortal_Update() methods are marked with the Transactional attribute, sharing the same database connection for all database interaction is necessary to avoid having System.Transactions accidentally use the DTC. In other words, reusing the existing context is a major boost to performance.

Updating Data

The method is very similar to Child_Insert(). It delegates the call to the UpdateAssignment() method in the Assignment class. This is because the data updated by ProjectResource is the same as ResourceAssignment, so the common behavior is factored out into the Assignment class.

Deleting Data

Finally, there's the Child_DeleteSelf() method. Like Child_Update() and Child_Insert(), it too delegates the work to the Assignment class.

This completes the ProjectResource class and really the whole Project object graph. You should now have an understanding of how to persist an editable root object, a child list, and an editable child, some of the most common stereotypes in most business applications.

RoleList

The RoleList object is used by Project, ProjectResources, ProjectResource, and Assignment. This is a name/value list based on the Roles table in Chapter 3. The name (key) values are of type int, while the values are the string names of each role.

The CSLA .NET framework includes the NameValueListBase class to help simplify the creation of name/value list objects. Such objects are so common in business applications that it is worth having a base class to support this one specialized scenario.

Factory Methods

As in the template in Chapter 5, RoleList implements a form of caching to minimize load on the database. The GetList() factory method stores the collection in a static field and returns it if the object has already been loaded. It only goes to the database if the cache field is null:

```
private static RoleList _list;

public static RoleList GetList()
{
  if (_list == null)
    _list = DataPortal.Fetch<RoleList>();
  return _list;
}
```

■ **Note** If you need to filter the name/value list results, you'll need to pass a criteria object as a parameter to the Fetch() method just like you would with any other root object.

In case the cache needs to be flushed at some point, there's also an InvalidateCache() method:

```
public static void InvalidateCache()
{
  _list = null;
}
```

By setting the static cache value to null, the cache is reset. The next time any code calls the GetList() method, the collection is reloaded from the database. This InvalidateCache() method will be called by the Roles collection later in the chapter.

Of course, there's also a non-public constructor in the class to enforce the use of the factory method to retrieve the object.

Data Access

Finally, there's the DataPortal_Fetch() method that loads the data from the database into the collection:

```
private void DataPortal_Fetch()
{
  this.RaiseListChangedEvents = false;
  using (var ctx =
    ContextManager<ProjectTracker.DalLinq.PTrackerDataContext>.
    GetManager(ProjectTracker.DalLinq.Database.PTracker))
  {
    var data = from role in ctx.DataContext.Roles
               select new NameValuePair(role.Id, role.Name);
    IsReadOnly = false;
    this.AddRange(data);
    IsReadOnly = true;
  }
  this.RaiseListChangedEvents = true;
}
```

As with the DataPortal_Fetch() method in Project, the code here gets a LINQ to SQL context object and uses it to define a LINQ query. This query is a bit different, however, because it directly creates a list of NameValuePair objects, populated with the data from the database. That list of objects is then added to the RoleList collection by calling the AddRange() method.

Since the collection is normally read-only, the IsReadOnly property is set to false before loading the data and then restored to true once the data has been loaded.

The result is a fully populated name/value list containing the data from the Roles table in the database.

At this point you should understand how a name-value list is loaded from the database and how you can use simple caching with a static field to improve performance.

ProjectList and ResourceList

The ProjectList and ResourceList classes are both read-only collections of read-only data. They exist to provide the UI with an efficient way to get a list of projects and resources for display to the user.

On the surface, it might seem that you could simply retrieve a collection of Project or Resource objects and display their data. But that would mean retrieving a lot of data that the user may never use. Instead, it's more efficient to retrieve a small set of read-only objects for display purposes and then retrieve an actual Project or Resource object once the user has chosen which one to use.

The CSLA .NET framework includes the ReadOnlyListBase class, which is designed specifically to support this type of read-only list. Such a collection typically contains objects that inherit from ReadOnlyBase.

Because these two read-only collections are so similar in implementation, I'm only going to walk through the ResourceList class in this chapter. You can look at the code for ProjectList in the code download for this book.

Factory Methods

The ResourceList collection exposes two factory methods, EmptyList() and GetResourceList():

```
public static ResourceList EmptyList()
{
  return new ResourceList();
}

public static ResourceList GetResourceList()
{
  return DataPortal.Fetch<ResourceList>();
}

private ResourceList()
{ /* require use of factory methods */ }
```

The GetResourceList() factory method simply uses the data portal to retrieve the list of data.

Data Access

The GetResourceList() factory method calls the data portal, which in turn ultimately calls the ResourceList object's DataPortal_Fetch() method to load the collection with data:

```
private void DataPortal_Fetch()
{
  RaiseListChangedEvents = false;
  using (var ctx =
    ContextManager<ProjectTracker.DalLinq.PTrackerDataContext>.
    GetManager(ProjectTracker.DalLinq.Database.PTracker))
  {
    var data = from r in ctx.DataContext.Resources
               select new ResourceInfo(r.Id, r.LastName, r.FirstName);
    IsReadOnly = false;
    this.AddRange(data);
    IsReadOnly = true;
  }
  RaiseListChangedEvents = true;
}
```

It gets a LINQ to SQL context object and uses it to define a LINQ query. Similar to the RoleList class, querying it directly creates a list of ResourceInfo objects. The ResourceInfo class has an internal constructor to make this easy:

```
internal ResourceInfo(int id, string lastname, string firstname)
{
  _id = id;
  _name = string.Format("{0}, {1}", lastname, firstname);
}
```

Those ResourceInfo objects are then added to the ResourceList collection using the AddRange() method.

Since ResourceList is a read-only collection, the IsReadOnly property is set to false before loading the data and true once the loading is complete.

The end result is a fully populated list of the resources in the database that can be displayed to the user by the UI.

Roles

The RoleList object provides a read-only, cached list of roles that a resource can hold when assigned to a project. But that list of roles needs to be maintained, and that is the purpose behind the Roles collection. This is an editable root collection that contains a list of editable child Role objects.

Factory Methods

The *Factory Methods* region implements a GetRoles() factory method, which just calls the data portal like the other factory methods you've seen. It also implements a non-public constructor to require use of the factory method.

But the constructor contains code that is quite important:

```
private Roles()
{
    this.Saved += Roles_Saved;
    this.AllowNew = true;
}
```

AllowNew is a protected property defined by BindingList, the base class of BusinessListBase. Setting this to true allows WPF and Windows Forms data binding to automatically add new child objects to the collection. Typically, this happens when the collection is bound to an editable grid control in the UI. Table 18-2 lists the properties you can use to control the behavior of an editable collection.

Table 18-2. *Properties Used to Control an Editable Collection*

Property	Description
AllowNew	If true, data binding can automatically add new child objects to the collection. It requires that you also override the AddNewCore() method. It defaults to false.
AllowRemove	If true, data binding can automatically remove items from the collection. It defaults to true.
AllowEdit	If true, data binding allows in-place editing of child objects in a grid control. It defaults to true.

Though a collection can opt to implement a static delete method to delete all the items in the database, that isn't a requirement for Roles, so it doesn't have such a method.

An event handler is also set up for the Saved event. This is so the RoleList cache can be invalidated any time the Roles collection has been saved. I discuss the Roles_Saved() method in the "Invalidating the Client-Side Cache" section.

Data Access

The *Data Access* region has some rather unique code. The reason for this is not that the collection is an editable root but rather that the Roles collection needs to invalidate the cache of any RoleList object when the list of roles is changed. In other words, when Save() is called on a Roles collection, any cached RoleList object must be reloaded from the database to get the new values.

Other than this requirement, the data access code is quite straightforward, so let's focus on the cache invalidation code.

Invalidating the Client-Side Cache

In the constructor, the Roles class hooks up the Roles_Saved() method to handle the Saved event. That event is raised when the Roles object has been saved, thus indicating that the list of role data has changed. In this event handler, the RoleList cache is invalidated:

```
private void Roles_Saved(
  object sender, Csla.Core.SavedEventArgs e)
{
  RoleList.InvalidateCache();
}
```

Obviously, changing the Roles collection also changes RoleList, so invalidating the cache ensures the application is using current values. This code ensures that the client-side cache is invalidated by calling RoleList.InvalidatedCache().

Invalidating the Server-Side Cache

It is important to realize that there could be a cached RoleList collection on both the client and the server. Keep in mind that CSLA .NET enables mobile objects and that means that business object code can run on the client and on the server. If a business object has server-side code that uses a RoleList, it will cause a RoleList object to be created and cached *on the server.*

If you look at the ValidRole() rule method in Assignment, you'll see that it calls the GetList() factory on RoleList, loading a list of roles. If any business rule validation occurs for either a ProjectResource or ResourceAssignment object on the server, it would cause the list to be loaded and cached on the server. Though this doesn't occur in ProjectTracker, it is a very common scenario in many applications.

The great thing about the way the mobile objects work is that caching the RoleList on the client and server is automatic. You'll note that there's no special code to make that happen. But it does mean a bit of extra work in the Roles collection to ensure that any server-side cache is also flushed.

Recall from Chapter 15 that the data portal optionally invokes DataPortal_OnDataPortalInvoke() and DataPortal_OnDataPortalInvokeComplete() methods if your business object implements them. The former is invoked before any DataPortal_XYZ method is called, and the latter is invoked afterward. You can use this method to run code on the server after the DataPortal_Update() method is complete:

```
protected override void DataPortal_OnDataPortalInvokeComplete(
  DataPortalEventArgs e)
{
  if (ApplicationContext.ExecutionLocation ==
      ApplicationContext.ExecutionLocations.Server &&
        e.Operation == DataPortalOperations.Update)
  {
    RoleList.InvalidateCache();
  }
}
```

Of course, the data portal could be configured to run the "server-side" code locally in the client process, in which case there's no point invalidating the cache here because the Saved event handler will take care of it. That's why the code checks the ExecutionLocation and Operation to see if it's actually an Update (which indicates an insert, update, or delete in the list) operation running on an application server. If so, it calls RoleList.InvalidateCache() to invalidate any server-side cache of role data.

Other than dealing with the RoleList cache, the data access code in Roles and Role is like the data access code you saw earlier in this chapter.

Implementing Exists Methods

I have covered all the code in the Project class except for the Exists() command implementation. Many objects can benefit from implementation of an Exists() command, as it allows the UI to quickly and easily determine whether a given object's data is in the database without having to fully instantiate the object itself. Ideally, a UI developer could write conditional code like this:

```
if (Project.Exists(productId))
```

Implementing an Exists() command also provides an opportunity to make use of Csla.CommandBase to create a command object. This makes sense because all an Exists() command needs to do is run a stored procedure in the database and report on the result.

Exists Method

The Project class itself has a static method called Exists(), which is public so it can be called from UI code:

```
public static bool Exists(Guid id)
{
  return ExistsCommand.Exists(id);
}
```

This method simply delegates all its work to a factory method in the ExistsCommand class. What is interesting is that the ExistsCommand class is private to Project. The only way for the UI or other code to interact with this command object is through the static method on the Project class. This allows the application to implement powerful functionality, without expanding its public API.

ExistsCommand Class

The real work occurs in the command object itself: ExistsCommand. The ExistsCommand class inherits from Csla.CommandBase and is declared as a private nested class within Project:

```
[Serializable]
private class ExistsCommand : CommandBase
```

Not all command objects are nested within other business classes, but in this case it makes sense. There's no need for UI developers to be aware of the ExistsCommand class or its implementation details; they only need to know about the Project.Exists() method.

In other cases, you may have public command objects that are directly used by the UI. A good example is a ShipOrder object that is responsible for shipping a sales order. It is quite realistic to expect that the UI would want to directly ship a sales order, so there's value in being able to call a ShipOrder.Ship(orderId) method.

Command objects, whether public or private, tend to be very simplistic in terms of their structure. ExistsCommand declares some instance fields, one property, and a constructor:

```
private Guid _id;
private bool _exists;

public bool ProjectExists
{
  get { return _exists; }
}
```

```
public ExistsCommand(Guid id)
{
  _id = id;
}
```

The constructor initializes the _id field so that value is available when the command is executed on the server. The _exists field is set as a result of the command running on the server and is exposed through the ProjectExists property.

Factory Methods

The Exists() factory method is much like the other factory methods in this chapter except that it calls the data portal's Execute() method:

```
public static bool Exists(Guid id)
{
  ExistsCommand result = DataPortal.Execute<ExistsCommand>(
    new ExistsCommand(id));
  return result.ProjectExists;
}
```

The data portal Execute() method invokes the DataPortal_Execute() method on the command object on the application server.

The parameter passed to the Execute() method is a new instance of ExistsCommand. In other words, this factory method creates an instance of the command object, sets its _id value through the constructor, and passes the command object to the application server through the data portal.

The result of Execute() is an updated command object that contains the result value in the ProjectExists property. That value is returned as the result of the static factory method, indicating whether the project exists or not.

Data Access

The code that runs on the server is entirely contained within the DataPortal_Execute() method:

```
protected override void DataPortal_Execute()
{
  using (var ctx =
    ContextManager<ProjectTracker.DalLinq.PTrackerDataContext>.
    GetManager(ProjectTracker.DalLinq.Database.PTracker))
  {
    _exists = ((from p in ctx.DataContext.Projects
                where p.Id == _id
                select p).Count() > 0);
  }
}
```

Of course, the code in DataPortal_Execute() could be as complex as you require. It might create and interact with business objects on the server, or it might use server-side resources such as the file system, a high-powered CPU, or specialized third-party hardware, or software installed on the server. In this case, the code works directly against the database to determine whether the data exists in the database:

```
_exists = ((from p in ctx.DataContext.Projects
                  where p.Id == _id
                  select p).Count() > 0);
```

Really, the data portal does most of the hard work with command objects. When DataPortal.Execute() is called on the client, the command object is copied to the server and its DataPortal_Execute() method is invoked. Once that method completes, the data portal copies the object back to the client, thus allowing the client to get any information out of the command object. This means that all instance fields declared in the class must refer to types that are Serializable.

The Exists() command in the Resource class is implemented in the same manner.

At this point, you should understand how all the business objects in ProjectTracker.Library are implemented.

Conclusion

This chapter completes the discussion of the ProjectTracker.Library code started in Chapter 17. The focus in this chapter was on data access and object persistence, exploring the various ways to use the CSLA .NET data portal, and walking through one sample implementation.

The ProjectTracker.Library business library supports all the interface projects included in the ProjectTracker solution:

- WPF
- Windows Forms
- Web Forms
- Web Services
- WCF services
- Workflow

This really illustrates the power of CSLA .NET by showing a single business library that supports all these different application types at the same time. The final chapters in this book focus on the WPF, Web Forms, and WCF services interfaces.

CHAPTER 19

Windows Presentation Foundation UI

Chapters 17 and 18 focused on creating business objects and enabling them with data access. The business objects, and the business logic they contain, are the centerpiece of any application, and those objects make the behaviors defined in your use cases (from Chapter 3) available for use when building applications.

But to the end user, the application is really more about the user interface than it is about data access or object-oriented design. The user experience is absolutely central to the application. So while the business logic and data access layers implement the majority of the application's functionality, it is the UI that makes or breaks the application.

In .NET 3.0, Microsoft introduced the WPF, which is the next-generation UI technology for the development of Windows applications.

Note Closely related to WPF, Silverlight is used for building rich client applications that deploy and execute within a web browser. You can get more information about CSLA .NET for Silverlight at `www.lhotka.net/cslalight`.

In this chapter, I assume you have a basic understanding of WPF. This includes the concepts of XAML programming, how code-behind works in a WPF application, and XML namespaces.

WPF provides many of the best features of both Windows and web development. It is a rich, interactive, event-driven environment similar to Windows Forms, yet it uses an XML-based, stylable tag markup language to describe the presentation, much like the Web.

The challenge with WPF is that it has aspects that are similar to both Windows Forms and Web Forms development, yet it is fundamentally different from both of those technologies. This leads to a learning curve that you must overcome before you can be productive in the new environment.

Like Windows Forms, WPF provides powerful data binding support, using an event-driven model for interaction between the UI controls and the business objects. Like Web Forms, WPF uses a data control model (called a data provider control) to load data into a form. And like its ASP.NET equivalent, the `ObjectDataProvider` control is too limited to work with CSLA .NET–style business objects. To address this, CSLA .NET includes a `CslaDataProvider` control for WPF.

This chapter will cover the basic process of building a WPF UI on top of the business objects created in Chapters 17 and 18. To do this, I will use data binding, along with several CSLA .NET controls from the `Csla.Wpf` namespace. The resulting WPF forms have little code-behind, because most of the work is done through XAML or by the CSLA .NET controls.

Before getting into the creation of the UI, it is important to discuss one higher-level issue regarding custom authentication.

Custom Authentication in WPF

WPF is not thread-safe. This means that all UI work must be done on the single UI thread. Nevertheless, WPF does use background threads behind the scenes. The security infrastructure in .NET is driven off the current principal object, which is associated with a specific thread. This means that you can run into cases where your code is running on a thread that doesn't have the right principal.

This issue only applies if you're using custom authentication. If you're using Windows authentication, then all threads will use the `WindowsPrincipal` for the user logged into the workstation, and there's no issue.

There are a number of possible scenarios with custom authentication and custom principal objects, but they all have the same issue: one or more threads end up with the incorrect principal. This is problematic, because the authorization and data portal subsystems of CSLA .NET rely on the .NET principal object to do their work. If you can't rely on having a valid principal, authorization is difficult to implement, and the data portal can't reliably impersonate the client user identity on the application server.

The behavior of WPF in this area is intentional; Microsoft is trying to protect the application from a scenario in which one thread accidentally changes the principal on other threads. The unfortunate side effect of this protection is that it is nearly impossible to build a WPF application that uses custom authentication.

The core issue is that WPF doesn't allow a thread to alter the current principal for other threads. Even if you attempt to do this, the WPF infrastructure will often reset the principal to a default value.

Microsoft's recommended solution is to set the default principal value on the `AppDomain`:

```
AppDomain.CurrentDomain.SetThreadPrincipal(principal);
```

Once this line of code runs, all threads created from that point forward will use the new default principal. However, that's a serious limitation, because it means you need to execute this line of code *before any background threads are created*, including those on the thread pool. This means your login process can't use any asynchronous behaviors (no async data portal or service calls), and it must occur very early in your application's lifetime to ensure no other async operations have occurred.

Also, this line of code can only be called one time during the application's lifetime. So if your application allows the user to log out and then log in later (without closing the application), you won't be able to use this technique at all.

The CSLA .NET `ApplicationContext` object has a partial workaround to this issue that solves the problem for all CSLA .NET code, as well as code that uses `ApplicationContext.User` to access the current principal. It is a *partial* solution, because CSLA .NET can't ensure that the actual `CurrentPrincipal` on each thread is always correct, so while all CSLA .NET code will work fine, some .NET features—most notably Code Access Security (CAS)—may not function at all times.

I'm discussing this issue because WPF developers commonly encounter it. While CSLA .NET addresses this issue to a large degree, you should understand that it exists and that it is caused by WPF working to prevent one thread from altering the principal used by other threads.

As long as you use `Csla.ApplicationContext.User` to access the principal, which is what CSLA .NET itself does, you should be able to alter the principal value during the lifetime of the application and have a consistent value available to all threads.

Interface Design

The UI application can be found within the `ProjectTracker` solution. The project is named `PTWpf`. The `PTWpf` interface contains a single main form with a set of navigation links on the left and a content area on the right. The main form loads user controls into the content area dynamically, displaying them to the user. Figure 19-1 shows what the main form looks like.

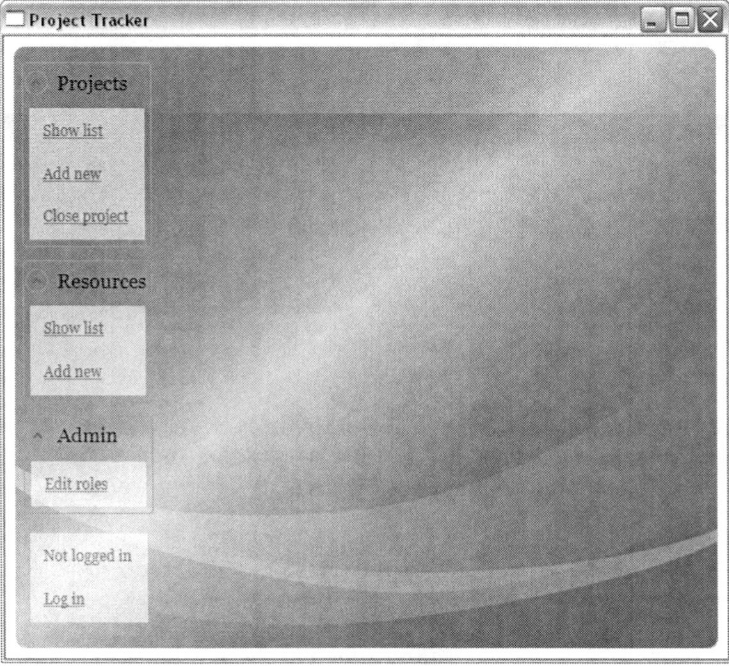

Figure 19-1. *Appearance of the main form*

Notice that the navigation items on the left deal with projects, resources, roles, and authentication. When the user clicks a link, a user control is loaded dynamically into the main area of the form. Figure 19-2 shows the application while the user is editing a project.

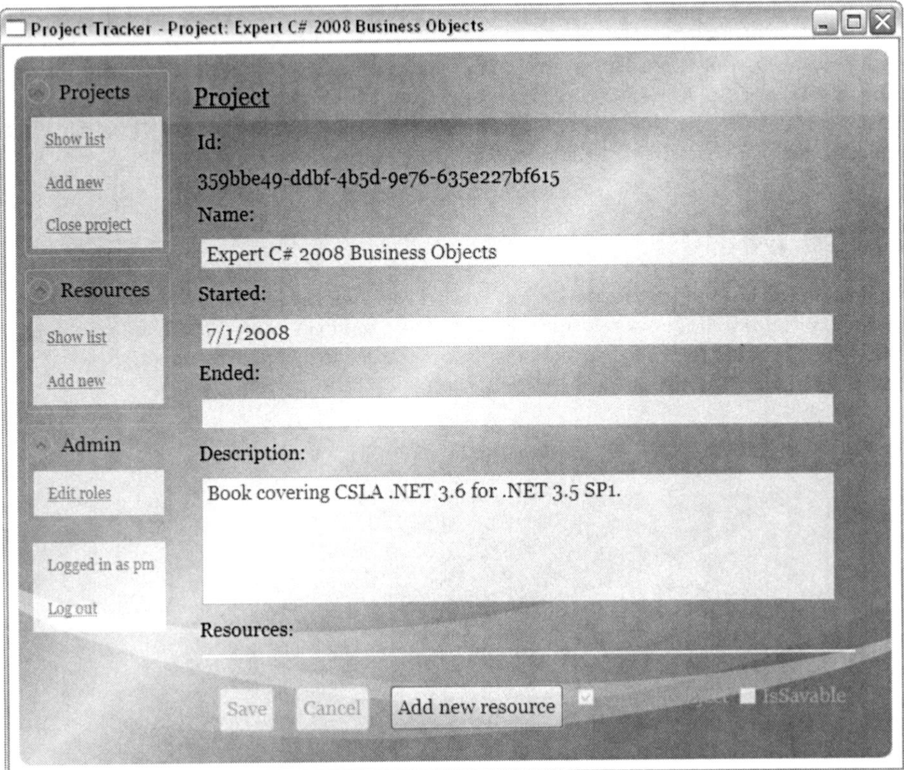

Figure 19-2. *Editing a project*

Of course, some dialog windows are used to collect input from the user as well, but the bulk of the application's functionality centers around the use of user controls hosted by the main form.

Table 19-1 lists the forms and controls that make up the interface.

Table 19-1. *Forms and User Controls in PTWpf*

Form/Control	Type	Description
`MainForm`	`Window`	The main form for the application
`EditForm`	`UserControl`	A custom base class for creating user controls
`ListTemplateConverter`	`IValueConverter`	Converts a Boolean value to a `DataTemplate` value
`Login`	`Window`	A login dialog to collect user credentials
`RolesEdit`	`EditForm`	Allows the user to edit the list of roles
`ProjectSelect`	`Window`	A dialog prompting the user to select from a list of projects
`ProjectList`	`EditForm`	Displays a list of projects
`ProjectEdit`	`EditForm`	Allows the user to view, add, or edit a project

Table 19-1. *Forms and User Controls in PTWpf*

Form/Control	Type	Description
ResourceSelect	Window	A dialog prompting the user to select from a list of resources
ResourceList	EditForm	Displays a list of resources
ResourceEdit	EditForm	Allows the user to view, add, or edit a resource
VisibilityConverter	IValueConverter	Converts a Boolean value to a Visibility value

The user control approach taken in this chapter gives you a great deal of flexibility. You can host the user controls in child forms in an MDI interface, as shown in this chapter, or you can host them in panes in a multipane interface. In short, by creating your "forms" as user controls, you gain the flexibility to use them in many different types of UI design.

User Control Framework

Loading a user control dynamically isn't difficult. The code needs to follow this basic process:

1. Create the EditForm control.
2. Remove any existing EditForm controls from view.
3. Add a new EditForm to the Children collection.
4. Hook the TitleChanged event for a new EditForm.

Although my intent with this chapter isn't for you to create a full-blown WPF UI framework, you must do some basic work to provide for a decent user experience.

The steps listed here require some interaction between each UserControl and the hosting MainForm. To standardize this process, I've created an EditForm class, which is a subclass of UserControl. This class provides some standard behaviors MainForm can count on for each control it hosts.

The EditForm Class

The primary purpose of the EditForm class is to standardize how each control is hosted in MainForm. However, it also provides some common behaviors that are useful to any data-bound form. Table 19-2 lists the behaviors provided by EditForm.

Table 19-2. *Behaviors Implemented in EditForm*

Behavior	Description
Principal changed	Enables a scheme by which MainForm can notify the active EditForm that the current .NET principal has changed
Provides a Title property	Extends UserControl by adding a Title property that can be set through XAML or code; includes an event so MainForm knows the Title has changed so it can update the main form caption
Error handling	Provides a standard way for any data provider to display exceptions that occur during data access

I'll discuss each behavior individually.

Principal Changed

When the current .NET principal changes, it means that the user has logged in or out of the application, so any authorization rules must be reapplied for the currently displayed `EditForm`. The exact impact of a user logging in or out is up to the individual `EditForm`, so the base class simply notifies the `EditForm` subclass by invoking a `virtual` method.

```
void EditForm_Loaded(object sender, System.Windows.RoutedEventArgs e)
{
  ApplyAuthorization();
}

void IRefresh.Refresh()
{
  ApplyAuthorization();
}

protected virtual void ApplyAuthorization()
{
}
```

The `ApplyAuthorization()` method is invoked both when the edit form is first loaded and then when `MainForm` calls the `Refresh()` method because the current principal has changed.

Each individual subclass can override `ApplyAuthorization()` to reapply authorization rules based on the new .NET principal. I'll show how this works when I discuss an actual edit form implementation.

Title Property

In this application, I want each edit form to be able to alter the top-level window caption. That caption is controlled by `MainForm`, so there needs to be some mechanism by which each edit control can ask `MainForm` to change the caption.

In WPF, data-bindable properties of controls are implemented as *dependency properties*. A dependency property is similar to a normal property, but it is tied into the WPF (and WF) infrastructure, so the property can be bound to values through XAML. Here's the `Title` property:

```
public event EventHandler TitleChanged;

public static readonly DependencyProperty TitleProperty =
    DependencyProperty.Register("Title", typeof(string),
                                typeof(EditForm), null);

public string Title
{
  get { return (string)GetValue(TitleProperty); }
  set
  {
    SetValue(TitleProperty, value);
    if (TitleChanged != null)
      TitleChanged(this, EventArgs.Empty);
  }
}
```

The `TitleChanged` event is a standard event, and `MainForm` handles this event so that it's notified when the value has been changed. The property declaration itself is a dependency property, so the value can be set through XAML. For example, here's how an `EditForm` instance is declared:

```
<local:EditForm x:Class="PTWpf.ProjectEdit"
    xmlns="http://schemas.microsoft.com/winfx/2006/xaml/presentation"
    xmlns:x="http://schemas.microsoft.com/winfx/2006/xaml"
    Title="Edit a Project">
```

The `Title` property can be set here in the XAML or in the code behind the form. Either way, the `TitleChanged` event is raised, so `MainForm` can update the main window caption.

Error Handling

When using a WPF data provider for data access, handling exceptions is a little tricky. The reason is that the data access is triggered by the control, not by your code, so there's no way for you to wrap the operation in a `try..catch` block to handle any exception.

The standard technique is to handle the `DataChanged` event of the data provider control and to see if the `Error` property of the data provider is anything other than `null`. If it is, then an exception occurred.

For this sample application, I've chosen to simply display the exception details to the user. Rather than repeating that code in each individual edit form, the `EditForm` base class provides an event handler to handle all such exceptions.

```
protected virtual void DataChanged(object sender, EventArgs e)
{
  var dp = sender as System.Windows.Data.DataSourceProvider;
  if (dp.Error != null)
    MessageBox.Show(
      dp.Error.ToString(),
      "Data error",
      MessageBoxButton.OK,
      MessageBoxImage.Exclamation);
}
```

Each edit form is responsible for hooking its data provider `DataChanged` events to this handler, which can be done through XAML or code-behind. I'll show how this is done when I discuss individual edit form implementations.

The MainForm Window

The other area of common plumbing code is in the `MainForm` class itself. `MainForm` acts as the overall application shell, hosting and coordinating all other windows and edit forms. In this section, I'll discuss only the code required for interaction with each `EditForm`, leaving discussion of the navigation and authentication for later in the chapter.

The content area of `MainForm` is a `DockPanel` control.

```
  <DockPanel Grid.Column="1" Name="contentArea"
             Margin="5,15,20,15" />
```

This `DockPanel` fills all the available space on the right-hand side of the form, maintaining a bit of a margin to keep the content inside the rounded corners (see Figure 19-1). By naming the control `contentArea`, the code behind the form is able to manipulate the control.

Moving from one edit form to another by showing the correct content in `contentArea`, `MainForm` implements a `ShowControl()` method to enable navigation:

```
public static void ShowControl(UserControl control)
{
  _mainForm.ShowUserControl(control);
}
```

```
private void ShowUserControl(UserControl control)
{
  UnhookTitleEvent(_currentControl);

  contentArea.Children.Clear();
  if (control != null)
    contentArea.Children.Add(control);
  _currentControl = control;

  HookTitleEvent(_currentControl);
}
```

The ShowControl() method is easily accessible to all code in the project, because it is a static method that is public. However, the actual instance of MainForm must display the user control, so the static method delegates to an instance method on the actual MainForm instance. The _mainForm field references the one instance of MainForm, and its value is set in the constructor of MainForm.

The ShowUserControl() method unhooks the TitleChanged event from any existing control.

```
private void UnhookTitleEvent(UserControl control)
{
  EditForm form = control as EditForm;
  if (form != null)
    form.TitleChanged -= new EventHandler(SetTitle);
}
```

The ShowUserControl() method then clears the Children collection of contentArea, ensuring the DockPanel is empty. Then it adds the new user control to the Children collection, effectively displaying the new content.

Finally, it hooks the TitleChanged event of the new control.

```
private void HookTitleEvent(UserControl control)
{
  SetTitle(control, EventArgs.Empty);
  EditForm form = control as EditForm;
  if (form != null)
    form.TitleChanged += new EventHandler(SetTitle);
}
```

This method also immediately sets the main window caption based on the current title of the new user control. This is done by calling the SetTitle() method.

```
private void SetTitle(object sender, EventArgs e)
{
  EditForm form = sender as EditForm;
  if (form != null && !string.IsNullOrEmpty(form.Title))
    _mainForm.Title =
      string.Format("Project Tracker - {0}", ((EditForm)sender).Title);
  else
    _mainForm.Title = string.Format("Project Tracker");
}
```

Notice how MainForm remains in control of the main window caption, using the Title property from the current user control to alter the overall value. This helps keep the application maintainable, because the window caption is controlled in a central location.

At this point, you should have an understanding of how MainForm hosts user controls and how the EditForm base class makes it easier to create standardized user controls for this purpose.

Value Converters

WPF allows you to do a great deal directly through XAML, minimizing code behind each window or user control. One powerful technique you can use to shift code into XAML is to implement a *value converter* control. These controls convert a value of one type, such as `bool`, to another type or value.

To create a value converter, you create a class that implements the `IValueConverter` interface from the `System.Windows` namespace. This interface requires that you implement the methods listed in Table 19-3. These methods are invoked by WPF data binding as needed.

Table 19-3. *Methods Defined by IValueConverter*

Method	Description
`Convert()`	Converts a data source value into a UI value
`ConvertBack()`	Converts a UI value into a data source value

One common use of a value converter is to change a `DateTime` property from a business object into a properly formatted `string` for display to the user. That fits into most people's conception of how data binding works.

However, in WPF, data binding is far more useful and widespread. You can use data binding to connect controls to other controls or objects. The potential is amazing. For example, in `PTWpf`, I use data binding and value converters so the UI responds to authorization rules automatically. Based on whether the user is authorized to create or edit the business object, I'll use data binding to enable or disable UI controls, hide some controls entirely, and even change the way data is displayed in a `ListBox` control.

Doing this requires a couple of value converters to convert a `bool` value to a `DataTemplate` (to change how a `ListBox` is displayed) or to a `Visibility` value (to show or hide parts of the UI).

I'll discuss the `VisibilityConverter` first, because it is the simpler of the two.

VisibilityConverter

The `VisibilityConverter` class implements `IValueConverter` and is designed to convert a `bool` value to a `Visibility` value. It is used when binding part of the UI to an authorization property such as `CanEditObject`. This way, when the user can edit the object, the `Visibility` value can return `Visible`, and if the user isn't allowed to edit the object, the `Visibility` value will return `Collapsed`.

```
public class VisibilityConverter : System.Windows.Data.IValueConverter
{
  public object Convert(object value, Type targetType,
    object parameter, System.Globalization.CultureInfo culture)
  {
    if ((bool)value)
      return System.Windows.Visibility.Visible;
    else
      return System.Windows.Visibility.Collapsed;
  }

  public object ConvertBack(object value, Type targetType,
    object parameter, System.Globalization.CultureInfo culture)
  {
    return false;
  }
}
```

Only the Convert() method is fully implemented in this case, because the converter is used to bind from an ObjectStatus control to a UI control. Changes to the UI control don't bind back to ObjectStatus.

In the Convert() method, the value parameter is cast to a bool, and that value is used to determine which Visibility value to return as a result.

You'll see how this is used when I discuss the RolesEdit form.

ListTemplateConverter

The ListTemplateConverter is a little more complex, because it defines a couple of properties as well as implements IValueConverter.

```
public class ListTemplateConverter : System.Windows.Data.IValueConverter
{
  public System.Windows.DataTemplate TrueTemplate { get; set; }

  public System.Windows.DataTemplate FalseTemplate { get; set; }

  #region IValueConverter Members

  public object Convert(object value, Type targetType,
    object parameter, System.Globalization.CultureInfo culture)
  {
    if ((bool)value)
      return TrueTemplate;
    else
      return FalseTemplate;
  }

  public object ConvertBack(object value, Type targetType,
    object parameter, System.Globalization.CultureInfo culture)
  {
    return value;
  }

  #endregion
}
```

Again, only the Convert() method is fully implemented, because the converter is used to bind from an ObjectStatus control to a UI control. If there are changes to the UI control, they don't bind back to ObjectStatus.

The TrueTemplate and FalseTemplate properties are used to define the DataTemplate values to be returned based on the input bool value. In your XAML, this converter is defined as a resource, like this:

```
<local:ListTemplateConverter x:Key="ListTemplateConverter"
    TrueTemplate="{StaticResource editableTemplate}"
    FalseTemplate="{StaticResource readonlyTemplate}" />
```

The two properties are set to DataTemplate items defined in that same XAML. You'll see an example of this when I discuss the RolesEdit form later in this chapter.

Like the VisibilityConverter, this converter's logic simply uses the value parameter to determine which result to return. The value converter concept in WPF is powerful, and you can use it to shift a lot of code behind each page into reusable controls that can be used from the XAML defining each page.

Application Configuration

The application needs to provide some basic configuration information through the application's configuration file. In the client application configuration file, either you can provide connection strings so that the application can interact with the database directly, or you can configure the data portal to communicate with a remote application server. I discussed this basic concept in Chapter 15 when I covered the channel adapter implementation. Recall that the data portal supports several channels, including WCF, Remoting, Enterprise Services, and Web Services. You can create your own channels as well if none of these meet your needs.

In Chapter 1, I discussed the trade-offs between performance, scalability, fault tolerance, and security that come with various physical n-tier configurations. The most scalable solution for an intelligent client UI is to use an application server to host the data access layer, while the most *performant* solution is to run the data portal locally in the client process. In this chapter, I'll show first how to run the data portal locally, and then remotely using the WCF channel.

The configuration is controlled by the application's configuration file. In the Visual Studio project, this is named `App.config`.

■ Note Naming the file `App.config` is important. Visual Studio 2008 will automatically copy the file into the appropriate bin directory, changing the name to match that of the program. In this case, it will change the name to `PTWin.exe.config` as it copies it into the bin directories. This occurs each time the project is built in Visual Studio.

Authentication

CSLA .NET controls authentication through the configuration file.

```
<?xml version="1.0" encoding="utf-8" ?>
<configuration>
  <appSettings>
    <add key="CslaAuthentication" value="Csla" />
    <add key="CslaPropertyChangedMode" value="Xaml" />
  </appSettings>
</configuration>
```

The `CslaAuthentication` key shown here specifies the use of custom authentication. Chapter 8 implemented the `PTPrincipal` and `PTIdentity` classes specifically to support custom authentication, and the UI code in this chapter will use custom authentication as well.

If you want to use Windows authentication, change the configuration to the following:

```
<add key="CslaAuthentication" value="Windows" />
```

Of course, this change requires coding changes. To start, remove the `PTPrincipal` and `PTIdentity` classes from `ProjectTracker.Library`, as they will no longer be needed. Also, the login/logout functionality implemented in this chapter will become unnecessary. Specifically, the `Login` form and the code to display that form should be removed from the UI project.

The `CslaPropertyChangedMode` key shown here causes CSLA .NET to use the XAML model for raising the `PropertyChanged` event from all business objects. Recall from Chapters 7 and 10 that the `PropertyChanged` event must be raised differently for WPF/XAML data binding than for Windows Forms data binding, because the two data binding infrastructures treat the event a little differently.

It's important that this value be set for WPF applications; otherwise, data binding won't update the UI properly based on underlying changes to the business object.

Local Data Portal

The configuration file also controls how the application uses the data portal. To make the client application interact directly with the database, use the following (with `your connection string` changed to the connection string for your database):

```
<?xml version="1.0" encoding="utf-8" ?>
<configuration>
  <appSettings>
    <add key="CslaAuthentication" value="Csla" />
    <add key="CslaPropertyChangedMode" value="Xaml" />
  </appSettings>
  <connectionStrings>
    <add name="PTracker" connectionString="your connection string"
      providerName="System.Data.SqlClient" />
    <add name="Security" connectionString="your connection string"
      providerName="System.Data.SqlClient" />
  </connectionStrings>
</configuration>
```

Because `LocalProxy` is the default for the data portal's `CslaDataPortalProxy` setting, no actual data portal configuration is required, so the only settings in the configuration file are to control authentication and to provide the database connection strings.

Remote Data Portal

To make the data portal use an application server and communicate using the WCF channel, use the following configuration:

```
<?xml version="1.0" encoding="utf-8" ?>
<configuration>
  <appSettings>
    <add key="CslaAuthentication" value="Csla" />
    <add key="CslaPropertyChangedMode" value="Xaml" />
    <add key="CslaDataPortalProxy"
      value="Csla.DataPortalClient.WcfProxy, Csla"/>
  </appSettings>
  <connectionStrings>
  </connectionStrings>
  <system.serviceModel>
    <client>
      <endpoint name="WcfDataPortal"
                address="http://localhost:4147/WcfHost/WcfPortal.svc"
                binding="wsHttpBinding"
                contract="Csla.Server.Hosts.IWcfPortal" />
    </client>
  </system.serviceModel>
</configuration>
```

The key lines for the WCF configuration are in bold. Of course, you need to change `localhost:4147` to the name of the application server on which the data portal host is installed. Also, the `WcfHost` text needs to be replaced with the name of your virtual root on that server.

Before using this configuration, you must create and configure the WCF host virtual root. I'll show how you do this in the next section.

The most important thing to realize about the application configuration is that the data portal can be changed from local to remote (using any of the network channels) with no need to change any UI or business object code.

Configuring the Data Portal Server

When using a remote data portal configuration, the client communicates with an application server. Obviously, this means that an application server must exist and be configured properly. When the client data portal is configured to use WCF, you must supply a properly configured WCF application server.

■ **Note** No data portal server is required when the data portal is configured for local mode. In that case, the "server-side" components run in the client process, and no application server is used or required.

The `WcfHost` website in the `ProjectTracker` download is an example of a WCF application server hosted in IIS. You may also choose to host the WCF server in a custom Windows service, in a custom EXE, or using WAS. These various hosts are similar to IIS in many ways, but are outside the scope of this book.

The `WcfHost` website is simple, because it relies on preexisting functionality provided by CSLA .NET, as discussed in Chapter 15. Table 19-4 lists the key elements of the website.

Table 19-4. *Key Elements of the WcfHost Website*

Element	Description
`WcfPortal.svc`	WCF service endpoint file, referencing the `Csla.Server.Hosts.WcfPortal` class
`bin`	Standard web `bin` folder containing `Csla.dll`, `ProjectTracker.Library.dll`, and any other assemblies required by the business library; the important thing is that your business assemblies and `Csla.dll` be present in this folder
`web.config`	Standard `web.config` file, but containing a `system.serviceModel` element to configure the WCF endpoint for the data portal

Any website containing the elements in Table 19-4 can act as a WCF data portal host. The `web.config` file must contain the configuration section for WCF, defining the endpoint for the data portal—for example:

```
<system.serviceModel>
  <services>
    <service name="Csla.Server.Hosts.WcfPortal">
      <endpoint address=""
                contract="Csla.Server.Hosts.IWcfPortal"
                binding="wsHttpBinding"/>
    </service>
  </services>
</system.serviceModel>
```

WCF services are defined by their address, binding, and contract.

For a WCF service hosted in IIS, the address is defined by IIS and the name of the `svc` file, so it is not specified in the `web.config` file. As shown here, you may provide a `""` address or no address at all.

If you use some other hosting technique, such as WAS or a custom Windows service, you may need to specify the server address.

In the case of a CSLA .NET data portal endpoint, the contract is fixed; it must be Csla.Server.Hosts.IWcfPortal. The contract is defined by the interface implemented in the data portal, as discussed in Chapter 15. It may not be different from this value.

The binding can be any synchronous WCF binding. The only requirement imposed by the data portal is that the WCF binding must be synchronous; beyond that, any binding is acceptable. You may choose to use HTTP, TCP, named pipes, or other bindings. You may choose to configure the binding to use SSL, X.509 certificates, or other forms of encryption or authentication. All the features of WCF are at your disposal.

Remember that the data access code for your business objects will run on the application server. This means that the application server's web.config file must define the connection strings required by your data access code.

```
<connectionStrings>
  <add name="PTracker" connectionString="your connection string"
    providerName="System.Data.SqlClient" />
  <add name="Security" connectionString="your connection string"
    providerName="System.Data.SqlClient" />
</connectionStrings>
```

This is the same configuration you'd put in the client's app.config file when using a local data portal configuration, but now these values must be on the server, because that is where the data access code will execute.

The CslaAuthentication value must be the same on both client and server. You can change it to Windows, as long as you make that change on both sides. If you do change this value to Windows, then you must ensure that the WCF host website is configured to require Windows authentication and to impersonate the calling user, because in that case, CSLA .NET will simply use the value provided by .NET.

At this point, you should understand how to configure the application and how to configure the data portal for either local (2-tier) or remote (3-tier) operation.

PTWpf Project Setup

The UI application can be found within the ProjectTracker solution. The project is named PTWpf and references the ProjectTracker.Library project, along with Csla.dll. ProjectTracker.Library is a project reference, while Csla.dll is a file reference.

When building applications using the CSLA .NET framework, it is best to establish a file reference to the framework assembly, but use project references between the UI and any business assemblies. This makes debugging easier overall, because it helps prevent accidental changes to the CSLA .NET framework project, while enabling fluid changes to both the business objects and UI code.

Let's go through the creation of the WPF UI. First, I'll discuss the layout and design of MainForm, then I'll cover the process of logging a user in and out.

With the common code out of the way, I'll discuss the process of maintaining the roles and project data in detail. At that point, you should have a good understanding of how to create lookup dialogs, as well as both grid-based and detail forms.

The MainForm Window

The MainForm form is the core of the application in that it provides navigation and hosts the user controls for display to the user. It coordinates the flow of the entire application.

As you can see from Figure 19-1 earlier in the chapter, the application has a graphic look and feel. This is implemented in MainForm by using a series of gradient-filled Rectangle and Path objects. All these graphic elements are contained in a Grid named BackgroundGrid; you can look at how this is done in the code download, which you can find either in the Source Code/Download area of the Apress website at www.apress.com/book/view/1430210192 or at www.lhotka.net/cslanet/download.aspx. My focus in this chapter is not on the graphics and layout concepts of WPF, so I'll focus on the navigation, data binding, and interaction with the business objects.

Navigation

The Grid named LayoutRoot contains the actual content of the form. This grid defines two columns: the left one contains the navigation controls, and the right one contains the contentArea control discussed earlier in this chapter.

Each section of the navigation area is contained in an Expander, which contains a list of Hyperlink controls—for example:

```
<Expander IsExpanded="True" Header="Projects"  >
  <ListBox>
    <ListBoxItem>
      <Hyperlink Name="ShowProjectListButton"
                 Click="ShowProjectList">Show list</Hyperlink>
    </ListBoxItem>
    <ListBoxItem>
      <Hyperlink Name="NewProjectButton"
                 Click="NewProject">Add new</Hyperlink>
    </ListBoxItem>
    <ListBoxItem>
      <Hyperlink Name="CloseProjectButton"
                 Click="CloseProject">Close project</Hyperlink>
    </ListBoxItem>
  </ListBox>
</Expander>
```

Each Hyperlink control has a Click event handler, which is implemented in the code behind the form. Each event handler is responsible for implementing the behavior required by the user. For example, the NewProject() event handler looks like this:

```
private void NewProject(object sender, EventArgs e)
{
  try
  {
    ProjectEdit frm = new ProjectEdit(Guid.Empty);
    ShowControl(frm);
  }
  catch (System.Security.SecurityException ex)
  {
    MessageBox.Show(ex.ToString());
  }
}
```

Creating a new project is a matter of displaying the ProjectEdit form to the user. You do this by creating a new instance of ProjectEdit with an empty Guid value (to indicate a new project should be added) and calling the ShowControl() method to display the form in the content area of MainForm. Any security exceptions are caught and displayed to the user in a dialog. Another example is the CloseProject() handler.

```
private void CloseProject(object sender, RoutedEventArgs e)
{
  ProjectSelect frm = new ProjectSelect();
  bool result = (bool)frm.ShowDialog();
  if (result)
  {
    Guid id = frm.ProjectId;
    ProjectCloser.CloseProject(id);
    MessageBox.Show("Project closed",
      "Close project", MessageBoxButton.OK, MessageBoxImage.Information);
  }
}
```

This method is a little more complex, because it displays the `ProjectSelect` dialog to the user to choose which project to close. If the user chooses a project, the `ProjectCloser` business class (a command object stereotype) closes the specified project. This is an example of a navigation link that executes a behavior without displaying a new edit form to the user.

All the `Click` handlers for the navigation items work in a similar manner to those shown here. If you prefer, you could route the click events to some class other than the form itself—possibly a controller or presenter class that is responsible for implementing the behaviors triggered by the user clicking each item.

In any case, the code would be similar to what I'm showing here. Regardless of your UI design pattern, you'll need some code that is responsible for implementing the requested UI behavior and does so by leveraging the preexisting functionality in the business objects.

Login and Logout

The final bit of common functionality implemented in `MainForm` allows the user to log into or out of the application. It is important to realize that the `ProjectTracker` application allows unauthorized or guest users to view certain data, so those users can interact with the application even if they haven't logged in.

The login process is triggered when the application first loads and when the user clicks the Login button on the menu. In both cases, a `LogInOut()` method is called to handle the actual login/logout behavior.

```
void LogInOut(object sender, EventArgs e)
{
  if (Csla.ApplicationContext.User.Identity.IsAuthenticated)
  {
    ProjectTracker.Library.Security.PTPrincipal.Logout();
    CurrentUser.Text = "Not logged in";
    LoginButtonText.Text = "Log in";
  }
  else
  {
    Login frm = new Login();
    frm.ShowDialog();
    if (frm.Result)
    {
      string username = frm.UsernameTextBox.Text;
      string password = frm.PasswordTextBox.Password;
      ProjectTracker.Library.Security.PTPrincipal.Login(
        username, password);
    }
```

```
    if (!Csla.ApplicationContext.User.Identity.IsAuthenticated)
    {
      ProjectTracker.Library.Security.PTPrincipal.Logout();
      CurrentUser.Text = "Not logged in";
      LoginButtonText.Text = "Log in";
    }
    else
    {
      CurrentUser.Text =
        string.Format("Logged in as {0}",
        Csla.ApplicationContext.User.Identity.Name);
      LoginButtonText.Text = "Log out";
    }
  }

  ApplyAuthorization();
  IRefresh p = _currentControl as IRefresh;
  if (p != null)
    p.Refresh();
}
```

If the current principal is authenticated, the following code will log that user out:

```
if (Csla.ApplicationContext.User.Identity.IsAuthenticated)
{
  ProjectTracker.Library.Security.PTPrincipal.Logout();
  CurrentUser.Text = "Not logged in";
  LoginButtonText.Text = "Log in";
}
```

On the other hand, if the current principal is not authenticated, then the following code will display the Login dialog to the user so he can enter his username and password:

```
Login frm = new Login();
frm.ShowDialog();
```

The Login dialog form is a modal dialog that prompts the user for his credentials and provides those values to the calling code.

Back in the LogInOut() method, if the user clicks the Login button on the dialog, the username and password values will call PTPrincipal.Login() to validate the credentials.

```
string username = frm.UsernameTextBox.Text;
string password = frm.PasswordTextBox.Password;
ProjectTracker.Library.Security.PTPrincipal.Login(
  username, password);
```

The result is that Csla.ApplicationContext.User will either be an authenticated PTPrincipal or an UnauthenticatedPrincipal. Then the status of the principal object will be used to determine whether the user is logged in or not.

```
if (!Csla.ApplicationContext.User.Identity.IsAuthenticated)
{
  ProjectTracker.Library.Security.PTPrincipal.Logout();
  CurrentUser.Text = "Not logged in";
  LoginButtonText.Text = "Log in";
}
```

```
else
{
  CurrentUser.Text =
    string.Format("Logged in as {0}",
    Csla.ApplicationContext.User.Identity.Name);
  LoginButtonText.Text = "Log out";
}
```

If the user was authenticated, then the button text will be changed to Log out, and the user's name will be displayed on the form. Otherwise, the button text will be changed to Log in, and text indicating that the user isn't logged in will be displayed.

In any case, an ApplyAuthorization() method is called so that MainForm can update its display based on the user's identity (or lack thereof). Then the current user control (if any) is notified that the principal has changed.

```
ApplyAuthorization();
IRefresh p = _currentControl as IRefresh;
if (p != null)
  p.Refresh();
```

Each user control is responsible for handling this event and responding appropriately. Recall that the EditForm base control defines the ApplyAuthorization() method, so each user control can override that method as necessary.

The ApplyAuthorization() method in MainForm is responsible for enabling and disabling navigation items.

```
private void ApplyAuthorization()
{
  this.NewProjectButton.IsEnabled =
    Csla.Security.AuthorizationRules.CanCreateObject(typeof(Project));
  this.CloseProjectButton.IsEnabled =
    Csla.Security.AuthorizationRules.CanEditObject(typeof(Project));
  this.NewResourceButton.IsEnabled =
    Csla.Security.AuthorizationRules.CanCreateObject(typeof(Resource));
}
```

Notice how the actual authorization check is delegated to the per-type authorization methods provided by CSLA .NET. These methods, which I discussed in Chapter 12, were implemented specifically to enable scenarios like this. The idea is that MainForm has no idea whether particular users or roles are authorized to add Project objects. Instead, the Project class itself has that knowledge, and MainForm simply asks the authorization subsystem whether the current user is authorized.

The end result is good separation of concerns: MainForm is concerned with the UI details of enabling and disabling controls, while the actual rules are contained within the business layer.

The Login Window

The LogInOut() method in MainForm calls a Login dialog form to collect and authenticate the user's credentials. After gathering credentials from the user, this dialog form calls PTPrincipal.Login() to do the authentication itself.

Figure 19-3 shows the Login form layout.

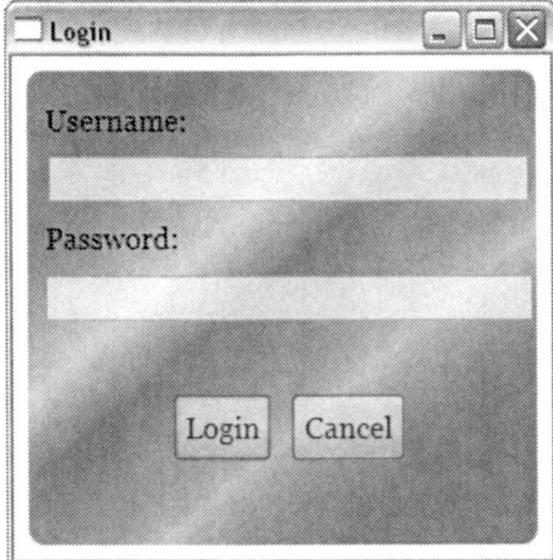

Figure 19-3. *Layout of the Login form*

The form defines a `Result` property, which is a `bool` that indicates whether the user clicked Login or not.

```
private bool _result;

public bool Result
{
  get { return _result; }
  set { _result = value; }
}

void LoginButton(object sender, EventArgs e)
{
  _result = true;
  this.Close();
}

void CancelButton(object sender, EventArgs e)
{
  _result = false;
  this.Close();
}
```

When the user clicks either Login or Cancel, the `Result` property is set to a corresponding value, and the dialog is closed. Even though the dialog is closed and disappears from the screen, the dialog *object* still exists in memory, and its properties are available to code in the application. The `LogInOut()` method relies on the `Result` property, as well as the values in the `UserNameTextBox` and `PasswordTextBox` controls, to do its work.

You've seen how the basic structure of the application works, from the `MainForm` and `Login` windows to the `EditForm` base class. I'll now move on and show how to implement a couple of the actual edit forms and dialogs. I won't cover all the elements in the UI, because they follow some basic themes; once you've seen a couple, you can understand the rest.

The RolesEdit Form

The `RolesEdit` user control allows an authorized user to edit the roles a resource can hold when assigned to a project. This is one of the simplest types of UIs to create, because the business objects and the controls in the `Csla.Wpf` namespace already handle most of the work.

Figure 19-4 shows the form with an authenticated user editing data.

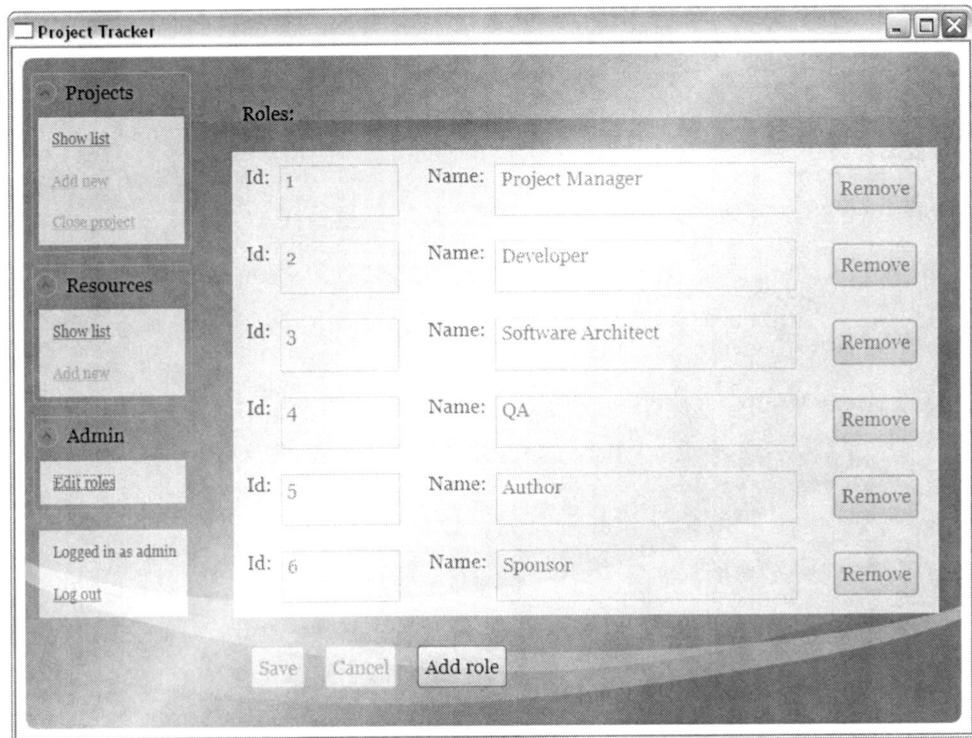

Figure 19-4. *Authenticated user using the RolesEdit form*

Most of the effort in building this form is in the XAML. I'll walk through it in some detail, since this is the first form I'm discussing.

Form Declaration

To start with, here's the form declaration:

```
<local:EditForm x:Class="PTWpf.RolesEdit"
    xmlns="http://schemas.microsoft.com/winfx/2006/xaml/presentation"
    xmlns:x="http://schemas.microsoft.com/winfx/2006/xaml"
    xmlns:local="clr-namespace:PTWpf"
    xmlns:csla="clr-namespace:Csla.Wpf;assembly=Csla"
    xmlns:ptracker=
"clr-namespace:ProjectTracker.Library.Admin;assembly=ProjectTracker.Library">
```

Rather than using a `Window` or `UserControl` base class, this uses `local:EditForm`, which is the `EditForm` class from earlier in this chapter. Notice that the `local:` prefix is defined in this header:

```
xmlns:local="clr-namespace:PTWpf"
```

You can think of this like a using statement, bringing a namespace into scope for use in this form. That's true for all the xmlns statements, so you can see the Csla.Wpf and ProjectTracker.Library.Admin namespaces are also made available.

Form Resources

The next section of XAML defines some global resources that are available to the entire form.

```
<local:EditForm.Resources>
  <local:VisibilityConverter x:Key="VisibilityConverter" />
  <csla:IdentityConverter x:Key="IdentityConverter" />
  <csla:CslaDataProvider x:Key="RoleList"
                         ObjectType="{x:Type ptracker:Roles}"
                         FactoryMethod="GetRoles"
                         DataChanged="DataChanged"
                         ManageObjectLifetime="True">
  </csla:CslaDataProvider>
  <csla:ObjectStatus x:Key="RoleListStatus"
                     DataContext="{StaticResource RoleList}" />
</local:EditForm.Resources>
```

I discussed the VisibilityConverter class earlier in the chapter; here you see how it is defined as a resource. The IdentityConverter, CslaDataProvider, and ObjectStatus classes were discussed in Chapter 10:

- IdentityConverter: Works around a data refresh issue with WPF data binding
- CslaDataProvider: Provides data binding access to the Roles business object
- ObjectStatus: Elevates the status properties of the business object as dependency properties so they can be bound to UI elements

CslaDataProvider

I want to focus more on the CslaDataProvider, because this is the first time you've seen it in action. Like the WPF ObjectDataProvider, the CslaDataProvider control allows data binding to access an object as a data source. However, the CslaDataProvider goes far beyond the simpler ObjectDataProvider. It can not only create or retrieve a business object, but it can also cancel edits to the object and save the object—all entirely through XAML. Let's go through the previous code.

The ObjectType property specifies the type of business object to be retrieved. The ptracker:Roles type corresponds to the Roles class from the ProjectTracker.Library.Admin namespace.

The FactoryMethod property specifies the name of the static factory method on the Roles class that should be invoked to create or retrieve the object. In this case, the GetRoles() method is invoked.

The DataChanged property specifies an event handler for the DataChanged event. Remember that this form inherits from EditForm, which defines a DataChanged() method to handle this event, so the event is routed to that handler.

Finally, the ManageObjectLifeTime property specifies that the data provider should manage the lifetime of this business object. Setting this to True tells the CslaDataProvider to enable the abilities to cancel edits, add new items to the collection, and remove items from the collection through WPF commanding.

Because IsInitialLoadEnabled is not specified, it defaults to True, which means that the data provider will invoke the factory method and load the business object when the form is loaded initially. This means the form will automatically populate with data as it is loaded, which is what we desire.

Because IsAsynchronous is not specified, it defaults to False, which means that the data provider invokes the factory method on the UI thread. Setting that value to True causes the data to load on a background thread, and the UI displays the values when they have been returned to the UI thread.

ObjectStatus

The ObjectStatus control is bound to the data provider, so its DataContext, or data source, is the business object returned by the provider. This means it exposes properties such as IsSavable and CanEditObject from the business object, so you can use those values to control the state of the UI elements as needed. These properties are used, along with the VisibilityConverter and ListTemplateConverter controls discussed earlier in this chapter, to control how the UI reacts as the user logs in and out of the application.

Setting the DataContext

With the CslaDataSource defined as a resource, it can be used to set the DataContext for part or all of the form. In this case, it is set for all content controls of the form by specifying the DataContext on the Grid control that contains all other controls.

```
<Grid Name="MainGrid"
        DataContext="{Binding Source={StaticResource RoleList}}">
```

The DataContext property is set to a binding expression, so the source object becomes the RoleList data provider from the Resources defined earlier. Data binding understands that when a data source is a data provider control, it should really bind to the Data property of that data provider, which will be the Roles business object in this case.

Grid Resources

The Grid also defines its own Resources, including two DataTemplate elements and a ListTemplateConverter. A DataTemplate defines how each row of data in a ListBox (or similar control) is to be displayed. The default template for a ListBoxItem simply displays the ToString() value of the data object, which is rarely the desired result. Defining a DataTemplate allows you to control exactly how each row of data is displayed.

Two templates are defined in order to deal with authorization. If the user is not authorized to edit the values, a read-only template is used. The read-write template is used if the user is allowed to edit the values. This technique means that the form can define a single ListBox control, but the actual display can be easily altered based on the user's permissions by using the ListTemplateConverter.

Read-Only Template

Each DataTemplate defines a self-contained section of UI. For example, the read-only template looks like this:

```
<DataTemplate x:Key="lbroTemplate">
  <Grid>
    <StackPanel Orientation="Horizontal">
      <TextBlock Text="{Binding Path=Name}" Width="250" />
    </StackPanel>
  </Grid>
</DataTemplate>
```

This means that each row of data in the ListBox will be displayed in a Grid control that contains a StackPanel that displays a TextBlock with a fixed width.

Read-Write Template

The read-write template is more complex, containing a couple of editable TextBox controls and a Button so the user can remove the item from the list.

```
<DataTemplate x:Key="lbTemplate">
  <Grid>
    <StackPanel Orientation="Horizontal">
      <TextBlock>Id:</TextBlock>
      <TextBox x:Name="IdTextBox"
                        Text="{Binding Path=Id,
                              Converter={StaticResource IdentityConverter}}"
                         Width="100" />
      <csla:PropertyStatus Source="{Binding}"
                           Property="Id" Grid.Column="1"
                           Target="{Binding ElementName=IdTextBox}" />
      <TextBlock>Name:</TextBlock>
      <TextBox x:Name="NameTextBox"
               Text="{Binding Path=Name,
                              Converter={StaticResource IdentityConverter}}"
               Width="250" />
      <csla:PropertyStatus Source="{Binding}"
                           Property="Name" Grid.Column="1"
                           Target="{Binding ElementName=NameTextBox}" />
      <Button
        Command="ApplicationCommands.Delete"
        CommandParameter="{Binding}"
        CommandTarget=
            "{Binding Source={StaticResource RoleList},
                               Path=CommandManager,
                               BindsDirectlyToSource=True}"
        HorizontalAlignment="Left">Remove</Button>
    </StackPanel>
  </Grid>
</DataTemplate>
```

There's a lot to this template, so I'll break it down.

Two TextBox controls allow the user to edit the Id and Name properties. Each TextBox has an associated PropertyStatus control, which provides visual cues for the authorization and validation rules associated with those business object properties. Let's look at the TextBox, which is bound to the Name property.

TextBox The TextBox bound to the Name property has an explicit name, because the PropertyStatus control will reference this control by its name. I'll discuss how that works when I cover the PropertyStatus control. Here's the TextBox control declaration:

```
<TextBox x:Name="NameTextBox"
         Text="{Binding Path=Name,
                        Converter={StaticResource IdentityConverter}}"
         Width="250" />
```

The Text property is bound to the business object's Name property using a Binding expression. Notice that this expression also uses the IdentityConverter. This is required to avoid the field refresh issue I discussed in Chapter 10, where changes made by the business object to the user-entered value aren't always reflected in the UI. Having a value converter on the binding avoids that issue, and

`IdentityConverter` should be used for any binding where you don't need a more specific value converter.

PropertyStatus The `NameTextBox` has an associated `PropertyStatus` control.

```
<csla:PropertyStatus Source="{Binding}"
                     Property="Name" Grid.Column="1"
                     Target="{Binding ElementName=NameTextBox}" />
```

As discussed in Chapter 10, the `PropertyStatus` control provides visual cues to the user based on the authorization and validation rules for the business object property. It enables and disables the target control (`NameTextBox`, in this case) depending on whether the user has read, write, or no access to the property. As shown in Figure 19-5, it displays any broken validation rule messages (for all three severities) for the property. Finally, if any async validation rules are being executed, it will display a busy animation so the user is aware that some background processing related to this property is underway.

Figure 19-5. *The PropertyStatus control displaying a validation error*

Notice how the control is bound to the current `DataContext` by setting its `Source` property to `{Binding}`, and the business object property name is specified through the `Property` property.

I typically associate a `PropertyStatus` control with every detail control bound to a business object property to gain the visual cues it provides.

Using ValidatesOnDataErrors You should be aware that WPF itself does provide a more limited way to leverage the validation rules for the business object property. You could choose to declare the `TextBox` control's binding expression using the `ValidatesOnDataErrors` property.

```
Text="{Binding Path=Name,
               Converter={StaticResource IdentityConverter},
               ValidatesOnDataErrors=True}"
```

The `ValidatesOnDataErrors` property specifies that WPF should check the `IDataErrorInfo` interface of the business object, and if any `Error` severity rules have been broken, it will alter the display of the `TextBox` control. By default, it simply adds a thin red border around the control, as shown in Figure 19-6, but you can override that style as you choose.

Figure 19-6. *WPF displaying a validation error with ValidatesOnDataErrors*

You can use this feature with or without a `PropertyStatus` control; the feature and the control are totally unrelated and compatible.

Button Control with Commanding The Remove button uses WPF commanding to interact with the CslaDataProvider control. This is controlled through the Command, CommandTarget, and CommandParameter properties.

```
<Button
  Command="ApplicationCommands.Delete"
  CommandParameter="{Binding}"
  CommandTarget=
       "{Binding Source={StaticResource RoleList},
                        Path=CommandManager,
                        BindsDirectlyToSource=True}"
  HorizontalAlignment="Left">Remove</Button>
```

These properties work as follows:

- Command: Specifies the command to be sent to the target when the button is clicked
- CommandParameter: Uses a binding expression to pass a reference to the current child object (the child object representing this one row of data in the ListBox) as a parameter
- CommandTarget: Uses a relatively complex binding expression to direct the command to the CommandManager of the CslaDataProvider

As discussed in Chapter 10, the CslaDataProvider control understands several standard commands, including Save, Undo, AddNew, and Delete. Of these, the only one that requires a parameter is Delete, because the CslaDataProvider needs to know which object to remove from the collection.

Also, recall from Chapter 10 that commands can only be handled by visual elements, and that a data provider is not a visual element. To support commanding, the CslaDataProvider exposes a CommandManager property, which is an object that is a visual element and can accept commands. The binding expression sets the target to this CommandManager object.

The BindsDirectlyToSource property must be set to True, because the RoleList resource is a data provider. WPF data binding would normally see that the resource is a data provider and would route all bindings to its Data property. However, in this case, the binding needs to actually go to the data provider itself, not the business object it is providing. The BindsDirectlyToSource property causes data binding to work directly against the resource, not the Data property.

You'll see other examples of Button controls using commanding later in this form.

Form Content

The form's content consists of a TextBlock label, a ListBox with the items to edit, and some button controls.

```
<StackPanel>
  <TextBlock>Roles:</TextBlock>
  <ListBox Name="RolesListBox"
           ItemsSource="{Binding}"
           ItemTemplate="{Binding Source={StaticResource RoleListStatus},
                          Path=CanEditObject,
                          Converter={StaticResource ListTemplateConverter}}" />
  <StackPanel Orientation="Horizontal"
              Visibility="{Binding Source={StaticResource RoleListStatus},
                           Path=CanEditObject,
                           Converter={StaticResource VisibilityConverter}}">
```

```
      <Button
            Command="ApplicationCommands.Save"
            CommandTarget="{Binding Source={StaticResource RoleList},
              Path=CommandManager, BindsDirectlyToSource=True}"
            HorizontalAlignment="Left" IsDefault="True">Save</Button>
      <Button
            Command="ApplicationCommands.Undo"
            CommandTarget="{Binding Source={StaticResource RoleList},
              Path=CommandManager, BindsDirectlyToSource=True}"
            HorizontalAlignment="Left" IsCancel="True">Cancel</Button>
      <Button Name="AddItemButton"
            Command="ApplicationCommands.New"
            CommandTarget="{Binding Source={StaticResource RoleList},
              Path=CommandManager, BindsDirectlyToSource=True}"
            HorizontalAlignment="Left" IsCancel="True">Add role</Button>
    </StackPanel>
  </StackPanel>
```

The core of the UI is the ListBox control, which displays the items from the Roles business object. It does this by specifying an ItemTemplate, which is a DataTemplate that defines how each item in the collection is to be displayed on the form.

As you've seen, two DataTemplate items are defined in the Grid.Resources element earlier in the XAML: one for a read-only display, and one for a read-write display. The ListTemplateConverter switches between those two templates automatically, based on the value of CanEditObject from the ObjectStatus control declared in the form's resources dictionary. That ObjectStatus control exposes the status properties from the business object being used by the form, so the result is that the user is shown the correct template (read-only or read-write) depending on whether she has permission to edit the data.

The various Button controls should also only be visible if the user is allowed to edit the data. Because these controls use WPF commanding to interact with the CslaDataProvider control, they'll automatically enable and disable based on whether the business object allows the user to save, cancel, or add a new item. Take the Save button, for example: the CslaDataProvider control uses the business object's IsSavable property to determine whether the object can be saved, so the button will only be enabled if the object's IsSavable property is true.

However, all the buttons are contained in a StackPanel control, and its Visibility property is bound to the CanEditObject property of the ObjectStatus control defined earlier in the form's resources. By using the VisibilityConverter control, the bool value of CanEditObject is converted to a Visibility value: either Visible or Collapsed.

```
<StackPanel Orientation="Horizontal"
            Visibility="{Binding Source={StaticResource RoleListStatus},
            Path=CanEditObject,
            Converter={StaticResource VisibilityConverter}}">
```

The result is that the user will only see the contents of the StackPanel if she's authorized to edit the business object.

Going back to the Button controls, I mentioned that they use WPF commanding to interact with the CslaDataProvider control, just like the Remove button discussed earlier.

```
<Button
      Command="ApplicationCommands.Save"
      CommandTarget="{Binding Source={StaticResource RoleList},
      Path=CommandManager, BindsDirectlyToSource=True}"
      HorizontalAlignment="Left" IsDefault="True">Save</Button>
```

In this case, the Save command is sent to the CommandManager of the data provider control, causing any changes to the business object (the Roles collection) to be saved.

At this point, you've seen all the XAML that defines the form. Nearly all the behaviors required for an edit form are handled purely through XAML, with just one bit of code required behind the form.

The ApplyAuthorization Method

The only code required behind the form is an override of the ApplyAuthorization() method. MainForm calls this method when the user logs in or out of the application, so this is the location where any changes must be made based on the new user identity.

When the current .NET principal changes, all authorization rules must be rechecked. The XAML elements handle all the UI changes, but something needs to trigger them to recheck the authorization rules. The simplest way to do this is to rebind them to the business object; that's the purpose of the Rebind() method on the CslaDataProvider control.

```
protected override void ApplyAuthorization()
{
  var dp = (Csla.Wpf.CslaDataProvider)this.FindResource("RoleList");
  dp.Rebind();
  if (!Csla.Security.AuthorizationRules.CanEditObject(dp.ObjectType))
    dp.Cancel();
}
```

There's one other bit of functionality in this method: a call to the CslaDataProvider control's Cancel() method. The Cancel() method is called if the new user is not authorized to edit the business object.

The reason for doing this is that the user could have been in the middle of editing the data when he logged out. The business object and UI could have a lot of changed data, but now that the user has logged out, those changes can't be saved and shouldn't be displayed. Calling Cancel() causes the object to return to an unchanged state, and data binding updates the UI, ensuring that the user isn't viewing partially edited and effectively invalid data.

This concludes the RolesEdit form. I've covered most of the important concepts required for any WPF data entry form. In the rest of the chapter, I'll discuss a couple of other forms in the application, focusing on slight variations for different UI requirements.

The ResourceList Form

It is common to build forms that display data, perhaps allowing the user to select an item from a list. By using data binding, building such a form is easy. The ResourceList form displays a list of resources from the database, allowing the user to select an item for editing. As with most WPF forms, most of the work is in the XAML.

The form defines a data provider resource.

```
<csla:CslaDataProvider x:Key="ResourceList"
                       ObjectType="{x:Type PTracker:ResourceList}"
                       FactoryMethod="GetResourceList"
                       IsAsynchronous="True"/>
```

This is different from the one used in RolesEdit, because IsAsynchronous is True, and IsInitialLoadEnabled isn't set (so it defaults to True). The result is that the data retrieval is started as soon as the form is loaded, but the data retrieval occurs on a background thread. To the user, the form displays almost immediately, and the data appears when it has been retrieved.

In the content of the form, a BusyAnimation control is used to give the user a visual cue that some background task is executing.

```
<csla:BusyAnimation Height="20" Width="20" Margin="5"
  IsRunning="{Binding Source={StaticResource ResourceList},
                      Path=IsBusy, BindsDirectlyToSource=True}" />
```

The IsRunning property is bound to the IsBusy property of the CslaDataProvider control, so, as shown in Figure 19-7, the animation turns on and off based on whether the data provider has an active query.

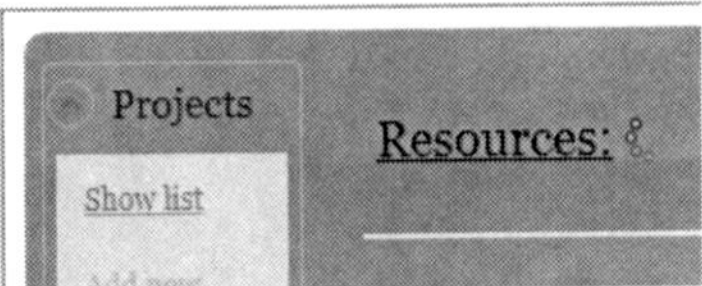

Figure 19-7. *Busy animation running while data is loading*

You can see part of the animation to the right of the Resources: label text.

The content of the form is displayed in a ListBox control, which has a simple DataTemplate to display each row. The ListBox control's MouseDoubleClick event is routed to an event handler, which is a method in the code behind the form.

```
<ListBox Name="listBox1"
         ItemsSource="{Binding}"
         MouseDoubleClick="ShowResource"/>
```

Here's the ShowResource() method:

```
void ShowResource(object sender, EventArgs e)
{
  ResourceInfo item =
    (ResourceInfo)this.listBox1.SelectedItem;

  if (item != null)
  {
    ResourceEdit frm = new ResourceEdit(item.Id);
    MainForm.ShowControl(frm);
  }
}
```

This is the only code behind the form. It retrieves the selected item (if any) from the ListBox control, and it passes the item's Id property to a new instance of the ResourceEdit form. Then it uses the ShowControl() method on MainForm to change the user's display to the new form, allowing the user to view or edit the selected item.

The ProjectList Form

The ProjectList form is nearly identical to ResourceList, with one slight twist. The ProjectList form allows the user to enter some filter criteria into a TextBox control. This value is used as a parameter to the GetProjectList() factory method for the ProjectList business object.

This is worth discussing, because I'm using data binding to connect the TextBox control to the parameter value in the CslaDataProvider control. In other words, no code behind the form is required to accept the user's input and use it as a parameter to the data provider.

Here's the data provider declaration with the parameter default highlighted:

```
<csla:CslaDataProvider x:Key="ProjectList"
                       ObjectType="{x:Type PTracker:ProjectList}"
                       FactoryMethod="GetProjectList"
                       IsAsynchronous="True"
                       IsInitialLoadEnabled="False">
  <csla:CslaDataProvider.FactoryParameters>
    <system:String>&lt;enter name&gt;</system:String>
  </csla:CslaDataProvider.FactoryParameters>
</csla:CslaDataProvider>
```

Figure 19-8 shows the form in the Visual Studio designer.

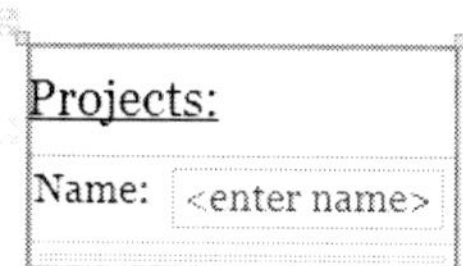

Figure 19-8. *ProjectList form in the designer*

The IsInitialLoadEnabled property is False, ensuring that the data provider won't try to load data from the database using <enter name> as a filter parameter. This also means that the user must enter *some filter value* to get any results at all.

The interesting part is the declaration of the TextBox control, because it is the TextBox that binds its input value to the data provider's parameter.

```
<TextBox Name="NameTextBox" AutoWordSelection="True">
  <TextBox.Text>
    <Binding Source="{StaticResource ProjectList}"
      Path="FactoryParameters[0]"
      BindsDirectlyToSource="true"
      UpdateSourceTrigger="PropertyChanged">
    </Binding>
</TextBox.Text>
```

I've highlighted the Binding element, because that's what is unusual in this case. The Text property has a binding that connects it to the ProjectList resource (the data provider), with its Path set to FactoryParameters[0], which is the first parameter in the list of parameters.

As with any binding expression that wants to interact with a data provider control, the BindsDirectlyToSource property is True. The UpdateSourceTrigger is set to PropertyChanged, which means the user doesn't need to tab out of the field for the update to occur. Figure 19-9 shows the result of a filtered query.

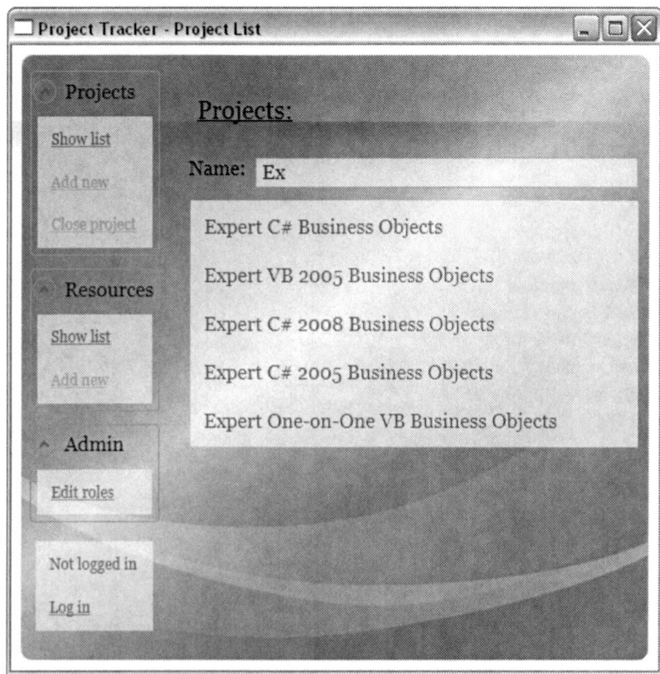

Figure 19-9. *ProjectList form displaying filtered results*

When the user double-clicks an item in the list, she's taken to the ProjectEdit form, using code just like that behind the ResourceList form.

The ProjectEdit Form

The final form I'll discuss in this chapter is the ProjectEdit form. This form allows the user to edit the details about a project and the list of resources assigned to the project. This form provides the opportunity to discuss both detail edit forms and master-detail relationships.

Figure 19-10 shows what the form looks like when the user is editing a project.

This form is constructed much like the others you've seen in this chapter. It uses a data provider control and data binding to enable viewing and editing of the data. It uses the ObjectStatus and PropertyStatus controls to enable visual cues for the user, and it uses commanding to implement the buttons.

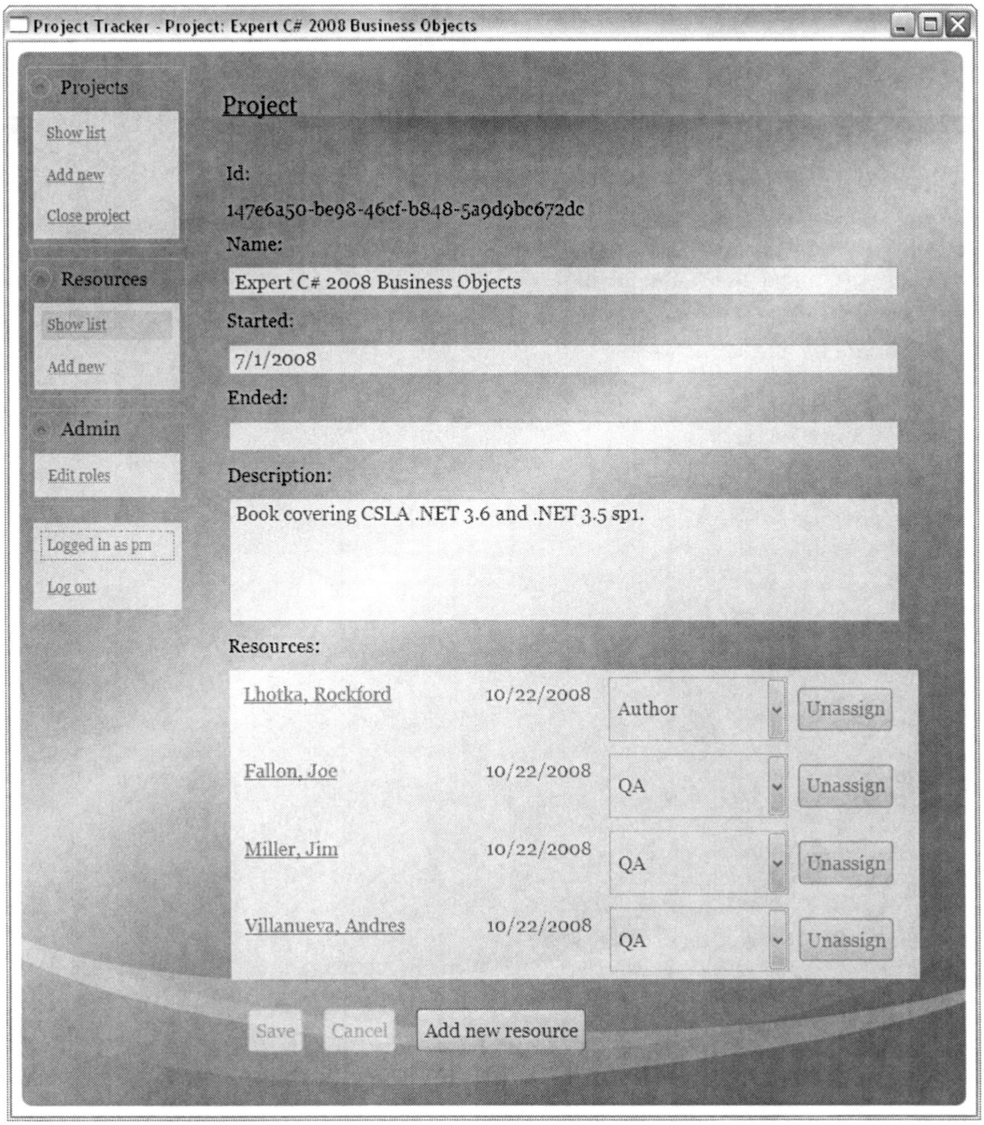

Figure 19-10. *ProjectEdit form*

Data Provider Controls and Data Retrieval

However, this form uses two data provider controls: one to populate the `ComboBox` controls in the resources list, and one to get the `Project` business object.

```
<csla:CslaDataProvider x:Key="RoleList"
                       ObjectType="{x:Type PTracker:RoleList}"
                       FactoryMethod="GetList"
                       IsAsynchronous="True" />
```

```
<csla:CslaDataProvider x:Key="Project"
                       ObjectType="{x:Type PTracker:Project}"
                       FactoryMethod="GetProject"
                       IsAsynchronous="False"
                       IsInitialLoadEnabled="False"
                       DataChanged="DataChanged"
                       ManageObjectLifetime="True"/>
```

The way the Project data provider is used is different from what you've seen so far. In this case, the Id value of the business object is passed into the form when it is created. That value is stored in a field and is then used in the form's Loaded event handler to retrieve the object. Here's the code with the relevant parts highlighted:

```
private Guid _projectId;
private Csla.Wpf.CslaDataProvider _dp;

public ProjectEdit()
{
  InitializeComponent();
  this.Loaded += new RoutedEventHandler(ProjectEdit_Loaded);
  _dp = this.FindResource("Project") as Csla.Wpf.CslaDataProvider;
}

public ProjectEdit(Guid id)
  : this()
{
  _projectId = id;
}

void ProjectEdit_Loaded(object sender, RoutedEventArgs e)
{
  using (_dp.DeferRefresh())
  {
    _dp.FactoryParameters.Clear();
    if (_projectId.Equals(Guid.Empty))
    {
      _dp.FactoryMethod = "NewProject";
    }
    else
    {
      _dp.FactoryMethod = "GetProject";
      _dp.FactoryParameters.Add(_projectId);
    }
  }
  if (_dp.Data != null)
    SetTitle((Project)_dp.Data);
  else
    MainForm.ShowControl(null);
}
```

The constructor puts the id parameter into a field, and that field is then used in the Loaded event as a parameter to the data provider control.

The fact that all code interacting with the data provider control is wrapped in a using block with a DeferRefresh() method is important. By default, each time a property of a data provider is changed, the data provider immediately refreshes its data from the database. If you need to set several properties at once, as in this case, you only want the control to go to the database once.

The using block with DeferRefresh() allows you to set many properties of the control, and only at the end of the using block will the control attempt to query the database.

Setting Up Data Binding

As with the other forms you've seen, this one uses data binding by setting a DataContext value for all the content of the form. This is done on the top-level Grid control, which contains all the other content.

```
<Grid Name="MainGrid"
      DataContext="{Binding Source={StaticResource Project}}"
      Margin="0 0 20 0">
```

However, this is a master-detail form. While the detail controls are bound to this DataContext (the Project object), items in the list of resources are bound to the ProjectResources collection of the project object.

In other words, the detail controls are bound like this:

```
<TextBox Name="NameTextBox" Grid.Column="0"
         Text="{Binding Name,
                Converter={StaticResource IdentityConverter}}" />
```

This kind of binding is used on the other forms in this chapter. However, the ListBox control that displays the ProjectResources collection is bound like this:

```
<ListBox ItemsSource="{Binding Resources}"
         ItemTemplate="{Binding Source={StaticResource ProjectStatus},
                       Path=CanEditObject,
                       Converter={StaticResource ListTemplateConverter}}"/>
```

In the Project class, the ProjectResources collection is exposed through a Resources property. Since the Project object has a Resources property, you can use that as the target for a binding expression, making the ListBox control bind to that property.

Each row of data in the ListBox control is one item from the ProjectResources collection: a single ProjectResource object. A DataTemplate is defined in the form to display the values for read-only use, and another is defined for read-write scenarios. This is no different from the previous forms in this chapter.

The only interesting thing in the DataTemplates is the use of a ComboBox control. Remember that this form has two data provider controls, and one returns the list of roles in the RoleList business object. This is used to populate the ComboBox control.

```
<ComboBox
  ItemsSource="{Binding Source={StaticResource RoleList}}"
  DisplayMemberPath="Value"
  SelectedValuePath="Key"
  SelectedValue="{Binding Path=Role}"
  Width="150" />
```

As with ComboBox controls in Windows Forms or Web Forms, the control is really bound to two data sources at once. One data source is used to populate the items in the list by setting the ItemsSource, DisplayMemberPath, and SelectedValuePath properties. The control is also bound to a single property on the current DataContext by setting the SelectedValue property—in this case, to the Role property for the current ProjectResource business object.

Navigation Through Commanding

Each item in the resources list can be clicked, allowing the user to navigate directly to the ResourceEdit form for that resource. You could do this navigation with a simple event handler, like I did in the ResourceList and ProjectList forms. In this case, however, I'm using commanding to illustrate a different technique you may choose.

The FullName property from the business object is bound to a Button control that is styled to appear like a hyperlink so the user knows to click on it. When the user clicks the control, it sends an Open command with the ResourceId property as a parameter.

```
<Button Style="{StaticResource LinkButton}"
        Margin="0" Width="200"
        Command="ApplicationCommands.Open"
        CommandParameter="{Binding Path=ResourceId}"
        Content="{Binding Path=FullName}" Foreground="Blue" />
```

The ProjectEdit form itself handles the command, because a CommandBinding has been defined on the form for this command.

```
<UserControl.CommandBindings>
  <CommandBinding Command="ApplicationCommands.Open"
                  Executed="OpenCmdExecuted"
                  CanExecute="OpenCmdCanExecute" />
</UserControl.CommandBindings>
```

A CommandBinding allows you to express, through XAML, that a command should be routed to a specific method. You also need to provide a CanExecute method that returns a Boolean through its CanExecuteRoutedEventArgs parameter, indicating whether the command can be executed at any point in time. If this returns false, the associated Button control is disabled automatically.

In the code behind the form, the two methods are implemented.

```
private void OpenCmdExecuted(object sender, ExecutedRoutedEventArgs e)
{
  if (e.Parameter != null)
  {
    ResourceEdit frm = new ResourceEdit(Convert.ToInt32(e.Parameter));
    MainForm.ShowControl(frm);
  }
}

private void OpenCmdCanExecute(
  object sender, CanExecuteRoutedEventArgs e)
{ e.CanExecute = true; }
```

The CommandParameter value is available in the OpenCmdExecuted() method through e.Parameter. In the XAML, the ResourceId value was passed as a parameter, so that value is available in the method. That value is used to create a new instance of the ResourceEdit form, which is then displayed to the user by calling the ShowControl() method.

This approach doesn't save any code over handling a Click event directly, but it can provide more flexibility. A full discussion of WPF commanding is outside the scope of this book, but you should know that commands can be routed to different locations, making them more flexible than tightly coupled event handlers.

Using a combination of data binding and the controls in the Csla.Wpf namespace, you can implement in XAML almost all common behaviors required for building a data display or entry form. In many cases, very little code is required behind any form, which improves maintainability of the application.

Conclusion

This chapter has walked through the process of creating a basic WPF UI using the business objects from Chapters 17 and 18. Obviously, there are many ways to create a UI using WPF, so the goal of this chapter was to highlight how you can use data binding to easily create forms to view and edit object data.

The key point to take from this chapter is that when you create your business layer using business objects, the UI developer doesn't need to worry about validation or authorization rules, data access, or most other complex issues. The UI developer can focus on user interaction, the look and feel of the application, and so forth. The result is a high degree of separation between the UI layer and the business layer.

At the same time, because the objects use the data portal mechanism to retrieve and update data, the application is able to exploit the capabilities of mobile objects: running business logic on both the client workstation and an application server as appropriate. Better still, you can simply change the application configuration file to switch between various physical n-tier configurations to meet different performance, scalability, reliability, and security requirements.

Chapter 20 will cover the implementation of a Web Forms UI based on the same set of business objects. Although there are obvious differences between the WPF and Web Forms environments, we'll achieve total reuse of the business logic and data access code when moving from one UI type to the next.

CHAPTER 20

Web Forms UI

Chapter 19 covered the creation of a WPF UI based on the `ProjectTracker` business objects. Microsoft .NET also supports web development through the ASP.NET Web Forms technology. In this chapter, the same business objects are used to create a Web Forms interface with functionality comparable to the WPF interface.

While Web Forms can be used to create many different user interfaces, web development in ASP.NET is not the core of this chapter. Instead, I focus on how business objects are used within a web application, including state management and data binding.

Tip ASP.NET is the .NET web server component that hosts web forms, web services, and other server-side handlers in IIS. ASP.NET is a very broad and flexible technology. Web forms are hosted within ASP.NET and provide one common approach to web development capabilities.

As in the WPF interface in Chapter 19, I won't cover the details of every web form in the application. Instead, I'll walk through a representative sample to illustrate key concepts.

In particular, I discuss the following:

- Basic site design
- The use of forms-based authentication
- Adding and editing roles
- Adding and editing project data

However, before getting into the design and development of the Web Forms UI itself, I need to discuss some of the basic concepts around the use of business objects in web development.

Web Development and Objects

Historically, the world of web development has been strongly resistant to the use of "stateful" objects behind web pages and not without reason. In particular, using such objects without careful forethought can be very bad for website performance. Sometimes, however, it's suggested that instead of a stateful object, you should use a `DataSet`, which is itself a very large, stateful object. Most people don't think twice about using it for web development.

Clearly then, stateful objects aren't inherently bad—it's how they're designed and used that matters. Business objects can be very useful in web development, but it is necessary to look carefully at how such objects are conceived and employed.

Note Objects can work very well in web development if they're designed and used properly.

In general terms, web applications can choose from three basic data access models, as shown in Figure 20-1. Notice how all options get their data through an ADO.NET `DataReader` object. The `DataReader` is the lowest level data access object in .NET.

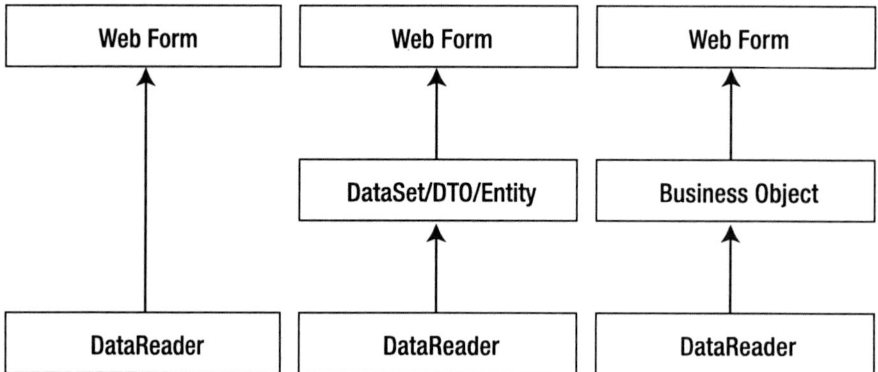

Figure 20-1. *The three basic data access models*

Using the DataReader directly can be very beneficial if the data set is relatively small and the page processing is fast because the data is taken directly from the database and put into the page. There's no need to copy the data into an in-memory container (such as a `DataSet` or object) before putting it into the page output. This is illustrated in Figure 20-2.

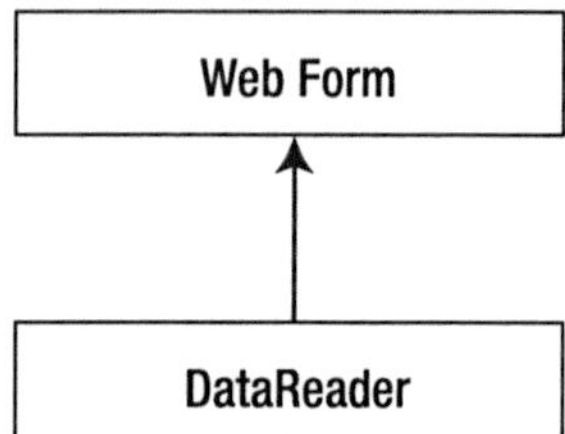

Figure 20-2. *Data flowing directly from a DataReader into a web form*

However, if the data set is large or the page processing is slow, using a DataReader becomes a less attractive option. Using one requires the database connection to remain open longer, causing an increase in the number of database connections required on the server overall and thereby decreasing scalability.

Direct use of a DataReader also typically leads to code that's harder to maintain. A DataReader doesn't offer the ease of use of the `DataSet` or an object. Nor does it provide any business logic or protection for the data, leaving it up to the UI code to provide all validation and other business processing.

■ **Note** In most cases, use of the `DataSet` or an object offers better scalability when compared to direct use of a DataReader and will result in code that's easier to maintain.

Having discounted the use of a DataReader in all but a few situations, the question becomes whether to use the `DataSet`, DTO (data transfer object), entity object, or a business object as a stateful, in-memory data container. These options are similar in that the data is loaded from a DataReader into the stateful object and from there into the page, as illustrated in Figure 20-3.

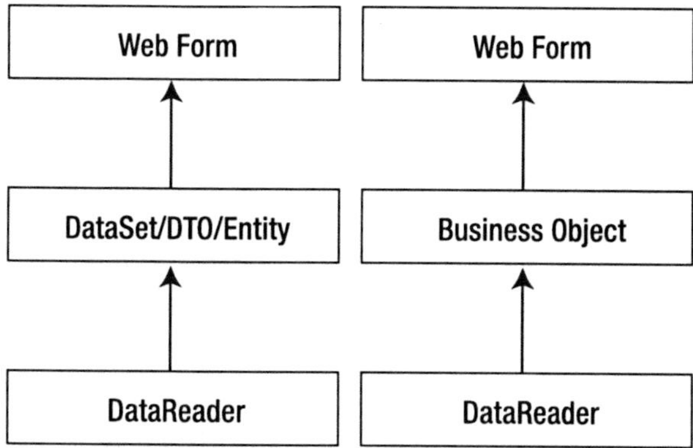

Figure 20-3. *Data is loaded into an intermediate object, followed by the web form.*

This means that in general you can expect similar performance characteristics from a `DataSet` and objects. However, objects are often actually more lightweight than the ADO.NET `DataSet` object. This is because most objects are specific to the data they contain and don't need to retain all the metadata required by the `DataSet` object.

So the question becomes whether to use data container objects, such as a DTO or entity object, or a business object. Generally speaking, there is little or no performance difference between these options because the data is loaded into object fields from a DataReader in all cases. This means the decision should be based on the functionality provided by the objects.

Data container objects are simple containers for data. They don't provide any business behaviors, only shaped data. In this regard they are much like a `DataSet`. And if your application has little or no business or validation logic, these objects are a good choice. However, if your application does have business logic, these objects leave you with no clear location for that logic. Too often the business logic ends up in the UI, behind the web forms, which breaks the discipline of layering that I discuss in Chapter 1.

Business objects provide access not only to the application's data but also to its *business logic*. As discussed in Chapter 1, business objects can be thought of as *smart data*. They encapsulate the business logic and the data so that the UI doesn't need to deal with potential data misuse.

Overall, business objects provide the high-scalability characteristics of the `DataSet` or data container objects, though without the overhead of the `DataSet`. They offer a better use of database connections than the DataReader, though at the cost of some performance in certain situations. When compared to both `DataSet` and DataReader, business objects enable a much higher level of reuse and easier long-term maintenance, making them the best choice overall.

State Management

The Achilles' heel of web development is state management. The original design of web technology was merely for document viewing, not the myriad purposes for which it's used today. Because of this, the issue of state management was never thought through in a methodical way. Instead, state management techniques have evolved over time in a relatively ad hoc manner.

Through this haphazard process, some workable solutions have evolved, though each requires trade-offs in terms of performance, scalability, and fault tolerance. The primary options at your disposal are as follows:

- State is maintained on the web server.
- State is transferred from server to client to server on each page request.
- State is stored in temporary files or database tables.

Whether you use a `DataSet`, a DataReader, or objects to retrieve and update data is immaterial here; ultimately, you're left to choose one of these three state management strategies. Table 20-1 summarizes the strengths and weaknesses of each.

Table 20-1. *State Management Strategies*

Approach	Strengths	Weaknesses
State stored on web server	Easy to code and use; works well with business objects	Use of global fields/data is poor programming practice; scalability and fault tolerance via a web farm requires increased complexity of infrastructure
State transferred to/from client	Scalability and fault tolerance easily achieved by implementing a web farm	Hard to code; requires a lot of manual coding to implement; performance a problem over slow network links
State stored in file/database	Scalability and fault tolerance easily achieved by implementing a web farm; a lot of state data or very complex data easily stored	Increased load on database server since state is retrieved/stored on each page hit; requires manual coding to implement; data cleanup must be implemented to deal with abandoned state data

As you can see, all of these solutions have more drawbacks than benefits. Unfortunately, in the many years that the Web has been a mainstream technology, no vendor or standards body has been able to provide a comprehensive solution to the issue of dealing with state data. All you can do is choose the solution that has the lowest negative impact on your particular application.

I will now go into some more detail on each of these techniques, in the context of using business objects behind web pages.

State on the Web Server

First, you can choose to keep state on the web server. This is easily accomplished through the use of the ASP.NET `Session` object, which is a name/value collection of arbitrary data or objects. ASP.NET manages the `Session` object, ensuring that each user has a unique `Session` and that the `Session` object is available to all Web Forms code on any page request.

This is by far the easiest way to program web applications. The `Session` object acts as a global repository for almost any data that you need to keep from page to page. By storing state data on the web server, you enable the type of host-based computing that has been done on mainframes and minicomputers for decades.

■ **Note** The `Csla.ApplicationContext` object provides `ClientContext` and `LocalContext` objects. Neither of these are a replacement for `Session`. No data in `Csla.ApplicationContext` survives between page requests. If you want to keep values in memory between page requests, `Session` is the tool you must use.

As I've already expressed, there are drawbacks. `Session` is a *global* repository for each user, but as any experienced programmer knows, the use of global fields is very dangerous and can rapidly lead to code that's hard to maintain. If you choose to use `Session` to store state, you must be disciplined in its use to avoid these problems.

The use of `Session` also has scalability and fault tolerance ramifications. Achieving scalability and fault tolerance typically requires implementation of a web farm: two or more web servers that are running exactly the same application. It doesn't matter which server handles each user's page request because all the servers run the same code. This effectively spreads the processing load across multiple machines, thus increasing scalability. You also gain fault tolerance because if one machine goes down, the remaining server(s) will simply take over the handling of user requests.

What I just described is a fully load-balanced web farm. However, because state data is often maintained directly on each web server, the preceding scenario isn't possible. Instead, web farms are often configured using "sticky sessions." Once a user starts using a specific server, he remains on that server because that's where his data is located. This provides *some* scalability because the processing load is still spread across multiple servers but it provides very limited fault tolerance. If a server goes down, all the users attached to that server also go down.

To enable a fully load-balanced web farm, *no* state can be maintained on *any* web server. As soon as user state is stored on a web server, users become attached to that server to the extent that only that server can handle their web requests. By default, the ASP.NET `Session` object runs on the web server in the ASP.NET process. This provides optimal performance because the state data is stored in process with the application's code, but this approach doesn't allow implementation of a fully load-balanced web farm.

■ **Caution** When the `Session` object runs inside the ASP.NET process, you can lose state without warning. ASP.NET may recycle the website `AppDomain` for many reasons, and when this happens the `Session` object is lost. Other `Session` configurations avoid this issue.

Instead, the `Session` object can be run in a separate process on the same web server. This can help improve fault tolerance because the ASP.NET process can restart and users won't lose their state data. However, this still doesn't result in a fully load-balanced web farm, so it doesn't help with scalability. Also, there's a performance cost because the state data must be serialized and transferred from the state management process to the ASP.NET process (and back again) on every page request.

As a third option, ASP.NET allows the `Session` object to be maintained on a dedicated, separate server rather than on any specific web server. This *state server* can maintain the state data for all users, making it equally accessible to all web servers in a web farm. This does mean that you can implement a fully load-balanced web farm, in which each user request is routed to the least loaded web server. As shown in Figure 20-4, no user is ever "stuck" on a specific web server.

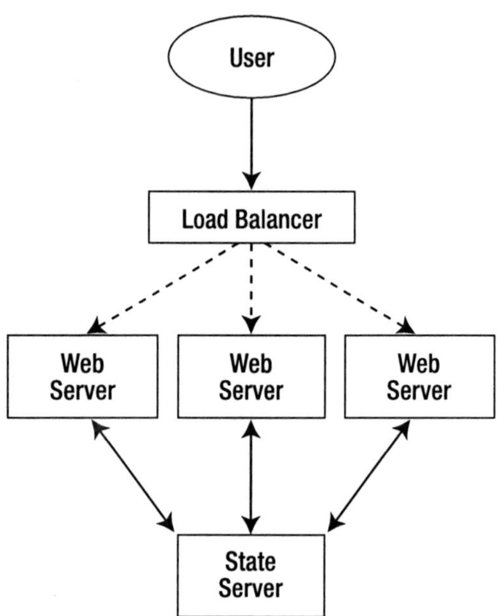

Figure 20-4. *Load-balanced web server farm with centralized state server*

With this arrangement, you can lose a web server with minimal impact. Obviously, users in the middle of having a page processed on that particular server will be affected, but all other users should be redirected to the remaining live servers transparently. All the users' `Session` data will remain available.

As with the out-of-process option discussed previously, the `Session` object is serialized so that it can be transferred to the state server machine efficiently. This means that all objects referenced by `Session` are also serialized—which isn't a problem for CSLA .NET–style business objects because they're marked as `Serializable`.

■ **Note** When using this approach, all state *must* be maintained in `Serializable` objects. Using the `DataContract` and `DataMember` attributes is not allowed because ASP.NET uses the `BinaryFormatter` to serialize the `Session` object.

In this arrangement, fault tolerance is significantly improved, but if the state server goes down, all user state is lost. To help address this, you can put the `Session` objects into a SQL Server database (rather than just into memory on the state server) and then use clustering to make the SQL Server fault-tolerant as well. In many cases, this SQL Server database is an entirely separate database from the application's database server.

Obviously, these solutions are becoming increasingly complex and costly, and they also worsen performance. By putting the state on a separate state server, the application will incur network overhead on each page request because the user's `Session` object must be retrieved from the state server by the web server so that the Web Forms code can use the `Session` data. Once each page is complete, the `Session` object is transferred back across the network to the state server for storage.

Table 20-2 summarizes these options.

Table 20-2. *Session Object Storage Locations*

Location of State Data	Performance, Scalability, and Fault Tolerance
`Session` in process	High performance; low scalability; low fault tolerance; web farms must use sticky sessions; fully load-balanced web farms not supported; state is lost when ASP.NET `AppDomain` recycles
`Session` out of process	Decreased performance; low scalability; improved fault tolerance (ASP.NET process can reset without losing state data); web farms must use sticky sessions; fully load-balanced web farms not supported
`Session` on state server	Decreased performance; high scalability; high fault tolerance

While storing state data on the web server (or in a state server) provides the simplest programming model, you must make some obvious sacrifices with regard to complexity and performance in order to achieve scalability and fault tolerance.

Transferring State to or from the Client

The second option to consider is transferring all state from the server to the client and back to the server again on each page request. The idea here is that the web server never maintains any state data—it gets all state data along with the page request, works with the data, and then sends it back to the client as part of the resulting page.

This approach provides high scalability and fault tolerance with very little complexity in your infrastructure: since the web servers never maintain state data, you can implement a fully load-balanced web farm without worrying about server-side state issues. On the other hand, there are some drawbacks.

First of all, all the state data is transferred over what is typically the slowest link in the system: the connection between the user's browser and the web server. Moreover, that state is transferred twice for each page: from the server to the browser and then from the browser back to the server. Obviously, this can have serious performance implications over a slow network link (like a modem) and can even affect an organization's overall network performance due to the volume of data being transferred on each page request.

The other major drawback is the complexity of the application's code. There's no automatic mechanism that puts all state data into each page; you must do that by hand. Often this means creating hidden fields on each page in which you can store state data that's required but that the user shouldn't see. The pages can quickly become very complex as you add these extra fields.

This can also be a security problem. When state data is sent to the client, that data becomes potentially available to the end user. In many cases, an application's state data includes internal information that's not intended for direct consumption by the user. Sometimes, this information may be sensitive, so sending it to the client could create a security loophole in the system. Although you could encrypt this data, it would incur extra processing overhead and could increase the size of the data sent to/from the client, so performance would be decreased.

To avoid such difficulties, applications often minimize the amount of data stored in the page by reretrieving it from the original database on each page request. All you need to keep in the page then is the key information to retrieve the data and any data values that have changed. Any other data values can always be reloaded from the database. This solution can dramatically increase the load on your database server but continues to avoid keeping any state on the web server.

In conclusion, while this solution offers good scalability and fault tolerance, it can be quite complex to program and can often result in a lot of extra code to write and maintain. Additionally, it can have a negative performance impact, especially if your users connect over low-speed lines.

State in a File or Database

The final solution to consider is the use of temporary files (or database tables of temporary data) in which you can store state data. Such a solution opens the door to other alternatives, including the creation of data schemas that can store state data so that it can be retrieved in parts, reported against, and so forth. Typically, these activities aren't important for state data, but they can be important if you want to keep the state data for a long period of time.

Most state data just exists between page calls or, at most, for the period of time during which the user is actively interacting with the site. Some applications, however, keep state data for longer periods of time, thereby allowing the user's "session" to last for days, weeks, or months. Persistent shopping carts and wish lists are examples of long-term state data that's typically stored in a meaningful format in a database.

Whether you store state as a single blob of data or in a schema, storing it in a file or a database provides good scalability and fault tolerance. It can also provide better performance than sending the state to and from the client workstation because communicating with a database is typically faster than communicating with the client. In situations like these, the state data isn't kept on the client or the web server, so you can create fully load-balanced web farms, as shown in Figure 20-5.

■ **Tip** As I mentioned earlier, one way to implement a centralized state database is to use the ASP.NET `Session` object and configure it so that the data is stored in a SQL Server database. If you just want to store arbitrary state data as a single chunk of data in the database, this is probably the best solution.

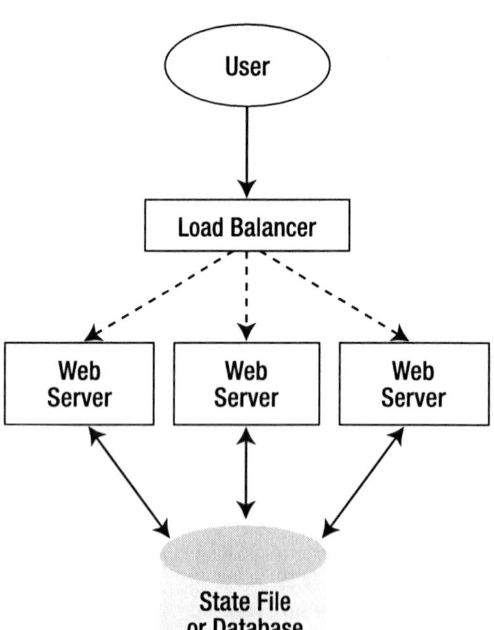

Figure 20-5. *Load-balanced web farm with centralized state database*

The first thing you'll notice is that this diagram is virtually identical to the state server diagram discussed earlier, and it turns out that the basic model and benefits are indeed consistent with that approach. The application gains scalability and fault tolerance because you can implement a web farm, whereby the web server that's handling each page request retrieves state from the central database. Once the page request is complete, the data is stored in the central state database. Using clustering technology, you can make the database server itself fault tolerant, thereby minimizing it as a single point of failure.

Though this approach offers a high degree of scalability and fault tolerance, if you implement the retrieval and storage of the state data by hand, it increases the complexity of your code. There are also performance implications because all state data is transferred across a network and back for each page request—and then there's the cost of storing and retrieving the data in the database itself.

In the final analysis, determining which of the three solutions to use depends on the specific requirements of your application and environment. For most applications, using the ASP.NET `Session` object to maintain state data offers the easiest programming model and the most flexibility. You can achieve optimal performance by running it in process with your pages or achieve optimal scalability and fault tolerance by having the `Session` object stored in a SQL Server database on a clustered database server. There are shades of compromise in between.

■ **Note** ASP.NET allows you to switch between three different state-handling models by simply changing the website's `Web.config` file (assuming you already have a SQL Server database server available in your environment).

The key is that CSLA .NET–style business objects are serializable, so the `Session` object can serialize them as needed. Even if you choose to implement your own BLOB-based file or data-storage approach, the fact that the objects are serializable means that the business objects can be easily converted to a byte stream that can be stored as a BLOB. If the objects were not serializable, the options would be severely limited.

For the sample application, I'll use the `Session` object to help manage state data; but I'll use it sparingly because overuse of global fields is a cardinal sin.

Interface Design

The UI application can be found within the `ProjectTracker` solution. The project is named `PTWeb`. The `PTWeb` interface uses a master page to provide consistency across all the pages in the site. The `Default.aspx` page provides a basic entry point to the website. Figure 20-6 shows what the page layout looks like.

Notice that the navigation area on the left provides links dealing with projects, resources, and roles. An authentication link is provided near the top right of the page. When the user clicks a link, she is directed to an appropriate content page. Figure 20-7 shows the user editing a project.

Figure 20-6. *Appearance of Default.aspx*

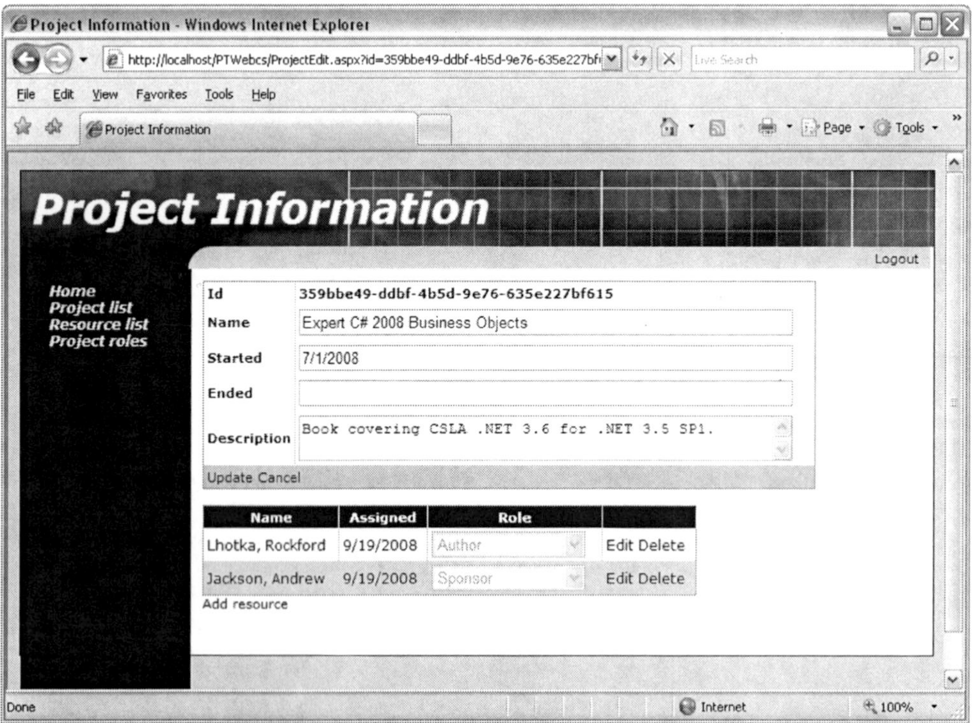

Figure 20-7. *Editing a project*

Table 20-3 lists the forms and controls that make up the interface.

Table 20-3. *Web Forms in PTWeb*

Form/Control	Description
`Default`	Represents the main page for the application
`Login`	Collects user credentials
`RolesEdit`	Allows the user to edit the list of roles
`ProjectList`	Allows the user to select and delete projects
`ProjectEdit`	Allows the user to view, add, or edit a project
`ResourceList`	Allows the user to select and delete resources
`ResourceEdit`	Allows the user to view, add, or edit a resource

All of the pages dealing with business data use the exact same objects as the WPF UI in Chapter 19. The same `ProjectTracker.Library` assembly created in Chapters 17 and 18 is used for the WPF, Web Forms, and WCF services interfaces in this book. The web forms using those objects are built using data binding, relying on the `CslaDataSource` control discussed in Chapter 10.

Application Configuration

The site needs to provide some basic configuration information through the `Web.config` file. This includes configuring the data portal or database connection strings. It also includes configuring the `CslaDataSource` control.

In the `Web.config` file, you can either provide connection strings so that the site can interact with the database directly, or you can configure the data portal to communicate with a remote application server. The basic concept was discussed in Chapter 15 when the channel adapter implementation was covered. Recall that the data portal supports several channels: WCF, Remoting, Enterprise Services, and Web Services. You can create your own channels as well if none of these meets your needs.

In Chapter 1, I discuss the trade-offs between performance, scalability, fault tolerance, and security that come with various physical n-tier configurations. In most cases, the optimal solution for a web UI is to run the data portal locally in the client process. However, for security reasons, it may be desirable to run the data portal remotely on an application server.

The `Web.config` file is an XML file that contains settings to configure the website. You use different XML depending on how you want the site configured.

CslaDataSource Control

The data binding in this chapter relies on the `CslaDataSource` control discussed in Chapter 10. In order to use this control in Web Forms, the site needs to define a control prefix for any controls in `Csla.dll`. I'll use the prefix `csla`.

This prefix is defined either in each web form or in `Web.config`. Since most pages use the control, it is best to define the prefix in `Web.config` so it is available sitewide. You should add this within the `<pages>` element:

```
<controls>
  <add tagPrefix="csla" namespace="Csla.Web" assembly="Csla"/>
</controls>
```

This globally defines the csla prefix to refer to the Csla.Web namespace from Csla.dll. With this done, all pages in the website can use the prefix like this:

```
<csla:CslaDataSource id="MyDataSource" runat="server"/>
```

Authentication

The way authentication is handled by CSLA .NET is controlled through Web.config:

```
<?xml version="1.0" encoding="utf-8" ?>
<configuration>
  <appSettings>
    <add key="CslaAuthentication" value="Csla" />
  </appSettings>
</configuration>
```

The CslaAuthentication key shown here specifies the use of custom authentication. The ProjectTracker.Library assembly includes the PTPrincipal and PTIdentity classes specifically to support custom authentication, and the UI code in this chapter uses custom authentication as well.

If you want to use Windows authentication, change the configuration to this:

```
<add key="CslaAuthentication" value="Windows" />
```

Of course, this change would require coding changes. To start, the PTPrincipal and PTIdentity classes should be removed from ProjectTracker.Library, as they would no longer be needed. Also, the login/logout functionality implemented in this chapter would become unnecessary. Specifically, the Login form and the code to display that form would be removed from the UI project.

Local Data Portal

The Web.config file also controls how the application uses the data portal. To have the website interact directly with the database, use the following (with your connection string changed to the connection string for your database):

```
<?xml version="1.0" encoding="utf-8" ?>
<configuration>
  <appSettings>
    <add key="CslaAuthentication" value="Csla" />
  </appSettings>
  <connectionStrings>
    <add name="PTracker" connectionString="your connection string"
      providerName="System.Data.SqlClient" />
    <add name="Security" connectionString="your connection string"
      providerName="System.Data.SqlClient" />
  </connectionStrings>
```

Because LocalProxy is the default for the data portal's CslaDataPortalProxy configuration setting, no actual data portal configuration is required, so the only settings in the configuration file are to control authentication and to provide the database connection strings.

■ **Tip** In the code download for this book, the PTracker and Security database files are in the solution directory, not in the website's App_Data directory. This means that you can't use a local data portal from the website without first copying the database files into the App_Data directory and changing the connection strings accordingly.

Remote Data Portal (with WCF)

To have the data portal use an application server and communicate using the WCF channel, the configuration would look like this:

```
<?xml version="1.0" encoding="utf-8" ?>
<configuration>
  <appSettings>
    <add key="CslaAuthentication" value="Csla" />
    <add key="CslaDataPortalProxy"
             value="Csla.DataPortalClient.WcfProxy, Csla"/>
  </appSettings>
  <connectionStrings>
  </connectionStrings>
  <system.serviceModel>
    <client>
      <endpoint name="WcfDataPortal"
                address="http://localhost:4147/WcfHost/WcfPortal.svc"
                binding="wsHttpBinding"
                contract="Csla.Server.Hosts.IWcfPortal"/>
    </client>
  </system.serviceModel>
```

The CslaDataPortalProxy setting indicates that the WcfProxy should be used to communicate with the application server. This requires that you define a client endpoint in the system.serviceModel element of the config file.

The only value you need to change in this element is the address property. Here you must change localhost:4147 to the name of the server on which the data portal host is installed. You also need to replace the WcfHost text with the name of the virtual root on that server.

Note You must create and configure the WCF host virtual root before using this configuration. I show how this is done in the next section.

As noted, the most important thing to realize about the site configuration is that the data portal can be changed from local to remote (using any of the network channels) with no need to change any UI or business object code.

Configuring the WCF Data Portal Server

The configuration of the remote data portal is the same for ASP.NET applications as it is for WPF applications, which is discussed in Chapter 19. For completeness and ease of reference, I'll cover it again here.

When using a remote data portal configuration, the client communicates with an application server. Obviously, this means that an application server must exist and be properly configured. When the client data portal is configured to use WCF, you must supply a properly configured WCF application server.

Note No data portal server is required when the data portal is configured for local mode. In this case, the "server-side" components run in the website's process and no application server is used or required.

The WcfHost website in the ProjectTracker download is an example of a WCF application server hosted in IIS. You may also choose to host the WCF server in a custom Windows service or a custom EXE or by using Windows Activation Service (WAS). These various hosts are similar to IIS in many ways but are outside the scope of this book.

The WcfHost website is very simple because it relies on preexisting functionality provided by CSLA .NET, as discussed in Chapter 15. Table 20-4 lists the key elements of the website.

Table 20-4. *Key Elements of the WcfHost Website*

Element	Description
WcfPortal.svc	WCF service endpoint file, referencing the Csla.Server.Hosts.WcfPortal class
Bin	Standard web Bin folder containing Csla.dll, ProjectTracker.Library.dll, and any other assemblies required by the business library; the important thing is that your business assemblies and Csla.dll be present in this folder
Web.config	Standard Web.config file but containing a system.serviceModel element to configure the WCF endpoint for the data portal

Any website containing the elements in Table 20-4 can act as a WCF data portal host. The Web.config file must contain the configuration section for WCF, defining the endpoint for the data portal:

```
<system.serviceModel>
  <services>
    <service name="Csla.Server.Hosts.WcfPortal">
      <endpoint address=""
                  contract="Csla.Server.Hosts.IWcfPortal"
                  binding="wsHttpBinding"/>
    </service>
  </services>
</system.serviceModel>
```

WCF services are defined by their address, binding, and contract.

For a WCF service hosted in IIS, the address is defined by IIS and the name of the svc file, so it is not specified in the Web.config file. As shown here, you may provide a "" address or provide no address at all. If you use some other hosting technique, such as WAS or a custom Windows service, you may need to specify the server address.

In the case of a CSLA .NET data portal endpoint, the contract is fixed; it must be Csla.Server.Hosts.IWcfPortal. The contract is defined by the interface implemented in the data portal, discussed in Chapter 15. It may not be different from this value.

The binding can be any synchronous WCF binding. The only requirement imposed by the data portal is that the WCF binding must be synchronous; beyond that, any binding is acceptable. You may choose to use HTTP, TCP, named pipes, or other bindings. You may choose to configure the binding to use SSL, x509 certificates, or other forms of encryption or authentication. All the features of WCF are at your disposal.

Remember that the data access code for your business objects will run on the application server. This means that the application server's Web.config file must define the connection strings required by your data access code:

```
<connectionStrings>
  <add name="PTracker" connectionString="your connection string"
    providerName="System.Data.SqlClient" />
  <add name="Security" connectionString="your connection string"
    providerName="System.Data.SqlClient" />
</connectionStrings>
```

This is the same configuration you'd put in the client's `app.config` file when using a local data portal configuration, but now these values must be on the server because that is where the data access code will execute.

The `CslaAuthentication` value must be the same on both client and server. You can change it to `Windows` as long as you make that change on both sides. If you do change this value to `Windows`, you must ensure that the WCF host website is configured to require Windows authentication and impersonate the calling user because in that case CSLA .NET will simply use the value provided by .NET.

At this point you should understand how to configure the application and how to configure the data portal for either local (2-tier) or remote (3-tier) operation.

PTWeb Site Setup

The UI application can be found within the `ProjectTracker` solution. The project is named `PTWeb`.

The site references the `ProjectTracker.Library` project, as shown in Figure 20-8. This causes Visual Studio to automatically put the associated `ProjectTracker.DalLinq` and `Csla.dll` files into the `Bin` directory as well, because those assemblies are referenced by `ProjectTracker.Library`.

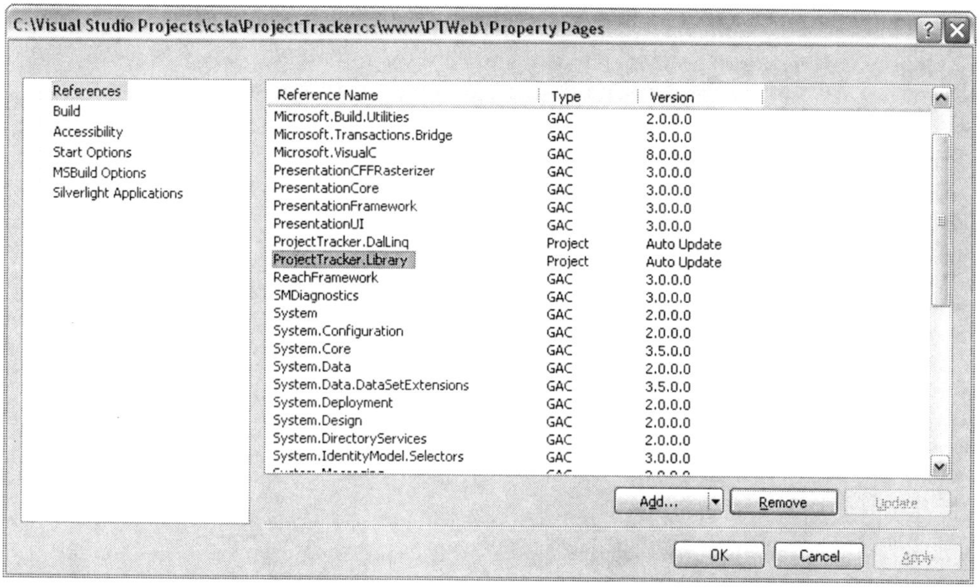

Figure 20-8. *Referencing ProjectTracker.Library*

The `PTWeb` website will only run within IIS, not within the ASP.NET Development Server (commonly known as Cassini or VS Host). The reason for this is explained later in the chapter in the "Forms-Based Authentication" section.

To host a website in IIS during development, you need to take the following steps:

1. Set up a virtual root in IIS that points to the directory containing the PTWeb project files.
2. Set the virtual root to use ASP.NET 2.0, using the ASP.NET tab of the virtual root properties dialog in the IIS management console.
3. Set the website's start options using the project properties dialog in Visual Studio 2008. Change the setting to use a custom server so it starts up using IIS with a URL such as http://localhost/PTWeb.

It may seem odd that step 2 sets the virtual root to use ASP.NET 2.0 when this is actually an ASP.NET 3.5 application. However, .NET 3.5 uses the core .NET 2.0 runtime and it is the core runtime that is set in step 2.

With the basic website setup complete, let's go through the creation of the Web Forms UI. First, I'll discuss the use of a master page and then I'll cover the process of logging a user in and out using forms-based authentication.

With the common code out of the way, I'll discuss the process of maintaining the roles and project data in detail. At that point, you should have a good understanding of how to create both grid-based and detail pages.

Master Page

To ensure that all pages in the site have the same basic layout, navigation, and authentication options, a *master page* is used. The master page provides these consistent elements, and all the rest of the pages in the site are *content pages*. This means they fit within the context of the master page itself, adding content where appropriate.

Look back at Figures 20-6 and 20-7 to see the visual appearance of the pages. Both Default.aspx and ProjectEdit.aspx are content pages, adding their content to that already provided by MasterPage.master:

```
<%@ Master Language="C#" CodeFile="MasterPage.master.cs"
  Inherits="MasterPage" %>
<!DOCTYPE html PUBLIC "-//W3C//DTD XHTML 1.1//EN"
  "http://www.w3.org/TR/xhtml11/DTD/xhtml11.dtd">
<html xmlns="http://www.w3.org/1999/xhtml" xml:lang="en">
<head id="Head1" runat="server">
  <title>Untitled Page</title>
  <meta http-equiv="Content-Type" content="text/html;
    charset=iso-8859-1" />
</head>
<body>
  <form id="form1" runat="server">
  <div id="mainTable">
    <div id="header">
      <asp:Label ID="PageTitle" runat="server">
      </asp:Label>
    </div>
    <div id="navigation">
      <div id="navigationContent">
```

```
            <asp:TreeView ID="TreeView1" runat="server"
              DataSourceID="SiteMapDataSource1"
              ShowExpandCollapse="False" SkipLinkText="" >
              <NodeStyle CssClass="nav" />
            </asp:TreeView>
          </div>
        </div>
        <div id="subnavigation">
          <div id="logout">
            <asp:LoginStatus ID="LoginStatus1"
              runat="server" OnLoggingOut="LoginStatus1_LoggingOut" />
          </div>
        </div>
        <div id="content">
          <asp:ContentPlaceHolder id="ContentPlaceHolder1"
            runat="server">
          </asp:ContentPlaceHolder>
        </div>
      </div>
      <asp:SiteMapDataSource ID="SiteMapDataSource1" runat="server"
        ShowStartingNode="False" />
    </form>
</body>
</html>
```

MasterPage.master defines the header/title bar at the top of the page. The area immediately beneath the header/title bar contains the Login button, and there is a navigation area down the left. Perhaps most importantly, it also defines a content area containing a ContentPlaceHolder control:

```
<asp:ContentPlaceHolder id="ContentPlaceHolder1"
  runat="server">
</asp:ContentPlaceHolder>
```

This is the area where content pages provide their content, and it is the main body of the page. You'll see how each content page provides content for this area later in the chapter.

Theme Support

ASP.NET supports the concept of the visual appearance of a website being defined by a *theme*: a group of files in a theme-specific subdirectory beneath the App_Themes directory in the virtual root. A theme is a group of style sheets, graphics, and control skins that describe the appearance of a site. A given site can have many themes, and you can even allow the user to choose between them if you so desire.

Note how all of the regions in the master page are set up using div tags. No appearance characteristics are specified in the page itself. Instead, the actual appearance is defined by a CSS style sheet contained within the current theme for the site. The PTWeb site includes and uses a Basic theme. The use of the Basic theme is set up in Web.config:

```
<pages theme="Basic" styleSheetTheme="Basic">
```

The theme property sets the default runtime theme, while styleSheetTheme sets the theme for use at design time in Visual Studio. The styleSheetTheme property should be removed when the website is deployed to a production server.

The files defining this theme are in the App_Themes/Basic folder beneath the virtual root. The files in this theme are listed in Table 20-5.

Table 20-5. *Files in the Basic Theme*

File	Description
Basic.css	The style sheet for the site
Basic.skin	The skins for GridView, DetailsView, and Login controls
Images\background.jpg	The background graphic for the header region
Images\corner.png	The graphic for the rounded corner in the upper left

Combined, these files define the look and feel of the site. This includes defining the appearance of the regions in MasterPage.master. For instance, the header region is defined in the css file like this:

```
#header
{
  background-image: url('images/background.jpg');
  background-repeat: no-repeat;
  height: 64px;
  line-height: 60px;
  text-align: left;
  color: #FFFFFF;
  font-family:
  Verdana, Arial, Helvetica, sans-serif;
  font-size: 36px;
  font-weight: bold;
  font-style: italic;
  padding-left: 10px
}
```

A control skin defines the appearance of specific controls in the website, such as GridView, TextBox, and so forth. For instance, the appearance of the Login control is defined in the skin file like this:

```
<asp:Login runat="server" BackColor="#DEDEDE" BorderColor="Black"
  BorderStyle="Solid" BorderWidth="1px" Font-Names="Verdana"
  Font-Size="10pt">
  <TitleTextStyle BackColor="Black" Font-Bold="True"
    Font-Names="Verdana" Font-Size="10pt"
    ForeColor="White" />
</asp:Login>
```

Each type of control in Web Forms has different options you can set in a skin file, allowing you to set the appearance of each control in many ways.

By making the site theme-enabled, you can easily change the appearance of the site later by creating a new theme directory and similar theme files and setting the theme property in Web.config to use the new theme.

Header Region

The header region of the page is the title area across the top. It contains a single Label control named PageTitle. This control displays the title of the current content page, based on the Title property set for that page. The following code is included in MasterPage.master to load this value:

```
protected void Page_Load(object sender, EventArgs e)
{
  PageTitle.Text = Page.Title;
}
```

As each content page loads, not only does the Load event for the content page run but so does the Load event for the master page. This means that code can be placed in the master page to run when any content page is loaded—in this case, to set the title at the top of the page.

Navigation Region

The navigation region displays the navigation links down the left side of each page. To do this, a web.sitemap file and associated SiteMapDataSource control are used to load the overall structure of the site into memory. This data is then data bound to a TreeView control for display to the user.

The web.sitemap file is an XML file that contains a node for each page to be displayed in the navigation region:

```
<?xml version="1.0" encoding="utf-8" ?>
<siteMap
  xmlns="http://schemas.microsoft.com/AspNet/SiteMap-File-1.0" >
  <siteMapNode url="" title=""  description="">
    <siteMapNode url="~/Default.aspx" title="Home"
                 description="Main page" />
    <siteMapNode url="~/ProjectList.aspx" title="Project list"
                 description="Project list" />
    <siteMapNode url="~/ResourceList.aspx" title="Resource list"
                 description="Resource list" />
    <siteMapNode url="~/RolesEdit.aspx" title="Project roles"
                 description="Project roles" />
  </siteMapNode>
</siteMap>
```

The site map concept can be used to define hierarchical website structures, but in this case, I use it to define a flat structure. Notice how each <siteMapNode> element defines a page—except the first one. That root node is required in the file, but since I'm defining a flat structure, it really doesn't represent a page and is just a placeholder. If you were to define a hierarchical page structure, that node would typically point to Default.aspx.

Notice that MasterPage.master includes a SiteMapDataSource control:

```
<asp:SiteMapDataSource ID="SiteMapDataSource1" runat="server"
  ShowStartingNode="False" />
```

This special data control automatically reads the data from the web.sitemap file and makes it available to controls on the page. The ShowStartingNode property is set to False, indicating that the root node in web.sitemap is to be ignored. That's perfect because that node is empty and shouldn't be displayed.

In this case, a TreeView control in the navigation region is bound to the SiteMapDataSource, so it displays the items listed in web.sitemap to the user.

LoginStatus Control

In the subnavigation region of MasterPage.master, you'll see a LoginStatus control:

```
<asp:LoginStatus ID="LoginStatus1"
  runat="server" OnLoggingOut="LoginStatus1_LoggingOut" />
```

This is one of the login controls provided with ASP.NET, and its purpose is to allow the user to log into and out of the site. The control automatically displays the word *Login* if the user is logged out and *Logout* if the user is logged in. When clicked, it also automatically redirects the user to a login web page defined in Web.config. I cover the Web.config options later in the "Configuring the Site" section.

Because the control automatically directs the user to the appropriate login page to be logged in, no code is required for that process. However, code is required to handle the case in which the user clicks the control to be logged out. This code goes in the master page:

```
protected void LoginStatus1_LoggingOut(
  object sender, LoginCancelEventArgs e)
{
  ProjectTracker.Library.Security.PTPrincipal.Logout();
  Session["CslaPrincipal"] =
    Csla.ApplicationContext.User;
  System.Web.Security.FormsAuthentication.SignOut();
}
```

This code covers a lot of ground.

First, the Logout() method of PTPrincipal is called, which sets the current principal on the current HttpContext and Thread objects to an UnauthenticatedPrincipal object. This is discussed in Chapter 12 and used in PTWpf in Chapter 19.

However, when users are logged in, their principal object is stored in a Session field so it can be easily reloaded on every page request. The details on how this works are discussed later in the "Reloading the Principal" section. When the user logs out, that Session field is updated to reference the new principal object.

Note If you want to avoid Session, you can choose to reload the user's identity and roles from the security database on every page request. While that avoids the use of Session, it can put a substantial workload on your security database server. In PTWeb, I have opted to use Session to minimize the load on the database.

The final step is to tell ASP.NET itself that the user is no longer authenticated. This is done by calling FormsAuthentication.SignOut(). This method invalidates the security cookie used by ASP.NET to indicate that the user has been authenticated. The result is that ASP.NET sees the user as unauthenticated on all subsequent page requests.

This covers the logout process, but the login process requires some more work. While the LoginStatus control handles the details of directing the user to a login page, that page must be created.

Login Page

Like the PTWpf smart client, the PTWeb site is designed to use custom authentication, so I can illustrate the custom authentication support provided by CSLA .NET. In this section, I briefly discuss the use of Windows integrated security and the ASP.NET membership service.

In Web Forms, when using custom authentication, you need to configure the site appropriately using `Web.config` and implement a login web page to collect and validate the user's credentials. That's the purpose behind `Login.aspx`.

Using Forms-Based Authentication

When using forms-based authentication, users are often automatically redirected to a login form before being allowed to access any other pages. Alternatively, anonymous users can be allowed to use the site and they can choose to log into the site to gain access to extra features or functionality. The specific behaviors are defined by `Web.config`.

Before moving on, remember that the following implementation only works within IIS. The ASP.NET Development Server provided with Visual Studio has various limitations; among them is the inability to load custom security objects from assemblies in the `Bin` directory. This means you can't use the ASP.NET Development Server to test or debug custom principal objects, custom membership providers, or other custom security objects if they're in an assembly referenced from the project.

Though this is an unfortunate limitation, it can be argued that the ASP.NET Development Server is not intended for anything beyond hobbyist or casual usage and that IIS should be used for serious business development.

Note An alternative solution is to install the assembly containing your custom principal and identity classes into the .NET GAC. For `PTWeb`, this would mean giving `ProjectTracker.Library` a strong name and using the `gacutil.exe` command line utility to install the assembly into the GAC. `ProjectTracker.Library` would need to be updated in the GAC after each time you build the assembly. I find that using IIS is a far simpler solution than using the GAC.

Configuring the Site

Using forms-based security in ASP.NET means that `Web.config` includes elements such as the following:

```
<authentication mode="Forms">
  <forms loginUrl="Login.aspx" name="ptracker"/>
</authentication>
<authorization>
  <allow users="*"/>
</authorization>
```

This tells ASP.NET to use forms-based authentication (`mode="Forms"`), yet to allow unauthenticated users (`<allow users="*"/>`).

Note To require users to log in before seeing any pages, replace `<allow users="*"/>` with `<deny users="?"/>`.

It is important that you also ensure that the security on the virtual root itself (within IIS) is configured to allow anonymous users. If IIS blocks anonymous users, it doesn't really matter what kind of security you use within ASP.NET.

Note Remember that IIS security runs *first*, and then any ASP.NET security is applied.

With the `Web.config` options shown previously, users can use the site without logging in, but the concept of logging in is supported. The goal is the same as with `PTWpf` in Chapter 19: allow all users to do certain actions, and allow authenticated users to do other actions based on their roles.

When users choose to log in, the `<forms>` tag specifies that they will be directed to `Login.aspx`, which will collect and validate their credentials. Figure 20-9 shows the appearance of `Login.aspx`.

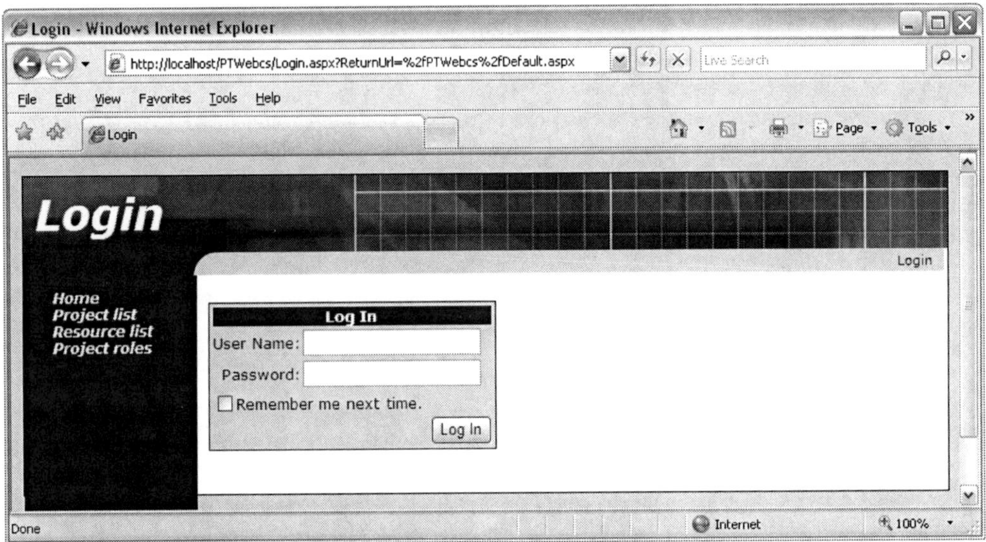

Figure 20-9. *Layout of the Login page*

Now this is where things get kind of cool. There is no code behind `Login.aspx`. This page uses the ASP.NET `Login` control:

```
<asp:Login ID="Login1" runat="server">
</asp:Login>
```

This control is designed to automatically use the default ASP.NET membership provider for the site.

■ **Caution** The user's credentials flow from the browser to the web server in clear text—they are not automatically encrypted. Due to this, it is recommended that `Login.aspx` be accessed over an SSL connection so that data traveling to and from the browser is encrypted during the login process.

You can write code to handle the events of the `Login` control if you desire, but a membership provider offers a cleaner solution overall. Of course, the membership provider that comes with ASP.NET doesn't understand `PTPrincipal` and `PTIdentity` objects, so `PTWeb` includes its own custom membership provider.

Implementing a Custom Membership Provider

A membership provider is an object that inherits from `System.Web.Security.MembershipProvider` to handle all aspects of membership. These aspects include the following:

- Validating user credentials
- Adding a new user
- Deleting a user
- Changing a user's password
- More

Of course, PTPrincipal doesn't understand all these things, and ProjectTracker.Library doesn't implement a full set of membership objects either. If you want to support all these capabilities, you should create your own security library with appropriate objects.

But PTPrincipal *does* understand how to validate a user's credentials. Fortunately, it is possible to implement a subset of the complete membership provider functionality, and that's what I do in PTWeb.

The PTMembershipProvider class is in the App_Code directory, so ASP.NET automatically compiles it and makes it available to the website. This class inherits from MembershipProvider and overrides the ValidateUser() method:

```
public class PTMembershipProvider : MembershipProvider
{
  public override bool ValidateUser(
    string username, string password)
  {
    bool result = PTPrincipal.Login(username, password);
    HttpContext.Current.Session["CslaPrincipal"] =
      Csla.ApplicationContext.User;
    return result;
  }
  // other methods …
}
```

All other methods are overridden to throw an exception indicating that they aren't implemented by this provider.

Notice how the ValidateUser() method already accepts username and password parameters. This is convenient because the Login() method of PTPrincipal accepts those parameters as well. The code simply calls the Login() method and records the result—true if the user is logged in, false otherwise.

The Login() method in PTPrincipal sets the User property of Csla.ApplicationContext, thus automatically setting both the Thread object's CurrentPrincipal property and the HttpContext.Current.User property to an authenticated PTPrincipal if the user's credentials are valid; otherwise, they are set to an UnauthenticatedPrincipal.

The code then sets a Session field, CslaPrincipal, to contain this principal value so it will be available to subsequent pages.

Then the result value is returned. The ASP.NET membership infrastructure relies on this return value to know whether the user's credentials are valid or not.

Before this custom membership provider can be used, it must be defined in Web.config as follows:

```
<membership defaultProvider="PTMembershipProvider">
  <providers>
    <add name="PTMembershipProvider"
      type="PTMembershipProvider"
      enablePasswordRetrieval="false"
      enablePasswordReset="false"
      requiresQuestionAndAnswer="false"
      applicationName="/"
```

```
            requiresUniqueEmail="false"
            passwordFormat="Clear"
            description="Stores and retrieves membership
              data using CSLA .NET business objects."
        />
      </providers>
    </membership>
```

By making PTMembershipProvider the default provider, this definition tells ASP.NET to automatically use it for any membership activities, including validating a user's credentials.

Reloading the Principal

At this point, you've seen how the user can log in or out using the LoginStatus control on the master page. And you've seen how Login.aspx and the custom membership provider are used to gather and validate the user's credentials.

But how does the principal object carry forward from page to page? Remember that the web technologies are stateless by default, and it is up to the web developer to manually implement state management as she chooses. Unfortunately, this extends to the user's identity as well.

The forms-based security infrastructure provided by ASP.NET writes an encrypted cookie to the user's browser. That cookie contains a security ticket with a unique identifier for the user, the user's name, and an expiration time. This cookie flows from the browser to the web server on each page request, so that basic information is available.

Notice, however, that the cookie doesn't include the principal and identity objects. That is because those objects could be quite large and in some cases might not even be serializable. Though PTPrincipal and PTIdentity are serializable, they could still be large enough to pose a problem if you try to write them to the cookie. Cookies have a size limit, and remember that PTIdentity contains an array with all the role names for the user. Given a large number of roles or lengthy role names, this could easily add up to a lot of bytes of data.

Note It is possible to serialize the principal and identity objects into the cookie (if the objects are serializable). Doing so isn't recommended, however, due to the size limitations on cookies.

It is quite possible to reload PTPrincipal and PTIdentity from the security database on every page request. Remember that the ASP.NET security cookie contains the username value, and you already know that the user was authenticated. You need another stored procedure in the database that returns the user information based on username alone; no password is provided or checked. Similarly, another static method such as Login() is required in PTPrincipal to load the objects based only on the username value. You can see an example of this by looking at the LoadPrincipal() method in the PTPrincipal class.

There are two drawbacks to this. First, reloading this data from the security database on every page request could cause a serious performance issue. The security database could get overloaded with all the requests. Second, there's an obvious security risk in implementing methods that allow loading user identities without having to supply the password. While that functionality wouldn't be exposed to the end user, it makes it easier for accidental bugs or malicious back-door code to creep into your website.

This is why I use Session to store the principal object in PTWeb. The user's credentials are validated, and the resulting principal object is placed in a Session field named CslaPrincipal. On all subsequent page requests, this value is retrieved from Session and is used to set both the current Thread and HttpContext object's principals.

The work occurs in Global.asax, as this file contains the event handlers for all events leading up to a page being processed. In this case, it is the AcquireRequestState event that is used:

```
protected void Application_AcquireRequestState(
  object sender, EventArgs e)
{
  if (HttpContext.Current.Handler is IRequiresSessionState)
  {
    if (Csla.ApplicationContext.AuthenticationType == "Windows")
      return;

    System.Security.Principal.IPrincipal principal;
    try
    {
      principal = (System.Security.Principal.IPrincipal)
        HttpContext.Current.Session["CslaPrincipal"];
    }
    catch
    {
      principal = null;
    }

    if (principal == null)
    {
      if (User.Identity.IsAuthenticated &&
        User.Identity is FormsIdentity)
      {
        // no principal in session, but ASP.NET token
        // still valid - so sign out ASP.NET
        FormsAuthentication.SignOut();
        Response.Redirect(Request.Url.PathAndQuery);
      }
      // didn't get a principal from Session, so
      // set it to an unauthenticated PTPrincipal
      ProjectTracker.Library.Security.PTPrincipal.Logout();
    }
    else
    {
      // use the principal from Session
      Csla.ApplicationContext.User = principal;
    }
  }
}
```

The reason for using the AcquireRequestState event, rather than the more obvious AuthenticateRequest event, is that Session isn't initialized when AuthenticateRequest is raised, but it usually is initialized when AcquireRequestState is raised.

The code shown here is relatively complex. This is because it must deal with a number of possible page request and Session time-out scenarios. Not all page requests are for Web Forms or initialize Session, so the code first ensures that this particular request requires Session. And if CSLA .NET is configured to use Windows authentication, there's no need to do any work to retrieve a custom principal. When using Windows authentication, CSLA .NET relies on ASP.NET and IIS to properly set the principal object based on the user's Windows credentials.

Assuming the request does use `Session`, and CSLA .NET is using custom authentication, the code attempts to retrieve the principal object from `Session`. This can result in an exception if `Session` doesn't exist (which can happen on some page requests), and so the value would end up being `null`. Also, if this is the first page request by the user, the `Session` field will return `null`. So the outcome is either a valid `PTPrincipal` object or `null`.

If the resulting `principal` value is `null`, the code deals with another possible scenario, where `Session` has timed out but the ASP.NET authentication security token is still valid. In other words, to ASP.NET, the user is still logged in but the user's `Session` state is expired. In this case I have chosen to sign the user out of ASP.NET:

```
FormsAuthentication.SignOut();
Response.Redirect(Request.Url.PathAndQuery);
```

You could choose instead to simply reload the principal object from the database, based on the username in the ASP.NET token:

```
ProjectTracker.Library.Security.PTPrincipal.LoadPrincipal(
  User.Identity.Name);
```

This second option keeps the user logged in as long as the ASP.NET authentication security token remains valid, even if `Session` expires first.

If no principal is retrieved from `Session`, and the ASP.NET authentication security token isn't active, the user simply hasn't logged in yet. In this case, `PTPrincipal.Logout()` is called to set the current principal as an unauthenticated `PTPrincipal`, and the `HttpContext` is set to use that same principal object. This supports the idea of an unauthenticated anonymous guest user.

Both the web and business library code have access to valid, if unauthenticated, principal objects and can apply authorization code as needed. Additionally, by having the current principal be a valid `PTPrincipal` object, a remote data portal can be invoked and the application server will impersonate the unauthenticated user identity so *that* code can apply authorization rules as well. On the other hand, if a principal object is retrieved from `Session`, that value is set as the current principal.

Using Windows Integrated Security

If you wanted to use Windows integrated security, you don't need `Login.aspx`, the custom membership provider, or the code in `Global.asax` because the user's identity is already known. The user provides his Windows credentials to the browser, which in turn provides them to the web server.

This means that the virtual root in IIS must be configured to disallow anonymous users, thus forcing the user to provide credentials to access the site. It is IIS that authenticates the user and allows authenticated users into the site.

To have ASP.NET use the Windows identity from IIS, you must configure `Web.config` correctly:

```
<authentication mode="Windows"/>
<identity impersonate="true"/>
```

The authentication mode is set to `Windows`, indicating that ASP.NET should defer all authentication to the IIS host. Setting the `impersonate` property to `true` tells ASP.NET to impersonate the user authenticated by IIS.

If you use Windows integrated security and you are using a remote data portal, you *must* make sure to change the application server configuration file to also use Windows security. If the data portal is hosted in IIS, the virtual root must be set to disallow anonymous access, thereby forcing the client to provide IIS with the Windows identity from the web server via integrated security.

However, you should also remember that Windows will limit how far a user's identity can go, from machine to machine. A Windows computer will only allow a user's identity to impersonate one network hop away from the user. So if you use Windows security with an application server, you are already two network hops away from the user. This means your application won't be able to use the user's identity for impersonation when connecting to the database, for example.

There are some advanced networking techniques you can implement to enable more complex impersonation scenarios. Windows and Active Directory network configuration is outside the scope of this book.

Fortunately most web applications are 2-tier, with the web server communicating directly with the database server, so impersonation works as desired.

Using the ASP.NET Membership Service

ASP.NET not only supports the broad concept of membership as used previously but it provides a complete membership service, including all the code to make it work. The membership service is most often used with the SQL membership provider that comes with ASP.NET. This provider requires that you use a predefined database schema along with the membership objects provided by Microsoft to manage and interact with the database. By default, ASP.NET uses a Microsoft SQL Server 2008 Express database in the virtual root's `App_Data` directory, but you can override that behavior to have it use another Microsoft SQL Server database if needed.

The other membership provider shipped with ASP.NET is a connector to Active Directory. It does the same thing but stores the user information in AD instead of a SQL database.

CSLA .NET includes the `MembershipIdentity` class in the `Csla.Security` namespace. If you want to use the membership service to authenticate your users and the associated provider to manage their roles, you can create a custom identity object by subclassing `MembershipIdentity`.

Instead of implementing `PTIdentity` to interact with a custom database table, you could choose to use the `MembershipIdentity` class. The `Login()` method in the `PTPrincipal` class needs to change in this case because the factory method provided by `MembershipIdentity` is slightly different from the one in the `PTIdentity` class:

```
public static MyPrincipal Login(
  string username, string password)
{
  var identity =
    MembershipIdentity.GetMembershipIdentity<MembershipIdentity>(
      username, password, true);
  return new MyPrincipal(identity);
}
```

The highlighted line of code shows how the `MembershipIdentity` object is created. The third parameter to the `GetMembershipIdentity()` factory method is `true`, indicating that the membership provider database is on the same machine where this code is running. In other words, the data portal shouldn't be used to move the request to the application server before attempting to access the membership database.

If you are logging in on a smart client, such as in a WPF application, you'd want to pass `false` so the request *is* transferred to the application server (which would be hosted in IIS) where the membership database exists.

The `PTWeb` application does not use the membership provider because `PTIdentity` uses a custom security database.

At this point, you should have an understanding of how the website is organized. It references ProjectTracker.Library and uses a master page and theme to provide a consistent, manageable appearance for the site. It also uses a mix of ASP.NET login controls and the prebuilt ProjectTracker security objects to implement custom authentication.

Now let's move on and discuss the pages that provide actual business behaviors.

Business Functionality

With the common functionality in the master page, Login.aspx, and Global.asax covered, it is possible to move on to the business functionality itself. As I mentioned earlier, I'll walk through the RolesEdit, ProjectList, and ProjectEdit web forms in some detail. ResourceList and ResourcEdit are available in the download available at www.apress.com/book/view/1430210192 or www.lhotka.net/cslanet/download.aspx and follow the same implementation approach.

All of these web forms are created using the data binding capabilities built into ASP.NET Web Forms and the CslaDataSource control discussed in Chapter 10. These capabilities allow the web developer to easily link controls on the form to business objects and their properties. The developer productivity gained through this approach is simply amazing.

Other key technologies I'll use are the MultiView control and the associated View control. These controls make it easy for a single page to present multiple views to the user and are often very valuable when building pages for editing data.

Finally, remember that all these pages are content pages. That means that they fit within the context of a master page—in this case, MasterPage.master. As you'll see, the tags in a content page are a bit different from those in a simple web form.

RolesEdit Form

The RolesEdit.aspx page is a content page, so its Page directive looks like this:

```
<%@ Page Language="C#" MasterPageFile="~/MasterPage.master"
  AutoEventWireup="true" CodeFile="RolesEdit.aspx.cs"
  Inherits="RolesEdit" title="Project Roles" %>
```

Notice the MasterPageFile property, which points to MasterPage.master. Also notice the Title property, which sets the page's title. It is this value that is used in the master page's Load event handler to set the title text in the header region of the page.

Figure 20-10 shows what the page looks like in Visual Studio.

The content title bar across the top of the main page body won't be visible at runtime. It is visible at design time to remind you that you are editing a content area in the page. If you look at the page's source, you'll see that all the page content is contained within a Content control:

```
<asp:Content ID="Content1"
  ContentPlaceHolderID="ContentPlaceHolder1" Runat="Server">
  <!-- page content goes here -->
</asp:Content>
```

The ContentPlaceHolderID property links this content to the ContentPlaceHolder1 control in the master page. This scheme means that a master page can define multiple content placeholders and a content page can have multiple Content controls—one for each placeholder.

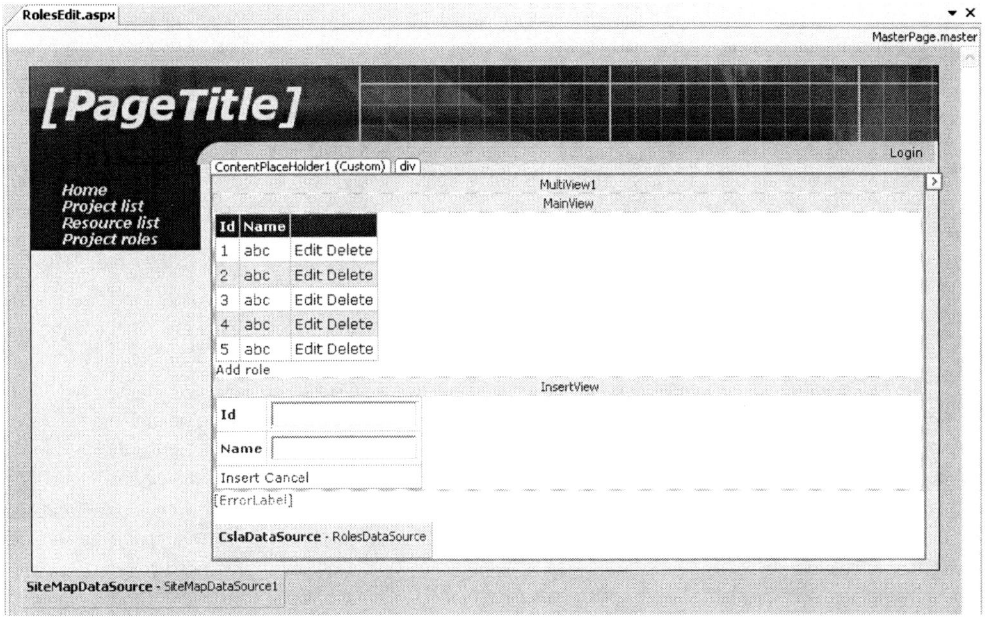

Figure 20-10. *Layout of the RolesEdit page*

Using the MultiView Control

The `MultiView` control contains two `View` controls named `MainView` and `InsertView`. Only one of these views is active (visible) at any time, so this form really defines two different views for the user.

Within your code, you select the view by setting the `ActiveViewIndex` property of the `MultiView` control to the numeric index of the appropriate `View` control. Of course, using a numeric value like this doesn't lead to maintainable code, so within the page, I define an enumerated type with text values corresponding to each `View` control:

```
private enum Views
{
  MainView = 0,
  InsertView = 1
}
```

The `Views` type is used to change the page view as needed.

Using ErrorLabel

Beneath the `MultiView` control in Figure 20-10 is a `Label` control with its `ForeColor` set to `Red`. The purpose behind this control is to allow the page to display error text to the user in the case of an exception.

As you'll see, the data access code uses `try...catch` blocks to catch exceptions that occur during any data updates (insert, update, or delete). The text of the exception is displayed in `ErrorLabel` so it is visible to the user.

Using a Business Object As a Data Source

In Chapter 10, I discuss the CslaDataSource control and how it overcomes the limitations of the standard ObjectDataSource control. The RolesEdit page uses this control, making it relatively easy to bind the Roles collection from ProjectTracker.Library to a GridView control on the page.

The RolesDataSource data source control is defined on the page like this:

```
<csla:CslaDataSource ID="RolesDataSource" runat="server"
  TypeName="ProjectTracker.Library.Admin.Roles, ProjectTracker.Library"
  OnDeleteObject="RolesDataSource_DeleteObject"
  OnInsertObject="RolesDataSource_InsertObject"
  OnSelectObject="RolesDataSource_SelectObject"
  OnUpdateObject="RolesDataSource_UpdateObject">
</csla:CslaDataSource>
```

The TypeName property defines the type and assembly containing the business class. The TypeAssemblyName property exists for backward compatibility and should not be used for new code. The TypeName property provides the control with enough information so that it can load the Roles type and determine the properties that will be exposed by child objects in the collection.

OnDeleteObject and similar properties link the control to a set of event handlers in the page's code. The code in those event handlers interacts with the business object to perform each requested action.

Of course, to get this data source control onto the web form, you can simply drag the CslaDataSource control from the toolbox onto the designer surface and set its properties through the Properties window in Visual Studio.

Then, when the GridView and DetailsView controls are placed on the form, you can use their pop-up tasks menu to select the data source control, as shown in Figure 20-11.

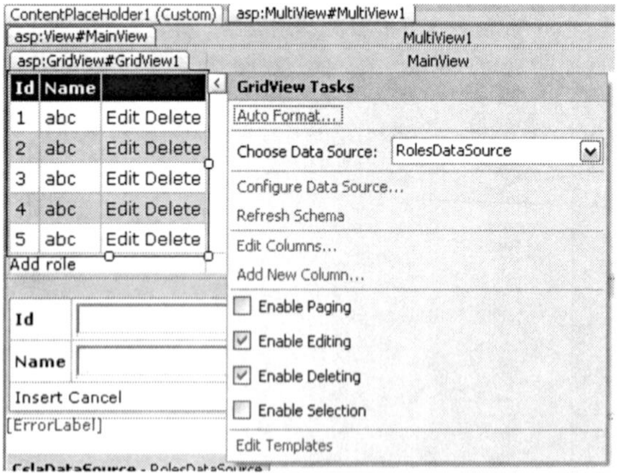

Figure 20-11. *Choosing a data source for a GridView or DetailsView*

You can either write the tags yourself or use the designer support built into Visual Studio as you choose. The one caveat to this is that you cannot use the <New data source...> option to create a CslaDataSource object using the Data Source Configuration Wizard. Due to some very complex issues with how this Visual Studio wizard creates the new control, a control added using this wizard won't work properly unless you close and reopen the page designer. So I recommend adding the CslaDataSource control first, then binding it to any UI controls.

Caching the Object in Session

To optimize the performance of the website, business objects are stored in Session. While they could be retrieved directly from the database when needed, storing them in Session reduces the load on the database server.

To minimize the number of objects maintained in Session, all pages use the same Session field to store their business objects: currentObject. This way, only one business object is stored in Session at any time, and that is the object being actively used by the current page.

Of course, browsers have a Back button, which means that the user could navigate back to some previous page that expects to be using a different type of object than the current page. For instance, the user could be editing a Project object and then start editing a Resource object. Session would have originally contained the Project but then would contain the Resource.

If the user then uses the Back button to return to the ProjectEdit page, Session could still have the Resource object in the currentObject field. This possibility is very real and must be dealt with by checking the type of the object retrieved from Session to see if it is the type the page actually needs. If not, the correct object must be retrieved from the database.

In RolesEdit, the GetRoles() method performs this task:

```
private ProjectTracker.Library.Admin.Roles GetRoles()
{
  object businessObject = Session["currentObject"];
  if (businessObject == null ||
    !(businessObject is ProjectTracker.Library.Admin.Roles))
  {
    businessObject =
      ProjectTracker.Library.Admin.Roles.GetRoles();
    Session["currentObject"] = businessObject;
  }
  return (ProjectTracker.Library.Admin.Roles)businessObject;
}
```

The code retrieves the currentObject item from Session. If the result is null, or if the resulting object isn't a Roles object, a new Roles object is retrieved by calling the Roles.GetRoles() factory method. That newly retrieved object is placed in Session, making it the current object.

In any case, a valid Roles object is returned as a result.

Selecting an Object

The SelectObject event is raised when the web page needs data from the data source—the Roles object in this case. The page must handle the event and return the requested data object:

```
protected void RolesDataSource_SelectObject(
  object sender, Csla.Web.SelectObjectArgs e)
{
  ProjectTracker.Library.Admin.Roles obj = GetRoles();
  e.BusinessObject = obj;
}
```

The GetRoles() helper method is called to retrieve the Roles collection object. Then the Roles object is returned to the RolesDataSource control by setting the e.BusinessObject property. The data source control then provides this object to the ASP.NET data binding infrastructure so it can be used to populate any UI controls bound to the data control. In this case, that's the GridView control in MainView. That control is declared like this:

```
<asp:GridView ID="GridView1" runat="server"
  AutoGenerateColumns="False"
  DataSourceID="RolesDataSource"
  DataKeyNames="Id">
  <Columns>
    <asp:BoundField DataField="Id" HeaderText="Id"
      ReadOnly="True" SortExpression="Id" />
    <asp:BoundField DataField="Name" HeaderText="Name"
      SortExpression="Name" />
    <asp:CommandField ShowDeleteButton="True"
      ShowEditButton="True" />
  </Columns>
</asp:GridView>
```

The `DataSourceID` property establishes data binding to the `RolesDataSource` control.

The `DataKeyNames` property specifies the name of the property on the business object that acts as a primary key for the object. For a `Role` object, this is `Id`. Remember the use of the `DataObjectField` attribute on the `Id` property in Chapter 17, which provides a hint to Visual Studio that this property is the object's unique key value.

The first two columns in the `GridView` control are bound to properties from the data source: `Id` and `Name`, respectively. The third column is a `CommandField`, which automatically adds Delete and Edit links next to each element in the list. The Delete link automatically triggers the `DeleteObject` event to delete the specified object. The Edit link puts the row into in-place edit mode, allowing the user to edit the data in the selected row. If the user accepts the updates, the `UpdateObject` event is automatically raised. No code beyond that, handling those events, is required to support either of these links.

Of course, you don't have to deal with all these tags if you don't want to. Most of the code in the `CslaDataSource` control exists to support the graphical designer support in Visual Studio. Look back at Figure 20-10 and notice how the `GridView` control displays the Id, Name, and command columns. I configured the control entirely using the Visual Studio designer and setting properties on the controls.

Figure 20-12 shows the Fields dialog for the `GridView` control.

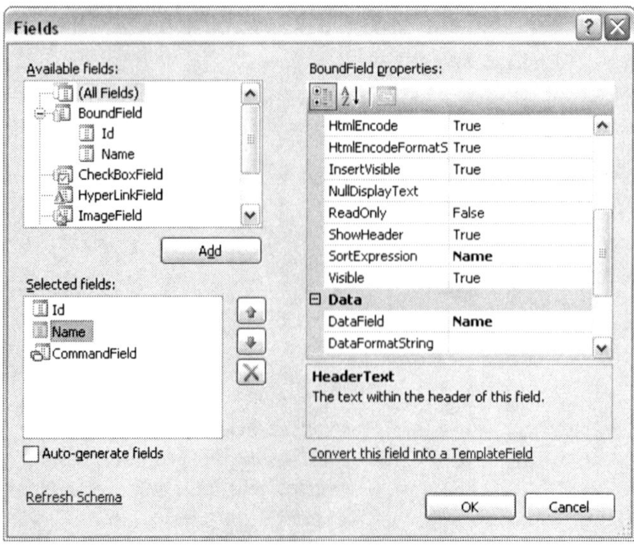

Figure 20-12. *Fields dialog for a GridView control*

Notice that the Available Fields box contains a list of the potentially bound fields from the data source: Id and Name. The `CslaDataSource` control's designer support returns this list by using reflection against the data source object, as discussed in Chapter 10. You can use this dialog to choose which columns are displayed, to control the way they are displayed, to rearrange their order, and more.

Inserting an Object

The `MainView` contains not only a `GridView` control but also a `LinkButton` control named `AddRoleButton`. This button allows the user to add a new `Role` object to the `Roles` collection. To do this, the `View` is changed to `InsertView`:

```
protected void AddRoleButton_Click(object sender, EventArgs e)
{
  this.DetailsView1.DefaultMode = DetailsViewMode.Insert;
  MultiView1.ActiveViewIndex = (int)Views.InsertView;
}
```

This changes the page to appear as in Figure 20-13.

Look at the address bar in the browser; see how it is still `RolesEdit.aspx` even though the display is entirely different from Figure 20-10. This illustrates the power of the `MultiView` control, which allows a user to remain on a single page to view, edit, and insert data.

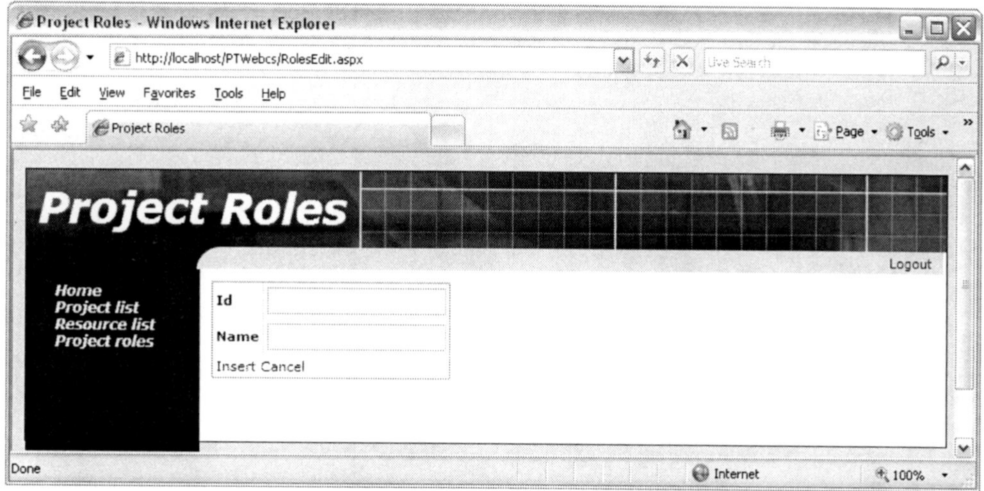

Figure 20-13. *The RolesEdit.aspx page when a new role is being added*

The control shown here is a `DetailsView` control, which is data bound to the same `RolesDataSource` control as the `GridView` earlier. This control is declared in a manner very similar to the `GridView`:

```
<asp:DetailsView ID="DetailsView1" runat="server"
  AutoGenerateRows="False" DataSourceID="RolesDataSource"
  DefaultMode="Insert" Height="50px" Width="125px"
  DataKeyNames="Id" OnItemInserted="DetailsView1_ItemInserted"
  OnModeChanged="DetailsView1_ModeChanged">
  <Fields>
    <asp:BoundField DataField="Id" HeaderText="Id"
      SortExpression="Id" />
    <asp:BoundField DataField="Name" HeaderText="Name"
```

```
            SortExpression="Name" />
          <asp:CommandField ShowInsertButton="True" />
        </Fields>
      </asp:DetailsView>
```

It is bound to RolesDataSource, and its DataKeyNames property specifies that the Id property is the unique identifier for the object. The <Fields> elements define the rows in the control much as columns are defined in a GridView.

If the user enters values for a new role and clicks the Insert link in the DetailsView control, the InsertObject event is raised by RolesDataSource. This event is handled in the page to add the new role to the Roles collection:

```
protected void RolesDataSource_InsertObject(
  object sender, Csla.Web.InsertObjectArgs e)
{
  try
  {
    ProjectTracker.Library.Admin.Roles obj = GetRoles();
    ProjectTracker.Library.Admin.Role role = obj.AddNew();
    Csla.Data.DataMapper.Map(e.Values, role);
    Session["currentObject"] = obj.Save();
    e.RowsAffected = 1;
  }
  catch (Csla.DataPortalException ex)
  {
    this.ErrorLabel.Text = ex.BusinessException.Message;
    e.RowsAffected = 0;
  }
  catch (Exception ex)
  {
    this.ErrorLabel.Text = ex.Message;
    e.RowsAffected = 0;
  }
}
```

This code retrieves the current Roles object and then calls its AddNew() method to add a new child Role object. Recall that in Chapter 17 the AddNewCore() method was implemented to enable easy adding of child objects to the collection. The public AddNew() method ultimately results in a call to AddNewCore(), which adds an empty child object to the collection.

This new child object is populated with data using the DataMapper object from the Csla.Data namespace:

```
Csla.Data.DataMapper.Map(e.Values, role);
```

All new values entered by the user are provided to the event handler through e.Values. The Map() method uses dynamic method invocation to copy those values to the corresponding properties on the object. Dynamic method invocation is only a little slower than directly setting the properties, but if you want to avoid that small bit of overhead, you can replace the use of DataMapper with code like this:

```
role.Id = Int32.Parse(e.Values["Id"].ToString());
role.Name = e.Values["Name"].ToString();
```

For this simple object, this code isn't too onerous, but for larger objects you could end up writing a lot of code to copy each value into the object's properties.

Either way, once the data from `e.Values` has been put into the object's properties, the object's `Save()` method is called to update the database.

■ **Note** This follows the typical web model of updating the database any time the user performs any action and results in a lot more database access than the equivalent WPF implementation from Chapter 19. You could defer the call to `Save()` by putting a Save button on the form and having the user click that button to commit all changes.

Once the `Save()` method is complete, the resulting (updated) `Roles` object is put into `Session`. This is very important because the result of `Save()` is a *new* `Roles` object, and that new object must be used in place of the previous one on subsequent pages. For instance, the newly added role data generates a new `timestamp` value in the database, which can only be found in this new `Roles` object.

This completes the insert operation, but the `MultiView` control is still set to display the `InsertView`. It needs to be reset to display `MainView`. That is done by handing the `ItemInserted` event from the `DetailsView` control:

```
protected void DetailsView1_ItemInserted(
  object sender, DetailsViewInsertedEventArgs e)
{
  MultiView1.ActiveViewIndex = (int)Views.MainView;
  this.GridView1.DataBind();
}
```

The `ActiveViewIndex` is changed so that the `MainView` is displayed when the page refreshes. Also, the `GridView` control in `MainView` is told to refresh its data by calling its `DataBind()` method.

Calling `DataBind()` causes the `GridView` to refresh its display so it shows the newly added `Role` object. Behind the scenes, this triggers a call to `RolesDataSource`, causing it to raise its `SelectObject` event.

Figure 20-13 also shows a Cancel link. If the user clicks that link, she likewise needs to be returned to `MainView`. When the user clicks Cancel, it triggers a `ModeChanged` event on the `DetailsView` control:

```
protected void DetailsView1_ModeChanged(
  object sender, EventArgs e)
{
  MultiView1.ActiveViewIndex = (int)Views.MainView;
}
```

So whether users click Insert or Cancel, they end up back at the main display of the list of roles.

Updating an Object

As shown in Figure 20-10, the `CommandField` column in the `GridView` control includes both Edit and Delete links for each row. I'll get to the Delete link shortly, but for now let's focus on the Edit link. When the user clicks the Edit link on a row, the `GridView` allows the user to edit that row's data, as shown in Figure 20-14.

The user can edit the Name column only. The Id column is set to read-only:

```
<asp:BoundField DataField="Id" HeaderText="Id"
  ReadOnly="True" SortExpression="Id" />
```

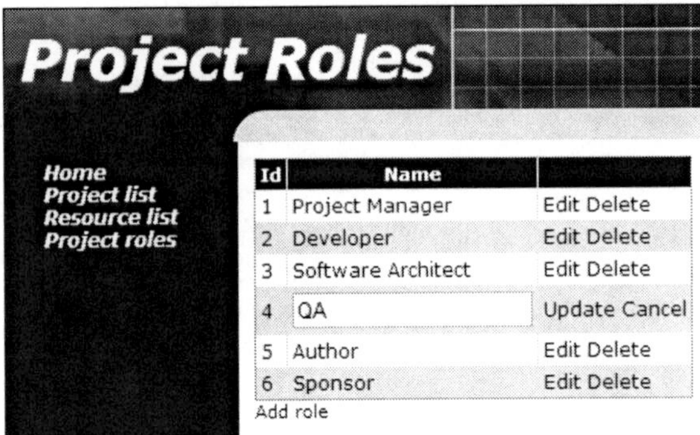

Figure 20-14. *The RolesEdit.aspx page when a role is being edited*

When done, users can either click the Update or Cancel links on the row. If they click Update, the `UpdateObject` event is raised by `RolesDataSource` to trigger the data update. This event is handled in the page:

```
protected void RolesDataSource_UpdateObject(
  object sender, Csla.Web.UpdateObjectArgs e)
{
  try
  {
    ProjectTracker.Library.Admin.Roles obj = GetRoles();
    ProjectTracker.Library.Admin.Role role =
      obj.GetRoleById(int.Parse(e.Keys["Id"].ToString()));
    role.Name = e.Values["Name"].ToString();
    Session["currentObject"] = obj.Save();
    e.RowsAffected = 1;
  }
  catch (Csla.DataPortalException ex)
  {
    this.ErrorLabel.Text = ex.BusinessException.Message;
    e.RowsAffected = 0;
  }
  catch (Exception ex)
  {
    this.ErrorLabel.Text = ex.Message;
    e.RowsAffected = 0;
  }
}
```

This code is quite similar to that for the insert operation discussed earlier, though in this case, the specific `Role` object that is edited is retrieved from the collection:

```
ProjectTracker.Library.Admin.Role role =
  obj.GetRoleById(int.Parse(e.Keys["Id"].ToString()));
```

`e.Keys` contains all the values from the page that correspond to the properties defined in the `GridView` control's `DataKeyNames` property. Recall that the only property set in `DataKeyNames` is `Id`, so that's the only value provided through `e.Keys`. This value is passed to the `GetRoleById()` method to retrieve the correct `Role` object.

■ **Note** Update and delete operations require that appropriate business object property names be specified in the GridView or DetailsView control's DataKeyNames property.

Since only one property can be edited, I opt to not use DataMapper and to set the property value manually. However, in a more complex edit scenario in which many properties are edited, you may choose to use DataMapper to simplify the code.

Finally, the Roles object's Save() method is called to commit the user's changes to the database. As with the insert process, the new Roles object returned from Save() is put into Session for use on all subsequent page requests.

Deleting an Object

Having seen how the update process works, you can probably guess how the delete process works. The user can click the Delete link next to a row in the GridView control. When they do so, RolesDataSource raises the DeleteObject event, which is handled in the page:

```
protected void RolesDataSource_DeleteObject(
  object sender, Csla.Web.DeleteObjectArgs e)
{
  try
  {
    ProjectTracker.Library.Admin.Roles obj = GetRoles();
    int id = (int)e.Keys["Id"];
    obj.Remove(id);
    Session["currentObject"] = obj.Save();
    e.RowsAffected = 1;
  }
  catch (Csla.DataPortalException ex)
  {
    this.ErrorLabel.Text = ex.BusinessException.Message;
    e.RowsAffected = 0;
  }
  catch (Exception ex)
  {
    this.ErrorLabel.Text = ex.Message;
    e.RowsAffected = 0;
  }
}
```

The Id value for the Role object to delete is retrieved from e.Keys and used to call the Remove() method on the Roles collection. Recall from Chapter 17 that this overload of Remove() accepts the Id value of the Role object.

Of course, the child object is merely marked for deletion and isn't removed until the Save() method is called on the Roles object itself. Again, the resulting Roles object returned from Save() is put into Session for use on subsequent page requests.

At this point, you should understand the basic process for creating a grid-based data form that supports viewing, inserting, editing, and deleting data. The only thing left to do in RolesEdit is to add support for authorization.

Authorization

The RolesEdit authorization code is perhaps the simplest in the application. If the user isn't authorized to edit the Roles object, the CommandField column in the GridView control shouldn't be shown; and if the user can't add a new role, the LinkButton for adding a new object shouldn't be shown.

When the page is loaded, an ApplyAuthorizationRules() method is called:

```
protected void Page_Load(object sender, EventArgs e)
{
  if (!IsPostBack)
    Session["currentObject"] = null;
    ApplyAuthorizationRules();
  else
    this.ErrorLabel.Text = "";
}

private void ApplyAuthorizationRules()
{
  bool canEdit =
    Csla.Security.AuthorizationRules.CanEditObject(
    typeof(ProjectTracker.Library.Admin.Roles));
  this.GridView1.Columns[
    this.GridView1.Columns.Count - 1].Visible = canEdit;
  this.AddRoleButton.Visible = canEdit;
}
```

The ApplyAuthorizationRules() method asks the CSLA .NET authorization subsystem whether the current user is authorized to edit an object of type Roles. If the user isn't authorized, the appropriate controls' Visible properties are set to false and the controls are thereby hidden.

Since the user is then unable to put the GridView control into edit mode or ask it to delete an item, the display effectively becomes read-only. Similarly, without the LinkButton for adding a new item, the user can't switch the MultiView to InsertView; so again the page becomes a simple read-only page.

As you can see, creating a simple grid-based edit page requires relatively little work. You add a data control, bind the GridView and possibly a DetailsView control to the data, and write a bit of code. Most of the code in this page exists to react to user actions as they indicate that data is to be inserted, edited, or deleted.

ProjectList Form

The ProjectList web form is responsible for displaying the list of projects to the user and allowing the user to choose a specific project to view or edit. From this page, the user can also delete a project and choose to add a new project. Figure 20-15 shows the layout of ProjectList.

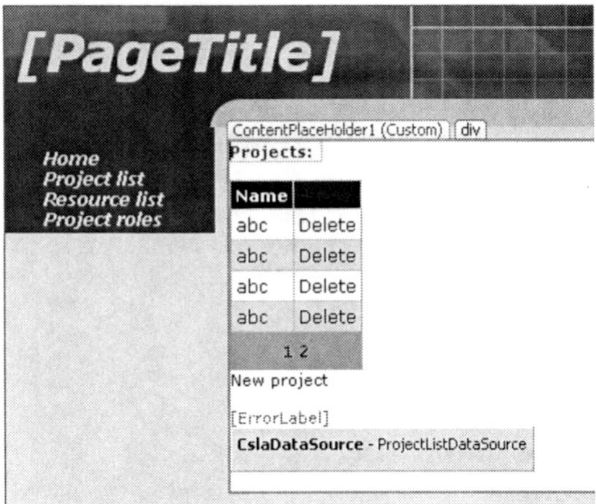

Figure 20-15. *Layout of ProjectList*

It is important to realize that the `GridView` control actually has three columns: `Id`, `Name`, and the `CommandField` column with the Delete links:

```
<Columns>
  <asp:BoundField DataField="Id" HeaderText="Id"
    SortExpression="Id" Visible="False" />
  <asp:HyperLinkField DataNavigateUrlFields="Id"
    DataNavigateUrlFormatString="ProjectEdit.aspx?id={0}"
    DataTextField="Name" HeaderText="Name" />
  <asp:CommandField ShowDeleteButton="True"
    SelectText="Edit" />
</Columns>
```

The `Id` column has its `Visible` property set to `False`, so it is there but invisible. Also notice that the `Name` column is a `HyperLinkField` not a simple `BoundField`. This makes each project name appear to the user as a hyperlink, though in reality it is more like a `LinkButton`—when the user clicks a project name, a `SelectedIndexChanged` event is raised from the `GridView` control.

Also of importance is the fact that the `GridView` control's `DataKeyNames` property is set to `Id`, so the `Id` property is specified as the unique identifier for each row of data:

```
<asp:GridView ID="GridView1" runat="server"
  AllowPaging="True" AutoGenerateColumns="False"
  DataSourceID="ProjectListDataSource" PageSize="4"
  OnRowDeleted="GridView1_RowDeleted"
  DataKeyNames="Id">
```

Without setting this property, the Delete link can't work.

The view, edit, and add operations are all handled by `ProjectEdit`, so `ProjectList` is really just responsible for redirecting the user to that other page as appropriate. The delete operation is handled directly from `ProjectList` through a `CommandField` column in the `GridView` control.

Notice that the `GridView` control displays paging links near the bottom. This is because paging is enabled for the control, as shown in Figure 20-16.

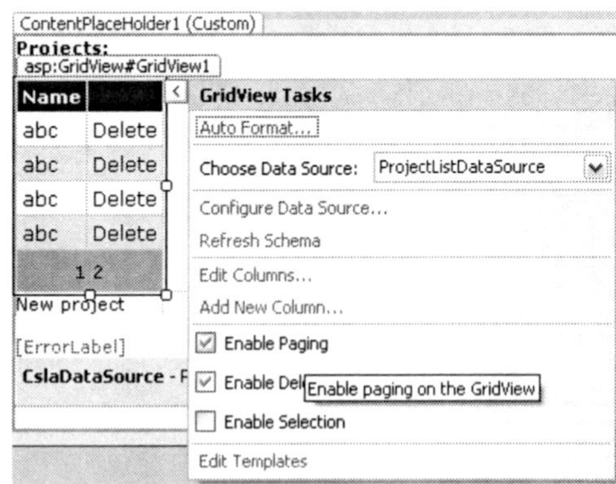

Figure 20-16. *Enabling paging for the GridView control*

You can also set the `GridView` control's `PageSize` property to control how many items are shown on each page. All the paging work is done by the `GridView` control itself, which is fine because the `ProjectList` business object is maintained in `Session`, so the user can move from page to page without hitting the database each time.

Figure 20-17 shows the properties of the `CslaDataSource` control used on the page.

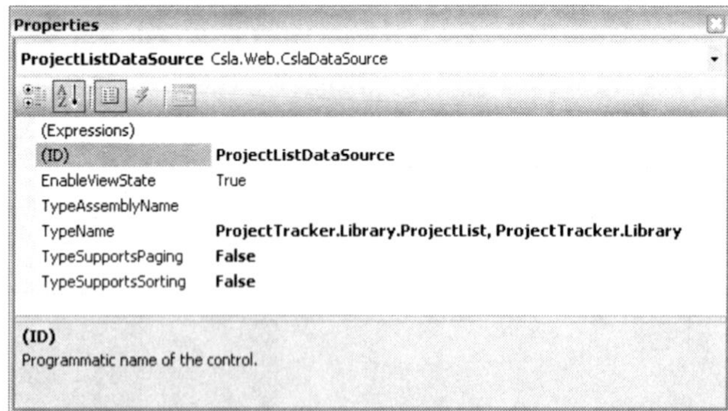

Figure 20-17. *Properties for the ProjectListDataSource control*

Like the `RolesDataSource` control in `RolesEdit`, the `TypeName` property is set to point to the appropriate class within `ProjectTracker.Library`. This data source control will be used to retrieve the list of projects and to delete a project if the user clicks a Delete link.

Since the `ProjectList` business object doesn't directly support paging or sorting, the `TypeSupportsPaging` and `TypeSupportsSorting` properties are left with `False` values. Paging and sorting are still possible but are handled by the `GridView` control itself, rather than by the business object. If the business object supports these concepts, the properties can be set to `True` and ASP.NET will automatically defer any paging or sorting to the business object.

Loading the Data

When the GridView control needs data, it asks the ProjectListDataSource for it. The data source control in turn raises its SelectObject event, which is handled in the page:

```
protected void ProjectListDataSource_SelectObject(
  object sender, Csla.Web.SelectObjectArgs e)
{
  e.BusinessObject = GetProjectList();
}
```

As in RolesEdit, this page caches the business object in Session. The details of that process are handled by GetProjectList():

```
private ProjectTracker.Library.ProjectList GetProjectList()
{
  object businessObject = Session["currentObject"];
  if (businessObject == null ||
    !(businessObject is ProjectTracker.Library.ProjectList))
  {
    businessObject =
      ProjectTracker.Library.ProjectList.GetProjectList();
    Session["currentObject"] = businessObject;
  }
  return (ProjectTracker.Library.ProjectList)businessObject;
}
```

This method is the same as the GetRoles() method discussed earlier except that it ensures that a valid ProjectList object is returned instead of a Roles object.

This code allows the GridView control to populate itself with pages of data for display as needed.

Viewing or Editing a Project

The Name column in the GridView control is set up as a HyperLinkField, meaning that the user sees the values as a set of hyperlinks. If the user clicks one of the project names, the browser directly navigates to the ProjectEdit.aspx page, passing the selected Id value as a parameter on the URL.

Adding a Project

The ProjectList page contains a LinkButton to allow the user to add a new project. If the user clicks this button, a Click event is raised:

```
protected void NewProjectButton_Click(object sender, EventArgs e)
{
  // allow user to add a new project
  Response.Redirect("ProjectEdit.aspx");
}
```

The ProjectEdit page takes care of viewing, editing, and adding Project objects, so all this code does is redirect the user to ProjectEdit. Notice that no parameter is provided to the page on the URL and this is what tells ProjectEdit to create a new Project rather than to view or edit an existing one.

Deleting a Project

The GridView control has a CommandField column, which automatically creates a Delete link for each row of data. If the user clicks a Delete link, the GridView deletes that row of data by calling its data source control, ProjectListDataSource. The result is a DeleteObject event handled in the page:

```
protected void ProjectListDataSource_DeleteObject(
  object sender, Csla.Web.DeleteObjectArgs e)
{
  try
  {
    ProjectTracker.Library.Project.DeleteProject(
      new Guid(e.Keys["Id"].ToString()));
    e.RowsAffected = 1;
  }
  catch (Csla.DataPortalException ex)
  {
    this.ErrorLabel.Text = ex.BusinessException.Message;
    e.RowsAffected = 0;
  }
  catch (Exception ex)
  {
    this.ErrorLabel.Text = ex.Message;
    e.RowsAffected = 0;
  }
}
```

Again, the DataKeyNames property being set in the GridView means that the Id column value from the row automatically flows into this event handler through e.Keys. The Project object uses a Guid value for its Id property value, and its factory methods accept a Guid value to identify the object. The Id column value is a string in the web page, so it is converted to a Guid object so that the static DeleteProject() method on the Project class can be called. The result is immediate deletion of the related project data.

Authorization

Having discussed all the core business functionality of the page, let's look at the authorization code. Like in RolesEdit, the authorization rules themselves are in the business class, and the UI code simply uses that information to enable and disable various UI controls as the page loads:

```
protected void Page_Load(object sender, EventArgs e)
{
  if (!IsPostBack)
    Session["currentObject"] = null;
    ApplyAuthorizationRules();
  else
    ErrorLabel.Text = string.Empty;
}

private void ApplyAuthorizationRules()
{
  this.GridView1.Columns[
    this.GridView1.Columns.Count - 1].Visible =
    Csla.Security.AuthorizationRules.CanDeleteObject(typeof(Project));
  NewProjectButton.Visible =
    Csla.Security.AuthorizationRules.CanCreateObject(typeof(Project));
}
```

When the page is loaded, the ApplyAuthorizationRules() method makes sure that the CommandField column in the GridView is only visible if the user is authorized to delete Project objects. It also hides the NewProjectButton control if the user isn't allowed to add Project objects.

The end result is that users who can't delete or add data are still allowed to view the list of projects, and they can even click a project's name to get more details in the ProjectEdit page.

ProjectEdit Form

At this point, you've seen how to create two different types of grid-based web forms. The pages so far have illustrated in-place editing, adding of new items, and displaying a list of items for selection or deletion. The final web form I discuss in this chapter is ProjectEdit, which is a detail form that allows the user to view and edit details about a specific object.

Like RolesEdit, this form uses a MultiView control. Figure 20-18 shows the MainView layout, and Figure 20-19 shows the AssignView layout. There's also a Label control and some CslaDataSource controls on the page itself, below the MultiView. These are shown in Figure 20-20.

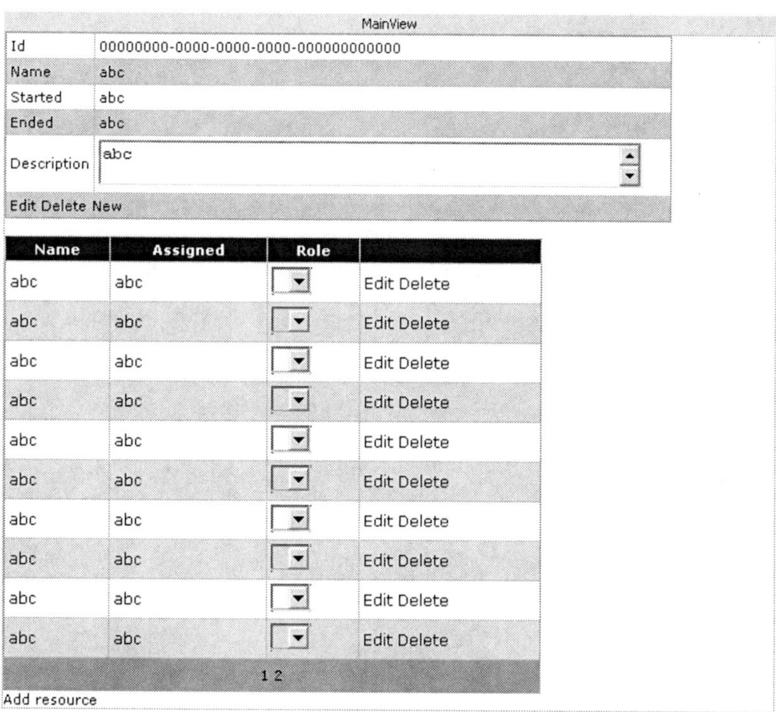

Figure 20-18. *Layout of MainView in ProjectEdit*

MainView includes a DetailsView control to allow display and editing of the Project object's properties. This control is data bound to the ProjectDataSource control shown in Figure 20-20, and so it is effectively data bound to the current Project object.

The Id row is set to read-only because the Project object's Id property is a read-only property. The Description row is a TemplateField, which allows the use of a TextBox control with its TextMode property set to MultiLine:

```
<asp:TemplateField HeaderText="Description"
  SortExpression="Description">
  <EditItemTemplate>
    <asp:TextBox ID="TextBox1" TextMode="MultiLine"
      Width="100%" runat="server"
      Text='<%# Bind("Description") %>'></asp:TextBox>
  </EditItemTemplate>
  <InsertItemTemplate>
    <asp:TextBox ID="TextBox1" TextMode="MultiLine"
      Width="100%" runat="server"
      Text='<%# Bind("Description") %>'></asp:TextBox>
  </InsertItemTemplate>
  <ItemTemplate>
    <asp:TextBox ID="TextBox1" TextMode="MultiLine"
      ReadOnly="true" Width="100%" runat="server"
      Text='<%# Bind("Description") %>'></asp:TextBox>
  </ItemTemplate>
</asp:TemplateField>
```

Notice that even the ItemTemplate, which controls what is displayed in view mode, uses a TextBox control, but with its ReadOnly property set to true. This allows the user to see the entire text of the Description property, even if it is quite long.

Finally, the DetailsView control has a CommandField row that allows the user to delete, edit, and add a Project.

Beneath the DetailsView control is a GridView to list the resources assigned to the project. This control is data bound to the ResourcesDataSource control shown in Figure 20-20. It is effectively data bound to the Resources property of the current Project object, meaning that it is bound to a collection of ProjectResource objects. Remember that each type of business object must have its own CslaDataSource control in order to act as a data source.

The GridView control also has a ResourceId column, which is not visible. Its DataKeyNames property is set to ResourceId, specifying that the ResourceId column contains the unique identifying value for each row. The Name and Assigned columns are read-only, while the Role column is a TemplateField:

```
<asp:TemplateField HeaderText="Role" SortExpression="Role">
  <EditItemTemplate>
    <asp:DropDownList ID="DropDownList1" runat="server"
      DataSourceID="RoleListDataSource"
      DataTextField="Value" DataValueField="Key"
      SelectedValue='<%# Bind("Role") %>'>
    </asp:DropDownList>
  </EditItemTemplate>
  <ItemTemplate>
    <asp:DropDownList ID="DropDownList2" runat="server"
      DataSourceID="RoleListDataSource"
      DataTextField="Value" DataValueField="Key"
      Enabled="False" SelectedValue='<%# Bind("Role") %>'>
    </asp:DropDownList>
  </ItemTemplate>
</asp:TemplateField>
```

Notice how the DropDownList controls are data bound to the RoleListDataSource control shown in Figure 20-20. This data source control provides access to a RoleList business object, so the DropDownList controls are populated with the list of roles a resource can play on a project. This way, ASP.NET does all the hard work of mapping the Key values for each role to the corresponding human-readable text value. The numeric Key values are stored in the business objects, while the text values are displayed on the page.

The GridView control also has a CommandField column so the user can edit or remove assignments. Of course, "remove" in this case really means unassign, but those details are handled by the business object, not the UI.

Finally, there's a LinkButton to allow the user to assign a new resource to the project. When users click that button, the view is switched so that they see AssignView, where they can select the resource to assign. The layout of that view is shown in Figure 20-19.

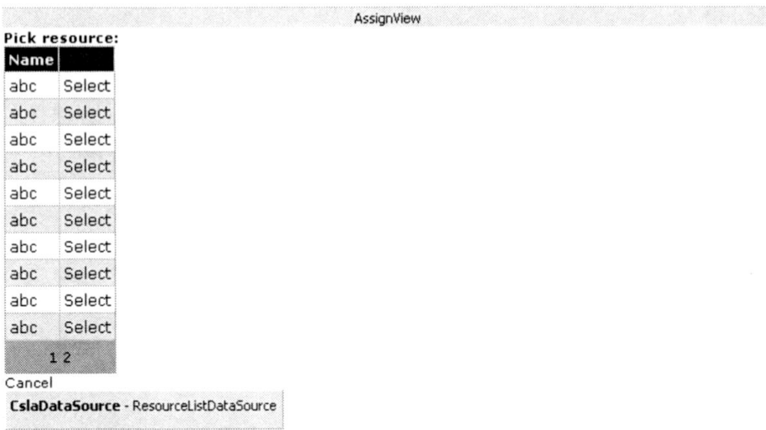

Figure 20-19. *Layout of AssignView in ProjectEdit*

AssignView is comparatively straightforward. It contains a GridView control that is data bound to the ResourceListDataSource control. Effectively, this means the GridView is bound to a ResourceList business object, so it displays the list of resources to the user. The CommandField column in the GridView provides a Select link, so the user can select the resource to be assigned.

There's also a LinkButton at the bottom to allow the user to cancel the operation and return to MainView without assigning a resource at all.

Finally, Figure 20-20 shows the bottom of the page, beneath the MultiView control.

Figure 20-20. *Other controls in ProjectEdit*

The CslaDataSource controls are used by the various DetailsView and GridView controls discussed previously. And, of course, the ErrorLabel control is a simple Label control that has its ForeColor property set to Red. The exception-handling code in the form uses this control to display details about any exceptions to the user.

Working, in the top left corner of Figure 20-20, comes from an UpdateProgress control, to go along with the UpdatePanel control that wraps the entire MultiView control to provide AJAX support to the page.

Now let's go through the implementation of the page. I'll do this a bit differently than with the previous pages because by now you should understand how the pieces fit together using data binding.

Caching the Project Object in Session

The RolesEdit and ProjectList forms implement methods to retrieve the central business object from Session or to retrieve it from the database as necessary. This not only implements a type of cache to reduce load on the database but it provides support for the browser's Back button as well. The same thing is done in ProjectEdit:

```
private Project GetProject()
{
  object businessObject = Session["currentObject"];
  if (businessObject == null ||
    !(businessObject is Project))
  {
    try
    {
      string idString = Request.QueryString["id"];
      if (!string.IsNullOrEmpty(idString))
      {
        Guid id = new Guid(idString);
        businessObject = Project.GetProject(id);
      }
      else
        businessObject = Project.NewProject();
      Session["currentObject"] = businessObject;
    }
    catch (System.Security.SecurityException)
    {
      Response.Redirect("ProjectList.aspx");
    }
  }
  return (Project)businessObject;
}
```

As before, if there's no object in Session, or if the object isn't a Project, a Project is retrieved from the database. But the code here is a bit more complex than that in the other forms.

Notice that the Request.QueryString property is used to get the id value (if any) passed in on the page's URL. If an id value is passed into the page, that value is used to retrieve an existing Project:

```
Guid id = new Guid(idString);
businessObject = Project.GetProject(id);
```

Otherwise, a new Project is created for the page:

```
businessObject = Project.NewProject();
```

Either way, the resulting object is placed into Session and is also returned as a result from the method.

It is possible for a user to navigate directly to ProjectEdit.aspx, providing no id value on the URL. In such a case, the user might not be authorized to add a Project, and so a SecurityException would result. In that case, users are simply redirected to the ProjectList page, where they can safely view the list of projects.

Creating a New Object

If users navigate to this page with no id value and they are authorized to add a new Project, they'd expect to see default values on the screen. Due to the way Web Forms works, this is harder than you might think.

It turns out that the DetailsView control, when in insert mode, doesn't ask its underlying data source control for any information. The assumption is that the user will enter all new values into an empty form. No provision is made to automatically load default values into the DetailsView control for a new object.

To overcome this, your page can handle the DetailsView control's ItemCreated event, where you can set default values. This is pretty ugly code because you need to manually index into the DetailsView control to find the detail controls it contains, so you can set their values:

```
protected void DetailsView1_ItemCreated(
  object sender, EventArgs e)
{
  if (DetailsView1.DefaultMode == DetailsViewMode.Insert)
  {
    Project obj = GetProject();
    ((TextBox)DetailsView1.Rows[1].Cells[1].Controls[0]).Text =
      obj.Name;
    ((TextBox)DetailsView1.Rows[2].Cells[1].Controls[0]).Text =
      obj.Started;
    ((TextBox)DetailsView1.Rows[3].Cells[1].Controls[0]).Text =
      obj.Ended;
    ((TextBox)DetailsView1.FindControl("TextBox1")).Text =
      obj.Description;
  }
}
```

This means that you must fully understand the row and column that contains each of the constituent controls, and you must know the type of each control. While this is not ideal, it is the solution for setting default values.

Notice how the GetProject() method is called first, so the code has access to a newly created Project object that automatically contains any required default values. The property values from that object are then used to set the control values in the web form.

This is not an issue when editing an existing object because the DetailsView control automatically invokes the data source control to retrieve an existing object.

Saving a Project

In this form, the Project object is saved in many scenarios, including the following:

- Inserting the project
- Editing the project
- Assigning a resource
- Unassigning a resource
- Deleting the project

To simplify the code overall, the `SaveProject()` method handles the common behaviors in all these cases:

```
private int SaveProject(Project project)
{
  int rowsAffected;
  try
  {
    Session["currentObject"] = project.Save();
    rowsAffected = 1;
  }
  catch (Csla.Validation.ValidationException ex)
  {
    System.Text.StringBuilder message = new System.Text.StringBuilder();
    message.AppendFormat("{0}", ex.Message);
    if (project.BrokenRulesCollection.Count > 0)
    {
      message.Append("<ul>");
      foreach (Csla.Validation.BrokenRule rule in project.BrokenRulesCollection)
        message.AppendFormat("<li>{0}: {1}</li>", rule.Property,
                             rule.Description);
      message.Append("</ul>");
    }
    this.ErrorLabel.Text = message.ToString();
    rowsAffected = 0;
  }
  catch (Csla.DataPortalException ex)
  {
    this.ErrorLabel.Text = ex.BusinessException.Message;
    rowsAffected = 0;
  }
  catch (Exception ex)
  {
    this.ErrorLabel.Text = ex.Message;
    rowsAffected = 0;
  }
  return rowsAffected;
}
```

This method accepts the `Project` as a parameter and calls its `Save()` method. As always, the resulting object is placed in `Session` to replace the old version of the object. In case of exception, the `ErrorLabel` text is updated.

The code here is the same as in the other pages but it is worth consolidating in this page (and in `ResourceEdit`) because of the many places the `Project` object is saved.

ProjectDataSource

The `ProjectDataSource` control takes care of data binding that deals with the `Project` object itself. The page handles its `DeleteObject`, `InsertObject`, `SelectObject`, and `UpdateObject` events. For instance, the `SelectObject` handler looks like this:

```
protected void ProjectDataSource_SelectObject(
  object sender, Csla.Web.SelectObjectArgs e)
{
  e.BusinessObject = GetProject();
}
```

Thanks to the GetProject() method discussed earlier, this method is very simple to implement. The delete, insert, and update events are also comparatively simple due to the SaveProject() method. For instance, here's the InsertObject event handler:

```
protected void ProjectDataSource_InsertObject(
  object sender, Csla.Web.InsertObjectArgs e)
{
  Project obj = GetProject();
  Csla.Data.DataMapper.Map(e.Values, obj, "Id");
  e.RowsAffected = SaveProject(obj);
}
```

The current Project object is retrieved from Session (or pulled from the database) and the new values entered by the user are mapped into the object's properties using the DataMapper from the Csla.Data namespace.

The Map() method requires two parameters. The first is the source object and the second is the target object. Any other parameters are the names of properties that should not be copied. So this code copies all the property values except the Id property. This is important because the Id property is read-only in the target object and an exception would result if the Map() method tried to copy the value.

Once the values are copied, the SaveProject() method is called to save the project and update Session with the newly updated data.

Once a new object is inserted, the user's display should be refreshed so it switches into edit mode. To do this, the page handles the DetailsView control's ItemInserted event:

```
protected void DetailsView1_ItemInserted(
  object sender, DetailsViewInsertedEventArgs e)
{
  Project project = GetProject();
  if (!project.IsNew)
    Response.Redirect("ProjectEdit.aspx?id=" + project.Id.ToString());
}
```

If the insert operation succeeds, the object's IsNew property is false and the user is redirected to the ProjectEdit web form, passing the newly created Id property as a parameter in the URL. This not only ensures that the page switches into edit mode (as opposed to insert mode) but the URL in the browser is also updated to reflect the object's Id value.

The update operation works in a similar manner, so I won't detail it here. The one thing I do want to point out is that once an update is complete, the authorization rules are rechecked:

```
protected void DetailsView1_ItemUpdated(
  object sender, DetailsViewUpdatedEventArgs e)
{
  ApplyAuthorizationRules();
}
```

This ensures that the UI properly responds to any changes in authorization rules based on the object's state. Some objects may have different authorization rules for a new or existing object.

DeleteObject is a bit different:

```
protected void ProjectDataSource_DeleteObject(
  object sender, Csla.Web.DeleteObjectArgs e)
{
  try
  {
    Project.DeleteProject(new Guid(e.Keys["id"].ToString()));
    Session["currentObject"] = null;
    e.RowsAffected = 1;
  }
  catch (Csla.DataPortalException ex)
  {
    this.ErrorLabel.Text = ex.BusinessException.Message;
    e.RowsAffected = 0;
  }
  catch (Exception ex)
  {
    this.ErrorLabel.Text = ex.Message;
    e.RowsAffected = 0;
  }
}
```

If the user clicks the link in the DetailsView control to delete the project, the DeleteObject event is raised. e.Keys contains the Id row value from the DetailsView because the DataKeyNames property on the control is set to Id. This value is used to create a Guid, which is then passed to the static DeleteProject() method to delete the project. Of course, this immediately deletes the Project using the data portal, and so proper exception handling is implemented to display any exception messages in ErrorLabel.

Once the Project has been deleted, it makes no sense to leave the user on ProjectEdit. If the delete operation is successful, the DetailsView control raises an ItemDeleted event:

```
protected void DetailsView1_ItemDeleted(
  object sender, DetailsViewDeletedEventArgs e)
{
  Response.Redirect("ProjectList.aspx");
}
```

The user is simply redirected to the ProjectList page, where he should no longer see the deleted project in the list. That is because the ProjectList page retrieves a new ProjectList business object each time the page is loaded.

ResourcesDataSource

The ResourcesDataSource control takes care of data binding dealing with the Resources collection from the Project object. The GridView control in MainView is bound to this control, and the page handles its DeleteObject, SelectObject, and UpdateObject events.

There's no need to handle the InsertObject event because the GridView isn't used to dynamically add ProjectResource objects to the collection. I discuss adding a new child object shortly.

The SelectObject event handler returns the collection of ProjectResource objects for the Project:

```
protected void ResourcesDataSource_SelectObject(
  object sender, Csla.Web.SelectObjectArgs e)
{
  Project obj = GetProject();
  e.BusinessObject = obj.Resources;
}
```

It first gets the current Project object by calling GetProject(). Then it simply provides the Resources collection to the data source control, which in turn provides it to any UI controls requiring the data.

The DeleteObject and UpdateObject event handlers are worth exploring a bit. The DeleteObject handler gets the ResourceId value from the GridView control through e.Keys and uses that value to remove the ProjectResource object from the collection:

```
protected void ResourcesDataSource_DeleteObject(
  object sender, Csla.Web.DeleteObjectArgs e)
{
  Project obj = GetProject();
  int rid = int.Parse(e.Keys["ResourceId"].ToString());
  obj.Resources.Remove(rid);
  e.RowsAffected = SaveProject(obj);
}
```

The current Project object is retrieved, and then the Remove() method is called on the Resources collection to remove the specified child object. SaveProject() is then called to commit the change.

UpdateObject is a bit more complex:

```
protected void ResourcesDataSource_UpdateObject(
  object sender, Csla.Web.UpdateObjectArgs e)
{
  Project obj = GetProject();
  int rid = int.Parse(e.Keys["ResourceId"].ToString());
  ProjectResource res =
    obj.Resources.GetItem(rid);
  Csla.Data.DataMapper.Map(e.Values, res);
  e.RowsAffected = SaveProject(obj);
}
```

In this case, the actual child object is retrieved from the Resources collection. Then the values entered into the GridView by the user are pulled from e.Values and are mapped into the child object using DataMapper. And finally, SaveProject() is called to commit the changes.

The GridView isn't used to insert new ProjectResource child objects, so ResourcesDataSource will never raise its InsertObject method. Users are allowed to assign a new user to the project by clicking a LinkButton control. In that case, the MultiView is changed to display AssignView so the user can select the resource to be assigned:

```
protected void AddResourceButton_Click(
  object sender, EventArgs e)
{
  this.MultiView1.ActiveViewIndex =
    (int)Views.AssignView;
}
```

Once AssignView is displayed, users can either select a resource or click the Cancel button. If they select a resource, the resource is assigned to the project:

```
protected void GridView2_SelectedIndexChanged(
  object sender, EventArgs e)
{
  Project obj = GetProject();
  try
  {
    obj.Resources.Assign(int.Parse(
      this.GridView2.SelectedDataKey.Value.ToString()));
    if (SaveProject(obj) > 0)
    {
      this.GridView1.DataBind();
      this.MultiView1.ActiveViewIndex = (int)Views.MainView;
    }
  }
  catch (InvalidOperationException ex)
  {
    ErrorLabel.Text = ex.Message;
  }
}
```

To make the assignment, the current Project object is retrieved. Then the Resources collection's Assign() method is called, passing the SelectedDataKey value from the GridView control as a parameter. This GridView control, which displays the list of resources, has its DataKeyNames property set to Id, so SelectedDataKey returns the Id value of the selected resource.

Once the assignment is made, SaveProject() is called to commit the change. If SaveProject() succeeds, it will return a value greater than 0. And in that case, the GridView control in MainView, which displays the list of assigned resources, is told to refresh its data by calling DataBind(). Remember that ASP.NET tries to optimize data access, and so GridView and DetailsView controls don't refresh their data from the data source on every postback. You need to explicitly call DataBind() to force this refresh to occur.

Several things could go wrong during this whole process. The resource might already be assigned or the SaveProject() method could fail due to some data error. Of course, SaveProject() already does its own exception handling and displays any exception messages to the user through the ErrorLabel control.

But if the user attempts to assign a duplicate resource to the project, the Assign() method will raise an InvalidOperationException. This is caught and the message text is displayed to the user. Notice that in that case, users are *not* sent back to MainView but remains on AssignView so that they can choose a different resource to assign if desired.

The simplest course of action occurs if the user clicks the Cancel LinkButton control:

```
protected void CancelAssignButton_Click(
  object sender, EventArgs e)
{
  this.MultiView1.ActiveViewIndex =
    (int)Views.MainView;
}
```

In that case, the user is simply directed back to the MainView display.

RoleListDataSource

The RoleListDataSource is used by the GridView control in MainView. It provides access to the list of roles a resource can play on a project. This data isn't cached in the UI because the RoleList object handles caching automatically (see Chapter 18 for details). Also, because RoleList is read-only, the only event that needs to be handled is SelectObject:

```
protected void RoleListDataSource_SelectObject(
  object sender, Csla.Web.SelectObjectArgs e)
{
  e.BusinessObject = RoleList.GetList();
}
```

The GetList() method returns the list of roles, either from the cache or the database. The beauty of this approach is that the UI code doesn't know or care whether the database was used to get the data; it just uses the result.

■ **Note** Because the RoleList object is cached in a static field, the cached object is shared by all users of the website. A static field is global to the AppDomain, and so is effectively global to the entire website. In this case, that's a good thing because it means the RoleList object is retrieved once for all users, but it is a detail you should keep in mind when working with data that should be per-user instead of shared.

ResourceListDataSource

The ResourceListDataSource is used by the GridView control in AssignView to display a list of resources in the database. It is bound to the ResourceList business object, which is read-only—meaning that only the SelectObject event needs to be handled:

```
protected void ResourceListDataSource_SelectObject(
  object sender, Csla.Web.SelectObjectArgs e)
{
  e.BusinessObject =
    ProjectTracker.Library.ResourceList.GetResourceList();
}
```

I'm making no special effort to cache the results of GetResourceList(), nor does that method do caching on its own. This is intentional.

Users will most likely come to ProjectEdit to view a project's details. A relatively small percentage of the time will they opt to assign a new resource to a project—so I made a conscious decision here to keep my code simple and just get the list each time it is needed.

If it turns out later that users are assigning far more resources than anticipated and that retrieving ResourceList is a performance bottleneck, the implementation can be changed to do some caching—in the UI, or in ResourceList itself.

Either way, I tend to default to implementing simpler code and only make it more complex when application usage patterns prove that some other solution is required.

Authorization

At this point, you've seen almost all the code in ProjectEdit. The rest of the code primarily deals with authorization, though there's a bit of UI magic as well.

When the page loads, an ApplyAuthorizationRules() method is called:

```
protected void Page_Load(object sender, EventArgs e)
{
  if (!Page.IsPostBack)
  {
    Session["currentObject"] = null;
    ApplyAuthorizationRules();
  }
```

```
    else
    {
      this.ErrorLabel.Text = string.Empty;
    }
  }

  private void ApplyAuthorizationRules()
  {
    Project obj = GetProject();
    // project display
    if (Csla.Security.AuthorizationRules.CanEditObject(typeof(Project)))
    {
      if (obj.IsNew)
        this.DetailsView1.DefaultMode = DetailsViewMode.Insert;
      else
        this.DetailsView1.DefaultMode = DetailsViewMode.Edit;
      this.AddResourceButton.Visible = !obj.IsNew;
    }
    else
    {
      this.DetailsView1.DefaultMode = DetailsViewMode.ReadOnly;
      this.AddResourceButton.Visible = false;
    }
    this.DetailsView1.Rows[
      this.DetailsView1.Rows.Count - 1].Visible =
      Csla.Security.AuthorizationRules.CanEditObject(typeof(Project));

    // resource display
    this.GridView1.Columns[
      this.GridView1.Columns.Count - 1].Visible =
      Csla.Security.AuthorizationRules.CanEditObject(typeof(Project));
  }
```

As with the previous forms, various controls, `GridView` columns, and `DetailsView` rows are made visible or invisible depending on the authorization values returned from the business objects.

Additionally, the mode of the `DetailsView` control is set based on the business object's `IsNew` property:

```
if (obj.IsNew)
  this.DetailsView1.DefaultMode = DetailsViewMode.Insert;
else
  this.DetailsView1.DefaultMode = DetailsViewMode.Edit;
```

This ensures that users get the right set of options in the `CommandField` row of the `DetailsView` control based on whether they are adding or editing the object.

As noted earlier in this chapter, the `ResourceEdit` and `ResourceList` forms are very comparable to `ProjectEdit` and `ProjectList`, so I won't cover them in this chapter. You can look at their code in the download for this book at `www.apress.com/book/view/1430210192` or `www.lhotka.net/cslanet/download.aspx`. This completes the `PTWeb` UI, so you should now have a good understanding of how to create both WPF and Web Forms interfaces based on business objects.

Conclusion

This chapter discussed the creation of a basic Web Forms UI based on the business objects in Chapters 17 and 18. As with the WPF technology in Chapter 19, there are many ways to create a Web Forms interface, and the one I've created here is just one of them.

The key is that the business objects automatically enforce all business rules and provide business processing so that the UI doesn't need to include any of that code. As you can see, it is very possible to create two very different user interfaces based on exactly the same set of business objects, data access code, and database design.

As shown here, the website is configured for optimal performance, running the `Session` and the data portal in the same process as the web forms. You could increase scalability and fault tolerance by moving `Session` into its own process or onto a state server. You could potentially increase security by running the data portal server components on a separate application server. In either case, all you need to do is change some settings in `Web.config`; the UI code and business objects will work in all these scenarios.

In Chapter 21, I wrap up the book by showing how you can create another type of interface to the business objects by using WCF.

CHAPTER 21

WCF Service Interface

Like the WPF technology discussed in Chapter 19, WCF is one of the pillars of the Microsoft .NET platform starting in version 3.0. WCF provides a unified approach to building service-oriented, client/server, messaging, and other distributed types of application. It effectively replaces or abstracts several older technologies:

- Web Services (`asmx` services)
- Remoting
- Enterprise Services
- MSMQ
- WSE

In Chapter 15, I discussed how the CSLA .NET data portal uses WCF to implement a powerful client/server model based on the mobile object concept. You can use XML services to build either client/server or service-oriented applications. My recommendation is that, when building an application interface using services, you follow a message-based, service-oriented architecture. This will result in looser coupling between your services and the applications that consume them, which in turn will increase the maintainability of your overall system and all the applications that interact using your services.

In this chapter, I'll provide a short overview of WCF as used to build XML services. Then I'll discuss the creation of a WCF service interface for the `ProjectTracker` business objects in order to illustrate how business objects can support the creation of XML services. First, however, we need to discuss the difference between the client/server and SOA models.

Choosing Between Client/Server and SOA

Terminology is important in any meaningful discussion about SOA. Table 21-1 defines the terms I'll be using in this chapter.

Table 21-1. *Important Service-Oriented Terms*

Term	Definition
Application	A set of behaviors implemented within a logical trust boundary. This term includes traditional single-, 2-, and n-tier applications, as well as applications that consume services, and applications that provide a service interface.
Edge application	An application that provides a user interface and consumes services from other applications. It sits on the "edge" of the system.
Logical trust boundary	A boundary describing both security and semantic trust. Data or messages crossing this boundary are going to or coming from code that is not trusted, either due to security or because you don't know if that code follows your semantic rules.
XML service (or just *service*)	An application that implements its interface layer in the form of XML messages that are received from, or returned to, a consuming application.
Consuming application	An application that interacts with one or more other applications using XML messages.
System	A group of two or more applications that interact with each other using XML messages.

In short, this means that an application is a self-contained entity. It might be a WPF application, a web application, or a service. Each application might be deployed using a single-, 2-, or n-tier physical model, and each application *should* be implemented using an n-layer logical model, as described in Chapter 1.

This also means that services are used for communication *between* applications, not inside them. Service communication is used to cross a trust boundary from one application to another application.

When you start connecting different applications to each other using services, you are creating a *system*. None of these applications should trust each other; each one has its own trust boundary. However, they can interact with each other by passing messages, resulting in a loosely coupled environment where (within reason) each application can be independently versioned and maintained without breaking the overall system.

The reality is that few organizations are building XML services or Web Services in a service-oriented manner. The vast majority of XML services are built using an n-tier client/server mindset.

There's nothing wrong with using XML services to build client/server applications. (I obviously think client/server is valuable; look at the data portal.) However, it is important to realize the strong difference between n-tier and SOA, so you can consciously choose which architecture you want to pursue.

In Chapter 15, I demonstrated one way to use WCF to implement client/server, so this chapter will focus on a message-based, service-oriented implementation. In this context, your application is either a service provider or a service consumer (or it could be both).

If your application is a service provider, you should understand that XML services are fundamentally just a text format for data interchange, much like HTML is for a web application. To be clear, I am suggesting that an XML service is merely another type of interface for an application. I've already discussed WPF and Web Forms interfaces, which allow a user to access an application. A service that accepts and returns XML messages is just another type of interface, as shown in Figure 21-1.

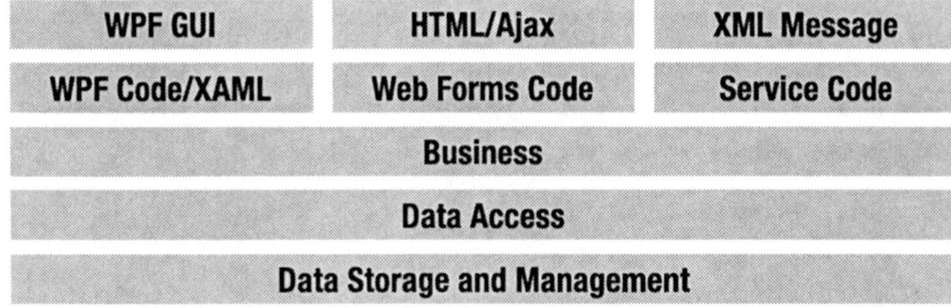

Figure 21-1. *Various types of application interface*

XML services are simply another type of interface that the application can make available. The primary difference is that an XML service interface is designed for use by other *applications*, not by users directly. Another application can use these services to get or update data in your application. This other application that's consuming your data may or may not have users of its own. This concept is illustrated in Figure 21-2, where you can see a consuming application without an end user, and an edge application that provides a user interface for some human end user.

End User
Consuming Application
Consuming Edge App
XML Message
Service Code
Business
Data Access
Data Storage and Management

Figure 21-2. *Consuming a service interface*

Overview of WCF Services

At an abstract level, XML services enable one application to call procedures or methods in another application. On the surface, this is similar to the aims of RPC, DCOM, RMI, IIOP, and .NET Remoting—all of these technologies enable one application to invoke procedures in another application.

Note It's also possible to view these technologies as a way for two components in the same application to interact with each other. While this is definitely a common use for the other technologies I mention, it isn't the intended use of XML services. XML services are designed for cross-application communication, not cross-component communication. This is because the focus is loosely coupled interoperability. Due to this focus, XML services don't offer the same performance or features as the other more platform-specific technologies listed.

The primary technology provided in .NET for creating and consuming XML services is the WCF, which enables the creation of services and consuming applications using a standardized API. It supports numerous network transport options, including

- HTTP
- TCP sockets
- Named pipes
- MSMQ

WCF also supports the WS-* standards, including

- Messaging
- Addressing
- Metadata exchange
- Policy
- Security policy
- Security
- Trust
- Secure conversation
- Reliable messaging
- Coordination
- Atomic transaction

WCF is also extremely extensible and continues to evolve. For example, while I use the term *XML services*, it is possible to build a service that accepts and returns messages encoded in the JavaScript Object Notation (JSON) format. Architecturally, there's no significant difference; the data on the network is simply in a different format. Another example is support for REST services. There are some design differences between traditional XML services and REST services, but architecturally they remain comparable.

Complete coverage of WCF requires entire books, so this chapter won't discuss all these features and options. My focus in this chapter is on the architecture and design you should use when building an XML service interface on top of your business objects.

Elements of a WCF Service

A WCF service consists of several elements. All the elements listed in Table 21-2 work together to implement the service and to expose it to consuming applications.

Table 21-2. *Elements of a WCF Service*

Element	Description
Endpoint configuration	Configuration settings in `web.config` defining the address, binding, and contract for the service
Service contract	Definition of the operations, data types, and fault types exposed to a consuming application
Endpoint definition	A `svc` file connecting the service's endpoint to a specific class that contains the service implementation
Service implementation	The implementation of the service contract and associated operations

I'll discuss each of these in more detail.

Endpoint Configuration

The three items listed in Table 21-3 define the configuration for a WCF service endpoint.

Table 21-3. *Definition of a WCF Service*

Element	Description
Address	A URI describing where to find the service. Often this is an `http://` URL, but there are URI formats describing TCP sockets, named pipes, and all other network transports supported by WCF.
Binding	Defines the transport technology and related options used to communicate between the consumer and provider of the service. The binding describes not only the transport technology, but also options such as encryption, authentication, and reliability.
Contract	Describes the specific service methods, data formats, and error formats accepted and returned by the WCF service.

Of these, the binding and contract are the most complex.

The address is usually an `http://` URL, such as

```
http://myserver/myroot/myservice.svc
```

The specific address format will vary slightly if you use a different network transport technology, but the basic concept is always the same: the address describes the location of the service.

Bindings are complex, because the binding describes the configuration for the technology used to transport messages to and from the service. Configuring bindings for various technologies, and all the related options such as security, can be complex and time consuming.

The configuration of bindings is outside the scope of this book. You should know, however, that the two most common bindings are `wsHttpBinding` and `basicHttpBinding`:

- `wsHttpBinding`: Allows you to use the features of WCF. This is the default binding for most WCF-to-WCF communication. It employs the WS-* standards, so it may work with other XML service technologies if they also fully support the standards.
- `basicHttpBinding`: Provides an older protocol that is compatible with `asmx` Web Services. It is also useful when working with Silverlight 2.0 clients and other client technologies that don't fully support the advanced WS-* standards.

Contracts can be complex, because they describe the shape of the WCF service itself. The contract for a service is really the definition of the service, and the contract contains the information required to create a consumer for the service. Much of the focus of this chapter is on the definition of contracts and how to implement a service that meets the contract's requirements.

These elements are expressed in `web.config` when configuring the WCF service endpoint—for example:

```
<system.serviceModel>
  <services>
    <service name="MyService">
      <endpoint address=""
                binding="wsHttpBinding"
                contract="IMyService" />
  </service>
</system.serviceModel>
```

When hosting your service in IIS, you don't need to provide the `address` property because it is calculated based on the server name and the virtual root name in IIS. However, you do need to specify the `binding` and `contract`.

Configuration is perhaps the most complex part of working with WCF. This example illustrates the simplest configuration of an address, binding, and contract. Most production applications will have a *lot* more XML to configure security, time-outs, message size limits, and many other features. Visual Studio will help you with some of this configuration, but you will need to read a book or two on WCF to fully understand all the options and how to use them.

The Microsoft Patterns and Practices group has created a guidance project to help address this complexity. You can find details at `www.codeplex.com/WCFSecurity`.

Service Contract

Table 21-4 lists the primary elements of a contract for a WCF service. Defining a contract requires that you think about all these elements.

All three of these elements work together to define the overall contract for a WCF service.

Table 21-4. *Primary Elements of a Service Contract*

Element	Description
Service contract	Defines the operations (service methods) exposed by the service that can be called by a consuming application
Data contract	Defines the shape of message data sent to or from the service
Fault contract	Defines any nonsuccessful responses that may be generated when a consuming application calls a service

ServiceContract Attribute

The service contract is implemented as a .NET interface, decorated with WCF-specific attributes—for example:

```
[ServiceContract]
public interface IMyService
{
  [OperationContract]
  ResultData[] MyOperation();
  [OperationContract]
  [FaultContract(typeof(AuthorizationFault))]
  ResultMessage OtherOperation(RequestMessage request);
}
```

The interface uses the `ServiceContract` attribute to indicate that it defines a service contract. Each method that is exposed to a consuming application is decorated with the `OperationContract` attribute. This means you can define an interface with some methods that are available only on the server, and with others that are available both on the server and to consuming applications. I recommend you avoid mixing those concepts and mark all methods in an interface with `OperationContract`. If you have methods that can be only called on the server, you should put them in a separate interface for clarity.

Also notice that the methods accept and return complex types, such as `ResultData`, `ResultMessage`, and `RequestMessage`. These are simple .NET classes, but they include attributes so they define specific data contracts. The service contract defines which data contracts are included as part of the overall contract for the WCF service.

The `FaultContract` attribute specifies the type `AuthorizationFault`. The `FaultContract` attribute is used to connect a fault contract to a service operation. This means that `OtherOperation()` can return a successful result or an `AuthorizationFault`. Both are valid responses that a consuming application should expect and handle properly.

DataContract Attribute

The service contract defines the operations, or service methods, that a consuming application can call. Operations often accept parameters and return results, and each of these parameter and result types are defined as a data contract.

Technically, it is possible for an operation to accept and return primitive types, but I strongly recommend against this. If your operation accepts a primitive type, such as `int`, you'll have a hard time versioning your service over time. Remember that the operations and their parameter/result types are all part of the contract. Changing them breaks the contract.

For example, you could define an operation like this:

```
CustomerData[] FindCustomers(string name);
```

This works great until you need to enhance the service to also find customers with sales less than some value. If you've used primitive types on your contract, all you can do is add a new method.

```
CustomerData[] FindCustomersBySales(double max);
```

This might not be so bad until you also have to find customers with sales *greater than* some value.

```
CustomerData[] FindCustomersBySales2(double min);
```

Pretty soon, you're reinventing the Win32 API or replicating many of the COM component APIs from the 1990s. No one wants that.

A better solution is to use data contract types for all parameter and return values. In that case, your operation is defined like this:

```
FindCustomerResponse[] FindCustomersBySales(FindCustomerRequest request);
```

Then you can define the two data contracts. `FindCustomerResponse` may look like this:

```
[DataContract]
public class FindCustomerResponse
{
  [DataMember]
  public int Id { get; set; }
  [DataMember]
  public string FirstName { get; set; }
  [DataMember]
  public string LastName { get; set; }
  [DataMember]
  public double SalesTotal { get; set; }
}
```

The `DataContract` attribute indicates that this class defines a data contract. The `DataMember` attribute, which you can apply to fields or properties, indicates that the element is part of the contract. When an instance of `FindCustomerResponse` is serialized, all `DataMember` elements are included in the resulting byte stream.

The `FindCustomerRequest` class may start like this:

```
[DataContract]
public class FindCustomerRequest
{
  [DataMember]
  public string Name { get; set; }
}
```

As you discover new requirements, you can add elements to the data contract without breaking the service contract (and thus without breaking existing consuming applications).

```
[DataContract]
public class FindCustomerRequest
{
  [DataMember]
  public string Name { get; set; }
  [DataMember(Order=2)]
  public double MaxSales { get; set; }
  [DataMember(Order=3)]
  public double MinSales { get; set; }
}
```

The `Order` parameter to the `DataMember` attribute indicates which version of the data contract introduced the new element. You can use this technique to extend the contract of your WCF service over time without needing to add new operations.

FaultContract Attribute

The final part of a contract for a WCF service is the fault contract. When an operation is called, it either succeeds or fails. If it succeeds, the operation will typically return some information through a defined data contract. Failure is more complex, because there are different kinds of failure.

Failure might be due to something entirely unexpected or exceptional. In that case, the operation will typically throw an exception, which flows back through WCF to the consuming application as an unexpected fault. An unexpected fault not only tells the consuming application that the operation failed, but it *faults the WCF channel*, which means that the network channel is no longer valid.

However, it is also possible that the operation could fail due to something you *do expect*. For example, your operation may do some authorization, and you may know ahead of time that the authorization could fail. Or the operation may include business rules, and if certain business rules or requirements aren't met, the operation could fail. These *expected failures* are also returned to the consuming application as faults, but they are expected faults that indicate a valid, though unsuccessful, response.

How does a consuming application know which faults are "normal"? These faults are described as a fault contract, so the consuming application knows they are a valid (if unsuccessful) result.

■ **Note** Not all XML service technologies support the concept of fault contracts. For example, the WCF implementation in Silverlight 2.0 doesn't support this concept, so Silverlight can't call operations decorated with the `FaultContract` attribute. Make sure your consuming applications can support fault contracts before you use them.

The `FaultContract` attribute is applied to an operation and defines a serializable type that is returned to contain information about the fault.

```
[FaultContract(typeof(MyFault))]
```

This serializable type is a data contract. Within the service implementation, the code may throw a fault using this type:

```
MyFault fault = new MyFault();
// set fault properties here
throw new FaultException<MyFault>(fault, "The code cannot run");
```

The information in the `MyFault` object is returned to the consuming application to indicate that the operation failed, but that it failed in an expected or valid manner. A responsible consuming application will be implemented to expect and properly handle any faults declared by a service.

If the consuming application is written using WCF, it'll get a `FaultException<T>` that contains a client-side representation of the `MyFault` object, along with the message text provided directly to the `FaultException` on the server. Again, a responsible consuming application will be expected to handle any faults declared as a `FaultContract` on each operation.

Endpoint Definition

A WCF service is exposed to consumers through an endpoint. This endpoint is expressed as a svc file that connects the endpoint to the code that implements the service contract. You can put the service code directly into the svc file, but I prefer to keep the code separate for clarity. Here's a typical svc file named `MyService.svc`:

```
<%@ ServiceHost Language=C#
                Debug="true"
                Service="MyService"
                CodeBehind="~/App_Code/MyService.cs" %>
```

The primary properties here are `Service` and `CodeBehind`. The `Service` property specifies the name of the class that implements the service. The `CodeBehind` property specifies the location of the code file containing the code for that class.

■ Note You could also put your service implementation in a separate Class Library assembly. In that case, you would not use the `CodeBehind` attribute; instead, you would provide the full type name of the class that implements the service in the `Service` property.

A consuming application will reference this `MyService.svc` as the entry point to the service implementation.

Service Implementation

At this point, most of the WCF-specific work is done. You've seen how to configure the endpoint, define the endpoint, and define the contract for the service. All that remains is to implement the service, which is pretty much all about your business and application requirements, not about WCF.

Remember that the service contract is defined as a .NET interface, with some WCF-specific attributes attached. Your service implementation is just a .NET class that implements that interface—for example:

```
public class MyService : IMyService
{
  public ResultData[] MyOperation()
  {
    // implement operation here
  }

  public ResultMessage OtherOperation(RequestMessage request)
  {
    // implement operation here
  }
}
```

The method implementations are typically business-focused. However, it is important to understand one key design issue: your internal implementation and data structures *should be separate* from the external data contract structures.

In other words, you shouldn't use `ResultData`, `ResultMessage`, or `RequestMessage` as business types or as types that are retrieved or stored directly into your database. These types are part of your public contract, and changing them is difficult and risky. Any change to these types risks breaking any consuming applications.

If you allow your business code to rely on these types directly, then changing your business code becomes difficult, because you are tying your external interface to your internal implementation. This is a direct violation of the concept of encapsulation, and encapsulation is one of the most powerful tools in the arsenal of object-oriented and service-oriented programming.

As you look at the `ProjectTracker` sample code later in this chapter, you'll see that I use the business object types from `ProjectTracker.Library` as my internal implementation, and I have *entirely separate* data contract types to define the public contract of the service. I do this specifically to achieve encapsulation and to preserve the maintainability of both my application and my service contract.

■ **Note** Business objects created using CSLA .NET cannot be directly exposed as part of a service contract. The serialization process used by WCF will not serialize a CSLA-style business object. When using CSLA .NET to create your business layer, you must plan to expose separate data contract types in your service contract, which is what you should do in any case.

At this point, you should understand how to define a service contract, define and configure an endpoint, and implement the service contract as a service implementation. In many cases, this is enough information to build your services.

The `ProjectTracker` application is a bit more complex, however, because it uses a custom authentication scheme, where the user's credentials are validated against data in a custom SQL Server database. Unfortunately, this turns out to be one of the most complex security scenarios to implement in WCF, so before I get into the `ProjectTracker` WCF service, you'll need to understand how the custom authentication process works in WCF.

Custom Authentication

If you're using custom authentication in your business objects, you'll typically want the client to pass a username and password to the service. The service can then authenticate those credentials and set up your custom principal object for use by the server code.

This section of the chapter is pretty intense. WCF configuration can get very complex. You should know that when using Windows AD authentication or the ASP.NET `MembershipProvider` model, things are much simpler and you can essentially skip this section of the chapter. However, the `ProjectTracker` application does use a custom username/password authentication model, as do many web applications in the world. If you have a similar situation, then buckle your seat belt and read on.

You can easily authenticate the credentials and set up the principal object using a CSLA .NET–style custom principal object. For example, in `ProjectTracker`, the `PTPrincipal` class has a `Login()` method to do this:

```
PTPrincipal.Login(username, password);
```

Unfortunately, getting the username and password from a client into a WCF service is challenging. Remember that this is a function of security, so a lot of infrastructure and configuration work is required to get all the security pieces set up before you can safely pass a username and password across the network.

WCF is designed to be secure, so it won't allow you to pass a username and password without first having a secure and encrypted binding. To do that, you first need a server certificate, either for SSL or for WCF's built-in, message-level security. Creating, installing, and configuring a test certificate is challenging. After that, some of the WCF configuration and code to *use* the certificate is also a bit complex.

Three steps are required:

1. Acquire or create an X.509 certificate.
2. Configure WCF to use message-level security.
3. Configure WCF to use username credentials.

I'll walk through each of these steps.

Acquiring an X.509 Certificate

Securing a service or a website is typically done with something commonly called an SSL certificate, which is more formally called an X.509 certificate. In a production Internet environment, a commercial firm like VeriSign or RapidSSL typically issues these certificates. These commercial certificates are cryptographically linked to a *trusted root certificate*, and all the major vendors have their root certificates installed automatically on Windows, so all Windows clients automatically trust the certificates they sell to their customers.

In a production intranet environment, the certificates might come from your organization itself. Many organizations have their own internal certificate authority and their own internally trusted root certificate. Certificates issued by an organization are trusted only by computers within the organization (because they install the organization's trusted root certificate), not by all computers in the world.

In a development or test environment, the developer often creates the certificates. A developer might use a tool like `makecert.exe`, which comes with the Microsoft .NET SDK. Such a certificate isn't linked to any trusted root certificate, so no one trusts it unless the user on a specific machine trusts it specifically.

Creating a Test Certificate

Since most of us do development without access to either production or corporate certificates, it is important to understand how to create and install a test certificate. This is the focus of the rest of this section.

■ **Note** If you do have access to the private key of a production or organizational certificate, you can use that instead of creating your own as discussed here.

Creating and installing a certificate is a multistep process:

1. Create the certificate using `makecert.exe`.
2. Install the certificate in the `LocalMachine` certificate store.
3. Grant IIS access to the certificate file.
4. Copy the certificate to the `TrustedPeople` certificate store on any test client machines.

Creating the Certificate

The Microsoft .NET SDK comes with a tool called makecert.exe. This complex tool has a lot of different uses and options. The article, "X.509 Certificate Validator" (MSDN, http://msdn2.microsoft.com/en-us/library/aa354512.aspx), describes in detail how to use the tool to create a certificate.

In summary, you can use the following command line to create a test certificate:

```
makecert -n CN=localhost localhost.cer -sky exchange -ss My -sr LocalMachine
```

Table 21-5 lists the arguments and their meaning.

Table 21-5. *Makecert.exe Arguments*

Argument	Meaning
-n CN=localhost	Defines the name of the certificate. If possible, this should be the network domain name of your server, but you can provide a name unique to your service if desired.
localhost.cer	This optional argument indicates that the certificate should be saved to a file named localhost.cer. This can simplify the process of installing the certificate on other test client machines.
-sky exchange	Specifies that the certificate should support key exchange. This is required for WCF, because a key-exchange process occurs as the secure channel is established.
-ss My	Indicates that the certificate should be installed to the certificate store named My.
-sr LocalMachine	Indicates that the certificate should be installed to the LocalMachine certificate store location.

It is important to realize that this command not only creates the certificate, but it also installs it for use by the server. This means that you should run this command on the machine that will be hosting your WCF service.

In my example, I use the name CN=localhost because I'm running both the client and service components on the same development machine. The machine's domain name is localhost for all code on the same machine, and having the certificate name match the machine's domain name simplifies WCF configuration.

If you plan to use test clients that are on different machines, you'll want to use a public machine name for your certificate name, or some arbitrary name such as the name of your service. That last option requires a little more configuration of WCF.

Granting Access to the Certificate to IIS

Even though the certificate is installed into the LocalMachine certificate store, it isn't entirely available to IIS without some extra work. The reason is that websites run under a limited user account on the server. They don't, by default, have access to the key file that contains the certificate's private key information.

Granting access to the key file is complicated by the fact that actually finding the key file can be challenging. To help address this, the WCF team at Microsoft has provided a sample application called FindPrivateKey. The "FindPrivateKey" article (MSDN, http://msdn2.microsoft.com/EN-US/library/aa717039.aspx) provides details and download information about FindPrivateKey.

Once you've downloaded and built the sample application, you can run it as follows:

```
findprivatekey My LocalMachine -n "CN=localhost" -a
```

The result is the full path to the certificate file corresponding to CN=localhost in the LocalHost/My certificate store.

You can then use the cacls.exe tool to grant access to the IIS account. For example, you'd enter the following command (on one line):

```
cacls.eXE " ??? C:\Documents and Settings\All Users\Application Data\Microsoft\Crypto\RSA
\MachineKeys\8aeda5eb81555f14f8f9960745b5a40d_38f7de48-5ee9-452d-8a5a-92789d7110b1"
/E /G "NETWORK_SERVICE":R
```

In this example, you can see both the full path to the certificate file (from the FindPrivateKey utility) and the account that is granted access (NETWORK_SERVICE). This is because I am working on Windows Server 2003, and it would be the same on Windows Vista. On Windows XP, however, you'd grant access to the ASPNET account.

The result is that your service, when hosted in IIS, will have access to the certificate's private key, so it can use that information to sign and encrypt messages.

Trusting the Certificate

Though the makecert.exe command shown earlier installs the certificate for server use, it doesn't make your machine trust the certificate. Because a trusted root authority didn't issue the certificate, you must manually establish that you trust the certificate.

To do this, you must copy the certificate into your TrustedPeople certificate store. You can do this using the certmgr.exe tool.

```
certmgr  -add -c -n localhost -r LocalMachine -s My -r CurrentUser -s
TrustedPeople
```

Table 21-6 lists the arguments to the command and their purpose. The article, "How to: Make X.509 Certificates Accessible to WCF" (MSDN, http://msdn2.microsoft.com/en-us/library/aa702621.aspx), discusses the process in more detail as it relates to WCF.

Table 21-6. *Certmgr.exe Arguments*

Argument	Meaning
-add	Specifies that the certificate should be added to a certificate store
-c	Indicates that the certificate should be copied from another certificate store
-n localhost	Specifies the name of the certificate to be copied
-r LocalMachine	Indicates the source certificate store location
-s My	Indicates the source certificate store name
-r CurrentUser	Indicates the target certificate store location
-s TrustedPeople	Indicates the target certificate store name

In short, this command copies the certificate from LocalMachine/My to CurrentUser/TrustedPeople. Server components use the LocalMachine/My certificate store, while interactive user applications use CurrentUser/TrustedPeople.

Manual Installation

Another way you can install the certificate is by double-clicking the `.cer` file. You need to use this technique to install the certificate onto other client machines. This brings up a dialog that allows you to view details about the certificate.

Click the Install Certificate button to bring up the Certificate Import Wizard. Figure 21-3 shows the key panel of the wizard, where you must specify to install the certificate into the Other People store, which corresponds to `CurrentUser/TrustedPeople`.

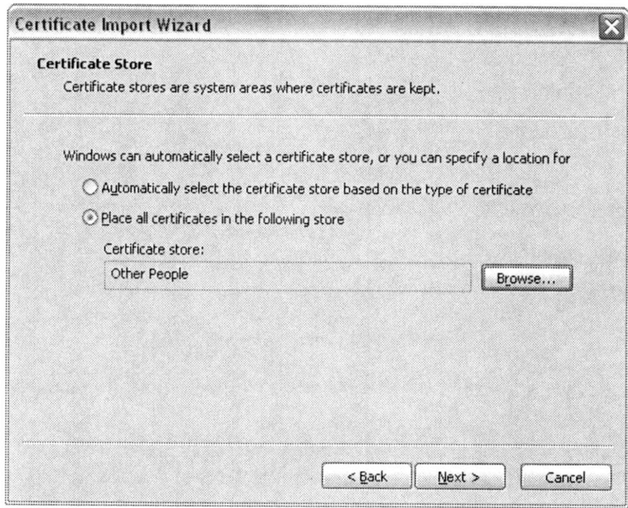

Figure 21-3. *Installing the certificate into the Other People store*

The result is the same: the current user can now use the certificate to communicate with the server.

Configuring WCF to Use Message Security

WCF can use transport-level security, like SSL; message-level security, like I'll discuss in this section; or a combination of both. The important thing is that you must use some form of security (encryption and signing of data) before you can send a custom username and password from the client to your service.

If you're already set up to use SSL security, you don't need to switch to message security. However, if you're not using any security, it is often simpler to set up message security as shown here. The process involves customizing the behavior for both the service endpoint and the corresponding client configuration.

Configuring the Service

By default, the `wsHttpBinding` uses message-level security, but you need to provide a certificate for the security to actually be enabled. Configuring the service to use a certificate is done through a behavior. As with everything in WCF, you can configure the behavior through code, but it is more commonly done through the configuration file.

The config file needs to now include a custom service behavior.

```
<system.serviceModel>
  <behaviors>
    <serviceBehaviors>
      <behavior name="ServiceCertificate">
        <serviceCredentials>
          <serviceCertificate
            findValue="localhost"
            storeLocation="LocalMachine"
            storeName="My"
            x509FindType="FindBySubjectName" />
        </serviceCredentials>
      </behavior>
    </serviceBehaviors>
  </behaviors>
  <services>
    <service name="MyService"
            behaviorConfiguration="ServiceCertificate">
      <endpoint address=""
                binding="wsHttpBinding"
                contract="IMyService" />
  </service>
</system.serviceModel>
```

Notice how the behaviorConfiguration property is now set on the service element to indicate that the service should use this custom behavior.

In the behavior element, the serviceCertificate element indicates how to find the certificate to be used to secure the communication channel. Table 21-7 lists the properties of this element.

Table 21-7. *Properties of the serviceCertificate Element*

Property	Description
findValue	The name of the certificate to find. This name must correspond to the name used earlier to name the certificate (CN=localhost).
storeLocation	The certificate store location containing the certificate.
storeName	The certificate store name containing the certificate.
X509FindType	Specifies which properties to use when searching for the certificate. In this case, the search is by subject name (the CN= value).

The result is that this behavior now requires that the communication be encrypted using the defined certificate.

Configuring the Client

All clients calling the service must also understand that a certificate is required for secure communication. On the client, you can configure WCF through code or in the client's config file. Typically, the configuration is through the config file, and that's what I'll show here.

As with the server, the client defines an endpoint with an address, binding, and contract. These properties must match those on the server, so both agree on the method of communication. Here's the simplest client configuration (prior to adding the requirement for encryption):

```
<system.serviceModel>
  <client>
    <endpoint name="MyService"
              address="http://localhost/MyService/MyService.svc"
              binding="wsHttpBinding"
              contract="MyService.IMyService">
    </endpoint>
  </client>
</system.serviceModel>
```

This is much like the configuration for a server, except the `endpoint` element is contained in a `client` element. If a custom behavior is added on the server, an equivalent change is required on the client. The following illustrates the changes required in the client's configuration file:

```
<system.serviceModel>
  <behaviors>
    <endpointBehaviors>
      <behavior name="ServiceCertificate">
        <clientCredentials>
          <serviceCertificate>
            <authentication certificateValidationMode="PeerTrust"/>
          </serviceCertificate>
        </clientCredentials>
      </behavior>
    </endpointBehaviors>
  </behaviors>
  <client>
    <endpoint name="MyService"
             behaviorConfiguration="ServiceCertificate"
              address="http://localhost/MyService/MyService.svc"
              binding="wsHttpBinding"
              contract="MyService.IMyService">
      <identity>
        <dns value="localhost"/>
      </identity>
    </endpoint>
  </client>
```

There are two important changes here. First, the client endpoint now uses a customized behavior named `ServiceCertificate`. This behavior specifies that the service requires a certificate and that the client should validate the certificate using `PeerTrust`.

The default is `ChainTrust`, meaning that trust flows down from a trusted root certificate. With a test certificate, however, there is no trusted root, so that would fail. The `PeerTrust` option indicates that trust flows from the `TrustedPeople` certificate store location, where the certificate was installed in the previous section.

Note This configuration setting is just for testing. In a production environment, you would typically use the default `ChainTrust`, because a production certificate would have a trusted root authority from a commercial vendor or from your organization itself.

Second, the `identity` element specifies the name of the certificate to use. This is not required here, because the certificate name, `localhost`, matches the domain name for the server, `http://localhost/<etc>`. However, if your certificate name does not match the server domain name, then you must use the `identity` element as shown to specify the name of the certificate.

At this point, the service and client are both configured to use message-level secure communications.

Configuring a Service to Use Username Credentials

By default, most common WCF bindings use Windows credentials from the client. This is true even if the client provides a username and password, as they are assumed to correspond to a Windows user account in the server's Windows domain.

If you want to use custom authentication and create a custom security principal object for your service, you need to configure WCF to use your authentication components instead of the defaults. You can do this in a couple of different ways:

- Create custom ASP.NET membership and role providers and configure WCF to use your custom providers.
- Create a custom WCF username/password validator and authorization policy object.

Both techniques are valid, but the second one is an entirely WCF solution, and it turns out to be relatively simple to implement. As a result, it is the second option I'll discuss in this section.

Using a custom principal object requires changes to the service, both in configuration and code. WCF allows customization for both authentication and authorization. In each case, a class must be created with a custom implementation of the required behavior. These two classes are invoked at different times during the WCF initialization process on every service call.

Unfortunately, the strong separation of these two concepts in WCF complicates matters a little. After the credential validation step, WCF clears the principal object from the current thread. Later in the process, the principal can be set for the service's thread, but at that point in time, the credentials are no longer available.

This means that the credential validation step must somehow cache the results of the `Login()` method in memory so that the principal object can be made current later in the process, as shown in Figure 21-4. This is the purpose behind the `PrincipalCache` object in `Csla.Security`.

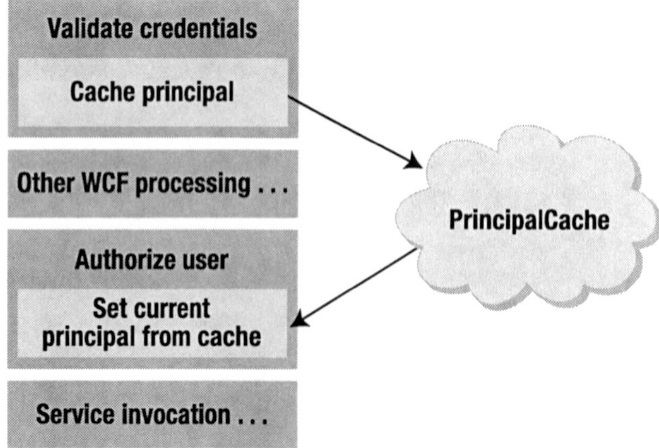

Figure 21-4. *Authentication and authorization during WCF initialization*

The PrincipalCache object caches principal objects at the AppDomain level. Since WCF guarantees that a consistent AppDomain is used throughout the life of a service call, this is a safe location for such a cache.

To minimize memory consumption, the PrincipalCache object is implemented as a circular list with a default size of ten items. Keep in mind that the principal object only needs to be cached for the fraction of a second it takes WCF to go through its initialization process prior to invoking the service itself, so the size of the cache should be roughly the same as the number of service requests you expect to occur at any instance in time.

You can control the size of the cache by using the CslaPrincipalCacheSize key in the server's web.config file.

```
<appSettings>
  <add key="CslaPrincipalCacheSize" value="20" />
</appSettings>
```

This overrides the default, expanding the cache to keep the most recent 20 principal objects in memory.

Without the PrincipalCache object, the authorization step would need to go back to the security database to reload the principal object. This would result in two hits to the security database for every service request.

Even with the PrincipalCache object, a second hit to the security database may be required. If the cache is configured to be too small, there's a chance that the principal object could be gone from the cache in the fraction of a second it takes to get from authentication to authorization. To prevent this unlikely occurrence from causing a failure, your authorization code should have the option of reloading the principal from the database if needed, and that's the approach I'll illustrate in this chapter.

Modifying PTPrincipal

Before I get into the WCF authorization and authentication code, it is necessary to modify PTPrincipal and PTIdentity to accommodate the separation between authentication and authorization.

WCF validates the user's credentials early in the process. Later in the process, WCF creates an authorization policy object that defines the principal and identity objects to be used as the service is executed. This authorization policy object is only provided with the username value, not the password, so PTPrincipal needs a way to load the principal and identity objects based purely on the username.

This requirement isn't unique to WCF. When creating a totally stateless web application, the custom principal can't be held in Session on the web server. Instead, it must be reloaded on each page request, based purely on the username. While ASP.NET forms authentication doesn't maintain the password, the username is provided on every page request. You can also use this LoadPrincipal() method to reload the principal from the database on every page request.

The LoadPrincipal() method is similar to the Login() method, except that it only requires a username, not a password. In fact, I've altered the Login() method to share some code.

```
public static bool Login(string username, string password)
{
  return SetPrincipal(PTIdentity.GetIdentity(username, password));
}

public static void LoadPrincipal(string username)
{
  SetPrincipal(PTIdentity.GetIdentity(username));
}
```

```
private static bool SetPrincipal(PTIdentity identity)
{
  if (identity.IsAuthenticated)
  {
    PTPrincipal principal = new PTPrincipal(identity);
    Csla.ApplicationContext.User = principal;
  }
  return identity.IsAuthenticated;
}
```

The highlighted line of code invokes a new overload of the GetIdentity() factory method on PTIdentity. This overload uses a different criteria object that contains only the username and calls an overload of DataPortal_Fetch() in PTIdentity:

```
private void DataPortal_Fetch(LoadOnlyCriteria criteria)
{
    using (var ctx = ContextManager<SecurityDataContext>.
      GetManager(ProjectTracker.DalLinq.Database.Security))
    {
      var data = from u in ctx.DataContext.Users
                 where u.Username == criteria.Username
                 select u;
      if (data.Count() > 0)
        Fetch(data.Single());
      else
        Fetch(null);
    }
}
```

The original login process is unchanged. The UI can either call Login(username, password) or LoadPrincipal(username), and the result will be the same. Of course, only the Login() method actually validates the user's credentials. I'll use the new LoadPrincipal() method in the implementation of the custom WCF authorization behavior.

Custom UserNamePasswordValidator

In WCF, custom username authorization is handled by subclassing UserNamePasswordValidator from the System.IdentityModel.Selectors namespace. The implementation of this class is not complex. If the user's credentials are valid, the method will return without an exception. If the credentials are invalid, the method must throw an exception. Only users with valid username/password combinations get past this point in the process.

It is important to realize that you cannot set the current principal at this point. WCF makes no guarantee that this code will run on the same thread as the actual service instance, and it explicitly resets the principal object at a point after this method completes. However, using the approach shown in Figure 21-4, it is possible to cache the principal in memory for use later by using the PrincipalCache object.

In this section of the chapter, I'm going to walk through the actual code used in the ProjectTracker application, because this will allow you to examine the code and configuration from the download in context. You can find the CredentialValidator class in the PTWcfServiceAuth project in ProjectTracker.

```
public class CredentialValidator : UserNamePasswordValidator
  {
    public override void Validate(string userName, string password)
    {
```

```
      if (userName != "anonymous")
      {
        PTPrincipal.Logout();
        if (!PTPrincipal.Login(userName, password))
          throw new FaultException("Unknown username or password");

        // add current principal to rolling cache
        Csla.Security.PrincipalCache.AddPrincipal(Csla.ApplicationContext.User);
      }
    }
  }
```

Notice the call to the `Logout()` method. This is required because the data portal must have a valid—even if unauthenticated—principal to work. Without the call to `Logout()`, the `Login()` call would throw a data portal exception due to having an invalid principal on the thread.

If the `Login()` call succeeds, the resulting principal (which is temporarily the current principal until this method completes) will be stored in the `PrincipalCache` object. This makes the principal object available for use later in the service initialization process.

Finally, notice that special consideration is made for the username `anonymous`. Remember that `ProjectTracker` allows unauthenticated users to access some information, so the application must allow anonymous users to at least make some service calls. This special username will get extra attention in the custom authorization policy class later.

I'll discuss how to configure WCF to use the `CredentialValidator` class later in the chapter. For now, it is enough to know that this code will be invoked early in the process as WCF initializes itself for every service call.

Custom Authorization Policy

During the initialization process for every service call, WCF creates an authorization policy object. This object is responsible for providing the principal and identity objects to be used during the service call itself, so this is the point at which the custom principal and identity objects must be set.

To implement a custom authorization policy, a class must implement the `IAuthorizationPolicy` interface from the `System.IdentityModel.Policy` namespace.

```
public class PrincipalPolicy : IAuthorizationPolicy
{
  private string _id = Guid.NewGuid().ToString();

  public string Id
  {
    get { return _id; }
  }

  public ClaimSet Issuer
  {
    get { return ClaimSet.System; }
  }

  public bool Evaluate(EvaluationContext context, ref object state)
  {
    // get the identities list from the context
    object obj;
```

```
      if (!context.Properties.TryGetValue("Identities", out obj))
        return false;
      IList<IIdentity> identities = obj as IList<IIdentity>;

      // make sure there is already a default identity
      if (identities == null || identities.Count <= 0)
        return false;

      // try to get principal from rolling cache
      string username = identities[0].Name;
      IPrincipal principal = Csla.Security.PrincipalCache.GetPrincipal(username);

      if (principal == null)
      {
        PTPrincipal.Logout();
        if (username != "anonymous")
        {
          // load principal based on username authenticated in CredentialValidator
          PTPrincipal.LoadPrincipal(username);
          // add current principal to rolling cache
          Csla.Security.PrincipalCache.AddPrincipal(Csla.ApplicationContext.User);
        }
        principal = Csla.ApplicationContext.User;
      }

      // tell WCF to use the custom principal
      context.Properties["Principal"] = principal;

      // tell WCF to use the custom identity
      identities[0] = principal.Identity;

      return true;
    }
  }
```

The Evaluate() method is called to evaluate the current context and set the principal and identity. The highlighted lines of code show how the principal is retrieved from the PrincipalCache object based on the username value available from the identity object, which is retrieved from the context.Properties dictionary.

```
string username = identities[0].Name;
IPrincipal principal =
  Csla.Security.PrincipalCache.GetPrincipal(username);
```

The identity object from context.Properties is typically a GenericIdentity that merely contains the name of the user, based on the credentials originally provided to CredentialValidator. WCF created this identity object, which should be replaced by the custom identity associated with the custom principal object.

It is possible that there is no cached principal object matching the username. This can happen for two reasons: because the anonymous username was used, or because a valid user's principal was flushed from the cache since CredentialValidator was called (meaning the cache size is too small). Either way, some valid custom principal object must be created and made current.

Notice that the Logout() method is called before LoadPrincipal(). Remember that WCF clears the principal object between authentication and setting the authorization policy, so when Evaluate() is called by WCF, the principal is not a valid principal from the data portal's perspective. In fact, it is just an authenticated GenericPrincipal at this point. The Logout() method makes sure there's a valid PTPrincipal on the thread before LoadPrincipal() tries to use the data portal.

If the anonymous username was used, then that unauthenticated custom principal is left as the current principal. However, if the anonymous username wasn't used, that indicates that the user's principal was flushed from the cache prematurely. The solution is to call the LoadPrincipal() method to reload the principal and identity objects from the security database.

■ **Note** You may also want to log that the anonymous username wasn't used, as it indicates that your cache size is too small to handle the number of service requests hitting your server.

The result is a valid custom principal that is current on the thread. You can use Csla.ApplicationContext.User to get at the principal like you would in any other environment.

Both the principal and identity must also be made available to WCF by setting values in context.Properties. The custom principal is provided to WCF through context.Properties.

```
context.Properties["Principal"] = principal;
```

The custom identity replaces the old GenericIdentity created by WCF.

```
identities[0] = principal.Identity;
```

This object is then used as the primary identity for the ServiceSecurityContext provided by WCF.

With these two classes defined in the PTWcfServiceAuth project, all that remains is to configure PTWcfService to use them.

Server Configuration

WCF allows the use of custom username validation and authorization policy objects through configuration. However, before changing web.config, it is important to reference the PTWcfServiceAuth project so that the assembly is available to the service. In the code download, look at the PTWcfService website to see the full web.config file.

The highlighted lines of code show the changes to web.config necessary to use the custom validation and authorization policy types.

```
<services>
  <service behaviorConfiguration="PTServiceBehavior" name="PTService">
    <endpoint address=""
              binding="wsHttpBinding" bindingConfiguration="UserNameWS"
              contract="IPTService" />
     <endpoint address="mex" binding="mexHttpBinding"
               contract="IMetadataExchange" />
  </service>
</services>

<bindings>
  <wsHttpBinding>
    <binding name="UserNameWS">
      <security mode="Message">
        <message clientCredentialType="UserName" />
      </security>
    </binding>
  </wsHttpBinding>
</bindings>
```

```
<behaviors>
  <serviceBehaviors>
    <behavior name="PTServiceBehavior">
      <serviceAuthorization principalPermissionMode="Custom">
        <authorizationPolicies>
          <add policyType="PTWcfServiceAuth.PrincipalPolicy,
                           PTWcfServiceAuth"/>
        </authorizationPolicies>
      </serviceAuthorization>

      <serviceCredentials>
        <serviceCertificate
          findValue="localhost"
          storeLocation="LocalMachine"
          storeName="My"
          x509FindType="FindBySubjectName" />
        <userNameAuthentication
          userNamePasswordValidationMode="Custom"
          customUserNamePasswordValidatorType=
                   "PTWcfServiceAuth.CredentialValidator, PTWcfServiceAuth" />
      </serviceCredentials>
      <serviceMetadata httpGetEnabled="true" />
      <serviceDebug includeExceptionDetailInFaults="true" />
    </behavior>
  </serviceBehaviors>
</behaviors>
```

The endpoint is configured to use a special `bindingConfiguration` named `UserNameWS`. That defines a custom version of `wsHttpBinding`.

```
<bindings>
  <wsHttpBinding>
    <binding name="UserNameWS">
      <security mode="Message">
        <message clientCredentialType="UserName" />
      </security>
    </binding>
  </wsHttpBinding>
</bindings>
```

It explicitly sets the security mode to `Message`, which is the default. More importantly, it specifies that the `clientCredentialType` is `UserName`, so the service will require that callers provide a username and password when calling the service.

Also, notice that the `PTServiceBehavior` behavior has been altered. A new `serviceAuthorization` element has been added.

```
<serviceAuthorization principalPermissionMode="Custom">
  <authorizationPolicies>
    <add policyType="PTWcfServiceAuth.PrincipalPolicy,
                     PTWcfServiceAuth"/>
  </authorizationPolicies>
</serviceAuthorization>
```

This specifies that the `principalPermissionMode` is `Custom`, which means that a custom authorization policy must be defined. It is set to use a `policyType` that references the `PrincipalPolicy` class discussed earlier in the chapter.

The behavior's serviceCredentials element has also been enhanced to define the customUserNamePasswordValidatorType that refers to the CredentialValidator class discussed earlier in the chapter.

```
<userNameAuthentication
  userNamePasswordValidationMode="Custom"
  customUserNamePasswordValidatorType=
          "PTWcfServiceAuth.CredentialValidator, PTWcfServiceAuth" />
```

With these changes, WCF will now invoke the CredentialValidator to authenticate the caller's username and password. Assuming that the method doesn't throw an exception, WCF will invoke the PrincipalPolicy to set up the authorization policy later in the process. This will include the custom principal and identity to be used by the service.

Providing a Username from the Client

The client application that calls the service must now provide a username with every call. It may also provide a password, but WCF will require that a username value be provided that is not empty or null. The client configuration also needs to change in order to reflect the changes made to the service's configuration.

In the client's code, setting the username and password values is relatively straightforward. You can see an example of the code in the PTWcfClient project.

```
PTWcfService.ProjectData[] list = null;
PTWcfService.PTServiceClient svc =
  new PTWcfClient.PTWcfService.PTServiceClient();
try
{
  svc.ClientCredentials.UserName.UserName = "pm";
  svc.ClientCredentials.UserName.Password = "pm";
  list = svc.GetProjectList();
}
finally
{
  svc.Close();
}
this.projectDataBindingSource.DataSource = list;
```

Because the service supports the special anonymous username, this will also work (for methods that don't require special roles):

```
PTWcfService.ProjectData[] list = null;
PTWcfService.PTServiceClient svc =
  new PTWcfClient.PTWcfService.PTServiceClient();
try
{
  svc.ClientCredentials.UserName.UserName = "anonymous";
  list = svc.GetProjectList();
}
finally
{
  svc.Close();
}
this.projectDataBindingSource.DataSource = list;
```

You might also use a channel factory to create the service proxy. In that case, you set the credentials on the factory.

```
PTWcfService.ProjectData[] list = null;
ChannelFactory<PTWcfService.IPTService> factory =
  new ChannelFactory<PTWcfService.IPTService>("WSHttpBinding_IPTService");
try
{
  factory.Credentials.UserName.UserName = "pm";
  factory.Credentials.UserName.Password = "pm";
  PTWcfService.IPTService proxy = factory.CreateChannel();

  using (proxy as IDisposable)
  {
    list = proxy.GetProjectList();
  }
}
finally
{
  factory.Close();
}
this.projectDataBindingSource.DataSource = list;
```

In this case, you can dispose the proxy, but you should call `Close()` on the factory object. Disposing the factory may result in an exception from WCF, because WCF treats a `Dispose()` as an abnormal scenario, whereas it treats `Close()`as a normal scenario.

Either way, the supplied values are passed securely to the service, where they are authenticated and then used to load the custom principal and identity objects.

Client Configuration

One change is required to the caller's WCF configuration, and it is highlighted here from the `app.config` file in `PTWcfClient`:

```
<bindings>
  <wsHttpBinding>
    <binding name="WSHttpBinding_IPTService" closeTimeout="00:01:00"
        openTimeout="00:01:00" receiveTimeout="00:10:00" sendTimeout="00:01:00"
        bypassProxyOnLocal="false" transactionFlow="false"
        hostNameComparisonMode="StrongWildcard"
        maxBufferPoolSize="524288" maxReceivedMessageSize="65536"
        messageEncoding="Text" textEncoding="utf-8" useDefaultWebProxy="true"
        allowCookies="false">
      <readerQuotas maxDepth="32"
                    maxStringContentLength="8192" maxArrayLength="16384"
        maxBytesPerRead="4096" maxNameTableCharCount="16384" />
      <reliableSession ordered="true" inactivityTimeout="00:10:00"
        enabled="false" />
      <security mode="Message">
        <transport clientCredentialType="Windows" proxyCredentialType="None"
            realm="" />
```

```
          <message clientCredentialType="UserName"
                   negotiateServiceCredential="true"
                   algorithmSuite="Default"
                   establishSecurityContext="true" />
        </security>
      </binding>
    </wsHttpBinding>
  </bindings>
  <behaviors>
    <endpointBehaviors>
      <behavior name="ServiceCertificate">
        <clientCredentials>
          <serviceCertificate>
            <authentication certificateValidationMode="PeerTrust"/>
          </serviceCertificate>
        </clientCredentials>
      </behavior>
    </endpointBehaviors>
  </behaviors>
  <client>
    <endpoint
        behaviorConfiguration="ServiceCertificate"
        address="http://localhost/PTWcfServicecs/PTService.svc"
        binding="wsHttpBinding" bindingConfiguration="WSHttpBinding_IPTService"
        contract="PTWcfService.IPTService" name="WSHttpBinding_IPTService">
    </endpoint>
  </client>
```

If you handcraft your client configuration, much of what you see here will be optional. However, if you allow Visual Studio to create the configuration for you, you'll see something similar to this. The highlighted lines of code merely specify that at the message level, the service expects a `UserName` type credential.

```
          <message clientCredentialType="UserName"
                   negotiateServiceCredential="true"
                   algorithmSuite="Default" establishSecurityContext="true" />
```

With this change, the client will now properly pass the credentials through to the service.

I realize this section of the chapter has been pretty intense. WCF configuration can get complex, and enabling some seemingly simple scenarios like passing a username/password combination to the server can be difficult to figure out. However, if you use Windows AD authentication or the ASP. NET `MembershipProvider` model, things will be much simpler.

Now that you have a basic understanding of the technologies behind WCF services, I'll discuss how to build an application interface using XML services.

Designing a WCF Service Interface

In many ways, a WCF service interface is easier to construct than a WPF or Web Forms interface, because you don't need to worry about any issues of display or user interaction. Those are the responsibilities of the calling application. All the service needs to worry about is providing an interface that allows the developer of a consumer application to access the information and functionality provided by *this* application's business logic and data.

Service Design

You could subdivide the ProjectTracker application's functionality in many different ways. For example, you could be specific and provide a set of discrete service operations, such as those listed in Table 21-8.

Table 21-8. *Possible Service Operations*

Add project	Get project	Remove project	Change project name
Change project start date	Change project end date	Add resource	Get resource
Remove resource	Change resource first name	Change resource last name	Get list of projects
Get list of resources	Change project description	Add resource to project	Remove resource from project
Add project to resource	Remove project from resource	Change role of resource on project	and so on . . .

Following this approach, you could end up writing a rather large number of service operations! Although it's perfectly possible to do that, you might instead consider consolidating some of these operations into methods with broader functionality, as follows:

- Get a list of projects
- Get details for a project
- Add or update a project
- Delete a project
- Get a list of resources
- Get details for a resource
- Add or update a resource
- Delete a resource

This is a smaller list of discrete operations, and by having fewer operations, there's less code to maintain. Moreover, this approach provides a higher level of abstraction—consumers have no idea what happens when they request details for a project, and over time you may change how that process works without having any impact on the consumers. Perhaps most importantly, having a small number of operations tends to improve performance, since a client application needs to make fewer cross-network method calls to get its work done.

The ProjectTracker WCF service interface, PTWcfService, implements the following set of operations:

- GetProjectList()
- GetProject()
- AddProject()
- UpdateProject()
- GetRoles()

Later in this chapter, I'll walk through GetProjectList(), AddProject(), and UpdateProject(), as they provide a good cross section of the concepts and implementation issues. The WCF service implementation can be found in the ProjectTracker solution. It is named PTWcfService.

Application Configuration

The website hosting the WCF service needs to provide some basic configuration information through the web.config file. In the web.config file, you can either provide connection strings so that the site can interact with the database directly, or you can configure the data portal to communicate with a remote application server.

I discussed the basic concept in Chapter 15 when I covered the channel adapter implementation. Recall that the data portal supports numerous communication channels, most notably Local and WCF.

In Chapter 1, I discussed the trade-offs between performance, scalability, fault tolerance, and security that come with various physical n-tier configurations. In most cases, the optimal solution for a web UI is to run the data portal locally in the client process. However, for security reasons, it may be desirable to run the data portal remotely on an application server.

The web.config file is an XML file that contains settings to configure the website. You use different XML depending on how you want the site configured.

The information in this section is much the same as that in Chapters 19 and 20. I'm repeating it here for completeness, so you don't need to refer back to those chapters if you are focused on creating a WCF service.

Authentication

CSLA .NET controls authentication through web.config.

```
<?xml version="1.0" encoding="utf-8" ?>
<configuration>
  <appSettings>
    <add key="CslaAuthentication" value="Csla" />
  </appSettings>
</configuration>
```

The CslaAuthentication key shown here specifies the use of custom authentication. The ProjectTracker.Library assembly includes the PTPrincipal and PTIdentity classes specifically to support custom authentication, and the UI code in this chapter will use custom authentication as well.

If you want to use Windows authentication, change the configuration to this:

```
<add key="CslaAuthentication" value="Windows" />
```

Of course, that change would require coding changes. To start, you would remove the PTPrincipal and PTIdentity classes from ProjectTracker.Library, as they would no longer be needed. Also, the virtual root would need to disallow anonymous users, and ASP.NET would need to be configured to impersonate the caller. If you use Windows authentication, you would not use the custom validation, authorization, and PrincipalCache code discussed earlier in the chapter.

Local Data Portal

The web.config file also controls how the application uses the data portal. To have the website interact directly with the database, use the following (with your connection string changed to the connection string for your database):

```
<?xml version="1.0" encoding="utf-8" ?>
<configuration>
  <appSettings>
    <add key="CslaAuthentication" value="Csla" />
  </appSettings>
  <connectionStrings>
    <add name="PTracker" connectionString="your connection string"
      providerName="System.Data.SqlClient" />
    <add name="Security" connectionString="your connection string"
      providerName="System.Data.SqlClient" />
  </connectionStrings>
```

Because LocalProxy is the default for the data portal, no actual data portal configuration is required, so the only settings in the configuration file are to control authentication and to provide the database connection strings.

■ **Tip** In the code download for this book (available at www.apress.com/book/view/1430210192 or www.lhotka.net/cslanet/download.aspx), the PTracker and Security database files are in the solution directory, not in the website's App_Data directory. This means that you can't use a local data portal from the website without first copying the database files into the App_Data directory and changing the connection strings accordingly.

Remote Data Portal (with WCF)

To have the data portal use an application server and communicate using the WCF channel, the configuration would look like this:

```
<?xml version="1.0" encoding="utf-8" ?>
<configuration>
  <appSettings>
    <add key="CslaAuthentication" value="Csla" />
    <add key="CslaDataPortalProxy"
              value="Csla.DataPortalClient.WcfProxy, Csla"/>
  </appSettings>
  <connectionStrings>
  </connectionStrings>
  <system.serviceModel>
    <client>
      <endpoint name="WcfDataPortal"
                address="http://localhost:4147/WcfHost/WcfPortal.svc"
                binding="wsHttpBinding"
                contract="Csla.Server.Hosts.IWcfPortal"/>
    </client>
  </system.serviceModel>
```

The CslaDataPortalProxy setting indicates the WcfProxy should be used to communicate with the application server. This requires that you define a client endpoint in the system.serviceModel element of the config file.

The only value you need to change in this element is the address property. You need to change localhost:4147 to the name of the application server on which the data portal host is installed. Also, you need to replace the WcfHost text with the name of your virtual root on that server.

Before using this configuration, you must create and configure the WCF host virtual root. I'll show how to do this in the next section.

The most important thing to realize about the site configuration is that the data portal can be changed from local to remote (using any of the network channels) without needing to change any UI or business object code.

PTWcfService Site Setup

The website references the `ProjectTracker.Library` project, as shown in Figure 21-5. This causes Visual Studio to automatically put the associated `Csla.dll` files into the `Bin` directory as well, because `Csla.dll` is referenced by `ProjectTracker.Library`.

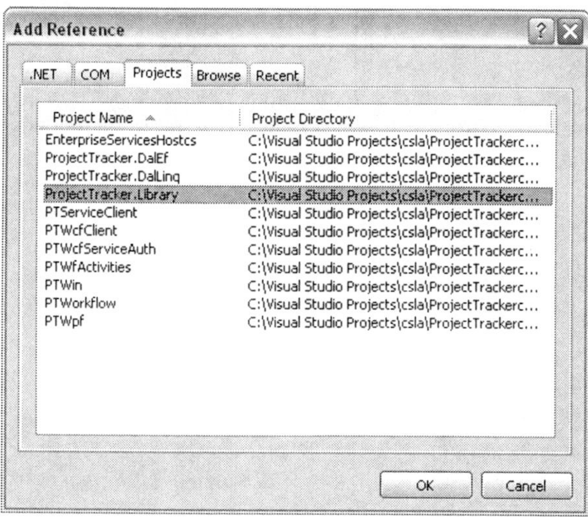

Figure 21-5. *Referencing ProjectTracker.Library*

The `PTWcfService` website will only run within IIS, not within ASP.NET Development Server (commonly known as Cassini or VS Host).

ASP.NET Development Server (provided with Visual Studio) has various limitations—among them, the inability to load custom security objects from assemblies in the `Bin` directory. This means you can't use ASP.NET Development Server to test or debug custom principal objects, custom membership providers, or other custom security objects if they are in an assembly referenced from the project.

Though this is an unfortunate limitation, it can be argued that ASP.NET Development Server is not intended for anything beyond hobbyist or casual usage, and that IIS should be used for any serious business development.

■ **Note** An alternative solution is to install the assembly containing your custom principal and identity classes into the .NET GAC. For `PTWcfService`, this would mean giving `ProjectTracker.Library` a strong name and using the `gacutil.exe` command-line utility to install the assembly into the GAC. You would need to update `ProjectTracker.Library` in the GAC after you build the assembly each time. I find that using IIS is a far simpler solution than using the GAC.

To host a website in IIS during development, you need to take the following steps:

1. Set up a virtual root in IIS, pointing to the directory containing the `PTWcfService` project files.
2. Set the virtual root to use ASP.NET 2.0 using the ASP.NET tab of the virtual root properties dialog in the IIS management console.
3. Set the website's start options using the project properties dialog in Visual Studio 2008. Change the setting to use a custom server, so it starts up using IIS with a URL such as `http://localhost/PTWcfService`.

As I mentioned in Chapter 20, it may seem odd that step 2 sets the virtual root to use ASP.NET 2.0 when this is actually an ASP.NET 3.5 application. However, .NET 3.5 uses the core .NET 2.0 runtime, and it is the core runtime that is set in step 2.

Now let's go through the creation of the WCF service interface. I'll start by discussing the structure of the service contract, data contract, and service implementation code. Then I'll walk through some of the methods that implement the service. Once I've covered the WCF service implementation, I'll briefly discuss the client application that calls the service.

Service Contract and Implementation

As I discussed earlier, a WCF service has four components: the `svc` file, an associated code file, the service contract, and the endpoint configuration. The `PTService.svc` file is really just a pointer to the code file.

```
<%@ ServiceHost Language=C# Debug="true"
    Service="PTService" CodeBehind="~/App_Code/PTService.cs" %>
```

All the interesting work happens in the code file, `PTService.cs`. You can find this file in the `App_Code` folder beneath the virtual root. It implements the service contract, which is defined in `IPTService.cs`. Here's the service contract:

```
[ServiceContract]
public interface IPTService
{
  [OperationContract]
  List<ProjectData> GetProjectList(ProjectListRequest request);
  [OperationContract]
  ProjectData GetProject(ProjectRequest request);
  [OperationContract]
  ProjectData AddProject(AddProjectRequest request);
  [OperationContract]
  ProjectData UpdateProject(UpdateProjectRequest request);
  [OperationContract]
  List<RoleData> GetRoles(RoleRequest request);
}
```

Of course, the contract for the service also includes the data contract definitions for all the types referenced in `IPTService`. For example, here's the `ProjectRequest` data contract:

```
[DataContract]
public class ProjectRequest
{
  [DataMember]
  public Guid Id { get; set; }
}
```

This data contract specifies the parameter value passed into the GetProject() operation. What is perhaps more interesting is the RoleRequest data contract.

```
[DataContract]
public class RoleRequest
{
}
```

This is an empty class, which might seem to make no sense. Why pass in an instance of an empty class as a parameter to an operation? The reason is versioning. As I discussed earlier in the chapter, it is difficult to change the signature of a service method after you've published your contract, because such a change would break all consuming applications. Someday this operation might need an input value, and by requiring even an empty object as a parameter today, it will become easy to add properties to the data contract in the future without breaking consuming applications. So as strange as it may be to define such empty data contracts, this technique directly addresses the issue of versioning and increases the maintainability of your service application.

The PTService class implements IPTService and thus is the implementation of the service itself.

```
public class PTService : IPTService
{
}
```

It contains the methods defined by the IPTService interface, each of which is defined as a service operation. I'll go through the details of three representative methods.

GetProjectList

The GetProjectList() operation is intended to return a list of the projects in the ProjectTracker application. A consumer application can use this data however it wishes, and this method will allow anonymous access with no authentication. Recall that the ProjectList business object applies no authorization rules, and both the PTWpf and PTWeb interfaces allow anonymous users access to the list of projects (and the list of resources through ResourceList).

This method provides an opportunity to see the simplest message-based implementation.

```
public List<ProjectData> GetProjectList(ProjectListRequest request)
{
  try
  {
    ProjectList list = null;
    if (string.IsNullOrEmpty(request.Name))
      list = ProjectList.GetProjectList();
    else
      list = ProjectList.GetProjectList(request.Name);

    List<ProjectData> result = new List<ProjectData>();
    foreach (ProjectInfo item in list)
    {
      ProjectData info = new ProjectData();
      Csla.Data.DataMapper.Map(item, info);
      result.Add(info);
    }
    return result;
  }
  catch (Csla.DataPortalException ex)
  {
    throw new FaultException(ex.BusinessException.Message);
  }
```

```
    catch (Exception ex)
    {
      throw new FaultException(ex.Message);
    }
  }
```

The method accepts a `ProjectListRequest` parameter, allowing the consuming application to provide a `Name` property to filter the results. If no `Name` property value is provided, then the operation will return all the projects in the database.

The result is returned as a list of `ProjectData` objects, though once the list is serialized, it appears in the XML as though it were an array. The `ProjectData` class defines a data contract for project data. You can examine the data contract definition in the code download for this book.

This list is populated by looping through all the items in a `ProjectList` object and using `DataMapper` to copy the properties from each `ProjectTracker.Library.ProjectInfo` child object in the collection to a `List<ProjectData>` object. That list is then returned as a result.

```
ProjectList list = ProjectList.GetProjectList();
List<ProjectData> result = new List<ProjectData>();
foreach (ProjectInfo item in list)
{
  ProjectData info = new ProjectData();
  Csla.Data.DataMapper.Map(item, info);
  result.Add(info);
}
return result;
```

It is important to realize that the business object is not being returned directly as a result. The `ProjectList` object can't be serialized into XML using the `DataContractSerializer` (the serializer used by WCF). Attempting to directly return the business object as a result will cause a serialization exception.

More importantly, returning a business object (the *internal implementation* of the service) as a result would make the business object itself part of the service contract. That would entirely eliminate the concept of encapsulation and would radically reduce the maintainability of your service and your application.

The approach shown here—where the internal business object is used to implement the service, and the data is copied into the formal data contract object that is part of the service contract—is correct. This approach preserves encapsulation and allows for independent versioning and enhancement of the business objects and the service interface.

AddProject

The `AddProject()` operation allows a caller to add a new project to the system. To avoid breaking encapsulation, the actual `Project` class is never exposed to the consumer of the service. Instead, a `ProjectData` data contract object is used to provide data to the method and to return any updates to the consuming application. The core of the operation implementation is highlighted here:

```
public ProjectData AddProject(AddProjectRequest request)
{
  try
  {
    ProjectData obj = request.ProjectData;
    var project = Project.NewProject();
    project.Name = obj.Name;
    project.Started = obj.Started;
    project.Ended = obj.Ended;
```

```
      project.Description = obj.Description;
      project = project.Save();

      ProjectData result = new ProjectData();
      Csla.Data.DataMapper.Map(project, result, "Resources");
      return result;
    }
    catch (Csla.DataPortalException ex)
    {
      throw new FaultException(ex.BusinessException.Message);
    }
    catch (Exception ex)
    {
      throw new FaultException(ex.Message);
    }
  }
```

By the time this code is running, WCF (with the custom validation and authorization components from the PTWcfServiceAuth project) will have verified the user's credentials and put a valid PTPrincipal class on the thread. The Project object will apply its normal authorization rules based on that user identity. In other words, the service code is *not* responsible for preventing an unauthorized user from adding a new project, because the Project object itself takes care of those details.

Thanks to the fact that all validation and authorization is in the Project object, the service method is straightforward. It creates a new Project, loads the parameter values from the caller into the object's properties, and then calls the Save() method to insert the data.

```
ProjectData obj = request.ProjectData;
var project = Project.NewProject();
project.Name = obj.Name;
project.Started = obj.Started;
project.Ended = obj.Ended;
project.Description = obj.Description;
project = project.Save();
```

This is all within a try...catch block. Notice that the catch block simply rethrows the exception as a FaultException. You could add logging code here if desired, but you should remember to rethrow the exception as a fault so the information will be returned properly through WCF to the consuming application. When an exception is wrapped in a FaultException, the message text from the exception is returned to the consumer automatically, so it gets some information about what went wrong.

I have chosen to copy each field from the data contract object to the business object explicitly. You could use DataMapper to do this instead, but I wanted to illustrate the different options available.

If no exception occurs and the Save() call succeeds, then the updated project data is returned to the caller. To do this, a ProjectData object is created, loaded with the data from the Project object, and returned as a result.

```
ProjectData result = new ProjectData();
Csla.Data.DataMapper.Map(project, result, "Resources");
return result;
```

The DataMapper is used to copy the values from Project into ProjectData. The first parameter is the source object, the second is the target object, and the Resources value indicates that the Resources property should be ignored so DataMapper won't try to copy that property value. Since the data contract doesn't have a Resources property, such an attempt would result in an exception.

The result is that the consuming application has access to the newly created Id value, along with any other changes that might have occurred to the data during the insert process.

UpdateProject

The UpdateProject() operation allows a caller to update data for an existing project in the system. To avoid breaking encapsulation, the actual Project class is never exposed to the consumer of the service. Instead, a ProjectData data contract object is used to provide data to the method and to return any updates to the consuming application. The core of the operation implementation is highlighted here:

```
public ProjectData UpdateProject(UpdateProjectRequest request)
{
  try
  {
    ProjectData obj = request.ProjectData;
    var project = Project.GetProject(obj.Id);
    project.Name = obj.Name;
    project.Started = obj.Started;
    project.Ended = obj.Ended;
    project.Description = obj.Description;
    project = project.Save();

    ProjectData result = new ProjectData();
    Csla.Data.DataMapper.Map(project, result, "Resources");
    return result;
  }
  catch (Csla.DataPortalException ex)
  {
    throw new FaultException(ex.BusinessException.Message);
  }
  catch (Exception ex)
  {
    throw new FaultException(ex.Message);
  }
}
```

As you can see, this method implementation is similar to the AddProject() method. The only real difference is that this method calls the GetProject() factory method to get an existing business object, while AddProject() uses the NewProject() factory method to create a new business object. This is necessary, because the Project object's IsNew property needs to be false for an update to occur, and retrieving an existing object makes that happen.

Stateless Update Alternative

There is an alternative, which uses an overload of the Save() method and would require changing the Project code to allow for setting the Id property through a new factory method called CreateUpdatableProject(). That factory in the Project class might look like this:

```
public static Project CreateUpdatableProject(Guid id)
{
  return DataPortal.Create<Project>(new SingleCriteria<Project, Guid>(id));
}
```

This would call a new `DataPortal_Create()` overload:

```
private void DataPortal_Create(SingleCriteria<Project, Guid> criteria)
{
  LoadProperty(IdProperty, criteria.Value);
  ValidationRules.CheckRules();
}
```

Notice how this new factory creates a new instance of the business object, but one where the `Id` property is set to some specific value.

The service code could then look like this:

```
var project = Project.CreateUpdatableProject(obj.Id);
project.Name = obj.Name;
project.Started = obj.Started;
project.Ended = obj.Ended;
project.Description = obj.Description;
project = project.Save(true);
```

The two highlighted lines are important. The first calls the new factory method to create a new object that has a specific `Id` value—namely, the value of some existing object. The object's property values are then all set, and the `Save()` method is called with a value of `true` for the `forceUpdate` parameter.

This `Save()` overload forces the data portal to perform an update operation, even if the object's `IsNew` value is `true`. It is included in CSLA .NET to enable stateless implementations of services and web pages, as shown here.

At this point, you've seen how to create service operations that retrieve, insert, and update information based on XML messages passed to and from a consuming application. The implementation shown here preserves encapsulation and decouples the service contract from the application's internal implementation, which increases the maintainability of both the service interface and the business layer.

The result is that there is now a WCF service interface to some of the `ProjectTracker` functionality. Consuming applications can now call these operations to interact with the application's business logic and data. These consumers may be running on any hardware platform or OS, and may be written in virtually any programming language. Those details don't matter in any meaningful way.

The important thing is that any consumers will interact with the `ProjectTracker` data *through* the business logic in the business objects, including validation, authentication, and authorization—thereby making it difficult for consumers to misuse the data or functionality.

Web Service Consumer Implementation

The thing about creating WCF services is that it's not a very satisfying experience. There's nothing to see—no visual reinforcement that you've accomplished anything. Luckily, we can generate an information page to check the service.

Generating a WCF Information Page

WCF includes functionality to generate an information page for WCF services automatically, and you can use this page to ensure that the basic configuration of your service is correct. You can't determine if the service will actually work without writing a consuming application.

Figure 21-6 shows the information page for PTWcfService.

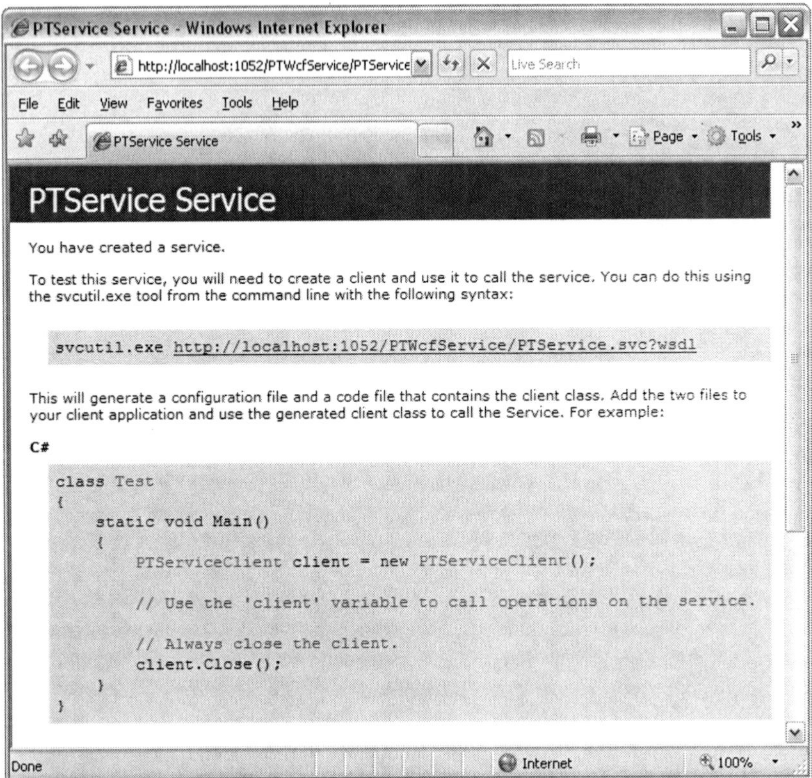

Figure 21-6. *Information page for a WCF service*

If this page displays properly, you'll know that IIS and ASP.NET are properly configured and that there are no major issues with the content of the `web.config` file, the `svc` file, or the service contract. Again, this doesn't mean that the service will actually work; it just means that there are no major configuration issues.

You can also click the link shown in the web page, which will display the WSDL for the service. This is a good idea, as it further tests the configuration and data contract definition for major issues. Figure 21-7 shows the resulting display.

To determine if your service implementation works, you need to create at least a simple consuming application. That's what I'll demonstrate in the rest of this chapter.

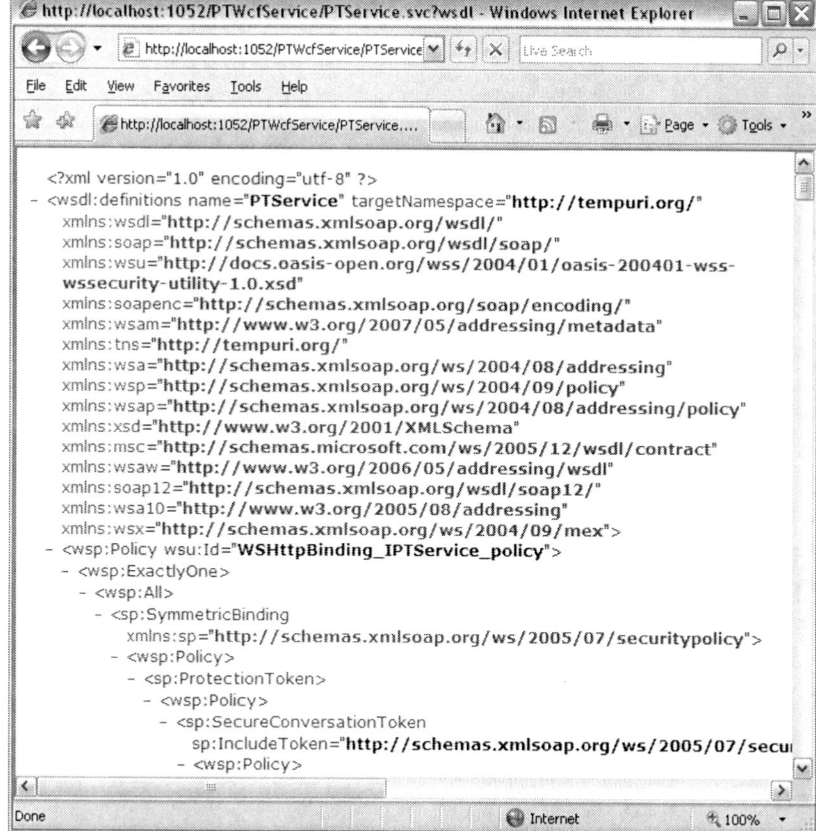

Figure 21-7. *WSDL display for a WCF service*

A Simple Smart Client

To illustrate how to call `PTWcfService`, the `ProjectTracker` solution contains a `PTWcfClient` project. This is a bare-bones Windows Forms application that acts as a consumer for `PTWcfService`. Figure 21-8 shows what the application looks like when running.

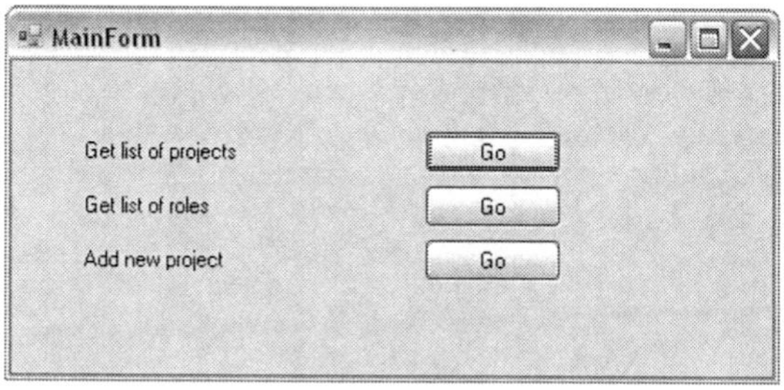

MainForm
Get list of projects Go
Get list of roles Go
Add new project Go

Figure 21-8. *The PTWcfClient application*

More interesting is Figure 21-9, which shows a simple `DataGrid` control bound to the results of the `GetProjectList()` operation.

Form1

Id	Name
b2503d89-3845-4cee-86b4-375ff97b747e	Expert C# Business Objects
bf3184f6-3055-46e2-9b76-59f0023ca2f9	Expert VB 2005 Business Objects
750a346c-6c08-48c8-9329-e306ce8c7299	Web site updates
c385607b-e7c9-43ad-9658-ea741634c6d0	Expert C# 2005 Business Objects
9c014795-2c1b-454d-91eb-edf79ba8e126	Expert One-on-One VB Business Objects

Figure 21-9. *The PTWcfClient application displaying a list of project data*

My goal with this application isn't to create a complete consumer. Rather, I'm using this application to show how to consume a basic web service and how to set up and pass credentials through the WCF proxy.

As shown in Figure 21-10, `PTWcfClient` has a service reference to `PTWcfService`.

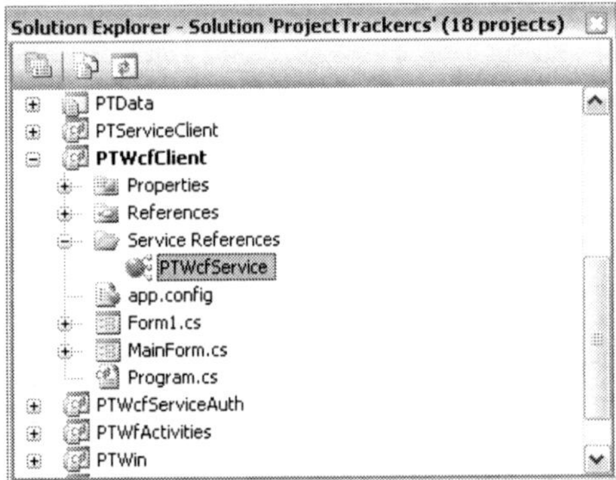

Figure 21-10. *Service reference to PTWcfService*

You can right-click the item in Solution Explorer and choose the Configure Service Reference menu option to see the dialog shown in Figure 21-11. This dialog allows you to control important elements of the service reference and also control how Visual Studio generates client-side proxy code so you can interact with the service.

Although you can override the service address in code, the default address is shown here. This address is important, because it is also the address used by Visual Studio if you ever right-click the service reference in Solution Explorer and choose the Update Service Reference menu option.

The remaining configuration values are the defaults. You may change them to suit your needs, but for this simple consuming application, the defaults are fine.

Notice the Collection type: option, which converts server-side collection or list types to an array on the client. The XML data transferred over the network is always the same format either way; this option simply controls whether "array data" from the server is expressed as an array or a list type on the client. This option controls the code generated by Visual Studio as it creates the service proxy classes, and it allows you to tell Visual Studio to insert code to convert array data into more complex types.

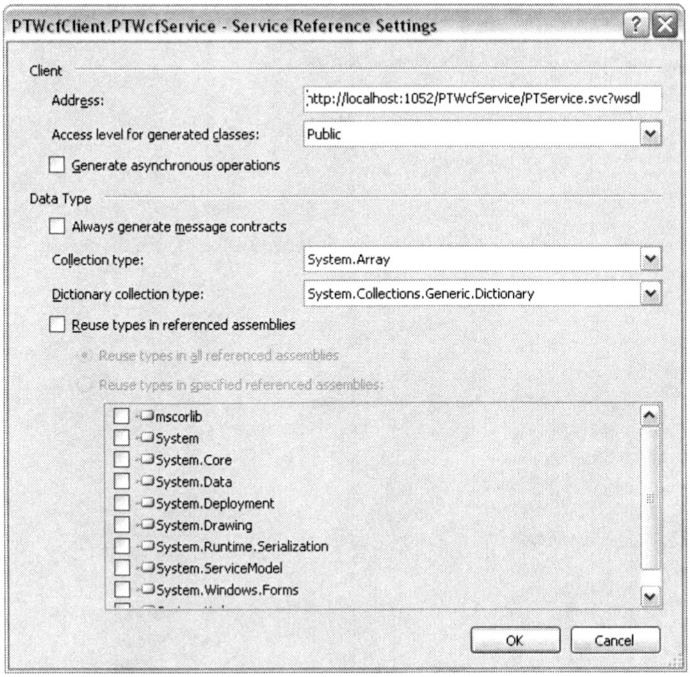

Figure 21-11. *Service Reference Settings dialog*

Client Configuration

When the service reference was added to the project, Visual Studio automatically retrieved the WSDL description for the service and used that information to generate a set of proxy types and other important information. It also added configuration information to the `app.config` file based on the WSDL.

■ **Note** You must create and install a test security certificate on your computer as described earlier in this chapter. If you do not create and install an X.509 certificate, the WCF service will be inaccessible to the client application.

You need to make a couple of changes to the generated configuration information. You need to add a custom behavior element to override the default certificate validation mode as discussed earlier in the chapter.

```
<behaviors>
  <endpointBehaviors>
    <behavior name="ServiceCertificate">
      <clientCredentials>
        <serviceCertificate>
          <authentication certificateValidationMode="PeerTrust"/>
        </serviceCertificate>
      </clientCredentials>
    </behavior>
  </endpointBehaviors>
</behaviors>
```

You also must change the endpoint to use this new behavior and to not use the hard-coded certificate value.

```
<client>
  <endpoint name="WSHttpBinding_IPTService"
         behaviorConfiguration="ServiceCertificate"
          bindingConfiguration="WSHttpBinding_IPTService"
          address="http://localhost:1052/PTWcfService/PTService.svc"
          binding="wsHttpBinding"
          contract="PTWcfService.IPTService">
    <!--<identity>
      <certificate encodedValue="AwAAAA ..." />
    </identity>-->
  </endpoint>
</client>
```

The reason for removing the identity element is that the encodedValue directly refers to the specific certificate used by the service. In the code download, this value corresponds to the test certificate I'm using on my computer, so it won't work with the certificate that you created and installed on your computer. The client will work without this value configured, so commenting it out is the simplest way to get the configuration to work.

You will probably also need to change the address property to match the specific address for your service.

Calling a Service Operation

The data binding support in Windows Forms works against the proxy classes generated for a WCF service. This means you can add a type like ProjectData to the Data Sources window. Figure 21-12 shows the Data Source Configuration Wizard listing all the types from the PTService service reference.

Once the types are in the Data Sources window, you can drag-and-drop these types onto a form just like you would with any business object. This is how the PTWcfClient UI was built.

For each type you drag onto the form, Visual Studio creates a corresponding BindingSource object in the form's component tray. The UI controls are bound to the BindingSource control, and that BindingSource control is bound to your data.

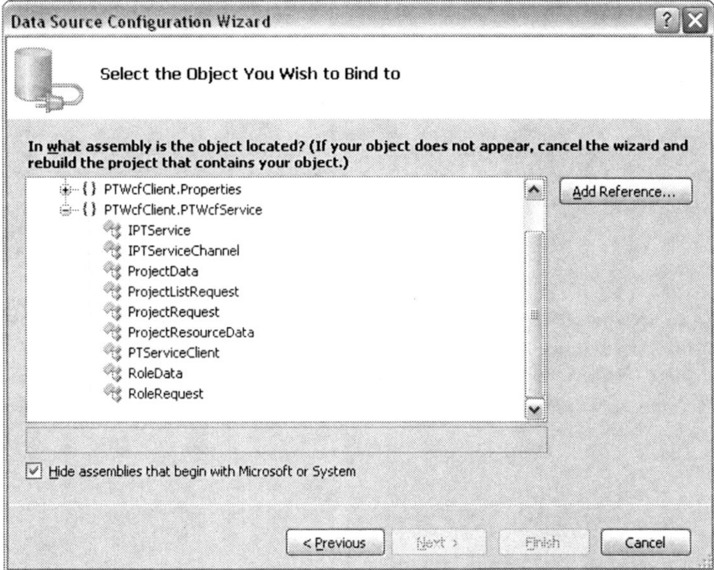

Figure 21-12. *Types available from the PTWcfService service reference*

You need to write a bit of code to set the DataSource property of the BindingSource object. For instance, when the client's form loads, the following code is run:

```
private void Form1_Load(object sender, EventArgs e)
{
  PTWcfService.ProjectData[] list;

  var svc = new PTWcfClient.PTWcfService.PTServiceClient(
    "WSHttpBinding_IPTService");
  try
  {
    svc.ClientCredentials.UserName.UserName = "anonymous";
    //svc.ClientCredentials.UserName.Password = "";
    list =
      svc.GetProjectList(new PTWcfClient.PTWcfService.ProjectListRequest());
  }
  finally
  {
    svc.Close();
  }

  this.projectDataBindingSource.DataSource = list;
}
```

First, an instance of PTServiceClient is created.

```
  var svc = new PTWcfClient.PTWcfService.PTServiceClient(
    "WSHttpBinding_IPTService");
```

This is a proxy object that allows the client code to interact with the WCF service. Because this service requires username/password credentials, those credentials must be set on the proxy.

```
svc.ClientCredentials.UserName.UserName = "anonymous";
//svc.ClientCredentials.UserName.Password = "";
```

In this case, the anonymous username with no password is used, but you can see how a user's actual credentials could be provided if necessary.

The service operation is then invoked to get the list of project data.

```
list =
  svc.GetProjectList(new PTWcfClient.PTWcfService.ProjectListRequest());
```

The consuming application then uses this value. In this example, it is used as the data source for the projectDataBindingSource, so the data is displayed to the user in a DataGrid control.

You can look through the rest of the client code in the code download for the book. All the forms in the consuming application follow the same basic structure for interacting with the WCF service operations.

Conclusion

XML services enable the creation of another type of interface for your business objects. Rather than exposing an interface directly to users like WPF or Web Forms, XML services expose an interface for use by other applications. Those applications can call your service methods to leverage the business functionality and data provided by your application and its business objects.

You can design your XML services using either n-tier client/server or service-oriented models. While the client/server approach works, it isn't ideal, and you should consider implementing message-based, service-oriented services as shown in this chapter.

Service-oriented design specifies that a service is an autonomous entity—an independent application, *not* a tier within a larger application. Service orientation also specifies that your service methods should communicate using a message-based approach, where the service methods accept a complex type as a message and return a complex type as a resulting message. Those complex types are defined as data contracts when using WCF.

Whether you use a remote data portal or not, the framework and concepts discussed in this book should enable you to create applications using object-oriented design concepts, while leveraging the power of .NET. Your objects will support data binding in WPF, Web Forms, and Windows Forms, along with support for the encapsulation of business, validation, and authorization logic in a clear and concise manner.

I've thoroughly enjoyed exploring these concepts with you, and I wish you the best as you develop your software.

Code well, have fun.

Index

C

F

H

I

M

N

P

T

Breinigsville, PA USA
20 September 2010

245649BV00005B/3/P